The Treasury
of Christian
Spiritual Classics

The Treasury of Christian Spiritual Classics

Complete and Unabridged with Contemporary Introductions

Introductions by Timothy P. Weber,
Southern Baptist Theological Seminary

THOMAS NELSON PUBLISHERS
Nashville • Atlanta • London • Vancouver

Published in Nashville, Tennessee, by Thomas Nelson, Inc., Publishers, and distributed in Canada by Word Communications, Ltd., Richmond, British Columbia, and in the United Kingdom by Word (UK), Ltd., Milton Keynes, England.

Scripture quotations are from the NEW KING JAMES VERSION of the Bible. Copyright © 1979, 1980, 1982, Thomas Nelson, Inc., Publishers.

Library of Congress Cataloging-in-Publication Data

The treasury of Christian spiritual classics : complete and unabridged with
  contemporary introductions / by Timothy P. Weber.
    p.   cm.
  Includes bibliographical references.
  ISBN 0-7852-8084-7
  1. Spiritual life—Catholic Church. 2. Catholic Church—Doctrines.
BX2349.T74 1994
248—dc20   94–33206
                                                  CIP

Printed in the United States of America
1 2 3 4 5 6 7 — 00 99 98 97 96 95 94

Contents

The Confessions of St. Augustine
1

On the Song of Songs, St. Bernard of Clairvaux
157

Revelations of Divine Love, Julian of Norwich
327

The Imitation of Christ, Thomas à Kempis
433

The Practice of the Presence of God, Brother Lawrence
555

Notes
585

The
Confessions
of
St. Augustine

Introduction

RELIGIOUS CONVERSIONS seem common these days, when religions abound and people feel free to switch as often as they like. That is the impression, at least, that comes with living in a free-market religious economy. Those experts who watch religious trends at the end of the twentieth century have noted the rapid decline in denominational "name-brand loyalty" which allows people raised in one kind of religious tradition to move to another with ease. People are now consumers about religion in much the same way that they are consumers about everything else. "Switching" occurs because a new congregation or religious group better meets a person's spiritual needs, not necessarily because he or she has undergone a radical change of life.

That is what "conversion" has historically meant—a significant change in life's direction, the trading of one set of ultimate allegiances for another. Such a major reorientation of one's life is what Jesus meant by being "born again" (John 3) and what Paul meant by becoming a "new creature." "Therefore, if anyone is in Christ, he is a new creation; old things have passed away; behold, all things have become new" (2 Cor. 5:17). From this biblical perspective, a conversion is more than a change in personal preference; it is a change of identity.

When seen from that point of view, it is safe to say that real conversions are relatively rare; and when they do occur, people take notice. Maybe that is why Augustine's *Confessions* is still read with such curiosity and interest. It contains the story of a notable conversion, the spiritual autobiography of one of the most amazing men in the history of the Christian movement.

One also suspects that any book entitled *Confessions* is bound to get at least a look in a society awash in tabloid journalism and tell-all "true confessions" by celebrities. It is now fashionable to "kiss and tell," to reveal one's most salacious secrets, in print and on television talk shows. People say in public today things that most people had difficulty discussing in private not all that long ago. Of course, most of those who engage in such self-disclosure do not usually do it because they are ashamed of what they have done. They "confess" in order to explain why there is nothing wrong with their behavior or why they should not be held accountable for it. In an age when everyone is a "victim," no one is personally responsible for anything. Without personal accountability and the willingness to admit personal wrongdoing, conversions hardly seem necessary.

People today who pick up Augustine's *Confessions* to find that kind of self-justifying self-disclosure are bound to be terribly disappointed. Though there is plenty of sin in Augustine's autobiography, he did not try to explain it away or blame it on somebody else. Though he often felt powerless to change his behavior, he felt personally responsible. He told the story of his life to show that God did for him what he could never do for himself, that when he was most incapable of changing himself, God intervened to change him through and through. But the *Confessions* also told the story of a person still in process, one who fully understood that conversion marked the beginning, not the end of the Christian life.

AUGUSTINE (354–430)

Augustine was born in 354 in Tagaste, a small North African town, in what is now Algeria, some forty years after Constantine became the first Roman emperor to call himself a Christian. Though Christianity was not declared the state religion until 380, by the time of Augustine's birth, it was receiving special privileges from the empire and growing rapidly. Augustine's mother Monica was a committed Christian; but his father Patricius was a pagan, and proud of it. Despite their religious differences, both parents were determined to give Augustine the best. In later years, he rarely mentioned his father; but Monica took an especially active role in her son's intellectual and spiritual development.

When he was seventeen, Augustine left home for Carthage, the center of Latin-speaking Roman culture in North Africa. There he intended to study rhetoric—how to speak and write with clarity and elegance—which would open doors for a career in law, public service, or teaching.

Like students in every age, Augustine experimented with new ideas and sensual pleasures. The more he studied rhetoric, the less satisfied he was with his mother's Christianity. Though Monica had provided him with basic instruction in the Christian faith during his boyhood, Augustine had never embraced it. Now he considered Christianity to be primitive and base, not suitable for a young scholar like himself, and a hindrance to the kind of life he wanted.

But he was not indifferent to certain philosophical issues, especially the problem posed by the existence of evil in a basically good world. The approach of the Manicheans appealed to him, at least for a while. Based on the teaching of Mani, a third-century Persian, the sect taught that there were two eternal but opposing principles at work in the universe, light (good) and darkness (evil). Drawing on the combined teachings of Buddha, Zoroaster, and Jesus, Mani argued that the two principles had become intermingled in human nature. Salvation, then, consisted of separating the elements of light and darkness in the human soul so that the darkness could eventually be absorbed by the light. Manicheism attracted well-educated people like Augustine. He joined and remained a "hearer" (i.e., learner) for nine years.

After completing his formal schooling in Carthage, he returned home to Tagaste and taught for a year (375–376). Then he went back to Carthage for another seven years. During that time he struggled with his sexuality. Unable to control his large sexual appetite, he took a mistress and fathered a son.

By 383, he had grown tired of both his unruly students in Carthage and his Manicheism, whose teachings he found less and less satisfying. He decided to take his mistress and son to Rome where he hoped to land a job teaching rhetoric. He liked his Roman students better, but they rarely paid him. Discouraged again, he moved on to Milan.

His three years in Milan proved to be the turning point in his life. Not long after his arrival, he heard about the rhetorical skills of Bishop Ambrose, the city's leading preacher. His mother, who had joined Augustine's family in Italy, urged him to go hear the man in person.

At first Augustine listened to the bishop for what he could teach him about public speaking and the art of persuasion; but after a while, he began to listen to the bishop's message. What he heard took away many of his old objections to Christianity, especially his complaints about the Bible. In comparison to what he was used to reading, the Bible seemed inferior, even crude. But Ambrose preferred to interpret the Bible allegorically, rather than literally, which allowed him to find a deeper, more spiritual message in the most problematic passages. Augustine was impressed by what he considered a perfectly acceptable academic approach to literature. He then began to reconsider his earlier views about Christianity.

What made this reappraisal even easier was Augustine's new-found Neoplatonism, a philosophy to which he had turned after rejecting Manicheism. Neoplatonism had significant religious overtones: through study, self-discipline, and mysticism, it tried to reach the One Source of all being, from which everything else had come. But if a single being of infinite goodness had created all things, where did evil come from? Unlike the Manicheans, who argued that evil had always existed alongside the good, the Neoplatonists believed that evil was merely a negation of the good, not a "thing" with its own independent existence. Evil was a corruption of the good and lacked equal standing with it. One might think of it this way: the One Source was like a stone dropped into a still pool of water. Where it splashes into the water the ripples are strong, but as they move away from the original splash, the weaker the ripples become. The "good" in the universe is everything close to the One Source; the evil is everthing moving away from it. Augustine found this explanation of good and evil much more to his liking and quite consistent with what he was hearing from Ambrose.

But one problem remained. He feared that becoming a Christian would force him to give up everything he loved and had worked for. Some of his closest friends had become Christians; and they had completely turned their backs on their old lives. Such radical transformation terrified Augustine. He especially did not want to give up his pursuit of pleasure and let go of his big ambitions.

Finally, in 386, he gave up. After months of torment, he decided to become a Christian. It happened in a friend's garden; and his life took an abrupt turn. He and his son were baptized by Bishop Ambrose. Then he decided to give up his teaching post and his mistress of many years (mainly his mother's idea) and return to North Africa. On the way home she became ill and suddenly died. Her death devastated him. When he was finally able to reach Tagaste, he sold nearly everything he owned and had inherited; then he, his son, and a few friends moved to Cassiciacum, where they intended to spend the rest of their lives as monks, studying the Scriptures and contemplating the mysteries of God. But soon after their move, Augustine's son died, leaving him shattered and broken again, but still intent on living out his life as a monk.

All those plans changed in 391. While visiting the city of Hippo, Augustine was commandeered by Bishop Valerius. Much against his better judgment, Augustine allowed himself to be ordained for service in the church. Four years later he became bishop alongside Valerius, then succeeded him after his death in 396. Life changed forever for Bishop Augustine, though he did his best to maintain his monastic lifestyle as much as possible.

It did not take long for Augustine to become a leading bishop in North Africa. Because of his learning and superior gifts, he found himself embroiled in a series of controversies, through which he helped to shape the Church of his own time and beyond.

He wrote books against the Manicheans, his old friends, and against the Donatists, who had left the Catholic Church over a dispute about leadership. When the Great Persecution had finally ended in 311, a new bishop was consecrated in Carthage whose loyalty during the persecution many questioned. Under Donatus's leadership, many Carthaginians protested the election. When the new bishop refused to step down, the Donatists, as they were then called, declared his ministry (and the sacraments he administered) to be invalid and withdrew from the church.

By the time Augustine came on the scene, Donatism was almost a hundred years old and extremely popular throughout North Africa.

At first Augustine tried to bring this long dispute to an end through debate and negotiation; but when the Donatists refused to return to the Church, he agreed that it was time to call in the imperial troops. He would have preferred it otherwise, but he was not afraid to use force if he thought it was necessary.

His next big controversy was over the teachings of Pelagius who had strenuously opposed Augustine's views about the human will and divine grace. The bishop had argued that because of the fall of Adam and Eve, all humans were born with original sin, that is, they had lost their ability *not to sin*. Consequently, the will was powerless to break sin's hold over it. Without the gift of God's grace, the sinner was hopelessly bound tight by sin. Augustine knew from his own experience that he had lacked the will even to desire to do the right thing.

Pelagius rejected these notions. He agreed with Augustine that God had made humanity free to choose to sin or not and that the evil that humans do originates in the will. But he denied Augustine's teaching that no one after Adam and Eve had the power to resist evil. Instead of blaming Adam and Eve for the mess they were in, people had no one to blame but themselves. If people did not retain the power to choose, then how could God hold them responsible for sinning?

From his study of the Bible and his recollection of his own experience, Augustine believed that Pelagius's views did not take sin seriously enough and dangerously downplayed the necessity of God's grace for salvation. The war was on; and it lasted for several years. In the end, the church judged Pelagianism to be inadequate; but it also gave a less than full endorsement to Augustine's views, which many believed were too innovative and out of balance.

After the city of Rome fell to invading barbarians in 410, Augustine published *The City of God*, which tried to answer the charge that Rome had fallen because it had become Christian. He argued that history was the story of two cities existing side by side: the city of God, which was built on love of God, and the earthly city, which was built on love of self. Throughout history the two cities war against each other; and versions of the earthly city rise and fall, brought down by their own corruption and divine judgment. In the end, the city of God will be victorious. Given this insight into God's plan in history, Augustine said that Rome's fall was due to its own shortcomings, while the city of God continued, unfazed by the fall of empires.

This perspective undoubtedly gave Augustine comfort at the end of his life. In his final days he watched the Vandals laying seige to Hippo; but mercifully, he died (430) before they breeched the walls.[1] Nevertheless, no one impacted Christian theology in the Latin-speaking world more than Augustine. His writings on the Trinity helped to define the doctrine for others. And for the next thousand years, no other theologian was so frequently quoted in western Catholicism. Twelve hundred years after his death, even the leading Protestant Reformers were proud to call themselves "Augustinians."

THE CONFESSIONS

Augustine wrote his spiritual autobiography in about 397, shortly after he became the bishop of Hippo, when he was about forty-three years old. If Augustine were living in the twentieth century, we would say that he was probably experiencing a mid-life crisis. Here he was, a bishop against his better judgment, trying to make sense of the many turns his life had taken.

Augustine's *Confessions* was not the first of its kind. In fact, there were many spiritual autobiographies around by the time Augustine wrote his. What made his different was its embarrassing candor. Those who read it at the end of the fourth century would have noticed its radically different approach. In other spiritual autobiographies, authors told how their lives had been rough sailing up to the point of conversion, then smooth sailing afterward. It was customary to see the conversion experience as a great dividing line between two separate lives—the former life of sin and struggle and the latter life of peace and rest. In Augustine's life story, conversion remained a turning point, but it was not the end of spiritual adventures. The bishop's struggles continued.

Augustine divided the *Confessions* into thirteen books. The first nine covered his life, from his boyhood in Tagaste to his conversion in Milan and his decision to return to North Africa. Book 10 contained an appraisal of his current spiritual condition, as Bishop of Hippo. Books 11–13, which are not included in this edition, included his exposition of the first chapter of Genesis, wherein he once again rejected the teachings of the Manicheans—by showing that "In the beginning God created the heavens and the earth . . . and called them *good*."

Augustine's motive for writing the *Confessions* was not just to tell his life story. He needed to understand the nature of his spiritual struggles. To put it in more modern terms, he wanted to come to terms with himself and what had happened to him. In order to arrive at self-understanding, he concentrated on his feelings of struggle and loss, of frustration and inadequacy. He analyzed his temptations and his inability to resist them and included in his work only those incidents that contributed to his knowledge of who he was and what God had done in his life. His desperate need to understand himself can be seen in the fact that he wrote the *Confessions* in the form of a prayer to God.

Some events he could not get out of his mind. For example, there was the time when he and a number of his boyhood friends stole pears out of a neighbor's orchard. What many people might consider a minor incident, Augustine saw as extremely important. Why had he done it? He was not hungry; he did not even like pears all that

much. He did it because he was with a group of friends and because he knew it was wrong. Looking back, he had to admit that it was the wrongness of it that appealed to him the most.[2] The episode stuck with him and seemed to symbolize his moral condition.

His life was filled with incidents like that of the stolen pears. He seemed unable to bridle his lusts. Though he knew his behavior was wrong, he could not help himself. There were times he could not even muster the desire not to do those things he knew were wrong. He was trapped and he knew it.

So what brought him freedom from his enslavement to sin? In a word, it was *confession*. When he was finally willing to admit that he could not help himself, then God could help him. Refusing to confront his inability to do the right thing had gotten him nowhere. Confession brought him to the throne of God.

Looking back, Augustine knew that it had not been his doing at all. God's grace had brought him to the moment in the garden when he despaired of himself and reached out to God. Held tight by his fallen nature, Augustine's redemption had to come from beyond himself. God did it all.

But what had God really done? Augustine had to spend the rest of his life finding an answer to that question. God had certainly forgiven him, restored his fallen will so that Augustine had the power for the first time in his life to choose not to sin. But the struggle remained. Along with the power *not to sin*, he still had the power *to sin*. To use the modern language of addiction, Augustine was a *recovering sinner*, not a *former sinner*. Being a sinner is what Augustine never got over. That is what was so striking about the *Confessions* when it first came out: a bishop who still marvelled at his ability to do the wrong thing, a Christian who still did not know or understand himself very well.[3]

When he became a Christian, he became a new man; but he was still Augustine too. His conversion marked a new beginning in his life, but it did not completely obliterate who he was or what had happened to him earlier. He still had sexual dreams and was bothered by his propensity for greed, both of which made him feel guilty. But there was a remedy for a guilty conscience—confession—which gave him the strength to stay on the strange road that his first confession had put him on.

It is Augustine's brutal honesty that has drawn seekers after God to the *Confessions* for the past sixteen centuries. In his experience many people have found their own. In his encounter with grace, they have found reason to trust God's grace for themselves.

NOTE: Augustine frequently quoted Scripture passages in the *Confessions*. These references are set in italic.

The First Book

GREAT ART THOU, O Lord, and *greatly to be praised; great is Thy power, and Thy wisdom infinite.* And Thee would man praise; man, but a particle of Thy creation; man, that bears about him his mortality, the witness of his sin, the witness that *Thou resistest the proud:* yet would man praise Thee; he, but a particle of Thy creation. Thou awakest us to delight in Thy praise; for Thou madest us for Thyself, and our heart is restless, until it repose in Thee.

Grant me, Lord, to know and understand which is first, to call on Thee or to praise Thee? and, again, to know Thee or to call on Thee? for who can call on Thee, not knowing Thee? for he that knoweth Thee not, may call on Thee as other than Thou art.

Or, is it rather, that we call on Thee that we may know Thee? But *how shall they call on Him in whom they have not believed? or how shall they believe without a preacher? and they that seek the Lord shall praise Him:* for *they that seek shall find Him,* and they that find shall praise Him.

I will seek Thee, Lord, by calling on Thee; and will call on Thee, believing in Thee; for to us hast Thou been preached. My faith, Lord, shall call on Thee, which Thou hast given me, wherewith Thou hast inspired me, through the Incarnation of Thy Son, through the ministry of the Preacher.

HOW SHALL I CALL UPON GOD?

And how shall I call upon my God, my God and Lord, since, when I call for Him, I shall be calling Him to myself? and what room is there within me, whither my God can come into me? whither can God come into me, God who made heaven and earth? is there, indeed, O Lord my God, aught in me that can contain Thee? do then heaven and earth, which Thou hast made, and wherein Thou hast made me, contain Thee? or, because nothing which exists could exist without Thee, doth therefore whatever exists contain Thee?

Since, then, I too exist, why do I seek that Thou shouldest enter into me, who were not, wert Thou not in me? Why? because I am not gone down in hell, and yet Thou art there also. For *if I go down into hell, Thou art there.* I could not be then, O my God, could not be at all, wert Thou not in me; or, rather, unless I were in Thee, *of whom are all things, by whom are all things, in whom are all things?* Even so, Lord, even so. Whither do I call Thee, since I am in Thee? or whence canst Thou enter into me? for whither can I go beyond heaven and earth, that thence my God should come into me, who hath said, *I fill the heaven and the earth.*

I PONDERED GOD'S IMMENSITY

Do the heaven and earth then contain Thee, since Thou fillest them? or dost Thou fill them and yet overflow, since they do not contain Thee? And whither, when the heaven and the earth are filled, pourest Thou forth the remainder of Thyself? or hast Thou no need that aught contain Thee, who containest all things, since what Thou fillest Thou fillest by containing it? for the vessels which Thou fillest uphold Thee not, since, though they were broken, Thou wert not poured out.

And when Thou art *poured out* on us, Thou art not cast down, but Thou upliftest us; Thou art not dissipated, but Thou gatherest us. But Thou who fillest all things, fillest Thou them with Thy whole self? or, since all things cannot contain Thee wholly, do they contain part of Thee? and all at once the same part? or each its own part, the greater more, the smaller less? And is, then, one part of Thee greater, another less? or, art Thou wholly everywhere, while nothing contains Thee wholly?

WHO IS LIKE OUR GOD?

What art Thou then, my God? what, but the Lord God? *For who is Lord but the Lord? or who is God save our God?* Most highest, most good, most potent, most omnipotent; most merciful, yet most just; most hidden, yet most present; most beautiful, yet most strong; stable, yet incomprehensible; unchangeable, yet all-changing; never new, never old; all-renewing, and *bringing age upon the proud, and they know it not;* ever working, ever at rest; still gathering, yet nothing lacking; supporting, filling, and overspreading; creating, nourishing, and maturing; seeking, yet having all things.

Thou lovest, without passion; art jealous, without anxiety; repentest, yet grievest not; art angry, yet serene; changest Thy works, Thy purpose unchanged; receivest again what Thou findest, yet didst never lose; never in need, yet rejoicing in gains; never covetous, yet exacting usury. Thou receivest over and above, that Thou mayest owe; and who hath aught that is not Thine? Thou payest debts, owing nothing; remittest debts, losing nothing. And what have I now said, my God, my life, my holy joy? or what saith any man when he speaks of Thee? Yet woe to him that speaketh not, since mute are even the most eloquent.

LET ME SEE THY FACE

Oh! that I might repose on Thee! Oh! that Thou wouldest enter into my heart, and inebriate it, that I may forget my ills, and embrace Thee, my sole good? What art Thou to me? In Thy pity, teach me to utter it. Or what am I to Thee that Thou demandest my love, and, if I give it not, art wroth with me, and threatenest me with grievous woes? Is it then a slight woe to love Thee not?

Oh! for Thy mercies' sake, tell me, O Lord my God, what Thou art unto me. *Say unto my soul, I am thy salvation.* So speak, that I may hear. Behold, Lord, my heart is before Thee; open Thou the ears thereof, and *say unto my soul, I am thy salvation.* After this voice let me haste, and take hold on Thee. Hide not Thy face from me. Let me die—lest I die—only let me see Thy face.

Narrow is the mansion of my soul; enlarge Thou it, that Thou mayest enter in. It is ruinous; repair Thou it. It has that within which must offend Thine eyes; I confess and know it. But who shall cleanse it? or to whom should I cry, save Thee? *Lord, cleanse me from my secret faults and spare Thy servant from the power of the enemy. I believe, and therefore do I speak.* Lord, Thou knowest. *Have I not confessed against myself my transgressions unto Thee, and Thou, my God, hast forgiven the iniquity of my heart? I contend not in judgment with Thee,* who art the truth; I fear to deceive myself; *lest mine iniquity lie unto itself.* Therefore I contend not in judgment with Thee; *for if Thou, Lord, shouldest mark iniquities, O Lord, who shall abide it?*

AN APPEAL FOR MERCY

Yet suffer me to speak unto Thy mercy, me, *dust and ashes.* Yet suffer me to speak, since I speak to Thy mercy, and not to scornful man. Thou too, perhaps, despisest me, yet wilt Thou *return and have compassion* upon me.

For what would I say, O Lord my God, but that I know not whence I came into this dying life (shall I call it?) or living death. Then immediately did the comforts of Thy compassion take me up, as I heard (for I remember it not) from the parents of my flesh, out of whose substance Thou didst sometime fashion me. Thus there received me the comforts of woman's milk. For neither my mother nor my nurses stored their own breasts for me; but Thou didst bestow the food of my infancy through them, according to Thine ordinance, whereby Thou distributest Thy riches through the hidden springs of all things.

Thou also gavest me to desire no more than Thou gavest; and to my nurses willingly to give me what Thou gavest them. For they, with a heaven-taught affection, willingly gave me what they abounded with from Thee. For this my good from them, was good for them. Nor, indeed, from them was it, but through them; for from Thee, O God, are all good things, and *from my God is all my health.* This I since learned, Thou, through these Thy gifts, within me and without, proclaiming Thyself unto me. For then I knew but to suck; to repose in what pleased, and cry at what offended my flesh; nothing more.

Afterwards I began to smile; first in sleep, then waking: for so it was told me of myself, and I believed it; for we see the like in other infants, though of myself I remember it not. Thus, little by little, I became conscious where I was; and to have a wish to express my wishes to those who could content them, and I could not; for the wishes were within me, and they without; nor could they by any sense of theirs enter within my spirit.

So I flung about at random limbs and voice, making the few signs I could, and such as I could, like, though in truth very little like, what I wished. And when I was not presently obeyed (my wishes being hurtful or unintelligible), then I was indignant with my elders for not submitting to me, with those owing me no service, for not serving me; and avenged myself on them by tears. Such have I learnt infants to be from observing them; and that I was myself such, they, all unconscious, have shown me better than my nurses who knew it.

And, lo! my infancy died long since, and I live. But Thou, Lord, who for ever livest, and in whom nothing dies: for before the foundation of the worlds, and before all that can be called "before," Thou art, and art God and Lord of all which Thou hast created: in Thee abide, fixed for ever, the first causes of all things unabiding; and of all things changeable, the springs abide in Thee unchangeable: and in Thee live the eternal reasons of all things unreasoning and temporal.

Say, Lord, to me, Thy suppliant; say, all-pitying, to me, Thy pitiable one; say, did my infancy succeed another age of mine that died before it? was it that which I spent within my mother's womb? for of that I have heard somewhat, and have myself seen women with child? and what before that life again, O God my joy, was I any where or any body? For this have I none to tell me, neither father nor mother, nor experience of others, nor mine own memory. Dost Thou mock me for asking this, and bid me praise Thee and acknowledge Thee, for that I do know?

I acknowledge Thee, Lord of heaven and earth, and praise Thee for my first rudiments of being, and my infancy, whereof I remember nothing; for Thou hast appointed that man should from others guess much as to himself; and believe much on the strength of weak females. Even then I had being and life, and (at my infancy's close) I could seek for signs whereby to make known to others my sensations. Whence could such a being be, save from Thee, Lord? Shall any be his own artificer? or can there elsewhere be derived any vein, which may stream essence and life into us, save from Thee, O Lord, in whom essence and life are one? for Thou Thyself art supremely Essence and Life.

For Thou art most high, and art not changed, neither in Thee doth to-day come to a close; yet in Thee doth it come to a close; because all such things also are in Thee. For they had no way to pass away, unless Thou upheldest them. And since *Thy years fail not,* Thy years are one to-day. How many of ours and our fathers' years have flowed away through Thy "to-day," and from it received the measure and the mould of such being as they had; and still others shall flow away, and so receive the mould of their degree of being. But *Thou art still the same,* and all things of to-morrow, and all beyond, and all of yesterday, and all behind it, Thou hast done to-day. What is it to me, though any comprehend not this? Let him also rejoice and say, *What thing is this.* Let him rejoice even thus; and be content rather by not discovering to discover Thee, than by discovering not to discover Thee.

MY SINFULNESS FROM INFANCY

Hear, O God. Alas, for man's sin! So saith man, and Thou pitiest him; for Thou madest him, but sin in him Thou madest not. Who remindeth me of the sins of my infancy? *for in Thy sight none is pure from sin, not even the infant whose life is but a day upon the earth.*

Who remindeth me? doth not each little infant, in whom I see what of myself I remember not? What then was my sin? was it that I hung upon the breast and cried? for should I now so do for food suitable to my age, justly should I be laughed at and reproved. What I then did was worthy reproof; but since I could not understand reproof, custom and reason forbade me to be reproved. For those habits, when grown, we root out and cast away. Now no man, though he prunes, wittingly casts away what is good. Or was it then good, even for a while, to cry for what, if given, would hurt? bitterly to resent, that persons free, and its own elders, yea, the very authors of its birth, served it not? that many besides, wiser than it, obeyed not the nod of its good pleasure? to do its best to strike and hurt, because commands were not obeyed, which had been obeyed to its hurt?

The weakness then of infant limbs, not its will, is its innocence. Myself have seen and known even a baby envious; it could not speak, yet it turned pale and looked bitterly on its foster-brother. Who knows not this? Mothers and nurses tell you that they allay these things by I know not what remedies. Is that too innocence, when the fountain of milk is flowing in rich abundance, not to endure one to share it, though in extremest need, and whose very life as yet depends thereon? We bear gently with all this, not as being no or slight evils, but because they will disappear as years increase; for, though tolerated now, the very same tempers are utterly intolerable when found in riper years.

Thou, then, O Lord my God, who gavest life to this my infancy, furnishing thus with senses (as we see) the frame Thou gavest, compacting its limbs, ornamenting its proportions, and for its general good and safety, implanting in it all vital functions, Thou commandest me to praise Thee in these things, *to confess unto Thee, and sing unto Thy name, Thou most Highest.* For Thou art God, Almighty and Good, even hadst Thou done nought but only this, which none could do but Thou; whose Unity is the mould of all things; who out of Thy own fairness makest all things fair; and orderest all things by Thy law.

This age, then, Lord, whereof I have no remembrance, which I take on others' word, and guess from other infants that I have passed, true though the guess be, I am yet loth to count in this life of mine which I live in this world. For no less than that which I spent in my mother's womb, is it hid from me in the shadows of forgetfulness. But if *I was shapen in iniquity, and in sin did my mother conceive me,* where, I beseech Thee, O my God, where, Lord, or when, was I Thy servant guiltless? But, lo! that period I pass by; and what have I now to do with that, of which I can recall no vestige?

MEMORIES OF MY BOYHOOD

Passing hence from infancy, I came to boyhood, or rather it came to me, displacing infancy. Nor did that depart—(for whither went it?)—and yet it was no more. For I was no longer a speechless infant, but a speaking boy. This I remember; and have since observed how I learned to speak. It was not that my elders taught me words (as, soon after, other learning) in any set method; but I, longing by cries and broken accents and various motions of my limbs to express my thoughts, that so I might have my will, and yet unable to express all I willed, or to whom I willed, did myself, by the understanding which Thou, my God, gavest me, practise the sounds in my memory.

When they named any thing, and as they spoke turned towards it, I saw and remembered that they called what they would point out by the name they uttered. And that they meant this thing and no other was plain from the motion of their body, the natural language, as it were, of all nations, expressed by the countenance, glances of the eye, gestures of the limbs, and tones of the voice, indicating the affections of the mind, as it pursues, possesses, rejects, or shuns.

And thus by constantly hearing words, as they occurred in various sentences, I collected gradually for what they stood; and having broken in my mouth to these signs, I thereby gave utterance to my will. Thus I exchanged with those about me these current signs of our wills, and so launched deeper into the stormy intercourse of human life, yet depending on parental authority and the beck of elders.

A DISOBEDIENT STUDENT

O God my God, what miseries and mockeries did I now experience, when obedience to my teachers was proposed to me, as proper in a boy, in order that in this world I might prosper, and excel in tongue-science, which should serve to the "praise of men," and to deceitful riches. Next I was put to school to get learning, in which I (poor wretch) knew not what use there was; and yet, if idle in learning, I was beaten. For this was judged right by our forefathers; and many, passing the same course before us, framed for us weary paths, through which we were fain to pass; multiplying toil and grief upon the sons of Adam. But, Lord, we found that men called upon Thee, and we learnt from them to think of Thee (according to our powers) as of some great One, who, though hidden from our senses, couldst hear and help us.

For so I began, as a boy, to pray to Thee, my aid and refuge; and broke the fetters of my tongue to call on Thee, praying Thee, though small, yet with no small earnestness, that I might not be beaten at school. And when Thou heardst me not *(not thereby giving me over to folly)* my elders, yea, my very parents, who yet wished me no ill, mocked my stripes, my then great and grievous ill.

Is there, Lord, any of soul so great, and cleaving to Thee with so intense affection (for a sort of stupidity will in a way do it); but is there any one who, from cleaving devoutly to Thee, is endued with so great a spirit, that he can think as lightly of the racks and hooks and other torments (against which, throughout all lands, men call on Thee with extreme dread), mocking at those by whom they are feared most bitterly, as our parents mocked the torments which we suffered in boyhood from our masters? For we feared not our torments less; nor prayed we less to Thee to escape them. And yet we sinned, in writing or reading or studying less than was exacted of us. For we wanted not, O Lord, memory or capacity, whereof Thy will gave enough for our age; but our sole delight was play; and for this we were punished by those who yet themselves were doing the like.

But elder folks' idleness is called

"business"; that of boys, being really the same, is punished by those elders; and none commiserates either boys or men. For will any of sound discretion approve of my being beaten as a boy, because, by playing at ball, I made less progress in studies which I was to learn, only that, as a man, I might play more unbeseemingly? and what else did he who beat me? who, if worsted in some trifling discussion with his fellow-tutor, was more embittered and jealous than I when beaten at ball by a play-fellow?

MY IDLE YOUTH

And yet, I sinned herein, O Lord God, the Creator and Disposer of all things in nature, of sin the Disposer (Ordinator) only, O Lord my God, I sinned in transgressing the commands of my parents and those my masters. For what they, with whatever motive, would have me learn, I might afterwards have put to good use. For I disobeyed, not from a better choice, but from love of play, loving the pride of victory in my contests, and to have my ears tickled with lying fables, that they might itch the more; the same curiosity flashing from my eyes more and more, for the shows and games of my elders.

Yet those who give these shows are in such esteem, that almost all wish the same for their children, and yet are very willing that they should be beaten, if those very games detain them from the studies, whereby they would have them attain to be the givers of them. Look with pity, Lord, on these things, and deliver us who call upon Thee now; deliver those too who call not on Thee yet, that they may call on Thee, and Thou mayest deliver them.

MY MOTHER'S DESIRE

As a boy, then, I had already heard of an eternal life, promised us through the humility of the Lord our God stooping to our pride; and even from the womb of my mother, who greatly hoped in Thee, I was sealed with the mark of His cross and salted with His salt. Thou sawest, Lord, how while yet a boy, being seized on a time with sudden oppression of the stomach, and like near to death—Thou sawest, my God (for Thou wert my keeper), with what eagerness and what faith I sought, from the pious care of my mother and Thy Church, the mother of us all, the baptism of Thy Christ my God and Lord. Whereupon the mother of my flesh, being much troubled (since, with a heart pure in Thy faith, she even more lovingly *travailed in birth* of my salvation), would in eager haste have provided for my consecration and cleansing by the health-giving sacraments, confessing Thee, Lord Jesus, for the remission of sins, unless I had suddenly recovered.

And so, as if I must needs be again polluted should I live, my cleansing was deferred, because the defilements of sin would, after that washing, bring greater and more perilous guilt. I then already believed: and my mother, and the whole household except my father: yet did not he prevail over the power of my mother's piety in me, that as he did not yet believe, so neither should I. For it was her earnest care that Thou my God, rather than he, shouldest be my father; and in this Thou didst aid her to prevail over her husband, whom she, the better, obeyed, therein also obeying Thee, who hast so commanded.

I beseech Thee, my God, I would fain know, if so Thou willest, for what purpose my baptism was then deferred? was it for my good that the rein was laid loose, as it were, upon me, for me to sin? or was it not laid loose? If not, why does it still echo in our ears on all sides, "Let him alone, let him do as he will, for he is not yet baptised"? but as to bodily health, no one says, "Let him be worse wounded, for he is not yet healed."

How much better then, had I been at once healed; and then by my friends' diligence and my own, my soul's recovered health had been kept safe in Thy keeping who gavest it. Better truly. But how many and great waves of temptation seemed to hang over me after my boyhood! These my mother foresaw; and preferred to expose to them the clay whence I might afterwards be moulded, than the very cast, when made.

I WAS FORCED TO STUDY

In boyhood itself, however (so much less dreaded for me than youth), I loved not study, and hated to be forced to it. Yet I was forced; and this was well done towards me, but I did not well; for, unless forced, I had not learnt. But no one doth well against his will, even though what he doth, be well. Yet neither did they well who forced me, but what was well came to me from Thee, my God. For they were regardless how I should employ what they forced me to learn, except to satiate the insatiate desires of a wealthy beggary, and a shameful glory.

But Thou, *by whom the very hairs of our head are numbered*, didst use for my good the error of all who urged me to learn; and my own, who would not learn, Thou didst use for my punishment—a fit penalty for one, so small a boy and so great a sinner. So by those who did not well, Thou didst well for me; and by my own sin Thou didst justly punish me. For Thou hast commanded, and so it is, that every inordinate affection should be its own punishment.

THE POWER TO READ AND WRITE

But why did I so much hate the Greek, which I studied as a boy? I do not yet fully know. For the Latin I loved; not what my first masters, but what the so-called grammarians taught me. For those first lessons, reading, writing, and arithmetic, I thought as great a burden and penalty as any Greek. And yet whence was this too, but from the sin and vanity of this life, because *I was flesh, and a breath that passeth away and cometh not again?*

For those first lessons were better certainly, because more certain; by them I obtained, and still retain, the power of reading what I find written and myself writing what I will; whereas in the others, I was forced to learn the wandering of one Æneas, forgetful of my own, and to weep for dead Dido, because she killed herself for love; the while, with dry eyes, I endured my miserable self dying among these things, far from Thee, O God my life.

For what more miserable than a miserable being who commiserates not himself; weeping the death of Dido for love to Æneas, but weeping not his own death for want of love to Thee, O God. Thou light of my heart, Thou bread of my inmost soul, Thou Power who givest vigour to my mind, who quickenest my thoughts, I loved Thee not. I committed fornication against Thee, and all around me thus fornicating there echoed, "Well done! well done!" *for the friendship of this world is fornication against Thee,* and "Well done! well done!" echoes on till one is ashamed to be thus a man.

And all this I wept not, I who wept for Dido slain, and "seeking by the sword a stroke and wound extreme," myself seeking the while a worse extreme, the extremest and lowest of Thy creatures, having forsaken Thee, earth passing into the earth. And if forbid to read all this, I was grieved that I might not read what grieved me. Madness like this is thought a higher and a richer learning, than that by which I learned to read and write.

But not, my God, cry Thou aloud in my soul; and let Thy truth tell me, "Not so, not so. Far better was that first study." For, lo, I would readily forget the wanderings of Æneas and all the rest, rather than how to read and write. But over the entrance of the Grammar School is a veil drawn! true; yet is this not so much an emblem of aught recondite, as a cloak of error. Let not those, whom I no longer fear, cry out against me, while I confess to Thee, my God, whatever my soul will, and acquiesce in the condemnation of my evil ways, that I may love Thy good ways. Let not either buyers or sellers of grammar-learning cry out against me. For if I question them whether it be true that Æneas came on a time

to Carthage, as the poet tells, the less learned will reply that they know not, the more learned that he never did. But should I ask with what letters the name "Æneas" is written, every one who has learnt this will answer me aright, as to the signs which men have conventionally settled.

If again, I should ask which might be forgotten with least detriment to the concerns of life, reading and writing or these poetic fictions? who does not foresee what all must answer who have not wholly forgotten themselves? I sinned, then, when as a boy I preferred those empty to those more profitable studies, or rather loved the one and hated the other. "One and one, two"; "two and two, four"; this was to me a hateful singsong: "the wooden horse lined with armed men," and "the burning of Troy," and "Creusa's shade and sad similitude," were the choice spectacle of my vanity.

THE VALUE OF CURIOSITY TO LEARNING

Why then did I hate the Greek classics, which have the like tales? For Homer also curiously wove the like fictions, and is most sweetly-vain, yet was he bitter to my boyish taste. And so I suppose would Virgil be to Grecian children, when forced to learn him as I was Homer. Difficulty, in truth, the difficulty of a foreign tongue, dashed, as it were, with gall all the sweetness of Grecian fable. For not one word of it did I understand, and to make me understand I was urged vehemently with cruel threats and punishments.

Time was also (as an infant) I knew no Latin; but this I learned without fear or suffering, by mere observation, amid the caresses of my nursery and jests of friends, smiling and sportively encouraging me. This I learned without any pressure of punishment to urge me on, for my heart urged me to give birth to its conceptions which I could only do by learning words not of those who taught, but of those who talked with me; in whose ears also I gave birth to the thoughts, whatever I conceived.

No doubt, then, that a free curiosity has more force in our learning these things, than a frightful enforcement. Only this enforcement restrains the rovings of that freedom, through Thy laws, O my God, Thy laws, from the master's cane to the martyr's trials, being able to temper for us a wholesome bitter, recalling us to Thyself from that deathly pleasure which lures us from Thee.

GOD'S DISCIPLINE

Hear, Lord, my prayer; let not my soul faint under Thy discipline, nor let me faint in confessing unto Thee all Thy mercies, whereby Thou hast drawn me out of all my most evil ways, that Thou mightest become a delight to me above all the allurements which I once pursued; that I may most entirely love Thee, and clasp Thy hand with all my affections, and Thou mayest yet rescue me from every temptation, even unto the end.

For, lo, O Lord, my King and my God, for Thy service be whatever useful thing my childhood learned; for Thy service, that I speak, write, read, reckon. For Thou didst grant me Thy discipline, while I was learning vanities; and my sin of delighting in those vanities Thou hast forgiven. In them, indeed, I learnt many a useful word, but these may as well be learned in things not vain; and that is the safe path for the steps of youth.

MY EARLY PROMISE RECALLED

But woe is thee, thou torrent of human custom! Who shall stand against thee? how long shalt thou not be dried up? how long roll the sons of Eve into that huge and hideous ocean, which even they scarcely overpass who climb the cross? Did not I read in thee of Jove the thunderer and the adulterer? both, doubtless, he could not be; but so the feigned thunder might countenance and pander to real adultery. And now which of our gowned masters lends a sober ear to one who from their own school cries out, "These were Homer's fictions, transferring things human to the gods; would he had brought down things divine to us!" Yet more truly had he said, "These are indeed his fictions; but attributing a divine nature to wicked men, that crimes might be no longer crimes, and whoso commits them might seem to imitate not abandoned men, but the celestial gods."

And yet, thou hellish torrent, into thee are cast the sons of men with rich rewards, for compassing such learning; and a great solemnity is made of it, when this is going on in the forum, within sight of laws appointing a salary beside the scholar's payments, and thou lashest thy rocks and roarest, "Hence words are learnt; hence eloquence; most necessary to gain your ends, or maintain opinions." As if we should have never known such words as "golden shower," "lap," "beguile," "temples of the heavens," or others in that passage, unless Terence had brought a lewd youth upon the stage, setting up Jupiter as his example of seduction.

> "Viewing a picture, where
>   the tale was drawn,
> Of Jove's descending in a
>   golden shower
> To Danae's lap, a woman
>   to beguile."

And then mark how he excites himself to lust as by celestial authority:

> "And what God? Great
>   Jove,
> Who shakes heaven's highest
>   temples with his
>   thunder,
> And I, poor mortal man, not
>   do the same!
> I did it, and with all my
>   heart I did it."

Not one whit more easily are the words learnt for all this vileness; but by their means the vileness is committed with less shame. Not that I blame the words, being, as it were, choice and precious vessels; but that wine of error which is drunk to us in them by intoxicated teachers; and if we, too, drink not, we are beaten, and have no sober judge to whom we may appeal. Yet, O my God (in whose presence I now without hurt may remember this), all this unhappily I learnt willingly with great delight, and for this was pronounced a hopeful boy.

MY GIFTS MISUSED

Bear with me, my God, while I say somewhat of my wit, Thy gift, and on what dotage I wasted it. For a task was set me, troublesome enough to my soul, upon terms of praise or shame, and fear of stripes, to speak the words of Juno, as she raged and mourned that she could not

> "This Trojan prince from
>   Latuim turn."

Which words I had heard that Juno never uttered; but we were forced to go astray in the footsteps of these poetic fictions, and to say in prose much what he expressed in verse. And his speaking was most applauded, in whom the passions of rage and grief were most pre-eminent, and clothed in the most fitting language, maintaining the dignity of the character.

What is it to me, O my true life, my God, that my declamation was applauded above so many of my own age and class? is not all this smoke and wind? and was there nothing else whereon to exercise my wit and tongue? Thy praises, Lord, Thy praises might have stayed the yet tender shoot of my heart by the prop of Thy Scriptures; so had it not trailed away amid these empty trifles, a defiled prey for the fowls of the air. For in more ways than one do men sacrifice to the rebellious angels.

THE RECORD OF CONSCIENCE

But what marvel that I was thus carried away to vanities, and went from Thy presence, O my God, when men were set before me as models, who, if in relating some action of theirs, in itself not ill, they committed some barbarism or solecism, being censured, were abashed; but when in rich and adorned and well-ordered discourse they related their own disordered life, being bepraised, they gloried?

These things Thou seest, Lord, and holdest Thy peace; *long-suffering, and plenteous in mercy and truth.* Wilt Thou hold Thy peace for ever? and even now Thou drawest out of this horrible gulf the soul that seeketh Thee, that thirsteth for Thy pleasures, *whose heart saith unto Thee, I have sought Thy face; Thy face, Lord, will I seek.* For *darkened* affections is removal from Thee. For it is not by our feet, or change of place, that men leave Thee, or return unto Thee.

Or did that Thy younger son look out for horses or chariots, or ships, fly with visible wings, or journey by the motion of his limbs, that he might in a far country waste in riotous living all Thou gavest at his departure? a loving Father, when Thou gavest, and more loving unto him, when he returned empty. So then in lustful, that is, in darkened affections, is the true distance from Thy face.

Behold, O Lord God, yea, behold patiently as Thou art wont, how carefully the sons of men observe the covenanted rules of letters and syllables received from those who spake before them, neglecting the eternal covenant of everlasting salvation received from Thee. Insomuch, that a teacher or learner of the hereditary laws of pronunciation will more offend men by speaking without the aspirate, of a *"uman* being," in despite of the laws of grammar, than if he, a "human being," hate a "human being" in despite of Thine. As if any enemy could be more hurtful than the hatred with which he is incensed against him; or could wound more deeply him

whom he persecutes, than he wounds his own soul by his enmity.

Assuredly no science of letters can be so innate as the record of conscience, "that he is doing to another what from another he would be loath to suffer." How deep are Thy ways, O God, Thou only great, *that sittest* silent on high and by an unwearied law dispensing penal blindness to lawless desires. In quest of the fame of eloquence, a man standing before a human judge, surrounded by a human throng, declaiming against his enemy with fiercest hatred, will take heed most watchfully, lest, by an error of the tongue, he murder the word "human being"; but takes no heed, lest, through the fury of his spirit, he murder the real human being.

I WAS ENSLAVED TO SIN

This was the world at whose gate unhappy I lay in my boyhood; this the stage where I had feared more to commit a barbarism, than having committed one, to envy those who had not. These things I speak and confess to Thee, my God; for which I had praise from them, whom I then thought it all virtue to please. For I saw not the abyss of vileness, wherein *I was cast away from Thine eyes.* Before them what more foul than I was already, displeasing even such as myself? with innumerable lies deceiving my tutor, my masters, my parents, from love of play, eagerness to see vain shows and restlessness to imitate them! Thefts also I committed, from my parents' cellar and table, enslaved by greediness, or that I might have to give to boys, who sold me their play, which all the while they liked no less than I.

In this play, too, I often sought unfair conquests, conquered myself meanwhile by vain desire of preeminence. And what could I so ill endure, or, when I detected it, upbraided I so fiercely, as that I was doing to others? and for which if, detected, I was upbraided, I chose rather to quarrel than to yield. And is this the innocence of boyhood? Not so, Lord, not so; I cry Thy mercy, O my God. For these very sins, as riper years succeed, these very sins are transferred from tutors and masters, from nuts and balls and sparrows, to magistrates and kings, to gold and manors and slaves, just as severer punishments displace the cane. It was the low stature then of childhood which Thou our King didst commend as an emblem of lowliness, when Thou saidst, *Of such is the kingdom of heaven.*

GIFTS OF GOD

Yet, Lord, to Thee, the Creator and Governor of the universe, most excellent and most good, thanks were due to Thee our God, even hadst Thou destined for me boyhood only. For even then I was, I lived, and felt; and had implanted providence over my well-being—a trace of that mysterious Unity whence I was derived: I guarded by the inward sense the entireness of my senses, and in these minute pursuits, and in my thoughts on things minute, I learnt to delight in truth, I hated to be deceived, had a vigorous memory, was gifted with speech, was soothed by friendship, avoided pain, baseness, ignorance. In so small a creature, what was not wonderful, not admirable?

But all are gifts of my God: it was not I who gave them me; and good these are, and these together are myself. Good, then, is He that made me, and He is my good; and before Him will I exult for every good which of a boy I had. For it was my sin, that not in Him, but in His creatures—myself and others—I sought for pleasures, sublimities, truths, and so fell headlong into sorrows, confusions, errors.

Thanks be to Thee, my joy and my glory and my confidence, my God, thanks be to Thee for Thy gifts; but do Thou preserve them to me. For so wilt Thou preserve me, and those things shall be enlarged and perfected which Thou hast given me, and I myself shall be with Thee, since even to be Thou hast given me.

The Second Book

THE PURPOSE OF MY CONFESSIONS

I WILL NOW CALL to mind my past foulness, and the carnal corruptions of my soul; not because I love them, but that I may love Thee, O my God. For love of Thy love I do it; reviewing my most wicked ways in the very bitterness of my remembrance, that Thou mayest grow sweet unto me (Thou sweetness never failing, Thou blissful and assured sweetness); and gathering me again out of that my dissipation, wherein I was torn piecemeal, while turned from Thee, the One Good, I lost myself among a multiplicity of things. For I even burnt in my youth heretofore, to be satiated in things below; and I dared to grow wild again, with these various and shadowy loves: *my beauty consumed away*, and I stank in Thine eyes; pleasing myself, and desirous to please in the eyes of men.

THE LUST OF THE FLESH

And what was it that I delighted in, but to love, and be beloved? but I kept not the measure of love, of mind to mind, friendship's bright boundary: but out of the muddy concupiscence of the flesh, and the bubblings of youth, mists fumed up which beclouded and overcast my heart, that I could not discern the clear brightness of love from the fog of lustfulness. Both did confusedly boil in me, and hurried my unstayed youth over the precipice of unholy desires, and sunk me in a gulf of flagitiousnesses.

Thy wrath had gathered over me, and I knew it not. I was grown deaf by the clanking of the chain of my mortality, the punishment of the pride of my soul, and I strayed further from Thee, and Thou lettest me alone, and I was tossed about, and wasted, and dissipated, and I boiled over in my fornications, and Thou heldest Thy peace, O Thou my tardy joy! Thou then heldest Thy peace, and I wandered further and further from Thee, into more and more fruitless seed-plots of sorrows, with a proud dejectedness, and a restless weariness.

Oh! that some one had then attempered my disorder, and turned to account the fleeting beauties of these, the extreme points of Thy creation! had put a bound to their pleasureableness, that so the tides of my youth might have cast themselves upon the marriage shore, if they could not be calmed, and kept within the object of a family, as Thy law prescribes, O Lord: who this way formest the offspring of this our death, being able with a gentle hand to blunt the thorns which were excluded from Thy paradise?

For Thy onmipotency is not far from us, even when we be far from Thee. Else ought I more watchfully to have heeded the voice from the clouds: *Nevertheless such shall have trouble in the flesh, but I spare you.* And *it is good for a man not to touch a woman.* And, *he that is unmarried thinketh of the things of the Lord, how he may please the Lord; but he that is married careth for the things of this world, how he may please his wife.*

To these words I should have listened more attentively, and being severed *for the kingdom of heaven's sake,* had more happily awaited Thy embraces; but I, poor wretch, foamed like a troubled sea, following the rushing of my own tide, forsaking Thee, and exceeded all Thy limits; yet I escaped not Thy scourges. For what mortal can? For Thou wert ever with me mercifully rigorous, and besprinkling with most bitter alloy all my unlawful pleasures: that I might seek pleasures without alloy. But where to find such, I could not discover, save in Thee, O Lord, who *teachest by sorrow,* and woundest us, to heal; and killest us, lest we die from Thee.

Where was I, and how far was I exiled from the delights of Thy house, in that sixteeneth year of the age of my flesh, when the madness of lust (to which human shamelessness giveth free license, though unlicensed by Thy laws) took the rule over me, and I resigned myself wholly to it? My friends meanwhile took no care by marriage to save my fall; their only care was that I should learn to speak excellently, and be a persuasive orator.

A BREAK FROM STUDIES

For that year were my studies intermitted; whilst after my return from Madaura (a neighbour city, whither I had journeyed to learn grammar and rhetoric), the expenses for a further journey to Carthage were being provided for me; and that, rather by the resolution than the means of my fa-

ther, who was but a poor freeman of Thagaste. To whom tell I this? not to Thee, my God; but before Thee to mine own kind, even to that small portion of mankind as may light upon these writings of mine. And to what purpose? that whosoever reads this, may think *out of what depths we are to cry unto Thee.* For what is nearer to Thine ears than a confessing heart, and a life of faith?

Who did not extol my father, for that beyond the ability of his means, he would furnish his son with all necessaries for a far journey for his studies' sake? For many abler citizens did no such thing for their children. But yet this same father had no concern how I grew towards Thee, or how chaste I were; so that I were but copious in speech, however barren I were to Thy culture, O God, who art the only true and good Lord of Thy field, my heart.

But while in that my sixteenth year I lived with my parents, leaving all school for a while (a season of idleness being interposed through the narrowness of my parents' fortunes), the briers of unclean desires grew rank over my head, and there was no hand to root them out. When that my father saw me at the baths, now growing towards manhood, and endued with a restless youthfulness, he, as already hence anticipating his descendants, gladly told it to my mother; rejoicing in that tumult of the senses wherein the world forgetteth Thee its Creator, and becometh enamoured of Thy creature, instead of Thyself, through the fumes of that invisible wine of its self-will, turning aside and bowing down to the very basest things.

But in my mother's breast Thou

hadst already begun Thy temple, and the foundation of Thy holy habitation, whereas my father was as yet but a catechumen, and that but recently. She then was startled with a holy fear and trembling; and though I was not as yet baptised, feared for me those crooked ways in which they walk who *turn their back to Thee, and not their face.*

Woe is me! and dare I say that Thou heldest Thy peace, O my God, while I wandered further from Thee? Didst Thou then indeed hold Thy peace to me? And whose but Thine were these words which by my mother, Thy faithful one, Thou sangest in my ears? Nothing whereof sunk into my heart, so as to do it. For she wished, and I remember in private with great anxiety warned me, "not to commit fornication; but especially never to defile another man's wife."

These seemed to me womanish advices, which I should blush to obey. But they were Thine, and I knew it not: and I thought Thou wert silent and that it was she who spake; by whom Thou wert not silent unto me; and in her wast despised by me, her son, *the son of Thy handmaid, Thy servant.* But I knew it not; and ran headlong with such blindness, that amongst my equals I was ashamed of a less shamelessness, when I heard them boast of their flagitiousness, yea, and the more boasting, the more they were degraded: and I took pleasure, not only in the pleasure of the deed, but in the praise.

What is worthy of dispraise but vice? But I made myself worse than I was, that I might not be dispraised; and when in any thing I had not sinned as the abandoned ones, I would say that I had done what I had not done, that I might not seem contemptible in proportion as I was innocent; or of less account, the more chaste.

Behold with what companions I walked the streets of Babylon, and wallowed in the mire thereof, as if in a bed of spices and precious ointments. And that I might cleave the faster to its very centre, the invisible enemy trod me down, and seduced me, for that I was easy to be seduced. Neither did the mother of my flesh (who had now *fled out of the centre of Babylon,* yet went more slowly in the skirts thereof), as she advised me to chastity, so heed what she had heard of me from her husband, as to restrain within the bounds of conjugal affection (if it could not be pared away to the quick) what she felt to be pestilent at present and for the future dangerous. She heeded not this, for she feared lest a wife should prove a clog and hindrance to my hopes. Not those hopes of the world to come, which my mother reposed in Thee; but the hope of learning, which both my parents were too desirous I should attain; my father, because he had next to no thought of Thee, and of me but vain conceits; my mother, because she accounted that those usual courses of learning would not only be no hindrance, but even some furtherance towards attaining Thee. For thus I conjecture, recalling, as well as I may, the disposition of my parents.

The reins, meantime, were slackened to me, beyond all temper of due severity, to spend my time in sport, yea, even unto dissoluteness in whatsoever I affected. And in all was a mist, intercepting from me, O my God, the brightness of Thy truth; and *mine iniquity burst out as from very fatness.*

STEALING PEARS

Theft is punished by Thy Law, O Lord, and the law written in the hearts of men, which iniquity itself effaces not. For what thief will abide a thief? not even a rich thief, one stealing through want. Yet I lusted to thieve, and did it, compelled by no hunger, nor poverty, but through a cloyedness of well-doing, and a pamperedness of iniquity. For I stole that, of which I had enough, and much better. Nor cared I to enjoy what I stole, but joyed in the theft and sin itself.

A pear tree there was near our vineyard, laden with fruit, tempting neither for colour nor taste. To shake and rob this, some lewd young fellows of us went, late one night (having according to our pestilent custom prolonged our sports in the streets till then), and took huge loads, not for our eating, but to fling to the very hogs, having only tasted them. And this, but to do what we liked only, because it was misliked.

Behold my heart, O God, behold my heart, which Thou hadst pity upon in the bottom of the bottomless pit. Now, behold let my heart tell Thee what it sought there, that I should be gratuitously evil, having no temptation to ill, but the ill itself. It was foul, and I loved it; I loved to perish, I loved mine own fault, not that for which I was faulty, but my fault itself, Foul soul, falling from Thy firmament to utter destruction: not seeking aught through the shame, but the shame itself!

WHY MAN SINS

For there is an attractivness in beautiful bodies, in gold and silver, and all things; and in bodily touch, sympathy hath much influence, and each other sense hath his proper object answerably tempered. Worldly honour hath also its grace, and the power of overcoming, and of mastery; whence springs also the thirst for revenge. But yet, to obtain all these, we may not depart from Thee, O Lord, nor decline from Thy law. The life also which here we live hath its own enchantment, through a certain proportion of its own, and a correspondence with all things beautiful here below. Human friendship also is endeared with a sweet tie by reason of the unity formed of many souls.

Upon occasion of all these, and the like, is sin committed, while through an immoderate inclination towards these goods of the lowest order, the better and higher are forsaken—Thou our Lord God, Thy truth, and Thy law. For these lower things have their delights, but not like my God, who made all things; for *in Him doth the righteous delight, and He is the joy of the upright in heart.*

When, then, we ask why a crime was done, we believe it not, unless it appear that there might have been some desire of obtaining some of those which we called lower goods, or a fear of losing them. For they are beautiful and comely; although compared with those higher and beatific goods, they be abject and low. A man hath murdered another; why? he loved his wife or his estate; or would rob for his own livelihood; or feared to lose some such things by him; or, wronged, was on fire to be revenged. Would any commit murder upon no cause, delighted simply in murdering? who would believe it? for as for that furious and savage man, of whom it is said that he was gratuitously evil and cruel, yet is the cause assigned; "lest" (saith he) "through idleness hand or heart should grow inactive." And to what end? that, through that practice of guilt, he might, having taken the city, attain to honours, empire, riches, and be freed from fear of the laws, and his embarrassments from domestic needs, and consciousness of villainies. So then, not even Catiline himself loved his own villainies, but something else, for whose sake he did them.

THE NATURE OF SIN

What then did wretched I so love in thee, thou theft of mine, thou deed of darkness, in that sixteenth year of my age? Lovely thou wert not, because thou wert theft. But art thou any thing, that thus I speak to thee? Fair were the pears we stole, because they were Thy creation, Thou fairest of all, Creator of all, Thou good God; God, the sovereign good and my true good. Fair were those pears, but not them did my wretched soul desire; for I had store of better, and those I gathered, only that I might steal.

For, when gathered, I flung them away, my only feast therein being my own sin, which I was pleased to enjoy. For if aught of those pears came within my mouth, what sweetened it was the sin. And now, O Lord my God, I enquire what in that theft delighted me; and behold it hath no loveliness; I mean not such loveliness as in justice and wisdom; nor such as is in the mind and memory, and senses, and animal life of man; nor yet as the stars are glorious and beautiful in their orbs; or the earth, or sea, full of embryo-life, replacing by its birth that which decayeth; nay, nor even that false and shadowy beauty which belongeth to deceiving vices.

For so doth pride imitate exaltedness; whereas Thou alone art God exalted over all. Ambition, what seeks it, but honours and glory? whereas Thou alone art to be honoured above all, and glorious for evermore. The cruelty of the great would fain be feared; but who is to be feared but God alone, out of whose power what can be wrested or withdrawn? when, or where, or whither, or by whom? The tendernesses of the wanton would fain be counted love: yet is nothing more tender than Thy charity; nor is aught loved more healthfully than that Thy truth, bright and beautiful above all. Curiosity makes semblance of a desire of knowledge; whereas Thou supremely knowest all. Yea, ignorance and foolishness itself is cloaked under the name of simplicity and uninjuriousness; because nothing is found more single than Thee: and what less injurious, since they are his own works which injure the sinner?

Yea, sloth would fain be at rest; but what stable rest besides the Lord? Luxury affects to be called plenty and abundance; but Thou art the fulness and never-failing plenteousness of incorruptible pleasures. Prodigality presents a shadow of liberality: but Thou art the most overflowing Giver of all good. Covetousness would possess many things: and Thou possessest all things. Envy disputes for excellency; what more excellent than Thou? Anger seeks revenge: who revenges more justly than Thou? Fear startles at things unwonted and sudden, which endanger things beloved, and takes forethought for their safety; but to Thee what unwonted or sudden, or who separateth from Thee what Thou lovest? Or where but with Thee is unshaken safety? Grief pines away for things lost, the delight of its desires; because it would have nothing taken from it, as nothing can from Thee.

Thus doth the soul commit fornication, when she turns from Thee, seeking without Thee, what she findeth not pure and untainted, till she returns to Thee. Thus all pervertedly imitate Thee, who remove far from Thee, and lift themselves up against Thee. But even by thus imitating Thee, they imply Thee to be the Creator of all nature; whence there is no place whither altogether to retire from Thee. What then did I love in that theft? and wherein did I even corruptly and pervertedly imitate my Lord? Did I wish even by stealth to do contrary to Thy law, because by power I could not, so that being a prisoner, I might mimic a maimed liberty by doing with impunity things unpermitted me, a darkened likeness of Thy Omnipotency? Behold, Thy servant, fleeing from his Lord, and obtaining a shadow. O rottenness, O monstrousness of life, and depth of death! could I like what I might not, only because I might not?

GOD'S GRACE AND MERCY EXTOLLED

What shall I render unto the Lord, that, whilst my memory recalls these things, my soul is not affrighted at them? *I will love Thee, O Lord, and thank Thee, and confess unto Thy name;* because Thou hast forgiven me these so great and heinous deeds of mine. To Thy grace I ascribe it, and to Thy mercy, that Thou hast melted away my sins as it were ice. To Thy grace I ascribe also whatsoever I have not done of evil; for what might I not have done, who even loved a sin for its own sake? Yea, all I confess to have been forgiven me; both what evils I committed by own wilfulness, and what by Thy guidance I committed not.

What man is he, who, weighing his own infirmity, dares to ascribe his purity and innocency to his own strength; that so he should love Thee the less, as if he had less needed Thy mercy, whereby Thou remittest sins to those that turn to Thee? For whosoever, called by Thee, followed Thy voice, and avoided those things which he reads me recalling and confessing of myself, let him not scorn me, who being sick was cured by that Physician, through whose aid it was that he was not, or rather was less, sick: and for this let him love Thee as much, yea and more; since by whom he sees me to have been recovered from such deep consumption of sin, by Him he sees himself to have been from the like consumption of sin preserved.

MY LOVE FOR SIN

What fruit had I then (wretched man!) *in those things, of the remembrance whereof I am now ashamed?* Especially, in that theft which I loved for the theft's sake; and it too was nothing, and therefore the more miserable I, who loved it. Yet alone I had not done it: such was I then, I remember, alone I had never done it. I loved then in it also the company of the accomplices, with whom I did it? I did not then love nothing else but the theft, yea rather I did love nothing else; for that circumstance of the company was also nothing.

What is, in truth? who can teach me, save He that enlighteneth my heart, and discovereth its dark corners? What is it which hath come into my mind to enquire, and discuss, and consider? For had I then loved the pears I stole, and wished to enjoy them, I might have done it alone, had the bare commission of the theft sufficed to attain my pleasure; nor needed I have inflamed the itching of my desires by the excitment of accomplices. But since my pleasure was not in those pears, it was in the offence itself, which the company of fellow-sinners occasioned.

EVIL COMPANIONS

What then was this feeling? For of a truth it was too foul: and woe was me, who had it. But yet what was it? *Who can understand his errors?* It was the sport, which as it were tickled our hearts, that we beguiled those who little thought what we were doing, and much disliked it. Why then was my delight of such sort that I did it not alone? Because none doth ordinarily laugh alone? ordinarily no one; yet laughter sometimes masters men alone and singly when no one whatever is with them, if any thing very ludicrous presents itself to their senses or mind. Yet I had not done this alone; alone I had never done it. Behold my God, before Thee, the vivid remembrance of my soul; alone, I had never committed that theft wherein what I stole pleased me not, but that I stole; nor had it alone liked me to do it, nor had I done it.

O friendship too unfriendly! thou incomprehensible inveigler of the soul, thou greediness to do mischief out of mirth and wantonness, thou thirst of others' loss, without lust of my own gain or revenge: but when it is said, "Let's go, Let's do it," we are ashamed not to be shameless.

I STRAYED FROM GOD

Who can disentangle that twisted and intricate knottiness? Foul is it: I hate to think on it, to look on it. But Thee I long for, O Righteousness and Innocency, beautiful and comely to all pure eyes, and of a satisfaction unsating. With Thee is rest entire, and life imperturbable. Whoso enters into Thee, *enters into the joy of his Lord:* and shall not fear, and shall do excellently in the All-Excellent. I sank away from Thee, and I wandered, O my God, too much astray from Thee my stay, in these days of my youth, and I became to myself a barren land.

The Third Book

I MOVE TO CARTHAGE

TO CARTHAGE I CAME, where there sang all around me in my ears a cauldron of unholy loves. I loved not yet, yet I loved to love, and out of a deep-seated want, I hated myself for wanting not. I sought what I might love, in love with loving, and safety I hated, and a way without snares. For within me was a famine of that inward food, Thyself, my God; yet, through that famine I was not hungered; but was without all longing for incorruptible sustenance, not because filled therewith, but the more empty, the more I loathed it. For this cause my soul was sickly and full of sores, it miserably cast itself forth, desiring to be scraped by the touch of objects of sense. Yet if these had not a soul, they would not be objects of love.

To love then, and to be beloved, was sweet to me; but more, when I obtained to enjoy the person I loved. I defiled, therefore, the spring of friendship with the filth of concupiscence, and I beclouded its brightness with the hell of lustfulness; and thus foul and unseemly, I would fain, through exceeding vanity, be fine and courtly. I fell headlong then into the love wherein I longed to be ensnared. My God, my Mercy, with how much gall didst Thou out of Thy great goodness besprinkle for me that sweetness? For I was both beloved, and secretly arrived at the bond of enjoying; and was with joy fettered with sorrow-bringing bonds, that I might be scourged with the iron burning rods of jealousy, and suspicion, and fears, and angers, and quarrels.

THE APPEAL OF TRAGEDIES

Stage-plays also carried me away, full of images of my miseries, and of fuel to my fire. Why is it, that man desires to be made sad, beholding doleful and tragical things, which yet himself would by no means suffer? yet he desires as a spectator to feel sorrow at them, and this very sorrow is his pleasure. What is this but a miserable madness? for a man is the more affected with these actions, the less free he is from such affections. Howsoever, when he suffers in his own person, it used to be styled misery; when he compassionates others, then it is mercy.

But what sort of compassion is this for feigned and scenical passions? for the auditor is not called on to relieve, but only to grieve: and he applauds the actor of these fictions the more, the more he grieves. And if the calamities of those persons (whether of old times, or mere fiction) be so acted, that the spectator is not moved to tears, he goes away disgusted and criticising; but if he be moved to passion, he stays intent, and weeps for joy.

Are griefs then too loved? Verily all desire joy. Or whereas no man likes to be miserable, is he yet pleased to be merciful? which because it cannot be without passion, for this reason alone

31

are passions loved? This also springs from that vein of friendship. But whither goes that vein? whither flows it? wherefore runs it into that torrent of pitch bubbling forth those monstrous tides of foul lustfulness, into which it is wilfully changed and transformed, being of its own will precipitated and corrupted from its heavenly clearness? Shall compassion then be put away? by no means. Be griefs then sometimes loved. But beware of uncleanness, O my soul, under the guardianship of my God, *the God of our fathers, who is to be praised and exalted above all for ever,* beware of uncleanness. For I have not now ceased to pity; but then in the theatres I rejoiced with lovers when they wickedly enjoyed one another, although this was imaginary only in the play. And when they lost one another, as if very compassionate, I sorrowed with them, yet had my delight in both.

But now I much more pity him that rejoiceth in his wickedness, than him who is thought to suffer hardship, by hissing some pernicious pleasure, and the loss of some miserable felicity. This certainly is the truer mercy, but in it grief delights not. For though he that grieves for the miserable, be commended for his office of charity; yet had he, who is genuinely compassionate, rather there were nothing for him to grieve for. For if good will be ill willed (which can never be), then may he, who truly and sincerely commiserates, wish there might be some miserable, that he might commiserate. Some sorrow may then be allowed, none loved. For thus dost Thou, O Lord God, who lovest souls far more purely than we, and hast more incorruptibly pity

on them, yet are wounded with no sorrowfulness. *And who is sufficient for these things?*

But I, miserable, then loved to grieve, and sought out what to grieve at, when in another's and that feigned and personated misery, that acting best pleased me, and attracted me the most vehemently, which drew tears from me. What marvel that an unhappy sheep straying from Thy flock, and impatient of Thy keeping, I became infected with a foul disease? And hence the love of griefs; not such as should sink deep into me; for I loved not to suffer, what I loved to look on; but such as upon hearing their fictions should lightly scratch the surface; upon which, as on envenomed nails, followed inflamed swelling, impostumes, and a putrified sore. My life being such, was it life, O my God?

A SACRILEGIOUS CURIOSITY

And Thy faithful mercy hovered over me afar. Upon how grievous iniquities consumed I myself, pursuing a sacrilegious curiosity, that having forsaken Thee, it might bring me to the treacherous abyss, and the beguiling service of devils, to whom I sacrificed my evil actions, and in all these things Thou didst scourge me! I dared even, while Thy solemnities were celebrated within the walls of Thy church, to desire, and to compass a business deserving death for its fruits, for which Thou scourgedst me with grievous punishments, through nothing to my fault, O Thou my exceeding mercy, my God, my refuge from those terrible destroyers, among whom I wandered with a stiff neck, withdrawing further from Thee, loving mine own ways, and not Thine; loving a vagrant liberty.

Those studies also, which were accounted commendable, had a view to excelling in the courts of litigation; the more bepraised, the craftier. Such is men's blindness, glorying even in their blindness. And now I was chief in the rhetoric school, whereat I joyed proudly, and I swelled with arrogancy, though (Lord, Thou knowest) far quieter and altogether removed from the subvertings of those "Subverters" (for this ill-omened and devilish name was the very badge of gallantry) among whom I lived, with a shameless shame that I was not even as they.

With them I lived, and was sometimes delighted with their friendship, whose doings I ever did abhor—*i.e.*, their "subvertings," wherewith they wantonly persecuted the modesty of strangers, which they disturbed by a gratuitous jeering, feeding thereon their malicious mirth. Nothing can be liker the very actions of devils than these. What then could they be more truly called than "subverters"? themselved subverted and altogether perverted first, the deceiving spirits secretly deriding and seducing them, wherein themselves delight to jeer at, and deceive others.

I STUDIED BOOKS OF ELOQUENCE

Among such as these, in that unsettled age of mine, learned I books of eloquence, wherein I desired to be eminent, out of damnable and vainglorious end, a joy in human vanity. In the ordinary course of study, I fell upon a certain book of Cicero, whose speech almost all admire, not so his heart. This book of his contains an exhorta-

tion to philosophy, and is called *Hortensius*. But this book altered my affections, and turned my prayers to Thyself, O Lord; and made me have other purposes and desires.

Every vain hope at once became worthless to me; and I longed with an incredibly burning desire for an immortality of wisdom, and began now to arise, that I might return to Thee. For not to sharpen my tongue (which thing I seemed to be purchasing with my mother's allowances, in that my nineteenth year, my father being dead two years before), not to sharpen my tongue did I employ that book; nor did it infuse into me its style, but its matter.

How did I burn then, my God, how did I burn to re-mount from earthly things to Thee, nor knew I what Thou wouldst do with me? For with Thee is wisdom. But the love of wisdom is in Greek called "philosophy," with which that book inflamed me. Some there be that seduce through philosophy, under a great, and smooth, and honourable name colouring and disguising their own errors: and almost all who in that and former ages were such, are in that book censured and set forth: there also is made plain that wholesome advice of Thy Spirit, by Thy good and devout servant: *Beware lest any man spoil you through philosophy and vain deceit, after the tradition of men, after the rudiments of the world, and not after Christ. For in Him dwelleth all the fulness of the Godhead bodily.*

And since at that time (Thou, O light of my heart, knowest) Apostolic Scripture was not known to me, I was delighted with that exhortation, so far only, that I was thereby strongly roused, and kindled, and inflamed to love, and seek, and obtain, and hold, and embrace not this or that sect, but wisdom itself whatever it were; and this alone checked me thus enkindled, that the name of Christ was not in it. For this name, according to Thy mercy, O Lord, this name of my Saviour Thy Son, had my tender heart, even with my mother's milk, devoutly drunk in, and deeply treasured; and whatsoever was without that name, though never so learned, polished, or true, took not entire hold of me.

I STUDIED THE SCRIPTURES

I resolved then to bend my mind to the holy Scriptures, that I might see what they were. But behold, I see a thing not understood by the proud, nor laid open to children, lowly in access, in its recesses lofty, and veiled with mysteries; and I was not such as could enter into it, or stoop my neck to follow its steps. For not as I now speak, did I feel when I turned to those Scriptures; but they seemed to me unworthy to be compared to the stateliness of Tully: for my swelling pride shrunk from their lowliness, nor could my sharp wit pierce the interior thereof. Yet were they such as would grow up in a little one. But I disdained to be a little one; and, swollen with pride, took myself to be a great one.

I KEPT COMPANY WITH EVIL MEN

Therefore I fell among men proudly doting, exceeding carnal and prating, in whose mouths were the snares of the Devil, limed with the mixture of the syllables of Thy name, and of our Lord Jesus Christ, and of the Holy Ghost, the Paraclete, our Comforter.

These names departed not out of their mouth, but so far forth as the sound only and the noise of the tongue, for the heart was void of truth. Yet they cried out "Truth, Truth," and spake much thereof to me, yet *it was not in them:* but they spake falsehood, not of Thee only (who truly art Truth), but even of those elements of this world, Thy creatures. And I indeed ought to have passed by even philosophers who spake truth concerning them, for love of Thee, my Father, supremely good, Beauty of all things beautiful. O Truth, Truth, how inwardly did even then the marrow of my soul pant after Thee, when they often and diversely, and in many and huge books, echoed of Thee to me, though it was but an echo?

And these were the dishes wherein to me, hungering after Thee, they, instead of Thee, served up the Sun and Moon, beautiful works of Thine, but yet Thy works, not Thyself, no nor Thy first works. For Thy spiritual works are before these corporeal works, celestial though they be, and shining. But I hungered and thirsted not even after those first works of Thine, but after Thee Thyself, the Truth, *in whom is no variableness, neither shadow of turning:* yet they still set before me in those dishes, glittering fantasies, than which better were it to love this very sun (which is real to our sight at least), than those fantasies which by our eyes deceive our mind.

Yet because I thought them to be Thee, I fed thereon; not eagerly, for Thou didst not in them taste to me as Thou art; for Thou wast not these emptinesses, nor was I nourished by them, but exhausted rather. Food in sleep shows very like our food awake; yet are not those asleep nourished by it, for they are asleep. But those were not even any way like to Thee, as Thou hast now spoken to me; for those were corporeal fantasies, false bodies, than which these true bodies, celestial or terrestrial, which with our fleshly sight we behold, are far more certain: these things the beasts and birds discern as well as we, and they are more certain than when we fancy them. And again, we do with more certainty fancy them, than by them conjecture other vaster and infinite bodies which have no being.

Such empty husks was I then fed on; and was not fed. But Thou, my soul's Love, *in looking for whom I fail*, that I may become strong, art neither those bodies which we see, though in heaven; nor those which we see not there; for Thou hast created them, nor dost Thou account them among the chiefest of Thy works. How far then art Thou from those fantasies of mine, fantasies of bodies which altogether are not, than which the images of those bodies, which are, are far more certain, and more certain still the bodies themselves, which yet Thou art not; no, nor the soul, which is the life of the bodies. So then, better and more certain is the life of the bodies than the bodies. But Thou art the life of souls, the life of lives, having life in Thyself; and changest not, life of my soul.

Where then wert Thou then to me, and how far from me? Far verily was I straying from Thee, barred from the very husks of the swine, whom with husks I fed. For how much better are the fables of poets and grammarians than these snares? For verses, and poems, and "Medea flying," are more profitable truly than these men's five elements, variously disguised, answering to five dens of darkness which have no being, yet slay the believer. For verses and poems I can turn to true food, and "Medea flying," though I did sing, I maintained not: though I heard it sung, I believed not; but those things I did believe.

Woe, woe, by what steps was I brought down to *the depths of hell!* toiling and turmoiling through want of Truth, since I sought after Thee, my God (to Thee I confess it, who hadst mercy on me, not as yet confessing), not according to the understanding by the mind, wherein Thou willedst that I should excel the beasts, but according to the sense of the flesh. But Thou wert more inward to me, than my most inward part; and higher than my highest. I lighted upon that bold woman, *simple and knoweth nothing*, shadowed out in Solomon, *sitting at the door, and saying, Eat ye bread of secrecies willingly, and drink ye stolen waters which are sweet:* she seduced me, because she found my soul dwelling abroad in the eye of my flesh, and ruminating on such food as through it I had devoured.

THE SOURCE OF EVIL

For other than this, that which really is I knew not; and was, as it were through sharpness of wit, persuaded to assent to foolish deceivers, when they asked me, "whence is evil?" "is God bounded by a bodily shape, and has hairs and nails?" "are they to be esteemed righteous who had many wives at once, and did kill men, and sacrificed living creatures?" At which I, in my ignorance, was much troubled, and departing from the truth, seemed to myself to be making towards it; because as yet I knew not that evil was nothing but a privation of good, until at last a thing ceases altogether to be; which how should I see, the sight of whose eyes reached only to bodies, and of my mind to a phantasm?

And I knew not *God to be a Spirit*, not one who hath parts extended in length and breadth, or whose being was bulk; for every bulk is less in a part than the whole: and if it be infinite, it must be less in such part as is defined by a certain space, than in its infinitude; and so is not wholly every where, as Spirit, as God. And what that should be in us, by which we were like to God, and might in Scripture be rightly said to be *after the image of God*, I was altogether ignorant.

Nor knew I that true inward righteousness which judgeth not according to custom, but out of the most rightful law of God Almighty, whereby the ways of places and times were disposed according to those times and places; itself meantime being the same always and every where, one thing in one place, and another in another; according to which Abraham, and Isaac, and Jacob, and Moses, and David, were righteous, and all those commended by the mouth of God; but were judged unrighteous by silly men, *judging out of man's judgment*, and measuring by their own petty habits, the moral habits of the whole human race. As if in an armory, one ignorant what were adapted to each part should cover his head with greaves, or seek to be shod with a helmet, and complain that they fitted not: or as if on a day when business is publicly stopped in the afternoon, one were angered at not being allowed to keep open shop, because he had been in the forenoon; or when in one house he observeth some servant take a thing in his hand, which the butler is not suffered to meddle with; or something permitted out of doors, which is forbidden in the dining-room; and should be angry, that in one house, and one family, the same thing is not allotted every where, and to all. Even such are they who are fretted to hear something to have been lawful for righteous men formerly, which now is not; or that God, for certain temporal respects, commanded them one thing, and these another, obeying both the same righteousness: whereas they see, in one man, and one day, and one house, different things to be fit for different members, and a thing formerly lawful, after a certain time not so; in one corner permitted or commanded, but in another rightly forbidden and punished.

Is justice therefore various or mutable? No, but the times, over which it presides, flow not evenly, because they are times. But men whose *days are few upon the earth*, for that by their senses they cannot harmonise the causes of things in former ages and other nations, which they had no experience of, with these which they have experience of, whereas in one and the same body, day, or family, they easily see what is fitting for each member, and season, part, and person; to the one they take exceptions, to the other they submit.

These things I then knew not, nor

observed; they struck my sight on all sides, and I saw them not. I indited verses, in which I might not place every foot every where, but differently in different metres; nor even in any one metre the self-same foot in all places. Yet the art itself, by which I indited, had not different principles for these different cases, but comprised all in one. Still I saw not how that rightousness, which good and holy men obeyed, did far more excellently and sublimely contain in one all those things which God commanded, and in no part varied; although in varying times it prescribed not every thing at once, but apportioned and enjoined what was fit for each. And I, in my blindness, censured the holy Fathers, not only wherein they made use of things present as God commanded and inspired them, but also wherein they were foretelling things to come, as God was revealing in them.

LOVING GOD

Can it at any time or place be unjust *to love God with all his heart, with all his soul, and with all his mind; and his neighbour as himself?* Therefore are those foul offences which be against nature, to be every where and at all times detested and punished: such as were those of the men of Sodom; which should all nations commit, they should all stand guilty of the same crime, by the law of God, which hath not so made men that they should so abuse one another. For even that intercourse which should be between God and us is violated, when that same nature, of which He is Author, is polluted by perversity of lust. But those actions which are offences against the

customs of men, are to be avoided according to the customs severally prevailing; so that a thing agreed upon, and confirmed, by custom or law of any city or nation, may not be violated at the lawless pleasure of any, whether native or foreigner. For any part which harmoniseth not with its whole, is offensive.

But when God commands a thing to be done, against the customs or compact of any people, though it were never by them done heretofore, it is to be done; and if intermitted, it is to be restored; and if never ordained, is now to be ordained. For lawful if it be for a king, in the state which he reigns over, to command that which no one before him, nor he himself heretofore, had commanded, and to obey him cannot be against the common weal of the state (nay, it were against it if he were not obeyed, for to obey princes is a general compact of human society); how much more unhesitatingly ought we to obey God, in all which He commands, the Ruler of all His creatures! For as among the powers in man's society, the greater authority is obeyed in preference to the lesser, so must God above all.

So in acts of violence, where there is a wish to hurt, whether by reproach or injury; and these either for revenge, as one enemy against another; or for some profit belonging to another, as the robber to the traveller; or to avoid some evil, as towards one who is feared; or through envy, as one less fortunate to one more so, or one well thriven in any thing, to him whose being on a par with himself he fears, or grieves at, or for the mere pleasure at another's pain, as spectators of gladiators, or deriders and mockers of others. These be the heads of iniquity, which spring from the lust of the flesh, of the eye, or of rule, either singly, or two combined, or all together; and so do men live ill against the three, and seven, that psaltery *of ten strings,* Thy Ten Commandments, O God, most high, and most sweet. But what foul offences can there be against Thee, who canst be defiled? or what acts of violence against Thee, who canst not be harmed?

But Thou avengest what men commit against themselves, seeing also when they sin against Thee, they do wickedly against their own souls, and *iniquity gives itself the lie,* by corrupting and perverting their nature, which Thou hast created and ordained, or by an immoderate use of things allowed, or in *burning* in things unallowed, *to that use which is against nature;* or are found guilty, raging with heart and tongue against Thee, *kicking against the pricks;* or when, bursting the pale of human society, they boldly joy in self-willed combinations or divisions, according as they have any object to gain or subject of offence. And these things are done when Thou art forsaken, O Fountain of Life, who art the only and true Creator and Governor of the Universe, and by a self-willed pride, any one false thing is selected therefrom and loved.

So then by a humble devoutness we return to Thee; and Thou cleansest us from our evil habits, and art merciful to their sins who confess, and *hearest the groaning of the prisoner,* and loosest us from the chains which we made for ourselves, if we lift not up against Thee the horns of an unreal liberty,

suffering the loss of all through covetousness of more, by loving more our own private good than Thee, the Good of all.

MAN'S WAYS ARE NOT GOD'S WAYS

Amidst these offences of foulness and violence, and so many iniquities, are sins of men, who are on the whole making proficiency; which by those that judge rightly, are, after the rule of perfection, discommended, yet the persons commended, upon hope of future fruit, as in the green blade of growing corn. And there are some, resembling offences of foulness or violence, which yet are no sins; because they offend neither Thee, our Lord God, nor human society; when, namely, things fitting for a given period are obtained for the service of life, and we know not whether out of a lust of having; or when things are, for the sake of correction, by constituted authority punished, and we know not whether out of a lust of hurting. Many an action then which in men's sight is disapproved, is by Thy testimony approved; and many, by men praised are (Thou being witness) condemned: because the show of the action, and the mind of the doer, and the unknown exigency of the period, severally vary.

But when Thou on a sudden commandest an unwonted and unthought of thing, yea, although Thou hast sometime forbidden it, and still for the time hidest the reason of Thy command, and it be against the ordinance of some society of men, who doubts but it is to be done, seeing that society of men is just which serves Thee? But blessed are they who know Thy commands! For all things were done by

Thy servants; either to show forth something needful for the present, or to foreshow things to come.

I SCOFFED AT GOD'S SERVANTS

These things I being ignorant of, scoffed at those Thy holy servants and prophets. And what gained I by scoffing at them, but to be scoffed at by Thee, being insensibly and step by step drawn on to those follies, as to believe that a fig-tree wept when it was plucked, and the tree, its mother, shed milky tears? Which fig notwithstanding (plucked by some other's, not his own, guilt) had some (Manichæn) saint eaten, and mingled with his bowels, he should breathe out of it angels, yea, there shall burst forth particles of divinity, at every moan or groan in his prayer, which particles of the most high and true God had remained bound in that fig, unless they had been set at liberty by the teeth or belly of some "Elect" saint!

And I, miserable, believed that more mercy was to be shown to the fruits of the earth than men, for whom they were created. For if any one an hungered, not a Manichæn, should ask for any, that morsel would seem as it were condemned to capital punishment, which should be given him.

MY MOTHER GRIEVED FOR ME

And Thou *sentest Thine hand from above*, and drewest my soul out of that profound darkness, my mother, thy faithful one, weeping to Thee for me, more than mothers weep the bodily deaths of their children. For she, by that faith and spirit which she had from Thee, discerned the death wherein I lay, and Thou heardest her, O Lord; Thou heardest her, and despisedst not her tears, when streaming down, they watered the ground under her eyes in every place where she prayed, yea Thou heardest her.

For whence was that dream whereby Thou comfortedst her; so that she allowed me to live with her, and to eat at the same table in the house, which she had begun to shrink from, abhorring and detesting the blasphemies of my error? For she saw herself standing on a certain wooden rule, and a shining youth coming towards her, cheerful and smiling upon her, herself grieving, and overwhelmed with grief. But he having (in order to instruct, as is their wont not to be instructed) enquired of her the causes of her grief and daily tears, and she answering that she was bewailing my perdition, he bade her rest contented, and told her to look and observe, "That where she was, there was I also." And when she looked, she saw me standing by her in the same rule. Whence was this, but that Thine ears were towards her heart? O Thou Good omnipotent, who so carest for every one of us, as if Thou caredst for him only; and so for all, as if they were but one!

Whence was this also, that when she had told me this vision, and I would fain bend it to mean, "That she rather should not despair of being one day what I was"; she presently, without any hesitation, replies: "No; for it was not told me that, 'where he, there thou also'; but 'where thou, there he also'"? I confess to Thee, O Lord, that to the best of my remembrance (and I have oft spoken of this), that Thy answer, through my waking mother,—that she was not perplexed by the plausibility of my false interpretation, and so quickly saw what was to be seen, and which I certainly had not perceived before she spake—even then moved me more than the dream itself, by which a joy to the holy woman, to be fulfilled so long after, was, for the consolation of her present anguish, so long before foresignified.

For almost nine years passed, in which I wallowed in the mire of that deep pit, and the darkness of falsehood, often assaying to rise, but dashed down the more grievously. All which time that chaste, godly and sober widow (such as Thou lovest), now more cheered with hope, yet no whit relaxing in her weeping and mourning, ceased not at all hours of her devotions to bewail my case unto Thee. And her *prayers entered into Thy presence,* and yet Thou sufferest me to be yet involved and reinvolved in that darkness.

MY MOTHER'S VISION

Thou gavest her meantime another answer, which I call to mind; for much I pass by, hasting to those things which more press me to confess unto Thee, and much I do not remember. Thou gavest her then another answer, by a Priest of Thine, a certain Bishop brought up in Thy Church, and well studied in Thy books. Whom when

this woman had entreated to vouchsafe to converse with me, refute my errors, unteach me ill things, and teach me good things (for this he was wont to do, when he found persons fitted to receive it), he refused, wisely, as I afterwards perceived. For he answered, that I was yet unteachable, being puffed up with the novelty of that heresy, and had already perplexed divers unskilful persons with captious questions, as she had told him: "but let him alone a while" (saith he), "only pray God for him, he will of himself by reading find what that error is, and how great its impiety."

At the same time he told her, how himself, when a little one, had by his seduced mother been consigned over to the Manichees, and had not only read, but frequently copied out almost all, their books, and had (without any argument or proof from any one) seen how much that sect was to be avoided; and had avoided it. Which when he had said, and she would not be satisfied, but urged him more, with entreaties and many tears, that he would see me and discourse with me; he, a little displeased at her importunity, saith, "Go thy ways, and God bless thee, for it is not possible that the son of these tears should perish." Which answer she took (as she often mentioned in her conversations with me) as if it had sounded from Heaven.

The Fourth Book

FOR THIS SPACE of nine years then (from my nineteenth year to my eight-and-twentieth) we lived seduced and seducing, deceived and deceiving, in divers lusts; openly, by sciences which they call liberal; secretly, with a false-named religion; here proud, there superstitious, every where vain! Here, hunting after the emptiness of popular praise, down even to theatrical applauses, and poetic prizes, and strifes for grassy garlands, and the follies of shows, and the intemperance of desires. There, desiring to be cleansed from these defilements, by carrying food to those who were called "elect" and "holy," out of which, in the workhouse of their stomachs, they should forge for us Angels and Gods, by whom we might be cleansed.

These things did I follow, and practise with my friends, deceived by me, and with me. Let the arrogant mock me, and such as have not been, to their soul's health, stricken and cast down by Thee, O my God; but I would still confess to Thee mine own shame in Thy praise. Suffer me, I beseech Thee, and give me grace to go over in my present remembrance the wanderings of my forepassed time, and *to offer unto Thee the sacrifice of thanksgiving.* For what am I to myself without Thee, but a guide to mine own downfall? or what am I even at the best, but an infant sucking the milk Thou givest, and feeding upon Thee, *the food that perishest not?* But what sort of man is any man, seeing he is but a man? Let now the strong and the mighty laugh at us, but let us *poor and needy* confess unto Thee.

I WAS A TEACHER OF RHETORIC

In those years I taught rhetoric, and, overcome by cupidity, made sale of a loquacity to overcome by. Yet I preferred (Lord, Thou knowest) honest scholars (as they are accounted), and these I, without artifice, taught artifices, not to be practised against the life of the guiltless, though sometimes for the life of the guilty. And Thou, O God, from afar perceivedst me stumbling in that slippery course, and amid much smoke sending out some sparks of faithfulness, which I showed in that my guidance of *such as loved vanity,* and *sought after leasing,* myself their companion.

In those years I had one, not in that which is called lawful marriage, but whom I had found out in a wayward passion, void of understanding; yet but one, remaining faithful even to her; in whom I in my own case experienced what difference there is betwixt the self-restraint of the marriage-covenant, for the sake of issue, and the bargain of a lustful love, where children are born against their parents' will, although, once born, they constrain love.

I remember also, that when I had settled to enter the lists for a theatrical prize, some wizard asked me what I would give him to win; but I, detesting and abhorring such foul mysteries, answered, "Though the garland were of imperishable gold, I would not suffer a fly to be killed to gain me it." For he was to kill some living creatures in his sacrifices, and by those honours to invite the devils to favour me. But this ill also I rejected, not out of a pure love for Thee, O God of my heart; for I knew not how to love Thee, who knew not how to conceive aught beyond a material brightness. And doth not a soul sighing after such fictions, commit fornication against Thee, trust in things unreal, and *feed the wind?* Still I would not forsooth have sacrifices offered to devils for me, to whom I was sacrificing myself by that superstition. For what else is it *to feed the wind*, but to feed them, that is, by going astray to become their pleasure and derision?

I CONSULTED ASTROLOGERS

Those imposters then, whom they style Mathematicians, I consulted without scruple; because they seemed to use no sacrifice, nor to pray to any spirit for their divinations: which art, however, Christian and true piety consistently rejects and condemns. For, *it is a good thing to confess unto Thee, and to say, Have mercy upon me, heal my soul, for I have sinned against Thee;* and not to abuse Thy mercy for a license to sin, but to remember the Lord's words, *Behold, thou art made whole, sin no more, lest a worse thing come unto thee.* All which wholesome advice they labour to destroy, saying, "The cause of thy sin is inevitably determined in heaven"; and "This did

Venus, or Saturn, or Mars": that man, forsooth, flesh and blood, and proud corruption, might be blameless; while the Creator and Ordainer of heaven and the stars is to bear the blame. And who is He but our God? the very sweetness and well-spring of righteousness, who *renderest to every man according to his works: and a broken and contrite heart wilt Thou not despise.*

There was in those days a wise man, very skilful in physic, and renowned therein, who had with his own proconsular hand put the Agonistic garland upon my distempered head, but not as a physician: for this disease Thou only curest, *who resistest the proud, and givest grace to the humble.* But didst Thou fail me even by that old man, or forbear to heal my soul? For having become more acquainted with him, and hanging assiduously and fixedly on his speech (for though in simple terms, it was vivid, lively, and earnest), when he had gathered by my discourse that I was given to the books of nativity-casters, he kindly and fatherly advised me to cast them away, and not fruitlessly bestow a care and diligence, necessary for useful things, upon these vanities; saying, that he had in his earliest years studied that art, so as to make it the profession whereby he should live, and that, understanding Hippocrates, he could soon have understood such a study as this; and yet he had given it over, and taken to physic, for no other reason but that he found it utterly false; and he, a grave man, would not get his living by deluding people. "But thou," saith he, "hast rhetoric to maintain thyself by, so that thou followest this of free choice, not of necessity: the more then oughtest thou to give me credit herein, who laboured to acquire it so perfectly as to get my living by it alone."

Of whom when I had demanded, how then could many true things be foretold by it, he answered me (as he could) "that the force of chance, diffused throughout the whole order of things, brought this about. For if when a man by haphazard opens the pages of some poet, who sang and thought of something wholly different, a verse oftentimes fell out, wondrously agreeable to the present business: it were not to be wondered at, if out of the soul of man, unconscious what takes place in it, by some higher instinct an answer should be given, by hap, not by art, corresponding to the business and actions of the demander."

And thus much, either from or through him, Thou conveyedst to me, and tracedst in my memory, what I might hereafter examine for myself. But at that time neither he, nor my dearest Nebridius, a youth singularly good and of a holy fear, who derided the whole body of divination, could persuade me to cast it aside, the authority of the authors swaying me yet more, and as yet I had found no certain proof (such as I sought) whereby it might without all doubt appear, that what had been truly foretold by those consulted was the result of haphazard, not of the art of the star-gazers.

THE DEATH OF A FRIEND

In those years when I first began to teach rhetoric in my native town, I had made one my friend, but too dear to me, from a community of pursuits, of mine own age, and, as myself, in the first opening flower of youth. He had grown up a child with me, and we had been both school-fellows and playfellows. But he was not yet my friend as afterwards, nor even then, as true friendship is; for true it cannot be, unless in such as Thou cementest together, cleaving unto Thee, by that *love which is shed abroad in our hearts by the Holy Ghost, which is given unto us.*

Yet was it but too sweet, ripened by the warmth of kindred studies: for, from the true faith (which he as a youth had not soundly and thoroughly imbibed), I had warped him also to those superstitious and pernicious fables, for which my mother bewailed me. With me he now erred in mind, nor could my soul be without him. But behold Thou wert close on the steps of Thy fugitives, at once *God of vengeance*, and Fountain of mercies, turning us to Thyself by wonderful means; Thou tookest that man out of this life, when he had scarce filled up one whole year of my friendship, sweet to me above all sweetness of that my life.

Who can recount all Thy praises, which he hath felt in his one self? What diddest Thou then, my God, and how unsearchable is the *abyss of Thy judgments?* For long, sore sick of a fever, he lay senseless in a death-sweat; and his recovery being despaired of, he was baptised, unknowing; myself meanwhile little regarding, and presuming that his soul would retain rather what it had received of me, not what was wrought on his unconscious body. But it proved far otherwise; for he was refreshed, and restored. Forthwith, as soon as I could speak with him (and I could, so soon as he was able, for I never left him, and we hung but too much upon each other), I essayed to jest with him, as though he would jest with me at that baptism which he had received, when utterly absent in mind and feeling, but had now understood that he had received.

But he so shrunk from me, as from an enemy; and with a wonderful and sudden freedom bade me, as I would continue his friend, forbear such language to him. I, all astonished and amazed, suppressed all my emotions till he should grow well, and his health were strong enough for me to deal with him as I would. But he was taken away from my frenzy, that with Thee he might be preserved for my comfort; a few days after, in my absence, he was attacked again by the fever, and so departed.

At this grief my heart was utterly darkened; and whatever I beheld was death. My native country was a torment to me, and my father's house a strange unhappiness; and whatever I had shared with him, wanting him, became a distracting torture. Mine eyes sought him every where, but he was not granted them; and I hated all places, for that they had not him; nor could they now tell me, "he is coming," as when he was alive and absent. I became a great riddle to myself, and I asked my soul, *why she was so sad, and why she disquieted me sorely:* but she knew not what to answer me. And if I said, *Trust in God,* she very rightly obeyed me not; because that most dear friend, whom she had lost, was, being man, both truer and better than that phantasm she was bid to trust in. Only tears were sweet to me, for they suc- ceeded my friend, in the dearest of my affections.

TIME HEALED MY WOUND

And now, Lord, these things are passed by, and time hath assuaged my wound. May I learn from Thee, who art Truth, and approach the ear of my heart unto Thy mouth, that Thou mayest tell me why weeping is sweet to the miserable? Hast Thou, although present every where, cast away our misery far from Thee? And Thou abidest in Thyself, but we are tossed about in divers trials. And yet unless we mourned in Thine ears, we should have no hope left.

Whence then is sweet fruit gathered from the bitterness of life, from groaning, tears, sighs, and complaints? Doth this sweeten it, that we hope Thou hearest? This is true of prayer, for therein is a longing to approach unto Thee. But is it also in grief for a thing lost, and the sorrow wherewith I was then overwhelmed? For I neither hoped he should return to life nor did I desire this with my tears; but I wept only and grieved. For I was miserable, and had lost my joy. Or is weeping indeed a bitter thing, and for very loathing of the things which we before enjoyed, does it then, when we shrink from them, please us?

THE FRIENDSHIP OF PERISHABLE THINGS

But what speak I of these things? for now is no time to question, but to confess unto Thee. Wretched I was; and wretched is every soul bound by the friendship of perishable things; he is torn asunder when he loses them, and then he feels the wretchedness which he had ere yet he lost them. So was it then with me; I wept most bitterly, and found my repose in bitterness. Thus was I wretched, and that wretched life I held dearer than my friend. For though I would willingly have changed it, yet was I more unwilling to part with it than with him; yea, I know not whether I would have parted with it even for him, as is related (if not feigned) of Pylades and Orestes, that they would gladly have died for each other or together, not to live together being to them worse than death.

But in me there had arisen some unexplained feeling, too contrary to this, for at once I loathed exceedingly to live and feared to die. I suppose, the more I loved him, the more did I hate, and fear (as a most cruel enemy) death, which had bereaved me of him: and I imagined it would speedily make an end of all men, since it had power over him. Thus was it with me, I remember. Behold my heart, O my God, behold and see into me; for well I remember it, O my Hope, who cleansest me from the impurity of such affections, directing *mine eyes towards Thee*, and *plucking my feet out of the snare*.

For I wondered that others, subject to death, did live, since he whom I loved, as if he should never die, was dead; and I wondered yet more that myself, who was to him a second self, could live, he being dead. Well said one of his friend, "Thou half of my soul"; for I felt that my soul and his soul were "one soul in two bodies": and therefore was my life a horror to me, because I would not live halved. And therefore perchance I feared to die, lest he whom I had much loved should die wholly.

I COULD NOT ESCAPE MYSELF

O madness, which knowest not how to love men, like men! O foolish man that I then was, enduring impatiently the lot of man! I fretted then, sighed, wept, was distracted; had neither rest nor counsel. For I bore about a shattered and bleeding soul, impatient of being borne by me, yet where to repose it, I found not. Not in calm groves, not in games and music, nor in fragrant spots, nor in curious banquetings, nor in the pleasures of the bed and the couch; nor (finally) in books or poesy, found it repose.

All things looked ghastly, yea, the very light; whatsoever was not what he was, was revolting and hateful, except groaning and tears. For in those alone found I a little refreshment. But when my soul was withdrawn from them a huge load of misery weighed me down. To Thee, O Lord, it ought to have been raised, for Thee to lighten; I knew it; but neither could nor would; the more, since, when I thought of Thee, Thou wert not to me any solid or substantial thing. For Thou wert not Thyself, but a mere phantom, and my error was my God. If I offered to discharge my load thereon, that it might rest, it glided through the void, and came rushing down again on me; and I had remained to myself a hapless spot, where I could neither be, nor be from thence.

For whither should my heart flee from my heart? Whither should I flee from myself? Whither not follow myself? And yet I fled out of my country; for so should mine eyes less look for him, where they were not wont to see him. And thus from Thagaste, I came to Carthage.

THE SOLACE OF FRIENDS

Times lose no time; nor do they roll idly by; through our senses they work strange operations on the mind. Behold, they went and came day by day, and by coming and going, introduced into my mind other imaginations and other remembrances; and little by little patched me up again with my old kind of delights, unto which that my sorrow gave way. And yet there succeeded, not indeed other griefs, yet the causes of other griefs. For whence had that former grief so easily reached my very inmost soul, but that I had poured out my soul upon the dust, in loving one that must die, as if he would never die? For what restored and refreshed me chiefly was the solaces of other friends, with whom I did love, what instead of Thee I loved; and this was a great fable, and protracted lie, by whose adulterous stimulus, our soul, which lay itching in our ears, was being defiled. But that fable would not die to me, so oft as any of my friends died.

There were other things which in them did more take my mind; to talk and jest together, to do kind offices by turns; to read together honied books; to play the fool or be earnest together; to dissent at times without discontent, as a man might with his own self; and even with the seldomness of these dissentings, to season our more frequent consentings; sometimes to teach, and sometimes learn; long for the absent with impatience; and welcome the coming with joy. These and the like expressions, proceeding out of the hearts of those that loved and were loved again, by the countenance, the tongue, the eyes, and a thousand pleasing gestures, were so much fuel to melt our souls together, and out of many make but one.

BLESSED IS HE WHO LOVETH THEE

This is it that is loved in friends; and so loved, that a man's conscience condemns itself, if he love not him that loves him again, or love not again him that loves him, looking for nothing from his person but indications of his love. Hence that mourning, if one die, and darkenings of sorrows, that steeping of the heart in tears, all sweetness turned to bitterness; and upon the loss of life of the dying, the death of the living. Blessed whoso loveth Thee, and his friend in Thee, and his enemy for Thee. For he alone loses none dear to him, to whom all are dear in Him who cannot be lost. And who is this but our God, the *God that made heaven and earth*, and *filleth them*, because by filling them He created them? Thee none loseth, but who leaveth. And who leaveth Thee, whither goeth or whither fleeth he, but from Thee well-pleased, to Thee displeased? For where doth he not find Thy law in his own punishment? *And Thy law is truth*, and truth Thou.

APART FROM GOD ONE FINDS SORROW

Turn us, O God of Hosts, show us Thy countenance, and we shall be whole. For whithersoever the soul of man turns itself, unless towards Thee, it is riveted upon sorrows, yea though it is riveted on things beautiful. And yet they, out of Thee, and out of the soul, were not, unless they were from Thee. They rise, and set; and by rising, they begin as it were to be; they grow, that they may be perfected; and perfected, they wax old and wither; and all grow not old, but all wither.

So then when they rise and tend to be, the more quickly they grow that they may be, so much the more they haste not to be. This is the law of them. Thus much hast Thou allotted them, because they are portions of things, which exist not all at once, but by passing away and succeeding, they together complete that universe, whereof they are portions. And even thus is our speech completed by signs giving forth a sound: but this again is not perfected unless one word pass away when it hath sounded its part, that another may succeed.

Out of all these things let my soul praise Thee, O God, Creator of all; yet let not my soul be riveted unto these things with the glue of love, through the senses of the body. For they go whither they were to go, that they might not be; and they rend her with pestilent longings, because she longs to be, yet loves to repose in what she loves. But in these things is no place of repose; they abide not, they flee; and who can follow them with the senses of the flesh? yea, who can grasp them, when they are hard by? For the sense of the flesh is slow, because it is the sense of the flesh; and thereby is it bounded. It sufficeth; for that it was made for; but it sufficeth not to stay things running their course from their appointed starting-place to the end appointed. For in Thy Word, by which they are created, they hear their decree, "hence and hitherto."

BE NOT FOOLISH

Be not foolish, O my soul, nor become deaf in the ear of thine heart with the tumult of thy folly. Hearken thou too. The Word itself calleth thee to return: and there is the place of rest imperturbable, where love is not forsaken, if itself forsaketh not. Behold, these things pass away, that others may replace them, and so this lower universe be completed by all his parts. But do I depart any whither? saith the Word of God.

There fix thy dwelling, trust there whatsoever thou hast thence, O my soul, at least now thou art tired out with vanities. Entrust Truth, whatsoever thou hast from the Truth, and thou shalt lose nothing; and thy decay shall bloom again, and *all thy diseases be healed*, and thy mortal parts be reformed and renewed, and bound around thee: nor shall they lay thee whither themselves descend; but they shall stand fast with thee, and abide for ever before God, *who abideth* and standeth fast *for ever.*

Why then be perverted and follow thy flesh? Be it converted and follow thee. Whatever by her thou hast sense of, is in part; and the whole, whereof these are parts, thou knowest not, and yet they delight thee. But had the sense of thy flesh a capacity for comprehending the whole, and not itself also, for thy punishment, been justly restricted to a part of the whole, thou wouldest, that whatsoever existeth at this present, should pass away, that so the whole might better please thee. For what we speak also, by the same sense of the flesh thou hearest; yet wouldest not thou have the syllables stay, but fly away, that others may come, and thou hear the whole. And so ever, when any one thing is made up of many, all of which do not exist together, all collectively would please more than they do severally, could all be perceived collectively. But far better than these is He who made all; and He is our God, nor doth He pass away, for neither doth aught succeed Him.

LET US LOVE GOD

If bodies please thee, praise God on occasion of them, and turn back thy love upon their Maker; lest in these things which please thee, thou displease. If souls please thee, be they loved in God: for they too are mutable, but in Him are they firmly stablished; else would they pass, and pass away. In Him then be they beloved; and carry unto Him along with thee what souls thou canst, and say to them, "Him let us love, Him let us love: He made these, nor is He far off. For He did not make them, and so depart, but they are of Him, and in Him. See there He is, where truth is loved. He is within the very heart, yet hath the heart strayed from Him. *Go back into your heart, ye transgressors*, and cleave fast to Him that made you. Stand with Him, and ye shall stand fast. Rest in Him, and ye shall be at rest. Whither go ye in rough ways? Whither go ye?

"The good that you love is from Him; but it is good and pleasant through reference to Him, and justly shall it be embittered, because unjustly is anything loved which is from Him, if He be forsaken for it. To what end then would ye still and still walk these difficult and toilsome ways? There is no rest, where ye seek it. Seek what ye seek; but it is not there where ye seek. Ye seek a blessed life in the land of death; it is not there. For how should there be a blessed life where life itself is not?"

"But our true Life came down hither, and bore our death, and slew him, out of the abundance of His own life: and He thundered, calling aloud to us to return hence to Him into that secret place, whence He came forth to us, first into the virgin's womb, wherein he espoused the human creation, our mortal flesh, that it might not be for ever mortal, and thence *like a bridegroom coming out of his chamber, rejoicing as a giant to run his course.* For He lingered not, but ran, calling aloud by words, deeds, death, life, descent, ascension; crying aloud to us to return unto Him. And He departed from our eyes, that we might return into our heart, and there find Him. For He departed, and lo, He is here.

"He would not be long with us, yet left us not; for He departed thither, whence He never parted, *because the world was made by Him.* And *in this world He was, and into this world He came to save sinners,* unto whom my soul confesseth, *and He healeth it, for it hath sinned against Him. O ye sons of men, how long so slow of heart?* Even now, after the descent of Life to you, will ye not ascend and live? But whither ascend ye, when ye are on high, and *set your mouth against the heavens?* Descend, that ye may ascend, and ascend to God. For ye have fallen, by ascending against Him." Tell them this, that they may weep *in the valley of tears,* and so carry them up with thee unto God; because out of His

Spirit thou speakest thus unto them, if thou speakest, burning with the fire of charity.

I WROTE ABOUT THE FAIR AND THE FIT

These things I then knew not, and I loved these lower beauties, and I was sinking to the very depths, and to my friends I said, "Do we love any thing but the beautiful? What then is the beautiful? and what is beauty? What is it that attracts and wins us to the things we love? for unless there were in them a grace and beauty, they could by no means draw us unto them." And I marked and perceived that in bodies themselves, there was a beauty, from their forming a sort of whole, and again, another from apt and mutual correspondence, as of a part of the body with its whole, or a shoe with a foot, and the like. And this consideration sprang up in my mind, out of my inmost heart, and I wrote "on the fair and fit," I think, two or three books. Thou knowest, O Lord, for it is gone from me; for I have them not, but they are strayed from me, I know not how.

HIERIUS, AN ORATOR OF ROME

But what moved me, O Lord my God, to dedicate these books unto Hierius, an orator of Rome, whom I knew not by face, but loved for the fame of his learning which was eminent in him, and some words of his I had heard, which pleased me? But more did he please me, for that he pleased others, who highly extolled him, amazed that out of a Syrian, first instructed in Greek eloquence, should afterwards be formed a wonderful Latin orator, and one most learned in things pertaining unto philosophy.

One is commended, and, unseen, he is loved: doth this love enter the heart of the hearer from the mouth of the commender? Not so. But by one who loveth is another kindled. For hence he is loved who is commended, when the commender is believed to extol him with an unfeigned heart; that is, when one that loves him praises him.

For so did I then love men, upon the judgment of men, not Thine, O my God, in whom no man is deceived. But yet why not for qualities, like those of a famous charioteer, or fighter with the beasts in the theatre, known far and wide by a vulgar popularity, but far otherwise, and earnestly, and so as I would be myself commended? For I would not be commended or loved, as actors are (though I myself did commend and love them), but had rather be unknown, than so known; and even hated, than so loved. Where now are the impulses to such various and divers kinds of loves laid up in one soul? Why, since we are equally men, do I love in another what, if I did not hate, I should not spurn and cast from myself?

For it holds not, that as a good horse is loved by him, who would not, though he might, be that horse, therefore the same may be said of an actor, who shares our nature. Do I then love in a man, what I hate to be, who am a man? Man himself is a great deep, whose very *hairs Thou numberest*, O Lord, *and they fall not to the ground without Thee*. And yet are the hairs of his head easier to be numbered than are his feelings, and the beatings of his heart.

But that orator was of that sort whom I loved, as wishing to be myself such; and I erred through a swelling pride, and *was tossed about with every wind,* but yet was steered by Thee, though very secretly. And whence do I know, and whence do I confidently confess unto Thee, that I had loved him more for the love of his commenders, than for the very things for which he was commended? Because, had he been unpraised, and these self-same men had dispraised him, and with dispraise and contempt told the very same things of him, I had never been so kindled and excited to love him. And yet the things had not been other, nor he himself other; but only the feelings of the relators.

See where the impotent soul lies along, that is not yet stayed up by the solidity of truth! Just as the gales of tongues blow from the breast of the opinionative, so is it carried this way and that, driven forward and backward, and the light is overclouded to it, and the truth unseen. And lo, it is before us. And it was to me a great matter, that my discourse and labours should be known to that man: which should he approve, I were the more kindled, but if he disapproved, my empty heart, void of Thy solidity, had been wounded. And yet the "fair and fit," whereon I wrote to him, I dwelt on with pleasure, and surveyed it, and admired it, though none joined therein.

THE NATURE OF THE MIND

But I saw not yet, whereon this weighty matter turned in Thy wisdom, O Thou Omnipotent, *who only doest wonders,* and my mind ranged through corporeal forms; and "fair," I defined and distinguished what is so in itself, and "fit," whose beauty is in correspondence to some other thing: and this I supported by corporeal examples. And I turned to the nature of the mind, but the false notion which I had of spiritual things, let me not see the truth. Yet the force of truth did of itself flash into mine eyes, and I turned away my panting soul from incorporeal substance to lineaments, and colours, and bulky magnitudes. And not being able to see these in the mind, I thought I could not see my mind.

And whereas in virtue I loved peace, and in viciousness I abhorred discord; in the first I observed a unity, but in the other, a sort of division. And in that unity I conceived the rational soul, and the nature of truth and of the chief good to consist; but in this division I miserably imagined there to be some unknown substance of irrational life, and the nature of the chief evil, which should not only be a substance, but real life also, and yet not derived from Thee, O my God, of whom are all things. And yet that first I called a Monad, as it had been a soul without sex; but the latter a Duad—anger, in deeds of violence, and in flagatiousness, lust; not knowing whereof I spake. For I had not known or learned that neither was evil a substance, nor our soul that chief and unchangeable good.

For as deeds of violence arise, if that emotion of the soul be corrupted, whence vehement action springs, stirring itself insolently and unrulily; and lusts, when that affection of the soul is ungoverned, whereby carnal pleasures are drunk in, so do errors and false opinions defile the conversation, if the reasonable soul itself be corrupted; as it was then in me, who knew not that it must be enlightened by another light, that it may be partaker of truth, seeing itself is not that nature of truth. *For Thou shalt light my candle, O Lord my God, Thou shalt enlighten my darkness: and of Thy fulness have we all received, for Thou art the true light that lighteth every man that cometh into the world, for in Thee there is no variableness, neither shadow of change.*

But I pressed towards Thee, and was thrust from Thee, that I might taste of death: for *thou resistest the proud.* But what prouder, than for me with a strange madness to maintain myself to be that by nature which Thou art? For whereas I was subject to change (so much being manifest to me, my very desire to become wise, being the wish, of worse to become better), yet chose I rather to imagine Thee subject to change, than myself not to be that which Thou art. Therefore I was repelled by Thee, and Thou resistedst my vain stiff-neckedness, and I imagined corporeal forms, and, myself flesh, I accused flesh; and, a *wind that passeth away, I returned not* to Thee, but I passed on and on to things which have no being, neither in Thee, nor in me, nor in the body. Neither were they created for me by Thy truth, but by my vanity devised out of things corporeal.

And I was wont to ask Thy faithful little ones, my fellow-citizens (from whom, unknown to myself, I stood exiled), I was wont, prating and foolishly, to ask them, "Why then doth the soul err which God created?" But I would not be asked, "Why then doth God

err?" And I maintained that Thy unchangeable substance did err upon constraint, rather than confess that my changeable substance had gone astray voluntarily, and now, in punishment, lay in error.

I was then some six or seven and twenty years old when I wrote those volumes; revolving within me corporeal fictions, buzzing in the ears of my heart, which I turned, O sweet truth, to thy inward melody, meditating on the "fair and fit," and longing to stand and hearken to Thee, and *to rejoice greatly at the Bridegroom's voice,* but could not; for by the voices of mine own errors, I was hurried abroad, and through the weight of my own pride, I was sinking into the lowest pit. For Thou didst not *make me to hear joy and gladness,* nor did *the bones exult which were not yet humbled.*

KNOWLEDGE WRONGLY APPLIED

And what did it profit me, that scarce twenty years old, a book of Aristotle, which they call the ten Predicaments, falling into my hands (on whose very name I hung, as on something great and divine, so often as my rhetoric master of Carthage, and others, accounted learned, mouthed it with cheeks bursting with pride), I read and understood it unaided? And on my conferring with others, who said that they scarcely understood it with very able tutors, not only orally explaining it, but drawing many things in sand, they could tell me no more of it than I had learned, reading it by myself.

And the book appeared to me to speak very clearly of substances, such as "man," and of their qualities, as the figure of a man, of what sort it is; and stature, how many feet high; and his relationship, whose brother he is; or where placed; or when born; or whether he stands or sits; or be shod or armed; or does, or suffers anything; and all the innumerable things which might be ranged under these nine Predicaments, of which I have given some specimens, or under that chief Predicament of Substance.

What did all this further me, seeing it even hindered me? when, imagining whatever was, was comprehended under those ten Predicaments, I essayed in such wise to understand, O my God, Thy wonderful and unchangeable Unity also, as if Thou also hadst been subjected to Thine own greatness or beauty; so that (as in bodies) they should exist in Thee, as their subject: whereas Thou Thyself art Thy greatness and beauty; but a body is not great or fair in that it is a body, seeing that, though it were less great or fair, it should notwithstanding be a body. But it was falsehood which of Thee I conceived, not truth, fictions of my misery, not the realities of Thy Blessedness. For Thou hadst commanded, and it was done in me, that the *earth should bring forth briers and thorns to me*, and that *in the sweat of my brows I should eat my bread*.

And what did it profit me, that all the books I could procure of the so-called liberal arts, I, the vile slave of vile affections, read by myself, and understood? And I delighted in them, but knew not whence came all, that herein was true or certain. For I had my back to the light, and my face to the things enlightened; whence my face, with which I discerned the things enlightened, itself was not enlightened.

Whatever was written, either on rhetoric, or logic, geometry, music, and arithmetic, by myself without much difficulty or any instructor, I understood, Thou knowest, O Lord my God; because both quickness of understanding, and acuteness in discerning, is Thy gift: yet did I not thence sacrifice to Thee. So then it served not to my use, but rather to my perdition, since I went about to get so good a *portion of my substance* into my own keeping; and I *kept not my strength for Thee*, but wandered from Thee *into a far country, to spend it upon harlotries*.

For what profited me good abilities, not employed to good uses? For I felt not that those arts were attained with great difficulty, even by the studious and talented, until I attempted to explain them to such; when he most excelled in them who followed me not altogether slowly.

But what did this further me, imagining that Thou, O Lord God, the Truth, wert a vast and bright body, and I a fragment of that body? Perverseness too great! But such was I. Nor do I blush, O my God, to *confess to Thee Thy mercies towards me*, and to call upon Thee, who blushed not then to profess to men my blasphemies, and to bark against Thee.

What profited me then my nimble wit in those sciences and all those most knotty volumes, unravelled by me, without aid from human instruction; seeing I erred so foully, and with such sacrilegious shamefulness, in the doctrine of piety? Or what hindrance was a far slower wit to Thy little ones, since they departed not far from Thee, that in the nest of Thy Church they might securely be fledged, and nourish the wings of charity, by the food of a sound faith.

O Lord our God, *under the shadow of Thy wings let us hope;* protect us, and carry us. Thou wilt carry us both when little, and *even to hoar hairs wilt Thou carry us;* for our firmness, when it is Thou, then is it firmness; but when our own, it is infirmity. Our good ever lives with Thee; from which when we turn away, we are turned aside. Let us now, O Lord, return, that we may not be overturned, because with Thee our good lives without any decay, which good art Thou; nor need we fear, lest there be no place whither to return, because we fell from it: for though our absence, our mansion fell not—Thy eternity.

The Fifth Book

LET MY SOUL PRAISE THEE

ACCEPT THE SACRIFICE of my confessions from the ministry of my tongue, which Thou hast formed and stirred up to confess unto Thy name. *Heal Thou all my bones, and let them say, O Lord, who is like unto Thee?* For he who confesses to Thee doth not teach Thee what takes place within him; seeing a closed heart closes not out Thy eye, nor can man's hardheartedness thrust back Thy hand: for Thou dissolvest it at Thy will in pity or in vengeance, *and nothing can hide itself from Thy heat.*

But let my soul praise Thee, that it may love Thee; and let it confess Thy own mercies to Thee, that it may praise Thee. Thy whole creation ceaseth not, nor is silent in Thy praises; neither the spirit of man with voice directed unto Thee, nor creation animate or inanimate, by the voice of those who meditate thereon: that so our souls may from their weariness arise towards Thee, leaning on those things which Thou hast created, and passing on to Thyself, who madest them wonderfully; and there is refreshment and true strength.

THE RESTLESS AND THE GODLESS

Let the restless, the godless, depart and flee from Thee; yet Thou seest them, and dividest the darkness. And behold, the universe with them is fair, though they are foul. And how have they injured Thee? or how have they disgraced Thy government, which, from the heaven to this lowest earth, is just and perfect? For whither fled they, when they fled from Thy presence? or where dost not Thou find them? But they fled, that they might not see Thee seeing them, and, blinded, might stumble against Thee (because *Thou forsakest nothing Thou hast made*); that the unjust, I say, might stumble upon Thee, and justly be hurt; withdrawing themselves from thy gentleness, and stumbling at thy uprightness, and falling upon their own ruggedness. Ignorant, in truth, that Thou art every where, Whom no place encompasseth! and Thou alone art near, even to those that *remove far from Thee.*

Let them then be turned, and seek Thee; because not as they have forsaken their Creator, hast Thou forsaken Thy creation. Let them be turned and seek Thee; and behold, Thou art there in their heart, in the heart of those that confess to Thee, and cast themselves upon Thee, and weep in Thy bosom, after all their rugged ways. Then dost Thou gently wipe away their tears, and they weep the more, and joy in weeping; even for that Thou, Lord—not man of flesh and blood, but—Thou, Lord, who madest them, re-makest and comfortest them. But where was I, when I was seeking Thee? And Thou wert before me, but I had gone away from Thee; nor did I find myself, how much less Thee!

MY TWENTY-NINTH YEAR

I would lay open before my God that nine-and-twentieth year of mine age. There had then come to Carthage a certain Bishop of the Manichees, Faustus by name, a great snare of the Devil, and many were entangled by him through that lure of his smooth language: which though I did commend, yet could I separate from the truth of the things which I was earnest to learn: nor do I so much regard the service of oratory as the science which this Faustus, so praised among them, set before me to feed upon. Fame had before bespoken him most knowing in all valuable learning, and exquisitely skilled in the liberal sciences.

And since I had read and well remembered much of the philosophers, I compared some things of theirs with those long fables of the Manichees, and found the former the more probable; even although they *could only prevail so far as to make judgment of this lower world, the Lord of it they could by no means find out. For Thou art great, O Lord, and hast respect unto the humble, but the proud Thou beholdest afar off.* Nor dost thou *draw near,* but to *the contrite in heart,* nor art found by the proud, no, not though by curious skill they could number the stars and the sand, and measure the starry heavens, and track the courses of the planets.

For with their understanding and wit, which Thou bestowedst on them, they search out these things; and much have they found out; and foretold, many years before, eclipses of those luminaries, the sun and moon—what day and hour, and how many dig-its—nor did their calculation fail; and it came to pass as they foretold; and they wrote down the rules they had found out, and these are read at this day, and out of them do others foretell in what year and month of the year, and what day of the month, and what hour of the day, and what part of its light, moon or sun is to be eclipsed and so it shall be, as it is fore-showed.

At these things men, that know not this art, marvel and are astonished, and they that know it, exult, and are puffed up; and by an ungodly pride departing from Thee, and failing of Thy light, they foresee a failure of the sun's light, which shall be, so long before, but see not their own, which is. For they search not religiously whence they have the wit, wherewith they search out this. And finding that Thou madest them, they give not themselves up to Thee, to preserve what Thou madest, nor sacrifice to Thee what they have made themselves; nor slay their own soaring imaginations, as *fowls of the air,* not their own diving curiosities (wherewith, like the *fishes of the sea* they wander over the unknown paths of the abyss), nor their own luxuriousness, as *beasts of the field,* that *Thou, Lord, a consuming fire,* mayest burn up those dead cares of theirs, and recreate themselves immortally.

But they knew not the way, Thy Word, by Whom Thou madest these things which they number, and themselves who number, and the sense whereby they perceive what they number, and the understanding, out of which they number; or that *of Thy wisdom there is no number.* But the Only Begotten is Himself *made unto us wisdom, and righteousness, and sanctification,* and was numbered among us, and *paid tribute unto Caesar.* They knew not this Way whereby to descend to Him from themselves, and by Him ascend unto Him. They knew not this way, and deemed themselves exalted amongst the stars and shining; and behold, they *fell upon the earth, and their foolish heart was darkened.*

They discourse many things truly concerning the creature; but Truth, Artificer of the creature, they seek not piously, and therefore find him not; or if they find him, *knowing Him to be God, they glorify Him not as God, neither are thankful, but become vain in their imaginations,* and *profess themselves to be wise,* attributing to themselves what is Thine; and thereby with most perverse blindness, study to impute to Thee what is their own, forging lies of Thee who art the Truth, and *changing the glory of the uncorruptible God into an image made like corruptible man, and to birds, and four-footed beasts, and creeping things, changing Thy truth into a lie, and worshipping and serving the creature more than the Creator.*

Yet many truths concerning the creature retained I from these men, and saw the reason thereof from calculations, the succession of times, and the visible testimonies of the stars; and compared them with the saying of Manichæus, which in his frenzy he had written most largely on these subjects; but discovered not any account of the solstices, or equinoxes, or the eclipses of the greater lights, nor whatever of this sort I had learned in the books of secular philosophy. But I was commanded to believe; and yet it corresponded not with what had been established by calculations and my own sight, but was quite contrary.

HAPPY IS THE MAN THAT KNOWETH THEE

Doth then, O Lord God of Truth, whoso knoweth these things, therefore please Thee? Surely unhappy is he who knoweth all these, and knoweth not Thee: but happy whoso knoweth Thee, though he know not these. And whoso knoweth both Thee and them is not the happier for them, but for Thee only, if, *knowing Thee,* he *glorifies Thee as God, and is thankful, and becomes not vain in his imaginations.*

For as he is better off who knows how to possess a tree, and return thanks to Thee for the use thereof, although he know not how many cubits high it is, or how wide it spreads, than he that can measure it, and count all its boughs, and neither owns it, nor knows or loves its Creator: so a believer, whose all this world of wealth is, and *who having nothing, yet possesseth all things,* by cleaving unto Thee, whom all things serve, though he know not even the circles of the Great Bear, yet is it folly to doubt but he is in a better state than one who can measure the heavens, and number the stars, and poise the elements, yet neglecteth Thee *who hast made all things in number, weight, and measure.*

SEEDS OF DOUBT

But yet who bade that Manichæus write on these things also, skill in which was no element of piety? For Thou hast said to man, *Behold piety and wisdom;* of which he might be ignorant, though he had perfect knowledge of these things; but these things, since, knowing not, he most impudently dared to teach, he plainly could have no knowledge of piety. For it is vanity to make profession of these worldly things even when known; but confession to Thee is piety. Wherefore this wanderer to this end spake much of these things, that convicted by those who had truly learned them, it might be manifest what understanding he had in the other abstruser things.

For he would not have himself meanly thought of, but went about to persuade men, "That the Holy Ghost, the Comforter and Enricher of Thy faithful ones, was with plenary authority personally within him." When then he was found out to have taught falsely of the heaven and stars, and of the motions of the sun and moon (although these things pertain not to the doctrine of religion), yet his sacrilegious presumption would become evident enough, seeing he delivered things which not only he knew not, but which were falsified, with so mad a vanity of pride, that he sought to ascribe them to himself, as to a divine person.

For when I hear any Christian brother ignorant of these things, and mistaken on them, I can patiently behold such a man holding his opinion; nor do I see that any ignorance as to the position or character of the corporeal creation can injure him, so long as he doth not believe any thing unworthy of Thee, O Lord, the Creator of all. But it doth injure him, if he imagine it to pertain to the form of the doctrine of piety, and will yet affirm that too stiffly whereof he is ignorant.

And yet is even such an infirmity, in the infancy of faith, borne by our mother Charity, till the newborn may *grow up unto a perfect man,* so as *not to be carried about with every wind of doctrine.* But in him who in such wise presumed to be the teacher, source, guide, chief of all whom he could so persuade, that whoso followed him thought that he followed, not a mere man, but Thy Holy Spirit; who would not judge that so great madness, when once convicted of having taught any thing false, were to be detested and utterly rejected?

But I had not as yet clearly ascertained whether the vicissitudes of longer and shorter days and nights, and of day and night itself, with the eclipses of the greater lights, and whatever else of the kind I had read of in other books, might be explained consistently with his sayings; so that, if they by any means might, it should remain a question to me whether it were so or no; but I might, on account of his reputed sanctity, rest my credence upon his authority.

THE ARRIVAL OF FAUSTUS

And for almost all those nine years, wherein with unsettled mind I had been their disciple, I had longed but too intensely for the coming of this Faustus. For the rest of the sect, whom by chance I had lighted upon, when unable to solve my objections about these things, still held out to me the coming of this Faustus, by conference with whom these and greater difficulties, if I had them, were to be most readily and abundantly cleared.

When then he came, I found him a man of pleasing discourse, and who could speak fluently and in better terms, yet still but the self-same things which they were wont to say. But what availed the utmost neatness of the cup-bearer to my thirst for a more precious draught? Mine ears were already cloyed with the like, nor did they seem to me therefore better, because better said; or therefore true, because eloquent; nor the soul therefore wise, because the face was comely, and the language graceful. But they who held him out to me were no good judges of things; and therefore to them he appeared understanding and wise, because in words pleasing.

I felt however that another sort of people were suspicious even of truth, and refused to assent to it, if delivered in a smooth and copious discourse. But Thou, O my God, hadst already taught me by wonderful and secret ways, and therefore I believe that Thou taughtest me, because it is truth, nor is there besides Thee any teacher of truth, where or whencesoever it may shine upon us. Of Thyself therefore had I now learned, that neither ought any thing to seem to be spoken truly, because eloquently; nor therefore falsely, because the utterance of the lips is inharmonious; nor, again, therefore true, because rudely delivered; or therefore false, because the language is rich; but that wisdom and folly are as wholesome and unwholesome food;

and adorned or unadorned phrases as courtly or country vessels; either kind of meats may be served up in either kind of dishes.

That greediness then, wherewith I had of so long time expected that man, was delighted verily with his action and feeling when disputing, and his choice and readiness of words to clothe his ideas. I was then delighted, and, with many others and more than they, did I praise and extol him. It troubled me, however, that in the assembly of his auditors, I was not allowed to put in and communicate those questions that troubled me, in familiar converse with him.

Which when I might, and with my friends began to engage his ears at such times as it was not unbecoming for him to discuss with me, and had brought forward such things as moved me; I found him first utterly ignorant of liberal sciences, save grammar, and that but in an ordinary way. But because he had read some of Tully's Orations, a very few books of Seneca, some things of the poets, and such few volumes of his own sect as were written in Latin and neatly, and was daily practised in speaking, he acquired a certain eloquence, which proved the more pleasing and seductive, because under the guidance of a good wit, and with a kind of natural gracefulness.

Is it not thus, as I recall it, O Lord my God, Thou Judge of my conscience? before Thee is my heart, and my remembrance, Who didst at that time direct me by the hidden mystery of Thy providence, and didst set those shameful errors of mine before my face, that I might see and hate them.

FAUSTUS DISCREDITED; MANICHÆUS IS FORSAKEN

For after it was clear that he was ignorant of those arts in which I thought he excelled, I began to despair of his opening and solving the difficulties which preplexed me (of which indeed however ignorant, he might have held the truths of piety, had he not been a Manichee). For their books are fraught with prolix fable, of the heaven, and stars, sun, and moon, and I now no longer thought him able satisfactorily to decide what I much desired, whether, on comparison of these things with the calculations I had elsewhere read, the account given in the books of Manichæus were preferable, or at least as good. Which when I proposed to be considered and discussed, he, so far modestly, shrunk from the burden.

For he knew that he knew not these things, and was not ashamed to confess it. For he was not one of those talking persons, many of whom I had endured, who undertook to teach me these things, and said nothing. But this man had a heart, though not right towards Thee, yet neither altogether treacherous to himself. For he was not altogether ignorant of his own ignorance, nor would he rashly be entangled in a dispute, whence he could neither retreat nor extricate himself fairly. Even for this I liked him the better. For fairer is the modesty of a candid mind, than the knowledge of those things which I desired; and such I found him, in all the more difficult and subtle questions.

My zeal for the writings of Manichæus being thus blunted, and despairing yet more of their other teachers, seeing that in divers things which perplexed me, he, so renowned among them, had so turned out; I began to engage with him in the study of that literature, on which he also was much set (and which as rhetoric-reader I was at that time teaching young students at Carthage), and to read with him, either what himself desired to hear, or such as I judged fit for his genius. But all my efforts whereby I had purposed to advance in that sect, upon knowledge of that man, came utterly to an end; not that I detached myself from them altogether, but as one finding nothing better, I had settled to be content meanwhile with what I had in whatever way fallen upon, unless by chance something more eligible should dawn upon me.

Thus that Faustus, to so many a snare of death, had now, neither willing nor witting it, begun to loosen that wherein I was taken. For Thy hands, O my God, in the secret purpose of Thy providence, did not forsake my soul; and out of my mother's heart's blood, through her tears night and day poured out, was a sacrifice offered for me unto Thee; and Thou didst deal with me by wondrous ways. Thou didst it, O my God: for *the steps of a man are ordered by the Lord, and He shall dispose his way.* Or how shall we obtain salvation, but from Thy hand, re-making what it made?

I ACCEPTED A POSITION AT ROME

Thou didst deal with me, that I should be persuaded to go to Rome, and to teach there rather, what I was teaching at Carthage. And how I was persuaded to this, I will not neglect to confess to Thee: because herein also the deepest recesses of Thy wisdom, and Thy most present mercy to us, must be considered and confessed.

I did not wish therefore to go to Rome, because higher gains and higher dignities were warranted me by my friends who persuaded me to this (though even these things had at that time an influence over my mind), but my chief and almost only reason was, that I heard that young men studied there more peacefully, and were kept quiet under a restraint of more regular discipline; so that they did not, at their pleasures, petulantly rush into the school of one whose pupils they were not, nor were even admitted without his permission. Whereas at Carthage there reigns among the scholars a most disgraceful and unruly license. They burst in audaciously, and with gestures almost frantic, disturb all order which any one hath established for the good of his scholars. Divers outrages they commit, with a wonderful stolidity, punishable by law, did not custom uphold them; that custom evincing them to be the more miserable, in that they now do as lawful what by Thy eternal law shall never be lawful; and they think they do it unpunished, whereas they are punished with the very blindness whereby they do it, and suffer incomparably worse than what they do.

The manners then which, when a student, I would not make my own, I was fain as a teacher to endure in others: and so I was well pleased to go where, all that knew it, assured me that the like was not done. But Thou, *my refuge and my portion in the land of the living;* that I might change my earthly dwelling for the salvation of my soul, at Carthage didst goad me, that I might thereby be torn from it; and at Rome didst proffer me allurements, whereby I might be drawn thither, by men in love with a dying life, the one doing frantic, the other promising vain, things; and, to correct my steps, didst secretly use their and my own perverseness. For both they who disturbed my quiet were blinded with a disgraceful frenzy, and they who invited me elsewhere savoured of earth. And I, who here detested real misery, was there seeking unreal happiness.

But why I went hence, and went thither, Thou knewest, O God, yet showedst it neither to me, nor to my mother, who grievously bewailed my journey, and followed me as far as the sea. But I deceived her, holding me by force, that either she might keep me back or go with me, and I feigned that I had a friend whom I could not leave, till he had a fair wind to sail. And I lied to my mother, and such a mother, and escaped: for this also hast Thou mercifully forgiven me, preserving me, thus full of execrable defilements, from the waters of the sea, for the water of Thy Grace; whereby when I was cleansed, the streams of my mother's eyes should be dried, with which for me she daily watered the ground under her face. And yet refusing to return without me, I scarcely persuaded her to stay that night in a place hard by our ship, where was an Oratory in memory of the blessed Cyprian.

That night I privily departed, but she was not behind in weeping and prayer. And what, O Lord, was she with so many tears asking of Thee, but that Thou wouldst not suffer me to sail? But Thou, in the depth of Thy counsels and hearing the main point of her desire, regardedst not what she then asked, that Thou mightest make me what she ever asked. The wind blew and swelled our sails, and withdrew the shore from our sight; and she on the morrow was there, frantic with sorrow, and with complaints and groans filled Thine ears, who didst then disregard them; whilst through my desires, Thou wert hurrying me to end all desire, and the earthly part of her affection to me was chastened by the allotted scourge of sorrows.

For she loved my being with her, as mothers do, but much more than many; and she knew not how great joy Thou wert about to work for her out of my absence. She knew not; therefore did she weep and wail, and by this agony there appeared in her the inheritance of Eve, with sorrow seeking what in sorrow she had brought forth. And yet, after accusing my treachery and hardheartedness, she betook herself again to intercede to Thee for me, went to her wonted place, and I to Rome.

A GRAVE ILLNESS

And lo, there was I received by the scourge of bodily sickness, and I was going down to hell, carrying all the sins which I had committed, both against Thee, and myself, and others, many and grievous, over and above that bond of original sin, whereby *we all die in Adam*. For Thou hadst not forgiven me any of these things in Christ, nor had He *abolished by His* cross *the enmity* which by my sins I

had incurred with Thee. For how should He, by the crucifixion of a phantasm, which I believed Him to be? So true, then, was the death of my soul, as that of His flesh seemed to me false; and how true the death of His body, so false was the life of my soul, which did not believe it.

And now the fever heightening, I was parting and departing for ever. For had I then parted hence, whither had I departed, but into fire and torments, such as my misdeeds deserved in the truth of Thy appointment? And this she knew not, yet in absence prayed for me. But Thou, everywhere present, heardest her where she was, and, where I was, hadst compassion upon me; that I should recover the health of my body, though frenzied as yet in my sacrilegious heart.

For I did not in all that danger desire Thy baptism; and I was better as a boy, when I begged it of my mother's piety, as I have before recited and confessed. But I had grown up to my own shame, and I madly scoffed at the prescripts of Thy medicine, who wouldest not suffer me, being such, to die a double death. With which wound had my mother's heart been pierced, it could never be healed. For I cannot express the affection she bare to me, and with how much more vehement anguish she was now in labour of me in the spirit, than at her childbearing in the flesh.

I see not then how she should have been healed, had such a death of mine stricken through the bowels of her love. And where would have been those her so strong and unceasing prayers, unintermitting to Thee alone? But wouldest Thou, God of mercies, *despise* the *contrite and humbled heart* of that chaste and sober widow, so frequent in alms-deeds, so full of duty and service to Thy saints, no day intermitting the oblation at Thine altar, twice a day, morning and evening, without any intermission, coming to Thy church, not for idle tattlings and old wives' *fables*, but that she might hear Thee in Thy discourses, and Thou her in her prayers.

Couldest Thou despise and reject from Thy aid the tears of such an one, wherewith she begged of Thee not gold or silver, nor mutable or passing good, but the salvation of her son's soul? Thou, by whose gift she was such? Never, Lord. Yea, Thou wert at hand, and wert hearing and doing, in that order wherein Thou hadst determined before that it should be done. Far be it that Thou shouldest deceive her in Thy visions and answers, some whereof I have, some I have not mentioned, which she laid up in her faithful heart, and ever praying urged upon Thee, as Thine own handwriting. For Thou, *because Thy mercy endureth for ever*, vouchsafest to those to whom Thou forgivest all their debts, to become also a debtor by Thy promises.

MY MISUNDERSTANDING OF THE CATHOLIC FAITH

Thou recoveredst me then of that sickness, and healedst the son of Thy handmaid, for the time in body, that he might live, for Thee to bestow upon him a better and more abiding health. And even then, at Rome, I joined myself to those deceiving and deceived "holy ones"; not with their disciples only (of which number was he, in whose house I had fallen sick and recovered); but also with those whom they call "The Elect." For I still thought "that it was not we that sin, but that I know not what other nature sinned in us"; and it delighted my pride, to be free from blame; and when I had done any evil, not to confess I had done any, *that Thou mightest heal my soul because it had sinned against Thee:* but I loved to excuse it, and to accuse I know not what other thing, which was with me, but which I was not.

But in truth it was wholly I, and mine impiety had divided me against myself: and that sin was the more incurable, whereby I did not judge myself a sinner; and execrable iniquity it was, that I had rather have Thee, Thee, O God Almighty, to be overcome in me to my destruction, than myself of Thee to salvation. Not as yet then hadst Thou *set a watch before my mouth, and a door of safe keeping around my lips, that my heart might not turn aside to wicked speeches, to make excuses of sins, with men that work iniquity: and,* therefore, was I still *united with their Elect.*

But now despairing to make proficiency in that false doctrine, even those (with which if I should find no better, I had resolved to rest contented) I now held more laxly and carelessly. For there half arose a thought in me that those philosophers, whom they call Academics, were wiser than the rest, for that they held men ought to doubt everything, and laid down that no truth can be comprehended by man: for so, not then understanding even their meaning, I also was clearly convinced that they thought, as they are commonly reported. Yet did I freely and openly discourage that host of mine from that over-confidence which I perceived him to have in those fables, which the books of Manichæus are full of. Yet I lived in more familiar friendship with them, than with others who were not of this heresy.

Nor did I maintain it with my ancient eagerness; still my intimacy with that sect (Rome secretly harbouring many of them) made me slower to seek any other way: especially since I despaired of finding the truth, from which they had turned me aside, in Thy Church, O Lord of heaven and earth, Creator of all things visible and invisible: and it seemed to me unseemly to believe Thee to have the shape of human flesh, and to be bounded by the bodily lineaments of our members. And because, when I wished to think on my God, I knew not what to think of, but a mass of bodies (for what was not such did not seem to me to be any thing), this was the greatest, and almost only cause of my inevitable error.

For hence I believed Evil also to be some such kind of substance, and to have its own foul and hideous bulk; whether gross, which they called earth, or thin and subtile (like the body of the air), which they imagine to be some malignant mind, creeping through that earth. And because a piety, such as it was, constrained me to believe that the good God never created any evil nature, I conceived two masses, contrary to one another, both unbounded, but the evil narrower, the good more expansive. And from this pestilent beginning, the other sacrilegious conceits followed on me.

For when my mind endeavoured to recur to the Catholic faith, I was driven back, since that was not the Catholic faith which I thought to be so. And I seemed to myself more reverential, if I believed of Thee, my God (to whom Thy mercies confess out of my mouth), as unbounded, at least on other sides, although on that where the mass of evil was opposed to Thee, I was constrained to confess Thee bounded; than if on all sides I should imagine Thee to be bounded by the form of a human body. And it seemed to me better to believe Thee to have created no evil (which to me ignorant seemed not some only, but a bodily substance, because I could not conceive of mind unless as a subtile body, and that diffused in definite spaces), than to believe the nature of evil, such as I conceived it, could come from Thee.

Yea, and our Saviour Himself, Thy Only Begotten, I believed to have been reached forth (as it were) for our salvation, out of the mass of Thy most lucid substance, so as to believe nothing of Him, but what I could imagine in my vanity. His Nature then, being such, I thought could not be born of the Virgin Mary, without being mingled with the flesh: and how that which I had so figured to myself could be mingled, and not defiled, I saw not. I feared therefore to believe Him born in the flesh, lest I should be forced to believe Him defiled by the flesh. Now will Thy spiritual ones mildly and lovingly smile upon me, if they shall read these my confessions. Yet such was I.

A WEAK ANSWER

Furthermore, what the Manichees had criticised in Thy Scriptures, I thought could not be defended; yet at times verily I had a wish to confer upon these several points with some one very well skilled in those books, and to make trial what he thought thereon: for the words of one Helpidius, as he spoke and disputed face to face against the said Manichees, had begun to stir me even at Carthage: in that he had produced things out of the Scriptures, not easily withstood, the Manichees' answer whereto seemed to me weak.

And this answer they liked not to give publicly, but only to us in private. It was, that the Scriptures of the New Testament had been corrupted by I know not whom, who wished to engraff the law of the Jews upon the Christian faith: yet themselves produced not any uncorrupted copies. But I, conceiving of things corporeal only, was mainly held down, vehemently oppressed and in a manner suffocated by those "masses"; panting under which after the breath of Thy truth, I could not breathe it pure and untainted.

EXPERIENCES AS A TEACHER

I began then diligently to practise that for which I came to Rome, to teach rhetoric; and first, to gather some to my house, to whom, and through whom, I had begun to be known; when lo, I found other offences committed in Rome, to which I was not exposed in Africa. True, those "subvertings" by profligate young men were not here practised, as was told me: but on a sudden, said they, to avoid paying their master's stipend, a number of youths plot together, and remove to another;—breakers of faith, who for love of money hold justice cheap. These also *my heart hated*, though not *with a perfect hatred:* for perchance I hated them more because I was to suffer by them, than becuase they did things utterly unlawful.

Of a truth such are base persons, and they go a whoring from Thee, loving these fleeting mockeries of things temporal, and filthy lucre, which fouls the hand that grasps it; hugging the fleeting world, and despising Thee, who abidest, and recallest, and forgivest the adulteress soul of man, when she returns to Thee. And now I hate such depraved and crooked persons, though I love them if corrigible, so as to prefer to money the learning which they acquire, and to learning, Thee, O God, the truth and fulness of assured good, and most pure peace. But then I rather for my own sake misliked them evil, than liked and wished them good for Thine.

I HEARD AMBROSE PREACH

When therefore they of Milan had sent to Rome to the prefect of the city, to furnish them with a rhetoric reader for their city, and send him at the public expense, I made application (through those very persons, intoxicated with Manichæan vanities, to be freed wherefrom I was to go, neither of us however knowing it) that Symmachus, then prefect of the city, would try me by setting me some subject, and so send me. To Milan I came, to Ambrose the Bishop, known to the whole world as among the best of men, Thy devout servant; whose eloquent discourse did then plentifully dispense unto Thy people the flour of Thy wheat, the gladness of Thy oil, and the sober inebriation of Thy wine.

To him was I unknowing led by Thee, that by him I might knowingly be led to Thee. That man of God received me as a father, and showed me an Episcopal kindness on my coming. Thenceforth I began to love him, at first indeed not as a teacher of the truth (which I utterly despaired of in Thy Church), but as a person kind towards myself. And I listened diligently to him preaching to the people, not with that intent I ought, but, as it were, trying his eloquence, whether it answered the fame thereof, or flowed fuller or lower than was reported; and I hung on his words attentively; but of the matter I was as a careless and scornful looker-on; and I was delighted with the sweetness of his discourse, more recondite, yet in manner less winning and harmonious, than that of Faustus. Of the matter, however, there was no comparison; for the one was wandering amid Manichæan delusions, the other teaching salvation most soundly. But *salvation is far from sinners*, such as I then stood before him; and as yet was I drawing nearer by little and little, and unconsciously.

I BECAME A CATECHUMEN

For though I took no pains to learn what he spake, but only to hear how he spake (for that empty care alone was left me, despairing of a way, open for man, to Thee), yet together with the words which I would choose, came also into my mind the things which I would refuse; for I could not separate them. And while I opened my heart to admit "how eloquently he spake," there also entered "how truly he spake"; but this by degrees. For first, these things also had now begun to appear to me capable of defence; and the Catholic faith, for which I had thought nothing could be said against the Manichees' objections, I now thought might be maintained without shamelessness; especially after I had heard one or two places of the Old Testament resolved, and ofttimes *"in a figure,"* which when I understood literally, I was slain spiritually.

Very many places then of those books having been explained, I now blamed my despair, in believing that no answer could be given to such as hated and scoffed at the Law and the Prophets. Yet did I not therefore then see that the Catholic way was to be held, because it also could find learned maintainers, who could at large and with some show of reason answer objections; nor that what I held was therefore to be condemned, because both sides could be maintained. For the Catholic cause seemed to me in such sort not vanquished, as still not as yet to be victorious.

Hereupon I earnestly bent my mind, to see if in any way I could by any certain proof convict the Manichees of falsehood. Could I once have conceived a spiritual substance, all their strongholds had been beaten down, and cast utterly out of my mind; but I could not. Notwithstanding, concerning the frame of this world, and the whole of nature, which the senses of the flesh can reach to, as I more and more considered and compared things, I judged the tenets of most of the philosophers to have been much more probable. So then after the manner of the Academics (as they are supposed) doubting of everything, and wavering between all, I settled so far, that the Manichees were to be abandoned; judging that, even while doubting, I might not continue in that sect, to which I already preferred some of the philosophers; to which philosophers notwithstanding, for that they were without the saving Name of Christ, I utterly refused to commit the cure of my sick soul. I determined therefore so long to be a Catechumen in the Catholic Church, to which I had been commended by my parents, till something certain should dawn upon me, whither I might steer my course.

The Sixth Book

MY MOTHER ARRIVED AT MILAN

O THOU, *my hope from my youth*, where wert Thou to me, and whither wert Thou gone? Hadst not Thou created me, and separated me from the beasts of the field, and fowls of the air? Thou hadst made me wiser, yet did I walk in darkness, and in slippery places, and sought Thee abroad out of myself, and found not the God of my heart; and had come into the depths of the sea, and distrusted and despaired of ever finding truth.

My mother had now come to me, resolute through piety, following me over sea and land, in all perils confiding in Thee. For in perils of the sea, she comforted the very mariners (by whom passengers unacquainted with the deep, use rather to be comforted when troubled), assuring them of a safe arrival, because Thou hadst by a vision assured her thereof. She found me in grievous peril, through despair of ever finding truth. But when I had discovered to her that I was now no longer a Manichee, though not yet a Catholic Christian, she was not overjoyed, as at something unexpected; although she was now assured concerning that part of my misery, for which she bewailed me as one dead, though to be reawakened by Thee, carrying me forth upon the *bier* of her thoughts, that Thou mightest say to the *son of the widow, Young man, I say unto thee, Arise; and he should revive,*

and begin to speak, and thou shouldest deliver him to his mother. Her heart then was shaken with no tumultuous exultation, when she heard that what she daily desired of Thee was already in so great part realised; in that, though I had not yet attained the truth, I was rescued from falsehood; but, as being assured, that Thou, who hadst promised the whole, wouldest one day give the rest, most calmly, and with a heart full of confidence, she replied to me, "She believed in Christ, that before she departed this life, she should see me a Catholic believer."

Thus much to me. But to Thee, Fountain of mercies, poured she forth more copious prayers and tears, that Thou wouldest hasten Thy help, and enlighten my darkness; and she hastened the more eagerly to the Church, and hung upon the lips of Ambrose, praying for *the fountain of that water, which springeth up unto life everlasting.* But that man she loved *as an angel of God,* because she knew that by him I had been brought for the present to that doubtful state of faith I now was in, through which she anticipated most confidently that I should pass from sickness unto health, after the access, as it were, of a sharper fit, which physicians call "the crisis."

MY MOTHER'S OBEDIENCE TO AMBROSE

When then my mother had once, as she was wont in Africa, brought to the Churches built in memory of the Saints, certain cakes, and bread and wine, and was forbidden by the door-keeper; so soon as she knew that the Bishop had forbidden this, she so piously and obediently embraced his wishes, that I myself wondered how readily she censured her own practice, rather than discuss his prohibition. For wine-bibbing did not lay siege to her spirit, nor did love of wine provoke her to hatred of the truth, as it doth too many (both men and women), who revolt at a lesson of sobriety, as men well-drunk at a draught mingled with water. But she, when she had brought her basket with the accustomed festival-food, to be but tasted by herself, and then given away, never joined therewith more than one small cup of wine, diluted according to her own abstemious habits, which for courtesy she would taste.

And if there were many churches of the departed saints that were to be honoured in that manner, she still carried round that same one cup, to be used every where; and this, though not only made very watery, but unpleasantly heated with carrying about, she would distribute to those about her by small sips; for she sought there devotion, not pleasure. So soon, then, as she found this custom to be forbidden by that famous preacher and most pious prelate, even to those that would use it soberly, lest so an occasion of excess might be given to the drunken; and for that these, as it were, anniversary funeral solemnities did much resemble the superstition of the Gentiles, she most willingly forbare it: and for a basket filled with fruits of the earth, she had learned to bring to the Churches of the martyrs a breast filled with more purified petitions, and to give what she could to the poor; that so the communication of the Lord's Body might be there rightly celebrated, where, after the example of His Passion, the martyrs had been sacrificed and crowned.

But yet it seems to me, O Lord my God, and thus thinks my heart of it in Thy sight, that perhaps she would not so readily have yielded to the cutting off of this custom, had it been forbidden by another, whom she loved not as Ambrose, whom, for my salvation, she loved most entirely; and he her again, for her most religious conversation, whereby in good works, *so fervent in spirit*, she was constant at church; so that, when he saw me, he often burst forth into her praises; congratulating me that I had such a mother; not knowing what a son she had in me, who doubted of all these things, and imagined the way to life could not be found out.

AMBROSE KNEW NOT MY PREDICAMENT

Nor did I yet groan in my prayers, that Thou wouldest help me; but my spirit was wholly intent on learning, and restless to dispute. And Ambrose himself, as the world counts happy, I esteemed a happy man, whom personages so great held in such honour; only his celibacy seemed to me a painful course. But what hope he bore within him, what struggles he had against the temptations which beset his very excellencies, or what comfort in adversities, and what sweet joys Thy Bread had for the hidden mouth of his spirit, when chewing the cud thereof, I neither could conjecture, nor had experienced.

Nor did he know the tides of my

feelings, or the abyss of my danger. For I could not ask of him, what I would as I would, being shut out both from his ear and speech by multitudes of busy people, whose weaknesses he served. With whom when he was not taken up (which was but a little time), he was either refreshing his body with the sustenance absolutely necessary, or his mind with reading. But when he was reading, his eye glided over the pages, and his heart searched out the sense, but his voice and tongue were at rest.

Ofttimes when we had come (for no man was forbidden to enter, nor was it his wont that any who came should be announced to him), we saw him thus reading to himself, and never otherwise; and having long sat silent (for who durst intrude on one so intent?) we were fain to depart, conjecturing that in the small interval which he obtained, free from the din of others' business, for the recruiting of his mind, he was loth to be taken off; and perchance he dreaded lest if the author he read should deliver any thing obscurely, some attentive or perplexed hearer should desire him to expound it, or to discuss some of the harder questions; so that his time being thus spent, he could not turn over so many volumes as he desired; although the preserving of his voice (which a very little speaking would weaken) might be the truer reason for his reading to himself. But with what intent soever he did it, certainly in such a man it was good.

I however certainly had no opportunity of enquiring what I wished of that so holy oracle of Thine, his breast, unless the thing might be answered briefly. But those tides in me, to be poured out to him, required his full leisure, and never found it. I heard him indeed every Lord's day, *rightly expounding the Word of truth* among the people; and I was more and more convinced that all the knots of those crafty calumnies, which those our deceivers had knit against the Divine Books, could be unravelled. But when I understood withal, that *"man, created by Thee after Thine own image,"* was not so understood by Thy spiritual sons, whom of the Catholic Mother Thou hast born again through grace as though they believed and conceived of Thee as bounded by human shape (although what a spiritual substance should be I had not even a faint or shadowy notion); yet, with joy I blushed at having so many years barked not against the Catholic faith, but against the fictions of carnal imaginations.

For so rash and impious had I been, that what I ought by enquiring to have learned, I had pronounced on, condemning. For Thou, Most High, and most near; most secret, and most present; Who hast not limbs some larger, some smaller, but art wholly every where, and no where in space, art not of such corporeal shape, yet hast Thou made man after Thine own image; and behold, from head to foot is he contained in space.

MY CONFUSION

Ignorant then how this Thy image should subsist, I should have knocked and proposed the doubt, how it was to be believed, not insultingly opposed it, as if believed. Doubt, then, what to hold for certain, the more sharply gnawed my heart, the more ashamed I was, that so long deluded and deceived by the promise of certainties, I had with childish error and vehemence, prated of so many uncertainties. For that they were falsehoods became clear to me later.

However I was certain that they were uncertain, and that I had formerly accounted them certain, when with a blind contentiousness, I accused Thy Catholic Church, whom I now discovered, not indeed as yet to teach truly, but at least not to teach that for which I had grievously censured her. So I was confounded, and converted; and I joyed, O my God, that the One Only Church, the body of Thine Only Son (wherein the name of Christ had been put upon me as an infant), had no taste for infantine conceits; nor in her sound doctrine maintained any tenet which should confine Thee, the Creator of all, in space, however great and large, yet bounded every where by the limits of a human form.

I joyed also that the old Scriptures of the law and the Prophets were laid before me, not now to be perused with that eye to which before they seemed absurd, when I reviled Thy holy ones for so thinking, whereas indeed they thought not so: and with joy I heard Ambrose in his sermons to the people, oftentimes most diligently recommend this test for a rule, *The letter killeth, but the Spirit giveth life;* whilst he drew aside the mystic veil, laying open spiritually what, according to the letter, seemed to teach something unsound; teaching herein nothing that offended me, though he taught what I knew not as yet, whether it were true.

For I kept my heart from assenting to any thing, fearing to fall headlong; but by hanging in suspense I was the worse killed. For I wished to be as assured of the things I saw not, as I was that seven and three are ten. For I was not so mad as to think that even this could not be comprehended; but I desired to have other things as clear as this, whether things corporeal, which were not present to my senses, or spiritual, whereof I knew not how to conceive, except corporeally.

And by believing might I have been cured, that so the eyesight of my soul being cleared, might in some way be directed to Thy truth, which abideth always, and in no part faileth. But as it happens that one who has tried a bad physician, fears to trust himself with a good one, so was it with the health of my soul, which could not be healed but by believing, and lest it should believe falsehoods, refused to be cured; resisting Thy hands, who hast prepared the medicines of faith, and hast applied them to the diseases of the whole world, and given unto them so great authority.

MY FAITH GROWS

Being led, however, from this to prefer the Catholic doctrine, I felt that her proceeding was more unassuming and honest, in that she required to be believed things not demonstrated (whether it was that they could in themselves be demonstrated but not to certain persons, or could not at all be), whereas among the Manichees our credulity was mocked by a promise of certain knowledge, and then so many most fabulous and absurd things were imposed to be believed, because they could not be demonstrated.

Then Thou, O Lord, little by little with most tender and most merciful hand, touching and composing my heart, didst persuade me—considering what innumerable things I believed, which I saw not, nor was present while they were done, as so many things in secular history, so many reports of places and of cities, which I had not seen; so many of friends, so many of physicians, so many continually of other men, which unless we should believe, we should do nothing at all in this life; lastly, with how unshaken an assurance I believed of what parents I was born, which I could not know, had I not believed upon hearsay—considering all this, Thou didst persuade me, that not they who believed Thy Books (which Thou hast established in so great authority among almost all nations), but they who believed them not, were to be blamed; and that they were not to be heard who should say to me, "How knowest thou those Scriptures to have been imparted unto mankind by the Spirit of the one true and most true God?" For this very thing was of all most to be believed, since no contentiousness of blasphemous questionings, of all that multitude which I had read in the self-contradicting philosophers, could wring this belief from me, "That Thou art" whatsoever Thou wert (what I knew not), and "That the government of human things belongs to Thee."

This I believed, sometimes more strongly, more weakly otherwhiles; yet I ever believed both that Thou wert, and hadst a care of us; though I was ignorant, both what was to be thought of Thy substance, and what way led or led back to Thee. Since then we were too weak by abstract reasonings to find out truth: and for this very cause needed the authority of Holy Writ; I had now begun to believe that Thou wouldest never have given such excellency of authority to that Writ in all lands, hadst Thou not willed thereby to be believed in, thereby sought.

For now what things, sounding strangely in the Scripture, were wont to offend me, having heard divers of them expounded satisfactorily, I referred to the depths of the mysteries, and its authority appeared to me the more venerable, and more worthy of religious credence, in that, while it lay open to all to read, it reserved the majesty of its mysteries within its profounder meaning, stooping to all in the great plainness of its words and lowliness of its style, yet calling forth the intensest application of such as are not light of heart; that so it might receive all in its open bosom, and through narrow passages waft over towards Thee some few, yet many more than if it stood not aloft on such a height of authority, nor drew multitudes within its bosom by its holy lowliness. These things I thought on, and Thou wert with me; I sighed, and Thou heardest me; I wavered, and Thou didst guide me; I wandered through the broad way of the world, and Thou didst not forsake me.

I DESIRED FAME, FORTUNE, AND MARRIAGE

I panted after honours, gains, marriage; and Thou deridest me. In these desires I underwent most bitter crosses, Thou being the more gracious, the less Thou sufferedst aught to grow sweet to me, which was not Thou. Behold my heart, O Lord, who wouldest I should remember all this, and confess to Thee. Let my soul cleave unto Thee, now that Thou hast freed it from that fast-holding birdlime of death. How wretched was it! and Thou didst irritate the feeling of its wound, that forsaking all else, it might be converted unto Thee, who art above all, and without whom all things would be nothing; be converted, and be healed.

How miserable was I then, and how didst Thou deal with me, to make me feel my misery on that day, when I was preparing to recite a panegyric of the Emperor, wherein I was to utter many a lie, and lying, was to be applauded by those who knew I lied, and my heart was panting with these anxieties, and boiling with the feverishness of consuming thoughts. For, passing through one of the streets of Milan, I observed a poor beggar, then, I suppose, with a full belly, joking and joyous: and I sighed, and spoke to the friends around me, of the many sorrows of our frenzies; for that by all such efforts of ours, as those wherein I then toiled, dragging along, under the goading of desire, the burden of my own wretchedness, and, by dragging, augmenting it, we yet looked to arrive only at that very joyousness whither that beggar-man had arrived before us, who should never perchance attain it. For what he had obtained by means of a few begged pence, the same was I plotting for by many a toilsome turning and winding; the joy of a temporary felicity.

For he verily had not the true joy; but yet I with those my ambitious designs was seeking one much less true. And certainly he was joyous, I anxious; he void of care, I full of fears. But should any ask me, had I rather be merry or fearful? I would answer, merry. Again, if he asked had I rather be such as he was, or what I then was? I should choose to be myself, though worn with cares and fears; but out of wrong judgment; for, was it the truth? For I ought not to prefer myself to him, because more learned than he, seeing I had no joy therein, but sought to please men by it; and that not to instruct, but simply to please. Wherefore also Thou didst break my bones with the staff of Thy correction.

Away with those then from my soul who say to her, "It makes a difference whence a man's joy is. That beggarman joyed in drunkenness; Thou desiredst to joy in glory." What glory, Lord? That which is not in Thee. For even as his was no true joy, so was that no true glory: and it overthrew my soul more. He that very night should digest his drunkenness; but I had slept and risen again with mine, and was to sleep again, and again to rise with it, how many days, Thou, God, knowest. But "it doth make a difference whence a man's joy is." I know it, and the joy of a faithful hope lieth incomparably beyond such vanity.

Yea, and so was he then beyond me: for he verily was the happier; not only for that he was thoroughly drenched in mirth, I disembowelled with cares: but he, by fair wishes, had gotten wine; I, by lying, was seeking for empty, swelling praise. Much to this purpose said I then to my friends: and I often marked in them how it fared with me; and I found it went ill with me, and grieved, and doubled that very ill; and if any prosperity smiled on me, I was loth to catch at it, for almost before I could grasp it, it flew away.

ALYPIUS FORSOOK THE CIRCUS

These things we, who are living as friends together, bemoaned together, but chiefly and most familiarly did I speak thereof with Alypius and Nebridius, of whom Alypius was born in the same town with me, of persons of chief rank there, but younger than I. For he had studied under me, both when I first lectured in our town, and afterwards at Carthage, and he loved me much, because I seemed to him kind, and learned; and I him, for his great towardliness to virtue, which was eminent enough in one of no greater years.

Yet the whirlpool of Carthaginian habits (amongst whom those idle spectacles are hotly followed) had drawn him into the madness of the Circus. But while he was miserably tossed therein, and I, professing rhetoric there, had a public school, as yet he used not my teaching, by reason of some unkindness risen betwixt his father and me. I had found then how deadly he doted upon the Circus, and was deeply grieved that he seemed likely, nay, or had thrown away so great promise: yet had I no means of advising or with a sort of constraint reclaiming him, either by the kindness of a friend, or the authority of a master. For I supposed that he thought of me as did his father; but he was not

such; laying aside then his father's mind in that matter, he began to greet me, come sometimes into my lecture-room, hear a little, and be gone.

I however had forgotten to deal with him, that he should not through a blind and headlong desire of vain pastimes, undo so good a wit. But Thou, O Lord, who guidest the course of all Thou hast created, hadst not forgotten him, who was one day to be among Thy children, Priest and Dispenser of Thy Sacrament; and that his amendment might plainly be attributed to Thyself, Thou effectedst it through me, but unknowingly. For as one day I sat in my accustomed place, with my scholars before me, he entered, greeted me, sat down, and applied his mind to what I then handled.

I had by chance a passage in hand, which while I was explaining, a likeness from the Circensian races occurred to me, as likely to make what I would convey pleasanter and plainer, seasoned with biting mockery of those whom that madness had enthralled; God, Thou knowest that I then thought not of curing Alypius of that infection. But he took it wholly to himself, and thought that I said it simply for his sake. And whence another would have taken occasion of offence with me, that right-minded youth took as a ground of being offended at himself, and loving me more fervently. For Thou hadst said it long ago, and put it into Thy book, *Rebuke a wise man and he will love thee.* But I had not rebuked him, but Thou, who employest all, knowing or not knowing, in that order which Thyself knowest (and that order is just), didst of my heart and tongue make burning coals, by which to set on fire the hopeful mind, thus languishing, and so cure it.

Let him be silent in Thy praises, who considers not Thy mercies, which confess unto Thee out of my inmost soul. For he upon that speech burst out of that pit so deep, wherein he was wilfully plunged, and was blinded with its wretched pastimes; and he shook his mind with a strong self-command; whereupon all the filths of the Circensian pastimes flew off from him, nor came he again thither. Upon this, he prevailed with his unwilling father that he might be my scholar. He gave way, and gave in. And Alypius beginning to be my hearer again, was involved in the same superstition with me, loving in the Manichees that show of continency which he supposed true and unfeigned. Whereas it was a senseless and seducing continency, ensnaring precious souls, unable as yet to reach the depth of virtue, yet readily beguiled with the surface of what was but a shadowy and counterfeit virtue.

ALYPIUS' LOVE FOR THE CIRCUS

He, not forsaking that secular course which his parents had charmed him to pursue, had gone before me to Rome, to study law, and there he was carried away incredibly with an incredible eagerness after the shows of gladiators. For being utterly averse to and detesting such spectacles, he was one day by chance met by divers of his acquaintance and fellow-students coming from dinner, and they with a familiar violence haled him, vehemently refusing and resisting, into the Amphitheatre, during these cruel and deadly shows, he thus protesting:

''Though you hale my body to that place, and there set me, can you force me also to turn my mind or my eyes to those shows? I shall then be absent while present, and so shall overcome both you and them.'' They hearing this, led him on nevertheless, desirous perchance to try that very thing, whether he could do as he said.

When they were come thither, and had taken their places as they could, the whole place kindled with that savage pastime. But he, closing the passages of his eyes, forbade his mind to range abroad after such evils; and would he had stopped his ears also! For in the fight, when one fell, a mighty cry of the whole people striking him strongly, overcome by curiosity, and as if prepared to despise and be superior to it whatsoever it were, even when seen, he opened his eyes, and was stricken with a deeper wound in his soul than the other, whom he desired to behold, was in his body; and he fell more miserably than he upon whose fall that mighty noise was raised, which entered through his ears, and unlocked his eyes, to make way for the striking and beating down of a soul, bold rather than resolute, and the weaker, in that it had presumed on itself, which ought to have relied on Thee.

For so soon as he saw that blood, he therewith drunk down savageness; nor turned away, but fixed his eye, drinking in frenzy, unawares, and was delighted with that guilty fight, and intoxicated with the bloody pastime. Nor was he now the man he came, but one of the throng he came unto, yea, a true associate of theirs that brought him thither. Why say more? He beheld, shouted, kindled, carried thence with him the madness which should goad him to return not only with them who first drew him thither, but also before them, yea and to draw in others. Yet thence didst Thou with a most strong and most merciful hand pluck him, and taughtest him to have confidence not in himself, but in Thee. But this was after.

ALYPIUS FALSELY ACCUSED

But this was already being laid up in his memory to be a medicine hereafter. So was that also, that when he was yet studying under me at Carthage, and was thinking over at midday in the market-place what he was to say by heart (as scholars use to practise), Thou sufferedst him to be apprehended by the officers of the market-place for a thief. For no other cause, I deem, didst Thou, our God, suffer it but that he who was hereafter to prove so great a man, should already begin to learn that in judging of causes, man was not readily to be condemned by man out of a rash credulity.

For as he was walking up and down by himself before the judgment-seat, with his note-book and pen, lo, a young man, a lawyer, the real thief, privily bringing a hatchet, got in, unperceived by Alypius, as far as the leaden gratings which fence in the silversmiths' shops, and began to cut away the lead. But the noise of the hatchet being heard, the silversmiths beneath began to make a stir, and sent to apprehend whomever they should find. But he hearing their voices, ran away, leaving his hatchet, fearing to be taken with it. Alypius now, who had not seen him enter, was aware of his going, and saw with what speed he made away. And being desirous to know the matter, entered the place; where finding the hatchet, he was standing, wondering and considering it, when behold, those that had been sent, find him alone with the hatchet in his hand, the noise whereof had startled and brought them thither. They seize him, hale him away, and gathering the dwellers in the market-place together, boast of having taken a notorious thief, and so he was being led away to be taken before the judge.

But thus far was Alypius to be instructed. For forthwith, O Lord, Thou succouredst his innocency, whereof Thou alone wert witness. For as he was being led either to prison or to punishment, a certain architect met them, who had the chief charge of the public buildings. Glad they were to meet him especially, by whom they were wont to be suspected of stealing the goods lost out of the market-place, as though to show him at last by whom these thefts were committed.

He, however, had divers times seen Alypius at a certain senator's house, to whom he often went to pay his respects; and recognising him immediately, took him aside by the hand, and enquiring the occasion of so great a calamity, heard the whole matter, and bade all present, amid much uproar and threats, to go with him. So they came to the house of the young man who had done the deed. There, before the door, was a boy so young as to be likely, not apprehending any harm to his master, to disclose the whole. For he had attended his master to the market-place. Whom so soon as

Alypius remembered, he told the architect: and he showing the hatchet to the boy, asked him "Whose that was?" "Ours," quoth he presently: and being further questioned, he discovered every thing. Thus the crime being transferred to that house, and the multitude ashamed, which had begun to insult over Alypius, he who was to be a dispenser of Thy Word, and an examiner of many causes in Thy Church, went away better experienced and instructed.

ALYPIUS—MAN OF CHARACTER

Him then I had found at Rome, and he clave to me by a most strong tie, and went with me to Milan, both that he might not leave me, and might practise something of the law he had studied, more to please his parents than himself. There he had thrice sat as Assessor, with an uncorruptness much wondered at by others, he wondering at others rather who could prefer gold to honesty.

His character was tried besides, not only with the bait of covetousness, but with the goad of fear. At Rome he was Assessor to the count of the Italian Treasury. There was at that time a very powerful senator, to whose favours many stood indebted, many much feared. He would needs, by his usual power, have a thing allowed him which by the laws was unallowed. Alypius resisted it: a bribe was promised; with all his heart he scorned it: threats were held out; he trampled upon them: all wondering at so unwonted a spirit, which neither desired the friendship, nor feared the enmity of one so great and so mightily renowned for innumerable means of doing good or evil.

And the very Judge, whose councillor Alypius was, although also unwilling it should be, yet did not openly refuse, but put the matter off upon Alypius, alleging that he would not allow him to do it: for in truth had the Judge done it, Alypius would have decided otherwise. With this one thing in the way of learning was he well-nigh seduced, that he might have books copied for him at Prætorian prices, but consulting justice, he altered his deliberation for the better; esteeming equity whereby he was hindered more gainful than the power whereby he were allowed. These are slight things, *but he that is faithful in little, is faithful also in much.* Nor can that any how be void, which proceeded out of the mouth of Thy Truth: *If ye have not been faithful in the unrighteous Mammon, who will commit to your trust true riches? And if ye have not been faithful in that which is another man's, who shall give you that which is your own?* He being such, did at that time cleave to me, and with me wavered in purpose, what course of life was to be taken.

Nebridius also, who having left his native country near Carthage, yea and Carthage itself, where he had much lived, leaving his excellent family-estate and house, and a mother behind, who was not to follow him, had come to Milan, for no other reason but that with me he might live in a most ardent search after truth and wisdom. Like me he sighed, like me he wavered, an ardent searcher after true life, and a most acute examiner of the most difficult questions.

Thus were there the mouths of three indigent persons, sighing out their wants one to another, and *waiting upon Thee that Thou mightest give them their meat in due season*. And in all the bitterness which by Thy mercy followed our worldly affairs, as we looked towards the end, why we should suffer all this, darkness met us; and we turned away groaning, and saying, *How long shall these things be?* This too we often said; and so saying forsook them not, for as yet there dawned nothing certain, which, these forsaken, we might embrace.

I HESITATED TO FOLLOW GOD

And I, viewing and reviewing things, most wondered at the length of time from that my nineteenth year, wherein I had begun to kindle with the desire of wisdom, settling when I had found her, to abandon all the empty hopes and lying frenzies of vain desires. And lo, I was now in my thirtieth year, sticking in the same mire, greedy of enjoying things present, which passed away and wasted my soul; while I said to myself, "To-morrow I shall find it; it will appear manifestly, and I shall grasp it; Faustus the Manichee will come, and clear every thing! O you great men, ye Academicians, it is true then, that no certainty can be attained for the ordering of life! Nay, let us search the more diligently, and despair not. Lo, things in the ecclesiastical books are not absurd to us now, which sometimes seemed absurd, and may be otherwise taken, and in a good sense.

"I will take my stand, where, as a child, my parents placed me, until the clear truth be found out. But where shall it be sought or when? Ambrose has no leisure; we have no leisure to read; where shall we find even the books? Whence, or when procure them? from whom borrow them? Let set times be appointed, and certain hours be ordered for the health of our soul.

"Great hope has dawned; the Catholic Faith teaches not what we thought, and vainly accused it of; her instructed members hold it profane to believe God to be bounded by the figure of a human body: and do we doubt to 'knock,' that the rest 'may be opened'? The forenoons our scholars take up; what do we during the rest? Why not this? But when then pay we court to our great friends, whose favour we need? When compose what we may sell to scholars? When refresh ourselves, unbending our minds from this intenseness of care?

"Perish every thing, dismiss we these empty vanities, and betake ourselves to the one search for truth! Life is vain, death uncertain; if it steals upon us on a sudden, in what state shall we depart hence? and where shall we learn what here we have neglected? and shall we not rather suffer the punishment of this negligence? What, if death itself cut off and end all care and feeling? Then must this be ascertained. But God forbid this! It is no vain and empty thing, that the excellent dignity of the authority of the Christian Faith hath overspread the whole world. Never would such and so great things be by God wrought for us, if with the death of the body the life of the soul came to an end.

"Wherefore delay then to abandon worldly hopes, and give ourselves wholly to seek after God and the blessed life? But wait! Even those things are pleasant; they have some, and no small sweetness. We must not lightly abandon them, for it were a shame to return again to them. See, it is no great matter now to obtain some station, and then what should we more wish for? We have store of powerful friends; if nothing else offer, and we be in much haste, at least a presidentship may be given us: and a wife with some money, that she increase not our charges: and this shall be the bound of desire. Many great men, and most worthy of imitation, have given themselves to the study of wisdom in the state of marriage."

While I went over these things, and these winds shifted and drove my heart this way and that, time passed on, but I delayed to turn to the Lord; and from day to day deferred to live in Thee, and deferred not daily to die in myself. Loving a happy life, I feared it in its own abode, and sought it, by fleeing from it. I thought I should be too miserable, unless folded in female arms; and of the medicine of Thy mercy to cure that infirmity I thought not, not having tried it.

As for continency, I supposed it to be in our own power (though in myself I did not find that power), being so foolish as not to know what is written, *None can be continent unless Thou give it;* and that Thou wouldest give it, if with inward groanings I did knock at Thine ears, and with a settled faith did cast my care on Thee.

ALYPIUS KEPT ME FROM MARRYING

Alypius indeed kept me from marrying; alleging that so could we by no means with undistracted leisure live together in the love of wisdom, as we had long desired. For himself was even then most pure in this point, so that it was wonderful; and that the more, since in the outset of his youth he had entered into that course, but had not stuck fast therein; rather had he felt remorse and revolting at it, living thenceforth until now most continently.

But I opposed him with the examples of those who as married men had cherished wisdom, and served God acceptably, and retained their friends, and loved them faithfully. Of whose greatness of spirit I was far short; and bound with the disease of the flesh and its deadly sweetness, drew along my chain, dreading to be loosed, and as if my wound had been fretted, put back his good persuasions, as it were the hand of one that would unchain me. Moreover, by me did the serpent speak unto Alypius himself, by my tongue weaving and laying in his path pleasurable snares, wherein his virtuous and free feet might be entangled.

For when he wondered that I, whom he esteemed not slightly, should stick so fast in the birdlime of that pleasure, as to protest (so oft as we discussed it) that I could never lead a single life; and urged in my defence when I saw him wonder, that there was great difference between his momentary and scarce-remembered knowledge of that life, which so he might easily despise, and my continued acquaintance whereto if but the honourable name of marriage were added, he ought not to wonder why I could not contemn that course; he began also to desire to be married; not as overcome with desire of such pleasure, but out of curiosity.

For he would fain know, he said, what that should be, without which my life, to him so pleasing, would to me seem not life but a punishment. For his mind, free from that chain, was amazed at my thraldom; and through that amazement was going on to a desire of trying it, thence to the trial itself, and thence perhaps to sink into that bondage wherat he wondered, seeing he was willing to *make a covenant with death; and he that loves danger, shall fall into it.*

For whatever honour there be in the office of well-ordering a married life, and a family, moved us but slightly. But me for the most part the habit of satisfying an insatiable appetite tormented, while it held me captive; him, an admiring wonder was leading captive. So were we, until Thou, O Most High, not forsaking our dust, commiserating us miserable, didst come to our help, by wondrous and secret ways.

MY MARRIAGE PLANS

Continual effort was made to have me married. I wooed, I was promised, chiefly through my mother's pains, that so once married, the health-giving baptism might cleanse me, towards which she rejoiced that I was being daily fitted, and observed that her prayers, and Thy promises, were being fulfilled in my faith. At which time verily, both at my request and her own longing, with strong cries of heart she daily begged of Thee, that Thou wouldest by a vision discover unto her something concerning my future marriage; Thou never wouldest.

She saw indeed certain vain and fantastic things, such as the energy of the human spirit, busied thereon, brought together; and these she told me of, not with that confidence she was wont, when Thou showedst her any thing, but slighting them. For she could, she said, through a certain feeling, which in words she could not express, discern betwixt Thy revelations, and the dreams of her own soul. Yet the matter was pressed on, and a maiden asked in marriage, two years under the fit age; and as pleasing, was waited for.

OUR PLANS COME APART

And many of us friends conferring about, and detesting the turbulent turmoils of human life, had debated and now almost resolved on living apart from business and the bustle of men; and this was to be thus obtained; we were to bring whatever we might severally procure, and make one household of all; so that through the truth of our friendship nothing should belong especially to any; but the whole thus derived from all, should as a whole belong to each, and all to all. We thought there might be some ten persons in this society; some of whom were very rich, especially Romanianus our townsman, from childhood a very familiar friend of mine, whom the grievous perplexities of his affairs had brought up to court; who was the most earnest for this project; and therein was his voice of great weight, because his ample estate far exceeded any of the rest.

We had settled also that two annual officers, as it were, should provide all things necessary, the rest being undisturbed. But when we began to consider whether the wives, which some of us already had, others hoped to have, would allow this, all that plan, which was being so well moulded, fell to pieces in our hands, was utterly dashed and cast aside. Thence we betook us to sighs, and groans, and our steps to follow the *broad and beaten ways* of the world; for many thoughts were in our heart, *but Thy counsel standeth for ever.* Out of which counsel Thou didst deride ours, and preparedst Thine own; purposing to *give us meat in due season, and to open Thy hand, and to fill our souls with blessing.*

I WAS A SLAVE OF LUST

Meanwhile my sins were being multiplied, and my concubine being torn from my side as a hindrance to my marriage, my heart which clave unto her was torn and wounded and bleeding. And she returned to Africa, vowing unto Thee never to know any other man, leaving with me my son by her. But unhappy I, who could not imitate a very woman, impatient of delay, inasmuch as not till after two years was I to obtain her I sought, not being so much a lover of marriage as a slave to lust, procured another, though no wife, that so by the servitude of an enduring custom, the disease of my soul might be kept up and carried on in its vigour, or even augmented, into the dominion of marriage. Nor was that my wound cured, which had been made by the cutting away of the former, but after inflammation and most acute pain, it mortified, and my pains became less acute, but more desperate.

MY MISERY INCREASED

To Thee be praise, glory to Thee, Fountain of mercies. I was becoming more miserable, and Thou nearer. Thy right hand was continually ready to pluck me out of the mire, and to wash me thoroughly, and I knew it not; nor did any thing call me back from a yet deeper gulf of carnal pleasures, but the fear of death, and of Thy judgment to come; which amid all my changes, never departed from my breast.

And in my disputes with my friends Alypius and Nebridius of the nature of good and evil, I held that Epicurus had in my mind won the palm, had I not believed that after death there remained a life for the soul, and places of requital according to men's deserts, which Epicurus would not believe. And I asked, "were we immortal, and to live in perpetual bodily pleasures, without fear of losing it, why should we not be happy, or what else should we seek?" not knowing that great misery was involved in this very thing, that, being thus sunk and blinded, I could not discern that light of excellence and beauty, to be embraced for its own sake, which the eye of flesh cannot see, and is seen by the inner man.

Nor did I, unhappy, consider from what source it sprung, that even on these things, foul as they were, I with pleasure discoursed with my friends, nor could I, even according to the notions I then had of happiness, be happy without friends, amid what abundance soever of carnal pleasures. And yet these friends I loved for themselves only, and I felt that I was beloved of them again for myself only.

O crooked paths! Woe to the audacious soul, which hoped, by forsaking Thee, to gain some better thing! Turned it hath, and turned again, upon back, sides, and belly, yet all was painful; and Thou alone rest. And behold, Thou art at hand, and deliverest us from our wretched wanderings, and placest us in Thy way, and dost comfort us, and say, "Run; I will carry you; yea I will bring you through; there also will I carry you."

The Seventh Book

I CONTINUED TO STRUGGLE
WITH GOD'S NATURE

DECEASED WAS NOW that my evil and abominable youth, and I was passing into early manhood; the more defiled by vain things as I grew in years, who could not imagine any substance, but such as is wont to be seen with these eyes. I thought not of Thee, O God, under the figure of a human body; since I began to hear aught of wisdom, I always avoided this; and rejoiced to have found the same in the faith of our spiritual mother, Thy Catholic Church. But what else to conceive Thee I knew not. And I, a man, and such a man, sought to conceive of Thee the sovereign, only, true God; and I did in my inmost soul believe that Thou wert incorruptible, and uninjurable, and unchangeable; because though not knowing whence or how, yet I saw plainly, and was sure, that that which may be corrupted must be inferior to that which cannot; what could not be injured I preferred unhesitatingly to what could receive injury; the unchangeable to things subject to change.

My heart passionately cried out against all my phantoms, and with this one blow I sought to beat away from the eye of my mind all that unclean troop which buzzed around it. And lo, being scarce put off, in the twinkling of an eye they gathered again thick about me, flew against my face, and beclouded it; so that though not under the form of the human body, yet was I constrained to conceive of Thee (that incorruptible, uninjurable, and unchangeable, which I preferred before the corruptible, and injurable, and changeable) as being in space, whether infused into the world, or diffused infinitely without it. Because whatsoever I conceived, deprived of this space, seemed to me nothing, yea altogether nothing, not even a void, as if a body were taken out of its place, and the place should remain empty of any body at all, of earth and water, air and heaven, yet would it remain a void place, as it were a spacious nothing.

I then being thus gross-hearted, nor clear even to myself, whatsoever was not extended over certain spaces, nor diffused, nor condensed, nor swelled out, or did not or could not receive some of these dimensions, I thought to be altogether nothing. For over such forms as my eyes are wont to range, did my heart then range: nor yet did I see that this same notion of the mind, whereby I formed those very images, was not of this sort, and yet it could not have formed them, had not itself been some great thing. So also did I endeavour to conceive of Thee, Life of my life, as vast, through infinite spaces on every side penetrating the whole mass of the universe, and beyond it, every way, through unmeasurable boundless spaces; so that the earth should have Thee, the heaven have Thee, all things have Thee, and they be bounded in Thee, and Thou bounded nowhere.

For that as the body of this air which is above the earth, hindereth not the light of the sun from passing through it, penetrating it, not by bursting or by cutting, but by filling it wholly: so I thought the body not of heaven, air, and sea only, but of the earth too, previous to Thee, so that in all its parts, the greatest as the smallest, it should admit Thy presence, by a secret inspiration within and without, directing all things which Thou hast created. So I guessed, only as unable to conceive aught else, for it was false. For thus should a greater part of the earth contain a greater portion of Thee, and a less, a lesser: and all things should in such sort be full of Thee, that the body of an elephant should contain more of Thee than that of a sparrow, by how much larger it is and takes up more room; and thus shouldest Thou make the several portions of Thyself present unto the several portions of the world, in fragments, large to the large, petty to the petty. But such are not Thou. But not as yet hadst Thou enlightened my darkness.

I WAS AIDED BY NEBRIDIUS

It was enough for me, Lord, to oppose to those deceived deceivers, and dumb praters, since Thy word sounded not out of them—that was enough which long ago, while we were yet at Carthage, Nebridius used to propound, at which all we that heard it were staggered: "That said nation of darkness, which the Manichees are wont to set as an opposing mass over against Thee, what could it have done unto Thee, hadst Thou refused to fight with it? For, if they answered, 'it would have done Thee some hurt,' then shouldest Thou be subject to injury and corruption: but if 'it could do Thee no hurt,' then was no reason brought for Thy fighting with it; and fighting in such wise, as that a certain portion or member of Thee, or offspring of Thy very Substance, should be mingled with opposed powers, and natures not created by Thee, and be by them so far corrupted and changed to the worse, as to be turned from happiness into misery, and need assistance, whereby it might be extricated and purified; and that this offspring of Thy Substance was the soul, which being enthralled, defiled, corrupted, Thy Word free, pure and whole might relieve; that Word itself being still corruptible because it was of one and the same Substance. So then, should they affirm Thee, whatsoever Thou art, that is, Thy Substance whereby Thou art, to be incorruptible, then were all these sayings false and execrable; but if corruptible, the very statement showed it to be false and revolting." This argument then of Nebridius sufficed against those who deserved wholly to be vomited out of the overcharged stomach; for they had no escape, without horrible blasphemy of heart and tongue, thus thinking and speaking of Thee.

THE PROBLEM OF EVIL

But I also as yet, although I held and was firmly persuaded that Thou our Lord the true God, who madest not only our souls, but our bodies, and not only our souls and bodies, but all beings, and all things wert undefilable and unalterable, and in no degree mutable; yet understood I not, clearly and without difficulty, the cause of evil. And yet whatever it were, I perceived it was in such wise to be sought out, as should not constrain me to believe the immutable God to be mutable, lest I should become that evil I was seeking out.

I sought it out then, thus far free from anxiety, certain of the untruth of what these held, from whom I shrunk with my whole heart: for I saw, that through enquiring the origin of evil, they were filled with evil, in that they preferred to think that Thy substance did suffer ill than their own did commit it.

And I strained to perceive what I now heard, that freewill was the cause of our doing ill, and Thy just judgment of our suffering ill. But I was not able clearly to discern it. So then endeavouring to draw my soul's vision out of that deep pit, I was again plunged therein, and endeavouring often, I was plunged back as often. But this raised me a little into Thy light, that I knew as well that I had a will, as that I lived: when then I did will or nill any thing, I was most sure that no other than myself did will and nill: and I all but saw that there was the cause of my sin. But what I did against my will, I saw that I suffered rather than did, and I judged not to be my fault, but my punishment; whereby however, holding Thee to be just, I speedily confessed myself to be not unjustly punished.

But again I said, Who made me? Did not my God, who is not only good, but goodness itself? Whence then came I to will evil and nill good, so that I am thus justly punished? who set this in me, and ingrafted into me this plant of bitterness, seeing I was wholly formed by my most sweet God? If the devil were the author, whence is that same devil? And if he also by his own perverse will, of a good angel became a devil, whence, again, came in him that evil will whereby he became a devil, seeing the whole nature of angels was made by that most good Creator? By these thoughts I was again sunk down and choked; yet not brought down to that hell of error (where no man confesseth unto Thee), to think rather that Thou dost suffer ill, than that man doth it.

GOD IS INCORRUPTIBLE

For I was in such wise striving to find out the rest, as one who had already found that the incorruptible must needs be better than the corruptible: and Thee therefore, whatsoever Thou wert, I confessed to be incorruptible. For never soul was, nor shall be able to conceive any thing which may be better than Thou, who art the sovereign and the best good. But since most truly and certainly, the incorruptible is preferable to the corruptible (as I did now prefer it), then, wert Thou not incorruptible, I could in thought have arrived at something better than my God. Where then I saw the incorruptible to be preferable to the corruptible, there ought I to seek for Thee, and there observe "wherein evil itself was"; that is whence corruption comes, by which Thy substance can by no means be impaired.

For corruption does no ways impair our God; by no will, by no necessity, by no unlooked-for chance: because He is

God, and what He wills is good, and Himself is that good; but to be corrupted is not good. Nor art Thou against Thy will constrained to any thing, since Thy will is not greater than Thy power. But greater should it be, were Thyself greater than Thyself. For the will and power of God is God Himself. And what can be unlooked for by Thee, who knowest all things? Nor is there any nature in things, but Thou knowest it. And what should we more say, "why that substance which God is should not be corruptible," seeing if it were so, it should not be God?

WHENCE IS EVIL?

And I sought "whence is evil," and sought in an evil way; and saw not the evil in my very search. I set now before the sight of my spirit the whole creation, whatsoever we can see therein (as sea, earth, air, stars, trees, mortal creatures); yea, and whatever in it we do not see, as the firmament of heaven, all angels moreover, and all the spiritual inhabitants thereof. But these very beings, as though they were bodies, did my fancy dispose in place, and I made one great mass of Thy creation, distinguished as to the kinds of bodies; some, real bodies, some, what myself had feigned for spirits. And this mass I made huge, not as it was (which I could not know), but as I thought convenient, yet every way finite.

But Thee, O Lord, I imagined on every part environing and penetrating it, though every way infinite: as if there were a sea, every where, and on every side, through unmeasured space, one only boundless sea, and it contained within it some sponge, huge, but bounded; that sponge must needs, in all its parts, be filled from that unmeasurable sea: so conceived I Thy creation, itself finite, full of Thee, the Infinite; and I said, Behold God, and behold what God hath created; and God is good, yea, most mightily and incomparably better than all these: but yet He, the Good, created them good; and see how He environeth and fulfils them.

Where is evil then, and whence, and how crept it in hither? What is its root, and what its seed? Or hath it no being? Why then fear we and avoid what is not? Or if we fear it idly, then is that very fear evil, whereby the soul is thus idly goaded and racked. Yea, and so much a greater evil, as we have nothing to fear, and yet do fear. Therefore either is that evil which we fear, or else evil is, that we fear. Whence is it then? seeing God, the Good, hath created all these things good. He indeed, the greater and chiefest Good, hath created these lesser goods; still both Creator and created, all are good.

Whence is evil? Or, was there some evil matter of which He made, and formed, and ordered it, yet left something in it which He did not convert into good? Why so then? Had He no right to turn and change the whole, so that no evil should remain in it, seeing He is Almighty? Lastly, why should He make any thing at all of it, and not rather by the same All-mightiness cause it not to be at all? Or, could it then be against His will? Or if it were from eternity, why suffered He it so to be for infinite spaces of times past, and was pleased so long after to make something out of it? Or if He were suddenly pleased now to effect somewhat, this rather should the All-mighty have effected, that this evil matter should not be, and He alone be, the whole, true, sovereign, and infinite Good. Or if it was not good that He who was good should not also frame and create something that were good, then, that evil matter being taken away and brought to nothing, He might form good matter, whereof to create all things. For He should not be All-mighty, if He might not create something good without the aid of that matter which Himself had not created.

These thoughts I revolved in my miserable heart, overcharged with most gnawing cares, lest I should die ere I had found the truth; yet was the faith of Thy Christ, our Lord and Saviour, professed in the Church Catholic, firmly fixed in my earth, in many points, indeed, as yet unformed, and fluctuating from the rule of doctrine; yet did not my mind utterly leave it, but rather daily took in more and more of it.

AN EXAMINATION OF ASTROLOGY

By this time also had I rejected the lying divinations and impious dotages of the astrologers. Let Thine own mercies, out of my very inmost soul, confess unto Thee for this also, O my God. For Thou, Thou altogether (for who else calls us back from the death of all errors, save the Life which cannot die, and the Wisdom which needing no light enlightens the minds that need it, whereby the universe is directed, down to the whirling leaves of trees?)—Thou madest provision for my obstinacy wherewith I struggled against Vindicianus, an acute old man, and Nebridius, a young man of admirable talents; the first vehemently affirming, and the latter often (though with some doubtfulness) saying, "That there was no such art whereby to foresee things to come, but that men's conjectures were a sort of lottery, and that out of many things which they said should come to pass, some actually did, unawares to them who spake it, who stumbled upon it, through their oft speaking."

Thou providest then a friend for me, no negligent consuler of the astrologers; nor yet well skilled in those arts, but (as I said) a curious consuler with them, and yet knowing something, which he said he had heard of his father, which how far it went to overthrow the estimation of that art, he knew not. This man then, Firminus by name, having had a liberal education, and well taught in Rhetoric, consulted me, as one very dear to him, what, according to his so-called constellations, I thought on certain affairs of his, wherein his worldly hopes had risen, and I, who had herein now begun to incline towards Nebridius' opinion, did not altogether refuse to conjecture, and tell him what came into my unresolved mind: but added, that I was now almost persuaded that these were but empty and ridiculous follies.

Thereupon he told me that his father had been very curious in such books, and had a friend as earnest in them as himself, who with joint study and conference fanned the flame of their affections to these toys, so that they would observe the moments whereat the very dumb animals, which bred about their houses, gave birth, and then observed the relative position of the heavens, thereby to make fresh experiments in this so-called art. He said then that he had heard of his father, that what time his mother was about to give birth to him, Firminus, a woman-servant of that friend of his father's was also with child, which could not escape her master, who took care with most exact diligence to know the births of his very puppies. And so it was that (the one for his wife, and the other for his servant, with the most careful observation, reckoning days, hours, nay, the lesser divisions of the hours) both were delivered at the same instant; so that both were constrained to allow the same constellations, even to the minutest points, the one for his son, the other for his new-born slave.

For so soon as the women began to be in labour, they each gave notice to the other what was fallen out in their houses, and had messengers ready to send to one another so soon as they had notice of the actual birth, of which they had easily provided, each in his own province, to give instant intelligence. Thus then the messengers of the respective parties met, he averred, at such an equal distance from either house, that neither of them could make out any difference in the position of the stars, or any other minutest points; and yet Firminus, born in a high estate in his parents' house, ran his course through the gilded paths of life, was increased in riches, raised to honours; whereas that slave continued to serve his masters, without any relaxation of his yoke, as Firminus, who knew him, told me.

Upon hearing and believing these things, told by one of such credibility, all that my resistance gave way; and first I endeavoured to reclaim Firminus himself from that curiosity, by telling him that upon inspecting his constellations, I ought, if I were to predict truly, to have seen in them parents eminent among their neighbours, a noble family in its own city, high birth, good education, liberal learning. But if that servant had consulted me upon the same constellations, since they were his also, I ought again (to tell him too truly) to see in them a lineage the most abject, a slavish condition, and every thing else utterly at variance with the former. Whence then, if I spake the truth, I should, from the same constellations, speak diversely, or if I spake the same, speak falsely: thence it followed most certainly that whatever, upon consideration of the constellations, was spoken truly, was spoken not out of art, but chance; and whatever spoken falsely, was not out of ignorance in the art, but the failure of the chance.

An opening thus made, ruminating with myself on the like things, that no one of those dotards (who lived by such a trade, and whom I longed to attack, and with derision to confute) might urge against me that Firminus had informed me falsely, or his father him; I bent my thoughts on those that are born twins, who for the most part come out of the womb so near one to other, that the small interval (how much force soever in the nature of things folk may pretend it to have) cannot be noted by human observation, or be at all expressed in those figures which the astrologer is to inspect, that he may pronounce truly. Yet they cannot be true: for looking into the same figures, he must have predicted the same of Esau and Jacob, whereas the same happened not to them. Therefore he must speak falsely; or if truly, then, looking into the same figures, he must not give the same answer. Not by art, then, but by chance, would he speak truly.

For Thou, O Lord, most righteous Ruler of the Universe, while consulters and consulted know it not, dost by Thy hidden inspiration effect that the consulter should hear what, according to the hidden deservings of souls, he ought to hear, out of the unsearchable depth of Thy just judgment, to Whom let no man say, What is this? Why that? Let him not so say, for he is man.

I WAS STILL PLAGUED BY THE SOURCE OF EVIL

Now then, O my Helper, hadst thou loosed me from those fetters: and I sought "whence is evil," and found no way. But thou sufferedst me not by any fluctuations of thought to be carried away from the Faith whereby I believed Thee both to be, and Thy substance to be unchangeable, and that Thou hast a care of, and wouldest judge men, and that in Christ, Thy Son, our Lord, and the holy Scriptures, which the authority of Thy Catholic Church pressed upon me, Thou hadst set the way of man's salvation, to that life which is to be after this death. These things being safe and immovably settled in my mind, I sought anxiously "whence was evil?"

What were the pangs of my teeming heart, what groans, O my God! yet even there were Thine ears open, and I knew it not: and when in silence I vehemently sought, those silent contritions of my soul were strong cries unto Thy mercy. Thou knewest what I suffered, and no man. For, what was that which was thence through my tongue distilled into the ears of my most familiar friends? Did the whole tumult of my soul, for which neither time nor utterance sufficed, reach them? Yet went up the whole to Thy hearing, all which I roared out from the groanings of my heart; and my desire was before Thee, and the light of mine eyes was not with me: for that was within, I without: nor was that confined to place, but I was intent on things contained in place, but there found I no resting-place, nor did they so receive me, that I could say, "It is enough," "it is well": nor did they yet suffer me to turn back, where it might be well enough with me.

For to these things was I superior, but inferior to Thee; and Thou art my true joy when subjected to Thee, and Thou hadst subjected to me what Thou createdst below me. And this was the true temperament, and middle region of my safety, to remain in Thy Image, and by serving Thee, rule the body. But when I rose proudly against Thee, and *ran against the Lord with my neck, with the thick bosses of my buckler,* even these inferior things were set above me, and pressed me down, and no where was there respite or space for breathing. They met my sight on all sides by heaps and troops, and in thought the images thereof presented themselves unsought, as I would return to Thee, as if they would say unto me, "Whither goest thou, unworthy and defiled?" And these things had grown out of my wound; for Thou "humbledst the proud like one that is wounded," and through my own swelling was I separated from Thee; yea, my pride-swollen face closed up mine eyes.

THOU BROUGHT ME TO THYSELF

But Thou, Lord, *abidest for ever,* yet not for ever art Thou angry with us; because Thou pitiest our dust and ashes and it was pleasing in Thy sight to reform my deformities and by inward goads didst Thou rouse me, that I should be ill at ease, until Thou wert manifested to my inward sight. Thus, by the secret hand of Thy medicining was my swelling abated, and the troubled and bedimmed eye-sight of my mind, by the smarting anointings of healthful sorrows, was from day to day healed.

I READ THE BOOKS OF THE PLATONISTS

And Thou, willing first to show me how Thou *resistest the proud, but givest grace unto the humble,* and by how great an act of Thy Mercy Thou hadst traced out to men the way of humility, in that Thy WORD was made flesh, and dwelt among men—Thou procuredst for me, by means of one puffed up with most unnatural pride, certain books of the Platonists, translated from Greek into Latin. And therein I read, not indeed in the very words, but to the very same purpose, enforced by many and divers reasons, that *In the beginning was the Word, and the Word was with God, and the Word was God: the Same was in the beginning with God: all things were made by Him, and without Him was nothing made: that which was made by Him is life, and the life was the light of men, and the light shineth in the* *darkness, and the darkness comprehended it not.*

And that the soul of man, though it *bears witness to the light,* yet itself *is not that light;* but the Word of God, being God, *is that true light that lighteth every man that cometh into the world.* And that *He was in the world, and the world was made by Him, and the world knew Him not.* But that *He came unto His own, and His own received him not; but as many as received Him, to them gave He power to become the sons of God, as many as believed in His name;* this I read not there.

Again I read there, that *God the Word was born not of flesh, nor of blood, nor of the will of man, nor of the will of the flesh, but of God.* But that *the Word was made flesh, and dwelt among us,* I read not there. For I traced in those books that it was many and divers ways said, that *the Son was in the form of the Father, and thought it not robbery to be equal with God,* for that naturally He was the Same Substance. But that *He emptied himself, taking the form of a servant, being made in the likeness of men, and found in fashion as a man, humbled Himself, and became obedient unto death, and that the death of the cross: wherefore God exalted Him* from the dead *and gave Him a name above every name, that at the name of Jesus every knee should bow, of things in heaven, and things in earth, and things under the earth; and that every tongue should confess that the Lord Jesus Christ is in the Glory of God the Father;* those books have not.

For that before all times and above all times Thy Only-Begotten Son remaineth unchangeable, co-eternal with Thee, and that of *His fulness souls receive,* that they may be blessed; and that by participation of wisdom abiding in them, they are renewed, so as to be wise, is there. But that *in due time He died for the ungodly;* and that *Thou sparedst not Thine Only Son, but deliveredst Him for us all,* is not there. *For Thou hiddest these things from the wise, and revealedst them to babes;* that they *that labour and are heavy laden might come unto Him, and He refresh them,* because *He is meek and lowly in heart; and the meek He directeth in judgment, and the gentle He teacheth His ways, beholding our loneliness and trouble, and forgiving all our sins.*

But such as are lifted up in the lofty walk of some would-be sublimer learning, hear not Him, saying, *Learn of Me, for I am meek and lowly in heart, and ye shall find rest to your souls. Although they knew God, yet they glorify Him not as God, nor are thankful, but wax vain in their thoughts; and their foolish heart is darkened; professing that they were wise, they became fools.*

And therefore did I read there also, that they had *changed the glory of Thy incorruptible nature* into idols and divers shapes, *into the likeness of the image of corruptible man, and birds, and beasts, and creeping things;* namely, into that Egyptian food for which Esau lost his birthright, for that Thy first-born people worshipped the head of a four-footed beast instead of Thee; turning in heart back towards Egypt; and bowing Thy image, their own soul, before the image of *a calf that eateth hay.* These things found I here, but I fed not on them.

For it pleased Thee, O Lord, to take away the reproach of diminution from Jacob, *that the elder should serve the younger:* and Thou calledst the Gentiles into Thine inheritance. And I had come to Thee from among the Gentiles; and I set my mind upon the gold which Thou willedst Thy people to take from Egypt, seeing Thine it was, wheresoever it were. And to the Athenians Thou saidst by Thy Apostle, *that in Thee we live, move, and have our being, as one of their own poets had said.* And verily these books came from thence. But I set not my mind on the idols of Egypt, *whom they served with Thy gold, who changed the truth of God into a lie, and worshipped and served the creature more than the Creator.*

LIGHT AND TRUTH

And being thence admonished to return to myself, I entered even into my inward self, Thou being my Guide: and able I was, for Thou wert become my Helper. And I entered and beheld with the eye of my soul (such as it was), above the same eye of my soul, above my mind, the Light Unchangeable. Not this ordinary light, which all flesh may look upon, nor as it were a greater of the same kind, as though the brightness of this should be manifold brighter, and with its greatness take up all space. Not such was this light, but other, yea, far other from all these. Nor was it above my soul, as oil is above water, nor yet as heaven above earth: but above to my soul, because It made me; and I below It, because I was made by It.

He that knows the Truth, knows what that Light is; and he that knows It, knows eternity. Love knoweth it. O Truth Who art Eternity! and Love Who art Truth! and Eternity Who art Love! Thou art my God, to Thee do I sigh night and day. Thee when I first knew, Thou liftedst me up, that I might see there was what I might see, and that I was not yet such as to see. And Thou didst beat back the weakness of my sight, streaming forth Thy beams of light upon me most strongly, and I trembled with love and awe: and I perceived myself to be far off from Thee, in the region of unlikeness, as if I heard this Thy voice from on high: "I am the food of grown men; grow and thou shalt feed upon Me; nor shalt thou convert Me, like the food of thy flesh, into thee, but thou shalt be converted into Me."

And I learned, that *Thou for iniquity chastenest man, and Thou madest my soul to consume away like a spider.* And I said, "Is Truth therefore nothing because it is not diffused through space finite or infinite?" And Thou criedst to me from afar: "Yea, verily, *I AM that I AM.*" And I heard, as the heart heareth, nor had I room to doubt, and I should sooner doubt that I live than that Truth is not, *which is clearly seen, being understood by those things which are made.*

ALL THINGS COME FROM GOD

And I beheld the other things below Thee, and I perceived that they neither altogether are, nor altogether are not, for they are, since they are from Thee, but are not, because they are not, what Thou art. For that truly is which remains unchangeably. *It is good then*

for me to hold fast unto God; for if I remain not in Him, I cannot in myself; but *He remaining in Himself, reneweth all things. And Thou art the Lord* my God since Thou *standest not in need of my goodness.*

CORRUPTION AND INCORRUPTION

And it was manifested unto me, that those things be good which yet are corrupted; which neither were they sovereignly good, nor unless they were good could be corrupted: for if sovereignly good, they were incorruptible, if not good at all, there were nothing in them to be corrupted. For corruption injures, but unless it diminished goodness, it could not injure. Either then corruption injures not, which cannot be; or which is most certain, all which is corrupted is deprived of good. But if they be deprived of all good, they shall cease to be. For if they shall be, and can now no longer be corrupted, they shall be better than before, because they shall abide incorruptibly. And what more monstrous than to affirm things to become better by losing all their good? Therefore, if they shall be deprived of all good, they shall no longer be. So long therefore as they are, they are good: therefore whatsoever is, is good.

That evil then which I sought, whence it is, is not any substance: for were it a substance, it should be good. For either it should be an incorruptible substance, and so a chief good: or a corruptible substance; which unless it were good, could not be corrupted. I perceived therefore, and it was manifested to me that Thou madest all things good, nor is there any substance at all, which Thou madest not;

and for that Thou madest not all things equal, therefore are all things; because each is good, and altogether very good, because our God *made all things very good.*

And to Thee is nothing whatsoever evil: yea, not only to Thee, but also to Thy creation as a whole, because there is nothing without, which may break in, and corrupt that order which Thou hast appointed it. But in the parts thereof some things, because unharmonising with other some, are accounted evil: whereas those very things harmonise with others, and are good; and in themselves are good. And all these things which harmonise not altogether, do yet with the inferior part, which we call Earth, having its own cloudy and windy sky harmonising with it.

Far be it then that I should say, "These things should not be": for should I see nought but these, I should indeed long for the better; but still must even for these alone praise Thee; for that Thou art to be *praised,* do show *from the earth, dragons, and all deeps, fire, hail, snow, ice, and stormy wind which fulfil Thy word; mountains and all hills, fruitful trees, and all cedars; beasts, and all cattle, creeping things, and flying fowls; kings of the earth, and all people, princes, and all judges of the earth; young men and maidens, old men and young, praise Thy Name.* But when, from heaven, these *praise Thee, praise Thee, our God, in the heights, all Thy angels, all Thy hosts, sun and moon, all the stars and light, the Heaven of heavens, and the waters that be above the heavens, praise Thy Name;* I did not now long for things better because I conceived of all: and with a sounder judgment I apprehended that the things above were better than these below, but all together better than those above by themselves.

MY FRENZY WAS LULLED TO SLEEP

There is no soundness in them, whom aught of Thy creation displeaseth: as neither in me, when much which Thou hast made, displeased me. And because my soul durst not be displeased at my God, it would fain not account that Thine, which displeased it. Hence it had gone into the opinion of two substances, and had no rest, but talked idly. And returning thence, it had made to itself a God, through infinite measures of all space; and thought it to be Thee, and placed it in its heart; and had again become the temple of its own idol, to Thee abominable. But after Thou hadst soothed my head, unknown to me, and closed *mine eyes that they should not behold vanity,* I ceased somewhat of my former self, and my frenzy was lulled to sleep; and I awoke in Thee, and saw Thee infinite, but in another way, and this sight was not derived from the flesh.

GOD ONLY IS ETERNAL

And I looked back on other things; and I saw that they owed their being to Thee; and were all bounded in Thee: but in a different way; not as being in space; but because Thou containest all things in Thine hand in Thy Truth; and all things are true so far as they be; nor is there any falsehood unless when that is thought to be, which is not.

And I saw that all things did harmonise, not with their places only, but with their seasons. And that Thou, who only art Eternal, didst not begin to work after innumerable spaces of times spent; for that all spaces of times, both which have passed, and which shall pass, neither go nor come, but through Thee, working, and abiding.

INIQUITY—PERVERSION OF THE WILL

And I perceived and found it nothing strange, that bread which is pleasant to a healthy palate is loathsome to one distempered: and to sore eyes light is offensive, which to the sound is delightful. And Thy righteousness displeaseth the wicked; much more the viper and reptiles, which Thou hast created good, fitting in with the inferior portions of Thy Creation, with which the very wicked also fit in; and that the more, by how much they be unlike Thee; but with the superior creatures by how much they become more like to Thee. And I enquired what iniquity was, and found it to be no substance, but the perversion of the will, turned aside from Thee, O God, the Supreme, towards these lower things, and *casting out its bowels*, and puffed up outwardly.

A REMEMBRANCE OF THEE

And I wondered that I now loved Thee, and no phantasm for Thee. And yet did I not press on to enjoy my God; but was borne up to Thee by Thy beauty, and soon borne down from Thee by mine own weight, sinking with sorrow into these inferior things. This weight was carnal custom. Yet dwelt there with me a remembrance of Thee; nor did I any way doubt that there was One to whom I might cleave, but that I was not yet such as to cleave to Thee: for that *the body which is corrupted presseth down the soul, and the earthly tabernacle weigheth down the mind that museth upon many things.*

And most certain I was, *that Thy invisible works from the creation of the world are clearly seen, being understood by the things that are made, even Thy eternal power and Godhead.* For examining whence it was that I admired the beauty of bodies celestial or terrestrial; and what aided me in judging soundly on things mutable, and pronouncing, "This ought to be thus, this not;" examining, I say, whence it was that I so judged, seeing I did so judge, I had found the unchangeable and true Eternity of Truth above my changeable mind. And thus by degrees I passed from bodies to the soul, which through the bodily senses perceives; and thence to its inward faculty, to which the bodily senses represent things external, whitherto reach the faculties of beasts; and thence again to the reasoning faculty, to which what is received from the senses of the body is referred to be judged.

Which finding itself also to be in me a thing variable, raised itself up to its own understanding, and drew away my thoughts from the power of habit, withdrawing itself from those troops of contradictory phantasms; that so it might find what that light was whereby it was bedewed, when, without all doubting, it cried out, "That the unchangeable was to be preferred to the changeable"; whence also it knew That Unchangeable, which, unless it had in some way known, it had had no sure ground to prefer it to the changeable. And thus with the flash of one trembling glance it arrived at THAT WHICH IS. And then I saw Thy *invisible things understood by the things which are made.* But I could not fix my gaze thereon; and my infirmity being struck back, I was thrown again on my wonted habits, carrying along with me only a loving memory thereof, and a longing for what I had, as it were, perceived the odour of, but was not yet able to feed on.

I SOUGHT STRENGTH TO ENJOY THEE

Then I sought a way of obtaining strength sufficient to enjoy Thee; and found it not, until I embraced *that Mediator betwixt God and men, the Man Christ Jesus, who is over all, God blessed for evermore,* calling unto me, and saying, *I am the way, the truth, and the life, and mingling that* food which I was unable to receive, with our flesh. *For, the Word was made flesh,* that Thy wisdom, whereby Thou createdst all things, might provide milk for our infant state. For I did not hold to my Lord Jesus Christ, I, humbled, to the humble; nor knew I yet whereto His infirmity would guide us.

For Thy Word, the Eternal Truth, far above the higher parts of Thy Creation, raises up the subdued unto Itself: but in this lower world built for Itself a lowly habitation of our clay, whereby to abase from themselves such as would be subdued, and bring them over to Himself; allaying their swelling, and fomenting their love; to the end they might go on no further in self-confidence, but rather consent to become weak, seeing before their feet the Divinity weak by taking our *coats of skin;* and wearied, might cast themselves down upon It, and It rising, might lift them up.

MY LIMITED UNDERSTANDING OF CHRIST

But I thought otherwise; conceiving only of my Lord Christ as of a man of excellent wisdom, whom no one could be equalled unto; especially, for that being wonderfully born of a Virgin, He seemed, in conformity therewith, through the Divine care for us, to have attained that great eminence of authority, for an ensample of despising things temporal for the obtaining of immortality. But what mystery there lay in *"The Word was made flesh,"* I could not even imagine. Only I had learnt out of what is delivered to us in writing of Him that He did eat, and drink, sleep, walk, rejoiced in spirit, was sorrowful, discoursed; that flesh did not cleave by itself unto Thy Word but with the human soul and mind. All know this who know the unchangeableness of Thy Word, which I now knew, as far as I could, nor did I at all doubt thereof. For, now to move the limbs of the body by will, now not, now to be moved by some affection, now not, now to deliver wise sayings through human signs, now to keep silence, belong to soul and mind subject to variation.

And should these things be falsely written of Him, all the rest also would risk the charge, nor would there remain in those books any saving faith for mankind. Since then they were written truly, I acknowledged a perfect man to be in Christ; not the body of a man only, nor, with the body, a sensitive soul without a rational, but very man; whom, not only as being a form of Truth, but for a certain great excellency of human nature and a more perfect participation of wisdom, I judged to be preferred before others.

But Alypius imagined the Catholics to believe God to be so clothed with flesh, that besides God and flesh, there was no soul at all in Christ, and did not think that a human mind was ascribed to him. And because he was well persuaded that the actions recorded of Him could only be performed by a vital and a rational creature, he moved the more slowly towards the Christian Faith. But understanding afterwards that this was the error of the Apollinarian heretics, he joyed in and was conformed to the Catholic Faith. But somewhat later, I confess, did I learn how in that saying, *The Word was made flesh*, Catholic Truth is distinguished from the falsehood of Photinus. For the rejection of heretics makes the tenets of Thy Church and sound doctrine to stand out more clearly. *For there must also be heresies, that the approved may be made manifest among the weak.*

THE BOOKS OF THE PLATONISTS NOT ENOUGH

But having then read those books of the Platonists, and thence been taught to search for incorporeal truth, I saw Thy *invisible things, understood by those things which are made;* and though cast back, I perceived what that was which through the darkness of my mind I was hindered from contemplating, being assured, "That Thou wert, and wert infinite, and yet not diffused in space, finite or infinite; and that Thou truly art who art the same ever, in no part nor motion vary-

ing; and that all other things are from Thee, on this most sure ground alone, that they are."

Of these things I was assured, yet too unsure to enjoy Thee. I prated as one well skilled; but had I not sought Thy way in Christ our Saviour, I had proved to be, not skilled, but killed. For now I had begun to wish to seem wise, being filled with mine own punishment, yet I did not mourn, but rather scorn, puffed up with knowledge. For where was that charity building upon the *foundation* of humility, *which is Christ Jesus?* or when should these books teach me it?

Upon these, I believe, Thou therefore willedst that I should fall, before I studied Thy Scriptures, that it might be imprinted on my memory how I was affected by them; and that afterwards when my spirits were tamed through Thy books, and my wounds touched by Thy healing fingers, I might discern and distinguish between presumption and confession; between those who saw whither they were to go, yet saw not the way, and the way that leadeth not to behold only but to dwell in the beatific country.

For had I first been formed in Thy Holy Scriptures, and hadst Thou in the familiar use of them grown sweet unto me, and had I then fallen upon those other volumes, they might perhaps have withdrawn me from the solid ground of piety, or, had I continued in that healthful frame which I had thence imbibed, I might have thought that it might have been obtained by the study of those books alone.

MY DIFFICULTIES VANISHED

Most eagerly then did I seize that verenable writing of Thy Spirit: and chiefly the Apostle Paul. Whereupon those difficulties vanished away, wherein he once seemed to me to contradict himself, and the text of his discourse not to agree with the testimonies of the Law and the Prophets. And the face of that pure word appeared to me one and the same; and I learned to *rejoice with trembling.* So I began; and whatsoever truth I had read in those other books, I found here amid the praise of Thy Grace; that whoso sees, may not *so glory as if he had not received*, not only what he sees, but also that he sees *(for what hath he, which he hath not received?)* and that he may be not only admonished to behold Thee, *Who art* ever *the same, but also healed*, to hold Thee, and that *he who cannot see afar off*, may yet walk on the way, whereby he may arrive, and behold, and hold Thee.

For, though a man *be delighted with the law of God after the inner man*, what shall he do with that *other law in his members which warreth against the law of his mind, and bringeth him into captivity to the law of sin which is in his members?* For, *Thou art righteous, O Lord, but we have sinned and committed iniquity, and have done wickedly*, and Thy hand is grown heavy upon us, and *we are justly delivered over* unto that ancient sinner, the king of death; because he persuaded our will to be like his will, whereby *he abode not in Thy truth. What shall wretched man do? who shall deliver him from the body of this death, but* only *Thy Grace, through Jesus Christ our Lord*, whom Thou hast begotten co-eternal, and *formedst in the beginning of Thy ways, in whom the prince of this world found nothing worthy of death*, yet killed he Him; and *the handwriting, which was contrary to us, was blotted out?*

This those writings contain not. Those pages present not the image of this piety, the tears of confession, *Thy sacrifice, a troubled spirit, a broken and a contrite heart*, the salvation of the people, the *Bridal City*, the earnest *of the Holy Ghost, the Cup of our Redemption.* No man sings there. *Shall not my soul be submitted unto God? for of Him cometh my salvation. For He is my God and my salvation, my guardian, I shall no more be moved.* No one there hears Him call, *Come unto Me, all ye that labour.* They scorn to *learn of Him, because He is meek and lowly in heart; for these things hast Thou hid from the wise and prudent, and hast revealed them unto babes.*

For it is one thing, from the mountain's shaggy top to see the land of peace, and to find no way thither; and in vain to essay through ways unpassable, opposed and beset by fugitives and deserters, under their captain *the lion and the dragon:* and another to keep on the way that leads thither, guarded by the host of the heavenly General; where they spoil not who have deserted the heavenly army; for they avoid it, as very torment. These things did wonderfully sink into my bowels, when I read that *least of Thy Apostles*, and had meditated upon Thy works, and trembled exceedingly.

The Eighth Book

I HESITATED TO BUY THE GOODLY PEARL

O MY GOD, let me, with thanksgiving, remember, and confess unto Thee Thy mercies on me. *Let my bones* be bedewed with Thy love, and let them *say unto Thee, Who is like unto Thee, O Lord? Thou hast broken my bonds in sunder, I will offer unto Thee the sacrifice of thanksgiving.* And how Thou hast broken them, I will declare; and all who worship Thee, when they hear this, shall say, "Blessed be the Lord in heaven and in earth, great and wonderful is His name."

Thy words had stuck fast in my heart, and *I was hedged round about on all sides by Thee.* Of Thy eternal life I was now certain, though I saw it in a figure and as *through a glass.* Yet I had ceased to doubt that there was an incorruptible substance, whence was all other substance; nor did I now desire to be more certain of Thee, but more steadfast in Thee. But for my temporal life, all was wavering, and *my heart had to be purged from the old leaven.*

The Way, the Saviour Himself, well pleased me, but as yet I shrunk from going through its straitness.

And Thou didst put into my mind, and it seemed good in my eyes, to go to Simplicianus, who seemed to me a good servant of Thine; and Thy grace shone in him. I had heard also that from his very youth he had lived most devoted unto Thee. Now he was grown into years; and by reason of so great age spent in such zealous following of Thy ways, he seemed to me likely to have learned much experience; and so he had. Out of which store I wished that he would tell me (setting before him my anxieties) which were the fittest way for one in my case to walk in Thy paths.

For, I saw the church full; and one went this way, and another that way. But I was displeased that I led a secular life; yea now that my desires no longer inflamed me, as of old, with hopes of honour and profit, a very grievous burden it was to undergo so heavy a bondage. For, in comparison of Thy sweetness, *and the beauty of Thy house which I loved,* those things delighted me no longer. But still I was enthralled with the love of woman; nor did the Apostle forbid me to marry, although he advised me to something better, chiefly wishing *that all men were as himself was.* But I being weak, chose the more indulgent place; and because of this alone, was tossed up and down in all beside, faint and wasted with withering cares, because in other matters I was constrained against my will to conform myself to a married life, to which I was given up and enthralled.

I had heard from the mouth of the Truth, *that there were some eunuchs which had made themselves eunuchs for the kingdom of heaven's sake: but,* saith He, *let him who can receive it, receive it. Surely vain are all men who are ignorant of God, and could not out of the good things which are seen, find out Him who is good.* But I was no longer in that vanity; I had surmounted it; and by the common witness of all Thy creatures had found Thee our Creator, and Thy Word, God with Thee, and together with Thee one God, by whom Thou createdst all things.

There is yet another kind of ungodly, *who knowing God, glorified Him not as God, neither were thankful.* Into this also I had fallen, but *Thy right hand upheld me,* and took me thence, and Thou placedst me where I might recover. For Thou hast said unto man, *Behold, the fear of the Lord is wisdom,* and, *Desire not to seem wise;* because they *who affirmed themselves to be wise, became fools.* But I had now *found the goodly pearl, which, selling all that I had,* I ought to have *bought,* and I hesitated.

SIMPLICIANUS TOLD ME OF THE CONVERSION OF VICTORINUS

To Simplicianus then I went, the father of Ambrose (a Bishop now) in receiving Thy grace, and whom Ambrose truly loved as a father. To him I related the mazes of my wanderings. But when I mentioned that I had read certain books of the Platonists, which Victorinus, sometime Rhetoric Professor of Rome (who had died a Christian, as I had heard), had translated into Latin, he testified his joy that I had not fallen upon the writings of other philosophers, full of *fallacies and deceits, after the rudiments of this world,* whereas the Platonists many ways led to the belief in God and His Word.

Then to exhort me to the humility of Christ, *hidden from the wise, and revealed to little ones,* he spoke of Victorinus himself, whom while at Rome he had most intimately known: and of him he related what I will not conceal. For it contains great *praise of Thy grace,* to be confessed unto Thee, how that aged man, most learned and skilled in the liberal sciences, and who had read, and weighed so many works of the philosophers; the instructor of so many noble Senators, who also, as a monument of his excellent discharge of his office, had (which men of this world esteem a high honour) both deserved and obtained a statue in the Roman Forum; he, to that age a worshipper of idols, and a partaker of the sacrilegious rites, to which almost all the nobility of Rome were given up, and had inspired the people with the love of

"Anubis, barking Deity, and all
The monster Gods of every
    kind, who fought
'Gainst Neptune, Venus, and
    Minerva":

whom Rome once conquered, now adored, all which the aged Victorinus had with thundering eloquence so many years defended;—he now blushed not to be the child of Thy Christ, and the new-born babe of Thy fountain; submitting his neck to the yoke of humility, and subduing his forehead to the reproach of the Cross.

O Lord, Lord, *Which has bowed the heavens and come down, touched the mountains and they did smoke,* by what means didst Thou convey Thyself into that breast? He used to read (as Simplicianus said) the holy Scripture, most studiously sought and searched into all the Christian writings, and said to Simplicianus (not openly, but privately and as a friend), "Understand that I am already a Christian." Whereto he answered, "I will not believe it, nor will I rank you among Christians, unless I see you in the Church of Christ."

The other, in banter replied, "Do walls then make Christians?" And this he often said, that he was already a Christian; and Simplicianus as often made the same answer, and the conceit of the "walls" was by the other as often renewed. For he feared to offend his friends, proud dæmon-worshippers, from the height of whose Babylonian dignity, as from *cedars of Libanus*, which *the Lord* had not *yet broken down*, he supposed the weight of enmity would fall upon him.

But after that by reading and earnest thought he had gathered firmness, and feared to be *denied by Christ before the holy angels, should he now be afraid to confess Him before men*, and appeared to himself guilty of a heavy offence, in being ashamed of the Sacraments of the humility of Thy Word, and not being ashamed of the sacrilegious rites of those proud dæmons, whose pride he had imitated and their rites adopted, he became bold-faced against vanity, and shame-faced towards the truth, and suddenly and unexpectedly said to Simplicianus (as himself told me), "Go we to the Church; I wish to be made a Christian."

But he, not containing himself for joy, went with him. And having been admitted to the first Sacrament and become a Catechumen, not long after

he further gave in his name, that he might be regenerated by baptism, Rome wondering, the Church, rejoicing. The proud *saw, and were wroth; they gnashed with their teeth, and melted away.* But the *Lord* God *was the hope* of Thy servant, and *he regarded not vanities and lying* madness.

To conclude, when the hour was come for making profession of his faith (which at Rome they, who are about to approach to Thy grace, deliver, from an elevated place, in the sight of all the faithful, in a set form of words committed to memory), the presbyters, he said, offered Victorinus (as was done to such as seemed likely through bashfulness to be alarmed) to make his profession more privately: but he chose rather to profess his salvation in the presence of the holy multitude. "For it was not salvation that he taught in rhetoric, and yet that he had publicly professed: how much less then ought he, when pronouncing Thy word, to dread Thy meek flock, who, when delivering his own words, had not feared a mad multitude!"

When, then, he went up to make his profession, all, as they knew him, whispered his name one to another with the voice of congratulation. And who there knew him not? and there ran a low murmur through all the mouths of the rejoicing multitude, Victorinus! Victorinus! Sudden was the burst of rapture, that they saw him; suddenly were they hushed that they might hear him. He pronounced the true faith with an excellent boldness, and all wished to draw him into their very heart: yea by their love and joy they drew him thither, such were the hands wherewith they drew him.

THE GREATER THE JOY, THE GREATER THE PAIN

Good God! what takes place in man that he should more rejoice at the salvation of a soul despaired of, and freed from greater peril, than if there had always been hope of him, or the danger had been less? For so Thou also, merciful Father, *dost more rejoice over one penitent than over ninety-nine just persons that need no repentance.* And with much joyfulness do we hear, so often as we hear with what joy *the sheep which had strayed is brought back upon the shepherd's shoulder,* and *the groat is restored to Thy treasury, the neighbours rejoicing with the woman who found it,* and the joy of the solemn service of Thy house forceth to tears, when in Thy house it is read of Thy *younger son, that he was dead, and liveth again; had been lost, and is found.* For Thou *rejoicest* in us, and in Thy holy angels, holy through holy charity. For Thou art ever the same; for all things which abide not the same nor for ever, Thou for ever knowest in the same way.

What then takes place in the soul, when it is more delighted at finding or recovering the things it loves, than if it had ever had them? yea, and other things witness hereunto; and all things are full of witnesses, crying out, "So is it." The conquering commander triumphant; yet had he not conquered unless he had fought; and the more peril there was in the battle, so much the more joy is there in the triumph. The storm tosses the sailors, threatens shipwreck; all wax pale at approaching death; sky and sea are calmed, and they are exceedingly joyed, as having been exceeding afraid.

A friend is sick, and his pulse threatens danger; all who long for his recovery are sick in mind with him. He is restored, though as yet he walks not with his former strength; yet there is such joy, as was not, when before he walked sound and strong.

Yea, the very pleasures of human life men acquire by difficulties, not those only which fall upon us unlooked for, and against our wills, but even by self-chosen, and pleasure-seeking trouble. Eating and drinking have no pleasure, unless there precede the pinching of hunger and thirst. Men, given to drink, eat certain salt meats, to procure a troublesome heat, which the drink allaying, causes pleasure. It is also ordered that the affianced bride should not at once be given, lest as a husband he should hold cheap whom, as betrothed, he sighed not after.

This law holds in foul and accursed joy; this in permitted and lawful joy; this in the very purest perfection of friendship; this, in him *who was dead, and lived again; had been lost and was found.* Every where the greater joy is ushered in by the greater pain. What means this, O Lord my God, whereas Thou art everlastingly joy to Thyself, and some things around Thee evermore rejoice in Thee? What means this, that this portion of things thus ebbs and flows alternately displeased and reconciled? Is this their allotted measure? Is this all Thou hast assigned to them, whereas from the highest heavens to the lowest earth, from the beginning of the world to the end of ages, from the angel to the worm, from the first motion to the last, Thou settest each in its place, and realisest each in their season, every thing good after its kind? Woe is me! how high art Thou in the highest, and how deep in the deepest! and Thou never departest, and we scarcely return to Thee.

THOSE KNOWN TO MANY INFLUENCE MORE TOWARDS SALVATION

Up, Lord, and do; stir us up, and recall us; kindle and draw us; inflame, grow sweet unto us; let us now love, *let us run.* Do not many, out of a deeper hell of blindness than Victorinus, return to Thee, approach, and are enlightened, receiving that *Light,* which *they who receive, receive power from Thee to become Thy sons?* But if they be less known to the nations, even they that know them, joy less for them. For when many joy together, each also has more exuberant joy; for that they are kindled and inflamed one by the other. Again, because those known to many, influence the more towards salvation, and lead the way with many to follow. And therefore do they also who preceded them much rejoice not in them, because they rejoice not in them alone. For far be it, that in Thy tabernacle the persons of the rich should be accepted before the poor, or the noble before the ignoble; seeing rather *Thou hast chosen the weak things of the world to confound the strong; and the base things of this world, and the things despised hast Thou chosen, and those things which are not, that Thou mightest bring to nought things that are.* And yet even that *least of* Thy *Apostles,* by whose tongue Thou soundedest forth these words, when through his warfare, Paulus the Proconsul, his pride conquered, was made to pass under the *easy yoke* of Thy Christ, and became a provincial of the great King; he also for his former name Saul, was pleased to be called Paul, in testimony of so great a victory.

For the enemy is more overcome in one, of whom he hath more hold; by whom he hath hold of more. But the proud he hath more hold of, through their nobility; and by them, of more through their authority. By how much the more welcome then the heart of Victorinus was esteemed, which the devil had held as an impregnable possession, the tongue of Victorinus, with which mighty and keen weapon he had slain many; so much the more abundantly ought Thy sons to rejoice, for that our King *hath bound the strong man,* and they saw his *vessels taken from him and cleansed,* and *made meet for Thy honour;* and become *serviceable for the Lord, unto every good work.*

TWO WILLS STRUGGLED WITHIN ME

But when that man of Thine, Simplicianus, related to me this of Victorinus, I was on fire to imitate him; for for this very end had he related it. But when he had subjoined also, how in the days of the Emperor Julian a law was made, whereby Christians were forbidden to teach the liberal sciences or oratory; and how he, obeying this law, chose rather to give over the wordy school than Thy *Word,* by which Thou *makest eloquent the tongues of the dumb;* he seemed to me not more resolute than blessed, in having thus found opportunity to wait on Thee only. Which thing I was sighing for, bound as I was, not with another's irons, but by my own iron will. My will the enemy held, and thence had made a chain for me, and bound me. For of a froward will, was a lust made; and a lust served, became custom; and custom not resisted, became necessity. By which links, as it were, joined together (whence I called it a chain) a hard bondage held me enthralled. But that new will which had begun to be in me, freely to serve Thee, and to wish to enjoy Thee, O God, the only assured pleasantness, was not yet able to overcome my former wilfulness, strengthened by age. Thus did my two wills, one new, and the other old, one carnal, the other spiritual, struggle within me; and by their discord, undid my soul.

Thus I understood, by my own experience, what I had read, how *the flesh lusteth against the spirit and the spirit against the flesh.* Myself verily either way; yet more myself, in that which I approved in myself, than in that which in myself I disapproved. For in this last, it was now for the more part not myself, because in much I rather endured against my will, than acted willingly. And yet it was through me, that custom had obtained this power of warring against me, because I had come willingly, whither I willed not.

And who has any right to speak against it, if just punishment follow the sinner? Nor had I now any longer my former plea, that I therefore as yet hesitated to be above the world and serve Thee, for that the truth was not altogether ascertained to me; for now it too was. But I, still under service to the earth, refused to fight under Thy banner, and feared as much to be freed of all encumbrances, as we should fear to be encumbered with it.

Thus with the baggage of this present world was I held down pleasantly, as in sleep; and the thoughts wherein I meditated on Thee were like the efforts of such as would awake, who yet overcome with a heavy drowsiness, are again drenched therein. And as no one would sleep for ever, and in all men's sober judgment waking is better, yet a man for the most part, feeling a heavy lethargy in all his limbs, defers to shake off sleep, and though half displeased, yet even, after it is time to rise, with pleasure yields to it, so was I assured that much better were it for me to give myself up to Thy charity, than to give myself over to mine own cupidity; but though the former course satisfied me and gained the mastery, the latter pleased me and held me mastered.

Nor had I any thing to answer Thee calling to me, *Awake thou that sleepest, and arise from the dead, and Christ shall give thee light.* And when Thou didst on all sides show me that what Thou saidst was true, I, convicted by the truth, had nothing at all to answer, but only those dull and drowsy words, "Anon, anon," "presently," "leave me but a little." But "presently, presently," had no present, and my "little while" went on for a long while; in vain *I delighted in Thy law according to the inner man, when another law in my members rebelled against the law of my mind, and led me captive under the law of sin which was in my members.* For the law of sin is the violence of custom, whereby the mind is drawn and holden, even against its will; but deservedly, for that it willingly fell into it. *Who then should deliver me thus wretched from the body of this death, but Thy grace only, through Jesus Christ our Lord?*

PONTITIANUS SPOKE OF ANTONY

And how Thou didst deliver me out of the bonds of desire, wherewith I was bound most straitly to carnal concupiscence, and out of the drudgery of worldly things, I will now declare, and confess unto Thy name, *O Lord, my helper and my Redeemer.* Amid increasing anxiety, I was doing my wonted business, and daily sighing unto Thee. I attended Thy Church, whenever free from the business under the burden of which I groaned. Alypius was with me, now after the third sitting released from his law business, and waiting to whom to sell his counsel, as I sold the skill of speaking, if indeed teaching can impart it.

Nebridius had now, in consideration of our friendship, consented to teach under Verecundus, a citizen and a grammarian of Milan, and a very intimate friend of us all; who urgently desired, and by the right of friendship challenged from our company, such faithful aid as he greatly needed. Nebridius then was not drawn to this by any desire of advantage (for he might have made much more of his learning had he so willed), but as a most kind and gentle friend, he would not be wanting to a good office, and slight our request. But he acted herein very discreetly, shunning to become known to personages great according to this world, avoiding the distraction of mind thence ensuing, and desiring to have it free and at leisure, as many hours as might be, to seek, or read, or hear something concerning wisdom.

Upon a day then, Nebridius being absent (I recollect not why), lo, there came to see me and Alypius, one Pontitianus, our countryman so far as being an African, in high office in the Emperor's court. What he would with us, I know not, but we sat down to converse, and it happened that upon a table for some game, before us, he observed a book, took, opened it, and contrary to his expectation, found it the Apostle Paul; for he had thought it some of those books which I was wearing myself in teaching. Whereat smiling, and looking at me, he expressed his joy and wonder that he had on a sudden found this book, and this only before my eyes. For he was a Christian, and baptised, and often bowed himself before Thee our God in the Church, in frequent and continued prayers.

When then I had told him that I bestowed very great pains upon those Scriptures, a conversation arose (suggested by his account) on Antony the Egyptian monk; whose name was in high reputation among Thy servants, though to that hour unknown to us. Which when he discovered, he dwelt the more upon that subject, informing and wondering at our ignorance of one so eminent. But we stood amazed, hearing Thy wonderful works most fully attested, in times so recent, and almost in our own, wrought in the true Faith and Church Catholic. We all wondered; we, that they were so great, and he, that they had not reached us.

Thence his discourse turned to the flocks in the monasteries, and their holy ways, a sweet-smelling savour unto Thee, and the fruitful deserts of the wilderness, whereof we knew nothing. And there was a monastery at Milan, full of good brethren, without the city walls, under the fostering care of Ambrose, and we knew it not. He went on with his discourse, and we listened in intent silence. He told us then how one afternoon at Triers, when the Emperor was taken up with the Circensian games, he and three others, his companions, went out to walk in gardens near the city walls, and there as they happened to walk in pairs, one went apart with him, and the other two wandered by themselves; and these, in their wanderings, lighted upon a certain cottage, inhabited by certain of Thy servants, *poor in spirit, of whom is the kingdom of heaven,* and there they found a little book containing the life of Antony.

This one of them began to read, admire and kindle at it; and as he read, to meditate on taking up such a life, and giving over his secular service to serve Thee. And these two were of those whom they style agents for the public affairs. Then suddenly, filled with an holy love, and a sober shame, in anger with himself he cast his eyes upon his friend, saying, "Tell me, I pray thee, what would we attain by all these labours of ours? what aim we at? what serve we for? Can our hopes in court rise higher than to be the Emperor's favourites? and in this, what is there not brittle, and full of perils? and by how many perils arrive we at a greater peril? and when arrive we thither? But a friend of God, if I wish it, I become now at once." So spake he. And in pain with the travail of a new life, he turned his eyes again upon the book, and read on, and was changed inwardly, where Thou sawest, and his mind was stripped of the world, as soon appeared.

For as he read and rolled up and down the waves of his heart, he stormed at himself a while, then discerned, and determined on a better course; and now being Thine, said to his friend, "Now have I broken loose from those our hopes, and am resolved to serve God; and this, from this hour, in this place, I begin upon. If thou likest not to imitate me, oppose not."

The other answered, he would cleave to him, to partake so glorious a reward, so glorious a service.

Thus both being now Thine, were *building* the *tower* at the necessary *cost*, the *forsaking all that they had, and following Thee.*

Then Pontitianus and the other with him, that had walked in other parts of the garden, came in search of them to the same place; and finding them, reminded them to return, for the day was now far spent. But they relating their resolution and purpose, and how that will was begun and settled in them, begged them, if they would not join, not to molest them. But the others, though nothing altered from their former selves, did yet bewail themselves (as he affirmed), and piously congratulated them, recommending themselves to their prayers; and so, with hearts lingering on the earth, went away to the palace. But the other two, fixing their heart on heaven, remained in the cottage. And both had affianced brides, who when they heard hereof, also dedicated their virginity unto God.

I WAS FORCED TO SEE HOW FOUL I WAS

Such was the story of Pontitianus; but Thou, O Lord, while he was speaking, didst turn me round towards myself, taking me from behind my back where I had placed me, unwilling to observe myself; and setting me before my face, that I might see how foul I was, how crooked and defiled, bespotted and ulcerous. And I beheld and stood aghast; and whither to flee from myself I found not. And if I sought to turn mine eye from off myself, he went on with his relation, and Thou again didst set me over against myself, and thrustedst me before my eyes, that *I might find out mine iniquity, and hate it.* I had known it, but made as though I saw it not, winked at it, and forgot it.

But now, the more ardently I loved those whose healthful affections I heard of, that they had resigned themselves wholly to Thee to be cured, the more did I abhor myself, when compared with them. For many of my years (some twelve) had now run out with me since my nineteenth, when, upon the reading of Cicero's Hortensius, I was stirred to an earnest love of wisdom; and still I was deferring to reject mere earthly felicity, and give myself to search out that, whereof not the finding only, but the very search, was to be preferred to the treasures and kingdoms of the world, though already found, and to the pleasures of the body, though spread around me at my will.

But I wretched, most wretched, in the very commencement of my early youth, had begged chastity of Thee, and said, "Give me chastity and continency, only not yet." For I feared lest Thou shouldest hear me soon, and soon cure me of the disease of concupiscence, which I wished to have satisfied, rather than extinguished. And I had wandered through crooked ways in a sacrilegious superstition, not indeed assured thereof, but as preferring it to the others which I did not seek religiously, but opposed maliciously.

I had thought that I therefore deferred from day to day to reject the hopes of this world, and follow Thee only, because there did not appear aught certain, whither to direct my course. And now was the day come wherein I was to be laid bare to myself, and my conscience was to upbraid me. "Where art thou now, my tongue? Thou saidst that for an uncertain truth thou likedst not to cast off the baggage of vanity; now, it is certain, and yet that burden still oppresseth thee, while they who neither have worn themselves out with seeking it, nor for ten years and more have been thinking thereon, have had their shoulders lightened, and received wings to fly away."

Thus was I gnawed within, and exceedingly confounded with a horrible shame, while Pontitianus was so speaking. And he having brought to a close his tale and the business he came for, went his way; and I into myself. What said I not against myself? with what scourges of condemnation lashed I not my soul, that it might follow me, striving to go after Thee! Yet it drew back; refused, but excused not itself. All arguments were spent and confuted; there remained a mute shrinking; and she feared, as she would death, to be restrained from the flux of that custom, whereby she was wasting to death.

I ASKED ALYPIUS, "WHAT AILS US?"

Then in this great contention of my inward dwelling, which I had strongly raised against my soul, in *the chamber* of my heart, troubled in mind and countenance, I turned upon Alypius. "What ails us?" I exclaim: "what is it? what heardest thou? The unlearned start up and *take heaven by force*, and we with our learning, and without heart, lo, where we wallow in flesh and blood! Are we ashamed to follow, because others are gone before, and not ashamed not even to follow?" Some such words I uttered, and my fever of mind tore me away from him, while he, gazing on me in astonishment, kept silence.

For it was not my wonted tone; and my forehead, cheeks, eyes, colour, tone of voice, spake my mind more than the words I uttered.

A little garden there was to our lodging, which we had the use of, as of the whole house; for the master of the house, our host, was not living there. Thither had the tumult of my breast hurried me, where no man might hinder the hot contention wherein I had engaged with myself, until it should end as Thou knewest, I knew not. Only I was healthfully distracted and dying, to live; knowing what evil thing I was, and not knowing what good thing I was shortly to become. I retired then into the garden, and Alypius, on my steps. For his presence did not lessen my privacy; or how could he forsake me so disturbed? We sate down as far removed as might be from the house. I was troubled in spirit, most vehemently indignant that I entered not into Thy will and covenant, O my God, which *all my bones cried out* unto me to enter, and praised it to the skies. And therein we enter not by ships, or chariots, or feet, no, move not so far as I had come from the house to that place where we were sitting. For, not to go only, but to go in thither was nothing else but to will to go, but to will resolutely and thoroughly; not to turn and toss, this way and that, a maimed and half-divided will, struggling, with one part sinking as another rose.

Lastly, in the very fever of my irresoluteness, I made with my body many such motions as men sometimes would, but cannot, if either they have not the limbs, or these be bound with bands, weakened with infirmity, or any other way hindered. Thus, if I tore my hair, beat my forehead, if locking my fingers I clasped my knees; I willed, I did it. But I might have willed, and not done it; if the power of motion in my limbs had not obeyed. So many things then I did, when "to will" was not in itself "to be able"; and I did not what both I longed incomparably more to do, and which soon after, when I should will, I should be able to do; because soon after, when I should will, I should will thoroughly. For in these things the ability was one with the will, and to will was to do; and yet was it not done: and more easily did my body obey the weakest willing of my soul, in moving its limbs at its nod, than the soul obeyed itself to accomplish in the will alone this its momentous will.

THE WORKING OF THE MIND

Whence is this monstrousness? and to what end? Let Thy mercy gleam that I may ask, if so be the secret penalties of men, and those darkest pangs of the sons of Adam, may perhaps answer me. Whence is this monstrousness? and to what end? The mind commands the body, and it obeys instantly; the mind commands itself, and is resisted. The mind commands the hand to be moved; and such readiness is there, that command is scarce distinct from obedience. Yet the mind is mind, the hand is body. The mind commands the mind, its own self, to will and yet it doth not. Whence this monstrousness? and to what end?

It commands itself, I say, to will, and would not command, unless it willed, and what it commands is not done. But it willeth not entirely: therefore doth it not command entirely. For so far forth it commandeth, as it willeth; and, so far forth is the thing commanded, not done, as it willeth not. For the will commandeth that there be a will; not another, but itself. But it doth not command entirely, therefore what it commandeth, is not. For were the will entire, it would not even command it to be, because it would already be. It is therefore no monstrousness partly to will, partly to nill, but a disease of the mind, that it doth not wholly rise, by truth up-borne, borne down by custom. And therefore are there two wills, for that one of them is not entire: and what the one lacketh, the other hath.

I STRUGGLED TO DO RIGHT

Let them perish from Thy presence, O God, as perish *vain talkers and seducers* of the soul: who observing that in deliberating there were two wills, affirm that there are two minds in us of two kinds, one good, the other evil. Themselves are truly evil, when they hold these evil things: and themselves shall become good when they hold the truth and assent unto the truth, that Thy Apostle may say to them, *Ye were sometimes darkness, but now light in the Lord.* But they, wishing to be light, not *in the Lord,* but in themselves, imagining the nature of the soul to be that which God is, are made more gross darkness through a dreadful arrogancy; for that they *went back farther from Thee, the true Light that enlighteneth every man that cometh into the world.* Take heed what you say, and blush for shame: *draw near unto Him and be enlightened, and your faces shall not be ashamed.*

Myself when I was deliberating upon the serving the Lord my God now, as I had long purposed, it was I who willed, I who nilled, I, I myself. I neither willed entirely, nor nilled entirely. Therefore was I at strife with myself, and rent asunder by myself. And this rent befell me against my will, and yet indicated, not the presence of another mind, but the punishment of my own. *Therefore it was no more I that wrought it, but sin that dwelt in me;* the punishment of a sin more freely committed, in that I was a son of Adam.

For if there be so many contrary natures as there be conflicting wills, there shall now be not two only, but many. If a man deliberate whether he should go to their conventicle or to the theatre, these Manichees cry out, Behold, here are two natures: one good, draws this way; another bad, draws back that way. For whence else is this hesitation between conflicting wills? But I say that both be bad: that which draws to them, as that which draws back to the theatre. But they believe not that will to be other than good, which draws to them. What then if one of us should deliberate, and amid the strife of his two wills be in a strait, whether he should go to the theatre or to our church? would not these Manichees also be in a strait what to answer? For either they must confess (which they fain would not) that the will which leads to our church is good, as well as theirs, who have received and are held by the mysteries of theirs: or they must suppose two evil natures, and two evil souls conflicting in one man, and it will not be true, which they say, that there is one good and another bad; or they must be converted to the truth, and no more deny that where one deliberates, one soul fluctuates between contrary wills.

Let them no more say then, when they perceive two conflicting wills in one man, that the conflict is between two contrary souls, of two contrary substances, from two contrary principles, one good, and the other bad. For Thou, O true God, dost disprove, check, and convict them; as when, both wills being bad, one deliberates whether he should kill a man by poison or by the sword; whether he should seize this or that estate of another's, when he cannot both; whether he should purchase pleasure by luxury, or keep his money by covetousness; whether he go to the circus or the theatre, if both be open on one day; or thirdly, to rob another's house, if he have the opportunity; or, fourthly, to commit adultery, if at the same time he have the means thereof also; all these meeting together in the same juncture of time, and all being equally desired, which cannot at one time be acted: for they rend the mind amid four, or even (amid the vast variety of things desired) more, conflicting wills, nor do they yet allege that there are so many divers substances.

So also in wills which are good. For I ask them, is it good to take pleasure in reading the Apostle? or good to take pleasure in a sober Psalm? or good to discourse on the Gospel? They will answer to each, "It is good." What then if all give equal pleasure, and all at once? Do not divers wills distract the mind, while he deliberates which he should rather choose? yet are they all good, and are at variance till one be chosen, whither the one entire will may be borne, which before was divided into many. Thus also, when, above, eternity delights us, and the pleasure of temporal good holds us down below, it is the same soul which willeth not this or that with an entire will; and therefore is rent asunder with grievous perplexities, while out of truth it sets this first, but out of habit sets not that aside.

I WAS SOUL-SICK AND TORMENTED

Thus soul-sick was I, and tormented, accusing myself much more severely than my wont, rolling and turning me in my chain, till that were wholly broken, whereby I now was but just, but still was, held. And Thou, O Lord, pressedst upon me in my inward parts by a severe mercy, redoubling the lashes of fear and shame, lest I should again give way, and not bursting that same slight remaining tie, it should recover strength, and bind me the faster. For I said within myself, "Be it done now, be it done now," and as I spake, I all but enacted it: I all but did it, and did it not: yet sunk not back to my former state, but kept my stand hard by, and took breath.

And I essayed again, and wanted somewhat less of it, and somewhat less, and all but touched, and laid hold of it; and yet came not at it, nor touched nor laid hold of it; hesitating to die to death and to live to life: and the worse whereto I was inured, prevailed more with me than the better whereto I was unused: and the very moment wherein I was to become other than I was, the nearer it approached me, the greater horror did it strike into me; yet did it not strike me back, nor turned me away, but held me in suspense.

The very toys of toys, and vanities of vanities, my ancient mistresses, still held me; they plucked my fleshly garment, and whispered softly, "Dost thou cast us off? and from that moment shall we no more be with thee for ever? and from that moment shall not this or that be lawful for thee for ever?" And what was it which they suggested in that I said, "this or that," what did they suggest, O my God? Let Thy mercy turn it away from the soul of Thy servant.

What defilements did they suggest! what shame! And now I much less than half heard them, and not openly showing themselves and contradicting me, but muttering as it were behind my back, and privily plucking me, as I was departing, but to look back on them. Yet they did retard me, so that I hesitated to burst and shake myself free from them, and to spring over whither I was called; a violent habit saying to me, "Thinkest thou, thou canst live without them?"

But now it spake very faintly. For on that side whither I had set my face, and whither I trembled to go, there appeared unto me the chaste dignity of Continency, serene, yet not relaxedly, gay, honestly alluring me to come and doubt not; and stretching forth to receive and embrace me, her holy hands full of multitudes of good examples: there were so many young men and maidens here, a multitude of youth and every age, grave widows and aged virgins; and Continence herself in all, not barren, but a *fruitful mother of children* of joys, by Thee her Husband, O Lord.

And she smiled on me with a persuasive mockery, as would she say, "Canst not thou what these youths, what these maidens can? or can they either in themselves, and not rather in the Lord their God? The Lord their God gave me unto them. Why standest thou in thyself, and so standest not? cast thyself upon Him, fear not He will not withdraw Himself that thou shouldest fall; cast thyself fearlessly upon Him, He will receive, and will heal thee." And I blushed exceedingly, for that I yet heard the muttering of those toys, and hung in suspense. And she again seemed to say, "Stop thine ears against *those* thy unclean *members on the earth,* that they may be *mortified. They tell thee of delights, but not as doth the law of the Lord thy God."* This controversy in my heart was self against self only. But Alypius sitting close by my side, in silence waited the issue of my unwonted emotion.

I HEARD A VOICE SAYING,
"TAKE UP AND READ"

But when a deep consideration had from the secret bottom of my soul drawn together and heaped up all my misery in the sight of my heart; there arose a mighty storm, bringing a mighty shower of tears. Which that I might pour forth wholly, in its natural expressions, I rose from Alypius: solitude was suggested to me as fitter for the business of weeping; so I retired so far that even his presence could not be a burden to me. Thus was it then with me, and he perceived something of it; for something I suppose I had spoken, wherein the tones of my voice appeared choked with weeping, and so had risen up.

He then remained where we were sitting, most extremely astonished. I cast myself down I know not how, under a certain fig-tree, giving full vent to my tears; and the floods of mine eyes gushed out an *acceptable sacrifice to Thee.* And, not indeed in these words, yet to this purpose, spake I much unto Thee: *and Thou, O Lord, how long? how long, Lord, wilt Thou be angry, for ever? Remember not our former iniquities,* for I felt that I was held by them. I sent up these sorrowful words: How long, how long, "to-morrow, and to-morrow?" Why not now? why not is there this hour an end to my uncleanness?

So was I speaking and weeping in the most bitter contrition of my heart, when, lo! I heard from a neighboring house a voice, as of boy or girl, I know not, chanting, and oft repeating, "Take up and read; Take up and read." Instantly, my countenance altered, I began to think most intently whether children were wont in any kind of play to sing such words: nor could I remember ever to have heard the like.

So checking the torrent of my tears, I arose; interpreting it to be no other than a command from God to open the book, and read the first chapter I should find. For I had heard of Antony, that coming in during the reading of the Gospel, he received the admonition, as if what was being read was spoken to him: *Go, sell all that thou hast, and give to the poor, and thou shalt have treasure in heaven, and come and follow me:* and by such oracle he was forthwith converted unto Thee.

Eagerly then I returned to the place where Alypius was sitting; for there had I laid the volume of the Apostle when I arose thence. I seized, opened, and in silence read that section on which my eyes first fell: *Not in rioting and drunkenness, not in chambering and wantonness, not in strife and envying; but put ye on the Lord Jesus Christ, and make not provision for the flesh, in concupiscence.* No further would I read; nor needed I: for instantly at the end of this sentence, by a light as it were of serenity infused into my heart, all the darkness of doubt vanished away.

Then putting my finger between, or some other mark, I shut the volume, and with a calmed countenance made it known to Alypius. And what was wrought in him, which I knew not, he thus showed me. He asked to see what I had read: I showed him; and he looked even further than I had read, and I knew not what followed. This followed, *him that is weak in the faith, receive;* which he applied to himself, and disclosed to me. And by this admonition was he strengthened; and by a good resolution and purpose, and most corresponding to his character, wherein he did always very far differ from me, for the better, without any turbulent delay he joined me.

Thence we go in to my mother; we tell her; she rejoiceth: we relate in order how it took place; she leaps for joy, and triumpheth, and blessed Thee, *Who art able to do above that which we ask or think;* for she perceived that Thou hadst given her more for me, than she was wont to beg by her pitiful and most sorrowful groanings. For thou convertedst me unto Thyself, so that I sought neither wife, nor any hope of this world, standing in that rule of faith, where Thou hadst showed me unto her in a vision, so many years before. And Thou didst *convert her mourning into joy* much more plentiful than she had desired, and in a much more precious and purer way than she erst required, by having grandchildren of my body.

The Ninth Book

MY SOUL WAS SET FREE

O LORD, *I am Thy servant; I am Thy servant, and the son of Thy handmaid. Thou has broken my bonds in sunder. I will offer to Thee the sacrifice of praise.* Let my heart and my tongue praise Thee; yea, let *all my bones say, O Lord, who is like unto Thee?* Let them say, and answer Thou me, and *say unto my soul, I am thy salvation?* Who am I, and what am I? What evil have not been either my deeds, or if not my deeds, my words, or if not my words, my will? But Thou, O Lord, art good and merciful, and Thy right hand had respect unto the depth of my death, and from the bottom of my heart emptied that abyss of corruption. And this Thy whole gift was, to nill what I willed, and to will what Thou willedst. But where through all those years, and out of what low and deep recess was my free-will called forth in a moment, whereby to submit my neck to Thy *easy yoke,* and my shoulders unto Thy *light burden, O Christ Jesus, my Helper and my Redeemer?*

How sweet did it at once become to me, to want the sweetness of those toys! and what I feared to be parted from, was now a joy to part with. For Thou didst cast them forth from me, Thou true and highest sweetness. Thou castest them forth, and for them enteredst in Thyself, sweeter than all pleasure, though not to flesh and blood; brighter than all light, but more hidden than all depths, higher than all honour, but not to the high in their own conceits. Now was my soul free from the biting cares of canvassing and getting, and weltering in filth, and scratching off the itch of lust. And my infant tongue spake freely to Thee, my brightness, and my riches, and my health, the Lord my God.

I DECIDED TO STOP TEACHING RHETORIC

And I resolved in Thy sight, not tumultuously to tear, but gently to withdraw, the service of my tongue from the marts of lip-labour: that the young, no students in Thy law, nor in Thy peace, but in lying dotages and law-skirmishes, should no longer buy at my mouth arms for their madness. And very seasonably, it now wanted but very few days unto the Vacation of the Vintage, and I resolved to endure them, then in a regular way to take my leave, and having been purchased by Thee, no more to return for sale. Our purpose then was known to Thee; but to men, other than our own friends, was it not known. For we had agreed among ourselves not to let it out abroad to any: although to us, now ascending from the *valley of tears,* and singing that *song of degrees,* Thou hadst given *sharp arrows,* and *destroying coals* against the *subtle tongue,* which as though advising for us, would thwart, and would out of love devour us, as it doth its meat.

Thou hadst pierced our hearts with

Thy charity, and we carried Thy words as it were fixed in our entrails: and the examples of Thy servants, whom for black hadst made bright, and for dead, alive, being piled together in the receptacle of our thoughts, kindled and burned up that our heavy torpor, that we should not sink down to the abyss; and they fired us so vehemently, that all the blasts of *subtle tongues* from gainsayers might only inflame us the more fiercely, not extinguish us. Nevertheless, because for *Thy Name's* sake which Thou hast hallowed throughout the earth, this our vow and purpose might also find some to commend it, it seemed like ostentation not to wait for the vacation now so near, but to quit beforehand a public profession, which was before the eyes of all; so that, all looking on this act of mine, and observing how near was the time of vintage which I wished to anticipate, would talk much of me, as if I had desired to appear some great one. And what end had it served me, that people should repute and dispute upon my purpose, and that *our good should be evil spoken of.*

Moreover, it had at first troubled me that in this very summer my lungs began to give way, amid too great literary labour, and to breathe deeply with difficulty and by the pain in my chest to show that they were injured, and to refuse any full or lengthened speaking; this had troubled me, for it almost constrained me of necessity to lay down that burden of teaching, or, if I could be cured and recover, at least to intermit it. But when the full wish for leisure, that I might see *how that Thou art the Lord*, arose, and was fixed, in me; my God, Thou knowest, I began

even to rejoice that I had this secondary, and that no feigned, excuse, which might something moderate the offence taken by those who, for their sons' sake, wished me never to have the freedom of Thy sons.

Full then of such joy, I endured till that interval of time were run; it may have been some twenty days, yet they were endured manfully; endured, for the covetousness which aforetime bore a part of this heavy business, had left me, and I remained alone, and had been overwhelmed, had not patience taken its place. Perchance, some of Thy servants, my brethren, may say that I sinned in this, that with a heart fully set on Thy service, I suffered myself to sit even one hour in the chair of lies. Nor would I be contentious. But hast not Thou, O most merciful Lord, pardoned and remitted this sin also, with my other most horrible and deadly sins, in the holy water?

I STAYED WITH VERECUNDUS

Verecundus was worn down with care about this our blessedness, for that being held back by bonds, whereby he was most strictly bound, he saw that he should be severed from us. For himself was not yet a Christian, his wife one of the faithful; and yet hereby, more rigidly than by any other chain, was he let and hindered from the journey which we had now essayed. For he would not, he said, be a Christian on any other terms than on those he could not.

However, he offered us courteously to remain at his country-house so long as we should stay there. Thou, O Lord, shalt reward him *in the resurrection of the just*, seeing Thou hast already given him *the lot* of the righteous. For although in our absence, being now at Rome, he was seized with bodily sickness, and therein being made a Christian, and one of the faithful, he departed this life; yet *hadst Thou mercy not on him only, but on us also:* lest remembering the exceeding kindness of our friend towards us, yet unable to number him among Thy flock, we should be agonised with intolerable sorrow.

Thanks unto Thee, our God, we are Thine: Thy suggestions and consolations tell us, Faithful in promises, Thou now requitest Verecundus for his country-house of Cassiacum, where from the fever of the world we reposed in Thee, with the eternal freshness of Thy Paradise: for that Thou hast forgiven him his sins upon earth, in that rich mountain, that mountain which yieldeth milk, Thine own mountain.

He then had at that time sorrow, but Nebridius joy. For although he also, not being yet a Christian, had fallen into the pit of that most pernicious error, believing the flesh of Thy Son to be a phantom: yet emerging thence, he believed as we did; not as yet endued with any Sacraments of Thy Church, but a most ardent searcher out of truth. Whom, not long after our conversion and regeneration by Thy Baptism, being also a faithful member of the Church Catholic, and serving Thee in perfect chastity and continence amongst his people in Africa, his whole house having through him first been made Christian, didst Thou release from the flesh; and now he lives in Abraham's bosom. Whatever that be, which is signified by that bosom,

there lives my Nebridius, my sweet friend, and Thy child, O Lord, adopted of a freed man: there he liveth.

For what other place is there for such a soul? There he liveth, whereof he asked much of me, a poor inexperienced man. Now lays he not his ear to my mouth, but his spiritual mouth unto Thy fountain, and drinketh as much as he can receive, wisdom in proportion to his thirst, endlessly happy. Nor do I think that he is so inebriated therewith, as to forget me; seeing Thou, Lord, Whom he drinketh, art mindful of us. So were we then, comforting Verecundus, who sorrowed, as far as friendship permitted, that our conversion was of such sort; and exhorting him to become faithful, according to his measure, namely, of a married estate; and awaiting Nebridius to follow us, which, being so near, he was all but doing: and so, lo! those days rolled by at length; for long and many they seemed, for the love I bare to the easeful liberty, that I might sing to Thee from my inmost marrow, *My heart hath said unto Thee, I have sought Thy face: Thy face, Lord, will I seek.*

I READ THE PSALMS OF DAVID

Now was the day come wherein I was in deed to be freed of my Rhetoric Professorship, whereof in thought I was already freed. And it was done. Thou didst rescue my tongue, whence Thou hadst before rescued my heart. And I blessed Thee, rejoicing; retiring with all mine to the villa. What I there did in writing, which was now enlisted in Thy service, though still, in this breathing-time as it were, panting from the school of pride, my books may witness, as well what I debated with others, as what with myself alone, before Thee: what with Nebridius, who was absent, my Epistles bear witness.

And when shall I have time to rehearse all Thy great benefits towards us at that time, especially when hasting on to yet greater mercies? For my remembrance recalls me, and pleasant is it to me, O Lord, to confess to Thee, by what inward goads Thou tamedst me; and how Thou hast evened me, *lowering the mountains and hills of my high imaginations, straightening my crookedness, and smoothing my rough ways;* and how Thou also subduest the brother of my heart, Alypius, unto the Name of Thy Only Begotten, our Lord and Saviour Jesus Christ, which he would not at first vouchsafe to have inserted in our writings. For rather would he have them savour of the lofty *cedars* of the Schools, which *the Lord* hath now *broken down,* than of the wholesome herbs of the Church, the antidote against serpents.

Oh, in what accents spake I unto Thee, my God, when I read the Psalms of David, those faithful songs, and sounds of devotion, which allow of no swelling spirit, as yet a Catechumen, and a novice in Thy real love, resting in that villa, with Alypius a Catechumen, my mother cleaving to us, in female garb with masculine faith, with the tranquillity of age, motherly love, Christian piety! Oh, what accents did I utter unto Thee in those Psalms, and how was I by them kindled towards Thee, and on fire to rehearse them, if possible, through the whole world, against the pride of mankind! And yet they are sung through the whole world, nor can *any hide himself from Thy heat.*

With what vehement and bitter sorrow was I angered at the Manichees! and again I pitied them for that they knew not those Sacraments, those medicines, and were mad against the antidote which might have recovered them of their madness. How I would they had then been somewhere near me, and without my knowing that they were there, could have beheld my countenance, and heard my words, when I read the fourth Psalm in that time of my rest, and how that Psalm wrought upon me, *When I called, the God of my righteousness heard me; in tribulation Thou enlargedst me. Have mercy upon me, O Lord, and hear my prayer.*

Would that what I uttered on these words, they could hear, without my knowing whether they heard, lest they should think I spake it for their sakes! Because in truth neither should I speak the same things, nor in the same way, if I perceived that they heard and saw me; nor if I spake them would they so receive them, as when I spake by and for myself before Thee, out of the natural feelings of my soul.

I trembled for fear, and again kindled with hope, and with rejoicing in Thy mercy, O Father; and all issued forth both by mine eyes and voice, when Thy good Spirit turning unto us, said, *O ye sons of men, how long slow of heart? why do ye love vanity, and seek after leasing?* For I had *loved vanity, and sought after leasing. And Thou, O Lord,* hadst already *magnified Thy Holy One, raising Him from the dead, and setting Him at Thy right hand,* whence *from on high* He should *send* His *promise, the Comforter, the Spirit of truth.*

And He had already sent Him, but I knew it not; He had sent Him, because He was now magnified, rising again from the dead, and ascending into heaven. For till then, *the Spirit was not yet given, because Jesus was not yet glorified.* And the prophet cries out, *How long, slow of heart? why do ye love vanity, and seek after leasing? Know this, that the Lord hath magnified His Holy One.* He cries out, *How long?* He cries out, *Know this:* and I so long, not knowing, *loved vanity, and sought after leasing:* and therefore I heard and trembled, because it was spoken unto such as I remembered myself to have been. For in those phantoms which I had held for truths, was there *vanity and leasing;* and I spake aloud many things earnestly and forcibly, in the bitterness of my remembrance. Which would they had heard, who yet *love vanity and seek after leasing!* They would perchance have been troubled, and have vomited it up; and *Thou wouldest hear them when they cried unto Thee;* for by a true death in the flesh did He die for us, who now *intercedeth unto Thee for us.*

I further read, *Be angry, and sin not.* And how was I moved, O my God, who had now learned to be angry at myself for things past, that I might not sin in time to come! Yea, to be justly angry; for that it was not another nature of a people of darkness which sinned for me, as they say who are not angry at themselves, and *treasure up* wrath *against the day of* wrath, *and of the revelation of Thy just judgment.* Nor were my *good things* now without, nor

sought with the eyes of flesh in that earthly sun; for they that would have joy from without soon become vain, and waste themselves on the things seen and temporal, and in their famished thoughts do lick their very shadows.

Oh that they were wearied out with their famine, and said, *Who will show us good things?* And we would say, and they hear, *The light of Thy countenance is sealed upon us.* For we are not *that light which enlighteneth every man,* but we are enlightened by Thee; that *having been sometimes darkness, we may be light in Thee.*

Oh that they could see the eternal Internal, which having tasted, I was grieved that I could not show It them, so long as they brought me their heart in their eyes roving abroad from Thee, while they said, *Who will show us good things?* For there, where I was *angry* within myself *in my chamber,* where I was inwardly pricked, where I had sacrificed, slaying my old man and commencing the purpose of a new life, *putting my trust in Thee,*—there hadst Thou begun to grow sweet unto me, and *hadst put gladness in my heart.* And I cried out, as I read this outwardly, finding it inwardly. Nor would I be multiplied with worldly goods; wasting away time, and wasted by time; whereas I had in Thy eternal Simple Essence other *corn, and wine, and oil.*

And with a loud cry of my heart I cried out in the next verse, O *in peace,* O for *The Self-same!* O what said he, *I will lay me down and sleep,* for who shall hinder us, when *cometh to pass that saying which is written, Death is swallowed up in victory?* And Thou surpassingly are the Self-same, Who *art not changed;* and in Thee is rest which forgetteth all toil, for there is none other with Thee, nor are we to seek those many other things, which are not what Thou art: but Thou Lord, *alone* hast *made me dwell in hope.* I read, and kindled; nor found I what to do to those deaf and dead, of whom myself had been, a pestilent person, a bitter and a blind bawler against those writings, which are honied with the honey of heaven, and lightsome with Thine own light: and I was consumed with zeal at the enemies of this Scripture.

When shall I recall all which passed in those holy-days? Yet neither have I forgotten, nor will I pass over the severity of Thy scourge, and the wonderful swiftness of Thy mercy. Thou didst then torment me with pain in my teeth; which when it had come to such height that I could not speak, it came into my heart to desire all my friends present to pray for me to Thee, the God of all manner of health. And this I wrote on wax, and gave it to them to read.

Presently so soon as with humble devotion we had bowed our knees, that pain went away. But what pain? or how went it away? I was affrighted, O my Lord, my God, for from infancy I had never experienced the like. And the power of Thy Nod was deeply conveyed to me, and rejoicing in faith, I praised Thy Name. And that faith suffered me not to be at ease about my past sins, which were not yet forgiven me by Thy baptism.

I WAS BAPTIZED WITH ALYPIUS AND ADEODATUS

The vintage-vacation ended, I gave notice to the Milanese to provide their scholars with another master to sell words to them; for that I had both made choice to serve Thee, and through my difficulty of breathing and pain in my chest was not equal to the Professorship. And by letters I signified to Thy Prelate, the holy man Ambrose, my former errors and present desires, begging his advice what of Thy Scriptures I had best read, to become readier and fitter for receiving so great grace. He recommended Isaiah the Prophet: I believe, because he above the rest is a more clear foreshower of the Gospel and of the calling of the Gentiles. But I, not understanding the first lesson in him, and imagining the whole to be like it, laid it by, to be resumed when better practised in our Lord's own words.

Thence, when the time was come wherein I was to give in my name, we left the country and returned to Milan. It pleased Alypius also to be with me born again in Thee, being already clothed with the humility befitting Thy Sacraments; and a most valiant tamer of the body, so as, with unwonted venture, to wear the frozen ground of Italy with his bare feet. We joined with us the boy Adeodatus, born after the flesh of my sin. Excellently hadst Thou made him. He was not quite fifteen, and in wit surpassed many grave and learned men. I confess unto Thee Thy gifts, O Lord my God, Creator of all, and abundantly able to reform our deformities: for I had no part in that boy, but the sin. For that we brought him up in Thy discipline, it was Thou, none else, had inspired us with it.

I confess unto Thee Thy gifts. There is a book of ours entitled *The Master;* it is a dialogue between him and me. Thou knowest that all there ascribed to the person conversing with me were his ideas, in his sixteenth year. Much besides, and yet more admirable, I found in him. That talent struck awe into me. And who but Thou could be the workmaster of such wonders?

Soon didst Thou take his life from the earth: and I now remember him without anxiety, fearing nothing for his childhood or youth, or his whole self. Him we joined with us, our contemporary in grace, to be brought up in Thy discipline; and we were baptised, and anxiety for our past life vanished from us. Nor was I sated in those days with the wondrous sweetness of considering the depth of Thy counsels concerning the salvation of mankind. How did I weep, in Thy Hymns and Canticles, touched to the quick by the voices of Thy sweet-attuned Church! The voices flowed into mine ears, and the Truth distilled into my heart, whence the affections of my devotion overflowed, and tears ran down, and happy was I therein.

THE BODIES OF TWO MARTYRS WERE FOUND

Not long had the Church of Milan begun to use this kind of consolation and exhortation, the brethren zealously joining with harmony of voice and hearts. For it was a year, or not much more, that Justina, mother to the Emperor Valentinian, a child, persecuted Thy servant Ambrose, in favour of her heresy, to which she was seduced by the Arians. The devout people kept watch in the Church, ready to die with their Bishop Thy servant. There my mother Thy handmaid, bearing a chief part of those anxieties and watchings, lived for prayer.

We, yet unwarmed by the heat of Thy Spirit, still were stirred up by the sight of the amazed and disquieted city. Then it was first instituted that after the manner of the Eastern Churches, Hymns and Psalms should be sung, lest the people should wax faint through the tediousness of sorrow: and from that day to this the custom is retained, divers (yea, almost all) Thy congregations, throughout other parts of the world, following herein.

Then didst Thou by a vision discover to Thy forenamed Bishop where the bodies of Gervasius and Protasius the martyrs lay hid (whom Thou hadst in Thy secret treasury stored uncorrupted so many years), whence Thou mightest seasonably produce them to repress the fury of a woman, but an Empress. For when they were discovered and dug up, and with due honour translated to the Ambrosian Basilica, not only they who were vexed with unclean spirits (the devils confessing themselves) were cured, but a certain man who had for many years been blind, a citizen, and well known to the city, asking and hearing the reason of the people's confused joy, sprang forth, desiring his guide to lead him thither. Led thither, he begged to be allowed to touch with his handkerchief the bier of Thy *saints, whose death is precious in Thy sight.* Which when he had done, and put to his eyes, they were forthwith opened. Thence did the fame spread, thence Thy praises glowed, shone; thence the mind of that enemy, though not turned to the soundness of believing, was yet turned back from her fury of persecuting.

Thanks to Thee, O my God. Whence and whither hast Thou thus led my remembrance, that I should confess these things also unto Thee? which great though they be, I had passed by in forgetfulness. And yet then, when *the odour of Thy ointments was so fragrant,* did we not *run after Thee.* Therefore did I more weep among the singing of Thy Hymns, formerly sighing after Thee, and at length breathing in Thee, as far as the breath may enter into this our house of grass.

MY MOTHER DIED IN OSTIA

Thou *that makes men to dwell of one mind in one house,* didst join with us Euodius also, a young man of our own city. Who being an officer of Court, was before us converted to Thee and baptised: and quitting his secular warfare, girded himself to Thine. We were together, about to dwell together in our devout purpose. We sought where we might serve Thee most usefully, and were together returning to Africa: whitherward being as far as Ostia, my mother departed this life. Much I omit, as hastening much. Receive my confessions and thanksgivings, O my God, for innumerable things whereof I am silent. But I will not omit whatsoever my soul would bring forth concerning that Thy handmaid, who brought me forth, both in the flesh, that I might be born to this temporal light, and in heart, that I might be born to Light eternal.

Not her gifts, but Thine in her, would I speak of; for neither did she make nor educate herself. Thou createdst her; nor did her father and mother know what a one should come from them. And the sceptre of Thy Christ, the discipline of Thine only Son, in a Christian house, a good member of Thy Church, educated her in Thy fear. Yet for her good discipline was she wont to commend not so much her mother's diligence, as that of a certain decrepit maid-servant, who had carried her father when a child, as little ones used to be carried at the backs of elder girls. For which reason, and for her great age, and excellent conversation, was she, in that Christian family, well respected by its heads. Whence also the charge of her master's daughters was entrusted to her, to which she gave diligent heed, restraining them earnestly, when necessary, with a holy severity, and teaching them with a grave discretion.

For, except at those hours wherein they were most temperately fed at their parents' table, she would not suffer them, though parched with thirst, to drink even water; preventing an evil custom, and adding this wholesome advice: "Ye drink water now, because you have not wine in your power; but when you come to be married, and be made mistreses of cellars and cupboards, you will scorn water, but the custom of drinking will abide." By this method of instruction, and the authority she had, she refrained the greediness of childhood, and moulded their very thirst to such an excellent moderation that what they should not, that they would not.

And yet (as Thy handmaid told me her son) there had crept upon her a love of wine. For when (as the manner was) she, as though a sober maiden, was bidden by her parents to draw wine out of the hogshead, holding the vessel under the opening, before she poured the wine into the flagon, she sipped a little with the tip of her lips; for more her instinctive feelings refused. For this she did, not out of any desire of drink, but out of the exuberance of youth, whereby, it boils over in mirthful freaks, which in youthful spirits are wont to be kept under by the gravity of their elders. And thus by adding to that little, daily littles *(for whoso despiseth little things shall fall by little and little)* she had fallen into such a habit as greedily to drink off her little cup brim-full almost of wine.

Where was then that discreet old woman, and that her earnest countermanding? Would aught avail against a secret disease, if Thy healing hand, O Lord, watched not over us? Father, mother, and governors absent, Thou present, who createdst, who callest, who also by those set over us, workest something towards the salvation of our souls, what didst Thou then, O my God? how didst Thou cure her? how heal her? didst Thou not out of another soul bring forth a hard and a sharp taunt, like a lancet out of Thy secret store, and with one touch remove all that foul stuff?

For a maid-servant with whom she used to go to the cellar, falling to words (as it happens) with her little mistress, when alone with her, taunted her with this fault, with most bitter insult, calling her wine-bibber. With which taunt, she, stung to the quick, saw the foulness of her fault, and instantly condemned and forsook it. As flattering friends pervert, so reproachful enemies mostly correct. Yet not what by them Thou doest, but what themselves purposed, dost Thou repay them. For she in her anger sought to vex her young mistress, not to amend her; and did it in private, for that the time and place of the quarrel so found them; or lest herself also should have anger, for discovering it thus late.

But Thou, Lord, Governor of all in heaven and earth, who turnest to Thy purposes the deepest currents, and the ruled turbulence of the tide of times, didst by the very unhealthiness of one soul heal another; lest any, when he observes this, should ascribe it to his own power, even when another, whom he wished to be reformed, is reformed through words of his.

I RECALLED MY MOTHER'S UPBRINGING

Brought up thus modestly and soberly, and made subject rather by Thee to her parents, than by her parents to Thee, so soon as she was of marriageable age, being bestowed upon a husband, she served him as her lord; and did her diligence to win him unto Thee, preaching Thee unto him by her conversation; by which Thou ornamentedst her, making her reverently amiable, and admirable unto her husband. And she so endured the wronging of her bed as never to have any quarrel with her husband thereon. For she looked for Thy mercy upon him, that believing in Thee, he might be made chaste. But besides this, he was fervid, as in his affections, so in anger: but she had learnt not to resist an angry husband, not in deed only, but not even in word. Only when he was smoothed and tranquil, and in a temper to receive it, she would give an account of her actions, if haply he had overhastily taken offence.

In a word, while many matrons, who had milder husbands, yet bore even in their faces marks of shame, would in familiar talk blame their husbands' lives, she would blame their tongues, giving them, as in jest, earnest advice: "That from the time they heard the marriage writings read to them, they should account them as indentures, whereby they were made servants; and so, remembering their condition, ought not to set themselves up against their lords." And when they, knowing what a choleric husband she endured, marvelled that it had never been heard, nor by any token perceived, that Patricius had beaten his wife, or that there had been any domestic difference between them, even for one day, and confidentially asking the reason, she taught them her practice above mentioned. Those wives who observed it found the good, and returned thanks; those who observed it not, found no relief, and suffered.

Her mother-in-law also, at first by whisperings of evil servants incensed against her, she so overcame by observance and persevering endurance and meekness, that she of her own accord discovered to her son the meddling tongues whereby the domestic peace betwixt her and her daughter-in-law had been disturbed, asking him to correct them. Then, when in compliance with his mother, and for the well-ordering of the family, and the harmony of its members, he had with stripes corrected those discovered, at her will who had discovered them, she promised the like reward to any who,

to please her, should speak ill of her daughter-in-law to her: and none now venturing, they lived together with a remarkable sweetness of mutual kindness.

This great gift also Thou bestowedst, O my God, my mercy, upon that good handmaid of Thine, in whose womb Thou createdst me, that between any disagreeing and discordant parties where she was able, she showed herself such a peace-maker, that hearing on both sides most bitter things, such as swelling and indigested choler uses to break out into, when the crudities of enmities are breathed out in sour discourses to a present friend against an absent enemy, she never would disclose aught of the one unto the other, but what might tend to their reconcilement.

A small good this might appear to me, did I not to my grief know numberless persons, who through some horrible and wide-spreading contagion of sin, not only disclose to persons mutually angered things said in anger, but add withal things never spoken, whereas to humane humanity, it ought to seem a light thing not to foment or increase ill will by ill words, unless one study withal by good words to quench it. Such was she, Thyself, her most inward Instructor, teaching her in the school of the heart.

Finally, her own husband, towards the very end of his earthly life, did she gain unto Thee; nor had she to complain of that in him as a believer, which before he was a believer she had borne from him. She was also the servant of Thy servants; whosoever of them knew her, did in her much praise and honour and love Thee; for that through the witness of the fruits of a holy conversation they perceived Thy presence in her heart. For she had been *the wife of one man*, had *requited her parents*, had *governed her house* piously, *was well reported of her good works*, had *brought up children*, so often *travailing in birth of them*, as she saw them swerving from Thee. Lastly, of all of us Thy servants, O Lord (whom on occasion of Thy own gift Thou sufferest to speak), us, who before her sleeping in Thee lived united together, having received the grace of Thy baptism, did she so take care of, as though she had been mother of us all; so served us, as though she had been child to us all.

I REMEMBERED A CONVERSATION WITH MY MOTHER

The day now approaching whereon she was to depart this life (which day Thou well knewest, we knew not), it came to pass, Thyself, as I believe, by Thy secret ways so ordering it, that she and I stood alone, leaning in a certain window, which looked into the garden of the house where we now lay, at Ostia; where removed from the din of men, we were recruiting from the fatigues of a long journey, for the voyage. We were discoursing then together, alone, very sweetly; and *forgetting those things which are behind, and reaching forth unto those things which are before*, we were enquiring between ourselves in the presence of the Truth, which Thou art, of what sort the eternal life of the saints was to be, *which eye hath not seen, nor ear heard, nor hath it entered into the heart of man*. But yet we gasped with the mouth of our heart, after those heavenly streams of Thy fountain, *the fountain of life*, which is *with Thee;* that being bedewed thence according to our capacity, we might in some sort meditate upon so high a mystery.

And when our discourse was brought to that point, that the very highest delight of the earthly senses, in the very purest material light, was, in respect of the sweetness of that life, not only not worthy of comparison, but not even of mention; we raising up ourselves with a more glowing affection towards the "Self-same," did by degrees pass through all things bodily, even the very heaven whence sun and moon and stars shine upon the earth; yea, we were soaring higher yet, by inward musing, and discourse, and admiring of Thy works; and we came to our own minds, and went beyond them, that we might arrive at that region of never-failing plenty, where *Thou feedest Israel* for ever with the food of truth, and where life is the *Wisdom by whom all* these *things are made*, and what have been, and what shall be, and she is not made, but is, as she hath been, and so shall she be ever; yea rather, to "have been," and "hereafter to be," are not in her, but only "to be," seeing she is eternal. For to "have been," and to "be hereafter," are not eternal.

And while we were discoursing and panting after her, we slightly touched on her with the whole effort of our heart; and we sighed, and there we leave bound *the first fruits of the Spirit;* and returned to vocal expressions of our mouth, where the word spoken has beginning and end. And what is like unto Thy Word, our Lord, who *endureth in Himself* without becoming old, and *maketh all things new?*

We were saying then: If to any the tumult of the flesh were hushed, hushed the images of earth, and waters, and air, hushed also the poles of heaven, yea the very soul be hushed to herself, and by not thinking on self surmount self, hushed all dreams and imaginary revelations, every tongue and every sign, and whatsoever exists only in transition, since if any could hear, all these say, *We made not ourselves, but He made us that abideth for ever*—If then having uttered this, they too should be hushed, having roused only our ears to Him who made them, and He alone speak, not by them, but by Himself, that we may hear His Word, not through any tongue of flesh, nor Angel's voice, nor sound of thunder, nor in the dark riddle of a similitude, but might hear Whom in these things we love, might hear His Very Self without these (as we two now strained ourselves, and in swift thought touched on that Eternal Wisdom which abideth over all)—could this be continued on, and other visions of kind far unlike be withdrawn, and this one ravish, and absorb, and wrap up its beholder amid these inward joys, so that life might be for ever like that one moment of understanding which now we sighed after; were not this, *Enter into thy Master's joy?* And when shall that be? When *we shall all rise again,* though we *shall not all be changed?*

Such things was I speaking, and even if not in this very manner, and these same words, yet Lord, Thou knowest that in that day when we were speaking of these things, and this world with all its delights became, as we spake, contemptible to us, my mother said, "Son, for mine own part I have no further delight in any thing in this life. What I do here any longer, and to what end I am here, I know not, now that my hopes in this world are accomplished. One thing there was for which I desired to linger for a while in this life, that I might see thee a Catholic Christian before I died. My God hath done this for me more abundantly, that I should now see thee withal, despising earthly happiness, become His servant: what do I here?"

MY MOTHER SAID, "LAY THIS BODY ANY WHERE"

What answer I made her unto these things, I remember not. For scarce five days after, or not much more, she fell sick of a fever; and in that sickness one day she fell into a swoon, and was for a while withdrawn from these visible things. We hastened round her; but she was soon brought back to her senses; and looking on me and my brother standing by her, said to us enquiringly, "Where was I?" And then looking fixedly on us, with grief amazed: "Here," saith she, "shall you bury your mother." I held my peace and refrained weeping; but my brother spake something, wishing, for her, as the happier lot, that she might die, not in a strange place, but in her own land.

Whereat, she with anxious look, checking him with her eyes, for that he still *savoured such things*, and then looking upon me: "Behold," saith she, "what he saith:" and soon after to us both, "Lay," she saith, "this body any where; let not the care for that any way disquiet you: this only I request, that you would remember me at the Lord's altar, wherever you be." And having delivered this sentiment in what words she could she held her peace, being exercised by her growing sickness.

But I, considering Thy gifts, Thou unseen God, which Thou instillest into the hearts of Thy faithful ones, whence wondrous fruits do spring, did rejoice and give thanks to Thee, recalling what I before knew, how careful and anxious she had ever been as to her place of burial, which she had provided and prepared for herself by the body of her husband. For because they had lived in great harmony together, she also wished (so little can the human mind embrace things divine) to have this addition to that happiness, and to have it remembered among men, that after her pilgrimage beyond the seas, what was earthly of this united pair had been permitted to be united beneath the same earth.

But when this emptiness had through the fulness of Thy goodness begun to cease in her heart, I knew not, and rejoiced admiring what she had so disclosed to me; though indeed in that our discourse also in the window, when she said, "What do I here any longer?" there appeared no desire of dying in her own country. I heard afterwards also, that when we were now at Ostia, she with a mother's confidence, when I was absent, one day discoursed with certain of my friends about the contempt of this life, and the blessing of death: and when they were amazed at such courage which Thou hadst given to a woman, and asked, "Whether she were not afraid to leave her body so far from her own city?"

she replied, "Nothing is far to God; nor was it to be feared lest at the end of the world, He should not recognise whence He were to raise me up." On the ninth day then of her sickness, and the fifty-sixth year of her age, and the three-and-thirtieth of mine, was that religious and holy soul freed from the body.

I WEPT FOR MY MOTHER

I closed her eyes; and there flowed withal a mighty sorrow into my heart, which was overflowing into tears; mine eyes at the same time, by the violent command of my mind, drank up their fountain wholly dry; and woe was me in such a strife! But when she breathed her last, the boy Adeodatus burst out into a loud lament; then, checked by us all, held his peace. In like manner also a childish feeling in me, which was, through my heart's youthful voice, finding its vent in weeping, was checked and silenced. For we thought it not fitting to solemnise that funeral with tearful lament, and groanings; for thereby do they for the most part express grief for the departed, as though unhappy, or altogether dead; whereas she was neither unhappy in her death, nor altogether dead. Of this we were assured on good grounds, the testimony of her good conversation and her *faith unfeigned*.

What then was it which did grievously pain me within, but a fresh wound wrought through the sudden wrench of that most sweet and dear custom of living together? I joyed indeed in her testimony, when, in that her last sickness, mingling her endearments with my acts of duty, she called me "dutiful," and mentioned, with great affection of love, that she never had heard any harsh or reproachful sound uttered by my mouth against her. But yet, O my God, Who madest us, what comparison is there betwixt that honour that I paid to her, and her slavery for me? Being then forsaken of so great comfort in her, my soul was wounded, and that life rent asunder as it were, which, of hers and mine together, had been made but one.

The boy then being stilled from weeping, Euodius took up the Psalter, and began to sing, our whole house answering him, the Psalm, *I will sing of mercy and judgment to Thee, O Lord*. But hearing what we were doing, many brethren and religious women came together; and whilst they (whose office it was) made ready for the burial, as the manner is, I (in a part of the house, where I might properly), together with those who thought not fit to leave me, discoursed upon something fitting the time; and by this balm of truth assuaged that torment, known to Thee, they unknowing and listening intently, and conceiving me to be without all sense of sorrow.

But in Thy ears, where none of them heard, I blamed the weakness of my feelings, and refrained my flood of grief, which gave way a little unto me; but again came, as with a tide, yet not so as to burst out into tears, nor to a change of countenance; still I knew what I was keeping down in my heart. And being very much displeased that these human things had such power over me, which in the due order and appointment of our natural condition must needs come to pass, with a new

grief I grieved for my grief, and was thus worn by a double sorrow.

And behold, the corpse was carried to the burial; we went and returned without tears. For neither in those prayers which we poured forth unto Thee, when the Sacrifice of our ransom was offered for her, when now the corpse was by the grave's side, as the manner there is, previous to its being laid therein, did I weep even during those prayers; yet was I the whole day in secret heavily sad, and with troubled mind prayed Thee, as I could, to heal my sorrow, yet Thou didst not; impressing, I believe, upon my memory by this one instance, how strong is the bond of all habit, even upon a soul, which now feeds upon no deceiving Word. It seemed also good to me to go and bathe, having heard that the bath had its name (balneum) from the Greek βαλανειον, for that it drives sadness from the mind.

And this also I confess unto Thy mercy, *Father of the fatherless*, that I bathed, and was the same as before I bathed. For the bitterness of sorrow could not exude out of my heart. Then I slept, and woke up again, and found my grief not a little softened; and as I was alone in my bed, I remembered those true verses of Thy Ambrose. For Thou art the

"Maker of all, the Lord,
  And Ruler of the height,
Who, robing day in light,
    hast poured
  Soft slumbers o'er the
    night,

"That to our limbs the power
  Of toil may be renew'd,

And hearts be rais'd that
    sink and cower,
And sorrows be subdu'd."

And then by little and little I recovered my former thoughts of Thy handmaid, her holy conversation towards Thee, her holy tenderness and observance towards us, whereof I was suddenly deprived: and I was minded to weep in Thy sight, for her and for myself, in her behalf and in my own. And I gave way to the tears which I before restrained, to overflow as much as they desired; reposing my heart upon them; and it found rest in them, for it was in Thy ears not in those of man, who would have scornfully interpreted my weeping.

And now, Lord, in writing I confess it unto Thee. Read it, who will, and interpret it, how he will: and if he finds sin therein, that I wept my mother for a small portion of an hour (the mother who for the time was dead to mine eyes, who had for many years wept for me that I might live in Thine eyes), let him not deride me; but rather, if he be one of large charity, let him weep himself for my sins unto Thee, the Father of all the brethren of Thy Christ.

I REFLECTED ON MY MOTHER'S GODLY LIFE

But now, with a heart cured of that wound, wherein it might seem blameworthy for an earthly feeling, I pour out unto Thee, our God, in behalf of that Thy handmaid, a far different kind of tears, flowing from a spirit shaken by the thoughts of the dangers of every soul *that dieth in Adam.* And although she having been quickened in Christ, even before her release from the flesh, had lived to the praise of Thy name for her faith and conversation; yet dare I not say that from what time Thou regeneratedst her by baptism, no word issued from her mouth against Thy Commandment. Thy Son, the Truth, hath said, *Whosoever shall say unto his brother, Thou fool, shall be in danger of hell fire.* And woe be even unto the commendable life of men, if, laying aside mercy, Thou shouldest examine it. But because Thou art not extreme in enquiring after sins, we confidently hope to find some place with Thee. But whosoever reckons up his real merits to Thee, what reckons he up to Thee but Thine own gifts? O that men would know themselves to be men; *and that he that glorieth would glory in the Lord.*

I therefore, O my Praise and my Life, God of my heart, laying aside for a while her good deeds, for which I give thanks to Thee with joy, do now beseech Thee for the sins of my mother. Hearken unto me, I entreat Thee, by the Medicine of our wounds, Who hung upon the tree, and now *sitting at Thy right hand maketh intercession to Thee for us.* I know that she dealt mercifully, and from her heart *forgave her debtors their debts;* do Thou also forgive her debts, what ever she may have contracted in so many years, since the water of salvation.

Forgive her, Lord, forgive, I beseech Thee; *enter not into the judgment with her. Let Thy mercy be exalted above Thy justice,* since Thy words are true, and *Thou hast promised mercy unto the merciful,* which thou gavest them to be, *who wilt have mercy on whom Thou wilt have mercy;* and wilt *have compassion on whom Thou hast had compassion.*

And, I believe, Thou hast already done what I ask; but *accept, O Lord, the free-will offerings of my mouth.* For she, the day of her dissolution now at hand, took no thought to have her body sumptuously wound up, or embalmed with spices; nor desired she a choice monument, or to be buried in her own land. These things she enjoined us not; but desired only to have her name commemorated at Thy Altar, which she had served without intermission of one day: whence she knew that holy Sacrifice to be dispensed, by which the *hand-writing that was against us is blotted out;* through which the enemy was triumphed over, who summing up our offences, and seeking what to lay to our charge, *found nothing in Him,* in Whom we conquer. Who shall restore to Him the innocent blood? Who repay Him the price wherewith He bought us, and so take us from Him. Unto the Sacrament of which our ransom, Thy handmaid bound her soul by the bond of faith.

Let none sever her from Thy protection: let neither *the lion nor the dragon* interpose himself by force or fraud. For she will not answer that she owes nothing, lest she be convicted and seized by the crafty accuser: but she will answer that *her sins are forgiven* her by Him, to Whom none can repay that price which He, Who owed nothing, paid for us.

May she rest then in peace with the husband before and after whom she had never any; whom she obeyed, *with patience bringing forth fruit* unto Thee, that she might win him also unto Thee. And inspire, O Lord my God, inspire Thy servants my brethren, Thy sons my masters, whom with voice and heart, and pen I serve, that so many as shall read these Confessions, may at Thy Altar remember Monnica Thy handmaid, with Patricius, her sometimes husband, by whose bodies Thou broughtest me into this life, how, I know not.

May they with devout affection remember my parents in this transitory light, my brethren under Thee our Father in our Catholic Mother, and my fellow-citizens in that eternal Jerusalem which Thy pilgrim people sigheth after from their Exodus, even unto their return thither. That so my mother's last request of me, may, through my Confessions, more than through my prayers, be, through the prayers of many, more abundantly fulfilled to her.

The Tenth Book

LET ME KNOW THEE

LET ME KNOW THEE, O Lord, who knowest me; *let me know Thee, as I am known*. Power of my soul, enter into it, and fit it for Thee, that Thou mayest have and hold it *without spot or wrinkle*. This is my hope, *therefore do I speak;* and in this hope do I rejoice, when I rejoice healthfully. Other things of this life are the less to be sorrowed for, the more they are sorrowed for; and the more to be sorrowed for, the less men sorrow for them. For behold, *Thou lovest the truth,* and *he that doth it, cometh to the light*. This would I do in my heart before Thee in confession: and in my writing, before many witnesses.

I CANNOT HIDE FROM THEE

And from Thee, O Lord, *unto whose eyes* the abyss of man's conscience is naked, what could be hidden in me though I would not confess it? For I should hide Thee from me, not me from Thee. But now, for that my groaning is witness, that I am displeased with myself, Thou shinest out, and art pleasing, and beloved, and longed for; that I may be ashamed of myself, and renounce myself, and choose Thee, and neither please Thee nor myself, but in Thee. To Thee therefore, O Lord, am I open, whatever I am; and with what fruit I confess unto Thee, I have said. Nor do I it with words and sounds of the flesh, but with the words of my soul, and the cry of the thought which Thy ear knoweth.

For when I am evil, then to confess to Thee is nothing else than to be displeased with myself; but when holy, nothing else than not to ascribe it to myself: because Thou, O Lord, *blessest the godly,* but first Thou *justifiest him when ungodly*. My confession then, O my God, in Thy sight, is made silently, and not silently. For in sound, it is silent; in affection, it cries aloud. For neither do I utter any thing right unto men, which Thou hast not before heard from me; nor dost Thou hear any such thing from me, which Thou hast not first said unto me.

WHAT IS THE VALUE OF MY CONFESSIONS TO OTHERS?

What then have I to do with men, that they should hear my confessions—as if they could *heal all my infirmities*—a race, curious to know the lives of others, slothful to amend their own? Why seek they to hear from me what I am; who will not hear from Thee what themselves are? And how know they, when from myself they hear of myself, whether I say true; seeing *no man knows what is in man, but the spirit of man which is in him?* But if they hear from Thee of themselves, they cannot say, "The Lord lieth." For what is it to hear from Thee of themselves, but to know themselves? and who knoweth and saith, "It is false," unless himself lieth? But because *charity believeth all things* (that is, among those whom knitting unto itself it maketh one), I also, O Lord, will in such wise confess unto Thee, that men may hear, to whom I cannot demonstrate whether I confess truly; yet they believe me, whose ears charity openeth unto me.

But do Thou, my inmost Physician, make plain unto me what object I may gain by doing it. For the confessions of my past sins, which Thou hast *forgiven and covered*, that Thou mightest bless me in Thee, changing my soul by Faith and Thy Sacrament, when read and heard, stir up the heart, that it sleep not in despair and say "I cannot," but awake in the love of Thy mercy and the sweetnes of Thy grace, whereby whoso *is weak, is strong*, when by it he became conscious of his own weakness. And the good delight to hear of the past evils of such as are now freed from them, not because they are evils, but because they have been and are not.

With what object, then, O Lord my God, to Whom my conscience daily confesseth, trusting more in the hope of Thy mercy than in her own innocency, with what object, I pray, do I by this book confess to men also in Thy presence what I now am, not what I have been? For that other object I have seen and spoken of. But what I now am, at the very time of making these confessions, divers desire to know, who have or have not known me, who have heard from me or of me; but their ear is not at my heart, where I am, whatever I am. They wish then to hear me confess what I am within; whither neither their eye, nor ear, nor understanding can reach; they wish it, as ready to believe—but will they know?

For charity, whereby they are good, telleth them that in my confessions I lie not; and she in them, believeth me.

THE OBJECT OF MY CONFESSIONS

But for what object would they hear this? Do they desire to joy with me, when they hear how near, by Thy gift, I approach unto Thee? and to pray for me, when they shall hear how much I am held back by my own weight? To such will I discover myself. For it is no mean object, O Lord my God, *that by many thanks should be given* to Thee *on our behalf,* and Thou be by many entreated for us. Let the brotherly mind love in me what Thou teachest is to be loved, and lament in me what Thou teachest is to be lamented. Let a brotherly, not a stranger, mind, not that of the *strange children, whose mouth talketh of vanity, and their right hand is a right hand of iniquity,* but that brotherly mind which when it approveth rejoiceth for me, and when it disproveth me, is sorry for me; because whether it approveth or disapproveth, it loveth me.

To such will I discover myself: they will breathe freely at my good deeds, sigh for my ill. My good deeds are Thine appointments and Thy gifts; my evil ones are my offences, and Thy judgments. Let them breathe freely at the one, sigh at the other; and let hymns and weeping go up into Thy sight out of the hearts of my brethren, Thy *censers.* And do Thou, O Lord, be pleased with the incense of Thy holy temple, *have mercy upon me according to Thy great mercy for Thine own Name's sake,* and no ways forsaking what Thou hast begun, perfect my imperfections.

This is the object of my confessions of what I am, not of what I have been, to confess this, not before Thee only, in a secret *exultation with trembling,* and a secret sorrow with hope; but in the ears also of the believing sons of men, sharers of my joy, and partners in my mortality, my fellow-citizens, and fellow-pilgrims, who are gone before, or are to follow on, companions of my way. These are Thy servants, my brethren, whom Thou willest to be Thy sons; my masters, whom Thou commandest me to serve, if I would live with Thee, of Thee. But this Thy Word were little, did it only command by speaking and not go before in performing. This then I do in deed and word, this I do *under Thy wings;* in over great peril, were not my soul subdued unto Thee under Thy wings, and my infirmity known unto Thee.

I am a little one, but my Father ever liveth, and my Guardian is *sufficient for me.* For he is the same who begat me, and defends me: and Thou Thyself art all my good; Thou, Almighty, Who art with me, yea, before I am with Thee. To such then whom Thou commandest me to serve will I discover, not what I have been, but what I now am and what I yet am. *But neither do I judge myself.* Thus therefore I would be heard.

MY SEARCH FOR GOD RECOUNTED

For Thou, Lord, dost judge me: because, although *no man knoweth the things of a man, but the spirit of a man which is in him,* yet is there something of man, which neither *the spirit of man that is in him,* itself *knoweth.* But Thou, Lord, knowest all of him, Who hast made him. Yet I, though in Thy sight I despise myself, and account myself *dust and ashes;* yet know I something of Thee, which I know not of myself. And truly, *now we see through a glass darkly,* not *face to face* as yet.

So long therefore as *I be absent from Thee,* I am more present with myself than with Thee, and yet know I Thee that Thou art in no ways passible; but I, what temptations I can resist, what I cannot, I know not. And there is hope, because *Thou art faithful, Who wilt not suffer us to be tempted above that we are able; but wilt with the temptation also make a way to escape, that we may be able to bear it.*

I will confess then what I know of myself, I will confess also what I know not of myself. And that because what I do know of myself, I know by Thy shining upon me; and what I know not of myself, so long know I not it, until *my darkness be made as the noon-day* in Thy countenance.

Not with doubting, but with assured consciousness, do I love Thee, Lord. Thou hast stricken my heart with Thy word, and I loved Thee. Yea also *heaven and earth, and all that therein is,* behold on every side they bid me love Thee; nor cease to say so unto all, *that they may be without excuse.* But more deeply *wilt Thou have mercy on whom Thou wilt have mercy, and wilt have compassion on whom Thou hast had compassion:* else in deaf ears do the heaven and the earth speak Thy praises.

But what do I love, when I love Thee? not beauty of bodies, nor the fair harmony of time, nor the brightness of the light, so gladsome to our eyes, nor sweet melodies of varied songs, nor the fragrant smell of flowers, and ointments, and spices, not manna and honey, not limbs acceptable to embracements of flesh. None of these I love, when I love my God; and yet I love a kind of light, and melody, and fragrance, and meat, and embracement when I love my God, the light, melody, fragrance, meat, embracement of my inner man: where there shineth unto my soul what space cannot contain and there soundeth what time beareth not away, and there smelleth what breathing disperseth not, and there tasteth what eating diminisheth not, and there clingeth what satiety divorceth not. This is it which I love when I love my God.

And what is this? I asked the earth, and it answered me, "I am not He;" and whatsoever are in it confessed the same. I asked the sea and the deeps, and the living creeping things, and they answered, "We are not Thy God, seek above us." I asked the moving air; and the whole air with his inhabitants answered, "Anaximenes was deceived, I am not God." I asked the heavens, sun, moon, stars, "Nor (say they) are we the God whom thou seekest." And I replied unto all the things which encompass the door of my flesh: "Ye have told me of my God, that ye are not He; tell me something of Him." And they cried out with a loud voice, "He made us."

My questioning them, was my thoughts on them: and their form of beauty gave the answer. And I turned myself unto myself, and said to myself, "Who art thou?" And I answered, "A man." And behold, in me there present themselves to me soul, and body, one without, the other within.

By which of these ought I to seek my God? I had sought Him in the body from earth to heaven, so far as I could send messengers, the beams of mine eyes. But the better is the inner, for to it as presiding and judging, all the bodily messengers reported the answers of heaven and earth, and all things therein, who said, "We are not God, but He made us."

These things did my inner man know by the ministry of the outer: I the inner knew them; I, the mind, through the senses of my body. I asked the whole frame of the world about my God; and it answered me, "I am not He, but He made me."

Is not this corporeal figure apparent to all whose senses are perfect? why then speaks it not the same to all? Animals small and great see it, but they cannot ask it: because no reason is set over their senses to judge on what they report. But men can ask, so that *the invisible things of God are clearly seen, being understood by the things that are made;* but by love of them, they are made subject unto them: and subjects cannot judge. Nor yet do the creatures answer such as ask, unless they can judge: nor yet do they change their voice (*i.e.*, their appearance), if one man only sees, another seeing asks, so as to appear one way to this man, another way to that; but appearing the same way to both, it is dumb to this, speaks to that; yea rather it speaks to all; but they only understand, who compare its voice received from without, with the truth within.

For truth saith unto me, "Neither heaven, nor earth, nor any other body is thy God." This, their very nature saith to him that seeth them: "They are a mass; a mass is less in a part thereof than in the whole." Now to thee I speak, O my soul, thou art my better part: for thou quickenest the mass of my body, giving it life, which no body can give to a body: but thy God is even unto thee the Life of thy life.

MY LOVE FOR GOD

What then do I love, when I love my God? who is He above the head of my soul? By my very soul will I ascend to Him. I will pass beyond that power whereby I am united to my body, and fill its whole frame with life. Nor can I by that power find my God; for so *horse and mule that have no understanding*, might find Him; seeing it is the same power, whereby even their bodies live.

But another power there is, not that only whereby I animate, but that too whereby I imbue with sense my flesh, which the Lord hath framed for me: commanding the eye not to hear, and the ear not to see; but the eye, that through it I should see, and the ear, that through it I should hear; and to the other senses severally, what is to each their own peculiar seats and offices; which, being divers, I the one mind, do through them enact. I will pass beyond this power of mine also; for this also have the horse and mule, for they also perceive through the body.

I EXPLORED THE MEMORY

I will pass then beyond this power of my nature also, rising by degrees unto Him who made me. And I come to the fields and spacious palaces of my memory, where are the treasures of innumerable images, brought into it from things of all sorts perceived by the senses. There is stored up, whatsoever besides we think, either by enlarging or diminishing, or any other way varying those things which the sense hath come to; and whatever else hath been committed and laid up, which forgetfulness hath not yet swallowed up and buried.

When I enter there, I require what I will to be brought forth, and something instantly comes; others must be longer sought after, which are fetched, as it were, out of some inner receptacle; others rush out in troops, and while one thing is desired and required, they start forth, as who should say, "Is it perchance I?" These I drive away with the hand of my heart, from the face of my remembrance; until what I wish for be unveiled, and appear in sight, out of its secret place. Other things come up readily, in unbroken order, as they are called for; those in front making way for the following; and as they make way, they are hidden from sight, ready to come when I will. All which takes place when I repeat a thing by heart.

There are all things preserved distinctly and under general heads, each having entered by its own avenue: as light, and all colours and forms of bodies by the eyes; by the ears all sorts of sounds; all smells by the avenue of the nostrils; all tastes by the mouth; and by the sensation of the whole body, what is hard or soft; hot or cold; smooth or rugged; heavy or light; either outwardly or inwardly to the body. All these doth that great harbour of the memory receive in her numberless secret and inexpressible windings, to be forthcoming, and brought out at need; each entering in by his own gate, and there laid up.

Nor yet do the things themselves enter in; only the images of the things perceived are there in readiness, for thought to recall. Which images, how they are formed, who can tell, though it doth plainly appear by which sense each hath been brought in and stored up? For even while I dwell in darkness and in silence, in my memory I can produce colours, if I will, and discern betwixt black and white, and what others I will: nor yet do sounds break in and disturb the image drawn in by my eyes, which I am reviewing, though they also are there, lying dormant, and laid up, as it were, apart. For these too I call for, and forthwith they appear.

And though my tongue be still, and my throat mute, so can I sing as much as I will; nor do those images of colour, which notwithstanding be there, intrude themselves and interrupt, when another store is called for, which flowed in by the ears. So the other things, piled in and up by the other senses, I recall at my pleasure, Yea, I discern the breath of lilies from violets, though smelling nothing; and I prefer honey to sweet wine, smooth before rugged, at the time neither tasting nor handling, but remembering only.

These things do I within, in that vast court of my memory. For there are present with me, heaven, earth, sea, and whatever I could think on therein, besides what I have forgotten. There also meet I with myself, and recall myself, and when, where, and what I have done, and under what feelings. There be all which I remember, either on my own experience, or others' credit. Out of the same store do I myself with the past continually combine fresh and fresh likenesses of things which I have experienced, or, from what I have experienced, have believed: and thence again infer future actions, events and hopes, and all these again I reflect on, as present. "I will do this or that," say I to myself, in that great receptacle of my mind, stored with the images of things so many and so great, "and this or that will follow." "O that this or that might be!" "God avert this or that!" So speak I to myself: and when I speak, the images of all I speak of are present, out of the same treasury of memory; nor would I speak of any thereof, were the images wanting.

Great is this force of memory, excessive great, O my God; a large and boundless chamber! who ever sounded the bottom thereof? yet is this a power of mine, and belongs unto my nature; nor do I myself comprehend all that I am. Therefore is the mind too strait to contain itself. And where should that be, which it containeth not of itself? Is it without it, and not within? how then doth it not comprehend itself?

A wonderful admiration surprises me, amazement seizes me upon this. And men go abroad to admire the heights of mountains, the mighty billows of the sea, the broad tides of rivers, the compass of the ocean, and the circuits of the stars, and pass themselves by; nor wonder that when I spake of all these things, I did not see them with mine eyes, yet could not have spoken of them, unless I then actually saw the mountains, billows, rivers, stars which I had seen, and that ocean which I believe to be, inwardly in my memory, and that, with the same vast spaces between, as if I saw them abroad. Yet did not I by seeing draw them into myself, when with mine eyes I beheld them; nor are they themselves with me, but their images only. And I know by what sense of the body each was impressed upon me.

HOW THE MEMORY WORKS

Yet not these alone does the unmeasurable capacity of my memory retain. Here also is all, learnt of the liberal sciences and as yet unforgotten; removed as it were to some inner place, which is yet no place: nor are they the images thereof, but the things themselves. For, what is literature, what the art of disputing, how many kinds of questions there be, whatsoever of these I know, in such manner exists in my memory, as that I have not taken in the image, and left out the thing, or that it should have sounded and passed away like a voice fixed on the ear by that impress, whereby it might be recalled, as if it sounded, when it no longer sounded; or as a smell while it passes and evaporates into air affects the sense of smell, whence it conveys into the memory an image of itself, which remembering, we renew, or as meat, which verily in the belly hath now no taste, and yet in the memory still in a manner tasteth; or as any thing which the body by touch perceiveth, and which when removed from us, the memory still conceives. For those things are not transmitted into the memory, but their images only are with an admirable swiftness caught up, and stored as it were in wondrous cabinets, and thence wonderfully by the act of remembering, brought forth.

THREE KINDS OF QUESTIONS

But now when I hear that there be three kinds of questions, "Whether the thing be? what it is? of what kind it is?" I do indeed hold the images of the sounds of which those words be composed, and that those sounds, with a noise passed through the air, and now are not. But the things themselves which are signified by those sounds, I never reached with any sense of my body, nor even discerned them otherwise than in my mind; yet in my memory have I laid up not their images, but themselves. Which how they entered into me, let them say if they can; for I have gone over all the avenues of my flesh, but cannot find by which they entered. For the eyes say, "if those images were coloured, we reported of them." The ears say, "if they sound, we gave knowledge of them." The nostrils say, "if they smell, they passed by us." The taste says, "unless they have a savour, ask me not." The touch says, "if it have not size, I handled it not; if I handled it not, I gave no notice of it."

Whence and how entered these things into my memory? I know not how. For when I learned them, I gave no credit to another man's mind, but recognized them in mine; and approving them for true, I commended them to it, laying them up as it were, whence I might bring them forth when I willed. In my heart then they were, even before I learned them, but in my memory they were not. Where then? or wherefore, when they were spoken, did I acknowledge them, and said, "So is it, it is true," unless that they were already in the memory, but so thrown back and buried as it were in deeper recesses, that had not the suggestion of another drawn them forth I had perchance been unable to conceive of them?

TO COLLECT AND RECOLLECT

Wherefore we find, that to learn these things whereof we imbibe not the images by our senses, but perceive within by themselves, without images, as they are, is nothing else, but by conception to receive, and by marking to take heed that those things which the memory did before contain at random and unarranged, be laid up at hand as it were in that same memory where before they lay unknown, scattered and neglected, and so readily occur to the mind familiarised to them.

And how many things of this kind does my memory bear which have been already found out, and as I said, placed as it were at hand, which we are said to have learned and come to know; which were I for some short space of time to cease to call to mind, they are again so buried, and glide back, as it were, into the deeper recesses, that they must again, as if new, be thought out thence, for other abode they have none: but they must be drawn together again, that they may be known: that is to say, they must as it were be collected together from their dispersion: whence the word "cogitation" is derived.

For *cogo* (collect) and *cogito* (recollect) have the same relation to each other as *ago* and *agito*, *facio* and *factito*. But the mind hath appropriated to itself this word (cogitation), so that,

not what is "collected" any how, but what is "recollected," *i.e.*, brought together, in the mind, is properly said to be cogitated, or thought upon.

THE SOUNDS OF WORDS

The memory containeth also reasons and laws innumerable of numbers and dimensions, none of which hath any bodily sense impressed; seeing they have neither colour, nor sound, nor taste, nor smell, nor touch. I have heard the sound of the words whereby when discussed they are denoted: but the sounds are other than the things. For the sounds are other in Greek than in Latin; but the things are neither Greek, nor Latin, nor any other language.

I have seen the lines of architects, the very finest, like a spider's thread; but those are still different, they are not the images of those lines which the eye of flesh showed me: he knoweth them, whosoever without any conception whatsoever of a body, recognises them within himself. I have perceived also the numbers of the things with which we number all the senses of my body; but those numbers wherewith we number are different, nor are they the images of these, and therefore they indeed are. Let him who seeth them not, deride me for saying these things, and I will pity him, while he derides me.

I REMEMBER HOW I REMEMBER

All these things I remember, and how I learnt them I remember. Many things also most falsely objected against them have I heard, and remember; which though they be false, yet is it not false that I remember them; and I remember also that I have discerned betwixt those truths and these falsehoods objected to them. And I perceive that the present discerning of these things is different from remembering that I oftentimes discerned them, when I often thought upon them.

I both remember then to have often understood these things; and what I now discern and understand, I lay up in my memory, that hereafter I may remember that I understood it now. So then I remember also to have remembered; as if hereafter I shall call to remembrance, that I have now been able to remember these things, by the force of memory shall I call it to remembrance.

THE BELLY OF THE MIND

The same memory contains also the affections of my mind, not in the same manner that my mind itself contains them, when it feels them; but far otherwise, according to a power of its own. For without rejoicing I remember myself to have joyed; and without sorrow do I recollect my past sorrow. And that I once feared, I review without fear; and without desire call to mind a past desire. Sometimes, on the contrary, with joy do I remember my fore-past sorrow, and with sorrow, joy. Which is not wonderful, as to the body; for mind is one thing, body another. If I therefore with joy remember some past pain of body, it is not so wonderful.

But now seeing this very memory itself is mind (for when we give a thing in charge, to be kept in memory, we say, "See that you keep it in mind;" and when we forget, we say, "It did not

come to my mind," and, "It slipped out of my mind," calling the memory itself the mind); this being so, how is it that when with joy I remember my past sorrow, the mind hath joy, the memory hath sorrow; the mind upon the joyfulness which is in it, is joyful, yet the memory upon the sadness which is in it, is not sad? Does the memory perchance not belong to the mind? Who will say so? The memory then is, as it were, the belly of the mind, and joy and sadness, like sweet and bitter food; which, when committed to the memory, are, as it were, passed into the belly, where they may be stowed, but cannot taste. Ridiculous it is to imagine these to be alike; and yet are they not utterly unlike.

But, behold, out of my memory I bring it, when I say there be four perturbations of the mind, desire, joy, fear, sorrow; and whatsoever I can dispute thereon, by dividing each into its subordinate species, and by defining it, in my memory find I what to say, and thence do I bring it: yet am I not disturbed by any of these perturbations, when by calling them to mind, I remember them; yea, and before I recalled and brought them back, they were there; and therefore could they, by recollection, thence be brought. Perchance, then, as meat is by chewing the cud brought up out of the belly, so by recollection these out of the memory. Why then does not the disputer, thus recollecting, taste in the mouth of his musing the sweetness of joy, or the bitterness of sorrow? Is the comparison unlike in this, because not in all respects like?

For who would willingly speak thereof, if so oft as we name grief or fear, we should be compelled to be sad or fearful? And yet could we not speak of them, did we not find in our memory, not only the sounds of the names according to the images impressed by the senses of the body, but notions of the very things themselves which we never received by any avenue of the body, but which the mind itself perceiving by the experience of its own passions, committed to the memory, or the memory of itself retained, without being committed unto.

IMAGES AND THE MEMORY

But whether by images or no, who can readily say? Thus, I name a stone, I name the sun, the things themselves not being present to my senses, but their images to my memory. I name a bodily pain, yet it is not present with me, when nothing aches: yet unless its image were present in my memory, I should not know what to say thereof, nor in discoursing discern pain from pleasure. I name bodily health; being sound in body, the thing itself is present with me; yet, unless its image also were present in my memory, I could by no means recall what the sound of this name should signify.

Nor would the sick, when health were named, recognise what were spoken, unless the same image were by the force of memory retained, although the thing itself were absent from the body. I name numbers whereby we number; and not their images, but themselves are present in my memory. I name the image of the sun, and that image is present in my memory. For I recall not the image of its image, but the image itself is present to me, calling it to mind. I name mem-

ory, and I recognize what I name. And where do I recognise it, but in the memory itself? Is it also present to itself by its image, and not by itself?

FORGETFULNESS AND MEMORY

What, when I name forgetfulness, and withal recognise what I name? whence should I recognise it, did I not remember it? I speak not of the sound of the name, but of the thing which it signifies: which if I had forgotten I could not recognise what that sound signifies. When then I remember memory, memory itself is, through itself, present with itself: but when I remember forgetfulness, there are present both memory and forgetfulness; memory whereby I remember, forgetfulness which I remember.

But what is forgetfulness, but the privation of memory? How then is it present that I remember it, since when present I cannot remember? But if what we remember we hold it in memory, yet, unless we did remember forgetfulness, we could never at the hearing of the name recognise the thing thereby signified, then forgetfulness is retained by memory. Present then it is, that we forget not, and being so, we forget. It is to be understood from this that forgetfulness, when we remember it, is not present to the memory by itself, but by its image: because if it were present by itself, it would not cause us to remember, but to forget. Who now shall search out this? who shall comprehend how it is?

Lord, I, truly, toil therein, yea and toil in myself; I am become a heavy soil requiring over much *sweat of the brow*. For we are not now searching out the regions of heaven, or measuring the distances of the stars, or enquiring the balancings of the earth. It is I myself who remember, I the mind. It is not so wonderful, if what I myself am not, be far from me. But what is nearer to me than myself? And lo, the force of mine own memory is not understood by me; though I cannot so much as name myself without it. For what shall I say, when it is clear to me that I remember forgetfulness? Shall I say that that is not in my memory, which I remember? or shall I say that forgetfulness is for this purpose in my memory, that I might not forget? Both were most absurd. What third way is there?

How can I say that the image of forgetfulness is retained by my memory, not forgetfulness itself, when I remember it? How could I say this either, seeing that when the image of any thing is impressed on the memory, the thing itself must needs be first present, whence that image may be impressed? For thus do I remember Carthage, thus all places where I have been, thus men's faces whom I have seen, and things reported by the other senses; thus the health or sickness of the body. For when these things were present, my memory received from them images, which, being present with me, I might look on and bring back in my mind, when I remembered them in their absence.

If then this forgetfulness is retained in the memory through its image, not through itself, then plainly itself was once present, that its image might be taken. But when it was present, how did it write its image in the memory, seeing that forgetfulness by its presence effaces even what it finds already noted? And yet, in whatever way, although that way be past conceiving and explaining, yet certain am I that I remember forgetfulness itself also, whereby what we remember is effaced.

THE POWER OF MEMORY

Great is the power of memory, a fearful thing, O my God, a deep and boundless manifoldness; and this thing is the mind, and this am I myself. What am I then, O my God? What nature am I? A life various and manifold, and exceeding immense. Behold in the plains, and caves, and caverns of my memory, innumerable and innumerably full of innumerable kinds of things, either through images, as all bodies; or by actual pesence, as the arts; or by certain notions or impressions, as the affections of the mind, which, even when the mind doth not feel, the memory retaineth, while yet whatsoever is in the memory is also in the mind—over all these do I run, I fly; I dive on this side and on that, as far as I can, and there is no end. So great is the force of memory, so great the force of life, even in the mortal life of man.

What shall I do then, O Thou my true life, my God? I will pass even beyond this power of mine which is called memory: yea, I will pass beyond it, that I may approach unto Thee, O sweet Light. What sayest Thou to me? See, I am mounting up through my mind towards Thee who abidest above me. Yea, I now will pass beyond this power of mine which is called memory, desirous to arrive at Thee, whence Thou mayest be arrived at; and to cleave unto Thee, whence one may cleave unto Thee.

For even beasts and birds have memory; else could they not return to their dens and nests, nor many other things they are used unto: nor indeed could they be used to any thing, but by memory. I will pass then beyond memory also, that I may arrive at Him who hath separated me from the four-footed beasts and made me wiser than the fowls of the air, I will pass beyond memory also, and where shall I find Thee, Thou truly good and certain sweetness? And where shall I find Thee? If I find Thee without my memory, then do I not retain Thee in my memory. And how shall I find Thee, if I remember Thee not?

LOST FROM SIGHT, NOT MEMORY

For the woman that had lost her groat, and sought it with a light; unless she had remembered it, she had never found it. For when it was found, whence should she know whether it were the same, unless she remembered it? I remember to have sought and found many a thing; and this I thereby know, that when I was seeking any of them, and was asked, "Is this it?" "Is that it?" so long said I "No," until that were offered me which I sought. Which had I not remembered (whatever it were) though it were offered me, yet should I not find it, because I could not recognise it. And so it ever is, when we seek and find any lost thing.

Notwithstanding, when any thing is by chance lost from the sight, not from the memory (as any visible body), yet its image is still retained within, and it is sought until it be restored to sight; and when it is found, it is recognized by the image which is within: nor do we say that we have found what was lost, unless we recognise it; nor can we recognise it, unless we remember it. But this was lost to the eyes, but retained in the memory.

SEARCHING THE MEMORY

But what when the memory itself loses any thing, as falls out when we forget and seek that we may recollect? Where in the end do we search, but in the memory itself? and there, if one thing be perchance offered instead of another, we reject it, until what we seek meets us; and when it doth, we say, "This is it"; which we should not unless we recognised it, nor recognise it unless we remembered it. Certainly then we had forgotten it. Or, had not the whole escaped us, but by the part whereof we had hold, was the lost part sought for; in that the memory felt that it did not carry on together all which it was wont, and maimed, as it were, by the curtailment of its ancient habit, demanded the restoration of what it missed?

For instance, if we see or think of some one known to us, and having forgotten his name, try to recover it; whatever else occurs, connects itself not therewith; because it was not wont to be thought upon together with him, and therefore is rejected, until that present itself, whereon the knowledge reposes equably as its wonted object. And whence does that present itself, but out of the memory itself? for even when we recognise it, on being reminded by another, it is thence it comes. For we do not believe it as something new, but, upon recollection, allow what was named to be right. But were it utterly blotted out of the mind, we should not remember it, even when reminded. For we have not as yet utterly forgotten that, which we remember ourselves to have forgotten. What then we have utterly forgotten, though lost, we cannot even seek after.

WHY DOES MAN LONG FOR A HAPPY LIFE?

How then do I seek Thee, O Lord? For when I seek Thee, my God, I seek a happy life. *I will seek Thee, that my soul may live.* For my body liveth by my soul; and my soul by Thee. How then do I seek a happy life, seeing I have it not, until I can say, where I ought to say it, "It is enough"? How seek I it? By remembrance, as though I had forgotten it, remembering that I had forgotten it? Or, desiring to learn it as a thing unknown, either never having known, or so forgotten it, as not even to remember that I had forgotten it? is not a happy life what all will, and no one altogether wills it not? where have they known it, that they so will it? where seen it, that they so love it?

Truly we have it, how, I know not. Yea, there is another way, wherein when one hath it, then is he happy; and there are, who are blessed in hope. These have it in a lower kind, than they who have it in very deed; yet are they better off than such as are happy neither in deed nor in hope. Yet even these, had they it not in some sort, would not so will to be happy, which that they do will, is most certain. They have known it then, I know not how, and so have it by some sort of knowledge, what, I know not, and am perplexed whether it be in the memory, which if it be, then we have been happy once; whether all severally, or in that man who first sinned, *in whom also we all died,* and from whom we are all born with misery, I now enquire not; but only, whether the happy life be in the memory?

For neither should we love it, did we not know it. We hear the name, and we all confess that we desire the thing; for we are not delighted with the mere sound. For when a Greek hears it in Latin, he is not delighted, not knowing what is spoken; but we Latins are delighted, as would he too, if he heard it in Greek; because the thing itself is neither Greek nor Latin, which Greeks and Latins, and men of all other tongues, long for so earnestly. Known therefore it is to all, for could they with one voice be asked, "would they be happy?" they would answer without doubt, "they would." And this could not be, unless the thing itself whereof it is the name were retained in their memory.

MEMORY AND THE HAPPY LIFE

But is it so, as one remembers Carthage who hath seen it? No. For a happy life is not seen with the eye, because it is not a body. As we remember numbers then? No. For these, he that hath in his knowledge, seeks not further to attain unto; but a happy life we have in our knowledge and therefore love it, and yet still desire to attain it, that we may be happy. As we remember eloquence then? No. For although upon hearing this name also, some call to mind the thing, who still are not yet eloquent, and many who desire to be so, whence it appears that it is in their knowledge; yet these have by their bodily senses observed others to be eloquent, and been delighted, and desire to be the like (though indeed they would not be delighted but for some inward knowledge thereof, nor wish to be the like, unless they were thus delighted); whereas a happy life, we do by no bodily sense experience in others.

As then we remember joy? Perchance; for my joy I remember, even when sad, as a happy life, when unhappy; nor did I ever with bodily sense see, hear, smell, taste, or touch my joy; but I experienced it in my mind, when I rejoiced; and the knowledge of it clave to my memory, so that I can recall it with disgust sometimes, at others with longing, according to the nature of the things, wherein I remember myself to have joyed. For even from foul things have I been immersed in a sort of joy; which now recalling, I detest and execrate; otherwise in good and honest things, which I recall with longing, although perchance no longer present; and therefore with sadness I recall former joy.

Where then and when did I experience my happy life, that I should remember, and love, and long for it? Nor is it I alone, or some few besides, but we all would fain be happy; which, unless by some certain knowledge we knew, we should not with so certain a will desire. But how is this, that if two men be asked whether they would go to the wars, one, perchance, would answer that he would, the other, that he would not; but if they were asked whether they would be happy, both would instantly without any doubting say they would; and for no other rea-son would the one go to the wars, and the other not, but to be happy.

Is it perchance that as one looks for his joy in this thing, another in that, all agree in their desire of being happy, as they would (if they were asked) that they wished to have joy, and this joy they call a happy life? Although then one obtains this joy by one means, another by another, all have one end, which they strive to attain, namely, joy. Which being a thing which all must say they have experienced, it is therefore found in the memory, and recognised whenever the name of a happy life is mentioned.

TRUE JOY

Far be it, Lord, far be it from the heart of Thy servant who here confesseth unto Thee, far be it, that, be the joy what it may, I should therefore think myself happy. For there is a *joy* which is *not* given *to the ungodly,* but to those who love Thee for Thine own sake, whose joy Thou Thyself art. And this is the happy life, to rejoice to Thee, of Thee, for Thee; this is it, and there is no other. For they who think there is another, pursue some other and not the true joy. Yet is not their will turned away from some semblance of joy.

JOY IN THE TRUTH

It is not certain then that all wish to be happy, inasmuch as they who wish not to joy in Thee, which is the only happy life, do not truly desire the happy life. Or do all men desire this, but *because the flesh lusteth against the Spirit, and the Spirit against the flesh, that they cannot do what they would,* they fall upon that which they can, and are content therewith; because, what they are not able to do, they do not will so strongly as would suffice to make them able?

For I ask any one, had he rather joy in truth, or in falsehood? They will as little hesitate to say "in the truth," as to say "that they desire to be happy," for a happy life is joy in the truth: for this is a joying in Thee, Who art *the Truth, O God my light, health of my countenance, my God.* This is the happy life which all desire; this life which alone is happy, all desire; to joy in the truth all desire. I have met with many that would deceive; who would be deceived, no one.

Where then did they know this happy life, save where they knew the truth also? For they love it also, since they would not be deceived. And when they love a happy life, which is no other than joying in the truth, then also do they love the truth; which yet they would not love, were there not some notice of it in their memory. Why then joy they not in it? why are they not happy? because they are more strongly taken up with other things which have more power to make them miserable, than that which they so faintly remember to make them happy. For there is yet a little light in men; let them walk, let them *walk,* that *the darkness overtake them not.*

But why doth "truth generate hatred" and the *man of thine,* preaching the truth, become an enemy to them? whereas a happy life is loved, which is nothing else but joying in the truth; unless that truth is in that kind loved, that they who love any thing else would gladly have that which they love to be the truth: and because they would not be deceived, would not be convinced that they are so? Therefore do they hate the truth for that thing's sake which they love instead of the truth. They love truth when she enlightens, they hate her when she reproves. For since they would not be deceived, and would deceive, they love her when she discovers herself unto them, and hate her when she discovers them. Whence she shall so repay them, that they who would not be made manifest by her, she both against their will makes manifest, and herself becometh not manifest unto them.

Thus, thus, yea thus doth the mind of man, thus blind and sick, foul and ill-favoured, wish to be hidden, but that aught should be hidden from it, it wills not. But the contrary is requited it, that itself should not be hidden from the Truth; but the Truth is hid from it. Yet even thus miserable, it had rather joy in truths than in falsehoods. Happy then will it be, when, no distraction interposing, it shall joy in that only Truth, by Whom all things are true.

THOU RESIDEST IN MY MEMORY

See what a space I have gone over in my memory seeking Thee, O Lord; and I have not found Thee, without it. Nor have I found any thing concerning Thee, but what I have kept in memory, ever since I learnt Thee. For since I learnt Thee, I have not forgotten Thee. For where I found Truth, there found I my God, the Truth Itself; which since I learnt, I have not forgotten. Since then I learnt Thee, Thou residest in my memory; and there do I find Thee, when I call Thee to remembrance, and delight in Thee. These be my holy delights, which Thou hast given me in

Thy mercy, having regard to my poverty.

WHERE IN MY MEMORY RESIDEST THOU?

But where in my memory residest Thou, O Lord, where residest Thou there? what manner of lodging hast Thou framed for Thee? what manner of sanctuary hast Thou builded for Thee? Thou hast given this honour to my memory, to reside in it; but in what quarter of it Thou residest, that am I considering. For in thinking on Thee, I passed beyond such parts of it as the beasts also have, for I found Thee not there among the images of corporeal things: and I came to those parts to which I committed the affections of my mind, nor found Thee there.

And I entered into the very seat of my mind (which it hath in my memory, inasmuch as the mind remembers itself also), neither wert Thou there: for as Thou art not a corporeal image, nor the affection of a living being (as when we rejoice, condole, desire, fear, remember, forget, or the like); so neither art Thou the mind itself; because Thou art the Lord God of the mind; and all these are changed, but Thou remainest unchangeable over all, and yet hast vouchsafed to dwell in my memory, since I learnt Thee. And why seek I now in what place thereof Thou dwellest, as if there were places therein? Sure I am, that in it Thou dwellest, since I have remembered Thee ever since I learnt Thee, and there I find Thee, when I call Thee to remembrance.

THERE ARE NO UNLEARNED MEMORIES

Where then did I find Thee, that I might learn Thee? For in my memory Thou wert not, before I learned Thee. Where then did I find Thee, that I might learn Thee, but in Thee above me? Place there is none; *we go backward and forward*, and there is no place. Every where, O Truth, dost Thou give audience to all who ask counsel of Thee, and at once answerest all, though on manifold matters they ask Thy counsel. Clearly dost Thou answer, though all do not clearly hear. All consult Thee on what they will, though they hear not always what they will. He is Thy best servant who looks not so much to hear that from Thee which himself willeth, as rather to will that which from Thee he heareth.

I BURNED FOR THY PEACE

Too late loved I Thee, O Thou Beauty of ancient days, yet ever new! too late I love Thee! And behold, Thou wert within, and I abroad, and there I searched for Thee; deformed I, plunging amid those fair forms which Thou hadst made. Thou wert with me, but I was not with Thee. Things held me far from Thee, which, unless they were in Thee, were not at all. Thou calledst and shoutedst, and burstest my deafness. Thou flashedst, shonest, and scatteredst my blindness. Thou breathedst odours, and *I drew in breath* and *pant for Thee*. I tasted, and *hunger and thirst*. Thou touchedst me, and I burned for Thy peace.

LAMENTABLE JOYS, JOYOUS SORROWS

When I shall with my whole self cleave to Thee, I shall no where have sorrow or labour; and my life shall wholly live, as wholly full of Thee. But now since whom Thou fillest, Thou liftest up, because I am not full of Thee I am a burden to myself. Lamentable joys strive with joyous sorrows: and on which side is the victory, I know not. Woe is me! Lord, have pity on me. My evil sorrows strive with my good joys; and on which side is the victory, I know not. Woe is me! Lord, have pity on me. Woe is me! lo! I hide not my wounds; Thou art the Physician, I the sick; Thou merciful, I miserable.

Is not the life of man upon earth all trial? Who wishes for troubles and difficulties? Thou commandest them to be endured, not to be loved. No man loves what he endures, though he love to endure. For though he rejoices that he endures, he had rather there were nothing for him to endure. In adversity I long for prosperity, in prosperity I fear adversity. What middle place is there betwixt these two, where *the life of man is* not *all trial?*

Woe to the prosperities of the world, once and again, through fear of adversity, and corruption of joy! Woe to the adversities of the world, once and again, and the third time, from the longing for prosperity, and because adversity itself is a hard thing, and lest it shatter endurance. Is not the *life of man upon earth all trial:* without any interval?

MY HOPE—THY MERCY

And all my hope is no where but in Thy exceeding great mercy. Give what Thou enjoinest, and enjoin what Thou wilt. Thou enjoinest us continency; and *when I knew,* saith one, *that no man can be continent, unless God give it, this also was a part of wisdom to know whose gift she is.* By continency verily are we bound up and brought back into One, whence we were dissipated into many. For too little doth he love Thee, who loves any thing with Thee, which he loveth not for Thee. O love, who ever burnest and never consumest! O charity, my God! kindle me. Thou enjoinest continency: give me what Thou enjoinest, and enjoin what Thou wilt.

CONTINENCE COMMANDED

Verily Thou enjoinest me continency from the *lust of the flesh, the lust of the eyes, and the ambition of the world.* Thou enjoinest continency from concubinage; and for wedlock itself, Thou hast counselled something better than what Thou hast permitted. And since Thou gavest it, it was done, even before I became a dispenser of Thy Sacrament. But there yet live in my memory (whereof I have much spoken) the images of such things as my ill custom there fixed, which haunt me, strengthless when I am awake: but in sleep, not only so as to give pleasure, but even to obtain assent, and what is very like reality. Yea, so far prevails the illusion of the image, in my soul and in my flesh, that, when asleep, false visions persuade to that which when waking, the true cannot.

Am I not then myself, O Lord my God? And yet there is so much difference betwixt myself and myself, within that moment wherein I pass from waking to sleeping, or return from sleeping to waking! Where is reason then, which, awake, resisteth such suggestions? And should the things themselves be urged on it, it remaineth unshaken. Is it clasped up with the eyes? is it lulled asleep with the senses of the body? And whence is it that often even in sleep we resist, and mindful of our purpose, and abiding most chastely in it, yield no assent to such enticements? And yet so much difference there is, that when it happeneth otherwise, upon waking we return to peace of conscience; and by this very difference discover that we did not, what yet we be sorry that in some way it was done in us.

Art Thou not mighty, God Almighty, so as to *heal all the diseases of my soul*, and by Thy more abundant grace to quench even the impure motions of my sleep! Thou wilt increase, Lord, Thy gifts more and more in me, that my soul may follow me to Thee, disentangled from the birdlime of concupiscence; that it rebel not against itself, and even in dreams not only not, through images of sense, commit those debasing corruptions, even to pollution of the flesh, but not even to consent unto them. For that nothing of this sort should have, over the pure affections even of a sleeper, the very least influence, not even such as a thought would restrain—to work this, not only during life, but even at my present age is not hard for the Almighty, Who art *able to do above all that we ask or think*.

But what I yet am in this kind of my evil, have I confessed unto my good Lord; *rejoicing with trembling*, in that which Thou hast given me, and bemoaning that wherein I am still imperfect; hoping that Thou wilt perfect Thy mercies in me, even to perfect peace, which my outward and inward man

shall have with Thee, when *death shall be swallowed up in victory*.

OF EATING AND DRINKING

There is another *evil of the day*, which I would were *sufficient for* it. For by eating and drinking we repair the daily decays of our body, until Thou *destroy both belly and meat*, when Thou shalt slay my emptiness with a wonderful fulness, and *clothe this corruptible with* an eternal *incorruption*. But now the necessity is sweet unto me, against which sweetness I fight, that I be not taken captive; and carry on a daily war by fastings; often *bringing my body into subjection*, and my pains are removed by pleasure. For hunger and thirst are in a manner pains; they burn and kill like a fever, unless the medicine of nourishments come to our aid. Which since it is at hand through the consolations of Thy gifts, with which land, and water, and air serve our weakness, our calamity is termed gratification.

This hast Thou taught me, that I should set myself to take food as physic. But while I am passing from the discomfort of emptiness to the content of replenishing, in the very passage the snare of concupiscence besets me. For that passing, is pleasure, nor is there any other way to pass thither, whither we needs must pass. And health being the cause of eating and drinking, there joineth itself as an attendant a dangerous pleasure, which mostly endeavours to go before it, so that I may for her sake do what I say I do, or wish to do, for health's sake.

Nor have each the same measure; for what is enough for health, is too little for pleasure. And oft it is uncertain whether it be the necessary care of the body which is yet asking for sustenance, or whether a voluptuous deceivableness of greediness is profferring its services. In this uncertainty the unhappy soul rejoiceth, and therein prepares an excuse to shield itself, glad that it appeareth not what sufficeth for the moderation of health, that under the cloak of health, it may disguise the matter of gratification. These temptations I daily endeavour to resist, and I call on Thy right hand, and to Thee do I refer my perplexities; because I have as yet no settled counsel herein.

I hear the voice of my God commanding, *Let not your hearts be overcharged with surfeiting and drunkenness.* Drunkenness is far from me; Thou wilt have mercy, that it come not near me. But full feeding sometimes creepeth upon Thy servant; Thou wilt have mercy, that it may be far from me. For *no one can be continent unless Thou give it.*

Many things Thou givest us, praying for them; and what good soever we have received before we prayed, from Thee we received it; yea to the end we might afterwards know this, did we before receive it. Drunkard was I never, but drunkards have I known made sober by Thee. From Thee then it was, that they who never were such, should not so be, as from Thee it was, that they who have been, should not ever so be; and from Thee it was, that both might know from Whom it was.

I hear another voice of Thine. *Go not after thy lusts, and from thy pleasure turn away.* Yea by Thy favour have I heard that which I have much loved;

neither if we eat, shall we abound; neither if we eat not, shall we lack; which is to say, neither shall the one make me plenteous nor the other miserable. I heard also another, *for I have learned in whatsoever state I am, therewith to be content; I know how to abound, and how to suffer need. I can do all things through Christ that strengtheneth me.*

Behold a soldier of the heavenly camp, not the dust which we are. But *remember,* Lord, *that we are dust,* and that of *dust Thou hast made man;* and he *was lost and is found.* Nor could he of himself do this, because he whom I so loved, saying this through the in-breathing of Thy inspiration, was of the same dust. *I can do all things* (saith he) *through Him that strengtheneth me.* Strengthen me, that *I can.* Give what Thou enjoinest, and enjoin what Thou wilt. He confesses to have received, and when *he glorieth, in the Lord he glorieth.*

Another have I heard begging that he might receive. *Take from me* (saith he) *the desires of the belly;* whence it appeareth, O my holy God, that Thou givest, when that is done which Thou commandest to be done. Thou hast taught me, good Father, that *to the pure, all things are pure;* but that *it is evil unto the man that eateth with offence;* and, that *every creature of Thine is good, and nothing to be refused, which is received with thanksgiving;* and that *meat commendeth us not to God;* and, that *no man should judge us in meat or drink;* and, that *he which eateth, let him not despise him that eateth not; and let him not that eateth not, judge him that eateth.* These things have I learned, thanks be to Thee, praise to Thee, my God, my

Master, knocking at my ears, enlightening my heart; deliver me out of all temptation.

I fear not uncleanness of meat, but the uncleanness of lusting. I know that Noah was permitted to eat all kind of flesh that was good for food; that Elijah was fed with flesh; that John, endued with an admirable abstinence, was not polluted by feeding on living creatures, locusts. I know also that Esau was deceived by lusting for lentiles; and that David blamed himself for desiring a draught of water; and that our King was tempted, not concerning flesh, but bread. And therefore the people in the wilderness also deserved to be reproved, not for desiring flesh, but because, in the desire of food, they murmured against the Lord.

Placed then amid these temptations, I strive daily against concupiscence in eating and drinking. For it is not of such nature that I can settle on cutting it off once for all, and never touching it afterward, as I could of concubinage. The bridle of the throat then is to be held attempered between slackness and stiffness.

And who is he, O Lord, who is not some whit transported beyond the limits of necessity? whoever he is, he is a great one; let him make Thy Name great. But I am not such, for *I am a sinful man.* Yet do I too magnify Thy Name; and *He maketh intercession to Thee* for my sins who *hath overcome the world;* numbering me among the *weak members of* His *body;* because *Thine eyes have seen* that of Him which is *imperfect, and in Thy book shall all be written.*

THE ALLUREMENTS OF SMELLS

With the allurements of smells, I am not much concerned. When absent, I do not miss them; when present, I do not refuse them; yet ever ready to be without them. So I seem to myself; perchance I am deceived. For that also is a mournful darkness whereby my abilities within are hidden from me; so that my mind making enquiry into herself of her own powers, ventures not readily to believe herself; because even what is in it is mostly hidden unless experience reveal it. And no one ought to be secure in that life, the whole whereof is called *a trial,* that he who hath been capable of worse to be made better, may not likewise of better be made worse. Our only hope, only confidence, only assured promise is Thy mercy.

THE DELIGHTS OF THE EAR

The delights of the ear had more firmly entangled and subdued me; but Thou didst loosen and free me. Now, in those melodies which Thy words breathe soul into, when sung with a sweet and attuned voice, I do little repose; yet not so to be held thereby, but that I can disengage myself when I will. But with the words which are their life and whereby they find admission into me, themselves seek in my affections a place of some estimation, and I can scarcely assign them one suitable.

For at one time I seem to myself to give them more honour than is seemly, feeling our minds to be more holily and fervently raised unto a flame of devotion, by the holy words themselves when thus sung, than when not;

and that the several affections of our spirit, by a sweet variety, have their own proper measures in the voice and singing, by some hidden correspondence wherewith they are stirred up. But this contentment of the flesh, to which the soul must not be given over to be enervated doth oft beguile me, the sense not so waiting upon reason as patiently to follow her; but having been admitted merely for her sake, it strives even to run before her, and lead her. Thus in these things I unawares sin, but afterwards am aware of it.

At other times, shunning over-anxiously this very deception, I err in too great strictness; and sometimes to that degree, as to wish the whole melody of sweet music which is used to David's Psalter, banished from my ears, and the Church's too; and that mode seems to me safer, which I remember to have been often told me of Athanasius, Bishop of Alexandria, who made the reader of the psalm utter it with so slight inflection of voice, that it was nearer speaking than singing. Yet again, when I remember the tears I shed at the Psalmody of Thy Church, in the beginning of my recovered faith; and how at this time I am moved not with the singing, but with the things sung, when they are sung with a clear voice and modulation most suitable, I acknowledge the great use of this institution.

Thus I fluctuate between peril of pleasure and approved wholesomeness; inclined the rather (though not as pronouncing an irrevocable opinion) to approve of the usage of singing in the church; that so by the delight of the ears the weaker minds may rise to the feeding of devotion. Yet when it befalls me to be more moved with the voice than the words sung, I confess to have sinned penally, and then had rather not hear music.

See now my state: weep with me, and weep for me, ye, whoso regulate your feelings within, as that good action ensues. For you who do not act, these things touch not you. But Thou, O Lord my God, hearken; behold, and see, and *have mercy and heal me*, Thou, in whose presence I have become a problem to myself; and *that is my infirmity*.

DISCUSSION OF THE LUST OF THE FLESH CONCLUDED

There remains the pleasure of these eyes of my flesh, on which to make my confessions in the hearing of the ears of Thy temple, these brotherly and devout ears: and so to conclude the temptations of the *lust of the flesh*, which yet assail me, *groaning earnestly, and desiring to be clothed upon with my house from heaven*. The eyes love fair and varied forms, and bright and soft colours. Let not these occupy my soul; let God rather occupy it, *who made these* things, *very good* indeed, yet is He my good, not they.

And these affect me, waking, the whole day, nor is any rest given me from them, as there is from musical, sometimes in silence, from all voices. For this queen of colours, the light, bathing all which we behold, wherever I am through the day, gliding by me in varied forms, soothes me when engaged on other things, and not observing it. And so strongly doth it entwine itself, that if it be suddenly withdrawn, it is with longing sought for, and if absent long, saddeneth the mind.

O Thou Light, which Tobias saw, when these eyes closed he taught his son the way of life; and himself went before with the feet of charity, never swerving. Or which Isaac saw, when his fleshly *eyes being heavy* and closed by old age, it was vouchsafed him, not knowingly, to bless his sons, but by blessing to know them. Or which Jacob saw, when he also, blind through great age, with illumined heart, in the persons of his sons shed light on the different races of the future people, in them foresignified; and laid his hands, mystically crossed upon his grandchildren by Joseph, not as their father by his outward eye corrected them, but as himself inwardly discerned.

This is the light, it is one, and all are one, who see and love it. But that corporeal light whereof I spake, it seasoneth the life of this world for her blind lovers with an enticing and dangerous sweetness. But they who know how to praise Thee for it, "O All-creating Lord," take it up in Thy hymns, and are not taken up with it in their sleep. Such would I be.

These seductions of the eyes I resist, lest my feet wherewith I walk upon Thy way be ensnared; and I lift up mine invisible eyes to Thee that Thou wouldest *pluck my feet out of the snare.* Thou dost ever and anon pluck them out, for they are ensnared. Thou ceasest not to pluck them out, while I often entangle myself in the snares on all sides aid: because *Thou that keepest Israel neither slumber nor sleep.*

What innumerable toys, made by divers arts and manufacures in our apparel, shoes, utensils and all sort of works, in pictures also in divers images, and these far exceeding all necessary and moderate use and all pious meaning, have men added to tempt their own eyes withal; outwardly following what themselves make, inwardly forsaking Him by whom themselves were made, and destroying that which themselves have been made! But I, my God and my Glory, do hence also sing a hymn to Thee, and do consecrate praise to Him who consecrateth me, because beautiful patterns which through men's souls are conveyed into their cunning hands, come from that Beauty, which is above our souls, which my soul day and night sigheth after.

But the framers and followers of the outward beauties derive thence the rule of judging of them, but not of using them. And He is there, though they perceive Him not, that so they might not wander, but *keep their strength for Thee,* and not scatter it abroad upon pleasurable wearinesses. And I, though I speak and see this, entangle my steps with these outward beauties; but Thou pluckest me out, O Lord, Thou pluckest me out; *because Thy lovingkindness is before my eyes.* For I am taken miserably, and Thou pluckest me out mercifully; sometimes not perceiving it, when I had but lightly lighted upon them; otherwhiles with pain, because I had struck fast in them.

THE LUST OF THE EYES

To this is added another form of temptation more manifoldly dangerous. For besides that concupiscence of the flesh which consisteth in the delight of all senses and pleasures, wherein it slaves, who *go far from Thee*, waste and *perish*, the soul hath, through the same senses of the body, a certain vain and curious desire, veiled under the title of knowledge and learning, not of delighting in the flesh, but of making experiments through the flesh. The seat whereof being in the appetite of knowledge, and sight being the sense chiefly used for attaining knowlege, it is in Divine language called *The lust of the eyes*.

For to see, belongeth properly to the eyes; yet we use this word of the other senses also, when we employ them in seeking knowledge. For we do not say, hark how it flashes, or smell how it glows, or taste how it shines, or feel how it gleams; for all these are said to be seen. And yet we say not only, see how it shineth, which the eyes alone can perceive; but also, see how it soundeth, see how it smelleth, see how it tasteth, see how hard it is. And so the general experience of the senses, as was said, is called *The lust of the eyes*, because the office of seeing, wherein the eyes hold the prerogative, the other senses by the way of similitude take to themselves when they make search after any knowledge.

But by this may more evidently be discerned, wherein pleasure and wherein curiosity is the object of the senses; for pleasure seeketh objects beautiful, melodious, fragrant, savoury, soft; but curiosity, for trial's sake, the contrary as well, not for the sake of suffering annoyance, but out of the lust of making trial and knowing them. For what pleasure hath it, to see in a mangled carcase what will make you shudder? and yet if it be lying near, they flock thither, to be made sad, and to turn pale. Even in sleep they are afraid to see it. As if when awake, any one forced them to see it, or any report of its beauty drew them thither! Thus also in the other senses, which it were long to go through.

From this disease of curiosity are all those strange sights exhibited in the theatre. Hence men go on to search out the hidden powers of nature (which is besides our end), which to know profits not, and wherein men desire nothing but to know. Hence also, if with that same end of perverted knowledge magical arts be enquired by. Hence also in religion itself, is God tempted, when signs and wonders are demanded of Him, not desired for any good end, but merely to make trial of.

In this so vast wilderness, full of snares and dangers, behold many of them, I have cut off, and thrust out of my heart, as Thou hast given me, O God of my salvation. And yet when dare I say, since so many things of this kind buzz on all sides about our daily life—when dare I say that nothing of this sort engages my attention or causes in me an idle interest? True, the theatres do not now carry me away, nor care I to know the courses of the stars, nor did my soul ever consult ghosts departed; all sacrilegious mysteries I detest.

From Thee, O Lord my God, to whom I owe humble and single-hearted service, by what artifices and suggestions doth the enemy deal with me to desire some sign! But I beseech Thee by our King, and by our pure and holy country, Jerusalem, that as any consenting thereto is far from me, so may it ever be further and further. But when I pray Thee for the salvation of any, my end and intention is far different. Thou givest and wilt give me *to follow Thee* willingly, doing what Thou *wilt*.

Notwithstanding, in how many most petty and contemptible things is our curiosity daily tempted, and how often we give way, who can recount? How often do we begin as it were tolerating people telling vain stories, lest we offend the weak; then by degrees we take interest therein! I go not now to the circus to see a dog coursing a hare; but in the field, if passing, that coursing peradventure will distract me even from some weighty thought, and draw me after it: not that I turn aside the body of my beast, yet still incline my mind thither. And unless Thou, having made me see my infirmity, didst speedily admonish me either through the sight itself, by some contemplation to rise towards Thee, or altogether to despise and pass it by, I dully stand fixed therein. What, when sitting at home, a lizard catching flies, or a spider entangling them rushing into her nets, ofttimes takes my attention? Is the thing different, because they are but small creatures? I go on from them to praise Thee the wonderful Creator and Orderer of all, but this does not first draw my attention. It is one thing to rise quickly, another not to fall. And of such things is my life full; and my one hope is Thy wonderful great mercy.

For when our heart becomes the receptacle of such things and is overcharged with throngs of this abundant vanity, then are our prayers also thereby often interrupted and distracted, and whilst in Thy presence we direct the voice of our heart to Thine ears, this so great concern is broken off, by the rushing in of I know not what idle thoughts. Shall we then account this also among things of slight concernment, or shall aught bring us back to hope, save Thy complete mercy, since Thou hast begun to change us?

DOES PRIDE EVER CEASE?

And Thou knowest how far Thou hast already changed me, who first healedst me of the lust of vindicating myself, that so Thou mightest *forgive all* the rest of my *iniquities, and heal all my infirmities*, and *redeem my life from corruption, and crown me with mercy and pity, and satisfy my desire with good things;* who didst curb my pride with Thy fear, and tame my neck to Thy *yoke*. And now I bear it and it is *light* unto me, because so hast Thou promised, and hast made it; and verily so it was, and I knew it not, when I feared to take it.

But, O Lord, Thou alone Lord without pride, because Thou art the only true Lord, who hast no Lord; hath this third kind of temptation also ceased from me, or can it cease through this whole life? To wish, namely, to be feared and loved of men, for no other end, but that we may have a joy therein which is no joy? A miserable life this and a foul boastfulness? Hence especially it comes that men do neither purely love nor fear Thee. And therefore *dost Thou resist the proud, and givest grace to the humble:* yea, Thou thunderest down upon the ambitions of the world, and *the foundations of the mountains tremble.*

Because now certain offices of human society make it necessary to be loved and feared of men, the adversary of our true blessedness layeth hard at us, every where spreading his snares of "well-done, well-done"; that greedily catching at them, we may be taken unawares, and sever our joy from Thy truth, and set it in the deceivingness of men; and be pleased at being loved and feared, not for Thy sake, but in Thy stead: and thus having been made like him, he may have them for his own, not in the bands of charity, but in the bonds of punishment: who purposed to *set his throne in the north,* that dark and chilled they might serve him pervertedly and crookedly imitating Thee.

But we, O Lord, behold we are Thy *little flock;* possess us as Thine, stretch Thy wings over us, and let us fly under them. Be Thou our glory; let us be loved for Thee, and Thy word feared in us. Who would be praised of men when Thou blamest, will not be defended of men when Thou judgest; nor delivered when Thou condemnest. But when—not *the sinner is praised in the desires of his soul,* nor he *blessed who doth ungodlily,* but—a man is praised for some gift which Thou hast given him, and he rejoices more at the praise for himself than that he hath the gift for which he is praised, he also is praised, while Thou dispraisest; and better is he who praised than he who is praised. For the one took pleasure in the gift of God in man; the other was better pleased with the gift of man, than of God.

WE ARE ASSAILED DAILY

By these temptations we are assailed daily, O Lord: without ceasing are we assailed. Our daily *furnace* is the tongue of men. And in this way also Thou commandest us continence. Give what Thou enjoinest, and enjoin what Thou wilt. Thou knowest on this matter the groans of my heart, and the floods of mine eyes. For I cannot learn how far I am more cleansed from this plague, and I much fear my *secret sins,* which Thine eyes know, mine do not. For in other kinds of temptations I have some sort of means of examining myself; in this, scarce any.

For, in refraining my mind from the pleasures of the flesh and idle curiosity, I see how much I have attained to, when I do without them; foregoing, or not having them. For then I ask myself how much more or less troublesome it is to me not to have them? Then, riches, which are desired, that they may serve to some one or two or all of the three concupiscences, if the soul cannot discern whether, when it hath them, it despiseth them, they may be cast aside, that so it may prove itself. But to be without praise, and therein essay our powers, must we live ill, yea so abandonedly and atrociously, that no one should know without detesting us? What greater madness can be said or thought of? But if praise useth and ought to accompany a good life and good works, we ought as little to forego its company, as good life itself. Yet I know not whether I can well or ill be without any thing, unless it be absent.

What then do I confess unto Thee in this kind of temptation, O Lord? What, but that I am delighted with praise, but with truth itself, more than with praise? For were it proposed to me, whether I would, being frenzied in error on all things, be praised by all men, or being consistent and most settled in the truth be blamed by all, I see which I should choose. Yet fain would I that the approbation of another should not even increase my joy for any good in me.

Yet I own, it doth increase it, and not so only, but dispraise doth diminish it. And when I am troubled at this my misery, an excuse occurs to me, which of what value it is, Thou God knowest, for it leaves me uncertain. For since Thou has commanded us not continency alone, that is, from what things to refrain our love, but righteousness also, that is, whereon to bestow it, and hast willed us to love not Thee only, but our neighbour also; often, when pleased with intelligent praise, I seem to myself to be pleased with the proficiency or towardliness of my neighbour, or to be grieved for evil in him, when I hear him dispraise either what he understands not, or is good.

For sometimes I am grieved at my own praise, either when those things be praised in me, in which I mislike myself, or even lesser and slight goods are more esteemed than they ought. But again how know I whether I am therefore thus affected, because I would not have him who praiseth me differ from me about myself; not as being influenced by concern for him, but because those same good things which please me in myself, please me more when they please another also? For some how I am not praised when my judgment of myself is not praised; forasmuch as either those things are praised, which displease me; or those more, which please me less. Am I then doubtful of myself in this matter?

Behold, in Thee, O Truth, I see that I ought not to be moved at my own praises, for my own sake, but for the good of my neighbour. And whether it be so with me, I know not. For herein I know less of myself than of Thee. I beseech now, O my God, discover to me myself also, that I may confess unto my brethren, who are to pray for me, wherein I find myself maimed. Let me examine myself again more diligently.

If in my praise I am moved with the good of my neighbour, why am I less moved if another be unjustly dispraised than if it be myself? Why am I more stung by reproach cast upon myself, than at that cast upon another, with the same injustice, before me? Know I not this also? or is it at last that I *deceive myself,* and do not the truth before Thee in my heart and tongue? This madness put far from me, O Lord, lest mine own mouth be to me the *sinner's oil to make fat my head.*

A MOST DANGEROUS TEMPTATION

I am poor and needy; yet best, while in hidden groanings I displease myself, and seek Thy mercy, until what is lacking in my defective state be renewed and perfected, on to that peace which the eye of the proud knoweth not.

Yet the word which cometh out of the mouth, and deeds known to men, bring with them a most dangerous temptation through the love of praise: which to establish a certain excellency of our own, solicits and collects men's suffrages. It tempts, even when it is reproved by myself in myself, on the very ground that it is reproved; and often glories more vainly of the very contempt of vainglory; and so it is no longer contempt of vainglory, whereof it glories; for it doth not condemn when it glorieth.

ANOTHER EVIL

Within also, within is another evil, arising out of a like temptation; whereby men become vain, pleasing themselves in themselves, though they please not, or displease or care not to please others. But pleasing themselves, they much displease Thee, not only taking pleasure in things not good, as if good, but in Thy good things, as though their own; or even if as Thine, yet as though for their own merits; or even if as though from Thy grace, yet not with brotherly rejoicing, but envying that grace to others. In all these and the like perils and travails, Thou seest the trembling of my heart; and I rather feel my wounds to be cured by Thee, than not inflicted by me.

TAUGHT BY TRUTH

Where hast Thou not walked with me, O Truth, teaching me what to beware, and what to desire; when I referred to Thee what I could discover here below, and consulted Thee? With my outward senses, as I might, I surveyed the world and observed the life, which my body hath from me, and these my senses. Thence entered I the recesses of my memory, those manifold and spacious chambers, wonderfully furnished with innumerable stores; and I considered, and stood aghast; being able to discern nothing of these things without Thee, and finding none of them to be Thee.

Nor was I myself, who found out these things, who went over them all, and laboured to distinguish and to value every thing according to its dignity, taking some things upon the report of my senses, questioning about others which I felt to be mingled with myself, numbering and distinguishing the reporters themselves, and in the large treasure-house of my memory revolving some things, storing up others, drawing out others.

Nor yet was I myself when I did this, *i.e.*, that my power whereby I did it, neither was it Thou, for Thou art the abiding light, which I consulted concerning all these, whether they were, what they were, and how to be valued; and I heard Thee directing and commanding me; and this I often do, this delights me; and as far as I may be freed from necessary duties, unto this pleasure have I recourse.

Nor in all these which I run over consulting Thee can I find any safe place for my soul, but in Thee; whither my scattered members may be gathered, and nothing of me depart from Thee. And sometimes Thou admittest me to an affection, very unusual, in my inmost soul; rising to a strange sweetness, which if it were perfected in me, I know not what in it would not belong to the life to come. But through my miserable encumbrances I sink down again into these lower things, and am swept back by former custom, and am held, and greatly weep, but am greatly held. So much doth the burden of a bad custom weigh us down. Here I can stay, but would not; there I would, but cannot; both ways, miserable.

THE SICKNESS OF MY SINS

Thus then have I considered the sicknesses of my sins in that threefold concupiscence, and have called Thy right hand to my help. For with a wounded heart have I beheld Thy brightness, and stricken back I said, "Who can attain thither? *I am cast away from the sight of Thine eyes."* Thou art the Truth who presidest over all, but I through my covetousness would not indeed forego Thee, but would with Thee possess a lie; as no man would in such wise speak falsely, as himself to be ignorant of the truth. So then I lost Thee, because Thou vouchsafest not to be possessed with a lie.

WHO CAN RECONCILE ME TO THEE?

Whom could I find to reconcile me to Thee? was I to have recourse to Angels? by what prayers, by what sacraments? Many endeavouring to return unto Thee, and of themselves unable, have, as I hear, tried this, and fallen into the desire of curious visions, and been accounted worthy to be deluded. For they, being high minded, sought Thee by the pride of learning, swelling out rather than smiting upon their breasts, and so by the agreement of their heart, drew unto themselves the *princes of the air,* the fellow-conspirators of their pride, by whom, through magical influences, they were deceived, seeking a mediator, by whom they might be purged, and there was none. For the devil it was, *transforming himself into an Angel of light.*

And it much enticed proud flesh, that he had no body of flesh. For they were mortal, and sinners; but Thou, Lord, to whom they proudly sought to be reconciled, art immortal, and without sin. But a mediator between God and man must have something like to God, something like to men; lest being in both like to man, he should be far from God: or if in both like God, too unlike man: and so not be a mediator. That deceitful mediator then, by whom in Thy secret judgments pride deserved to be deluded, hath one thing in common with man, that is sin; another he would seem to have in common with God; and not being clothed with the mortality of flesh, would vaunt himself to be immortal. But since *the wages of sin is death,* this hath he in common with men, that with them he should be condemned to death.

THE TRUE MEDIATOR

But the true Mediator, Whom in Thy secret mercy Thou hast showed to the humble, and sentest, that by His example also they might learn that same humility, that *Mediator between God and man, the Man Christ Jesus,* appeared betwixt mortal sinners and the immortal Just One; mortal with men, just with God: that because the wages of righteousness is life and peace, He might by a righteousness conjoined with God make void that death of sinners, now made righteous, which He willed to have in common with them. Hence He was showed forth to holy men of old; that so they, through faith in His Passion to come, as we through faith of it passed, might be saved. For as Man, He was a Mediator; but as the

Word, not in the middle between God and man, because equal to God, and God with God, and together one God.

How hast Thou loved us, good Father, who *sparedst not Thine only Son, but deliveredst Him up for us ungodly!* How hast Thou loved us, for whom *He that thought it no robbery to be equal with Thee, was made subject even to the death of the cross,* He alone, *free among the dead, having power to lay down his life, and power to take it again:* for us to Thee both Victor and Victim, and therefore Victor, because the Victim; for us to Thee Priest and Sacrifice, and therefore Priest because the Sacrifice; making us to Thee, of servants, sons, by being born of Thee, and serving us.

Well then is my hope strong in Him, that Thou *wilt heal all my infirmities,* by Him Who *sitteth at Thy right hand and maketh intercession for us;* else should I despair. For many and great are my infirmities, many they are, and great; but Thy medicine is mightier.

We might imagine that Thy Word was far from any union with man, and despair of ourselves, unless He had been *made flesh and dwelt among us.*

Affrighted with my sins and the burden of my misery, I had cast in my heart, and had purposed to *flee to the wilderness:* but Thou forbadest me, and strengthenedst me, saying, *Therefore Christ died for all, that they which live may now no longer live unto themselves, but unto Him that died for them.* See, Lord, I *cast my care upon Thee,* that I may live, and *consider wondrous things out of Thy law.*

Thou knowest my unskilfulness, and my infirmities; teach me, and heal me. He, Thine only Son, *in Whom are hid all the treasures of wisdom and knowledge,* hath redeemed me with His blood. *Let not the proud speak evil of me;* because I meditate on my Ransom, and eat and drink, and communicate it; and *poor,* desired to be *satisfied* from Him, amongst those that *eat and are satisfied, and they shall praise the Lord who seek Him.*

On the Song
of Songs

St. Bernard
of Clairvaux

Introduction

SOME HISTORICAL PERIODS are more passionate than others; and the twelfth century was one of the most passionate of them all. It was a time of courtly love, when knights and their ladies dreamed of love in its most idealized form and, it seems, rarely did much about it. Passion could also be seen in the way thousands of people—from serfs to nobles—strapped on armor and headed East to fight in Crusades against the Moslems in the Holy Land. Their enthusiasm for holy war was amazing, even by our modern standards.

Other kinds of passion were evident in the twelfth century. Western Christianity had finally emerged from a long night of the soul, the period historians call the Dark Ages. The glories of the Roman Empire were long gone, as were the brilliant, but brief achievements of its successor, the empire of Charlemagne. In the ninth century, the sons of Charlemagne saw the remains of their father's empire fall to civil war and invading barbarians. Life in western Europe degenerated into chaos. Without centralized government, all power passed to those who had the means and the will to take it. Aggressive local lords established huge feudal estates which were protected by private armies of hired knights.

There was also a deep longing for God and the reform of the church. During the tenth century, the Roman papacy bottomed out morally. Peter's throne became a prize dearly sought by powerful Italian families, which meant that few men who sat on it were spiritually qualified to do so. Popes during this period lived like kings and openly consorted with mistresses and prostitutes, which is why some historians have called this phase of papal history the "pornocracy."

Finally people demanded change. German emperors, who ruled over the beginnings of a new empire, decided to take over the process for selecting popes. They saw to it that reform-minded Germans were put into office, so the moral stock of the papacy skyrocketed. These Gregorians, as the reforming popes were called, undertook the spiritual regeneration of the western church in the eleventh century.

They were helped by a new wave of renewal within monasticism. By the tenth century, even the Benedictine movement had fallen on hard times, so reformers based at a new monastery at Cluny, in central France, worked to revive monastic life. They succeeded in impressive ways. Lay people looked to the Cluniacs for spiritual leadership and even protection from warring local lords. Because of them the whole church experienced a surge of new life.

Even the theologians got passionate about reform. The entire theological enterprise was rejuvenated when scholars like Anselm, Abelard, and Peter Lombard began asking new kinds of questions and using a daring "scholastic" method to answer them. They sought to marry faith and reason in new ways and were not afraid to challenge the tradition while remaining fiercely loyal to it.

Piety also was full of intensity in the 1100s. People went on pilgrimages, feasted on holy days, felt a fervent affection for the Virgin Mary, venerated religious relics of the saints, and even volunteered for Crusades. One could not find a better example of the century's passion and piety than St. Bernard of Clairvaux. Throughout his life, he was consumed by love.

ST. BERNARD OF CLAIRVAUX
(1090–1153)

Bernard has been called the most influential Christian of the twelfth century because he seemed to be involved in all the major events and issues of his time. Bernard was born in Fontaines, near Dijon, France, in 1090. His parents were part of the nobility, which meant that Bernard and his brothers had every advantage that came with rank and class. The family was both prosperous and pious, and Bernard's religious commitments were formed early, when he felt a call to the monastic life. Never willing to do alone what he could do in a crowd, in 1112 he and thirty of his friends, including his own brothers, entered the monastery at Citeaux.

His new monastic home had been founded in 1097 by Robert of Molesme who hoped to spur monastic reform. By his time, even the Cluniacs were in decline. Robert had been a Benedictine monk in Burgundy, but had grown weary of what he considered low standards and lack of discipline.

He started a new monastery at Citeaux in hopes of doing better. Because the Latin version of Citeaux was *Cistercium*, Robert's monks were called Cistercians.

Almost immediately the Cistercians became models of religious zeal and monastic discipline. The third abbot of Citeaux was Stephen Harding, who drew up a new rule for the order. It stressed hard work more than scholarship. Instead of relying on the gifts of others for their support, the Cistercians took care of themselves. They built their monasteries in out-of-the-way places and did all their own cooking, cleaning, weaving, farming, and carpentry. Their churches were plain, without elaborate ornamentation. They ate sparingly (once daily during the summer and twice daily during the winter) and slept only six hours a night (seven during the cold winter months). They denied themselves every pleasure for Jesus' sake, though they did allow themselves the luxury of a warm fire on Christmas day.

Bernard, the son of French nobility, was willing to give up his privileges for the Cistercian way of life, which he embraced with unqualified enthusiasm. When Abbot Stephen decided to open another monastery at Clairvaux, he put Bernard in charge, even though he had been a Cistercian only three years.

From that time on, he was known as Bernard of Clairvaux. Eventually he became the most influential Cistercian of them all. His monastery became a model of Cistercian rigor. Despite their reputation for toughness and even excessive asceticism, Bernard thought life with the Cistercians was heaven. In fact, he became such an enthusiastic recruiter for the order that when he came to call, women hid their sons and husbands, in fear that Bernard would convince them to follow him back to the monastery.

Bernard's influence extended far beyond Clairvaux and the monastic movement. He got embroiled in church politics. In 1128 he served as secretary to the Synod of Troyes and wrote the rule for the Knights Templar, one of the military orders of monks who fought during the Crusades. Then in 1130, he took sides in a disputed papal election. He backed Innocent II against his rival Anacletus, arguing that he was morally superior. Bernard's influence helped Innocent to gain the upper hand. When one of his former students became Pope Eugenius III in 1145, his access to the highest levels of the church increased. When it came time to stir up the masses for a Second Crusade to the Holy Land, the pope called on Bernard. He traveled all over Europe, preaching combat as a Christian duty. On account of his spiritual powers of persuasion, thousands volunteered to fight; no one knows for sure how many ever made it home alive.

Even this brief overview demonstrates that Bernard seemed to show up in all the important places. He dominated his times by joining together a deep spirituality and an iron will. His self-discipline and self-righteousness gave him an edge over everybody else. He was so certain of being right that few people thought of opposing him. He had a good nose for heresy and brought charges against some leading theologians, including Abelard at the Council of Sens in 1140.

At the same time, Bernard was famous for his abundant tenderheartedness. He stressed two themes in his personal theology: the humanity of Jesus and the suffering of the Virgin Mary. His hymns about Christ are still sung today, including "Jesus, the Very Thought of Thee" and "O Sacred Head Now Wounded." His devotion to the Virgin Mary was legendary. Through his influence she came to play a much more significant role in the popular piety of the Middle Ages than she ever had before. For Bernard, Mary was both the Mother of God and the perfect human mother who combined holiness, love, and beauty. The example of her virginity, which was so important to a monk like Bernard, spurred thousands of women to enter the monastic life. Though his stress on Mary's motherhood and virginity provided a mixed message of sorts, thanks to Bernard, women emulated her and men adored her.

When Bernard died in 1153, worn out by three decades of rigorous asceticism, he was the most admired Christian in Europe. Only twenty-one years later, the Catholic Church declared him a saint.

ON THE SONG OF SONGS

Famous as a preacher of the Bible, Bernard's favorite source for sermons was the Song of Songs. A small book in the Old Testament, it has baffled readers and commentators for centuries.

Setting aside the question of authorship (according to tradition, it was King Solomon), the book appears to be nothing more than an erotic love poem describing the longing of two lovers for each other. In typical Semitic fashion, each praises the other's beauty and desirability. He says: "Your hair is like a flock of goats, / Going down from Mount Gilead. / Your teeth are like a flock of shorn sheep / Which have come up from the washing, . . . Your lips are like a strand of scarlet, / And your mouth is lovely. . . . Your two breasts are like two fawns, / Twins of a gazelle, / Which feed among the lilies" (4:1–5). She says of her lover: "His head is like the finest gold; / His locks are wavy, / And black as a raven. . . . His hands are rods of gold / Set with beryl. His body is carved ivory / Inlaid with sapphires. / His legs are pillars of marble / Set on bases of fine gold" (5:11–15). The two lovers pine for each other, visit each other in the dead of night, search high and low for each other in the city and the fields. One does not even have to read between the lines to feel the poem's passion. It is the steamiest stuff to be found in the Scriptures.

At first reading, it is curious that a celibate monk like Bernard of Clairvaux would find the Song of Songs so appealing. Modern people who are used to interpreting everything in sexual terms might suppose that Bernard was drawn to it for obvious reasons. But they would probably be wrong. Bernard did not think for a minute that the Song of Songs was an erotic poem about human love. He thought the book was about God—and God's love for humanity.

Of course, Bernard was not the only one to read the Song of Songs in a non-literalistic way. Even Jewish commentators preferred to understand it as an allegorical poem about God's love for Israel. Most early Christian commentators interpreted it as a description of God's love for the church. Whereas Bernard could—and did—understand the Song of Songs in that way, he preferred to see it as a picture of the love that exists between God and the individual human soul.

Biblical interpreters in the Middle Ages believed that they were well within their rights to read the Scriptures in this way. Each biblical text, they were convinced, could be read from four different perspectives. According to this fourfold approach, one could take a text literally, allegorically, morally, and tropologically. In a literal interpretation, one looked for the basic, straightforward, "historical" facts of the text. In an allegorical approach, one sought to find beneath the text's words a deeper spiritual meaning. To understand a text morally was to determine its application to real life (what humans *ought to do* in light of the passage); while to understand it tropologically was to find in the passage a spiritual direction to pursue.

Using this widely approved fourfold method, Bernard spent a lifetime trying to understand his favorite book. After years of studying the Song of Songs for himself, in about 1135 he began to preach it to his fellow monks at Clairvaux. Over the next nineteen years, he preached eighty-six sermons from the Song of Songs—and in all that time he got through less than half the book! (The edition that follows is a rearranged digest of his sermons.)

The first thing that strikes modern

readers about Bernard's sermons is his use of the fourfold method of interpretation. He turned each text this way and that, until he believed he had exhausted all interpretive possibilities. For example, in his sermon on "Behold, He standeth behind the wall, looking though the windows, looking out from the lattices," Bernard said, "The *literal meaning* of the Bride's next words would seem to be that He, Whom she described before as hastening towards her, has now approached her dwelling and stands looking in through windows in the wall, restrained by modesty from coming in. The *spiritual sense*, however, requires another manner of approach, worthy both of the Spouse Who makes it and of the Holy Spirit Who describes it in these words. The 'wall' is human flesh; the Bridegroom's drawing near denotes the Incarnation of the Word. The lattices and windows are, I think, the bodily senses and the human feelings, though which He gained experience of our needs."[1]

Twentieth-century readers are usually surprised by such inventiveness. Evidently there were no limits to what he could do with a text. For example, in his sermon on "For thy breasts are better than wine, and their fragrance than the choicest perfumes," he applied the words to different human subjects. First, he considered the breasts of the *bridegroom:* "We may take the two Breasts of the Bridegroom [i.e., Christ] to mean the two ways in which He shows His essential clemency—namely, His Patience in waiting for the sinner, and His Mercy in receiving the penitent." Then he

considered the breasts of the *bride:* "And that holy kiss has such creative power that she, receiving it, conceives, and her breasts fill with milk. Those who are frequently at pains to pray know full well what I mean." Then he tried out a number of other interpretations.[2] Most readers today will think this approach far-fetched, even ludicrous. But in Bernard's day, it seemed the height of sophistication and spirituality.

What, then, is *On the Song of Song's* enduring value? Today's readers should keep in mind that Bernard preached these sermons to monks and geared his approach to their needs. Though his allegorical approach to the text often led him down strange paths, Bernard never lost sight of the Song's consistent theme—the power and glory of love. He understood full well that the only thing that could sustain monks over the long haul was a growing relationship with God that was based on love, not fear. Under the constant strain of soul and body, deprived and often exhausted by strenuous self-discipline, monks needed ways to rejuvenate themselves. The regular ebb and flow of monastic life—working and praying—helped; but Bernard understood that even more important was an ongoing spiritual life in which intimacy with God was central.

This is the reason Bernard was so drawn to the Song of Songs. In the poetic words of one lover to another he heard the echoes of his own relationship to God. In the anticipation of the Bride for the Bridegroom, he detected his own longing after God. That much still comes through, after eight centuries. Bernard's bottom line, the point that will shock modern readers more than anything else is this: There is something even more powerful and passionate than the love between a man and woman—the love between God and a human soul. The surprising thing is that it took a twelfth century French monk to make the point so well.

Chapter One

"The Song of Songs, which is Solomon's"

OBSERVE HOW FITTING is the name of Solomon to head this book; for Solomon means Peaceful, and the book begins by speaking of the sign of peace—that is to say, the kiss. And notice at the same time that only the peaceful are invited to consider this scripture—namely, those who have mastered their passions and freed their hearts from thronging cares.

Do not suppose either that it is without significance that this scripture is called *The Song of Songs*, and not merely *A Song*. There are many songs in the scriptures, but I do not recall that any other song is styled like this. Israel sang to the Lord to celebrate the twofold miracle of their avenging and deliverance at the Red Sea; but that, if I remember rightly, is simply called "this Song." Deborah too, and Judith, and Samuel's mother, each sang a song, some of the prophets did the same; but none of them called what they sang *The Song of Songs*. Moreover, you will find, I think, that all these sang to celebrate some benefit bestowed upon themselves or on their people—a victory in battle or something of that kind.

OF SOLOMON'S PRAISES OF CHRIST AND HIS CHURCH

But King Solomon had wisdom, glory, wealth and peace all in abundance; he had no need like that to give him cause to sing when it was satisfied. No. He was inspired by God to sing the praises of Christ and of His Church, to hymn the grace of holy love, the mysteries of the eternal marriage; and at the same time he gave expression to the longing of the holy soul. What he has written, therefore, is a nuptial song, in figurative style; and it is called *The Song of Songs* because of its unique excellence; which is the reason also why He to Whom it is addressed alone is called the King of kings and Lord of lords.

The anointing of grace alone can teach a man this Song of Songs; experience alone can make him understand it. It is a joyful utterance, not of the lips but of the heart, and of harmonious wills. Its accents are not heard abroad by everyone, but only by those two whom it concerns, the Bridegroom and the Bride, the singer and the Sung.

Chapter Two

"Let Him kiss me with the kiss of His Mouth"

OF THE INCARNATION OF THE WORD

THIS VERSE EXPRESSES, so it seems to me, the ardent longing of the Fathers for the coming of the Christ in flesh. It is as though each holy soul were saying, "What good is there for me in all the prophets' words? I find Moses now of stammering speech, Isaiah's lips unclean, and Jeremiah cannot speak because he is a child. They are dumb, all of them. Let Him, to Whom they testify, speak Himself to me. Let *Him* kiss me with the kiss of His Mouth."

But notice this. It is the Word assuming Manhood Who is the Mouth that gives the kiss; it is the Manhood taken that receives it. The Kiss, which is perfected equally by Him Who gives and Him Who takes, is the Person compacted of both natures, the Mediator between God and Man, the Man Christ Jesus.

No saint therefore ever dared to say, "Let Him kiss me with His Mouth," but only "with the kiss of His Mouth." They recognized the unique prerogative of that Manhood upon which the Mouth of the Word was once for all impressed, when the Fullness of the Godhead was united corporeally with it. It was for this kiss that every saint of old time yearned, sensing beforehand that all the treasures of wisdom and of knowledge were hidden in Him, and longing to receive of His Fullness.

Further, it was not hidden from the saints of old that God was meditating counsels of peace towards this mortal race; and they foretold that Christ would bring peace when He came. But, as the Fount of Peace delayed to come and people's faith grew weak, men cried out for God to support the prophecies by action, to give the sign of peace—that is, the holy Kiss, the mystery of the Incarnation of the Word. O Root of Jesse, Who standest for an ensign of the peoples, how many prophets and kings desired to see Thee and yet saw Thee not! How happy Simeon, above all, who in his old age saw the sign so long desired, received the kiss of peace and in peace departed, yet not before he had declared that Jesus was born to be a sign that should be spoken against!

And so indeed it was. Those who hated peace opposed it from the first; it was peace only for men of goodwill. So to the happy shepherds the angel said, "This shall be a sign unto you"— to you who are humble, obedient, watchful—"ye shall find the Babe wrapped in swaddling clothes and lying in a manger." Yet God in Him was "reconciling the world unto Himself."

WHAT IT IS TO KISS THE FEET, THE HAND, AND THE MOUTH OF THE LORD

We read today from the book of experience. It is not given to everyone to say, "Let Him kiss me with the kiss of His Mouth"; but he who has but once received that spiritual kiss from the Mouth of Christ is urged by the experience most ardently to seek its repetition, and longs to taste the hidden manna once again. A soul like mine, on the other hand, laden with sins, enslaved by fleshly passions and lacking experience of the sweetness of the Holy Spirit and of inward joys, can make no smallest claim to such a grace.

Such a one, none the less, I counsel thus. Do not presume to lift yourself so high as to the Mouth of the Divine Bridegroom, but lie along with me before the Feet of the Lord most stern, afraid (as was the publican) to lift your eyes to heaven, lest you be blinded by excess of light. It is not for you, soul of this sort, whoever you may be, to scorn the place where once that holy sinner laid down her sins and put on holiness, where the Ethiopian changed her skin and, being restored to a new whiteness, with confidence and truth could answer her reproachers, "I am black but comely, O daughters of Jerusalem."

You, O unhappy soul, if you would cease to be unhappy, must imitate this happy penitent, prostrate upon the ground, kissing His Feet and washing them with tears. Nor must you dare to lift your shamed and tear-stained face until you also hear, "Arise, arise, O captive daughter of Sion. Shake thyself from the dust!"

OF THE NEED TO CONFESS
OUR WRONGS

When you have imprinted this first kiss upon His Feet, do not forthwith presume to raise yourself to kiss His Mouth. There is an intermediate stage—to kiss His Hand. And notice why. If Jesus shall have said to me, "Thy sins are forgiven thee," what good is it, unless I cease from sinning? Long have I wallowed in the mire of vice; if I fall back therein, when once escaped, then I shall be in worse case than before. So what I need is this: that He Who moved my will to penitence should further give me power to persevere. For woe is me indeed if He, without Whom I can do nothing, should suddenly withdraw His Hand, even while I repent!

So between Feet and Mouth you need this half-way house—His Hand, which first must cleanse you and then raise you up. How shall it raise you up? By giving you the grace of self-control, the fruits of penitence, which gifts will of themselves incite you to aspire to blessings greater still. And, in receiving these gifts from His Hand, you ought to kiss it—that is, give glory to His Name, not to yourself. Give Him one kiss because He has forgiven you; another, for the virtues that He has bestowed.

When in those two kisses you have received twin proofs of the Divine condescension, you may perhaps be bold enough to seek yet holier things. For your confidence will strengthen as you grow in grace; and you will love more fervently and knock with more assurance at His door for that which you still lack. And, what is more, to him who knocks it shall be opened; I think He will not then refuse to you that final kiss, that crowning act of condescension on His part, unutterably sweet.

OF THE ORDER WE MUST FOLLOW

So this, then, is the way, the order we must follow. First, we fall at the Lord's feet and bewail to Him Who made us the wrong things we have done. Next, we seek His Hand to lift us up and strengthen our weak knees, that we may stand upright. And, when we have won these two graces by many prayers and tears, we may at last, perhaps, dare to lift up our heads to that all-glorious Mouth, not only to behold it but to kiss. For the Spirit Whom we thus behold is Christ the Lord, Who deigns to make us of one spirit with Himself when we cleave to Him in this holy kiss.

Rightly, Lord Jesus, rightly has my heart said to Thee, "My face has sought Thee: Thy Face, Lord, will I seek." Thou madest me to hear Thy mercy in the morning of my life, when Thou didst pardon me my evil living even as I lay, kissing Thy sacred footsteps in the dust. And, as its day went on, Thou hast rejoiced my soul by giving me the grace to live well, through the kiss of Thy Hand. What remains now, good Lord, save that Thou shouldst fill me full with the joy of Thy Countenance, by deigning to admit me to the kiss of Thy Mouth? Show me, most sweet, most lovely One, where Thou dost feed Thy flock and dost repose at noon.

OF THE SOUL'S BURNING LOVE FOR GOD, AND OF THE ATTENTION WE SHOULD PAY TO PRAYER AND PSALMODY

The scripture we have undertaken to expound begins with the last of the aforesaid stages in the progress of the soul. "Let Him kiss me with the kiss of His Mouth." Who is it says these words? It is the Bride. And who is she? The soul athirst for God.

You must consider other relationships if you would understand that which is proper to the Bride. A slave feels fear before his lord; a hireling looks for wages; a pupil gives attention to his teacher; a son honours his father. But she who asks a kiss, she *loves*. Love is the highest of all our natural gifts, supremely so when it is rendered back to God, Who is its Source. And the mutual sweet affection between the Word and the soul cannot more sweetly be expressed than by thus calling them the Bridegroom and the Bride. For between bride and bridegroom all is held in common; neither calls anything their own or possesses a single thing the other does not share. They have but one inheritance, one home, one table, and one couch; they are in fact one flesh. Fitly, then, the soul who loves is called the Bride.

OF THE DESIRE OF THE SOUL ATHIRST FOR GOD

And notice how abruptly she comes out with her request! From the Great One she has a great boon to ask; but she employs no flatteries to get what she desires, nor does she beat about the bush. Bluntly, boldly, out of her full heart she blurts it out, "Let Him kiss me with the kiss of His Mouth!" Is it not as if she said, "Whom have I in heaven but Thee? And there is none upon earth that I desire in comparison of Thee?"

Her love is chaste, assuredly, for she seeks only the Object of her love, not anything that He may have to give. Her love is holy, for it is spiritual, not after the flesh. And it is burning, eager, for she is so absorbed in it that she forgets the majesty of Him to Whom she speaks. What? "The earth shall tremble at the look of Him," and she asks for a kiss! Is she inebriated? Yes, indeed she is. And perhaps, when she burst forth like this, she had come from the banqueting-house, whither she rejoices so greatly later that she has been led. For this is what David referred to when he said to God, concerning some, "They shall be satisfied with the pleasures of Thy House: and Thou shalt give them drink of Thy pleasures, as out of the river." How mighty is the strength of love! What perfect confidence the Spirit of liberty inspires! How plainly do we see that "perfect love casteth out fear!"

OF ANGELIC INTERVENTION IN MAN'S PRAYERS

Yet it is modesty that leads her to address her words, not to the Spouse Himself but to others, as though He were not there. "Let Him kiss me," she says, "with the kiss of His Mouth." It is a great thing that she asks, and there is need that the request be made with modesty and she who asks commended. So she asks the friends of Him Whom she desires, the members of His household, to commend her to Him; and by those I think we are to understand the holy angels who, so Scripture teaches, are ever present when we mortals pray. And for that reason I very much regret that some of you are so weighed down with sleep during the holy Vigils; I am afraid lest your sloth should drive away the an-

gels in disgust—and if good spirits thus depart from us, how shall we bear the onslaughts of the evil?

You should give heed to your leaders in heaven when you engage in prayer or psalmody, and perform the work with reverence and discipline, rejoicing to remember that your angels do always behold the Face of the Father. "Sing ye praises with understanding," therefore, together with the heavenly choir, since you yourselves are "fellow-citizens with the saints and of the household of God." The Psalms are tasty to the heart, as food is to the mouth; but the wise and faithful soul must be careful to chew them, as it were, between the teeth of his intelligence; lest, if he bolt them whole and chew them not, his palate be defrauded of their sweetness, which excels that of honey and the honeycomb.

The Bride, then, makes known her desire to the Bridegroom's attendants—that is, the heavenly powers; she longs most ardently to receive that kiss, and yet she does not name Him Whom she loves. "Let *Him* kiss me——" that is all she says, like Mary Magdalene who said to Him she thought to be the gardener, "If thou have borne Him hence——" taking for granted that everybody must know Whom she meant, seeing that He was never absent from her heart. So is it with the Bride. Speaking to the companions of the Spouse, as those to whom her own heart's thoughts are open, she names not her Beloved's Name but just blurts out the words, "Let Him kiss me with the kiss of His Mouth!"

What that kiss means I will explain

to-morrow, according as God's goodness shall enable me, in answer to your prayers.

THE KISS OF GOD'S MOUTH SIGNIFIES THE HOLY SPIRIT

Now, as I promised yesterday, I will discuss the highest kiss, that of the Mouth of God. Give all heed to this mystery, for it is passing sweet, but seldom known and hard to understand.

"No man knoweth the Son, but the Father; neither knoweth any man the Father, save the Son, and he to whomsoever the Son will reveal Him." It seems to me that He Who spoke these words denoted by them a certain kiss, transcending not words only but also the experience of all created beings, the angels not excluded. For the love of the Father for the Son is a love quite unique; it is the Most High embracing His Co-equal, the Eternal His Co-eternal, the One the Only One. And that the Son, for his part, reciprocates no less a love, He Himself attests. "That the world may know that I love the Father," He declares, "arise, and let us go"—meaning, beyond all doubt, go to His Passion. That mutual love between Begetter and Begotten, what is it but a kiss, mysterious as sweet?

The Bride, though she asks much, is not so bold as to ask that which is kept only for the Father: hers is a lesser plea. See her, new-made the Bride, receiving a new kiss, not from the Mouth but from the Kiss of it. "He [Jesus] breathed on them"—that is, on the apostles, on the nascent Church—"and said, Receive ye Holy Spirit." That was a kiss that was bestowed, assuredly—not His bodily breath, but the unseen Spirit given through the breath; that from that action we might understand that He proceeds from the Son equally as from the Father, just as a kiss is common to the person kissing and the person kissed.

THE CHURCH ASKS FOR THE KISS THAT SHE MAY HAVE THE KNOWLEDGE OF THE HOLY TRINITY

It is, then, through the Spirit that the Bride dares to ask, under the figure of a kiss, that the same Holy Spirit may be poured upon her. The statement of the Son, quoted just now, justifies her request: He has promised to reveal the Father and she is sure, if He do so to any, He will do so to her. So she asks boldly for the Kiss, which is that Spirit in Whom both Son and Father are revealed. In asking for this Kiss, she prays she may be given grace to know the Holy Trinity, to have the threefold knowledge of Father, Son and Holy Spirit, so far as in this mortal flesh it may be had.

Chapter Three

"For thy breasts are better than wine, and their fragrance than the choicest perfumes"

OF THE BREASTS OF THE BRIDEGROOM— THAT IS, OF CHRIST

"**T**HY BREASTS ARE BETTER than wine." As the author does not say by whom these words are spoken, we are free to assign them to whomever we think fit. Reasons are, in fact, not lacking for attributing them either to the Bridegroom, or to the Bride, or to the Bridegroom's companions. If we take the first, this is the situation: the Bride is conversing with the Bridegroom's friends about Him and, while she does so, He Himself draws near. He is wont thus willingly to join Himself to those who speak of Him; it was so with the two disciples going to Emmaus, who found in Him a pleasant and eloquent companion.

This very thing is promised in the Gospel, when He says, "Where two or three are gathered in My Name, there am I in their midst." And it is promised also through the prophet, in the words, "Before they call, I will answer: and while they are yet speaking, I will hear." I think, moreover, that sometimes He does not wait for words but lets Himself be called by thoughts alone, as the man who was after God's own heart declares, "Lord, Thou hast heard the desire of the poor." The Bride, then, conscious of His Presence, breaks off her conversation and turns to Him, wanting to excuse the boldness of the request she thought to make by intermediaries. "Thy breasts," she says, "are better than wine." Which is as if she said, "It is Thy doing that I aspire so high, for Thou hast so fed me with the milk of Thy lovingkindness that I have laid aside all fear."

OF GOD'S PATIENCE AND MERCY

We may take the two Breasts of the Bridegroom to mean the two ways in which He shows His essential clemency—namely, His Patience in waiting for the sinner, and His Mercy in receiving the penitent. This is no discovery of mine: you read in Scripture of His patience, "Despisest thou the riches of His goodness and forbearance and longsuffering, not knowing that the goodness of God leadeth thee to repentance?" and of His readiness to pardon it is written, "Let the wicked forsake his way and the unrighteous man his thoughts; and let him return unto the Lord, and He will have mercy upon him, and to our God, for He will abundantly pardon." David sums up both attributes beautifully in the words, "Longsuffering and of great goodness."

OF THE BREASTS OF THE BRIDE

The Bridegroom, coming suddenly while the Bride spoke of Him, gives her the kiss for which she asked, and so fulfils in her the Scripture, "Thou hast given him his heart's desire, and hast not denied him the request of his lips." And that holy kiss has such creative power that she, receiving it, conceives, and her breasts fill with milk. Those who are frequently at pains to pray know full well what I mean. We go to the altar and begin our prayer with hearts dried up and cold, but, if we persevere, quite suddenly grace flows in like a flood, enriching our whole being. Then it is the Bridegroom, speaking to the Bride, Who says, "Thou hast that thou didst ask for; in consequence, thy breasts are better than wine." That is to say, "Thy fruitfulness is proof of what thou hast received."

Or you may take those words as spoken by the Bridgroom's friends. In that case they will mean, "You should not grumble at your Spouse for further gifts, for what He has already given you—namely, breasts full of nourishment for babes—is better and more needful than the wine of contemplation that you seek. For many are made happy by your breasts, while contemplation is for yourself alone. Rachel is the fairer, certainly, but Leah is more fruitful."

Another interpretation has only just occurred to me. Do not the words "Thy breasts are better than wine" befit the lips of little children addressing their mother or their nurse? For young and tender souls take it ill if they see their guides and teachers seeking for leisure for their own souls' rest. "Do not do so," they say, "for the spiritual delights which we draw from your breasts subdue the fleshly lust with which we used to be intoxicated, as with wine." And wine is a good metaphor for fleshly lust; for the pressed grape is dry and finished with, as is the flesh in death.

"All flesh is grass," the prophet says, and the apostle, "Meats for the belly and the belly for meats, but God shall destroy both it and them." The world also passes away and all that is therein, and their end is unending. But the breasts of the Bride never run dry, however many nurslings she may have; for the well-spring of Charity supplies them unfailingly, and they flow ever new.

OF COMPASSION AND CONGRATULATION

I draw what I would say next concerning the breasts of the Bride from the great and inexhaustible fountain of Paul. "Rejoice with them that do rejoice," he says, "and weep with them that weep." So feels a mother for her children; so, then, I call the Bride's two breasts Compassion and Congratulation; and no one who has not these things should have the oversight of souls. Congratulation, sharing another's joy, yields the milk of encouragement; Compassion, sharing others' suffering, that of consolation. The mother's bosom flows afresh with these, whenever she receives the kiss.

OF THE SPIRITUAL PERFUMES PROPER TO THE BRIDE

Now I will show you what the perfumes are with which those breasts are fragrant. The chief ones are Contrition, Devotion and Piety. The first of these is pungent, and gives pain; the second soothes and eases it; the third is healing and drives out disease.

OF THE PERFUME OF CONTRITION

The sinful soul compounds the perfume of Contrition for itself, when it begins to take stock of its ways, to pound its many sins in the mortar of conscience, and to cook them in the cauldron of a troubled heart over the fire of repentance, as the Psalmist says, "My heart was hot within me, and while I was thus musing the fire kindled." This first most needful unguent of the sinful soul was typified by the actual ointment wherewith the sinful woman anointed the bodily Feet of God. Of that ointment we are told that "the house was filled with the odour of it." And the odour of penitence reaches even to the mansions of the blesséd; so that, as the Truth Himself declares, "there is joy in the presence of the angels of God over one sinner that repenteth." Rejoice, O penitents! Be strong, ye feeble souls! The ointment that not only leads men to amend their lives but also moves the very angels to rejoice is not to be despised.

OF THE PERFUME OF DEVOTION

We find the material for the first perfume growing in plenty in our own little gardens. But the sweet spices which compose the second, that is to say, Devotion, grow not on earth at all and must be sought from very far away. For "every good gift and every perfect gift is from above, and cometh down from the Father of lights," and this perfume is made up of the benefits bestowed by the good God on the human race. Happy the man who collects and ponders these, and renders worthy thanks to God for them!

Pounded in his heart by the pestle of meditation, brought to a great heat upon the fire of holy longing, and enriched lastly with the oil of joy, they will make a perfume far finer and more precious than the first. Moreover, whereas the first ointment was poured upon the Feet of Christ, this one anoints His Head. For "whoso offereth Me thanks and praise, he honoureth Me," says God; and Paul says that "the Head of Christ is God." So without doubt he who gives God thanks anoints Christ's Head. Not of course that He Who is God is not also Man, for God and Man is one Christ; but every good thing comes from God, and not from man, even when it is through men that it is ministered.

This perfume, compounded of the remembered benefits of God, cannot be made by souls still taken up with bitter thinking on their past offences. On this account I counsel you, my friends, to leave those painful paths sometimes for the smoother and more pleasant road of calling God's lovingkindnesses to mind. "Delight thou in the Lord," the Psalmist says, "and He shall give thee thy heart's desire." Sorrow for sin is necessary indeed, but it should not be our sole preoccupation. Remembrance of God's goodness should be mingled with it, as honey is with wormwood; so that the bridle of God's mercy may restrain us from despair.

Meditate, then, upon these things— God's goodness in creating you and all the world, the Lord's Self-emptying for our redemption, His taking flesh, His bearing of the cross, His death. Steep yourselves in odours such as these, that by them the foul stench of your sins may be dispelled and your own hearts be rendered redolent of these same fragrances, which are as strong to save as they are sweet.

OF THE PERFUME OF PIETY

The third perfume, which I call Piety, is far more precious than the former two. It is compounded of the necessities of the poor, the cares of the oppressed, the troubles of the sorrowful, the shortcomings of sinners, and indeed of all the tribulations of all the wretched people in the world, even although they be our enemies. These ingredients seem things to be despised; but the perfume made from them is the sweetest that there is, worthy of the Bride, agreeable to her Spouse.

"Blesséd are the merciful, for they shall obtain mercy"; this, therefore, is a healing balm. Happy is the soul who has made it her business to collect miseries, to pour on them the oil of mercy and heat them on the fire of love! Happy is the man who is ever quick to sympathize and help, who counts it better to give than to receive, who finds it easy to forgive, hard to be angry, and quite impossible to take revenge! O happy soul, whoever thou mayst be, who art of such a disposition, imbued with piety, making thyself all things to all men, dead to thyself and living but for others! Thou plainly hast this third, most perfect perfume; thy hands are fragrant with it, nor shall it ever dry up in the evil day.

EXAMPLES OF PIETY

Such a soul was Paul, who was to God "a sweet savour of Christ in every place," great-hearted as he was, tending all the churches with such devoted care. Job was another, who tells us of himself, "I was eyes to the blind, and feet was I to the lame; I was a father to the poor." Joseph in his treatment of those who had sold him into slavery, and Samuel, mourning for Saul who sought his life, showed a like disposition; as also did Moses, that meekest of men, who interceded for his people, saying, "Forgive their sin, if Thou wilt; but, if not, blot me out of the book that Thou hast written"; and David, who so lamented for Saul and Absalom, who both had tried to kill him. All these had this best of perfumes, and all the churches are fragrant with it still. And not they only, but all who have shown themselves kind and loving in this life, who have striven to use all their endowments for the common good, who put themselves at everybody's service and were humble under all conditions, are held in fragrant and blesséd memory.

And thou likewise, my brother, whoever thou art, if thou share with us thy fellows the gifts that God has given thee, if thou show thyself always obliging, loving, agreeable, tractable and humble, wilt have like testimony borne to thee by all of us—namely, that thou art fragrant with the best perfume of all. For everyone who not only bears with the infirmities of others, both physical and mental, but—if he may—affords them active help or at the least upholds their weakness by his prayers, is as a sweet odour among brethren. We say in a Community of such an one, "This is a lover of the brethren, who prayeth much for the people, and for the Holy City."

THE SUPERIORITY OF THE PERFUME OF PIETY

Of the two former perfumes we found mention in the Gospels; of the first, that a woman kissed the Lord's Feet and anointed them with it; of the second, that she or another poured it upon His Head. The passage which refers to the third perfume is this: "Mary Magdalene and Mary of James and Salome had bought sweet spices, that they might come and anoint Jesus." Notice that they bought *spices* only, not ointment ready-made for His embalming; and that they bought them to anoint *Jesus*. His whole Body, not a part only, as the Head or Feet.

You also, if you study to do good to all men, as Paul enjoins, for God's sake not refusing service even to your enemies, you also will be fragrant with this perfume, and will have taken on yourself, so far as in you lies, to anoint the Lord's whole Body—that is to say, the Church. He would not let those spices be used on His dead Body: was that perhaps because He willed that they should be reserved for use upon the Church, which is His living Body, fed by the Living Bread? That is the Body that the Lord wants cherished and anointed, and its weak members carefully restored to health.

You see, then, how this perfume of Piety is to be preferred far above the rest. And, in conclusion, I would point out this. The words "Thy breasts are better than wine, and their fragrance than the choicest perfumes" apply in some sense to every holy soul. But they belong absolutely only to the Church, who in one or other of her members finds all the qualities that we have spoken of, "according to the measure of the gift of Christ," and the good pleasure of the Holy Spirit, "dividing unto every man severally as He will." So thanks be to Thee, Lord Jesus, that Thou hast deigned to join us to Thy Church, not only that we may be found among the faithful, but also that we may be united to Thee as Thy Bride in bonds most blissful, chaste and neverending, when at the last with unveiled face we shall behold Thy glory, the which Thou sharest with the Father and the Holy Ghost, world without end, Amen.

Chapter Four

"Thy Name is as oil poured forth: therefore do the maidens love Thee exceedingly"

OF THE DUTY OF GRATITUDE TO GOD

WE SPOKE LAST of the perfumes proper to the Bride. In the next words she herself recognizes that her fragrance is not of herself, but is hers only by the Bridegroom's gift. "It comes not of my own desert or effort," she declares, "But from Thy bounty, O my Spouse. Thy Name is as oil poured forth." She speaks truth. As the sea is the source of all the springs and rivers, so is the Lord Jesus the fount of all virtues and knowledge, of all our intellectual powers and personal holiness.

Let then these streams of grace return whence they came; let the heavenly shower be rendered to its Source again, that it may be poured out once more upon the earth in even greater plenty. Do you ask how this shall be done? I tell you, as the apostle says: "In everything give thanks." Whatever you depend on in yourself of wisdom or of power, attribute it to Him Who is the Wisdom and the Power of God—that is, to Christ.

Further, after the Bride has said, "Thy Name is as oil poured forth," she adds "therefore do the maidens love Thee exceedingly." With these young, untried souls we may compare ourselves. So, if the Bride dares take no credit to herself for any of her powers or her graces, how much less should we! Let us, then, follow in her steps

and say right from our hearts, "Not unto us, O Lord, not unto us, but unto Thy Name give the praise." "Deliver us, O Lord our God, and gather us from among the heathen: that we may give thanks unto Thy holy Name and make our boast of Thy praise."

OF THE NAME OF THE BRIDEGROOM

Many different names are given to the Bridegroom in the Holy Scriptures; but they all, I think, fall into one or other of two categories. They all express either His mercy or His majesty. "Holy and reverend is His Name"; and yet "there is none other Name under heaven given among men whereby we must be saved." "I am the LORD," the thunderous Voice of old proclaimed; but I am given a prayer to say beginning with the tender name of "Father." And servants are called friends, and Jesus' Resurrection is announced not merely to disciples but to brethren. It is no wonder that this outpouring of the Name came at the fullness of the time, when God fulfilled what He had promised by the prophet Joel and poured out His Spirit upon all flesh.

Something akin to this, you will remember, had happened of old time. When Moses asked what was His Name Who spoke with him, the answer was "I AM WHO AM," and that he was to tell his people "HE WHO IS has sent me unto you." Heaven was in possession of that Name already; the angels had already received the revelation of it. But now, at Moses' question, the Name of which the knowledge was inpoured to the angels is outpoured upon men; so that the cry may arise from the earth, "Thy Name is as oil poured forth."

SALVATION IS FOUND IN HIS NAME

Draw near, ye nations! Your salvation is at hand. The Name is poured forth, upon which whosoever calls, he shall be saved. The God of angels names Himself also the God of men; He has shed oil on Jacob, it has fallen on Israel. Say ye to your brethren, therefore, "Give us of your oil!" O God of Abraham, of Isaac, and of Jacob, pour forth, pour forth, open Thy Hand yet wider and fill all things living with Thy plenteousness! Let them come from the east and from the west and sit down with Abraham, with Isaac, and with Jacob in the heavenly kingdom! Let the tribes of the Lord come to confess His Name, and let the song of them that feast resound, "Thy Name is as oil poured forth!" And I am sure of this, at any rate: if Philip and Andrew are the porters at the gate of heaven, they will not shut it in the face of anyone at all who seeks this oil, who would see Jesus. For Philip will tell Andrew straight away, and they will both tell Jesus.

But what will Jesus say?

Surely, just what He said before. "Except a corn of wheat fall into the ground and die, it abideth alone. But, if it die, it bringeth forth much fruit." It behooves the Christ to suffer and to rise from the dead; and repentance

and the remission of sins must be preached in His Name, not only in Judaea but to all the nations; in order that, from the One Name of *Christ*, thousands of thousands of believers may be called *Christians* and may say, "Thy Name is as oil poured forth."

WHY THE NAME OF THE BRIDEGROOM IS COMPARED TO OIL

There is undoubtedly a resemblance between oil and the Bridegroom's Name; not without reason has the Holy Spirit compared one with the other. And I should say the likeness consists in these three things:

1. As oil, by feeding flame, gives light, so does the Bridegroom's Name, when preached, enlighten souls.

2. As oil nourishes the flesh, so does the Bridegroom's Name feed those who meditate upon it.

3. As oil, when used as medicine, eases pain, so does the Bridegroom's Name heal us when we invoke it.

HIS NAME GIVES LIGHT

Let us consider these things one by one. When has so sudden and so bright a light of faith been kindled in the world, as by the preaching of the Name of Jesus? By it, God called us out of darkness into His marvellous light; in that light we see light, so that Paul can say, "Ye were sometime darkness, but now are ye light in the Lord." Paul's preaching of Jesus and Him crucified in every place was as a lamp set on a pedestal for all to see. And how that Name, flashing like lightning from the lips of Peter, set the lame man soundly on his feet!

HIS NAME PROVIDES NOURISHMENT

But Jesus' Name is food as well as light. Are you not strengthened, as often as you think of it? Does anything revive your flagging powers, confirm your virtues, quicken your good habits and foster you in purity of heart as does that Name? What book is worth the reading, what conversation worthy to be heard, that does not name that Name? "Jesus" is honey to the lips, and music to the ears, and gladness to the heart.

HIS NAME BRINGS HEALING

That Name is also medicine. Is any of you sad? Let "Jesus" come into his heart and leap thence to his lips, and lo! that Name, arising like the sun, dispels the clouds and all is peace again! Is any sinning—even, it may be, in his despair upon the brink of mortal sin? If he call on that Name of life, are not his life and health restored forthwith? When dangers threaten, who has not known his fears dispelled by uttering that Name of power? Whose doubts has it not driven away, leaving instead the shining certitude of faith? Who has not found new courage in that saving Name, when almost overwhelmed with troubles and distresses? Such are the soul's diseases; such the remedy, as God's own words prove, "Call upon Me in the time of trouble: so will I hear thee and thou shalt praise Me."

Nothing restrains anger, curbs pride, heals the wound of malice, bridles self-indulgence, quenches the passions, checks avarice and puts unclean thoughts to flight, as does the Name of Jesus. For, when I name His Name, I call to mind a Man meek and lowly of heart, generous, reasonable, pure, merciful—a Man conspicuous, in fact, for everything in which integrity and holiness consist; and, at the same time, in the same Lord Jesus, I see Almighty God. As Man, He heals me by His example; as God, He strengthens me by His aid.

Hidden in this Name of Jesus, O my soul, as in a vessel, thou hast a sovereign remedy against every ill. Keep it in thy bosom always, ready to thy hand; so that all thine affections and actions may be centred upon Him.

OF THE TWOFOLD OPERATION OF THE HOLY SPIRIT

"Thy Name is as oil poured forth." The operation of the Holy Spirit is twofold: first, He grounds us in the virtues, inwardly, for our own salvation's sake; next, He decks us outwardly with profitable gifts. We receive the former unction for ourselves, the latter for our neighbours. For instance, faith, hope and charity are given us for ourselves, because without them we cannot be saved. But the gifts of wise or learned speech, of healing, prophecy and the like, which we may lack entirely without the smallest detriment to our own salvation, all these undoubtedly are given us to use to forward the salvation of our neighbours.

We may name these operations Infusion and Effusion, after their effects; and it is to Effusion that the words refer about which we are speaking, "Thy Name is as oil poured forth." For it is with reference to the fragrance she derives from Him that the Bride speaks thus to her Spouse; and anyone who feels himself endued with any outward grace, which he can pour back in his turn on others, can make her words his own.

OF DANGERS TO GUARD AGAINST

There are two dangers here that we must guard against. We must not give to others what we have received for ourselves; nor must we keep for ourselves that which we have received to spend on others. You fall into the latter error, if you possess the gift of eloquence or wisdom, and yet—through fear or sloth or false humility—neglect to use the gift for others' benefit. And, on the other hand, you dissipate and lose what is your own, if without right intention and from some wrong motive you hasten to outpour yourself on others, when your own soul is only half-filled.

If you are wise, therefore, you will show yourself a tank, and not a pipe. For a pipe pours out as fast as it takes in; but a tank waits till it is full before it overflows, and so communicates its surplus without loss to itself. We have all too few such tanks in the Church at present, though we have pipes in plenty. Of so great charity are those who mediate the heavenly waters to us, that they desire to pour out when they themselves have not yet been in-poured; they are readier to speak than to listen, eager to teach that which they do not know, and most anxious to exercise authority on others, although they have not learnt to rule themselves!

You cannot, then, do better than follow the Wise Man's advice, "Have pity on thine own soul, pleasing God." If—like the widow—I have just a little oil for my own use, do you think I ought to give it to you and myself go empty? No, I keep it for mine own anointing, and will not bring it forth save at the prophet's bidding. If some of you, esteeming me as other than I am, importune still, I shall reply, "Not so, lest there be not enough for us and you; but go ye rather unto them that sell, and buy for yourselves."

But "Charity seeks not her own," you say? Do you know why? Because she does not lack it! Nobody seeks what they already have; and Charity is always in possession of her own—that is to say, of all things needful to salvation. In these her will is to abound, that all may do the same; and she keeps what is needful for herself, that no one else may lack. In other words, she is not perfect except she be full.

But thou, my brother, whose own salvation is hardly yet assured, whose charity is feeble and unstable if it exists at all, thou must learn not to give except when thou art full; thou must not try to be more generous than God. Let the tank, of which we spoke just now, take pattern from the spring; for the spring does not form a stream or spread into a lake until it is brim full. And He Who is Himself the Fount of life, full in and of Himself, did He not fill the heavens first with every excellence, before He let His overflowing mercy gush out on the earth, to save both man and beast? Do thou likewise.

Be filled thyself; then—but discreetly, mind—pour out of thy fullness. Charity which is thus discreet as well as generous does not waste itself by giving out, but rather gains in depth. "My son," says Solomon, "do not be wasteful." And the apostle tells us "we ought therefore to give heed to the things we hear, lest we forget them." What then? Art thou holier than Paul, wiser than Solomon? And, what is more, *I* have no wish to be enriched at thy expense; for, if thou be injurious to thyself, to whom shalt thou do good? Out of thy fullness help me, if thou canst; and, if not, spare thyself.

OF THINGS NEEDFUL FOR SALVATION

Now listen while I tell you what things, what mighty things are needful for our own salvation, and how great grace must be inpoured upon ourselves, before we dare to give ourselves to others. To the soul that says "My wounds stink and are corrupt," there comes the Doctor—that is, the Holy Spirit. What has He got to do? Well, first the ulcer of inveterate bad habit must be cut away with the sharp knife of *Compunction.* That hurts; the ointment of *Devotion,* which is nought else but joy born of the hope of pardon, must be applied to ease the pain; and from this in turn will spring self-discipline and victory over sin. "Thou hast broken my bonds asunder," the soul cries at this stage, "I will offer to Thee the sacrifice of praise."

It must be given next the physic of *Repentance,* and the poultice of all the exercises proper to the penitent—fasting, prayers, watches and the rest. In this travail it must be sustained by the food of *Good Works,* so that it may not faint. That good works are food, the Lord Himself has told us. "My meat," He says, "is to do the will of My Father." That is why the strengthening toils of penitence must be accompanied by works of piety. But food arouses thirst, so drink also is needed—the draught of *Prayer,* that wine that maketh glad the heart of man, that moistens the dry conscience, assimilates good actions to nourish the whole soul, strengthens faith, confirms hope, quickens and orders charity, enriches and develops the entire character.

Thus fed and given to drink, what needs the sick man more, except to rest after his active labours? In *Contemplation's* sleep he dreams of God, beholding Him darkly, as in polished metal, not yet face to face. Yet even that dim, transient vision of His glory kindles love—love that is full of zeal and worthy of the Bridegroom's friend, that fills and warms the soul, that bubbles up and now at last can safely overflow. The man whom *Love* thus holds completely in possession may freely preach, bear fruit, work signs and miracles; no vanity will find a place in him. For Love, if it be full, is the perfection of the Law and of the heart; for God is Love and only God can satisfy the creature created in God's Image, since God alone is greater than the creature He has made. It is very dangerous to put a person who has not this perfect love into a prominent position, however gifted he may be in other ways. Though he have all knowledge, though he have given his substance to the poor and handed over his body to be burned, without love he is empty.

So you see with what great graces we need to be inpoured before we venture to give out to others—if indeed our self-giving is to be out of our fullness, not our poverty! First, we need Compunction; then Devotion; thirdly, the travail of Repentance; fourthly, Good Works; fifthly, faithful Prayer;

sixthly, leisure for Contemplation; and, in the seventh place, the fullness of Love. All these things are the work in us of One and the Same Spirit, according to the operation that we have called Infusion; to the end that the other, which is called Effusion, may be exercised with purity of heart—and therefore safely—to the praise and glory of our Lord Jesus Christ, Who with the Father and the Holy Spirit liveth and reigneth, God to the ages of ages, Amen.

ON LOVING GOD

"Therefore do the maidens love Thee exceedingly," says the loving Bride; meaning that on the maidens, that is to say, the immature girls who need to keep close to their mother, the fragrance of the Name inpoured on her has been outpoured; and therefore they have loved Him. Souls of this kind, indeed, cannot receive the Name except by such effusion; and, when it is received, it cannot but be loved. Those of greater capacity do not need this effusion; such, each in their degree, are the Nine Orders of the Holy Angels. It is the babes in Christ who must be fed with oil and milk drawn from the Bride's bosom, that they may know how gracious the Lord is. And when she sees their ardent love, she turns to Him and says, "Thy Name is as oil poured forth: therefore do the maidens love Thee exceedingly."

Exceedingly. What does that mean? With vehemence or ardour, yes—and also to excess. So, indirectly, there is a message here for you who have but lately come, a word reproving the unwise, immoderate zeal to which you cling so stubbornly, in spite of our repeated efforts to repress it. The common life is not enough for you! The fasts and solemn vigils, the penances, the measure of food and clothing appointed by the Rule for all, do not content you; you want your private rules! Why do you thus take back into your own hands the guidance of your souls which you have put in ours? It is your self-will that you are following, not me—that self-will which, as your consciences testify, has so often led you into sin before.

Do you not know that "to obey is better than sacrifice"? Have you not read in the Rule that whatever is done without the approval of your spiritual father must be imputed to vainglory and therefore has no merit? Have you not read in the Gospel how the boy Jesus set an example to dedicated youth, not disdaining to follow His parents to Nazareth, though He was Master and they learners, He God and they but human beings, He the Word and Wisdom and they only a carpenter and his wife? "And He was subject unto them," the sacred history adds! How long will you be wise in your own eyes? God entrusts Himself to mortals and submits to them, and do you still walk in your own ways? You had received a good spirit, but you use it ill; and I am fearful lest Satan should overthrow you through this lack of prudence. I purpose, therefore, to give you certain rules, which it is very important for those who love God to observe.

OF CHRIST'S LOVE FOR US

I will base what I have to say on the words of a master. "If any man love not the Lord Jesus Christ, let him be anathema." Assuredly I ought to love Him utterly, from Whom I have my being, life, and reason. He who refuses to live for Thee, Lord Jesus, is plainly worthy of death; indeed he *is* dead. For Thou hast made all things for Thyself; and to try to exist for one's own self is the negation of one's very being. "Fear God and keep His commandments. This"—the Wise Man says—"is the whole man." If this is the whole man, without it man is nothing.

I must be grateful, then, for all God's gifts. But there is something that kindles and moves me even more. It is the cup that Thou didst drink, Lord Jesus, more than ought else, that renders thee love-worthy; it is the work of our redemption that supremely claims our love. The Creator bestowed not so much labour on making the whole world, as did our Saviour in redeeming us! In the first work "He spake and it was done"; but in the second He put up with people who tried to catch Him in His talk, carped at His actions, mocked His sufferings, and even upbraided Him in death.

Moreover, He was not returning any love of ours in this; but, as St. John says, "Not that we loved God, but that He first loved us." Indeed He loved us, not only when we did not exist but when we were opposed to Him, as Paul says, "while we were yet enemies, we were reconciled to God through the Blood of His Son." In other words, if He had not loved us when we were enemies, He would not now possess us for His friends; just as, if He had not loved those who did not yet exist, they would not be existing now for Him to love.

This love of His is tender, wise, and strong. Tender, in that He took on Him our flesh; careful and wise, in that He guarded against sin; and strong, in that He suffered death. It is a thing beyond all measure sweet to look upon man's Maker as a Man. His wisdom took our nature free from sin; His power drove death from it. In taking flesh, He stooped to me; in shunning sin, He acted in a manner concordant with Himself; by undergoing death, He satisfied the Father. A loving Friend, a prudent Counsellor, a mighty Helper He! I trust myself entirely to Him Who willed to save me, knew the way to do it, and had the power to carry out the work. He has both sought me out and called me by His grace; if I come to Him, will He cast me out? No, indeed He will not; and, what is more, there is no power or deceit that I need fear, lest it should pluck me from His Hand. For He, in conquering death, has conquered everything.

Taking our actual flesh, He ministered sweet comfort to the weak. Taking the likeness only of our sinfulness, He wisely hid from the Seducer of the world the snare that was to take Him; and thereby showed Himself more prudent than the devil, and mightier in the holier stratagem He used. To reconcile us to the Father, bravely He suffered death and conquered it, shedding His Blood as price of our redemption. Had He not loved me tenderly, that Majesty would not have sought me in my prison. To love He conjoined wisdom to deceive the tyrant; to wisdom, longsuffering endurance to placate God His Father, outraged by our sins. Thus, as I said, His love is tender, wise and strong.

CHRIST'S LOVE FOR US SHOWS US HOW TO LOVE HIM

Learn then from Christ, O Christian, how Christ should be loved. Learn to love Him tenderly, prudently, and with all thy might. Tenderly, that nothing may seduce us from Him; prudently, that no deceit turn us aside; and mightily, that nothing may swamp our love for Him. Let Christ, Who is God's Wisdom, be thy joy, that carnal pleasures part thee not from Him. Let Christ, Who is the Truth, enlighten thee, that thou be not misled. Let Christ, Who is the Power of God, be strength to thee, so that thou be not hindered by adversity. Let love inflame thy zeal, wisdom inform it, and perseverance make it permanent; so that it be at once ardent, and circumspect, and undefeated, with nothing lukewarm in it, yet discreet, though never cowardly.

And are not these three things just what the Law requires, when God says, "Thou shalt love the Lord thy God with all thy heart, and with all thy soul, and with all thy strength"? Love of the heart, it seems to me, stands for the eager aspect, the zealous side of love; love of the soul for the painstaking side, where reason operates; loving with all one's strength denotes the steadfastness and vigour of the mind. Do thou then love the Lord thy God with the full, unreserved affection of thy heart, with all thy reason's watchfulness and care, and with all the strength thou hast; so that for love of Him thou wilt not fear to die, as it is written later in this Song, "Love is strong as death."

Let the Lord Jesus be thy heart's delight, driving from it delight in the allurements of the flesh, as one nail drives another. Let Him be light and leading to thine understanding, not only to preserve thee in the purity of faith against all heresies, but also to restrain thee from excesses in thy way of life. And let thy love be also strong and steadfast, unyielding before fear and resolute in suffering. So let us love with generous affection, with circumspection and with doggedness, knowing that the heart's emotion, sweet as it is, goes easily astray if the soul's love go not along with it; which love again, though it is rational, is weak unless it be supported by the brave and persevering love of all one's strength.

EXAMPLES OF IMPERFECT LOVE

Let us take some examples to prove the truth of this. The disciples, grieving because their Master said that He must go away, loved Him after a fashion only—that is, tenderly; but in another sense they loved Him not at all. Wherefore He said to them, "If ye loved Me, ye would rejoice because I said, I go to the Father." Their love was in fact against the interests of their own salvation; in other words, it was not wise. Wherefore He said to them, "It is expedient for you that I go away."

Peter also loved, but loved not wisely, when he rebuked the Saviour for foretelling His death. When, having been corrected, he declared his readiness to die with Him, his love was wise; but he could not fulfill his promise because he had not yet attained the third degree of love, the love of all one's strength. But afterwards, when he had been endued with power from on high, and was forbidden by the Sanhedrin to preach the Holy Name, his love *was* strong; for he made firm reply, "We ought to obey God, rather than men."

OF CARNAL LOVE

And notice that the love of the heart is carnal, in a sense, because it is directed mainly to the Humanity of Christ and the things that He did or commanded in the flesh. A person who is filled with this love is readily moved by any discourse on these matters, meditates upon them with greater sweetness than on any others, and in his prayer has the picture of the God-Man in His Birth, His Infancy, His Ministry of teaching, His Death, His Resurrection or Ascension, ever before his eyes, inciting him to holiness of life and driving out his vices.

Indeed I think myself that the chief reason why the unseen God willed to appear in flesh and mix with men was that He might draw to Himself in flesh the love of those who were not able yet to love save in carnal manner, and so to lead them gradually on to spiritual love. Those who said, "Behold, we have left all and followed Thee," were they not in this first degree of love? They had left all, simply from devotion to His bodily presence, so that not only they could not endure to hear of His approaching sufferings and death for our redemption, but a little later they faced even the prospect of His glorious Ascension only with deepest grief.

Such devotion to the Humanity of Christ is a gift of the Holy Spirit, and a great gift too; yet, relatively, we must call it carnal. Compare with it that other love, which had regard not to the Word made Flesh so much as to the Word as Wisdom, Righteousness, Truth, Goodness, Strength and all else that is perfect. Suppose there are two people, both of whom love Christ. One is sustained by sweet devotion to His Passion and moved by that to carry out his duty; the other has a flaming zeal for righteousness, desires wisdom, longs earnestly for holiness of life and perfect self-control, blushes at ostentation, abominates detraction, is innocent of envy, hates pride, avoids and honestly despises human glory, is relentlessly severe in curbing his fleshly imperfections; in a word, as though by inborn instinct he rejects all evil and cleaves only to the good. What of these two? Think you they have an equal love for Christ? Or would you not say rather that the second plainly loves Him the best, and that the former, by comparison, loves in a carnal manner?

OF SPIRITUAL LOVE

And yet the love, that shuts the door on fleshly pleasures and overcomes the world, is good, for all that it is carnal in a sense. Those who progress in it attain to rational love; and this is perfected when it becomes spiritual. By rational love I mean that which keeps a perfect balance between the different elements of the Church's faith in Christ, and therefore is secure against all heresy. A like moderation ought to be observed in our personal lives, so that neither scrupulosity nor instability nor unregulated zeal should lead us to excess. And to love like this is, as I said before, to love with all one's soul.

And if the Holy Spirit so enable us that no afflictions or toils or fear of death, however fierce, can turn us from the path of righteousness, then we have come to love with all our strength; and that is spiritual love—fitly so-called, I think, because the fullness of the Spirit is so marked in it.

I have now said enough about the saying of the Bride, "Therefore do the maidens love Thee exceedingly." And, that I may be able to expound the words that follow, may the Lord Jesus Christ our Guardian deign to unlock for us the treasures of His mercy, Who liveth and reigneth with the Father in the unity of the Holy Spirit, throughout all ages, Amen.

Chapter Five

"Draw me after Thee; we will run in the odour of Thy perfumes"

WHY THE BRIDE MAKES THIS PRAYER

DRAW ME AFTER THEE; we will run in the odour of Thy perfumes." What? Does the Bride need to be drawn after her Spouse, as though she followed Him unwillingly? Yet, when you come to think of it, not everybody who is drawn is drawn against their will. A sick man, for example, who cannot walk alone, is glad if someone takes him to the bath or to his dinner; although a criminal is far from glad if he be drawn to judgment or to punishment. She who speaks here desires to be drawn, and would not ask to be, had she the power to follow of herself. Why so? Must we admit that even she is weak? Had one of her maidens made this prayer, we could have understood it; but that the Bride, who seemed so strong and perfect, so able to draw others, should need thus to be drawn, seems strange indeed!

OF THE BRIDE'S WEAKNESS

If we admit her weakness, where shall we find strength? Or can it be that the Church speaks these words, as she sees her Belovéd ascending into heaven and yearns to follow Him and share His glory? And indeed every soul, however far advanced, as long as it groans in this mortal body and is held captive in this wicked world, harassed by limitations and pestered by shortcomings, is inevitably less quick to rise to heavenly contemplation than it would like to be, and is not altogether free to follow the Bridegroom "whithersoever He goeth." Hence comes the anguished cry of the apostle, "O wretched man that I am, who shall deliver me from the body of this death?"; hence also the petition, "Bring my soul out of prison." It may be that the Bride cries "Draw me after Thee" with a like groaning beneath the burden of the flesh. Or it may be that she desires to depart and be with Christ all the more ardently, because she sees her maidens established in charity, as she said before, and therefore needing her in flesh no more.

But she says "Draw me *after* Thee"—not "to Thee," as this interpretation surely would require; and this suggests rather that she is asking for grace to follow in His footsteps, so that her life may be conformed to His. The soul indeed needs help supremely to deny herself and take up her cross, and so to follow Christ; and the Bride needs to be drawn by no one save by Him Who says, "Without Me ye can do nothing." "I know," she says, "I cannot come to Thee except I follow Thee; nor can I even follow, unless I have Thine aid. Therefore I pray that thou wouldst draw me after Thee."

FEW DESIRE TO FOLLOW CHRIST

Lord Jesus, how few souls there are who want to follow Thee! Everyone wants to reach Thee in the end, because they know that "at Thy right Hand are pleasures for evermore." They want to have the happiness that Thou canst give, but not to imitate Thee; they want to reign with Thee, but not to suffer. Even the carnal-minded would like a holy death, although they cannot stand a holy life! But it was otherwise with those to whom Thou saidst, "Ye are they who have continued with Me in My temptations." Blesséd were they to whom Thou spakest thus! They followed after Thee in truth, with their feet *and* their hearts. Thou madest known to them the ways of life, in calling them to follow Thee Who art both Life and Way. And it is thus that Thy Belovéd, having left all for Thee, desires always to go after Thee, knowing that Thy ways are ways of pleasantness, and all Thy paths are peace.

THE SPIRITUAL WALK IS NOT STATIC

You know well from your own experience that he who walks in the Spirit does not remain always in one state, but progresses now with alacrity, now at a snail's pace. When therefore you are in the latter case, afflicted with [boredom] and weariness, do not give up, but seek your Helper's Hand, as does the Bride. And in your day of strength, when grace is present with you, rejoice in it, but do not be puffed up or rest in it as though it were your rightful property; lest you be cast into excessive sorrow if God should suddenly withdraw His gift. Here too we may take pattern from the Bride; for she is free in heart and persevering and, being schooled in wisdom, knows how to bear both poverty and wealth.

So she says, "Draw me after Thee; we will run in the odour of Thy perfumes." Small wonder she needs drawing, seeing it is a Giant after Whom she runs and she is trying to catch up with One Who springs upon the mountains and leaps upon the hills! "His Word," the Psalmist says, "runneth very swiftly." The Bride cannot keep pace with Him Who "rejoiceth as a giant to run His course." So she prays, "I am tired, leave me not; but draw me after Thee. Draw me, albeit in some sort against my will, that Thou mayst make me willing. Draw me, slow as I am, that Thou mayst make me swift. And"—she adds—"let me not run alone, but let the maidens run along with me—I, in the odour of Thy perfumes; they, roused by my example and behest. For in this way they will be running in the odour of Thy perfumes too."

OF THE PERFUMES PROPER TO THE BRIDEGROOM

We have already spoken of the perfumes proper to the Bride, and found them precious and superb. That being so, what must the Bridegroom's be? Their very fragrance stirs not the maidens only but the Bride herself to run; and, if she had received an actual anointing with them, it were a wonder if she did not fly! I cannot possibly expound these perfumes worthily; I am not even sure, as yet, whether my thoughts about them are such as should be uttered. But it does seem to me that the Bridegroom possesses a variety of perfumes and balms, and that some of them delight the Bride more than the others, and delight her alone, since she is closer to Him;

whereas others reach as far as to the maidens, and some even to strangers far away, so that no one can go wholly unwarmed by His fire. Nevertheless the Lord, though gracious to all men, shows special favour to the members of His household; and the nearer anyone approaches Him by worthy living and purity of heart, the sweeter and the fresher fragrances will he perceive.

OF MAN'S LIMITED UNDERSTANDING

A person's understanding of these matters is limited by his experience; and it is not for me to claim the special privilege accorded to the Bride. Only the Bridegroom knows with what joys He regales, revives, and soothes her whom He loves. "A garden enclosed, a fountain sealed" He calls her later in this Song; and such she is for us. Yet from the fountain streams flow to the streets, whence people draw for common uses, drinking, washing, cooking; so you of more profound experience must bear with me while I set forth the simpler truths suited to simpler people, and speak of God the Bridegroom, not as the High and Holy, but in His lowliness as Man, anointed by the Spirit and sent to preach the Gospel to the poor.

"God," the apostle tells us, "hath made Him to be Wisdom, and Righteousness, and Sanctification, and Redemption." From these four, as from perfumes very precious, so sweet a fragrance has filled the nostrils of the Church that, moved thereby, people have hastened to the Bridegroom from the four quarters of the earth, even as the queen of the east hastened to hear the wisdom of Solomon, drawn by the fragrance of his reputation.

The Church, however, could not run in the sweet odour of her Solomon, until such time as He, Who was the Wisdom of the Father from all eternity, was made by Him to be Wisdom in time; so that His fragrance might be sensed by her. And equally was He then made for her Righteousness, Sanctification, and Redemption, that she might run enveloped by the sweetness of these too, all of which were in Him before creation was. "In the beginning was the Word," says John; but the shepherds hastened to behold Him only when they heard the tidings of His birth. When the Word was with God alone, they did not stir; but, when the Word, Who was, was *made*, when the Lord wrought His Incarnation and made it known to men, they hastened then, they ran!

OF WISDOM, RIGHTEOUSNESS, SANCTIFICATION, AND REDEMPTION

Wisdom, Righteousness, Sanctification, and Redemption, all these He was from the beginning to the angels—even Redemption, since He granted them the grace to keep from sinning. And He was made to be these same four things for men, who cannot look upon the unseen things of God save through that which is made. All that He was already for the angels He was made for us: Wisdom, declared in preaching; Righteousness, in loosing sinners from their chains; Sanctification, in the life He lived among them; Redemption, in the Passion He suffered for their sakes. And since the time God made Him to be these for us, the Church has smelled His fragrance and has followed Him.

Consider this fourfold anointing. Thou wast a prisoner, O Man, bound with the chains of sin and ignorance. He came down to thy prison, not to torment thee but to rescue thee. By Wisdom He drove away thy darkness with the Truth; by Righteousness, which is of faith, He freely justified thee, loosing the bands of sin; by His own Holiness of life He set thee an example and pointed out to thee thy homeward road. And, to crown all, He gave up His own soul to death and paid the price of our Redemption out of His own pierced Side.

What has He left undone for thee, that He ought to have done? He has restored sight to the blind, released the captive, led back the wanderer to the road, pardoned the criminal. Who will not run willingly, eagerly, after the Doer of these things? What possible excuse has anyone for not running in the odour of perfumes such as these, unless maybe he scarcely is as yet aware of them?

Chapter Six

"The King led me into His store-houses. We will be glad and rejoice in thee, remembering thy breasts more than wine"

WHO SPEAK THESE WORDS, AND WHY

THE KING HAS LED ME into His store-houses." The Bride had told us we must run, but she had not said whither. Now she explains. Our goal is the King's store-place, those fragrant chambers where all the choicest fruits of garden and of field are treasured up. Thither she runs, and thither run the maidens; but she, because she loves more ardently than they, runs faster and arrives more speedily. And, on arrival, she is not refused admittance, not even made to wait. The door is opened to her on the spot, as to a member of the household and one particularly welcome and beloved. The maidens, lacking her fervour, follow on more slowly; when later they arrive, they stay outside. But the Bride is not made proud or selfish by success, as are so many of us; and she is not forgetful of her maidens now. Rather, she turns to them and says, "Take courage and rejoice! The King has brought me into His store-houses!"—meaning thereby, "I seem to have come in alone, but the blessing is not mine in isolation. You share it, as indeed you share all that I have. You must regard yourselves as entering in with me."

And the maidens answer, "We will be glad and rejoice *in thee*"—that is, not in our own merits. They add "remembering thy breasts," by which

they mean "we shall wait patiently until thou comest, knowing thou wilt return with thy breasts full of milk to nourish us. So we look forward to our own time of joy, meanwhile remembering thy breasts more than wine"; by which last words they signify (as I have said before) that the desires of the flesh, which they still feel sometimes, have been overmastered by the surprising sweetness that they have drawn from her.

You see, then, how the maidens trust their mother, counting her blessings and her joys as theirs and drawing comfort in their own exclusion from the fact that she has been admitted! Let those in high position who, instead of ministering to those under them, prefer to have them go in dread of them take this to heart! Learn from the Bride's example to be as mothers to your subjects; seek rather to be loved than feared and, if severity be needed towards any, let it be meted by a Father's hand and not a tyrant's.

THE MEANING OF THE KING'S STORE-HOUSES, GARDEN, AND CHAMBER

Now let us see what is the spiritual meaning of the *store-houses*. Later on, mention is made both of the *garden* and the *chamber*, and these throw light upon each other, if they are taken together. They all have reference to the Holy Scriptures; for with the Scriptures the soul athirst for God delights to occupy herself, pondering them long because she knows that in them she is sure to find Him Whom she seeks. So we will take the garden to represent the simple *history*, the store-houses the *moral sense* of Scripture, and the chamber the *mystical and inmost meaning*, reached through contemplation.

OF THE KING'S GARDEN

The garden is a good metaphor for history, for the noble characters with which history abounds resemble fruitful trees set in the Bridegroom's garden and the paradise of God, from whose lives one may take example as a man picks fruit. Does not holy David sing, concerning a good man, "He shall be like a tree planted by the waterside, that will bring forth his fruit in due season"? And again, "The righteous shall flourish like a palm tree; he shall spread abroad like a cedar in Libanus."

History, then, is a garden; and it is threefold. For it includes three periods: first, the Creation of both heaven and earth; then the Reconciliation; lastly, the Restoration. The Creation is the sowing and planting of the garden; the Reconciliation is its burgeoning, when the heavens dropped down from above in dew and the clouds rained down the Righteous One, and so the earth opened and brought forth the Saviour, by Whom the Reconciliation of heaven and earth was brought about. And the Restoration is still to come, at the end of the age; for then there will be a new heaven and a new earth, and the good shall be gathered from among the wicked, as fruits from a garden, to be laid up safely in the barns of God. "In that Day," as Isaiah says, "shall the branch of the Lord be beautiful and glorious, and the fruit of the earth shall be excellent and comely." You have thus three periods in the garden of the historic sense.

OF THE KING'S STORE-HOUSES

The word "store-rooms" is in the plural; and this, I think, betokens that the moral sense of Scripture also is threefold. The Bride rejoices, a little later on, because she has been led into the cellar (or store-house) of *wine;* and, as the Holy Spirit has seen fit to give this room a name, I am going to call the other two respectively the storehouses of *perfumes* and of *unguents*, both of these being, as is wine, both sweet and salutary, as everything around the Bridegroom cannot help but be.

I have, however, other and perhaps better names for these three rooms. I call the first the cell of *Discipline*, the second that of *Nature*, and the third that of *Grace*. In the first you learn to be a learner—that is, to be subject to another and to take the lowest place. In the second you learn to live on an equality with others, as a man with his fellows; and in the third you learn to be a master and rule over other men. Nature has indeed made all men equal; but pride has corrupted this essential good, so that men have grown impatient of equality and are for ever striving to exalt themselves over one another: hence the necessity for the threefold system that I have just outlined.

And, if you consider the properties

of the first two cells that I described, you will see that there is a correspondence between the two sets of names. For in the cell of Discipline the latent goodness in the characters of those held in subjection is brought out by the rigorous means employed, just as the strength and sweetness are expressed out of the raw materials of perfumes, when they are crushed and pounded in the mortar. And in the cell of Nature the ready and as it were inborn affection between those who have learnt to live in unity as equals is like the unguent on the head which, at the slightest touch of warmth, runs sweetly down, anointing the whole body. As for the third, the cell of Grace, that must be called the wine-cellar, because in it is stored the wine of zeal fervent with charity.

OF THE KING'S CHAMBER

Let us now think about the chamber of the King. Only the blesséd Bride herself is really competent to speak of this experience. If I knew nothing of it, I would say nothing; but I will gladly share with you the little I do know, and may "He that teacheth man knowledge" instruct you in the rest. I said, you will remember, that the King's Bedchamber denotes the secret mysteries attained through contemplation; and I think this chamber of the King is multifold, in the same manner the His perfumes are. For He has many queens and many loves and maidens without number; and each of these has her own secret with Him, as Isaiah says, "My secret for myself." Souls do not all enjoy the Bridegroom's secret and belovéd presence in one situation; we have not chosen

Him but He has chosen us, and set us in the place appointed of the Father, and He is with us in the place where He has put us.

One woman, grieving for her sins, found hers beside His Feet; the devotion of another (if it was another) was crowned beside His Head. Thomas attained his special revelation at his Master's side, John on His breast, and Paul in the third heaven. I cannot attempt to distinguish between these different varieties of merits, or rather of rewards. I would only point out that the first woman got her blessing through humility, the second through hope, Thomas through faith, John through love, and Paul in the depths of wisdom.

There are, then, many mansions in the Bridegroom's house; and every soul finds lodging there according to its merits, not stopping in one place but moving on through contemplation to further exploration of the secrets of the Spouse. But no one is admitted to the inmost chamber, except the Bride herself, His dove, His beautiful, His only perfect one. And, even for the Bride, I think there are some mysteries she still desires to know. Does she not ask Him where He feeds His flock and where He rests at noon?

A PLACE OF RESTLESSNESS

Now in the Bridegroom's house there is a special place where He, the Ruler of the universe, issues His orders and His laws for all creation. Lofty and secret is this place; and for the soul admitted to it there is but small repose, for God does not allow her to rest in contemplation of His wondrous ways, but fires her with longing to know more. The Bride expresses this tension beautifully when she says, a little further on, "I sleep, but my heart waketh"—the sleep denoting the entranced, adoring stillness in which she marvels at God's works, the waking, the weariness she suffers in her restless, eager quest. Compare the words of Job, "When I lie down I say, 'When shall I arise and the night be gone?'" This place, where complete repose is not attained, is not the Bridegroom's chamber.

There is, however, another room, where the soul sees God as the Judge, Most Just and Terrible, Whose penetrating gaze is ever fixed upon His unrepentant creatures. He who beholds this vision is awe-stricken. There is nothing of the security of the bed-chamber here, only the terror of judgment. It is a fearful place, devoid of all repose; and I am overcome with dread when I am brought to it. And yet this too is an abode of God, even the gate of heaven; for in it God is *feared*, and "the fear of the Lord is the beginning of wisdom."

Do not be surprised that I put the beginning of wisdom here, and not in the first room. For in the first we listen as it were to Wisdom giving lectures, and we acquire knowledge. But in the second room we take to heart what we perceive, and so are rendered wise. Yet (as I said) in neither does the soul find perfect rest; for in the one it beholds God in His activity, and in the other it sees Him in His wrath.

A PLACE OF REST

And yet there is a place where God is seen as truly tranquil and at rest, where He appears neither as Teacher nor as Judge but as the Spouse. I do not know how it may be with you; but I have been admitted to this place sometimes, though all too seldom and but for a short space. I have seen then most vividly the mercy of the Lord from everlasting unto everlasting upon them that fear Him. And I have looked upon the bléssed as though they had been sinless from the first; for, though they sinned in time, their sins appear not in eternity at all, being all covered by the mantle of their Father's love. And at that sight I have felt suddenly so great a joy and confidence that it surpassed the fear that I experienced in the former place, and I myself appeared to be one of that company! O visit me with Thy salvation, Lord, again and yet again!

O place of true repose, meet to be called the chamber of the King! The tranquil God here renders all things tranquil; perceiving Him at rest, the soul herself reposes. It is as though one saw a king, after a busy day spent in adjudicating cases and so forth, put up his work, dismiss his servants and, entering his own private room, enjoy his rest the more because he sees around him only the faces of those dear to him. If it should ever be the happy lot of one of you to be withdrawn a while into this secret place, and not recalled from it by the obtrusion of the senses, or by some vexing care, or haunting sin, or—harder than anything to banish—by the inrush of concrete images upon his consciousness, he will be able, when he returns to us, to say, "The King led me into His chamber."

And yet I would not dare to say that even this is the same chamber as that to which the Bride rejoices that she has been led.

Chapter Seven

"The upright love thee"

THE MAIDENS HAVE just said, "We will rejoice and be glad in thee, remembering thy breasts more than wine"; and they are unquestionably referring to their mother. Now they add, "The upright love thee." I think they say this, because some of their number are of another mind. They are not honest and sincere, as are the speakers, but seek their own advantage and are jealous of the special privilege accorded to the Bride, in that she only was admitted into the store-houses. This is no other thing than that of which Paul speaks, "Peril among false brethren"; and these are the people against whom the Bride has to defend herself in the ensuing words, "I am black but comely, O daughters of Jerusalem." So now, against those evil tongues, the good, straightforward, humble, gentle souls essay to comfort her with the assurance, "The upright love thee."

There is, I think, no incongruity in thus interpreting these words. For almost everywhere among the maidens such souls are found, who watch the actions of the Bride for the sake not of imitation but of finding fault, who are tormented by the good deeds of their elders but feast upon the bad. You see them walking together or sitting in close groups, letting their shameless tongues wag freely in hateful whisperings. They are so avid both to speak and hear evil of others that nothing can escape them. They form cliques in order to speak evil, and join together to promote disunion. They strike up friendships with each other that are instinct with enmity, and are united in an odious fellowship by the bond of spite.

So were Herod and Pilate "made friends together in that day"—the day of the Lord's Passion. Such come together, not to eat the Supper of the Lord, but to drink the cup of devils; and death comes in through our windows, as Jeremiah says, when we open wanton lips and ears to share the poisonous chalice of scandal and detraction with another in this way. Let not my soul be of their company, for, as the apostle says, "Detractors are hateful to God." And God Himself corroborates this statement in the psalm, "On him that slandereth his neighbour will I be avenged." Nor is this surprising; because, as you can plainly see, this vice is above all opposed to Charity, the which God is.

DETRACTORS LACK CLARITY

He who speaks evil of another shows that he himself is void of charity. And, further, what object has he in so doing, save to make others hate and scorn the one of whom he speaks? His spiteful tongue thus strikes a deadly blow at charity in all who hear him speak and, so far as it can, destroys it root and branch, not only in the immediate hearers but also in all others to whom the slander, flying from lip to lip, is afterwards repeated. You see how easily and in how short a time detractive speech infects a multitude of souls.

This pest of backbiting takes several forms. Some people vomit forth the poison nakedly and as it were unthinkingly, just as it comes up on their tongues. Others, however, try to hide the malice that they have conceived and must somehow bring forth, under the pretext of unwillingness to mention it. "Ah yes," sighs such an one, with spurious regret, "I am dreadfully sorry about this, for I love him dearly; but I have never been able to get him to amend his ways." "Oh yes, of course I knew about it," says another, "but I would never have allowed myself to be the one to make it known. Now that the truth is out, however, alas, I can't deny it." And he adds, "It's such a pity! He has such good points in his character; but this, of course, is inexcusable."

IN PRAISE OF UPRIGHTNESS

Let us return now to the words about which we are speaking, "The upright love thee." Nobody is so foolish as to think that "uprightness" in those who love the Bride is to be taken in a bodily sense; we must therefore explain it spiritually, as meaning rectitude of heart and mind. The Spirt, nonetheless—for it is He Who speaks—means us to see a parallel between the two. God made man upright in the latter sense, in that He made him after His own Image; for, as the psalmist says, "The Lord our God is upright, and there is no iniquity in Him." God, therefore, made man upright as He is Himself—that is, without iniquity. And iniquity comes from the heart, not from the flesh; so it is in the spiritual part of you, not in your mortal clay, that the Likeness of God has got to be either preserved or restored.

Yet God has given man an upright body too; and it may be that He means this outward and lower rectitude to serve as a reminder of the higher, and make us strive for it; the beauty of the earthly rebuking—so to speak—the soul's deformity. For nothing could be more incongruous than a bent spirit in an upright body; and it is altogether wrong that our bodily eyes should take delight in looking at the heavens, when our spiritual senses are directed to the things of earth, so that we love to wallow in the mud like pigs.

"Look at me," says the body to the soul, "and blush for shame! You were created upright in your Creator's Image, and you had me given as your helper, made in the likeness of *your* rectitude. Whichever way you look, therefore, whether to God above you or to me beneath you, you see what you were made for. Are you not covered with confusion thus to have lost your glorious gift of uprightness, when I have kept mine that once mirrored yours? Why should our Maker, Who has preserved your likeness whole in me, have to behold His Likeness marred in you?"

Souls thus deformed cannot love the Bride, because they are the friends, not of the Spouse but of the world and therefore (as James says) the enemies of God. To seek and to love the things of earth is therefore to deform the soul; and, on the other hand, to ponder and desire the things that are above is uprightness. And perfect uprightness consists in thinking rightly first, and then acting in accordance with your thoughts. Consider him upright, whom you have found to be both Catholics in faith and righteous in his works. You do right when you offer faith to God; you do right when you offer works. But, if you separate the two, then you do wrong. For "faith without works is dead"; and lack of charity in action murders faith, just as Cain murdered Abel, so that God cannot respect your offering.

OF FAITH AND WORKS

Do you believe in Christ? Then do the works of Christ, so that your faith may live! Let love be to your faith as soul to body, and let your conduct prove that your faith is real. You who say that you abide in Christ ought to walk as He walked. But if you seek your own glory, envy the prosperous, slander the absent, and render back evil for evil—Christ did not act like that! Your lips confess that you know God, yet you deny Him by your actions. You have acted not uprightly but wickedly, for you have given your tongue to Christ but your heart to the devil. Iniquity rules over you, so that you cannot stand upright.

Let us then, brethren, who believe in Christ, study to make our actions and our thoughts upright. Let us lift up our hearts, together with our hands, that we may be found upright through and through, approving the rightness of our faith by upright actions, lovers of the Bride, and beloved of the Bridegroom, Jesus Christ our Lord, Who is God blesséd for ever. Amen.

Chapter Eight

"I am black but comely, O ye daughters of Jerusalem, as the tents of Kedar, as the curtains of Solomon. Look not upon me for that I am black, because the sun has tanned me"

WHY THE BRIDE SPEAKS THESE WORDS

WE HAVE ALREADY SEEN that the Bride numbers among her maidens some who are of very different spirit from herself. These, envying her glory, have disparaged her and called her black. And she replies, "I am black but comely, O ye daughters of Jerusalem!"

Observe her patience and good humour! Not only does she not return railing for railing, but she blesses them, calling them "daughters of Jerusalem" who by their naughtiness had merited to be called rather daughters of Babylon, or any other such reproachful term as might occur to her! She has learned not to break the bruiséd reed nor quench the smoking flax; she will not further irritate those vexed already by the pangs of jealousy, but rather seeks to soothe them by her winning words, remembering (as all should do who have the care of souls) that her first business is their salvation, not her own revenge. That is why she calls them "daughters of Jerusalem," which in a sense in no misnomer. For these bad souls receive the Sacraments and profess the Faith together with the good, and outwardly at least are members of the Church. Moreover, hope of their salvation must still be entertained. So they are not unfittingly addressed as "daughters of Jerusalem."

IN WHAT SENSE THE BRIDE IS BLACK BUT COMELY

You must not think that "black but comely" is a contradiction; for the form or essence of a thing can be beautiful, even though its colour, which is but a quality, be black. And in some things, such as eyes and hair, for instance, blackness itself is far from unbecoming.

In regard to the Bride, however, note that she says "I am black," not "I was." Had she said "I was," she might have been referring to her former life, when as a subject of the prince of this world she still bore the image of the earthly; and she would then be contrasting that blackness with the beauty that is hers, now that she bears the image of the heavenly and walks in newness of life. But as she says, "I am black," we shall do better to interpret both blackness and comeliness with reference to her present, higher state; and if we consider the contrast between the outward mean appearance of the saints and the inward glory that is working in them, we shall see well what she means.

PAUL WAS BLACK BUT COMELY

Here, for instance, is a soul "black, yet beautiful"—St. Paul. "His letters are weighty and powerful, but his bodily presence is weak and his speech contemptible," they say. That is how you size up Paul, you daughters of Jerusalem! You judge from his exterior, and you call him black, because you see he is a little man with manifold afflictions. Yet was it not he who was caught up into Paradise, even to the third heaven? That is the soul that you call black; and outwardly it is so; but in the eyes of God and of the angels it is beautiful.

O happy blackness, that begets integrity of mind, the light of knowledge, and purity of conscience such as his! The glory of the saints is inward, because it is the inward man that bears God's Likeness; which Likeness they daily labour to renew. "The King's daughter is all glorious *within*," the psalmist says. And yet the outward blackness is cause for glory too; for the saints reckon nothing valueless, knowing that all things work together for their good. "Most gladly, therefore," says the apostle, "will I rather glory in my infirmities, that the power of Christ may rest upon me. For strength is perfected in weakness and, when I am weak, then am I strong." The Bride is right, then, to account as glory not her beauty only but her blackness too, which those who envy her reckon as shame. She does not blush for it, because her Spouse bore it before her; and that which makes her like Him is the greatest glory she can have. "God forbid," she cries exultantly, "that I should glory save in the cross of my Lord Jesus Christ!"

He was, the prophet says, "a Man of sorrows and acquainted with grief; He had no form nor comeliness." And he goes on, "We did esteem Him as a leper, stricken of God and humbled. But He was wounded for our iniquities and bruised for our misdeeds, and with His stripes we are healed." You see, then, what has made Him black! And if you take along with this last passage what David says of Him, "Thou art fairer than the children of men," you have in the Bridegroom everything which the Bride says here about herself.

JESUS, TOO, WAS BLACK BUT COMELY

Might He not, then, have answered fitly to the envious Jews, "I am black but comely, O ye sons of Jerusalem"? Black indeed was He Who had "no form nor comeliness," Who was "a worm and no man, a very scorn of men and the outcast of people," Who was even made to be sin for our sakes. But ask the apostles how they saw Him on the mount, or ask the angels what He is like on Whom they yearn to look; and they will tell you He is beautiful. He is, then, beautiful in Himself, and black but for thy sake.

How beautiful art Thou, Lord Jesus, in the humanity that Thou dost share with me, how beautiful not only in Thy deeds of wonder but in Thy truth, Thy gentleness, Thy righteousness! Blesséd is he who, pondering Thy life as Man with men, sets out with all his might to copy Thee! For the Bride, Thy fair one, has received this very blessedness from Thee as firstfruits of her dowry; and she is neither slow to imitate Thy beauty nor ashamed to bear with Thee the things that made Thee black. Wherefore she says, "I am black but comely, O ye daughters of Jerusalem!"

THE MEANING OF THE TWO COMPARISONS

To the words "I am black but comely" the Bride adds, "as the tents of Kedar, as the curtains of Solomon." It is not clear whether the former figure only has reference to her blackness, the latter to her beauty; or whether both are illustrations of the first. Kedar itself means blackness; and in the tents of Kedar we fitly see the body of our present pilgrimage and warfare which, like a tent, surrounds the soul and, for the time, deprives it of the light. That is why souls desire to be delivered from the body, that they may speed to the embrace of Christ. He who cries out with Paul, "O wretched man that I am, who shall deliver me from the body of this death?" knows well that in this tent of Kedar he cannot be entirely exempt from spot and wrinkle and some degree, however small, of blackness; and he desires to go forth from thence in order to divest himself of all these things. That clearly is the reason why the Bride says she is black, as are the tents of Kedar.

The second figure is more difficult, although I am convinced that there is something both high and holy hidden under it. Suppose we take it first with reference to her beauty. "The curtains of Solomon" must then be something pertaining to *her* Solomon, her Peaceful One—that is, to Christ. Now in a psalm the words occur, with reference to God, "Who spreadest out the heavens *like a curtain*"; and the Eternal Wisdom says elsewhere, "When He prepared the heavens, I was there." Lastly, He says, "What things soever the Father doeth, these also doeth the Son likewise." He, then, spread out the heavens like a curtain; and it is heaven that is symbolized by "the curtains of Solomon." Thus it is with the loveliness of heaven that the Bride compares her own.

OF THE BEAUTY OF THE HEAVENS

A beautiful curtain indeed is that which, like a tent, spreads over the whole earth and rejoices the eyes of men with sun and moon and stars, each after its own manner! Yet the beauty of this material and transitory heaven is quite inadequate as a simile for the Bride's loveliness, which is of a rational, spiritual and eternal nature and consists in charity, righteousness, patience, poverty, humility, holy fear and all the other virtues. We must look further for the heaven worthy for this purpose, even to that of which the psalmist speaks, "Sing ye to the Lord, Who goeth up over the heaven to the east." This spiritual heaven He, Who by His wisdom made the heavens, created for His own abode. The longing of the Bride cannot stop short of this, where her Belovéd dwells; and it is with the beauty of this heaven that she compares her own. (It has, moreover, certain points of likeness with the material firmament of which we spoke just now. Does it not spread out like a tent, not spatially but over the whole world of man's desire? Has it not varying degrees of blessedness, like divers colours? Is it not studded with angels, as with stars?)

OF THE BEAUTY OF THE BRIDE

Think now about the beauty of the Bride, compared with that of heaven in this sense. Her soul is heavenly by origin, and therefore worthy of comparison with heaven; just as her body, being of the earth, is fitly likened to the tents of Kedar. She worships God, just as the angels do, and loves Christ above all, even as they. And she is chaste as they are; and that, moreover, in weak and sinful flesh, which they have not. What further proof is needed of her heavenliness? And Scripture puts it with the utmost plainness, "I saw the Holy City, New Jerusalem," it says, "coming down from God out of heaven, prepared as a bride adorned for her husband." And it goes on, "And I heard a great voice out of the Throne, saying, 'Behold, the tabernacle of God is with men, and He will dwell with them.'"

You see, then, that the Bridegroom, Who is Jesus, and the Bride, who is Jerusalem, both come from heaven. And, when our Immanuel came down to earth, He brought with Him the culture, so to speak, of that Jerusalem which is above, the mother of us all. In Him, therefore, we see the Bridegroom and the Bride in one, the crowned Head and the Body beautified. Nor has the heavenly Man come down in vain; for the celestial culture is already taking root on earth, wherever people strive to live after the heavenly pattern.

OF HEAVEN ON EARTH

I think, moreover, that every holy soul is itself heaven in a sense—a heaven with Understanding for its sun, Faith for its moon, and Virtues for its stars, a heaven where God dwells, according to His faithful promise, "We will come unto him and make Our abode with him." Nor is it surprising that the Lord Jesus should gladly make this heaven His dwelling-place, seeing that He did not bring it into being merely by a word, as He did the others, but fought to gain possession of it and died in order to redeem it. That is why He declares, when it is His at last, "This shall be My rest for ever: here will I dwell, for I have a delight therein."

How roomy is the soul, how highly privileged, which is found worthy to receive the Divine Presence in itself and able to contain It! It must go on becoming ever roomier by charity, for if it have not charity, then it is nought. Let it but grow in charity, however, in all-embracing love extending even to its enemies, and the saying "He spreadeth out the heavens like a curtain" will apply even to it; God will not merely have His dwelling in it, but will have room to move within its spacious bounds.

What lowliness, what loftiness, to be at once the tent of Kedar and the shrine of God, an earthly dwelling and a heavenly palace, a clay hut and a royal hall, a mortal body and a temple wherein dwells the Light, scorned by the proud and yet the Bride of Christ! She is black but comely, O ye daughters of Jerusalem; and though the toils of exile darken her complexion she has a sort of heavenly loveliness, like the curtains of Solomon. You must admire and reverence her loftiness, therefore, however much her lowliness displeases you. How marvellously are these two opposites combined, moreover, to further her salvation; for her sublimity supports her in her troubles, while her humility keeps her from pride when things go well!

Thus far we have interpreted the "curtains of Solomon" with reference to the beauty of the Bride, and as denoting heaven. But, as I said at the beginning, this figure may be meant to illustrate her blackness, as do the tents of Kedar. In this case we must suppose that King Solomon on occasion used a tent, which became blackened by exposure to sun and wind, yet served to keep intact the beauty of his person, who was sheltered by it. The Bride will then mean by this comparison that she has become black through her zeal for whiteness.

HE BECAME BLACK THAT WE MIGHT BE WHITE

The blackening of One renders many white, not because He is tainted with their failure but because He suffers with their suffering. "It is expedient that one man should die for the people, and that the whole nation perish not." It is expedient that One should be blackened in the likeness of sinful flesh on behalf of all, rather than that the whole race be condemned for their black sin. It is expedient that God's glory should be hidden beneath a servant's form, that the slaves may live; that the purity of life eternal should be blackened in the flesh, to purify the flesh; and that the beauty of Him Who is fairer than the sons of men should be outraged in the Passion, shamed upon the Cross, and rendered pale in death until no form nor comeliness remain, in order that the Bridegroom may obtain for His Bride the Church that she be beautiful and glorious, without spot or wrinkle.

I recognize this "curtain of Solomon"; and beneath its blackness I embrace Solomon Himself. His blackness is external only. He is black in the sight of the unwise, but the faithful perceive Him to be passing fair—black, yet beautiful, black in Herod's eyes but beautiful to the thief's penitence and the centurion's faith. "Truly this was the Son of God," the latter cried. Assuredly he did not judge by what he saw, but (as the Gospel says) from hearing of the Voice. Hearing discovered what sight failed to find. Outward appearances deceived the eyes; but through the ears the Truth poured itself in. It is right that this should be so. The ear was the first gate to be unlocked to death; let it then be the first to open to the Life; and let the hearing restore to us the power of vision which it took away! For we shall never understand, unless we first believe.

You see now with what wisdom the Bride has discerned God in the flesh, the Life in death, under this figure of "the curtains of Solomon." The centurion knew Him to be the Son of God, and the Church knows Him now and emulates His blackness, that she may share His glory too. She is not put off by His appearing black or being called so; rather she says to Him, "The rebukes of them that rebuked Thee are fallen upon me." But notice that she does not say, "I am black as Solomon," but only "as the curtains of Solomon." For this Solomon is black only on the surface; there is nothing of the inward defilement of sin in Him Who bears the sins of the world, that He may be found fit to reconcile sinners and justify His title of the Peaceful One.

OF THE BLACKNESS OF PENITENCE AND PERSECUTION

There is a further blackness of penitence, when one laments one's sins; and I trust Solomon will not abhor that in me, for God does not despise a broken, contrite heart. There is also the blackness of sympathy, when one man makes another's grief his own; and this our Peaceful One has not disdained to take upon Himself. And, finally, there is the blackness of persecution, which ranks as the most glorious ornament of all, when suffered for the sake of righteousness and truth. It is with reference to this that the Bride adds, "Look not upon me for that I am black, because the sun has tanned me." She means, "Do not blame me for being blackened by the fires of persecution." Or maybe the fire that she has in mind is her own zeal for righteousness; or possibly she means it is the Sun of Righteousness Himself Whose rays have tanned her skin. But the words which follow, "My mother's sons were angry with me," agree better with the first sense; and these shall be the subject of our next discourse.

Chapter Nine

"My mother's sons fought against me"

THE CHURCH COMPLAINS OF THOSE
WHO VEX HER FROM WITHIN

ANNAS AND CAIAPHAS and Judas Iscariot were sons of the Synagogue, as the Church was its daughter. And Annas and Caiaphas and Judas fought bitterly against the Church, when they hanged Jesus, in Whom she was contained, upon the Tree. These and others of that nation who are known to have gainsaid the Christian name are the "mother's sons" to whom the Bride refers.

She mentions these alone, ignoring the many things she has endured from strangers. She laments more explicitly that which she feels most keenly and deems that we should be most careful to avoid—that is to say, discord within a family, such as the psalmist speaks of when he says, "Mine own familiar friend hath laid great wait for me," and in another place, "Had it been mine enemy that spake evil of me, then I could have borne it; but it was thou, my companion, my guide, mine own familiar friend."

You, whom experience has taught and daily teaches how good and joyful a thing it is to dwell together in unity, I do implore to shun this vile and hateful thing! I would die rather than hear one of you cry out with justice, "My mother's sons fought against me!" Are not all you of this Community like sons of the same mother, and brothers to each other? What is there, coming from without, that can disturb or sadden you, if only your common life is healthy and you rejoice as brothers in the bond of peace?

BE AT PEACE AMONG YOURSELVES

Have peace, then, among yourselves, belovéd, and do not vex each other either by word or deed or even by a look; lest some poor tempest-driven soul be brought to such a pitch of helpless fury as to complain of you in these same words, "My mother's sons fought against me!" For if you sin thus against your brother, you sin against Christ, Who says, "That which you have done to one of the least of those who belong to Me, you have done to Me Myself." Nor is it enough to abstain only from the more serious offences, such as open insult and abuse; you must refrain from secret and envenomed whisperings too. Even to keep one's lips from everything like this will not suffice; the slightest injuries must be avoided—if indeed anything can be termed slight, when it is done deliberately to hurt a brother.

Moreover, what you think slight and therefore do all too readily, the other person sees quite differently, as one who judges by appearances is apt to think a mote a beam and to mistake one spark for a blazing fire. For the charity which "believeth all things" is not in everyone, and the hearts of men are readier to suspect evil than to believe good. With us, moreover, the Rule of Silence both forbids you to excuse yourself, when someone else has anything against you, and also will not suffer him who nurses the suspicion to say it openly, and so get it cleared up. In consequence, it consumes him inwardly, making him like a person dying of some internal wound. He groans within himself, unable to refrain from churning on his trouble or think of anything except the wrong he has received. He cannot pray, he cannot read, he cannot meditate on any sacred or spiritual subject.

And while this soul, for whom Christ died, is thus cut off from all grace and travelling towards death, what of yourself? What is *your* state of mind, what good can *you* get out of prayer or work or any occupation, while Christ holds it against you that you have brought your brother to this pass? "My mother's son," He says, "is fighting against Me; and I am filled with bitterness by him who shares the dainties of My table."

You will say, perhaps, that your brother ought not to let himself be so upset about so small a matter. My answer is: the smaller the occasion of offence, so much the easier for you to keep from giving it; though, as I said, I do not know how you can reckon anything as slight or small which is more than anger; seeing that the Judge Himself has told us that even anger makes us liable to judgment. Do you call that a little thing, by which Christ is offended, and on account of which you stand for judgment before God?

When, therefore, you receive an injury (which is almost bound to happen sometimes in a Religious House) you must not answer back in haste and savagely, as people in the world are wont to do; nor must you ever dare to pierce your brother's soul, for which Christ deigned to hang upon the cross, with cutting and infuriating words. You must not grunt in surly wise, as though imputing blame, nor grumble under your breath, nor put on sneering airs, nor laugh derisively, nor knit your brows in wrath or threatening. Let the disturbance in you die where it arose; you must not let it out, for it is deadly and may kill somebody if it escapes. Be as the psalmist says, "I was upset: and I spoke not."

OTHER INTERPRETATIONS

There are two other possible interpretations of the words, "My mother's sons fought against me." They may be taken as referring to the devil and his angels, who are sons of the Jerusalem which is above, even as we ourselves, and cease not to make war against the Church their sister. Or they may be taken in a good sense, of spiritual persons in the Church who wield the sword of the Spirit, which is the Word of God, against their carnal brethren, wounding them thereby for their salvation.

If I myself have sometimes put some of you to grief after this fashion, I do not regret it, for it has ministered to your souls' health. And, what is more, I do not think that I have ever acted thus without great sorrow to myself; as it is written, "A woman, when she is in travail, hath sorrow." But God forbid that I should hug the memory of my pangs, now that I see my labor's fruit, Christ formed in you, my children! And somehow I feel even more tenderly towards those of you whom my correction has helped to overcome some fault, than towards those who have been stable from the outset and never needed such a remedy.

The Word of God is indeed a living and effective arrow, sharper than any two-edged sword to pierce the hearts of men. There is another, chosen dart—the love of Christ. This did not only pierce the heart of Mary, but pierced it through and through, leaving no corner of that virgin bosom void of love; so that she loved with all her heart and soul and strength, and was filled full with grace. And surely she was pierced like this, that the same love might reach even to us, and we receive of that same fullness; so that she might be made mother of love to us, as God, Who is Love, is its Father. Mary indeed received the deep, sweet wound of love in her entire being. How happy should I be if I might feel the lightest prick from that same dart of love!

Chapter Ten

"They made me keeper of the vineyards. Mine own vineyard have I not kept"

OF THE GROWTH OF THE CHURCH

"THEY MADE ME KEEPER of the vineyards." Who gave the Bride this charge, if not her mother's sons, of whom she spoke just now? This will hold good whichever meaning we attach to them; for the Church has never lacked either for persecutors or for those who have attacked her for her good, and both forms of trial have turned out to her profit. Her gains, that is to say, have been more than her losses; or, as she puts it here, in place of her own vineyard which her opponents took away from her, she finds herself to her delight set over many. And by these vineyards we must understand the churches, the nations that accept the Faith.

You read in Acts how this happened. The sons of her own mother attacked her and drove her from Jerusalem; that was the vineyard that she lost. Yet that same vineyard was not so ruined by the persecution but that it could be planted elsewhere and under other husbandmen, who would render its fruits in due season. It did not perish, it migrated; and, blessed by the Lord, it grew. That Vine, which is the Lord Himself, Whose branches are the apostles, Whose Keeper is the Father, cannot be allowed to perish. It is planted in faith and it takes root in love; the soil in which it grows is hoed by discipline of life, fertilized by tears of penitence, and watered by the preaching of the Word. Thus it yields wine in plenty, wine wholly sweet and pure, that maketh glad the hearts of men and angels too; for angels, yearning for mankind's salvation, rejoice when sinners turn then and repent.

How many vineyards have been planted from that one, which the fierce persecution seemed to have destroyed! And the Bride has been put in charge of all of them, so that she shall not grieve because she lost the first. Take comfort, O daughter of Sion! Reverence the mystery and do not mourn it as a loss. Open thine arms, and take the fullness of the Gentiles to thine heart!

OF THE CARE OF ONE'S OWN SOUL

"Mine own vineyard have I not kept." If vines are souls, with faith for root, virtues for branches, and good works for grapes, then I must make these words my own, but in another sense. I have received the oversight of souls, and yet I know not how to guard mine own. While I lived in the world, I cared for mine own vineyard not at all, for faith was dead in me and virtues and good works were lacking. I did a little better after my conversion to the Lord, but not very much. And yet they made me keeper of the vineyards, not considering all that!

And in what peril do I stand in consequence! Engrossed with care for the many, inevitably I give less thought to the one. I have no chance to build a hedge around my vineyard or to dig out a press; its wall is broken down and all the passers-by pluck off the grapes. It lies open on all sides to sadness, anger, and impatience. Certain little foxes of urgent necessities cease not to lay it waste; anxieties, suspicions, cares burst in on it from every quarter; there is scarcely an hour when I am not settling differences or dealing with troubles of some kind. I cannot stop the people or refuse to see them; and they do not leave me time even to pray. My vineyard is dried up and barren for lack of moisture. Good Jesus, Thou knowest how it is with me. Receive, I pray Thee, my troubled spirit as a sacrifice. Despise not, O God, a broken, humbled heart.

"Mine own vineyard have I not kept." I have used these words to express my own imperfection. But they can be used also in the same sense as our Saviour's words in the Gospel. "He that loseth his life for My sake shall find it"; and he who can say them in this sense will be perfect. He will moreover be a really fit person to be made keeper of the vineyards, for the care of them will never hinder his keeping of his own! Such a one was Peter, such a one was Paul. And you, too, can show yourself an imitator of Paul and a disciple of Christ, if you give up your own will and make complete renunciation of your bodily desires, crucifying the flesh with its vices and lusts. You will be wiser if you thus lose your life in order to keep it, than if you lose it by keeping it.

Chapter Eleven

"Tell me, O Thou Whom my soul loveth, where Thou feedest Thy flock, where Thou reposest at noon, lest I begin to wander after Thy companions' flocks"

THE WORD, Who is the Bridegroom, often appears to faithful souls; but always, in this life, He does so under some appearance. For we are no more able yet to see Him as He is, than we can see the sun as it is with our bodily eyes. For we see the sun really only as it lights up other things, such as the air, a mountain, or a wall. Our bodily eyes, moreover, have this power of sight because they, alone of all our members, have a certain inborn affinity with light; and if they are disturbed and lose that likeness, they can no longer see. In the same way the man who is enlightened by the Sun of Righteousness, that lighteneth every man that cometh into this world, is able to see Him in proportion to the degree of his enlightenment, because that constitutes a certain likeness to Him. The likeness is, however, not yet perfect; therefore he can by no means see Him as He is.

OF THE BRIDEGROOM

His Majesty is therefore to be approached, not rashly but with utmost reverence; and we must seek Him, not from place to place but from stage to stage of spiritual purity. For the purer the soul, the closer will it come to God; and when we are *wholly* pure, then we shall have arrived. We shall be in His Presence then, and we shall see Him as He is; and yet we shall not be confounded by any lack of likeness to Him in ourselves. But that, as I have said, will only be hereafter. Here and now, we see Him in all created things; and that mode of perceiving the invisible things of God beneath the things that He has made is common to all rational creatures, as the apostle says.

With the Fathers God used another mode of manifesting Himself, a knowledge of His Presence given through the senses, but not given to all, nor even identical for all who did receive it, but "at sundry times and in divers manners." And God used also another, a different and inward way, when He deigned to reward the utmost ardent longing of the soul with the awareness of Himself. The psalmist tells us from his own experience the sign that marks a coming of this sort. "There shall go," he says, "a fire before Him, and burn up His enemies on every side." This fire of holy longing must always precede God's visitation in a soul, to burn up its impurities and so prepare His place. But when at last the Lord so ardently desired has pity and vouchsafes His Presence, the soul can say with Jeremiah, "Good art Thou, Lord, to them that hope in Thee, and to the soul that seeks Thee."

OF THE FRIEND OF THE BRIDEGROOM

And the soul's angel, that one of the Bridegroom's friends whose special business it is to promote this secret intercourse between Him and it, and watch it taking place, he dances with delight in sharing of its joy! And he says, turning to the Lord, "I thank Thee, Lord of majesty, that Thou hast granted to this soul its heart's desire, and hast not denied it to the request of its lips."

He is faithful, this friend of the Bridegroom! He knows about this mutual love between Him and the soul, but is not jealous of it; for he seeks his Lord's advantage, not his own. He goes and comes between Belovéd and belovéd, presenting Him with the outpourings of her heart and bringing back His gifts; he urges one and reconciles the Other. And sometimes, though not often, he actually effects their introduction, drawing her forward or bringing Him to meet her; for he is a member of the household, well known in the palace; every day he sees the Father's Face, and he fears no repulse.

OF THE JOY OF UNION WITH CHRIST

This commingling of the Word with the soul is purely spiritual, and has nothing corporeal or concrete in it. The rapture of the pure soul into God, and God's most blest descent into the soul, these constitute a union which takes place in the spirit, because God is a Spirit and He is moved with love towards the soul whom He knows to be walking in the spirit, especially if He sees it burning with love towards Himself. A soul in this condition, so loving and so loved, will not be satisfied with the sort of manifestation through created things that is given to everyone, nor even with the dreams and visions granted to the few. It will demand a special privilege—not an outward appearance but an inward inpouring. It will desire Him not merely to appear to it but to act upon it, and the more interior His operation is, the happier it will be.

For He is the Word: He does not merely sound in ears, He enters hearts. What He says is effective, not just empty sound. He does not beat upon our ears, but woos our hearts. His Features we see not; and yet they mould us, not by their outward beauty striking on our bodily sight, but by the love and joy they kindle in our hearts.

OF THE PHYSICIAN

God shows Himself after this mode in different ways to different people, and differently also to the same at different times, according to their longings and their needs. Sometimes He is the Bridegroom, tenderly longing to take the holy soul in His arms, delighting in her love; and this experience, granted from time to time even in our present pilgrimage, crowns all the heart's desires. At other times He comes as the Physician, with remedies for those immature and feeble souls whom we have called the "maidens." Do we not often find ourselves like that in prayer—we who are daily disquieted by our present failings and gnawed with shame for those gone by?

From what great bitterness hast Thou delivered me, good Jesu, by coming in this way! How often, when I have poured out my grief and shame, hast Thou anointed my sore conscience with Thy mercy and poured the oil of gladness on my wounds! How often has the prayer that I began, almost despairing of salvation, sent me back full of joy and confident of pardon! Those in like case know well that the Lord Jesus is a doctor Who heals the contrite-hearted and remedies their sickness. Those who lack this experience, let them believe His own words when He says, "The Lord hath anointed Me to preach good tidings to the meek, to bind up the broken-hearted." Let them come and prove Him for themselves, that they may learn the meaning of that saying, "I will have mercy and not sacrifice."

OF THE COMPANION

Sometimes, again, He joins the Bride and her young maidens as their Companion by the way, a Fellow-traveller Whose conversation so rejoices them and takes away their weariness that, when He goes, they say, "Did not our hearts burn within us concerning Jesus, when He talked with us by the way?" He deals thus in His compassion with souls whose hearts, weary of spiritual exercises, have grown dry and sad and turned back on the things of time. He Who is from heaven meets us, when we are like this, upon our way, and begins to speak of heaven, to sing some lovely sing of Sion to us, it may be, or tell us of the peace, the endless peace, that obtains ever in the City of God. And the hearing of that tale, I tell you, will be as good as a lift on the road to that drowsy, plodding soul; it will drive away all the distaste from his mind and all the fatigue from his body!

Do you not think that he who wrote, "My soul has gone to sleep for weariness: strengthen me with Thy words" was experiencing just this trial and asking for this very help? How delightful a Companion is He, Whose speech and manners are so pleasing that they make everyone run after Him! Wherefore they say, "We will run in the odour of Thy perfumes."

He appears, then, as Bridegroom, as Physician, and as Companion by the way. And I think sometimes He appears also as the wealthy Father, Whose house is stored with food for all the family; or as a mighty King, Who wants to show His timid Bride the riches of His winepresses and barns, His gardens and His fields, so that she may desire them and He lead her at last into His secret chamber.

BY FAITH ONLY

In all these manifestations He is kind and gentle and very merciful; yet in them all we see Him by faith only, the thing that we see is but the shadow of truth. For faith *is* a shadow; and yet faith is good, because it mitigates the light to our weak eyes and prepares them to behold it. It preserves the light; it does not put it out. That which lies open to an angel's sight is preserved for me by the shadow of faith, enfolded in a faithful bosom, as it were, until the time for it to be revealed. Is it not better for you thus to hold, wrapped up, that which you could not grasp if it were bare?

Even the Lord's own Mother lived in the shadow of faith, for it was said of her, "Blessèd is she that believed." She lived also in the shadow of the Body of Christ, for it was said to her, "The power of the Most High shall over-shadow thee." And the power which overshadowed the Virgin was surely in the Flesh of Christ; it was the sheltering shadow of that life-giving Body which enabled her to do what mortal woman could not do—to bear the Presence of Majesty and to sustain the unapproachable Light.

We, then, who walk by faith, live in Christ's shadow; and we are fed with His own Flesh, that we may live. That is perhaps the reason why the Bride addresses Him as though He were a shepherd, saying, "Tell me where Thou feedest Thy flock, where Thou reposest at noon." He is the Good Shepherd, Who gives His life for the sheep—His life *for* them, His flesh *to* them, the one for their redemption, the other for their food. O mighty marvel! He is Himself the Shepherd of the sheep, their Pasturage and their Redemption's Price!

Such are the treasures of wisdom and of knowledge hidden in the Bridegroom, such is the life-giving Food prepared to refresh holy souls. Bléssed is the man whose heart's desire has been fully satisfied thereby. But he must beware of taking for himself alone what would suffice for many; and I think it may be for this reason that the Spouse is represented lastly as a Shepherd, to remind him who has received so much that duty bids him feed the simpler of the flock, who cannot by themselves attain to knowledge of these things, just as sheep dare not go without their shepherd to the feeding-grounds.

That, too, is why the Bride asks where the Bridegroom feeds His flock and rests during the midday heat: She wants to feed herself and feed her flock, with Him and under Him; for she knows that the sheep cannot safely stray far from their Chief Shepherd, lest wolves attack them, and especially wolves in sheep's clothing. This motive she expresses in words, "Lest I begin to wander after Thy companions' flocks." By "Thy companions" she means those who pretend to be His friends but are not really so; who go about saying, "Lo, here is Christ!" or "Lo, He is there!" that they may draw sheep from His flock and add them to their own.

OF THE SIGNIFICANCE OF HIS REPOSE AT NOON

"Tell me, O Thou Whom my soul loveth, where Thou feedest Thy flock, where Thou reposest at noon." Notice first how beautifully the Bride distinguishes spiritual love from the affection of the flesh. She says not merely "Thou Whom I love," but "Thou Whom *my soul* loveth." Consider secondly what it is that delights her in His place of pasturage; and do not overlook the fact that she speaks of "noon." I take it that the mention of His reposing denotes great security; in that land, the Shepherd needs not to stand ever on the watch to keep the sheep from harm, but can Himself repose beneath the trees, while they roam freely in the meadows.

O happy country, where the sheep go in and out at will, and none makes them afraid! Who will vouchsafe me to behold them, and myself among them, those ninety-and-nine whom the Shepherd left in safety while He went humbly after that one that had strayed? The Bride is right to yearn and sigh for that sweet place of pasturage and peace, of rest and safety, of wonderment and joy! And woe is me to be so far from it, to hail it only from afar! A safe abode is Paradise, a sweet Food is the Word, Eternity is boundless wealth for evermore.

OF THE SACRAMENT

And yet I also have the Word, but in the flesh; the Truth is set before me too, but in the Sacrament. An angel feeds and waxes fat upon the finest wheat-flour, the very grain itself; I, in this life, must be contented with the husk—that is, the Sacrament; with the flesh, as with bran; with the chaff of the letter; and with the veil of faith. And all such things as these bring death in the tasting, unless the first-fruits of the Spirit season them at least in some degree. I shall find death surely in the pottage, unless the prophet's flour sweeten it.

Even the Sacrament, without the Spirit, is received but to condemnation; the flesh profiteth nothing, and faith itself is dead. It is the Spirit Who quickens all these things, that I may live by them. Yet, even so, however rich the Spirit make them, I cannot find the same delight in husks as in the grain, in faith as in vision, in remembrance as in Presence, in time as in eternity, in the reflection as in the Face Itself, or in the servant's form as in God's very Image.

OF GOD'S PLACE OF REPOSE

So, then, my children, let us make all speed towards the safer place, the sweeter pasturage, the richer and more fruitful field! Let us make haste, I say, that we may dwell where none makes us afraid, where wealth fails not and feasting never palls. For Thou, O Lord of Hosts, art also Shepherd of the sheep; therefore Thou dost both feed them and Thyself take rest—only not here. Wherefore Thou *stoodest*, when Thou sawest Stephen Thy sheep beset by wolves on earth. I pray Thee, therefore, tell me where Thou feedest and takest rest at noon, for that noonday is the whole day, the day that knows no evening, the day that in Thy courts is better than a thousand because it knows no set of sun. It had perhaps a morning, though, when first the hallowed Day arose on us and through the tender mercy of our God the Dayspring from on high visited us.

How many kings and prophets desired to see that glory, and yet saw it not! For they lived in the night; the Dawn began when Gabriel announced the rising of the Sun of Righteousness; yet was its light but feeble while Christ lived on earth, so feeble that hardly anybody knew the Day had dawned at all. For they would not have crucified the Lord of glory, had they known. But, with His rising from the dead, the morning broke, and night was swallowed up in victory. "Very early in the morning, the first day of the week, they came to the sepulchre at the rising of the sun," the Gospel says. It was indeed the morning, when the Sun was risen! It drew new splendour from the Resurrection and shone with a serener light than we had known before; for He then laid aside the weakness of the flesh and decked Himself with glory.

Yet, however much He may increase His light and warmth upon us as the day goes on, He will not shed His *noonday* glory on us in this mortal life.

He feeds us, yes—but does not satisfy; He Himself may not rest, for He must stand to guard us against the perils of the night. All that is mine here falls short of perfection, much is beyond my prayer, nothing is safe. When wilt Thou fill me with joy with Thy Countenance, Thy Face that is the Noon-day? "Tell me where Thou feedest Thy flock, where Thou reposest at noon." I know well enough, my Shepherd, where Thou feedest them but dost not Thyself repose, for I have visited those pastures when I followed Thee. I want to know where Thou dost both feed Thy flock and take Thine own repose!

OF THE FOUR TEMPTATIONS
THAT LIE IN WAIT FOR US

The Bride, as we have seen, entreats her Spouse to tell her where He feeds His flock and rests at noon, so that she be not led astray by His so-called companions. It seems to me that we should make this prayer, not only lest we be seduced by heretics, but also that the clear light of His noon-day may make us able to discern the wiles of those invisible powers, which always lie in ambush to deceive us. For Satan transforms himself sometimes into an angel of light; and only the true Noon-day Light can guard us from the Noon-day Demon that simulates the day. How often, for example, has this tempter made sport of someone who slumbered at Night Office by suggesting that it ought to be recited at an earlier hour! How often, looking with baleful eye at those who made good progress in the common life, has he suggested to them that they would achieve perfection far better in a her-

mit's cell! And how those poor wretches have then learned the truth of the saying (which before they heard in vain), "Woe to him who is alone for, if he fall, he has no one to lift him up!"

How many has not the same demon urged on to bodily exertion beyond their strength, thus cheating them of the power to perform their duty! And do not many of you know, out of your own experience—I say it to your shame—how, to begin with, no one could hold you back, so full were you of zeal; but, after a time, you fell into such sloth that, as the apostle puts it, having begun in the Spirit you finished in the flesh! You see such people—O the shame of it!—whining for superfluities who once would not accept necessities! Those who persist in fasting indiscreetly, and gravely upset others by their singularity, seem to me to have departed altogether from their duty. They should reflect how they must give account, not to me but to Him Who says, "Rebellion is as the sin of witchcraft, and to refuse obedience is like committing idolatry."

OF THE TERROR BY NIGHT

But I do not want to encourage the greedy by thus condemning those who fast too much! Let both give ear! There are four sorts of temptations described in the psalm—the Terror by Night, the Arrow that Flies by Day, the Thing that Walks in Darkness and the Noon-day Demon. All of us who have been converted to the Lord know that we must expect temptation, as the Scripture says. And, at the outset, the thing that troubles us is *fear*—fear of the unwonted strictness of the life that we are entering.

This fear is called the Terror by Night, either because in Scripture night is a figure for things contrary, or else because the reward for which we set out to endure such things has not yet been revealed. In point of fact "the sufferings of this present time are not worthy to be compared with the glory that shall be revealed in us." But, at the moment, that truth is hidden from us, night is all around, the present evils block the future good from view and frighten us. Newcomers therefore ought to watch and pray against this first temptation, lest—which God forbid—some sudden weakness in face of difficulty should make them draw back from the good work that they have begun.

OF THE ARROW THAT FLIES BY DAY

But when we have vanquished that temptation, let us arm ourselves no less against the praise of men, who flatter us about the holy life we lead! For otherwise we shall be wounded by the Arrow that Flies by Day—that is, by *vainglory*. Reports of that sort are rightly said to fly, and in the day; for it is from the works of light that they arise. And if you blow them aside as empty air, something more solid remains to be offered you in the shape of worldly riches and preferment; for a man who is indifferent to praise may still be greedy of position.

OF THE THING THAT WALKS IN DARKNESS

The Lord Himself was tempted in this order, according to Matthew; for after it was suggested to Him that He should throw Himself down, from motive of vainglory, He was shown and offered all the kingdoms of this world. Do you follow His example in resisting this temptation; for otherwise you will find yourself caught in the toils of the Thing that Walks in Darkness—that is, *hypocrisy*. Hypocrisy issues from ambition; and it has its dwelling in darkness, for it hides what it is and pretends to be what it is not. Hypocrisy is always up to something and, while retaining the appearance of piety, it is engaged in selling virtue itself while it is buying honours.

OF THE NOON-DAY DEMON

The last temptation is the Noon-day Demon. He usually lies in ambush for the perfect, for stalwart souls, that is, who have already overcome the snares of pleasure, flattery and ambition. He comes disguised, not daring to appear in his true colours to a man who, as he knows full well, abhors all open evils, but hoping (as I said before) to work his victim's overthrow by simulating good.

The more advanced souls are, so much the more will they be on their guard against such *delusion*. That was why Mary was troubled at the angel's greeting, I believe; she feared that it might be a trick. And Joshua did not receive the angel as a friend, until he knew for sure he was a friend indeed. And I think the apostles also suspected a delusion of the Noon-day Demon, when they saw the Lord walking on the sea. Let us too fear this fourth and last temptation, and watch out for it all the more alertly, the further we seem to have progressed. But the true Noon-day revealed Himself to the disciples, saying, "It is I; be not afraid," and their doubt was dispelled. May He send forth His light and truth on us in the same way, whenever the masked falsehood tries to take us by surprise.

OF THE FOUR TEMPTATIONS AND THE CHURCH

Lastly, consider briefly how these four temptations, in their order, may be seen in Christ's own Body, that is, in the Church. Look at the early Church: Did she not suffer from the Terror by Night in a most marked degree? It was indeed a night, when everyone who slew the saints thought that he did God service! When that storm passed, her enemy, baulked of his prey, changed his weapon and wounded certain of her members with the Arrow that Flies by Day. And these vainglorious persons, wanting to make a name for themselves, left the Church their Mother, and long afflicted her with their various perversions of her teaching. This plague, however, was routed by the wisdom of the saints, as the first one had been by the endurance of the martyrs.

At the present time, the Church is free from both these evils, but is obviously infected through and through with the Thing that Walks in Darkness. For hypocrisy, which is the leaven of the Pharisees, is so widespread that there is no hiding it, and so barefaced that it does not try to hide! The whole body of the Church is poisoned with it; the evil is as desperate to cure as it is deeply seated. A heretic or persecutor would be recognized for what he was and driven away.

But now whom shall the Church exclude or shun? All are her friends, all are her enemies; all are her patrons, all are her opponents; all are of her household, and none at peace with her; all are her neighbours, and all of them are seeking their own ends.

The ministers of Christ serve Antichrist. They come to honour through the good things of the Lord, and give no honour to the Lord Himself. They want to be made deacons, archdeacons, bishops, archbishops, simply for worldly wealth and worldly pleasure. These offices are not bestowed as the reward of merit; it is the Thing that Walks in Darkness that dispenses them.

It was said once, and now the saying is fulfilled upon the Church, "Behold, in peace my bitterness is bitterest." It was bitter in the death of the martyrs, still more bitter in the struggle with the heretics; but it is bitterest of all now, in the lives of the Church's members. She can neither put them to flight nor herself flee from them, so firmly entrenched, so numerous are they. The plague of the Church is inward and incurable; therefore is her bitterness most bitter in her peace. But in what peace? It is, and is not peace. There is peace from the heathen and the heretic, but not from her own sons. "I have nourished and brought up children," she laments, "and they have rebelled against me."

OF THE ANTICHRIST

There is only one thing left to happen, and that is for the Noon-day Demon to appear, to seduce those who still abide in Christ and His simplicity.

The Noon-day Demon will be Antichrist himself; and he will simulate not the day only but the very Noon, and will exalt himself above all that is called or is adored as God. And the Lord Jesus will slay him with the breath of His mouth and destroy him in the brightness of His Coming; for He is the true and the eternal Noonday, the Church's Bridegroom and her Advocate, Who is God blesséd above all for ever, Amen.

Chapter Twelve

"If thou knowest not thyself, O fair one among women, go forth and depart after thy companions' flocks, and feed thy kids beside the shepherds' tent"

OF HUMILITY AND PATIENCE

"SHOW ME THYSELF," prayed holy Moses once, emboldened by the favour he had already found with God. He received a vision far less than that for which he prayed; yet that which he did get gave him the means by which to reach the one that he desired, later on. The sons of Zebedee, in the same way, asked a great thing in their simplicity, and were directed to the step from which they might advance. So is it with the Bride. She has asked for a tremendous thing, as we have seen; and by way of answer she gets a stern reproof, which is none the less faithful and wholly for her good.

Great graces cannot be obtained without humility; so those who are to have them must be humiliated, that they may be made worthy by humility to receive the grace. When you yourself experience humiliation, you should take it as a sure sign that some grace is in store.

It is a small thing, however, that we should willingly endure humiliation which comes direct from God Himself; we must bear it just as readily when He inflicts it through some other person, as David did when cursed by Shimei. For, as the psalmist says, "It is good for me that Thou hast humbled me: that I may learn Thy jus-

tifications." It is humility, you see, that justifies, that makes us righteous, not humiliation. How many people are humiliated, and yet are not humble! Some resent humiliation, some take it patiently, and others willingly. The first are blameworthy, the second innocent, the last are righteous. Innocence is of course a part of righteousness; but only the humble man, he who can say "It is good for me that Thou hast humbled me," has righteousness in its entirety. And he who bears humiliation unwillingly cannot use those words, much less he who makes complaint of it. Different as these two are, neither gets any grace out of humiliation; for God gives grace only to the humble, not merely to those who are humiliated.

The humble person is he who has turned humiliation into humility; for God loves a cheerful giver, and only joyful and complete humility deserves the grace of God, which indeed it displays. The constrained humility of him who merely endures will win him life, because of the endurance; but, because of the sadness mixed with it, it will not win him grace.

FROM HUMILIATION TO HUMILITY

Would you like to see a humble man, glorying rightly, and indeed worthy of glory? "Willingly will I glory," he declares, "in my infirmities, that the strength of Christ may dwell in me." He does not say he bears them patiently, but that he glories in them, and that willingly; and so he shows that it is good for him that he is being humbled. "He who humbles himself shall be exalted": That is the general rule about this matter. It does not mean that every humility will be exalted, but only that which issues from the will and not from sadness or necessity. And, on the other hand not everyone who is exalted will be humiliated, but only he who out of vanity exalts himself.

In humility it is the willingness that constitutes the merit. Other people provide you with the material for your humility, in reproaches, injuries, sufferings, and the like; but you cannot be said to be made humble by other people, in the same sense that you are made humble by yourself, if you make up your mind to suffer all these things gladly and in silence, for the sake of God.

But where am I getting to? All this about humility and patience came out of the reply made by the Bridegroom to the Bride. To that let us return.

OF THE BRIDEGROOM'S REPROOF OF THE BRIDE

"If thou knowest not thyself," He says, "go forth——" "Go forth, get out of My sight, out of My house"—a stern reproof indeed, such as a servant gets from an offended master! And this reproof the Bridegroom gives to His beloved; but it applies on one condition only—"*if thou know not thyself.*"

Nothing could terrify her more than this threat that she shall be sent away from Him. It means that she would have to leave the spirit for the flesh, the good things of the soul for temporal desires, and go from inward peace into the world's unrest! And this, for a soul that has once learned to seek God's Presence deep within itself, would be worse than if it had to suffer for a time the very pains of hell.

OF RETURNING TO THE WORLD

Terrible and terrifying, then, is this command, "Go forth and feed thy kids." It is as if He said, "You are unworthy of the sweet, familiar contemplation of heavenly mysteries, which you now enjoy, and you must face the fact. You must leave your heart, which is My shrine, where you have been so happy, and go back to the pleasures of the world." These last are what is meant by "kids," which in the Judgment will be set on God's left Hand. And the next words, "beside the shepherds' tent," bring out this meaning further; for kids are pastured, not above the shepherds' tent, as are the lambs, but by the side of them; which signifies that they, the senses of the body, seek not their pasture in the heavenly meadows but find their satisfaction in material things.

What an appalling change of interests! And notice that the Bridegroom says, not just "Go forth," but "go forth after thy companions' flocks." This noble creature, once a member of the flock but now rushing to ruin, is not allowed to stay with it, but told to fall behind. For, as the psalmist says, "Man, when he was in honour, did not understand: he was coupled with the senseless beasts and made like unto them." Indeed I think the beasts, if they could speak, would say, "Behold, the Man is made as one of us!" For Adam was "in honour": He dwelt in Paradise, that place of pleasure, knowing no pain nor deprivation, and having dominion over all the works of his Creator's Hands. And—greater glory still—he bore God's Likeness; his lot was with the angels and the hosts of heaven were his friends.

OF THE WORD MADE FLESH

But he turned that glory "into the likeness of a calf that eateth hay." Therefore the Bread of Angels is made to be hay in the manger for the cattle that we are! "The Word was made Flesh," and the prophet says, "All flesh is grass." But that grass which the Word was made withered not into hay, nor did its flower fall, for the Spirit of the Lord rested upon it. And, because "the Word of the Lord abideth for ever," so must the grass, the Flesh, that He is made be likewise everlasting. For how shall He bestow eternal life, if He Himself do not abide for ever? And He says expressly, "If any man eat of this Bread, he shall love for ever," and explains moreover, "The Bread which I will give is My Flesh, for the life of the world."

The food of man, then, has been turned to cattle fodder, because man himself has turned into a beast. O lamentable change, that paradisal Man, the lord of earth, the citizen of heaven, the member of the household of the Lord of Hosts, the brother of the blessèd spirits, the fellow-citizen with the heavenly powers, should of a sudden find himself, through his own frailty, imprisoned in a stable and tethered in a stall! But know, O ox, thine Owner, and thou, ass, thy Master's crib, that the prophets of God may be found faithful who thus foretold these His wondrous doings! Recognize, now that thou art a beast, Him Whom thou didst not recognize when thou wast yet a man. Adore Him in the stable, from Whom in paradise thou fleddest away. Reverence the manger of Him Whose rule thou didst defy; and eat the "grass" for which thou hadst no taste when it was bread, and angels' bread at that!

OF THE CAUSE OF MAN'S DOWNFALL

Consider now the cause of this so great downfall. It happened because "when man was in honour, he did not understand." What did he fail to understand? We can supply the explanation which the psalmist does not give. When man was placed in honour, he was delighted with his high estate, and did not understand that he was clay. And forthwith he experienced the truth of what one of his sons, who knew the same enslavement, long after wisely said, "If a man think himself to be something, when he is nothing, he deceives himself." That is how the superexcellent creature came to be mingled with the flock, and to exchange God's Image for the likeness of a beast, and angels' company for that of animals! You see how it behoves us to avoid this ignorance, through which such countless evils have come upon our race.

OF MAN'S TWOFOLD IGNORANCE

Consider further why the Bridegroom bids the Bride go forth, not with or to the flocks, but *after* her companions' flocks. He means by this to indicate a second kind of ignorance, which is an even greater ground for fear and shame than is the first; for the first kind put man on a level with the beasts, but this one even puts him after them. For those whom God rejects by reason of their ignorance, saying to them, "I know you not," will have to stand before His fearful bar and be delivered to the endless fire; which animals will not. "It had been better for him," Scripture says of such an one, "if he had not been born a man." Not, you observe, if he had not been born at all; but if he had been born, not as a man but as a beast of some kind or any other creature which, lacking reason, is liable neither to judgment nor to punishment.

The rational soul which blushed for the former ignorance will, therefore, have the animals for its companions in enjoying the good things of earth. But it will lack even their company if it incurs the pains of hell; it will be driven away in disgrace from the flocks of its beast companions then, and will go no more along *with* them, but *after* them; for they will have no suffering to bear, but the soul will know nothing but pain for evermore, if it has added this second ignorance to that which went before. Indeed, if you come to think of it, even in this life the creature which has reason but does not live by it, is in a sense more beast-like than the beasts themselves. Their lack of rational behaviour is excused on the ground of their nature: the gift of reason has been denied to them. But man, who has received it by an unique prerogative, has no excuse.

OF MAN'S DESERVED CONDEMNATION

Deservedly, therefore, must he go forth and take his place behind his fellow-beasts, because he is the only animal which, though rational itself, has so lapsed from its proper way of life and broken the law of its nature, that it feels and behaves like the irrational creatures. Both now in his depravity, and hereafter in his final punishment, man's place is obviously "after the flocks."

See how accursed is the man found ignorant of God! Of God? Or of himself? Which should I say? Unquestionably both, for either ignorance is damnable and of itself sufficient to bring us to perdition. You cannot doubt this as regards ignorance of God, if you accept the statement that eternal life consists in nothing but in knowing the Father as true God and Jesus Christ Whom He has sent. And the Bridegroom Himself expressly condemns the soul's self-ignorance, for He tells the Bride to go forth, not if she knows not God but if she knows not herself. There is more that I could profitably say about these two kinds of ignorance, but I will not keep you now.

OF THE TWO KINDS OF IGNORANCE AND KNOWLEDGE

Before I speak further about these two kinds of ignorance, of God and of ourselves, which lead to condemnation, I must make it clear that some kinds of ignorance are not culpable at all. It is no obstacle whatever to your salvation, for instance, if you are ignorant of some craft, such as carpentry or building. And plenty of people, Peter and Andrew, James and John, and the other disciples among them, have found acceptance with God, who were unacquainted with the liberal arts, though these are of a higher order and more profitable both to learn and to practise than are the practical.

OF THE VALUE OF KNOWLEDGE

But you must not think that I am scoffing at knowledge or blaming the learned and forbidding the study of letters! Far from it! I know well what service her scholars have rendered and are rendering to the Church, both by refuting her enemies and by instructing the simple. But it is written that "knowledge puffeth up," and in another place, "He that addeth knowledge addeth also grief." There is a difference, you see, between these two: One knowledge fills a man with pride; the other saddens him. And obviously the latter is that which ministers to our salvation, for God heals the broken-hearted but abhors the proud.

All knowledge which is founded on the truth is indeed good in itself. But you, who are set on working out your own salvation with fear and trembling, and with all speed, because the time is short, must give priority to the studies which most nearly concern it. Doctors tell us—do they not?—that part of the art of medicine consists in knowing what foods should be taken, and in what order and manner they are best consumed. For, though all foods God has created are good in themselves, you may easily make them far from good *for you*, if you do not take them in the proper order and the proper way. And the same applies to the various branches of knowledge.

OF TRUE MOTIVATION FOR SEEKING KNOWLEDGE

But I had better send you to the master, for this teaching is not ours but his, though it is ours too, because it is the Truth's. "If any man," he says, "thinks that he knows anything, he does not yet know it as he ought to know." It is the manner of knowing that he singles out as the important thing; and that includes the order of our study, the effort we devote to it, and the end we have in view in undertaking it. As to the order, that must come first which will forward our salvation; as to the effort, the most must be expended on the studies that kindle us to love; and, as to the object that we have in view, we must seek to acquire knowledge, not from vainglory or curiosity or anything like that, but only for the sake of our own edification or that of our neighbor.

For there are some who desire knowledge merely for its own sake; and that is shameful curiosity. And there are others who desire to know, in order that they may themselves be known; and that is vanity, disgraceful too. Others, again, desire knowledge in order to acquire money or preferment by it; that too is a discreditable quest. But there are also some who desire knowledge, that they may build up others' souls with it; and that is charity. Others, again, desire it that they themselves may be built up thereby; and that is prudence.

OF KNOWING ONESELF

Out of all these types, the last two only put knowledge to right use. All the others merely illustrate the truth of the apostle's saying that "knowledge puffeth up." I would have the soul begin by getting knowledge of itself. This is required by the natural order, because the fact of our own existence is the first fact in our experience; it is dictated also by our own advantage, because such knowledge does not puff us up but humbles us, and thereby lays the only safe foundation for the building of our souls. There is indeed no means of getting humble so lively and effective as finding out what oneself really is; but to get this result the soul must be honest and sincere, and look itself squarely in the face, not averting its gaze from anything that it may see. Will it not find itself in the Land of Unlikeness when it thus sees itself in the clear light of truth? And, in the misery it can no longer hide, will it not cry to the Lord, "In Thy truth Thou hast humbled me"?

How shall he not be humbled, who thus perceives his state, laden with sins, burdened with his mortal body, involved in earthly cares, tainted with the corrupt desires of the flesh, blind, bent, weak, enmeshed in countless errors, exposed to many dangers, vexed by a host of fears, harassed by innumerable troubles, prone to vices, and feeble in the virtues? How shall he lift his head and stand erect? Will he not rather turn humbly to the Lord and cry, "Heal my soul, for I have sinned against Thee"? And when he turns to the Lord, he will be comforted; for the Lord is the Father of mercies and the God of all consolation.

KNOWLEDGE OF SELF LEADS
TO KNOWLEDGE OF GOD

Personally, as long as I look at myself, I see cause for nothing but sorrow. But if I raise my eyes and look at the Divine Compassion, that happy sight tempers the grimness of the other, and I say to Him, "My soul was troubled to me-ward: therefore will I remember Thee." It is by such an experience and in that order—following, that is to say, our recognition of our need and our appeal to Him—that God makes Himself known to us for our soul's good. The knowledge of yourself is thus the first step towards the knowledge of God; He will become visible to you through His own Image which is being renewed in you, the while you are being transformed from splendour unto splendour, by beholding boldly and with open face the glory of the Lord.

Observe that both these kinds of knowledge are necessary to salvation. For, if you do not know yourself, you have in you neither the fear of God nor yet humility, and how can you be saved if you lack those? For humility is the mother of salvation, and the fear of the Lord is the beginning of wisdom. And if you lack the knowledge of God, there is no hope for you either; for you cannot love Him Whom you do not know, nor possess Him Whom you have not loved. Know yourself, therefore, that you may fear God; know Him, that you may love Him even as you fear. In the one is the beginning of wisdom, as I have just said; in the other its perfecting, for love is the fulfilling of the Law. You must beware, therefore, of both ignorance of self and ignorance of God, because salvation is not possible without the fear and love of God. Other things do not matter one way or the other; you will not be saved because you know them, nor damned because you do not.

OF THE VALUE OF OTHER FORMS OF KNOWLEDGE

I must not be thought, however, to underrate booklearning, which both adorns and instructs the soul and makes it able to instruct other people. I may safely apply myself to the acquisition of this sort of knowledge, provided I have already acquired these other two which are essential to salvation. I think the prophet had this sequence in his mind, when, after saying, "Sow to yourselves for righteousness, reap the hope of life," he added "and kindle for yourselves the light of knowledge." You have sown to yourself for righteousness, if your genuine self-knowledge has taught you to fear God, if you have humbled yourself and wept and given alms, if you have fasted and kept vigil and wearied heaven with your prayers.

"They went along and wept," the psalmist says, "sowing their seed." What? Shall they weep for ever? God forbid! "They shall come again with exultation, carrying their sheaves." But that, you say, will be at the Resurrection, in the Last Day, and that is a long time to wait! Do not be discouraged and fainthearted; you reap the firstfruits of the Spirit even now. The joy and exultation in that Day, when life is ours in fact and not in hope alone, will be very great—so great that surely the very hope of it must itself be joyful! "Rejoicing in hope," says the apostle. And David did not say he *would be* glad when he got to the House of the Lord, but that he *was* glad to be on his way there! He was experiencing the truth of the saying that "the expectation of the righteous is gladness."

THE KNOWLEDGE OF GOD BRINGS HOPE AND JOY

And, in the soul of him who has sown to himself for righteousness, that gladness is born of the assurance of forgiveness, attested by the grace he is receiving to live more holily; as those of you who have passed the painful first stages of conversion know quite well. How sweet, how gracious does the soul find Thee, Lord Jesus, when Thou hast given it not only pardon for its sins but also the reward of holiness! How true the saying is that "they that sow in tears shall reap in joy!" And in it the two kinds of knowledge are put into a nutshell; for knowledge of ourselves makes us to sow in tears, and knowledge of God makes us to reap in joy.

Provided, then, that we acquire this twofold knowledge first, we shall run no risk of being puffed up by any other knowledge we may subsequently gain; for no worldly honour or advantage can compare with the hope we have conceived and the joy, born of that hope, which is already so deeply rooted in our souls. And hope itself comes from knowing God; for, if we know not God, how shall we hope in Him? And, if we do not know ourselves, how shall we be humble? For we shall think ourselves to be something, when in point of fact we are nothing at all!

OF PRIDE AND DESPAIR

These two kinds of ignorance it behoves us at all costs to avoid; because they produce respectively the beginning of sin and its consummation. For, just as the fear of the Lord is the beginning of wisdom, so is pride the starting-point of every sin; and as the love of God is the perfecting of wisdom, so is despair the final wickedness. And pride (as I have said) comes from ignorance of self, and despair comes from ignorance of God.

As regards the former, we must watch out very carefully not to exalt ourselves in the very least degree. But, however much we may humble ourselves, we run no risk at all of thinking ourselves less than we really are! It is like going through a low doorway; you can stoop as low as you like without coming to harm, but raise your head but a fingerbreadth too high and you knock it against the lintel. So beware, O man, of comparing thyself with others; for the one whom thou regardest, perhaps, as the vilest of all men may turn out better than thou one day and may even be so now!

And as pride comes from ignorance of self, so does ignorance of God beget despair. For a man turning from an evil life is bound to be rendered desperate by the knowledge of his sins, if he does not also know how good God is, how kind and gentle, and how ready to forgive. And in this case, imagining that God is harsh and terrible when really He is merciful and to be loved, he will be easily persuaded by his carnal reason to return to all his former sins. Thus it is that from the ignorance of God there comes the final, crowning sin, which is despair.

And yet, O ye of little faith, what is it that ye fear? That He will not forgive your sins? Never! He nailed them to the cross with His own Hands! Because your flesh is tender and delicate? Ah, but He knoweth whereof we are made. Because you are grown used to evil and fettered by your sins? But the Lord Jesus looses them that are bound! Are you afraid, perhaps, that He is angry at the multitude of your transgressions, and will not extend a helping hand to you? But "where sin abounded, grace did much more abound!" Are you anxious about food and clothing and such like? But He knows that you have need of all these things! What more do you want? What is it that still keeps you back from being saved? It is because you know not God, and will not credit what we tell you of Him.

God keep us from such ignorance as this!

WHY THE BRIDEGROOM CALLS THE BRIDE THE "FAIR ONE AMONG WOMEN"

The Bride, who has been given not knowledge merely but friendship and familiarity with Him Who is at once her Bridegroom and her God, has boldly asked that He will show her where His glory dwells; and verily His dwelling and His glory are no other than Himself. He finds her boldness worthy of reproof, reminding her that she must know herself. He thunders thus at His belovéd, not in anger but that by fear she may be purified, and so made able for the vision after which she longs.

Aptly, then, He calls her fair, not absolutely but with a qualification—"thou fair one *among women*"—that He may humble her still more by showing her wherein she is deficient. For I think that by "women" in this passage He means worldly souls, who live according to the flesh, and consequently lack stability and manly force. The spiritual soul is fair compared with these, because it lives according to the Spirit, not the flesh. But it is not so absolutely: There is no perfect beauty for those still in the body. Fair among women, among souls that are not spiritually minded, that she is. But fair among the blesséd angels and the heavenly spirits, that the Bride is not.

Let the soul, then, be not too eager, while it is still on earth among the "women," to search out heavenly things, lest glory overwhelm it. "The vision you demand, O Bride, in asking where I feed My flock, where I repose at noon," the Bridegroom says, "is too sublime for you. While you are in the body, you have not strength to look upon the marvelous noon-day light wherein I dwell. You must wait till the very last for that, when I shall have made you glorious before Me, without spot or wrinkle or any such thing. And then, when I shall have appeared, you will be wholly fair, as I am wholly fair; you will be altogether like Me, for you will see Me as I am. And you will hear Me say, 'Thou art all fair, My love, and there is no spot in thee.'"

Chapter Thirteen

"I have likened thee, My love, to My horsemen among the chariots of Pharaoh"

THE SPIRITUAL MEANING OF THE EXODUS

THE TWOFOLD MARVEL of Israel's Exodus from Egypt, their passage of the Sea and the retribution that overtook their enemies, was a clear type of the grace of Baptism, by whose waters men are saved and their offences drowned. The Bridegroom reminds the Bride of these blessings which she has received already, so that she may not remain unduly saddened by His previous rebuke; and (in the words that follow) He promises to give her other blessings too. Further, He testifies again that she is beautiful, and calls her His love.

Let us examine the gifts of which He here reminds her. Firstly, He has freed her from the yoke of sin, by destroying all the works of the flesh, just as He saved Israel from slavery in Egypt by overturning and swamping Pharaoh's chariots. Secondly, having thus stooped to set her free, He taker her for His friend. Thirdly, He adorns her with the beauty that befits His Bride, though as yet only on the cheeks and neck. And finally He promises to give her necklaces of gold picked out with silver, with which to deck herself—of gold, by reason of its preciousness, and silver-studded, for the sake of elegance. Is not the order of these gifts delightful? First in His mercy He frees her; then in His lowliness He loves her; next in His kindness He purges and cleanses her; lastly He promises to give her the richest and most precious ornaments.

THE HORSEMEN OF THE LORD AND PHARAOH'S CHARIOTS

These two armies are compared, not with each other but each with something else; for light has no fellowship with darkness, nor has the believer anything in common with the infidel. "The horsemen of the Lord" denote the holy, spiritual soul; "Pharaoh" denotes the devil. You will not think it strange that a single soul should be compared to a whole troop of cavalry, if you think of the array of virtues that are found in it—how regulated its affections are, how disciplined its habits, how armed it is with prayer, how vigorious in its actions, how frightening in its zeal, how unremitting in its struggles with the Enemy himself, how numerous its victories over him! "Terrible as an army set in array for battle" is the description of it later on.

OF THE MINISTRY OF ANGELS

If this interpretation does not please you, then there is another. You know that such a soul is never without a guard of angels, who are jealous over it with God's own jealousy, that they may keep it safe for its Husband and present it as a chaste virgin to Christ. Now do not say, "Where are these angels? Who has ever seen them?" The prophet Elisha saw them, and obtained by his prayers that his servant should see them too. If you do not see them, it is because you are neither a prophet nor a prophet's servant. The patriarch Jacob also saw them, and said, "This is God's host." The Teacher of the Gentiles saw them too, and said of them, "Are they not all ministering spirits, sent forth to serve those who are inheriting salvation?"

Upheld, therefore, by angel ministries, marching surrounded by a heavenly troop, the Bride is like those horsemen of the Lord who triumphed amid Pharaoh's chariots by such a marvelous miracle of God's aid. Consider in detail the parallel between the type and its fulfilment. In the one you have the people brought out of Egypt; in the other man led from the world. In the former, the combat is with flesh and blood, and Pharaoh and his chariots are overwhelmed by salty waves; in the latter, the battle is against the devil and the powers of darkness, and the desires of the flesh and of the world, which war against the soul, are overcome by floods of penitential tears. I think that, even now, the devil, meeting such a soul, cries out, "Let us flee from Israel, for the Lord fights for him!"

OF WICKEDNESS, SENSUALITY, AND AVARICE

Would you like me to name a few of Pharaoh's captains and describe their chariots? One great captain of the spiritual and unseen king of Egypt is Wickedness; another is Sensuality; a third is Avarice. Each of these has charge of a particular area: Wickedness commands in the region of crimes and misdeeds; Sensuality rules in the land of uncleanness and fleshly impurity; and Avarice is allotted the district of robbery and fraud.

Wickedness has a four-wheeled chariot with which to chase God's People; and those wheels are Cruelty, Impatience, Presumption, and Shamelessness. Very swift indeed is this chariot to shed blood, for it is not stayed by Innocence, nor held back by Patience, nor refrained by Fear, nor checked by Shame. It is drawn by two extremely vicious and aggressive horses, earthly Power and worldly Pomp. These two have separate drivers, Pomp being driven by Arrogance and Power by Envy. The latter urges Power with two spurs, Dread lest it should fail and Fear lest it should have to be surrendered.

The chariot of Sensuality likewise has four wheels, and these are Gluttony, Lust, Luxury, and Sloth. Its horses are Prosperity, whose driver is inglorious Ease, and Plenty, whose driver is treacherous Security. Ease and Security employ no spurs or whip; they use instead the canopy Dissimulation to give them shade, and the fan Extravagance to stir the cooling breeze of Adulation.

Avarice also has four wheels to his chariot, namely Timidity, Meanness, Contempt of God, and Forgetfulness of Death. He likewise has two horses, Niggardliness and Greed; but these are driven by a single driver, Desire for Gain; for Avarice will not run to the expense of two! This one servant, however, is indefatigable in his master's service, and he urges on his horses with two stinging whips, Craving to Acquire and Fear of Losing.

The king of Egypt has other captains besides these, Pride and Ungodliness among the chief, and other chariots too. He also has innumerable officers of lower rank; and I leave you to think out for yourselves their names and functions, their weapons and equipment. The unseen Pharaoh, confident in the strength of this great army, charges about attacking God's family on every side; he pursues Israel coming out of Egypt even to this day. The People of God, on the other hand, have neither chariots nor weapons; their confidence is in the Lord alone.

WHY THE BRIDEGROOM CALLS THE BRIDE HIS LOVE

He calls her "love"—that is to say, His friend. He was *her* friend before He set her free; for, if He had not loved her, He would not have rescued her. And she, for her part, was drawn to love Him and to be His friend by the boon of liberation which He had given her. "We love Him," she says, "because He first loved us." This union of the Word with the sinful soul is prefigured in the story of Moses and the Ethiopian woman. What is it in that loveliest of mysteries that delights you most? Is it the kindness of the Word in stooping thus? Or the inestimable glory conferred upon the soul? Or the unlooked-for confidence the sinner feels? Ah, but Christ did something Moses could not do! *He* had the power to change the Ethiopian's skin! For He goes on to say, "Thy cheeks are beautiful as are the turtle-dove's." Those are the next words that we must discuss.

Chapter Fourteen

"Thy cheeks are beautiful as are the turtle-dove's, thy neck as neck-laces. We will make thee ear-rings of gold, inlaid with silver"

OF THE CONSTITUENTS OF A RIGHT INTENTION

I THINK THAT IT WAS His reproof, making her blush and so more lovely in His eyes, that called forth from the Bridegroom this utterance of praise, "Thy cheeks are beautiful as the turtle-dove's." You must not take this in a phyical sense: it is the soul's face, not the body's, that is meant; and the soul's face is the mind's intention, for from that you judge the rightness of a person's actions, just as you judge a body beautiful according to the face.

I wonder, however, why He speaks of "cheeks" rather than "face"? There must be some good reason and, if you have nothing better to suggest, I will tell you my idea. In an intention there are two elements—the thing you mean to do and your reason for doing it. The beauty or ugliness of a soul is judged by these two things; so that to a person in whom both are good it may be fitly said, "Thy cheeks are beautiful as are the turtle-dove's." Where one of them is bad, however, this cannot be said; still less when both are so. Thus the words will apply to one who seeks truth simply from love of it, but not to one who seeks it from motive of vainglory or for some temporal end; the latter is, so to speak, beautiful on one side only. And a person who has no creditable interests at all but is wholly ensnared by the flesh must of course be adjudged as ugly altogether.

OF WRONG INTENTIONS

To have one's heart set on the world, and not on God, is thus to have none of this beauty of the "cheeks" at all. And to be set on God to some extent, yet not for God's own sake, is to be a hypocrite; in which case the insincerity of the motive vitiates whatever beauty there might be in the act, and spreads its foulness over the whole face. And if a person directs his intention Godwards solely or chiefly in order to obtain the necessities of this present life, though he is not a hypocrite, he shows a lack of generosity but little acceptable to God. Further, if the intention be directed on something other than God, for the sake of God, that is to have Martha's busyness instead of Mary's ease!

Far be it from me to say that such a soul is ugly! Yet, all the same, I cannot call it wholly beautiful: careful and troubled as it is about so many things, it is inevitably somewhat bespattered with the dust of earth. Yet this defilement will be quickly and easily removed, by a pure intention and good conscience towards God, in the hour of holy death.

It is therefore only if the soul seeks God alone and only for God's sake that its "face" will be wholly beautiful, both elements in its intention being wholly good. That twofold beauty is the Bride's special quality, which makes her worthy of the words of praise, "Thy cheeks are beautiful as are the turtle-dove's."

OF SPIRITUAL SOLITUDE

But why "the turtle-dove's"? It seems to be a modest little bird, which goes about, not in a flock but with a single mate; and, if it lose its mate, it does not seek another but henceforth lives alone. You, whom the Holy Spirit is urging so to act that your soul may become the Bride of God, must imitate this chaste little bird. "Sit alone and keep silence," as the prophet says; sit solitary, like the turtle-dove; withdraw yourself from people. Do you not know you have a Bridegroom Who is diffident, and will not grant you the honour of His presence with other people there? Get away, then, I tell you, not physically but in mind and in intention, in spirit and devotion; for the Lord Christ is Himself a Spirit, and it is spiritual solitude that He requires of you, though bodily withdrawal is not without its uses, when it may be had, especially in time of prayer.

You have His own commandment in the matter. "Thou, when thou wilt pray, enter into thy chamber, and when thou hast shut the door, pray." He Himself practised what He preached; He would spend all the night in prayer, not only hiding from the crowds but not allowing any even of His closest friends to come with Him. Even at the last, when He was hastening to His willing death, though He had taken three of those with Him, He withdrew even from them when He desired to pray. You must do likewise, when you want to pray.

Be quite clear that the only solitude required of you is that of mind and spirit. You are alone in spirit, if you are not thinking about ordinary matters, if you are not interested in things present, if you reject worldly values, if you keep out of quarrels, if you do not resent injuries or hug grievances. Otherwise you are not really alone, even when you are alone in body. Do you see that it is possible both to be alone in a crowd, and to be in a crowd when you are alone?

No matter how many people there may be around you, you are alone, if only you do not pry eagerly into their conversation or judge it harshly. Even if you see a wrong thing done, you must not judge your neighbour, but rather must make excuses at least for his intention, if not for his action. Suppose that it was done in ignorance, or that he was startled into it, or that he did it by mistake. If the thing is too blatant to be explained away like this, you must still try to think that there was some excuse, and should say to yourself, "The temptation surely was very fierce. How should *I* have acted, had I been so assailed?"

OF THE BRIDE'S INTELLIGENCE OF HEAVENLY THINGS

"Thy neck is beautiful as necklaces." The neck is wont to be adorned with necklaces, not compared to them. But whereas necklaces are worn in order that the wearer may beg from the jewels a beauty lacking to herself, the Bride's neck is so naturally lovely that it requires no embellishment.

The Holy Spirit helping us, we have already seen that the Bride's cheeks denote the mind's intention. As far as I can see, her neck denotes the soul's intelligence. You will agree to this, I think, if you consider the functions of the two; for the neck in the body transmits nourishment to the internal organs, just as the understanding conveys the spiritual food needful for life to all the faculties. And the Bride's simple, pure intelligence is radiant with plain truth; it is a neck that needs no ornament, but is itself a decoration for the soul. Hence its comparison with necklaces.

FIRST COMES HEARING THEN SEEING

"We will make thee ear-rings of gold, inlaid with silver." I think these words are spoken by the Bridegroom's companions: they are promising to make her beautiful and costly earrings, to comfort her till she attains the sight of Him for Whom she longs so greatly. For "faith cometh by hearing"; and, as long as we walk by faith and not by sight, we have to learn by listening, rather than by trying to see. For it is faith alone that purifies the heart and so prepares for sight.

"You yearn to see your Bridegroom in His glory," the companions say, "but that is not for now. So we are giving you these ear-rings, to comfort you meanwhile, and to prepare you for that for which you crave." It is as though they used the prophet's words, "Hearken, O daughter, and see!" "You want to see," they tell her, "but you must listen first; for hearing is the step by which you mount to sight. So listen and give heed to the ornaments that we are giving you, so that by the

obedience of hearing you may pass to the glory of vision. We bestow joy and gladness on your hearing. For the vision itself (in which are the fullness of joy and the fulfilment of desire) is not ours to give, but His Whom your soul loves: He Himself will fill you with the joy of His countenance. Accept these ear-rings at our hand, for comfort's sake, meanwhile; but, from His right Hand afterwards, comforts for evermore."

OF EAR-RINGS FOR THE BRIDE

Consider now what kind of ear-rings they are giving her—of gold, inlaid with silver. Gold is the glory of the Godhead; gold is the wisdom that is from above. The heavenly craftsmen, whose work it is, promise to fashion from this gold of Truth some shining tokens, and to insert them in the soul's inward ears. In other words, they will construct some likenesses of spiritual things and will present them to the contemplative soul, so that it may perceive as it were in reflection and by analogy something of that most pure Divine Reality, which it is not able yet to behold face to face.

We are speaking here of things Divine, which only those who have experienced them can understand. They alone know how, although still in the body, walking by faith and without any revelation yet of what the Light consists in, they do somehow behold the lineaments of Truth sometimes, and so can say with the apostle, "Now I know in part." But, when this has happened, when in a moment of the spirit's ecstasy some lightning flash like this has shone upon the mind, pictures forthwith present themselves, similitudes taken from lower things, which adumbrate to some extent the pure and dazzling ray of Truth, making its splendour at once more tolerable to the soul itself and easier to express. I believe that these are suggested to us by the holy angels, just as bad and harmful images are without doubt due to the agency of evil spirits.

There is another reading in this passage which seems to emphasize this fact. "We the artificers," it says, "will make for thee similitudes of gold, with garnishings of silver." ("Garnishings of silver" and "inlaid with silver" mean the same.) I think this means that the holy angels not only provide us with the images but also enable us to express them convincingly, so that our hearers may better understand and enjoy them. And if you ask me why silver should be a figure for eloquence, the prophet answers you, "The words of the Lord are pure words, as silver tried in the fire." That, then, is how the heavenly and ministering spirits fashion for the Bride, while she is still on earth, ear-rings of gold, inlaid with silver.

OF A REQUEST FULFILLED

But notice how she asks for one thing and receives another. She begs for the repose of contemplation, and the labor of preaching is laid upon her. She thirsts for the presence of her Spouse, and is given the task of bringing forth and nourishing His children. We noticed the same thing once before, you will remember; when she was longing for His kisses and embraces, the answer she received was "Thy breasts are better than wine"—a reminder of her motherhood and her duty to her sons. So now, when she has asked to be shown where the Bridegroom feeds His flock and where He rests at noon, she receives, instead of that vision, "ear-rings of gold, inlaid with silver"—that is to say, wisdom with eloquence, for teaching other people.

Chapter Fifteen

"While the King reclined at His table, my spikenard gave forth its sweet smell"

ON RECEIVING REPROOF

WHILE THE KING reclined at His table, my spikenard gave forth its sweet smell." This is the Bride's reply to the Bridegroom's reproof; but it is clear that she is speaking of Him, and not to Him. Her manner of receiving it had pleased Him; so, having praised her beauty, one may think that He withdrew, so that she might more freely speak her feelings to those who stayed with her. It is to them, to the companions of the Bridegroom who, knowing His will, are offering her gifts, that these words are addressed.

That is their outward context. But, before I proceed to extract the spiritual kernel from this nut, I have one thing to say. Happy is he who takes reproof as well as did the Bride on this occasion! It would of course be better still if no reproof were needed. But, as we all offend in many ways, I am required by my office to reprove transgressors, and charity urges me further to fulfil my duty.

But how do you think I feel if a reproof is so taken that it fails of its purpose and returns to me empty, so to speak, like a dart that rebounds from the board to the thrower's hand? Am I not troubled and distressed? Indeed, to borrow the words of a master, "I am in a strait betwixt two things, and know not which to choose"—whether to be glad that at any rate I have done my duty, or sad because my words have failed of their desired effect. For I sought to destroy an enemy and rescue a brother, and the opposite has ensued: I have wounded a soul and increased its guilt, for to its previous fault it has now added scorn.

"They will not hearken unto thee," the prophet says, "because they will not hearken unto Me." You see what Majesty it is that you despise. It was the Lord Who spoke to you, not I—the Lord Who said to His apostles, "He that despiseth you, despiseth Me." I am neither prophet nor apostle; but, though I lack their merits, none the less I hold an apostolic and prophetic office, with all the load of care that it entails. What then? Is the seat of authority to be held in no respect, because it has an unworthy occupant? Even of the Scribes and Pharisees in Moses' seat the Lord enjoined, "What things they tell you, do."

ON THE DANGER OF DEFENDING SIN

Very often impatience is combined with scorn, so that the person reproved not only makes no effort to amend, but is angry with his reprover, like a madman who repels his doctor's hand. A strange perversion, truly! And sometimes shameless insolence is added too; not only is the reproof resented but the fault itself is brazenly defended. Do you realize how dangerous, how terrible a thing it is to defend sin? Is it not tantamount to calling evil good and good evil? Must not such brazenness quickly beget impenitence, which is the mother of despair? For who repents for that which he thinks good? "Woe to them," says the prophet. And that woe is eternal. For it is one thing for a person to be led astray by concupiscence, and another deliberately to choose the evil as though it were the good, and so in false security to hasten on to death, as though to life. I assure you that I have preferred sometimes to say nothing and take no notice of the evil I observed, rather than give occasion for so great an ill.

You will tell me, perhaps, that if I but do my duty, my good action will return into mine own bosom, and that I shall be innocent of the blood of him whom I vainly tried to turn from his evil course, that he might live. But say what you will, it will be no comfort to me, if I have to watch a son of mine in spiritual death! Would not any mother weep to see her child in mortal sickness of the body, in spite of all the cares and pains that she had lavished on him? How much more, then, ought I to weep for my son's spiritual death, even though I know I have done all I could to warn him!

You see what great evils you avoid both for yourself and us if, when you are reproved, you take it humbly. Such a soul puts me altogether in his debt. I serve him as my Lord's most worthy Bride, who truthfully can say, "While the King reclined at His table, my spikenard gave forth its sweet smell."

OF THE TWO KINDS OF HUMILITY

Humility is a fragrant virtue. The odour of it, rising from this vale of tears, spreads all about; its grateful sweetness reaches even to the nostrils of the King, reclining at His table. Spikenard is a lowly plant and of a warm nature, so they tell us who are versed in herbs. It is therefore a fit symbol of that kind of humility which is aflame with holy love. I say this, because there is another kind of humility, produced by truth, which has no warmth. This truth-born humility is rooted in knowledge and the understanding; but the seat of the other, which is produced and warmed by love, is in the affections. A true knowledge of yourself will make you vile in your own sight, though you will perhaps be hardly ready yet to have others hold you in the same esteem. You will then be humble; but only by the working of truth. If, however, love acts upon you equally with truth, you will be certain to desire that others should esteem you as you really are.

AN APPEAL TO FOLLOW THE EXAMPLE OF CHRIST

You see, then, that to hold a low opinion of yourself through conviction of the truth is something quite different from the willing acceptance of humbling conditions through the further gift of love; for the one is forced upon us and the other is a free-will act. "He emptied Himself," says the apostle, "and took on Him the form of a servant," thus giving us the pattern of humility. He emptied Himself, He humbled Himself, not because He was obliged to do so, but out of love for us. He let Himself seem vile to men, although He knew that He was not; though not forgetting that He was the Highest, He willed to be esteemed the lowest and the least. And He said, "Learn of Me, for I am meek and lowly in heart"—in heart, you notice, that is to say, in will. He was humble with the sort of humility that springs from the affection of the heart. It was love that motivated His Self-emptying, that led Him to become a little lower than the angels, to be subject to His parents, to bow His Head beneath the Baptist's hands, to endure the weakness of the flesh, and to submit to death, even upon the cross.

Was I not right in taking spikenard, that warm and lowly herb, as a type of this humility which is warmed by love? If, then, you have the other kind, which truth enforces on you, exert your will and make a virtue out of this necessity; for without the will's consent no virtue is possible at all. You will have achieved this, if you do not want to appear outwardly otherwise than as you find yourself within. Submit yourself to God, and subdue your will wholeheartedly to truth. "Shall not my soul," the psalmist says, "be subject unto God?"

It is, however, a small thing to subject yourself to God, if you do not submit yourself also to every human creature for the sake of God—whether to the Abbot, as your Superior, or to the priors, as appointed by him. I say further, submit yourself to old and young alike, defer to your inferior, respect your junior. For "thus it becometh us to fulfil all righteousness"; thus will you make the Bride's words your own, "My spikenard gave forth its sweet smell."

OF THE SWEET SMELL OF HUMILITY

That fragrance is devotion, the odour of a good repute, the sweet savour of Christ which reaches everyone in every place, which is perceived and loved by all. He whom truth alone forces to be humble cannot achieve this; for his humility is only for himself; it does not spread abroad to give delight to others; in short, it has no fragrance because it lacks devotion and is not voluntary but enforced. The Bride's humility, on the other hand, is willing, lasting, fruitful. Its fragrance is unaffected by rebuke or praise. She says with blesséd Mary, "God hath regarded the lowliness of His handmaiden," for what is the meaning of the words, "My spikenard gave forth its sweet smell," if not "My humility has found favour in His sight"?

"Not my wisdom," she says, "not my nobility, not my beauty, for those are not by own, but my humility—the only thing that really belongs to me—that was the thing that gave forth its sweet smell." Humility is always pleasing to God, and the Lord that sitteth on high is wont to have respect to lowly things. Therefore, while the King reclines at His table—that is, in His heavenly dwelling-place, the Bosom of the Father—the fragrance of humility is wafted up to Him. "He dwells on high," the psalmist says, "and He beholdeth humble things in heaven and in earth."

Chapter Sixteen

"A little bunch of myrrh is my Belovéd unto me. He shall abide between my breasts. My Belovéd is to me as a cluster of Cyprus grapes in the vineyards of En-gedi"

ON THE FELLOWSHIP OF CHRIST'S SUFFERINGS AND THE POWER OF HIS RESURRECTION

HE WAS CALLED the king before; now He is the Belovéd. He was reclining at His table last; now the Bride says He is between her breasts. Humility is a great virtue; even God's Majesty inclines to it. The title of respect is quickly turned into the term of friendship; and He Who was far off is speedily brought near.

OF THE MEANING OF MYRRH

"A little bunch of myrrh is my Belovéd unto me." Myrrh, which is bitter, denotes the hard, harsh facts of trouble and distress. The Bride, seeing that she is about to endure these things for the Belovéd's sake, says these words with joy, trusting that she will bear them manfully. Like the apostles, she rejoices that she is counted worthy to suffer shame for Jesus' Name. That is why she speaks of her Belovéd, not as a big bundle but as a little bunch; whatever toil and sorrow may be in store for her, she makes but little of them, for the love of Him.

She fitly uses the diminutive; for a Child is born to us. She rightly says, "a little bunch," because "the sufferings of this present time are not worthy to be compared with the future glory that shall be revealed in us." And "our light affliction, that is but for a moment, worketh for us a far more exceeding and eternal weight of glory." And is He not "a little bunch," Whose yoke is easy and Whose burden light? Not that the burden is light in itself, for suffering and death are bitter, heavy things; it is the love of him who carries it that makes it light. Wherefore the Bride does not say merely that her Belovéd is a little bunch of myrrh, but adds *"to me,"* that is, to me who love Him. For the same reason she calls Him her Belovéd, to show us that her love has power to surmount all vexations and is as strong as death. And to show you that she does not glory in herself not trust in her own strength, but only in His help, she adds, "He shall abide between my breasts." "Though I walk through the midst of the shadow of death," she confidently sings, "I fear no evil, for Thou art with me."

In an earlier discourse, I explained the Bride's two breasts as being Congratulation and Compassion, according to Paul's teaching, "Rejoice with them that do rejoice, and weep with them that weep." It is because she knows that adversity and prosperity both have their dangers, that she desires thus to have her Belovéd between her breasts, so that, strengthened by His continual protection, she may be neither unduly elated by the one nor cast down by the other. You will copy her, if you are wise: you will not let this precious little bunch of myrrh be torn out of your bosom even for an hour, but will cherish the thought of all His bitter sufferings for you unceasingly, so that you can say with the Bride, "A little bunch of myrrh is my Belovéd unto me; He shall abide between my breasts."

BERNARD'S PRACTICE

My own practice, from the beginning of my conversion, has been to gather for myself this little bunch of myrrh, out of all my Lord's troubles and distresses, and keep it ever in my bosom to supply the countless merits that I know I lack. Out of the hardships of His infancy, His labours of preaching, His fatigues in travelling, His nights of prayer, His temptations when fasting, His tears of sympathy, the snares of those who tried to catch Him in His talk, the perils He endured among false brethren, the insults and the spitting and the blows, the piercing of the nails, and all the other things He bore for our salvation, out of all these, as from a wood, I gather for myself this little bunch of myrrh. Nor do I overlook the fact that it was myrrh He drank upon the cross, and myrrh with which He was anointed in the tomb; for by the first He made His own the bitterness of my sin, and by the second He declared the future incorruption of my body.

Precious is this little bunch of myrrh; no one shall take it from me, it shall abide between my breasts. In meditating on these things is wisdom, the perfecting of righteousness, full-ness of knowledge, the riches of salvation, abundant store of merit. In adversity they raise me up, in prosperity they keep me steady, enabling me to walk between the two in safety, along the royal road that leads to life. You know how often these things are on my lips; God knows that they are always present to my heart. To know Jesus and Him crucified is my philosophy, and there is none higher. I do not ask Him where He rests at noon, for He dwells ever in my breast and heart. Nor do I ask Him where He feeds His flock, as does the Bride; for I behold Him as my Saviour on the cross.

A CALL TO FELLOWSHIP WITH CHRIST

Do you, then, gather for yourselves, brethren belovéd, this precious little bunch, and take it to your heart and guard it there. Carry it, not on your shoulders where you cannot see it, but in front of you, before your eyes; lest, if you carry it and do not smell its fragrance, its load should weigh you down. Remember how Simeon took Him in his arms, how Mary bore Him in her womb and nursed Him in her lap, how Joseph also must often have dandled Him upon his knee. All these bore Him *before* them, not behind. Do you likewise. For if your eyes are fixed upon Him Whom you bear, by looking at the straitening He endured, you will more easily sustain your own afflictions, He helping you Who is the Bridegroom of the Church, God above all, blesséd for evermore. Amen.

If the Belovéd was in the myrrh, much more will He be in the sweetness of the grape. My Lord Jesus is therefore myrrh to me in His Death, grapes in His Resurrection; for my benefit He has made of Himself a most health-giving draught, mingled with tears. He died for our sins and rose again for our justification, that we being dead to sin might live to righteousness. If, then, you have mourned for your sins, you have tasted the bitter myrrh. And if the hope of holier living has refreshed you, you have exchanged that bitterness for the wine that maketh glad the heart of man, and may say without presumption, "My Belovéd is to me as a cluster of Cyprus grapes in the vineyards of En-gedi."

Chapter Seventeen

"Lo, thou art fair, My love, lo, thou art fair! Thou hast doves' eyes. Lo, Thou art fair, my Belovéd, and comely!"

OF THE TWOFOLD BEAUTY OF THE SOUL

HOW ALTOGETHER LOVELY is the sequence here! The Bride's presumption and the Bridegroom's anger both came from love. And, as the fault was followed by reproof, and the reproof by amendment, so now amendment meets its recompense. Only the Belovéd is here not: the Master and the King have disappeared; majesty is doffed and awed respect remitted; aloofness must give way before the waxing tide of love. And as Moses spoke to God of old, as one friend to Another, and the Lord answered him, so now between the soul and God the Word there is established a relationship as homely and as close as that between two neighbours. Nor is that surprising. Their holy love, deriving from a single source, is mutual, and is expressed in words and looks full of the utmost sweetness. He calls her, finally, His love, and tells her twice that she is beautiful. She says the same to Him.

OF HUMILITY AND INNOCENCE

This twofold beauty of the soul consists first in humility, and then in innocence conjoined with it; for the humility of one who has greatly offended cannot be admired, though it is lovable. The King desired the beauty of blessèd Mary, because she kept her purity, yet was not lacking in humility. Any soul who, like her, unites the beauty of simplicity and innocence with that of lowliness, will hear the Bridegroom say, "Lo, thou art fair, My love; lo, thou art fair!" Lord Jesus! If only *I* might hear Thee say but once, "Lo, thou art fair!" If thou wouldst but preserve my lowliness, for I have ill-kept my primal innocence! I am Thy servant. I dare not call myself Thy friend, since there is in me no twofold beauty for Thee to attest. It is enough for me to hear Thee say but once, "Lo, thou art fair!" But what if there be doubt, even of that?

I know what I will do. I, who am Thy servant only, will reverence her whom Thou hast called Thy love; I, a misshapen little man, will gaze in wonder at her perfect beauty; I will rejoice to hear the Bridegroom's voice admiring it. Who knows but that in this way I may find favour in her eyes, so that she may obtain for me a place among His friends? The friend of the Bridegroom stands and rejoices to hear the Bridegroom's Voice. That Voice speaks here in His belovéd's ear. Let us, then, hear it and rejoice. They are together; they are talking to each other. Let us stand by and listen; and let no worldly care nor fleshly lure entice us from that sacred colloquy.

OF THE COLLOQUY BETWEEN THE WORD AND THE SOUL

"Lo, thou art fair, My love," He says, "lo, thou art fair!" "Lo" or behold" expresses admiration; the rest is praise. She merits admiration, for her humility is born of holiness preserved, not of repentance for its loss. And she deserves that He should call her fair, for she lacks neither kind of spiritual beauty. This is proved by the fact that she accepts His reproof with equanimity, although her conscience tells her of no failure; whereas we ourselves can scarcely endure to be chidden, even for great faults. For it is not wrong of her to want to see the Bridegroom's glory, but praiseworthy. Yet, when she is rebuked, she penitently says, "A little bunch of myrrh is my Belovéd unto me. He shall abide between my breasts." That is to say, "Enough! I ask for nothing but to know Jesus and Him crucified." What great humility!

She has done nothing wrong, yet she assumes the disposition of a penitent; she has no cause for penitence, and yet she can repent! You ask, Why is she chidden, if she had done no wrong? Here lies the Bridegroom's wisdom. As once He tried and tested Abraham's obedience, so now He tests the Bride's humility. And, as He said to Abraham of old, "Now I know that thou fearest God," so now He says to her, "I know that thou art humble," for that is what He means by saying, "Lo, thou art fair!" He says it twice, to show that to this beauty of humility is added the glory of her holiness. And He no longer calls her "thou fair one among women," but absolutely fair, without comparison.

OF THE MEANING OF DOVES' EYES

He adds, "Thou hast doves' eyes." This plainly is a further praise of her humility. He means that she no longer occupies herself with lofty matters that are too high for her, but is content, like unassuming doves that nest in hollows of the rock, to remain hidden in His wounds and willingly to contemplate the things relating to His Incarnation and His Passion. Or it may be that the reference in "doves' eyes" is to the Holy Spirit, Whose symbol the bird is. "Thou hast doves' eyes" will then be a commendation of the Bride's spiritual insight, and will carry on the thought expressed before by the "earrings of gold." For it is the faith that comes by hearing that has quickened her spiritual sight, and so made her pleasing in the Bridegroom's eyes.

I am sure that we must not belittle this sort of vision, which is all that is possible for us at present, in spite of its inferiority to that which is to come; nor must we think that everybody has it. For notice that the Bride now says, "Lo, Thou art fair, my Belovéd!"—*my* Belovéd, not "belovéd" only! She is indeed highly exalted to be able thus to address the Lord of all! For I suppose that, in the mode of seeing to which she refers, no image of Him in the flesh or even on the cross is present to her senses: "He hath no form nor comeliness," yet she, beholding Him, declares Him fair and comely, for He is seen by her after a better mode.

"Mouth to mouth" God speaks with her, as once He spoke with Moses; she beholds Him undisguised, not in types or symbols; and she declares Him with her mouth to be such as her vision shows her. Her eyes have seen the King in His beauty, yet not as King but as her Belovéd. One prophet saw Him high and lifted up upon His throne; another said he saw Him face to face;

but I think the Bride, seeing the Lord and calling Him Belovéd, surpasses both of them. For fear accompanied the prophets' visions, but the Bride's brings love. Fear indeed hath torment, but perfect charity casts fear out of doors. "Lo, Thou art fair, my Belovéd, and comely!" It is love that echoes in those words, not fear.

OF THE COMMUNICATION BETWEEN THE WORD AND THE SOUL

Perhaps you ask, How can this colloquy take place at all between the Word and the soul? It is a reasonable question; the answer is that, when you hear or read of the Word and the soul beholding and conversing with each other, the language must be taken in a spiritual sense. It is not corporeal images that are beheld, nor words spoken by the body's lips that are exchanged between them. The Word is a Spirit; the soul also is a spirit; and in lieu of tongues they have means of communication proper to themselves—the Word His condescension, the soul her devotion.

A soul without devotion is like a tongueless person or a wordless babe; it is incapable of converse with the Word. But, when the Word speaks by His tongue of condescension to the soul, that soul cannot but hear, for "the Word of God is living and effective." And again, when the soul speaks with its devotion to the Word, it is impossible that He should not hear, and that so much the more because devotion's tongue can never speak at all, except when moved by Him.

Therefore, for the Word to say to a soul, "Thou art fair," and to call it His love, is to invest it with the power of loving and of knowing itself loved. Similarly, when the soul calls the Word Belovéd and says that He is fair, she is simply ascribing to Him the grace of loving and of being loved that He has given her, and marvelling at the condescension and the favour that He shows in giving it. His fairness *is* His love; and it is all the greater in His case because it was the earlier. And she, out of her inmost heart, cries out that He deserves from her a fuller and a more consuming love, because He first loved her. What the Word says, therefore, is in itself a gift inpoured, and the soul's answer is her marvelling thankfulness for it; the more she realizes how He first loved her, so much the more she marvels. So she is not content to say just once, "Lo, Thou art fair!" but emphasizes it by telling Him that He is "comely" too.

OF THE SPLENDOURS OF THE WORD

Or we may surely take the twofold phrase of the two Substances in Christ, the one His by nature, the other His by grace. How fair art Thou, Lord Jesus, to Thine angels in Thy Form of God, in Thine eternity, amid the splendours of the holy ones begotten ere the morning star, the Splendour of the Father, the Image of His Being, the endless Brightness of eternal life! How fair art Thou to me, my Lord, in that Thy glorious estate! But, when Thou emptiedst Thyself, when Thou, the Light Unfailing, didst put off Thy glory, then did Thy kindness shine forth still more clearly, Thy love was still more gloriously displayed, Thy grace blazed brighter yet!

O Star of Jacob, how radiant is Thy rising! How beautiful a Flower art

Thou, from Jesse's Root! O Dayspring from on High, how joyful is the light wherewith Thou visitest my darkness! How marvelous, how wonderful art Thou even to the heavenly powers, in Thy Conception by the Holy Spirit, Thy Birth of Mary Virgin, Thy spotless Life, Thy teaching, Thy miracles, Thy showing forth of holy mysteries! In what a blaze of glory dost Thou rise, O Sun of Righteousness, after Thy setting, from the heart of the earth! How glorious is Thine apparel when at last the heights of heaven receive Thee, King of glory! In face of all these things, how can I otherwise than say, "Lord, who is like unto Thee?"

We may believe, then, that these matters, and others like them which are beyond our present knowledge and experience, were what drew from the Bride her twofold cry, "Lo, Thou art fair, my Belovéd, and comely!" and that the repetition denoted His beauty in each of His two Natures. And now, dancing for joy at the sight of Him and the hearing of His words, she sings to Him a marriage-song,

"Our bed is decked with flowers,
   the rafters of our houses are
    of cedar,
   the panels of the ceiling are
    of fir."

Chapter Eighteen

"Our bed is strewn with flowers. The rafters of our houses are of cedar, the panels of the ceilings are of fir"

SHE SINGS A MARRIAGE-SONG, describing gracefully the bridal couch and quarters, by way of invitation to her Spouse to come and rest therein. For it is better for the Bride to rest and be with Christ; she goes forth only for the sake of saving souls. Now, therefore, thinking that the time is opportune and yearning with intolerable love, she tells Him that their chamber is prepared and, pointing to the couch, begs Him to rest, as once the two disciples at Emmaus begged, "Abide with us, O Lord!"

Let us consider now the meaning of these things. They all have reference to the Church; and I should say the bed, where rest is taken, denoted the Religious Houses, where people live a quiet life, unvexed by worldly cares. That bed is "strewn with flowers," because the brethren's way of life reflects the brightness and exudes the fragrance of the examples and instructions given by the Fathers. The "houses," on the other hand, will be the Christian congregations; and the "rafters" the Christian princes of both orders, who hold them all together by their righteous laws, as beams retain the walls. And the "panels," which are fixed to the beams and decorate so nobly the houses of the great, I take to be the gentle and good lives of a well-ordered clergy, and their faithful discharge of their official duties.

There is doubtless something relevant to this interpretation in the fact that the rafters are said to be of cedar wood and the panels of fir. The lofty cedar, with its imperishable, fragrant wood, aptly denotes the qualities required in those who are the rafters of the Church; for those set over others need to be strong and steadfast, with eyes uplifted to the things above, and their faith and life diffusing the sweet savour of Christ. The fir also is a fragrant wood that never rots; and that declares with equal fitness the character that should be borne by everyone in Holy Orders, that he may worthily adorn the House of God.

This brief verse gives you a comprehensive picture of the Church in all its parts—the authority of the prelates, the reverend estate of the clergy, the orderly living of the Christian people, and the quiet of the monks. When each of these is as it should be, holy Mother Church rejoices at the sight of them, and presents them for her Belovéd also to behold; for she refers all to His goodness, Who is the Author of all, and takes no credit to herself at all. Her saying *our* bed" and *our* houses" is a sign of love, not of possessiveness.

OF THE ACTIVE LIFE UNDER OBEDIENCE AS THE MEANS TO CONTEMPLATION

Do some of you, who hear or read these utterances of the Spirit, think they apply to you? Do you, perhaps, desire the repose of contemplation, like the Bride? You do well, if it is so. But you must not forget the flowers with which she strews her bed. You must take care that yours is likewise strewn with flowers of good works; for the practice of the virtues must precede that holy rest, as surely as the flower precedes the fruit. It would be a complete inversion of the proper order to ask for the reward before you had earned it, and to seize your dinner before you had done your work! So do not imagine that your love of quiet and repose may be allowed to interfere with the activities obedience lays on you, or with your observance of Community traditions.

The Bridegroom will certainly not share with you a couch strewn, not with flowers of obedience but with hemlock and nettles of disobedience! He will not heed your prayers when it is thus with you, nor come when He is called: He, Who so loved obedience that He preferred to die rather than disobey, will most assuredly refuse His blessings to a disobedient man. Nor will the empty idleness that you call contemplation find favour in the sight of Him Who, as an exile from His heavenly fatherland of perfect rest, wrought in the midst of earth the work of our salvation.

OF THE NEED FOR PURIFICATION

I am even afraid lest that fearful judgment should be pronounced on some of you, which once He thundered at the faithless Jews, "Your new moons and your sabbaths I cannot abide!" For some of you have so upset us all by your self-choosing ways, so angered us by your intolerance and set us all at nought by your rebelliousness, that the bed whereon you have the effrontery to ask the Lord of purity to rest, so far from being strewn with flowers, is defiled with filth! The centurion prayed the Lord not to come under his roof, because he was not worthy to receive Him; the prince of the apostles cried, "Depart from me, O Lord, for I am a sinful man!"—and do *you* say, "Come to me, Lord, for I am holy," with your soul reeking as it is with sin?

You say, What would I have you do? First, I would have you cleanse your conscience from all the anger, argumentativeness, grumbling, and jealousy that now defile it—from everything, in short, that is opposed to peace among the brethren and obedience to your elders. Then I would have you devote yourself to good works and praiseworthy pursuits. You will call safely on your Spouse when you have done all that; you too can say to Him, "Our bed is strewn with flowers."

So much, then, for the bed. As to the house, I think that everyone who walks according to the Spirit should look upon himself as a spiritual house of God, according to the words of the apostle, "The temple of God is holy; which temple ye are." You must take heed, therefore, to this building, which is your own self, using such sound, enduring beams for it as the fear of the Lord, patience, longsuffering, and especially charity, of which this Song says that it is "strong as death." And for the panelling between the rafters you may, if you have got them, use such precious woods as wisdom, knowledge, prophecy, the gift of healing, interpretation of the Scriptures and such like, which are recognized as being useful for adornment, though not essential to our soul's salvation.

A FINAL WORD OF ADVICE

About this I have no precept to give you, only this advice: These timbers are obviously scarce and difficult to come by; you should therefore not seek for them too eagerly, but should be satisfied with humbler woods for panelling your ceilings. A roof skilfully panelled with plenty of such timbers as peace, goodness, gentleness, joy in the Holy Ghost, showing mercy with cheerfulness, giving with simplicity, and a ready sympathy with others' weal and woe, all of which grow so freely in the Bridegroom's garden, is surely beautiful enough for anyone!

Chapter Nineteen

"I am the Flower of the Field and the Lily of the Valleys"

I AM THE FLOWER of the field," He says, referring, so it seems to me, to the Bride's saying that their couch was strewn with flowers, and so reminding her that that of which she boasts derives from Him.

OF THE THREE PLACES WHERE FLOWERS ARE FOUND

Notice, first of all, that flowers are mentioned in three situations—the field, the garden and the couch or chamber; so that you may understand presently why He chooses to describe Himself as the Flower of the Field. In fields and gardens flowers grow; in chambers they do not. To get them thither, they must be picked and carried; and, though they show their beauty and exhale their sweetness there, they must be put in water and frequently renewed. So if the couch strewn with flowers denotes the soul full of good works, it follows from this extension of the metaphor that fresh good works must constantly be done.

In the garden and the field, as we have said, the flowers grow; but with this difference, that the garden requires cultivation and the field, the meadow-land, produces flowers of its own accord, without the help of man. Now do you see what that Field is, unploughed, unhoed, unfed, unsown by man, yet lovely with that noble Flower, on which assuredly God's Spirit rests? The Bridegroom could not fitly have described Himself as the Flower of the Chamber, because He is a Flower that never fades. Nor could He call Himself the Flower of the Garden, lest it should seem He was engendered by the will of man. But He can rightly call Himself the Flower of the Field, for He sprang up without the aid of human industry; and, having sprung up, He can never wither, for God will not allow His Holy One to see corruption, as the psalmist says.

THE MEANING OF THE THREE FLOWERS

There is another explanation of this passage, which is worth considering. We may understand the flower of the garden as Virginity, the flower of the field as Martyrdom, and the flower of the bridal couch as Good Works, as I have said before. Virginity, related as it is to modesty, shunning publicity, rejoicing in seclusion, docile and biddable, is fitly called the flower of the garden, for in a garden flowers are enclosed. Indeed, the Bride is likened to a garden such as this a little further on. Martyrdom, again, is fitly called the flower of the plain, since martyrs are exposed to the mockery of all, and made a spectacle for angels and for men: theirs is the pitiable state of which the psalmist speaks, "We are become a reproach to our neighbours, a scorn and derision unto them that are round about us."

Good actions are similarly well described as flowers of the chamber or the couch, because they make the conscience easy and at rest. Moreover, contemplation is embarked upon more safely, when some good action has been done; and a man will set out with confidence to search the things of God, in proportion as he knows that he has not allowed his love of rest to hinder him from any act of love.

THESE THREE FLOWERS
REPRESENT OUR LORD

This passage is patent also of a meaning, by which all the flowers represent our Lord. Being Himself a virgin *(virgo)*, and a shoot *(virga)*, and virgin-born, He is the Flower of the Garden. Being Himself a Martyr, led forth to die outside the city walls, uplifted on the cross, gazed at and mocked of men; being Himself the martrys' Crown and their Exemplar too, He is the Flower of the Field. Again, He is the Flower of the Chamber or the Couch, in that He is the mirror and the pattern of good action, as He says Himself, "Many good works have I shown you from My Father."

But (we may ask) if each of these three flowers represents the Lord, why did He choose to call Himself the Flower of the Field? He did so, doubtless, that He might inspire the Church to bear the persecution, which He knew must come upon her, to show her in what respect He most desired that she should follow in His steps,

and to urge her on to labour in spite of her desire for rest.

OF THE LILY OF THE VALLEYS

"I am the Flower of the Field and the Lily of the Valleys." She points to the couch, He calls her to the field; that is, He summons her to enter on the struggle, setting Himself before her as her Pattern and Reward. "I am the Flower of the Field," He says, "let him who loves Me come into the field, let him not shrink to enter on the fight with Me and for My sake." He adds, "I am the Lily of the Valleys"—that is, the Crown of the humble. For the time is coming when "every valley shall be filled up and every mountain and hill shall be brought low," and then the Splendour of the life eternal, the Lily not of the hills but of the Valleys, will be made manifest.

"The righteous shall grow as the lily," says the prophet, and who is righteous, if he be not humble? The Lord Himself showed that He regarded humility as the perfection of righteousness, when He bowed His Head beneath the hands of His servant John the Baptist, saying, "Suffer it now, for thus it becometh us to fulfil all righteousness." The righteous man is humble; he is a lily of the valleys too. We also, if we are found humble, shall grow as the lily and flower before the Lord to all eternity. Will He not then finally prove Himself to be the Lily of the Valleys, when He shall re-fashion the body of our humility, making it like the body of His glory? The apostle's saying, not "our body," but "the body of our humility" shows that it is only the humble who will thus be glorified.

POSTSCRIPT ON THE RECITATION OF THE DIVINE OFFICE

I should like to go straight on now to consider what the Bridegroom says about His most dear Bride; but the hour forbids it. For, according to our Rule, nothing is to be put before the Work of God. That (the Work of God) was the name by which our father Benedict desired that we should call the solemn praises which are rendered to God daily in the oratory; which fact shows clearly how greatly he desired that we should give ourselves to the performance of that Work with our whole hearts. I exhort you, therefore, beloved, to apply yourselves to the Divine praises with *complete attention*, and with *energy*. When I say energy, I mean that you should wait upon the Lord with zest as well as reverence; you should not be lazy and drowsy, yawning and sparing your voices, lopping your words off short in the middle or leaving whole words out; you must not sing through your noses, in a soft, feeble, womanish voice, but must pronounce the utterances of the Holy Spirit with the manly voice and disposition that their dignity requires.

ADVICE FOR WORSHIPERS

And when I say that you should recite your Office with complete attention, I mean that, while you chant, you should think of nothing except what you are chanting. It is not only empty, idle thoughts that I am bidding you avoid; at that time and in that place, you should repress also all thoughts about the work which some of you are given for the common good, though at other times such thoughts must often occupy your minds. I would even advise you not to take with you, when you go to choir, the thoughts which were suggested to you by the books you were reading in the cloister just before, or those which you may get from hearing me discourse, here in this place of listening to the Holy Spirit. They are profitable thoughts; but they will be of small profit to you, if you turn them over while you sing the psalms! For the Holy Spirit does not like you to bring forward at that time something other than your duty, which makes you neglect the thing that it is your duty to do.

Chapter Twenty

"As the lily among the thorns, so is My love among the daughters. As the apple-tree among the trees of the wood, so is my Belovéd among the sons. I sat down under the shadow of Him for Whom I had longed, and His fruit was sweet to my taste"

THE MEANING OF THE LILY AMONG THORNS

DAUGHTERS WHO PRICK like thorns are not good daughters. But the earth has borne an accurséd stock of plants since it was said to Adam, "Thorns and thistles shall it bring forth to thee"; and, as long as the soul remains in the body, its life is lived in a thicket of thorns and it must endure the sharp discomforts of trouble and temptation. So, if the Bride is a lily, as the Bridegroom says, she has need to watch carefully against the thorns around her; for the tender substance of a flower cannot sustain the slightest puncture without injury. That is why the psalmist exhorts us to serve the Lord with fear, and the apostle bids us work out our own salvation with fear and trembling. They knew from their own experience that the friends of the Bridegroom are indeed as lilies among thorns.

OF THE UNIVERSITY OF THORNS

Yet it is well for us to have been wounded by the thorns, if the pain bring us to repentance; and many do correct their fault when they experience its penalty. The fault itself, the penalty thereof, a treacherous brother and a hostile neighbour, all of these are thorns. Indeed the world is full of thorns: They are on the earth, and in the air, and in our own flesh. No one can live entirely unscathed among all these in his own strength; only the power of God can keep him safe. But "be of good cheer," says the Lord, "for I have overcome the world." Do not be frightened at the troubles that you see ahead, for "tribulation worketh patience" and "the Lord preserveth all them that love Him."

To live godly among the ungodly, to maintain innocence and gentleness in face of jealousy and spite is no small proof of virtue; and it is a still greater one persistently to seek peace among those who oppose it, and to behave as a friend to those who act towards you as your enemies. Indeed, this last constitutes a special likeness to the lily, whose beauty sheds a lustre on the very thorns that pierce it. For is not such conduct a fulfilment of the perfection counselled in the Gospel, that we should pray for those that despitefully use us and do good to them that hate us? Do you likewise; and then the Lord will say to you also, "As the lily among the thorns, so is My love among the daughters."

THE MEANING OF THE APPLE-TREE, ITS SHADOW, AND ITS FRUIT

The Bride, having received the Bridegroom's commendation, praises

Him in return; and, as He compared her to a lovely flower, she now compares Him to a beautiful tree. Yet it seems to me that the apple-tree is inadequate as a simile here, for there are other trees much more outstanding. And it appears that the Bride herself did not think so very highly of it; for she contrasts it only with the wild trees of the wood, which do not bear fruit fit for human food.

Why, then, are better, nobler trees omitted and this insignificant one adduced to tell the Bridegroom's praise? Should He, to Whom the Spirit was not given by measure, receive such measured praise? For to compare Him Who has no equal with the apple-tree sounds as though there might be somebody superior to Him! The answer is, I think, that small praise is given, because it is His smallness, not His greatness, that is praised. It is not as the great Lord, highly to be praised, that He is spoken of, but as the small Lord, greatly to be loved, the "little Child" Who, as the prophet says, "is born to us."

OF OUR LORD'S HUMILITY

It is, therefore, His humility, and not His majesty, that is here extolled; and it is right and reasonable that this should be so; for the weakness and foolishness of God are better than the wisdom and the strength of men. Men are indeed like the woodland trees that bear no fruit; for, as the prophet says, "they are become unprofitable altogether." Among them all, only the Lord Jesus is, as Man, a fruitful Tree. He is preferred before all men, yet made a little lower than the angels; for, by a marvellous mystery, in His

Incarnation He at once put Himself into a lower state than theirs and kept His domination over them. So the Bride finds Him sweetest when He thus renders Himself weak and little; she extols His grace and mercy all the more, and marvels at His condescension. She would rather gaze in wonder at Him as Man among men, than as God amid the angel hosts; she loves most to behold Him as the apple-tree that surpasses all the wild trees of the woodland, but is inferior to other cultivated trees.

OF THE TREE OF LIFE

"As the apple-tree among the trees of the wood, so is my Belovéd among the sons." It is well said, "among the sons"; for the Only Begotten of the Father, knowing no jealousy, had made it His business to provide Him with many sons; and He is not ashamed to call these sons His brethren, so that He Himself may be the Firstborn among many. But He Who is the Son by nature of course takes precedence of the adopted sons, the sons by grace. The figure of the apple-tree, which gives both grateful shade and pleasant food, befits Him too; for He, and He alone, is verily the Tree of Life to them that lay hold upon Him; He only is the Living Bread that came down from heaven and gives life to the world.

RESTING IN HIS SHADOW

The Bride, therefore, goes on to say, "I sat down under the shadow of Him for Whom I had longed, and His fruit was sweet to my taste." She did well to long thus for His shadow, seeing she was to find it in both shade and food at once. His shadow is His Flesh, in one sense; in another, it is faith. It was the Flesh of Him, her Son, that overshadowed Mary; it is my faith in Him that overshadows me, although I too am overshadowed by His Flesh, in that I eat It in a mystery. And we must needs come to the shadow first, so as to pass on from it to that which casts it; as the prophet says, "If ye have not believed, ye will not understand."

Another prophet says, "Under His shadow we shall live"; but the Bride says, "I sat down." To sit down is to rest; and it is more to rest in His shadow than to live in it, just as it is more to live in it than merely to be in it. The prophet speaks of an experience shared by many—"*we* shall live"; but the Bride, in saying "*I* sat down,"

is glorying in a privilege bestowed on her alone. For while we live laboriously, serving God with fear because of our offences, she, loving and devoted, takes her sweet repose.

So the next thing she tells us is, "His fruit was sweet to my taste," meaning the experience of contemplation which she attained in this sweet state of loving exaltation. That, even that, is "in the shadow," in a glass and darkly. But a time is coming when the shadows will wane before the waxing light of day, until they vanish altogether; and, in their place, a vision shall steal in, as clear as it is lasting, a vision bringing not just sweetness to the palate, but full, unwearying satisfaction to the inmost man.

Chapter Twenty-One

"The King led me into the wine-cellar. He set in order charity within me"

THE SWEET, FAMILIAR converse between the Bridegroom and the Bride is over. He leaves her; and the maidens, to whom she now returns, marvel to see her uplifted and refreshed, as though with wine, and wonder what has happened. She tells them in these words, "The King led me into the wine-cellar. He set in order charity within me." She is inebriated, she explains, with love.

I will not repeat what I have already said about the wine-cellar in an earlier discourse. I would have you notice now how the Bride's words fit the Church on the Day of Pentecost. The people thought that the disciples must be drunk; but Peter, the friend of the Bridegroom, answered on the Bride's behalf that they were not drunk with wine, as was supposed, but were inebriated by the Holy Spirit, in fulfilment of Joel's prophecy, "'In the last days,' saith God, 'I will pour out My Spirit upon all flesh!'"

ALL ARE WELCOME IN THE WINE-CELLAR

Each of those disciples could have said with truth, "The King has led me into the wine-cellar." And I am confident that you too, if you persevere in faithful, humble prayer, will receive that for which you ask. The door will certainly be opened to you, if you go on knocking; and you will not be sent away empty. And, when you return to us from this experience, full of grace and love, unable in the fervour of your spirit to conceal the grace you have received, you will unselfishly impart the same to us, and we shall give joyful thanks for the grace that has been given to you.

Moreover, you yourself will then be able truthfully to say, "The King led me into the wine-cellar"; only you must be careful to glory only in the Lord, not in yourself. I am not saying that every spiritual gift comes from the wine-cellar. The Bridegroom, as I said before, has other store-houses than this, and gives therefrom to each man as He will. But if it should be given to anyone to go forth from himself in prayer and enter into something of God's hidden mysteries; and if, when presently he comes back to himself, he is on fire with the love of God, aflame with zeal for righteousness, and eager to fulfil his spiritual duties, such an one may say with truth that the King has led him into the wine-cellar.

OF THE ORDERING OF CHARITY, WHICH IS DISCRETION

The Bride goes on to say, "He set in order charity within me." This was absolutely necessary; for zeal without knowledge is unbearable. The more assiduous the effort, the greater is the need for discretion; and discretion is the regulation, the setting in order of love. Zeal without knowledge is always less useful and effective than regulated zeal, and very often it is highly dangerous. The more fervent the zeal, the more eager the disposition, the more profuse the love, so much the more essential is it that a watchful knowledge should control the zeal, refrain the natural eagerness and regulate the love. Discretion is the virtue that keeps the rest in order; it ensures both their fitness in given circumstances and their permanence. In fact, it is not so much a virtue in itself, as the helmsman, the charioteer of the virtues, the controller of the affections and the instructor in all the ways of life. Without Discretion, virtue becomes vice and the natural impulses serve only to upset and wreck the personality.

"He set in order charity within me." That is what happened when, within the Church, "He gave some to be apostles, and some prophets, and some evangelists, and some pastors and teachers, for the perfecting of the saints." But a single love must bind all these together and weld them into the unity of the Body of Christ; and that it obviously cannot do, if it is not in an ordered state itself. For if everybody follows his own impulses and inclinations, and does just what he likes, without regard to reason, so that no one is content with what he has been given to do, but everybody interferes with everybody else's work, confusion, not unity, will certainly result.

DOING THE WORK GOD HAS GIVEN YOU TO DO

"He set in order charity within me." O that the Lord Jesus would set in or-

der in me too such little charity as I possess, in such a way that I might make all His concerns my own, while diligently caring for my own office first! I should of course be plainly wrong if I preferred some other task to that, even though charity appeared to be my motive in so doing. But, equally of course, my charity is not yet wholly ordered if, having done my special work as well as I am able, I do not joyfully behold the greater services that others do for God. My charity will be perfectly in order, only if I put my own work first and, at the same time, appreciate another's work still more. Then and then only will there be nothing to prevent my saying, "He has set in order charity in me."

The sighs I hear and the downcast faces in front of me show that you are well aware of the difficulty of rejoicing more in someone else's great achievement than in one's own small one! That being so, you can appreciate the excellence of the grace which the Bride has received, and will understand that it is not given to everyone to make these words his own.

ON ADVANCING IN THE CHRISTIAN LIFE

When we look into our hearts, we realize our imperfection, and how rare a thing it is for anyone not to be envious of another's good, but rather to rejoice in it, and to praise him the more generously in proportion as one feels oneself surpassed. There is some light in us, brethren, when we feel like that. Let us walk while we have the light, lest darkness come upon us. To walk is to go forward, to advance. The apostle was advancing when he said, "I count not myself to have apprehended," and added, "this one thing I do: forgetting those things that are behind and reaching forth unto those that are before, I press towards the mark."

That "one thing," that ceaseless pressing forward, is at once a remedy, a hope, and a consolation; the danger is lest we should be overtaken by the darkness of death, when we are not advancing but are sitting still. But those whom death finds going forward will be perfected in respect of all that now they lack. They will be put into shape; not one of them will be left in his deformity.

But, you say, how can I advance when I *am* envious of my brother's progress? If you grieve for the envy you feel, though you feel it, you do not consent to it. It is a sickness to be cured, rather than a deed to be condemned. What you must not do is to give into it, meditating evil designs upon your bed, hugging your sickness, as it were, and fostering the disease by venting your jealousy in action. If you keep clear of this, if you are spiritually on the move and reaching after better things, your envy will not hurt your soul; for it will be not you that does the wrong but sin that dwelleth in you.

There is no condemnation for him who yields not his members as instruments of iniquity, who gives not his tongue to detraction, nor any part of himself to do any hurt or harm whatever; but, on the contrary, is ashamed of his evil feelings and tries hard to eradicate the ingrained vice by confessing and bewailing it in prayer, becoming moreover all the gentler towards others and humbler about himself, if he fails to do so. Who, with

any sense, would condemn a man who has thus learnt from the Lord to be "meek and lowly in heart"? God forbid that any imitator of the Saviour, the Bridegroom of the Church, our Lord Jesus Christ, should come short of salvation!

OF THE TWO KINDS OF CHARITY, AND HOW THEY ARE COMBINED

There is charity in action, and there is charity in feeling. I think the law concerning charity, which had been given to men, has reference to the former, for who could keep it, if feelings were meant? It is charity in action that is commanded; charity in feeling is given as its reward. We do not deny that, by the grace of God, we can begin to have charity in feeling, even in this life, and may even make some progress in it; but we are positive that its perfection belongs only to our future bliss.

Why, then, is it commanded, if we cannot have it? But, if you insist that the commandment must refer to charity in feeling, I will not dispute it, provided you agree that nobody is or ever has been able to fulfil it perfectly. For who would dare to say that he achieved what Paul himself confessed that he had failed to do? And He Who gave the commandment did not conceal the fact that its fulfilment was beyond the powers of men. He saw fit thus to make them realize their own insufficiency, so that they might know the precise goal of righteousness that they were aiming at. And so, by commanding the impossible, He made them not trangressors of the Law, but humble, "that every mouth may be stopped and the whole world made answerable to God, because by the works of the Law no flesh shall be accounted righteous in His sight."

OF CHARITY IN ACTION

That is what I would say about it, if we were all agreed that the commandment refers to charity in feeling. But what makes me think that it refers to charity in action is, that when the Lord had said, "Love your enemies," He at once added the practical injunction, "Do good to them that hate you." It is written also in another place, "If thine enemy hunger, feed him; if he be thirsty, give him to drink." And the Lord Himself said, "If ye love Me, keep My commandments''; and again, "Whatsoever ye would that men should do unto you, that do ye unto them." All these are practical commands.

OF THREE KINDS OF AFFECTION

And yet I do not say that we ought to be without affection, doing things with our hands only, out of a withered heart. The apostle reckons lack of affection among man's most serious offences. But there is one kind of affection which is begotten by the flesh, another which is ruled by reason and a third which is seasoned by wisdom. The first, as the apostle says, neither is nor can be subject to the law of God; the second, on the other hand, accords with it, for it is good. These two are obviously opposites; but the third is quite distinct from both of them, for it is the affection which tastes and knows how gracious the Lord is; this third kind banishes the first and rewards the second. For the first is sweet but shameful; the second is jejune but strong; the last alone is rich as well as sweet. It is, then, by the second that good works are done, and in it charity consists—not indeed the affective charity which is seasoned with wisdom and fills the mind with Divine sweetness, but the practical sort which kindles in the soul the love of that other love, though it cannot afford the same refreshment of itself.

"Let us not love in word, neither in tongue, but in deed and in truth"— that is to say, let it be the living truth that impels us to good works, and not our emotions. "He set in order charity within me." Which kind of charity? Both, but in opposite ways. For active charity is concerned with the lower things of life, affective with the higher. For instance, a well-disposed person will put the love of God before the love of man; he will prefer heaven to earth, eternity to time, and soul to body. But, where his actions are concerned, he will nearly always put things the other way about; for he will be much more often occupied with caring for the temporal needs of his neighbour, and will find himself obliged to labour more for the peace of earth than for the glory of heaven.

Our Lord's words, "The last shall be first, and the first last," apply here in a sense. A man, when he is praying, speaks to God; yet how often does charity itself tear us away from prayer, because somebody needs our help or our advice? How often does a godly motive require us to exchange godly quiet for the tumult of affairs? How often do we lay down our book with a good conscience, to go and sweat at manual work? How often, even, do we quite rightly omit to celebrate Mass, that we may see to temporal affairs? It is an inversion of the proper order; but necessity knows no law. Active charity follows its own order, "beginning with the last," as the Master of the household bade.

OF CHARITY IN FEELING

With affective charity, however, it is otherwise; that puts first things first. For wisdom assesses everything at its true value; and it is truth that determines the order followed by affective charity. If, then, you love God with all your heart and soul and strength, outpassing in your greater fervour that mere love of love which was enough for active charity, and are set all on fire with the Divine love that you receive, you certainly have such knowledge of God as you are able for. And you also have knowledge of yourself, when you realize that you have nothing in yourself that merits love, except what comes from God.

Your neighbour, whom it is your duty to love as you love yourself, is a man, as you are; if, then, you know yourself, you will know him too. So, if you love yourself only because you love God, you will love as you love yourself all others who love Him. Further, though you, who love God, cannot love an enemy "as yourself," because he who loves not God is nothing, you can nevertheless love him with the intent that he may learn to love.

OF THE MAN WHO LOVES
GOD SUPREMELY

Give me, then, a man who loves God before all things, and with his whole being, who loves himself and his neighbors in proportion as he and they respectively love God, and his enemies as those who may love Him some day; who loves his kindred truly, his spiritual teachers even more; who looks away from earth to heaven, and uses this world without abusing it, employing transitory means for transitory ends but yearning ceaselessly for things eternal—give me, I say, a man like this, who sees things as they really are; and without hesitation I will say that God has set in order charity in him.

Chapter Twenty-Two

"Stay me with flowers, encompass me with fruit, for I languish with love. His left Hand is under my head, and His right Hand will embrace me"

OF FAITH AND WORKS

STAY ME WITH FLOWERS, encompass me with fruit; for I languish with love." The Bride's love has grown since she rested in the Bridegroom's shade, ate of His fruit and drank out of His cup. While she was in the wine-cellar, her thirst was satisfied; but, now that He has gone, she thirsts again. She feels His absence the more keenly, from having so delighted in His presence; for losing what you love makes you desire it still more, and the more you long for it, the more you miss it. So the Bride asks now that she may be comforted with fragrant flowers and fruit, till He returns.

ON THE MEANING OF FLOWERS AND FRUIT

If we take it that these words are spoken by the Church, the flowers and fruit will be the faithful in every age, our own included—the flowers standing for beginners in the way, the fruit for mature souls. Surrounded by these, our pilgrim Mother, to whom to live is Christ, to die is gain, is better able to sustain the trials of delay, as Scripture says, "Give her of the fruit of her hands, and let her own works praise her in the gates." If, however, the words are taken of the soul, according to the moral sense, the flowers denote faith and the fruit good works; and fitly so, for, just as flowers always come before the fruit, so must faith always come before good works. For "without faith it is impossible to please God"; and again, "Whatsoever is not of faith is sin."

As, therefore, there is no fruit without a flower first, so is there no good action without faith. Further, "faith without works is dead," just as a flower blooms in vain if it produce no fruit. The soul accustomed to repose finds comfort, therefore, in good works rooted in faith unfeigned, whenever, as so often happens, the light of contemplation is withdrawn. No one enjoys that light for long on end while he is in the body; but the contemplative soul, as often as it falls from that estate, betakes itself to action, as the next best thing and that from which it may most easily return to contemplation.

For Action and Contemplation are very close companions; they live together in one house on equal terms; Martha is Mary's sister. But, though such a soul falls from the light of contemplation, it never lets itself fall into sin or sloth, but maintains itself in the light of good deeds. The Lord Himself has told us that such works are light. "Let your light so shine before men,"

He says, "that they may see your good works."

OF UNSATISFIED DESIRE

"Stay me with flowers, encompass me with fruit; for I languish with love." Love waxes strong when its object is present; when that is removed, it languishes. The languishing, of which the Bride speaks here, is simply the weariness of eager and unsatisfied desire, which she who loves cannot but feel when her Belovéd is not there. However much He hastens, she still thinks He tarries; and that is why she asks that the fruit of good works and the sweet odours of the flowers of faith may be piled around her, that she may rest in them while He delays.

I tell you this out of my own experience. For I assure you, brethren, that I am not sorry to have put the preparation of my sermon before my own repose and ease, if I find afterwards that someone has been helped by it—that an ill-tempered man, for instance, has grown gentle, a proud one humble or a coward brave, or that someone who is gentle, brave, and humble has made further progress in the virtues he already has. I do not regret the interruption to my own quest for contemplative rest at all, when I am compassed with such flowers and fruits of holiness as these. With patience do I let myself be taken from the arms of barren Rachel, if Leah can make the fruits of your advancement to abound! For Charity, which "seeketh not her own," had long since won me to put your advantage before all else that I desire to do. Prayer, reading, writing, meditation, and the rest, I count them all as loss on your account.

OF THANKFULNESS

"His left Hand is under my head, and His right Hand will embrace me." It appears that the Bridegroom has at last returned, to raise His drooping Bride. He could not bear to see His loved one in such sorrow; He could not tarry when she called Him with such great desire. And, as He found her faithful in good works while He was absent from her, He comes back now with greater blessings than He gave before.

Happy the soul that thus reposes in Christ's bosom, and rests between the two Arms of the Word! "His left Hand is under my head, and His right Hand will embrace me." She says, not "doth" but "will embrace"; that you may know she is so grateful for the former grace, that she returns thanks for the second before He gives it her.

OF INGRATITUDE

Learn from this not to be slack or slow in giving thanks; learn to thank God for every gift of His, however small. "Consider diligently," says the Scripture, "what is put before thee," so that God may not be defrauded of the thanks you owe Him for any gift of His, however small. Are we not told to "gather up the fragments that remain, that nothing may be lost"—that is to say, not to forget the smallest benefits? For that assuredly *is* lost, which is bestowed on an ingrateful person.

Ingratitude is the soul's enemy; it empties it of merit, scatters its virtues, and deprives it of graces. Like a hot, parching wind, it dries up the wellspring of holiness, the dew of mercy, and the streams of grace. The Bride, therefore, returns thanks for the blessing which she has received from the Bridegroom's left Hand, without waiting for the further grace she looks for from His right.

OF FEAR AND HOPE

In what sense may we understand the left and right Hands of the Word of God? We have the authority of Scripture and the Fathers for the use of analogies in such a matter; and it seems to me that, as the right and left hand are commonly taken to denote respectively things prosperous and things adverse, we may take the Word's left Hand as meaning the threat of punishment, and His right as meaning the promise of the Kingdom. There are times when the fear of punishment weighs heavily upon us; we must say then that His left Hand is resting *on* our head, not under it.

But, when we get beyond this servitude of spirit into a freer, worthier disposition, in which the hope of future recompense has greater influence with us than the fear of punishment, then we may truly say, "His left Hand is under my head." For he who has overcome his servile fear by this better, nobler attitude of hope has by the very worthiness of his desires brought closer to himself the Word's right Hand, which contains all the promises, as the prophet says, "In Thy right Hand are pleasures for evermore." That is why the Bride, in the full confidence of hope, boldly declares, "His right Hand will embrace me."

With that disposition, and in that happy situation, she can appropriate the words, "I will sleep in peace and take my rest." The soul oppressed by servitude of spirit has much fear and little hope; it neither sleeps in peace nor takes its rest, for it is ever hesitating between hope and fear and is perpetually tortured by the latter, because it is the stronger of the two. But if, as it progresses in the life of grace, its fear decreases and its hope grows stronger, charity with all its powers will arise to help it, and will cast fear out of doors. And, thus confirmed in hope, it will sleep in peace and take its rest at last.

Chapter Twenty-Three

"I charge you, O ye daughters of Jerusalem, by the roes and the harts of the plains, that ye stir not up nor awake the belovéd, until she please"

OF CONTEMPLATION'S SLEEP

IT IS TO THE MAIDENS that this prohibition is addressed; and He calls them "daughters of Jerusalem" because, for all their present weakness of purpose and performance, they are attached to the Bride with the hope of advance and of going with her to Jerusalem. He tells them they must not disturb His sleeping spouse, until such time as she herself desires to awake; and in His mighty love and condescension He mounts guard over her Himself, lest she should be roused to attend to their frequent small demands.

OF THE NATURE OF THE BRIDE'S SLEEP

Let us consider the nature of this sleep, which the Bridegroom wills His loved one to enjoy undisturbed. It is not bodily repose, however peaceful; nor yet the sleep of death, that Lazarus slept. Still less is it the sleep of sin, that kills the soul. Rather, it is a sleep instinct with life and ever on the watch, a sleep that enlightens the interior sense, banishes death, and imparts life eternal. It does not lull the spiritual sense into unconsciousness; it lifts it to a higher plane. And yet it is a death, in the same sense in which the apostle said, commending some still living in the flesh, "Ye are dead, and your life is hid with Christ in God."

I am justified, then, in calling the Bride's ecstasy a death; but it is a death that snatches her, not out of life itself but out of its pitfalls, so that she can say, "Our soul is escaped, even as a bird out of the snare of the fowler." We spend our whole life in the midst of snares; but, when the soul is rapt out of itself by the compulsion of some holy thought that lifts it far above its ordinary mode of thinking, they lose their terror. The soul flies free; it is withdrawn. "Surely in vain the net is spread in the sight of any bird!"—who fears to fall into temptation or excess, who is no longer conscious even that he lives? Who will give me such wings, wings as a dove, that I may flee away and be at rest? Would that I might often thus fall dead, and so fall not into the snares of death, ceasing to hear the deadly blandishments of self-indulgence, or feel the promptings of the flesh, the heat of avarice, the provocations to anger and impatience, the pressure of anxieties, and the vexations that my responsibilities entail! May my soul die this death of the righteous, that no deceit may trap it nor wickedness delight it!

OF THE "DEATH" OF THE RIGHTEOUS

It is a good death indeed, that does not take away life but translates it to a better state; that does not kill the body but does uplift the soul. This sort of death, however, is a human death. I long to die (if I may use the term) the death that angels die, the death by which the soul passes beyond awareness of the present and is completely stripped not only of desire for corporeal things but also of all images derived from them, and enters into a pure communion with those who bear the image of Purity Itself.

Such is, in my opinion, that exodus from self, which is generally known as contemplation—at least when it occurs in this degree. For to be freed from the bonds of one's passions while one is yet alive belongs indeed to human excellence; but to be loosed from the toils of material images in one's interior seeing is proper rather to angelic purity. Both are, however, gifts of God; in both the soul goes forth from and transcends itself, though in the latter case it goes much further.

Blesséd is he who can say, "Behold, I got me away far off an abode in the wilderness." If you have mastered the pleasures of the flesh, you have indeed made progress; but you have not gone far. You have not gotten you away far off, until your inward purity is such, that you can wing your flight above the thronging crowd of concepts and appearances based on material things. You are in error, if you think you have already found the place of rest, of light, of peace, of safe, remote retreat. Give me a man, however, who has been to this place, and I will forthwith admit that he has found repose, and has the right to say, "Return, my soul, unto thy rest, for the Lord has blessed thee." This place is truly a solitary

place and the abode of light, "a tabernacle for a shadow in the day-time from the heat, a place of refuge, and a covert from the storm and rain."

OF ROES AND HARTS OF THE PLAINS

This, then, is the retreat to which the Bride has withdrawn, in which she sweetly rests in the Bridegroom's embrace, from which the maidens are forbidden to arouse her, till she please. I think the adjuration "by the roes and by the harts of the plains," with which this prohibition is accompanied, refers to the holy souls who have put off the body, and to the angels, who are with God. The point of the comparison lies partly in the keenness of sight with which these animals are gifted, and partly in their speed; for both the angels and the holy souls rise easily and swiftly to the contemplation of the loftiest truths.

The open plains, moreover, over which they roam, plainly suggest the freedom with which contemplation moves. The Bride is in these blesséd spirits' company; her maidens, therefore, must not disturb their mother without pressing need. Some of you sitting here might well take this to heart. They might at least consider the respect due to those set over them, and reflect that, in disturbing them without due cause, they are incurring the displeasure also of heaven's citizens.

As you know, there is scarcely an hour when people are not dropping in on me, even when those who come are not such as try my patience. Yet I reproach myself for making this complaint, lest some weak soul should hide his needs too long, for fear of troubling me. Such brethren will best spare me, if they spare me not at all; and I shall be more at rest if I know that they are not afraid to come and ask for what they need. I will do everything I can for them; and in them I shall serve my God with charity unfeigned.

Chapter Twenty-Four

"The Voice of my Belovéd! Behold, He cometh leaping upon mountains, overleaping hills! My Belovéd is like a roe or a young hart"

THE BRIDE SEES in her maidens a new reluctance to intrude upon her peace; and in the words "The Voice of my Belovéd!" she declares with joy that it is He Who has restrained them in this way, and guarded her repose. She adds, "Behold, He cometh leaping upon mountains, overleaping hills!" Having heard Him, that is to say, she turns forthwith to see Him. Hearing leads to sight, because faith comes by hearing, and it is faith that purifies the heart and makes it capable of seeing God. The Bride thus follows the order indicated by the psalm, "Hearken, O daughter, and see!" It is observed also by holy Job, where he says to God, "I have heard of Thee by the hearing of the ear; but now mine eye seeth Thee"; and on the Day of Pentecost also hearing preceded sight, as it is written, "Suddenly there came a sound from heaven, as of a rushing mighty wind," and afterwards, "there appeared unto them cloven tongues, like as of fire."

OF MOUNTAINS AND HILLS

Now let me try to explain what are those "mountains and hills," upon and over which the Church rejoiced to see the Bridegroom leaping. She speaks (so I believe) of the time when she saw Him hastening to redeem her, whose beauty He desired; for there is another passage which foretells the Saviour's Coming in a similar way. "He set His tabernacle in the sun," it says. "He coming forth out of His chamber like a bridegroom. He rejoiced as a giant to run His course." It is quite obvious what going and returning are here intended, and it is no less clear whence He went forth and with what intent the circuit was begun and ended. How great a leap was that, from highest heaven to earth! And "in the sun," on earth before the eyes of men, "He set His tabernacle"—that is, the Body which He deigned to take, out of a Virgin's body, for Himself, that He, the Unseen, might be seen in it and that all flesh might see the salvation of our God, made manifest in flesh.

The "mountains and hills" are less easy to interpret; but I think they may be taken in either of two ways. You may say that they signify collectively the heavenly, blesséd spirits, through whose ranks He passed to come to earth and Himself be made "a little lower than the angels." Or you may take only the mountains, upon which He leaps, as meaning the angelic host; and the hills, which He overleaps, as denoting the devil and the fallen angels, whom He passes over because of their pride. He deals, you see, with angels as He deals with us; among the humble He leaps in, the proud He passes over. He hates pride, even in angels. And, when I read this verse, and then look at myself, I find I am infected with the same disease that made Him turn away from Satan, when He vouchsafed the grace of His visitation to angels and to men.

OF THE PENALTY FOR PRIDE

With trembling do I say then to myself, "If He acted thus with an angel, what will He do with me, who am but dust and ashes?" Satan waxed proud in heaven; I have done so on a dunghill. And everybody finds pride more tolerable in the rich than in the poor! What penalty, then, can be in store for me? Yet, truly, I am being punished now; I am stricken with many stripes already. It is not without reason that, for days past, my spirit had been unwontedly languid and heavy. I had been running well; but there was a stone of stumbling in the way. I tripped and fell. Pride has been found in me, and the Lord has turned away in anger from His servant. Hence come the barrenness of soul and the lack of devotion, from which I now suffer. That is why my heart is withered, curdled like milk, dried up like earth without water.

Chanting the psalms has lost its savour for me, I do not want to read, prayer gives me no delight, I cannot meditate. Where are the spiritual exaltation, the mental calm, the peace, the joy in God the Holy Spirit that I used to have? For the same reason I am slothful at manual labour, drowsy at Night Office, easily made angry, obstinate in hatred, unguarded in speech, self-indulgent at table, and lifeless and dull when I preach! Alas, the Lord visits all the mountains on His circuit, but He does not come near me; I am the one hill that He overleaps.

All round me I see people outstanding in their abstinence, their patience, their humility, their gentleness, their piety or mercy, or spending hours in contemplation; and these are mountains which receive the visits of the Bridegroom frequently. But I, who find nothing of this sort in myself at all, am forced to regard myself as one of those mountains of Gilboa, which the Saviour in His wrath and indignation passes over, though He rains down His abundant goodness upon all the rest.

OF THE ANTIDOTE FOR PRIDE

My little children, thinking on these lines takes away pride and disposes us for the reception of grace and the Bridegroom's visitations. I put myself in your place just now, to teach you to do the same thing for yourselves. For I have learnt for a fact that nothing so effectively obtains, retains, and regains grace, as that we should be found always not high-minded before God, but filled with holy fear. "Happy is the man that feareth alway." Fear, when grace smiles upon you. Fear, when it goes away. Fear, when at last it comes to you again. Let these three fears succeed each other in your soul, according to your state. While grace is with you, fear lest you be found unworthy of it. When it departs, fear even more; for He Who gives it says, "Without Me ye can do nothing"; and do not fail to blame its loss upon your pride. And, if grace mercifully be restored to you, fear most of all, lest you should fall again, according to the saying in the Gospel, "Behold thou art made whole. Go thou, and sin no more, lest a worse thing befall thee."

If your heart is filled with this three-fold fear, for grace received and lost and given again, you will be like the waterpot at Cana, filled to the brim, not with two measures but with three; and will deserve Christ's blessing to turn the waters of your fear into the wine of gladness, and that perfect charity should cast fear out of doors.

OF THE ROE OR YOUNG HART

"My Belovéd is like a roe or a young hart," the Bride goes on. It is a fitting simile for Him Whom she described just now as leaping on the mountains; for deer are swift and agile animals, and it is of the Word of God, that "runneth very swiftly," that she speaks. The roebuck is, moreover, a creature noted for the keenness of its sight, and this too fits what went before; for, if the Bridegroom had not the most piercing vision, He could not have distinguished in His rapid course between the mountains upon which He should alight and those He should pass over.

His longing for the Bride does indeed make Him haste to come to her; but, all the same, He moves with circumspection and looks before He leaps. For Christ is just and merciful at once, Saviour and Judge together. Because He is the Lover of mankind, He wills that all men should be saved and come to knowledge of the truth. Because He is the Judge, He knows His own, whom He had chosen from the first. And these two attributes of Mercy and of Judgment are commended to us by the Holy Spirit under

the figure of the roe and the young hart.

There is a further beauty in the fact that the comparison is with a *young* hart—a fawn, that is to say, not with a stag. It recalls the Fathers of whom, according to the flesh, the Bridegroom came, and brings to mind the Saviour's Infancy; for the Child born to us, of Whom the prophet speaks, was like a little fawn. Tremble for fear before the Judge's scrutiny, you who desire the Coming of the Saviour; stand in awe before the roebuck's piercing gaze, and be afraid of Him of Whom the prophet says that He shall search Jerusalem with candles. His keen eyes see everything; nothing can escape Him. He will try the very hearts and reins, and even a man's thoughts are known to Him.

What safety is there in Babylon, if even Jerusalem be so searched out? For I think that by "Jerusalem" in this passage the prophet means the Religious, whose ordered, honourable mode of life is modelled on that of Jerusalem which is above; whereas that of the citizens of Babylon is a disordered wilderness of crime. The sins of the latter are obvious and judged already; they call for punishment, not scrutiny. But mine are different. I look like a monk and seem to belong to Jerusalem; the monastic name and habit cloak my sins, so that they require very subtle investigation—searching with candles, as it were—to bring them to the light.

OF THE SEARCHING GAZE OF GOD

We may well fear that so searching a scrutiny will reveal as sins many things which we look upon as acts of righteousness. But "if we shall have used discernment on ourselves, we shall not suffer judgment." It is a good exercise of judgment on myself, that withdraws and hides me from God's Judgment. I am afraid to fall into the Hands of the Living God; I would rather be brought before the presence of His wrath already judged, than meet my judgment there. "The spiritual man discerneth all things, and he himself is judged of no man." I will judge my bad qualities and actions, then, and my good ones also. I will take pains to correct the bad with better, to purge them with tears and punish them with fasts and other acts of holy discipline.

I will hold myself in low esteem regarding my good points, counting myself, according to the Lord's command, as an unprofitable servant who has done no more than he was bound to do. I will try not to offer Him tares instead of wheat, or chaff mixed with the grain. I will search out my ways and my pursuits, that He Who comes to search Jerusalem with candles may find in me nothing unsifted or unsearched. For He will not pass a second judgment on one already judged.

Who will enable me so to get right to the bottom of my faults, that I may have no cause to fear those piercing Eyes nor blush beneath His candlelight? At present I am seen, but I do not see: His unseen Eyes are on me all the time. He knows me wholly, through and through; but I have only partial knowledge of myself. A time is coming, though, when I shall know myself, even as I am known. The Bride, His love, His dove, His fair one, she has nought to fear. But I—I am afraid before the searching gaze of Him Who stands behind a wall, the hidden Searcher out of hidden things.

Chapter Twenty-Five

"Behold, He standeth behind the wall, looking through the windows, looking out from the lattices"

OF THE WORD'S DRAWING NEAR

THE LITERAL MEANING of the Bride's next words would seem to be that He, Whom she described before as hastening towards her, has now approached her dwelling and stands looking in through windows in the wall, restrained by modesty from coming in. The spiritual sense, however, requires another manner of approach, worthy both of the Spouse Who makes it and of the Holy Spirit Who describes it in these words. The "wall" is human flesh; the Bridegroom's drawing near denotes the Incarnation of the Word. The lattices and windows are, I think, the bodily senses and the human feelings, through which He gained experience of our needs. For "He hath borne our griefs and carried our sorrows." He knew all these before, of course, but in a different manner.

The Lord of virtues knew the virtue of obedience; yet, as the apostle says, "He learned obedience by the things that He suffered." In the same manner He learned mercy, although the mercy of the Lord is from everlasting. And the statement that "He was in all points tempted like as we are, yet without sin, that He might be made merciful" teaches the same thing. Do you see how it was that He was made what He already was, and learnt what He

already knew, how He sought out for Himself windows and apertures with us, through which He might obtain more intimate acquaintance with our troubles?

His own experience, as Man, of human weakness and corruption were as so many cracks and fissures in our ruined nature, through which He looked in. And He is well said to be standing as He looks, for He alone *stood* in the flesh Who never sinned in it. He stood, moreover, in the power of His Godhead, even when His Body was broken and laid low upon the cross. And for each of us who desire His coming He still, I think, stands behind the wall, as long, in fact, as our sin-tainted body hides His Face from us; for "while we are in the body, we are absent from the Lord."

But would to God that my sinful body were the only such barrier between me and Him! Would that there were not many more such walls, raised by my own sin!

THE WORD IS EVER NEAR HIS SAINTS

But let me explain more clearly what is meant by speaking of the Bridegroom's drawing near. In His Divine majesty and power, He is indeed equally and indifferently present everywhere. But, in the manifestation of His grace, He is rightly said to be nearer to some of His rational creatures, angels, and men, than He is to others. Salvation is always far from the wicked; but the Lord is near His saints and His chosen ones, even when He seems to be far off. He is not, however, equally near to all of them, but to some more and to others less, according to their merits. For, though He is near to all who call upon Him in truth, and is close to those who are troubled at heart, He is not so near to all such as to enable them to say with the Bride that He stands behind the wall. To her He is near indeed; for only the one wall comes between them. She longs, therefore, that she may be loosed from the body and the wall broken down, so that she may be with Him Who stands behind it.

OF BARRIERS AND OPENINGS BETWEEN THE SOUL AND HIM

I, on the other hand, because I am a sinner, do not desire thus to be dissolved, but dread it, knowing how dreadful is a sinner's death. I am afraid to go forth from the body; I tremble at the very entrance of the harbour, as long as I lack certainty that He Who is the Life is waiting to receive me as I pass. How can my going out be safe, unless the Lord preserve it? Alas, the evil spirits will waylay me and make a mock of me, unless He stands by to redeem and save!

The soul of Paul was not afraid like this; he (like the Bride) had but one wall to keep him from the sight and the embrace of the Belovéd—namely, the law of sin which he found in his members. That was why he cried,

"Who shall deliver me from the body of this death?" But who resembles Paul? Who has not sometimes consented with his will to sin, and so raised up another wall between himself and God? And, if the will has been translated into action, a third wall has been raised; a fourth, if repetition converts the sin into a habit; a fifth, if habit harden you into contempt.

Take care, then, to resist concupiscence, which is the root of all, with all your strength. For, if your will keeps true, the whole fabric of evil which would otherwise result just disappears; and there is nothing but your body to hinder the Bridegroom's drawing near to you. You will then glory with the Bride and say, "Behold He stands behind the wall!"

OF OPENING THE LATTICES (CONFESSING SIN)

You must take care also that He always finds your windows and lattices—that is, your confessions of sin—open for Him to look through at your inmost soul; for His look spells your progress. I take it that lattices (cancelli) are those narrow windows, under which scribes sit, so that the light may fall upon their work; and I suppose that is why those who draw up charters are called chancellors. And, as there are two kinds of compunction, the one proceeding from sorrow for sin and the other from joy at the Divine gifts, it seems to me that, when I confess my sins, I open as it were the narrow lattice; and when my heart swells with love at the thought of God's mercy and goodness and I ease it by singing His praise, then, I think, I open a much bigger window, through which the Bridegroom looks (if I am not mistaken) with greater willingness, because the sacrifice of praise redounds more to His glory than penitence for sin.

Chapter Twenty-Six

"Lo, my Belovéd saith to me, Arise, make haste, My love, My dove, My fair one, and come. For lo! the winter is past, the rain is over and gone, the flowers have appeared in our land, the time of pruning has come"

OF THE SUCCESSIVE STAGES OF THE BRIDEGROOM'S COMING

LO, MY BELOVÉD SAITH to me——" Notice the stages of the Divine grace and condescension, and with what watchful care the Bride observes them all. He comes, He hastens, He draws near, He is present, He looks at her, and finally He speaks; and she takes note of all. He comes to the Church in the angels, He hastens in the patriarchs, He draws near in the prophets, He is present in the Incarnation, He looks upon her in the miracles, He speaks in the apostles. Or you may say that He comes in His desire to show mercy, hastens in His zeal to help, draws near to her in His Self-humiliation, is present in things present with the present generation, looks on those that are yet for to come, and speaks by teaching and convincing her concerning the Kingdom of God.

Such, therefore, is the Bridegroom's Coming. He brings the blessings and the riches of salvation with Him; and all things that are His are brim full of delights and abound in joyful and health-giving pledges. And she who loves watches all this, and takes it in. Blesséd is she whom the Lord finds watching! He will not pass her over, but will stay and speak to her sweet words of love. For it is as her Belovéd that He speaks, and she is right thus to call Him here, for it is words of love that He will speak to her, not words of blame.

She hears Him speaking now, as a reward for the great devotion and the religious care she showed before. Had He not spoken, but only looked at her, she might have thought His look was such as that He gave to Peter when He "turned and looked" at him. But the sound of His voice fills the Bride's heart with joy; for His words show that it was tender love that lay behind His look.

OF THE TESTIMONIES

The words He speaks are these: "Arise, make haste, My love, My dove, My fair one!" Happy the soul that deserves to hear such words as these! For they refer not only to the Church as a whole, but also to ourselves, her individual members; we are all called to inherit blessings, every one of us, and that is why the psalmist dares say to the Lord, "I have gained possession of Thy testimonies as mine inheritance for ever: for they are my heart's joy." He speaks, I think, of the inheritance by reason of which he claims to be a son of his Heavenly Father. And if a son, then an heir—God's heir and joint-heir with Christ! And he glories in the fact that his inheritance has brought him that great treasure, the testimonies of the Lord. "Testimonies," he says—not "testimony" only; for he exults in many such, "as much as in all riches," as he says elsewhere. And wherein do the riches of salvation, the heart's delights, and the true safety of the soul consist, save in these testimonies, these attestations, which it receives from God?

OF HIS VISITATIONS

Why, then, do we hitherto defraud ourselves of these divine communications, and deprive ourselves of our paternal heritage? Does not the apostle say, "The Spirit itself beareth witness, that we are the sons of God"? But how can you be a son, if you have no inheritance? Our poverty in this respect clearly convicts us of negligence and lack of care; for any one of us, who watches for the Lord Who made him with a pure and perfect heart, seeking to prepare his ways before Him, as the prophet says, will doubtless often be visited by Him; nor will he ever fail to know the time of His visitation, however hiddenly his Lover comes.

The watchful soul will note His Coming from afar in every detail, even as does the Bride. The strong desire that speeds Him on His way, His drawing near, His presence, all these it will perceive; it will observe with bliss His look that falls upon it like a sunbeam through a crack; and, finally, that soul will hear Him call it His love, His dove, His fair one, in tones of love and joy.

OF RIGHTEOUSNESS AND THE BRIDEGROOM'S COMING

I would rather listen to someone more experienced talking about these things, than deal with them myself. But, as such persons usually prefer to keep silence about the things that they have learned in silence, and as my office obliges me to speak, I will do what I can. I shall, however, confine myself to such matters as you can easily verify in your own experience, leaving the profounder ones to those who can understand them.

In the first place, then, if I receive an admonition to righteousness, whether from without from a man, or by the inward prompting of the Holy Spirit, I must consider that salutary counsel as a sign that the Bridegroom is on His way to come to me, and as a warning to prepare myself to receive my heavenly Guest. For it is written that "righteousness shall go before Him." And this will be especially the case if the counsel given be of humility or patience, of brotherly love or of obedience to authority, or—above all—of holiness and peace and purity of heart. For the Scripture says, "Holiness becometh the House of the Lord," and "His place is in peace," and again, "the pure in heart shall see God."

OF THE REPROOF OF A RIGHTEOUS MAN

Further, if in a spirit of mercy a righteous man rebukes me, I must take that in the same way; for it is a happy fall from which a man picks himself up and overcomes his fault, when he has been corrected. The reproof of the righteous should therefore never be despised; for it is the downfall of sin, the health of the heart, and the path of God to the soul. We should indeed neglect no edifying word of any sort; for, if you put distaste away and listen willingly, you may then take it that the Bridegroom is not merely coming but is hastening to you. For we did not first love Him, but "He first loved us." And if the words you hear make your heart burn at the thought of your sins, remember that "a fire goeth before Him," and do not doubt that He is close at hand.

OF THE FIRE THAT CLEANSES

If, however, you are not only moved to compunction by what you hear, but are converted wholly to the Lord, and vow and are determined henceforth to keep His righteous judgments, then you may know that He is present with you. This will especially be so, if you find yourself glowing with love for Him. For Scripture says, not only that a fire goes before Him, but that He *is* a fire. The fire that goes before Him has ardour but not love; it burns but does not melt, it moves but does not cause us to advance. It is sent by God to arouse you and make you realize what you are in yourself, so that you may afterwards taste more sweetly what you are soon to become by the power of God.

But the Fire which God is consumes indeed, but without causing pain; sweet is the burning, blissful devastation that its flames effect. For it is truly a "hot burning coal," but it acts like fire on our faults, only in order that it may act as unction to the soul. Recognize, then, in the power that changes your heart and the love that inflames you the Presence of the Lord.

When every taint and stain of sin and vice has been burnt up, there follows for the soul thus cleansed and calmed a sudden and unwonted broadening of the mind, and an influx of light upon the understanding, which gives it a new insight into the Holy Scriptures or a fresh apprehension of the mysteries. And this experience is undoubtedly His look upon the soul, bringing forth "thy righteousness as the light and thy judgments as the noon-day," according to Isaiah's prophecy, "Then shall thy light break forth as the morning." And yet, however great the purity of heart you may attain, that ray of the Infinite Brightness will not inpour itself through open doors; but, while the body's ruined, tottering wall still stands, only through narrow cracks.

OF THE VOICE OF GOD

After this look of God, so full of condescension and compassion, there comes the voice, that gently intimates His will, and is none other than Love's Self and cannot fail of its effect. Thus the Bride hears that she is to arise and hasten, no doubt to labour for the good of souls. It is a property of true, pure contemplation that it sometimes enkindles the soul with such fervent zeal to win others to love God that it gladly exchanges its rest for the labor of preaching; and then again, when something of this task had been accomplished, it returns to the delights of contemplation, and thence again, with all its former eagerness, to work for souls with even greater power than before. Often, however, it hesitates between the two, fearful lest the very strength of the attraction which it feels for either should distract it even by a hairsbreadth from following God's Will.

It was perhaps something like that which Job meant when he said, "When I lie down, I say, When shall I arise? And again, I will look for the evening." That is to say: when I am at rest, I accuse myself of neglecting my work; and when I am at work, of having disturbed my repose. The only remedy in these uncertainties is prayer, entreating to be shown God's holy Will at every moment, that He may tell us what to do and when and how to do it.

OF PREACHING, PRAYER, AND
CONTEMPLATION

The Bridegroom calls the Bride "My love, My dove, My fair one"; and I think these titles answer to preaching, prayer, and contemplation. For she is fitly called His love, who labours faithfully, by exhorting and counselling and serving others, to bring about the ends that He desires; and fitly also is she called His dove, who does not cease to mourn her sins and to entreat His mercy in her prayer. Fitly, again, does He call her His fair one; for the supernal contemplation, to which she gives herself as often as she may, makes her bright and beautiful with heavenly desire.

Any one soul may gain this threefold good; but I think its three parts are represented by the three close friends who lived together in one house. For Martha served, Lazarus groaned as it were beneath the stone that sealed his tomb, entreating the grace of resurrection; and Mary did nothing but attend to Christ. I said—boldly, perhaps—that any soul as watchful as the Bride would be greeted, consoled, and embraced by the Bridegroom as His love and His dove and His fair one. But who, in fact, achieves it?

And yet, even if after long years we still fail of this as individuals, we have among us Martha, the Saviour's friend, in those who faithfully discharge our temporal affairs; we have Lazarus, the mourning dove, in our novices who, until recently, were dead in sin and still go in fear of judgment till the assurance of Christ's pardon rolls away the stone and they can breathe again. And we have also contemplative Mary in those who, by the help of grace and after a long time, have reached at last that better, happier state in which they meditate with unwearying delight, not on their sins but on the law of God; and sometimes, gazing with open face upon the Bridegroom's glory, they are themselves transformed into the same Image, from brightness unto brightness, as by the Lord the Spirit.

OF THE TASK LAID UPON THE BRIDE

"Arise, make haste, My love, My dove, My fair one, and come." Just now the bridegroom forbade the Bride to be aroused; now He arouses her Himself, and tells her to make haste. And yet He does not go against her will in doing this; for, if the Bride but knows a wish of His, she instantly desires to fulfil it. It is, moreover, no small comfort to her that He says "Come," not "Go"; because she understands from this that she is being led, not merely sent, and He is coming with her. What task can she find difficult, with that Companion? "Set me alongside Thee," she says with Job, "and let any man's hand fight against me!" And again, "Though I walk through the midst of

the shadow of death, I will fear no evil: for Thou art with me."

THE TIME OF PRUNING HAS COME

The Bridegroom rouses her, because the time has come for active work. "The winter, in which nobody can work," He says, "is past; the rain, which hindered cultivation, also has departed; the flowers have appeared on our earth—in brief, the spring is here!" And then He tells her what she must do first. "The time of pruning has come": she must see to the vines.

I have already told you that the vines denote souls or churches. You see here a more perfect soul invited to look after others; and that not by the prompting of its own ambition but by the call of God. Moreover, this same invitation is nothing other than a certain inward urge of holy charity, impelling us to seek our brethren's salvation, and to adorn the Lord's House with the fruits of righteousness, to the praise and glory of His Name. Whenever a person finds himself thus moved, he may be certain that the Bridegroom is Himself present with him, inviting Him to tend His vines.

OF PRUNING, JESUS, AND THE APOSTLES

He says moreover, "The time of pruning has come"; for not every time is suitable for this or any other task. As to the winter, which He says is past, I think it means the time when the Lord Jesus did not walk openly among the Jews, because they sought to kill Him. Was it not winter when Peter sat beside the fire of coals, as frozen in his heart as in his limbs? The Scripture says expressly, "It was cold." But neither he who then denied his Lord nor his brethren, whom he had been forewarned to strengthen, had then received the Spirit. They had not yet been filled with power from on high; they could not yet go safely out to hoe and prune the vines with their inspired preaching, so that they might bear fruit.

And, further, the Lord Himself kept silence in His Passion and, when interrogated, answered not a word. Why? Because it was still winter in the faithless hearts around Him; and winter's muddying rain of evil, harmful doctrine had not ceased to fall. But when these passed, and the dry land appeared and flowers bloomed upon it, showing that pruning time had come at last, when do you think *that* was? When indeed could it be, save when the Flesh of Christ blossomed anew in the Resurrection? For He is the first, the greatest Flower to blossom on our earth; Christ is the Firstfruits of them that are asleep; Jesus of Nazareth (which name itself means "flower") is the Flower of the Field and the Lily of the Valleys.

But this first Flower did not come alone; for many bodies of the saints arose with Him, appearing on our earth as bright and shining flowers. And they were flowers, too, who first believed among the people, the firstfruits of the saints. For after that rain of unbelief of which we spoke had somewhat abated, God Himself sent a gracious rain in His inheritance, and flowers began to appear. The Lord gave His blessing and the earth yielded her increase; so that in one day three thousand souls believed, and in another five. And, as time went on, the tempest ceased, and with the return of peace the vines grew and were propagated and spread and increased beyond number; so that to-day the Bride is invited, not to plant vines but to prune those already under cultivation; and that is a task that can be performed only in time of peace.

OF THE NEED FOR CONSTANT PRUNING

So much for that. But I would point out also that, where your own soul is concerned, it is no good pruning only once; you must do it often—always, if possible. For, if you are honest with youself, there will always be something that needs cutting back; for whatever progress you may make while you are still in the body, you are mistaken if you think your faults are dead, rather than merely repressed.

The Jebusite dwells within your borders, whether you like it or not; he can be subdued but not exterminated. In view of this great danger, I can only advise you to watch yourself most carefully and to cut away all offending growths as soon as they appear. For virtues and vices cannot grow together; if your virtues are to grow, your faults must be prevented from making any development at all.

So it is always pruning time with us, brethren, because there is always need for it. But "the winter is past" for us too; I am sure of that. Do you know what I mean? I mean the winter of fear, which is driven away by the summer of charity. Summer indeed has its showers; but the tears of charity are sweet, because it weeps for love and not for sorrow, it weeps with longing, weeps with them that weep. It is with such a shower that your acts of obedience are bedewed; of that I am convinced. And I observe with joy that you do not befoul them with murmuring or cloud them with sadness, but make a gay and happy thing of them, full of a certain spiritual joy. It is as if your hands were always full of flowers.

Chapter Twenty-Seven

"The voice of the turtle-dove is heard in our land. The fig-tree hath put forth her green figs. The vines in flower yield their fragrant odour"

THE VOICE OF the turtle-dove is heard in our land." This is the second time that He Who is from heaven speaks of earth as courteously and as companionably as though it were indeed our home as much as His. "*Our* land, *our* earth," He says. How kind it is of God to speak like that! Listen, you earthborn sons of men! The Lord hath done great things for us. He has a very close relationship with earth, and with the Bride whom it has pleased Him to take thence for Himself; and that is why, speaking familiarly as Bridegroom, not as Lord, He says "our land."

What? He is Creator, and He speaks as Partner? Yes; for it is Love that speaks, which knows not the word "lord"; and this Song is a song of love, rightly containing only loving words. And it is God Who loves, and is Himself the Source of His own love; which makes His love so much the mightier, in that Himself and it are one. Those whom God loves He reckons as His friends, not as His servants; the Master thus becomes the Friend, and He would not have called His disciples friends, if they were not so in fact.

OF OUR EARTH

Do you see how even majesty gives way to love? It is so, indeed, brethren: love looks up to none and down on none. It regards as equals all those who love each other perfectly, and it harmonizes high and low in its own self, making them not merely equal but actually one. You think perhaps that God is excepted from this rule of love; but "he that is joined to God is one spirit." What is there surprising about this? He has become as one of us—or rather, not *as* one but actually one. For to be made man's equal was not enough for Him: He is a Man. That is the reason why He claims our earth as His, not indeed as His fatherland, but as His possession. Why should He not so claim it? From it He takes His Bride; from it He takes the substance of His Body; from it He takes His status as the Bridegroom; from it the Bride and He are made one flesh. And if they have one flesh, why not one country?

"The heaven of heavens is the Lord's," the psalmist says, "but the earth hath He given to the children of men." It is, then, as Son of Man that He inherits the earth; as Lord that He has it in subjection; as Creator that He governs and directs it; as Bridegroom that He shares it with the Bride. For by calling it so graciously "our earth" He repudiates exclusive ownership, and does not disdain to be allied with others in calling it His own.

OF SIGHING SAINTS

"The voice of the turtle-dove is heard in our land." The voice of this little bird is more of a moan than a song, and thus reminds us that we are but pilgrims on the earth and have here no continuing city. So when a holy soul sighs for the presence of Christ, grieving that the coming of the Kingdom is so long delayed, and hailing from afar its longed-for fatherland with plaints and sighs, do you not think that such a soul is like the turtle-dove, that chaste and mournful bird?

How should Christ's absence move me, if not to tears and plaints? "Lord, all my desire is before Thee, and my groaning is not hid from Thee." Nor am I alone in this; for all those who love His appearing moan along with me, even as He said, "Can the children of the bridechamber mourn while the Bridegroom is with them? But the days will come when the Bridegroom shall be taken away from them; and then shall they mourn." It is as if He said, "Then shall the voice of the turtle-dove be heard."

And so it is, Lord Jesus! Those days have come. For creation itself groaneth and travaileth until now, awaiting the revelation of the sons of men; and not creation only, but also we ourselves, waiting for the adoption of the sons of God (that is, the redemption of our body), for we know that while we are at home in the body, we are absent from the Lord.

But if there are many who groan thus, why is there mention here of only one? "The voice of the turtle-dove," He says—why not "of turtle-doves"? Perhaps the apostle explains this for us, in the place where he says, "The Spirit Himself maketh intercession for us, with groanings that cannot be uttered." And so indeed it is. He, Who inspires us to groan, Himself groans in us. It is His Voice in every mouth; so that, however many lips there be that utter, one sound proceeds from all. For the manifestation of the Spirit is given to every man, that He may profit by it.

A COMMENDATION OF VIRGINITY AND HOLY WIDOWHOOD

The turtle-dove has something else to recommend it, besides its plaintive voice. It is a chaste bird, content with one mate and living in solitary widowhood, if that mate dies; therefore its voice may be regarded as enjoining chastity. In the beginning that injunction was not heard. The command then was rather to "increase and multiply and replenish the earth." And that obtained under the patriarchs as well, for they had many wives; and the Law of Moses also required that a man whose brother had died childless should take the wife himself and give seed to his brother. The injunction to chastity was heard first from the lips of the heavenly Turtle-dove Himself, when He commended those who had renounced their generative powers for the Kingdom of Heaven's sake. And when that other turtle-dove's counsel concerning virginity was everywhere accepted, then at last it could be said with truth that the voice of the turtle-dove had been heard in our land.

The flowers have appeared in our land, and the voice of the turtle-dove has been heard; the Truth, that is to say, has been both seen and heard; and eye and ear corroborate each other's witness. When He was transfigured on the mount, for instance, a Voice from heaven also witnessed to Him; as also at the Jordan the Voice confirmed the token of the dove. And the apostles likewise "went forth and *preached* everywhere, the Lord working with them and confirming the word with *signs* following." Thus God in His bounty makes the voice and the sign to concur in founding the Faith; so that the truth may have an ample ingress to the soul, through these two windows of the ear and eye.

OF THE UNBELIEF OF THE JEWS AND THE FAITH OF THE EARLY CHURCH

"The fig-tree has put forth her green figs." This also is a sign of spring, according to the literal sense. The fig-tree, however, puts forth fruit at the time when other trees flower; but these, which are unfit for eating, fall prematurely and give place to others which ripen properly. As only one fig-tree is mentioned here, I think it means the nation of the Jews which, though sprung from a good root, failed to bear fruit. But "the vines in flower," the Bridegroom goes on, "give forth their fragrant odour," and that betokens fruit to come. (It is said, by the way, that the scent of flowering vines drives away snakes and poisonous reptiles; and I should like our novices to take note of that and act with corresponding confidence, considering what kind of spirit it is which they have received, and of which even the evil spirits cannot endure so much as the first tokens! What will a man's absolute perfection be, if his first fervour as a novice is like that?) But to return to my text: if the fig-tree denotes the Jews, the "vines in flower" will be those who believed the preaching of the new grace of Jesus Christ, who had their conversation honest among the Gentiles and were a sweet odour of Christ in every place. And, if the vines are faithful souls and their flowers are good works, their fruit is martyrdom; for the martyr's blood is truly "the fruit of the vine."

Chapter Twenty-Eight

"Arise, My love, My Bride, and come. O My dove in the clefts of the rock, in the hollows of the wall, show Me thy face and let Me hear thy voice. For sweet is thy voice and thy face is comely"

OF THE RICHES OF GOD'S MERCY IN THE OPEN WOUNDS OF CHRIST

"ARISE, MY LOVE, my bride, and come." This repetition of the Bridegroom's invitation shows the strength of His love. Notice, moreover, that all through this Song He never names her Bride except when calling her to work among the vines—that is, with souls—and drink the wine of love. When at His bidding she has come and has been perfected, she will be spiritually wedded to Him; they two will be not one flesh but one spirit, as the apostle says.

OF THE ROCK

"O My dove in the clefts of the rock, in the hollows of the wall, show Me thy face and let Me hear thy voice." So He goes on wooing and claiming her. The literal meaning does not yield us much; but someone has interpreted "the clefts of the rock" as meaning the Wounds of Christ, and fitly too, for Christ is the Rock. Blesséd are the clefts which proved to Thomas that Christ was risen, and that He was God! In those "the sparrow hath found her an house and the turtle-dove a nest, where she may lay her young"; in these the dove finds safety too, from them she looks forth fearlessly at the hawk that flies around. "He hath exalted me upon a rock," she says; and

again, "He hath set my feet upon a rock."

A wise man builds his house upon a rock, for neither wind nor waves can harm it there. What is there about a rock that is not good? Raised on a rock, safe on a rock, on it I stand firmly; I am safe from the enemy, secure against falling, and all because I am raised up above the earth. For everything belonging to the earth is shifting and unstable; but our Rock is in heaven, and from it all our safety and stability derive.

"The rock is a refuge for the conies," and where indeed are there complete security and rest for us frail men, save in the Saviour's Wounds? The measure of my safety there is as the measure of His power to save. The world rages, the body presses, the devil lies in wait; and yet I do not fall, for I am founded on the stable Rock.

I have perhaps done some great sin; my conscience will be troubled, but not discomposed, for I will remember the Wounds of the Lord, "wounded for our transgressions." What sin is there so "unto death," that Christ's Death does not loose it? If I but keep in mind this potent and effective remedy, no malady however sore can frighten me. For what is wanting in myself I boldly claim out of my Lord's Heart, whence mercy flows, nor does that mercy lack for clefts through which it may flow forth.

They pierced His Hands and His Feet and thrust His Heart with a spear; and through those openings I may suck honey from the rock and oil from the hard stone—that is, I taste and see how gracious the Lord is. He was thinking thoughts of peace, and I knew it not; for who hath known the Mind of the Lord or who hath been His counsellor? But the piercing nail *(clavus)* had been turned for me into a master key *(clavis)*, to show me the Will of the Lord. How should I not see, through that opening?

Both nail and wound proclaim that, of a truth, God was in Christ, reconciling the world unto Himself. The iron entered into His own soul and drew near to His Heart, that He might know our weakness from His own experience. His Body's open Wounds lay bare the secret of His Heart, that mighty mystery of love, the tender mercy of our God whereby the Dayspring from on High hath visited us. Never, O kind and gentle Lord, hast Thou more clearly shown Thine inmost Heart, than through Thy Wounds. For there is no greater proof of pitying mercy possible, than that a man should lay down his own life for those condemned to death.

OF THE "TREASURES OF THY LOVE"

The mercy of the Lord, then, is my merit; and truly I am not devoid of merit while His mercies do not fail. What if my sins are many? "Where sin abounded, grace doth much more abound." And, if the mercies of the Lord are from everlasting unto everlasting, I likewise will sing them everlastingly. Shall I sing my own righteousness? No, Lord. I will make mention only of Thy righteousness. Need I be afraid lest there should not be enough of it to cover both of us? No; for Thine is the everlasting righteousness, and there is nothing longer than eternity. Thy broad and endless righteousness will cover me and Thee alike, cloaking in me a multitude of sins, in Thee what but the treasures of Thy love, the riches of Thy goodness? These are the things that are laid up for me "in the clefts of the rock."

ON THE STRENGTH OF MARTYRS

It is because the Bride is thus devoted to the Wounds of Christ and meditates on them continually, that the Bridegroom calls her "My dove in the clefts of the rock." It is from this devotion that the endurance of the martyrs comes. The martyr does not feel his own wounds, while he looks at the Lord's. With body gashed and torn, he stands exultant and triumphant; for his soul is hidden safely in the Rock—that is, the Wounds of Christ. Left to himself, he could not bear the pain; he would go under and deny his Lord. But, hidden in the Rock, what wonder is it that he endures like rock? It is love that effects this endurance, not lack of sensibility; the senses are not annihilated but controlled. The pain is there, but it is overcome and set at nought.

So from the Rock the martyrs draw their courage, and from the Rock there gushes forth the spring, whence they drink the Cup of the Lord. And how exhilarating, how splendid that Cup is! Splendid I say, and joyful, and that no less for the Captain Who watches the fight than for the soldier who is triumphing; for "our courage is the joy of the Lord." How should He not rejoice to hear the martyr's brave confession? That is just what He asks for when He says, "Let Me hear thy voice." Nor will He delay to repay it according to His promise; He will Himself confess before His Father those who have confessed Him before men.

ON TAKING REFUGE WITH THE
SAINTS AND ANGELS

"O My dove in the clefts of the rock, in the hollows of the wall——" The dove finds safety in the hollows of the wall, as well as in the clefts of the rock; and by the wall we may understand the Communion of Saints, and the hollows therein as the places vacated by the fallen angels, which are to be filled up by men, as ruins are repaired with fresh-cut stones. And we shall not be far out if we regard this wall as standing round the vineyard of the Lord, and signifying therefore the angels' guardianship.

The Church will thus have two things to console her on her pilgrimage—the memory of Christ's Passion in the past, and the prospect of being received among the saints hereafter. Back and forth she looks between the two, with insatiable longing. Each of them is lovely in her eyes; each is a refuge from the troubling of the wicked and from pain. The consolation is complete in either case, for she knows not only what she has to look for but from Whom it must be claimed. She has no doubt regarding one thing or the other, but looks for both joyfully; for all her expectation is founded on Christ's Death.

How gladly she searches out the clefts whence flowed the precious Blood, the Price of our Redemption! How gladly she explores the hollows, the wayside inns and the abidingplaces in the Father's House, in which He puts His children according to their several deserts! For the present, of course, she visits this heavenly habitation only in the spirit. But the time is coming when she will dwell therein in body too, when all those long-deserted hollows will be filled, and she herself in her entirety will make their darkness light. There will be then no hollows in the heavenly wall at all, and no room left for anything but joy in its complete perfection.

There is also a sense in which these hollows are not found but *made* by pious souls, whose ardent thought and longing acts like a chisel on the wall of heaven, and carves out havens for them where they will, among the saints and angels, even now. I am sure that a person who goes on knocking, so to speak, wherever he be guided by the Holy Spirit, will find a place of refuge opened to him by those holy ones, where he may rest among them for a little while. Both face and voice of such a soul will always be acceptable to God—the face, because of its purity, and the voice because of the witness of adoration and thanksgiving which it gives.

OF THE TWO KINDS OF CONTEMPLATION

Happy is the soul which has made a practice of hollowing such caves of refuge for itself; but happier still is the soul which has made its cave in the Rock! For we are permitted to hollow out such hiding-places for ourselves in the Rock, as well as in the wall. But sharper tools are needed for the latter—a greater purity of heart, intenser application and personal holiness such as John had, who plunged himself into the mystery of the Word and from the heart thereof brought forth the holiest wisdom, and Paul who, seeking wisdom, heard in the third heaven, to which he was caught up, things which it is not lawful for a man to utter.

You see, then, that there are two kinds of contemplation—one of the state, the happiness, the glory of the Heavenly City, the other of the majesty, eternity and Godhead of its King; and that the first of these is represented by the wall, the other by the rock. The latter is the harder to dig into, but also the more rewarding in the results it gives. Be not afraid. Bring to the work a pure heart and a single mind, to seek God's glory only, not your own, and you may safely search in the Rock, wherein are hidden the treasures of wisdom and knowledge. If you still hesitate, listen to the Rock's own words, "They that work in Me shall not do amiss." O that I had wings like a dove, that I might flee away and be at rest!

The Church is like a dove in her innocence and her continual plaint of prayer, and therefore she finds rest—rest in the Word Who is the Rock. She looks out from the cleft and sees the glory of her Spouse, but is not overwhelmed by it, because she does not claim it for herself. Moreover, the object of her searching is His will, not His majesty. For though she does venture to contemplate His majesty sometimes, it is only to worship, not to examine it. And if it ever falls to her lot to be snatched out of herself in ecstasy, it is then God Himself Who lifts her to Himself, not she who insolently dares to intrude on Him.

OF SEEKING THE WILL OF GOD

To seek to know the will of God, therefore, is not fraught with danger as is the searching of His majesty, but is a safe and duteous pursuit. How can I do otherwise than try my hardest to find out the glorious will of Him to Whom I owe obedience in all things? That aspect of His glory does not overwhelm me, however much I ponder it; for it is wholly kind and fatherly, the glory truly "as of the Sole-Begotten of the Father." It does not crush me, but it sets its stamp on me; for when we behold His glory openly, we are transformed into the same Image from brightness to brightness, as by the Lord of the Spirit.

We are transformed, when we are conformed; and the conformity of man to the Image of God consists in our alignment with His will, not with His majesty. *My* glory, then, will be if ever He says of me, "I have found a man after Mine own Heart." His Heart is as His Father's—merciful. When He says, "Let Me see thy face," He means that He would have the Church be merciful and gentle as He is, uplifting fearlessly to Him a face resembling His own.

Chapter Twenty-Nine

"Catch us the little foxes that are spoiling the vines, for our vineyard has flowered"

OF THE CARE THAT IS NEEDED FOR THE VINEYARD OF THE SOUL

A WISE MAN regards his life and soul and conscience as a vineyard, and will leave nothing in it uncared for. Not so the fool; you will find everything neglected in his vineyard, the vines all lying flat, and everything disordered and untended. Can you call it a vineyard at all, when it is just a waste of thorns and thistles? It was a vineyard once, but it is not so now; it has gone back to wilderness. The vine of virtue, the grapes of good works, the wine of spiritual joy, where are they all? The fool has let his vineyard go, the vineyard that God planted and perhaps gave him at the font; now it is not a vineyard any more. For the fool, because his life is not directed to any profitable end, is dead while he lives; and where there is no life, there is no vineyard.

It is, then, only of the wise man, who has life, that we can rightly say that he has—or rather is—a vineyard. He is a fruitful tree in the House of the Lord, and therefore a live tree; for the very wisdom whence he is called wise is a tree of life to them that lay hold upon her. His wisdom is indeed his faith; for the wise man is the just, the righteous man, and the just live by faith. And he will always have—or rather be—a vineyard, for he will always have life. He is a good vineyard too, complete with vines and shoots and wine and press. For nothing in his life is wasted; his words and thoughts, his occupations and relationships, are all God's husbandry, God's building; his whole life is the vineyard of the Lord of Hosts.

OF CATCHING THE LITTLE FOXES

Such a vineyard will, however, never lack for pests and hidden dangers; for "when goods increase, they are increased that eat them." The wise man will, therefore, be as careful to protect his vineyard as to cultivate it, and will not allow the foxes to devour it. The worst fox is the backbiter, but the fawning flatterer is almost as bad. The wise man will beware of these. He will do his best to catch them—catch them for God, that is, by kindness and by courteous service, by wholesome counsel and by prayers on their behalf. He will not cease to pour such coals of fire on their heads, till he succeeds, if possible, in drawing out the envy from the slanderer's heart and the insincerity from the flatterer's, and so fulfils the Bridegroom's bidding, "Catch for us the little foxes that are spoiling the vines." Is not a person truly "caught" for God, when he is brought to blush like this for what he has done wrong? If only I could catch like that all who oppose me causelessly, that I might give them back to Christ or win them for Him!

"Catch for us the little foxes that are spoiling the vines." According to the moral sense, the vines—as we have seen—are spiritual men whose inward faculties are cultivated, so that they sprout and bring forth fruit; and it can then be truly said of them that the Kingdom of God is within them. And Paul enumerates the fruit they bear as follows: "The fruit of the Spirit is love, joy, peace, patience, forbearance, goodness, kindness, gentleness, faith, moderation, self-control and chastity." These are the things in which our progress consists; those are the fruits which the Bridegroom accepts. He watches diligently for them to appear, smiles when they do so, and is most anxious that we should not lose them; for that would be His loss as well as ours, so closely does He identify our interests with His own. So when the vine has flowered and the fruit first appears, His foreseeing wisdom bids us catch the little foxes for Him, lest they should ravage the undeveloped grapes.

OF THE TEMPTATIONS
THAT BESET NOVICES

This parable applies to us to-day. You see those novices? They have but lately come, but lately been converted. We cannot say of them that our vine has flowered, for it is flowering now. Their flower is their recently adopted mode of life, the rule for better living that they have just accepted. They have assumed a general look of discipline; they display a well-regulated exterior; and these outward appearances are pleasing, I admit. For they are less concerned about their looks and clothes than they used to be, they talk less, they look more cheerful, their demeanour is more modest and their gait more demure. These recent acquisitions are, however, flowers that give hope of fruit to come, rather than fruits themselves.

It is not the foxes that I fear for you, my children, for foxes damage only fruit and do not hurt the flowers. Your danger is the searing cold, the north wind, and the morning frosts that cut the early blooms and kill the unformed fruit. If once this deadly chill invades the soul, and there is nobody (which God forbid!) at hand to check it, it penetrates right to the very heart, numbs the soul's affections, prevents it from listening to advice, dims the light of its judgment and cramps its liberty of spirit.

It is then with the soul as with the body when suffering from a fever: It gets a shivering fit, its strength is sapped, languour creeps over all the faculties, it dreads austerity, is scared of poverty, the spirit shrinks, grace is withdrawn, life becomes a burden, reason goes out of action, courage is quenched, the novice's first fervour dies away, tepidity and distaste for spiritual things weigh on the soul increasingly, its love for others waxes cold, pleasure fascinates, security deceives it, and the force of old habit calls it back. Need I say more?

The law is evaded, duty is rejected, obligations are disregarded, the fear of the Lord is abandoned. Then comes the final plunge, the most reckless, the most shameful of all, a leap indeed from the height to the pit, from the roof to the gutter, from the sky to the dunghill, from the cloister to the world, from heaven to hell!

OF THE TEMPTATIONS OF MATURER MONKS

We must return now to the vines that have flowered—that is to say, to riper souls, whose danger is from foxes, not from frost. We must consider why those foxes are called little, and why we are told to catch them, and not to kill them or to drive them off.

Foxes denote temptations; and temptations must come. For who receives the victor's crown, who has not striven fairly? And what strife can there be, without an adversary? So, when you come to serve the Lord, prepare your soul for temptation, knowing assuredly that they who would live holily in Christ must suffer persecution. There are, moreover, different temptations at different times and stages of our life. Of those that beset us at the outset of our course I have already spoken; and they are obvious. But those which attack maturer souls are subtle, hidden ones, like cunning little foxes; for in them vice is made to look like virtue.

EXAMPLES OF VICES MADE TO LOOK LIKE VIRTURES

For instance, I have seen a man running his course well; and then, quite suddenly, a thought—a little fox, I think—occurs to him. "If I were back at home," he thinks, "I could impart the good I here enjoy alone to many of my family and friends! They love me and would listen readily. Why is this waste made? I will go, and save them and myself along with them. There is nothing to be dreaded in a change of place. It does not matter where I am, if I am doing good." You know the rest. He

goes, poor wretch, not as an exile to his home, but as a dog returning to his vomit of the flesh—and perishes. He loses his own soul and he wins no other. That is one little fox—the illusive hope of gaining other souls.

Shall I tell you some more? Sometimes a man, who is advancing well, is moved with a desire to preach, not to his kindred but to seculars outside. He argues that he will incur a curse if he withholds corn from the people; and that the Gospel bids us tell out from the house-tops what we have heard in the ear. Another little fox, more plausible than the first and all the worse for that. But I will catch him for you. First, Moses says, "Thou shalt not plough with the firstling of thy bull," and Paul interprets it "not a novice, lest being lifted up with pride he fall into the condemnation of the devil." And again, "No man taketh this honour unto himself, but he that is called of God, as was Aaron," and "how shall they preach, except they be sent?" Out of considerations such as these I weave my net and take the little fox, so that he cannot spoil the vines. For obviously it is not fitting for a monk to preach in public, and it is not expedient for a novice; nor is it permissible for anyone, unless he be expressly sent to do it.

Here is another of them. How many fervent souls has the desire for solitude lured from their monasteries into a hermitage, with one of two results: Either the hermitage has spewed them out again with all their fervour gone; or else it has brought them to careless and even abandoned ways, quite contrary to hermit law? A fox's work indeed! The man thought he would be richer in spiritual fruits alone, than in Community, where he had (so it seemed to him) only the ordinary gifts of grace; he thought that he was right to go. But the event proved that a little fox had been at his destructive work again.

What shall I say of the excessive abstinence, by which some people in this house make themselves a nuisance to the rest of us and cause a grave disquiet? Do not the resultant discord and the perversion of conscience in those who do these things destroy the unanimity that ought to be between us, and with it this great vineyard which God planted with His own right Hand?

Let us now consider what the Bridegroom says about these wily little animals that spoil the vines. Little in badness they are not; it is their craftiness that makes Him call them so. For while other vices are, as one might say, portly, and loom large to the view, these are so slim and small and hard to see that none perfect and experienced souls have keen enough eyes to detect them. Perhaps that also is the reason why the Bridegroom commands that these little beasts are to be caught, not driven off or killed; for once their falsity is demonstrated, they can do no more harm. No one who is not out of his mind would step into a trap when he knew it was there!

OF HIS ONENESS WITH US

And He says, "Catch *for us* the foxes." "For us"—making as though we were His equals, although He has no peer! He might have said "for Me," but He prefers "for us," for His delights are with the sons of men. What graciousness, what sweetness, what mighty love He shows! Is the Highest of all indeed made one of the many? Who has done this? Love has done it. Love which regards not its own worth. Love which is rich in condescension, strong in its attachments and effective in its power to persuade. What is there that has greater force than Love? It prevails even with God! Yet what is there so gentle? What other force is there so irresistibly compelling, and yet so unresisting when itself compelled?

The Lord emptied Himself that you might see Love's plenitude outpoured, Love's loftiness abased to your own level, and Love's uniqueness made to be your fellow. Who then is it, O admirable Spouse, whom Thou thus linkest with Thyself in such a homely fashion? "Catch *for us*," Thou sayest; dost Thou mean for the Church, as well as Thee? We know what she is—gathered from the nations, composed of sinners and of mortal men. But who art Thou, that Thou shouldst love this Ethiopian woman so devotedly? Not another Moses, verily, but One greater than he. Art Thou not He Who is fairer than all the children of men? But I have said too little. Thou art the Brightness of eternal life, the Splendour and the Image of God's Being; Thou art Thyself God above all, blessèd for evermore. Amen.

Chapter Thirty

"My Belovéd is mine, and I am His Who feeds among the lilies, until the Day breathe and the shadows be turned back"

OF THE UNSPEAKABLE LOVE BETWEEN THE CHURCH AND CHRIST

THE NEXT WORDS are the Bride's, and every utterance of hers is as rich in meaning and as mysterious as it is gracious to the ears. "My Belovéd," she says now, "is mine, and I am His"; and the words sound abrupt, as though she spoke to herself, from which we must conclude that He has now withdrawn Himself again from her, though still remaining present to her mind. What does she mean? Speak, holy soul, and tell us what is this intimate relationship, this give-and-take between yourself and Him. Does He belong to and exist for you in the same way that you belong to Him, or in a different way? Explain the mystery for us in plain words, that we may understand.

OF THE BRIDE'S BOUNDLESS LOVE FOR THE BRIDEGROOM

But this, I think, she cannot do. It was her heart that spoke, not her intellect. She spoke out of the fullness of her heart, because she had to speak; but what she really feels defies expression. For love, like fear and joy, must find outlet in words; but what comes out is much less full than that which forced it out. The Bride, aflame with holy love, seeks for relief in speech; but, in so seeking, she does not stop to think what she shall say or how it is best put. She simply blurts out the first words that rise to her lips. How should she do otherwise, seeing how feasted and how filled she is?

Look back over this marriage-song from the beginning to this point, and think of all the blesséd converse the Spouse has held with her! Do you then wonder at her spontaneous burst of joy? Do you yourself stop and choose your words, under the influence of strong emotion? No, you come out with it, not only willy-nilly, but even without knowing that you are going to speak at all. You are like a vessel which must give off the odour of its contents, good or bad according to what those contents are. And the Bride of my Lord is a good vessel, and sweet is the odour that proceeds from her.

I thank Thee, Lord Jesus, that Thou hast deigned to admit me to perceive at least that fragrant odour. Most gratefully do I receive this fragment of her fullness, even as dogs eat the crumbs that fall from their lords' table. Let her feast at Thy board and rejoice in the sight of Thee; let her be rapt out of herself and filled with the good things of Thine House, as indeed is fitting; but, when she gives vent to her deep satisfaction, grant some faint odour of her riches to my poverty.

EXAMPLES OF RIGHTEOUS MEN

For I am a sinner, with a long way still to go before I reach salvation. But

I will not grumble; its fragrance from afar shall comfort me. That which I call the fragrance of salvation is the expectation of it; for the sinner can only look forward to that which the righteous actually beholds. Such a righteous one was Simeon, who looked for and adored the Christ, before he saw Him in the flesh. Righteous also was Abraham, who desired to see the Day of the Lord and was not disappointed of his hope, for "he saw it and was glad." The apostles too were righteous, to whom it was said, "Ye yourselves are like to men that wait for their Lord."

And was not David righteous, when he said, "I waited patiently for the Lord"? He "opened his mouth and drew in his breath," and when he was filled full, he did not merely speak his joy, he sang! Good Jesu! What sweetness have I tasted through his singing! O that Thou wouldest deign to let me meet that friend of Thine, that mighty prophet, in the day of solemnity and rejoicing, when he shall come forth from Thy bridal chamber, singing his marriage-song with psaltery and harp, and shedding all around the fragrance of his own delight and blessedness! In that day—or rather in that hour, or maybe I should say in that half-hour, for the space of which the Scripture says that there was silence in heaven—my mouth shall be filled with joy and my tongue with exultation; for then not merely every psalm but every verse of Scripture will yield me perfumes of surpassing sweetness.

What could be sweeter than the fragrance that exhales from what John says about the mystery of the Eternal Word? Paul's utterances, too, have spread their fragrance over all the world; and I am permitted to desire even the unspeakable words which I may not hear and to sense their sweetness from afar. I do not know how it is, but the more mysterious things are, so much the more are we attracted to them; we long to plumb them the more avidly when they are hidden from us. And so indeed it is with these words of the Bride, "My Belovéd is mine, and I am His." Like Paul she does not reveal her secret; but she lets us know that it exists, so that we may get as it were a whiff of its perfume, though she accounts us unworthy or unable as yet to taste the mystery itself.

OF THE MUTUAL LOVE OF THE BRIDEGROOM AND THE BRIDE

This much at least, however, is quite clear; these words express an ardent mutual love between two persons; yet not between two equals, for the one finds in that love supremest bliss, and the Other shows in it amazing condescension. We cannot fathom the mystery the words enshrine; but I think we shall get as much of it as our dull intellects can grasp, if we take them as meaning "My Belovéd inclines—gives His attention and His thought—to me, and I incline to Him." They will then mean the same as David's words, "I waited patiently for the Lord and He inclined to me"; only the order is reversed, and the Bride's is the more correct, for "herein is love, not that we loved God, but that He loved us." And yet a little further on she herself follows David's order, for she says, "I am my Belovéd's and He is mine." Why so? Surely to show that she is more full of grace when she attributes all to grace, from first to last. For the full acknowledgment of grace is itself a sign of the fullness of grace in the soul that makes it.

OF THE BRIDEGROOM'S CARE FOR HIS BRIDE, THE CHURCH

But to return to the interpretation, "My Belovéd inclines to me, to me He gives attention, and I incline to Him." We are the Bride; it is our glory to be among those to whom the Bridegroom, the Eternal God, the Majesty that rules the universe, attends, in spite of the disparity between us and Him. And His inclining precedes ours; as the apostle Peter teaches when he says, "casting all your care upon Him"—that is to say, attending to Him—not in order that He may care for and attend to you, but "*for* He careth"—He cares now—"for you." He did indeed attend to her, His Bride the Church, whom He loved and for whom He gave Himself.

For was she not that wandering sheep, to rescue which He left His heavenly flock and came to earth? He sought her diligently and, when He had found her, He did not lead her back; He carried her! And He invited all the angels to celebrate the new and joyous festival, which He kept with her and on her account.

OF THE CHURCH'S ATTENTION TO THE BRIDEGROOM

But the Church attends to Him, as well as He to her, just as she says here. "He is mine," she says, "for He is kind and merciful; and I am His, for I am not ungrateful. He gives me grace out of His graciousness; I give Him gratitude for grace received. He is concerned to set me free and save me, I to promote His honour and to do His Will. He is mine, and mine alone; for I am His sole dove. I am His, and not another's, for I hear not the voice of strangers, and pay no heed to those who tell me, 'Lo, here is Christ!' or 'Lo, there He is!' "

Thus speaks the Church. For God had wrought salvation in the midst of the earth at such great cost, not for one soul alone but for the many whom He would gather into His one Church, His only Bride. He and she are therefore uniquely and supremely dear to each other; she has no other Bridegroom, and He no other Bride. What may she not expect from such a Lover? For what may she not hope from Him Who came from heaven to seek her and called her to Him from the ends of the earth and purchased her with His own Blood?

OF THE CONTRIBUTION OF THE CHURCH

And, looking to the future, she knows, moreover, that the Lord has need of her, that He may see the felicity of His chosen and rejoice in the gladness of His people, so that He may be praised with His inheritance. You must not think that this is a small matter; for I assure you that none of His works will reach perfection, if this one fail of it. Does not the end of all things depend on the condition and consummation of the Church? In vain does the lower creation await the revelation of the sons of God, if that be lacking! In vain do the patriarchs and prophets await their perfecting; for God has ordained that "they without us shall not be made perfect." And even the glory of the holy angels will be defective if their number be not made up, nor will the City of God be able to rejoice in its integrity.

For the Church, and the Church alone, furnishes those babes and sucklings, out of whose mouths God's praise is perfected. The children of the Church, the babes in Christ, supply heaven with a kind of happiness it would not otherwise have known; for no one who has never been unhappy can know such happiness as theirs. Joy after sorrow, rest after toil, the haven after shipwreck are very opportune. Everyone likes to feel secure; but most of all the man who has known fear of danger. And everyone enjoys the light; but none so much as he who has escaped from darkness. And to have passed to life from death doubles the grace of life.

All this is my contribution to the common life of heaven; and it is something which the blessèd spirits have not got. Even the blessèd life is incomplete without my blessedness; and I would even dare to say that something is added to the angels' joy when they, through charity, enjoy my bliss in me. For if the angels rejoice over a sinner's penitence, if my tears are a delight to them, what then is my delight? Everything that they do is directed to the praise of God; but there is something lacking to that praise if there is no one present who can say, "We went through fire and water, and Thou broughtest us out into a wealthy place."

OF THE SOUL'S LOVE FOR CHRIST, AS MEMBER OF HIS CHURCH

"My Belovèd is mine, and I am His." We have attributed these words so far to the whole Church, by reason of the promises which God has given her, both for this present life and for that which is to come. But may the individual soul appropriate them? I think the answer here is "yes," but with some qualification. The member is entitled to a share in the Body's privileges, but not all members use them. There are, however, some among the Church's children—God alone knows who they are—who are indeed His friends and so may use these words.

Give me a soul that loves nothing except God and that which merits love on His account, a soul to whom to live is Christ and has been for a long time, who has the Lord always before his eyes, whatever he is doing, desiring always only to fulfill His will and implementing his desire—give me, I say, a soul like that, and I at any rate will not deny that it is worthy of the Bridegroom's care, of God's regard. And that is the sort of person you must be, if you would say, "My Belovèd is mine, and I am His."

OF THE BASIS OF THE BELIEVER'S CONFIDENCE

The confidence of such an individual rests upon two grounds. The first is the essential simplicity of the Godhead, which enables the Bridegroom to regard many as one, and one as many, without extending His attention for the many or restricting it for one, but giving it entire to each and all alike. The second is a certain rare but very sweet experience of the Presence of the Word and of His Father in the soul, according to His promise, "If a man love Me, he will keep My words, and My Father will love him, and We will come unto him and make Our abode with him"; which indwelling is attested by the great wisdom and the equally great love with which the soul feels itself infused. It is these two together that are the hall-mark of this experience; for if we were merely instructed by the Word, we should be puffed up, and the love of the Father would lead us astray if we were uninstructed, like those of whom the apostle said that they had "a zeal of God, but not according to knowledge."

OF THE PROOF OF GOD'S LOVE FOR BELIEVERS

How great a grace of holy intimacy must spring from this indwelling, and from the intimacy what a confidence! The soul knows that she loves the Word, and loves Him ardently; she does not doubt that He attends with equal care to her. For she is mindful of His promise, "With what measure ye mete it shall be meted unto you again"; and yet she recognises that, in loving Him, she but returns His love, because He first loved her.

And so indeed it is! God's love begets the soul's and comes before it; His interest and care for her evoke her care for Him. For God always displays Himself to usward in the same sort as we have made ourselves to Him. That is the psalmist's meaning when he says, "With the holy Thou shalt be holy," and so forth; and we might say with equal truth "With the loving Thou shalt be loving, for such as give their leisure to attend to Thee Thou wilt be at leisure, Thou wilt attend to such as attend to Thee, and be tenderly concerned for those who show a like concern for Thee."

You see, then, that not only your love but also your interest and care for Him are proof of His for you. Do you keep watch? He watches too. So get up in the night, even before the time for Vigils, and you will find Him there and waiting for you. He loves you more than you love Him, and He loved you before your love for Him was born. O Lord, how good art Thou to the soul that seeks Thee! Thou runnest to meet her. Thou embracest her. Thou showest that Thou art her Spouse—Thou, Who art the Lord over all things, God blesséd for ever.

WHY CHRIST IS CALLED BELOVÉD, AND IS SAID TO FEED AMONG THE LILIES

"My Belovéd is mine, and I am His, Who feeds among the lilies." No one could accuse the Bride of presumption when she can speak thus of her Spouse. For even had she said He fed among the stars, feeding itself is something so commonplace and humble that it acquits her forthwith of forwardness in claiming thus to be allied with Him. But He, like the Lamb that He is, "feeds among the lilies," among the grass of the field which to-day is and to-morrow is cast into the oven. Notice, however, that He feeds among, not on them. He does not eat grass like the ox; but He walks and lies down in it as though He were one of the herd.

Nevertheless the Bride is not unmindful that He Who feeds is also He Who makes His flock to feed; and that He Who abides among the lilies is the Same as He Who reigns above the stars. But she prefers to call His humbleness to mind, not only because she loves humility, but also because it was when He began to feed as one of the flock that He first became her Belovéd; it was indeed the fact of His doing so that made Him dear to her. For He is her Lord in His loftiness and her Belovéd in His lowliness; He reigns above the stars and loves among the lilies. Even above the stars He loved; for He is Love, and never and nowhere can He do otherwise than love. But until He came down and fed among the lilies, He was not the Belovéd, for His love was not returned. For even the patriarchs and prophets loved Him only because they foresaw Him feeding thus; He could not be beloved till He was known.

OF THE SHEPHERD'S IDENTIFICATION WITH HIS SHEEP

The Bride, then, is quite right to mention here the fact to which she owes both her knowledge and her love of Him. For he Who is the universal Shepherd emptied Himself even to this extent, that He became as one of His own sheep. He fed and He was found among the lilies; there the Church saw and loved Him, because she found Him poor and needy as herself, a bird of her own feather. She loved Him also for His truth and gentleness and righteousness; because He has fulfilled the promises, and purged iniquities, and judged the evil spirits and their prince. He showed Himself love-worthy in these ways—true in Himself, gentle towards men, righteous on their behalf.

O Bridegroom most truly worthy of the utmost love, how should the Church delay to trust herself entirely to One so faithful to His word, so ready to forgive, so just in her defense? The prophet, before naming the three qualities, had said, "In Thy splendour and Thy beauty set Thou forth, proceed prosperously and reign!" Whence come this splendour and this beauty? Surely from lilies, the loveliest of flowers. "Proceed and reign," he says, "because of Truth and Gentleness and Righteousness." These are the lilies that have sprung up out of the earth, and are fairer than any other flowers and sweeter than the sweetest perfumes.

As long as the earth lay under the curse, it brought forth thorns and thistles; but now Truth has sprung up out of it, a glorious Flower of the Field and Lily of the Valleys. It was the dazzling beauty of this Flower at its first opening that made the glory that the shepherds saw at Bethlehem; it was the fragrance of the same that drew the Magi from afar. And have you ever noticed how apt a symbol the lily is for Truth? For the golden stamens in its centre are surrounded by a crown of petals of the purest white; the gold denoting Christ's Divinity and the white crown His Manhood's purity—the diadem indeed "with which His Mother crowned Him," for in that wherewith His Father crowned Him He dwelleth in light inaccessible and we cannot see Him in it in this life. But of that more anon.

OF LILIES IN THE BRIDEGROOM'S GARDEN

Truth, then, is a lily; and so is Gentleness—a lovely lily, too, having the purity of innocence and the fragrance of hope. And doubtless Gentleness, as well as Truth, springs from the earth, since from earth springs the Lamb Who was led to the slaughter and opened not His mouth. Righteousness, too, arises from the earth, according to the prophet's words, "Drop down, ye heavens, from above, and let the skies pour down the Righteous One; let the earth open and bring forth the Saviour and let Righteousness arise together." And this is not a lily which to-day is and to-morrow is cast into the oven; for it is written, "The righteous shall spring up as the lily: he shall flourish for ever before the Lord."

The Belovéd has many other lilies in His garden besides Truth and Gentleness and Rightousness; for the virtues of the Lord of virtues have no end. Perhaps that is why He calls Himself the Lily, because He is so wholly surrounded by them, and everything to do with Him resembles one. His Conception, His Birth, His way of life, His miracles, His signs, His Passion, His Death, His Resurrection, His Ascension, are lilies, all of them.

Even the holy Virgin could not have sustained the blinding glory of conceiving Him, had not the power of the Highest overshadowed her; and her inviolate virginity made of His Birth a thing of dazzling whiteness. So with the other mysteries: each one is lustrous in its purity and gives off a fragrance even to us to-day, who know them but by faith. "Blesséd are they who have not seen but have believed." My portion in these lilies is the odour of life that they distil; by faith I inhale it, and in this way I both mitigate the harshness of my exile here and renew my longing for my heavenly homeland in my inmost heart.

OF THE LILIES NEEDED IN OUR GARDENS

Some of the Bridegroom's friends have lilies, but not in plenty, as He has; for it is He alone to Whom the Spirit is not given by measure. It is one thing to have lilies; and another to have nothing but lilies. It is much if a man can grow three or four of them, among all the thorns and thistles of the ancient curse that have possessed his ground so long. As for myself, poor as I am, I shall do well if I succeed some day in clearing enough space to grow a single lily, so that He Who feeds among the lilies may perhaps condescend to feed sometimes even along with me.

But I am wrong in speaking as though one lily was enough. We must have two at least; and they are Self-control and Innocence, whereof the one without the other will not suffice to save us. So I must cultivate Innocence first; and if later on I contrive to grow Self-control as well, I shall consider myself a rich man. But I shall be a very king if to these two lilies I can add the third of Patience, which is the guardian of the other two. And I am sure that if that Lover of lilies comes and finds these three, He will not scorn to feed and keep the [Passover] with us.

OF LILIES IN THE GARDEN OF THE SOUL, AND OF THE BRIDEGROOM'S FEEDING

The Bridegroom calls the Bride a "lily among thorns." He also is a Lily; but He has no thorns, because He did no sin. He alone of men needs not to say, "I am turned in my anguish, while the thorn is transfixed." He, therefore, is never without lilies, because He is always without faults; He shines always in unsullied whiteness, fairer than the sons of men. So if you, who hear or read these words, would have the Dweller among lilies dwell in you, your character must have the lily's purity and fragrance too.

OF WHITENESS IN THE SOUL

This is an apt comparison, for scent and colour are as distinct in spiritual things as in material. Colour, in the former, depends upon intention, and is judged by conscience; whereas the scent or odour of our actions is the repute they gain and the impression they produce. So vice is black and virtue white, because virtue proceeds from a pure heart and a good conscience. And, if the virtue wins a good report as well, it is a lily, because it has the lily's whiteness and its fragrance as well.

There are, however, other sorts of whiteness in the soul, besides this whiteness of a pure intention. One is the whiteness which results from God's forgiveness; as He Himself says through the prophet, "Though your sins be as scarlet, they shall be white as snow." Another is the whiteness with which a person clothes himself, when he shows mercy with cheerfulness; this whiteness shines out in his face as well as in his actions, whereas when a person gives a gloomy and reluctant service, his face and hands alike are blackened by the feelings of his heart. So "God loveth a cheerful giver"; and He also loves him who gives with simplicity. For simplicity also is a whiteness of the soul, as is proved by the fact that its opposite, duplicity, is a spot or a stain. That is why he is called blessèd to whom the Lord imputes no sin, and in whose spirit there is no deceit. And the Lord Himself says, "Be not as the hypocrites, of a sad countenance," thus briefly warning us against these blemishes of sadness and deceit.

OF THE BRIDEGROOM'S DELIGHT IN VIRTUE

Perhaps, then, the meaning of His feeding among the lilies is that He delights in the whiteness and the fragrance of virtues. When in the days of His flesh He fed in the house of Martha and Mary, He was at the same time refreshed in spirit by their virtues and their loving service; and that while He Himself was nourishing their souls, giving them courage in their fearfulness, cheering their lowliness, enriching their devotion. For with Him to nourish others and Himself to feed are one.

To Him my penitence and my salvation, and indeed I myself, are food; I am made one with Him when I am assimilated to Him. Were this not so, our union with Him would be less than perfect. For, if I feed on Him but He feeds not on me, although He is in me, yet am I not in Him. But if He so feeds on me that I am in Him; and I in turn on Him, that He may be in me, how firmly and completely are we made one together, since I shall be in Him, and He in me! It was indeed in order thus to unite sinners to Himself, that He Himself was made sin, who did none; so that the body of sin, in which sinners were hitherto implanted, might be destroyed, and that by His righteousness they might be freely justified.

There is a further explanation of this passage that I should like to give before I stop. The Word of God, the Bridegroom, is the Truth. When the Truth speaks, and he who hears does not obey, the Truth is left, as you might say, empty and hungry, unsatisfied and sad, because It has gone forth and met with no response. But, if the hearer has obeyed, does it not seem to you that, in some sense, the Truth is fed and puts on flesh, because action has issued from the Word and it is strengthened by the fruits of obedience and the produce of righteousness?

So He says in the Apocalypse, "Behold, I stand at the door and knock; if any man hear My voice and open Me the door, I will come in to him, and will sup with him, and he with Me." And He seems Himself to sanction this interpretation when He says by the prophet that His word shall not return unto Him void, but shall prosper and effect the purpose for which He sent it forth. It shall not return unto Him void or empty or, as you might say, hungry, but shall be full-filled.

OF UNACCEPTABLE GIFTS TO THE BRIDEGROOM

But hear the Word's own word about His food. "My meat," He says, "is to do the Will of Him that sent Me." His food, then, is good works, and He finds it among the lilies—that is, among the virtues. Nor will He take it elsewhere, however good it may seem to be in itself. For instance, He will not accept an alms from the hand of a thief, nor from that of a hypocrite who has a trumpet blown in front of him to win the praise of men.

And I am afraid there may be some among ourselves whose gifts the Bridegroom will not accept, because they lack the fragrance of the lily. If, for example, my fasting is done to please myself, it can give Him no pleasure; for He detects the stink of self-will in it, instead of the sweet odour of obedience. And I think this applies not to fasting only, but also to silence, vigils, prayer, reading, manual labour, in short to everything that a monk does, when self-will is found in it and not obedience to his master. Self-will is a great evil; for it makes your good works *not* good for yourself. When they are like that, they need to be turned into lilies; for He Who feeds among the lilies will taste of nothing that is tainted with self-will.

OF THE DAY THAT IS COMING

"My Belovéd is mine, and I am His, Who feeds among the lilies, until the day breathe and the shadows be turned back." Only the last part of this text remains to be considered; and the question is to which of the two preceding clauses it should be attached, for either yields a reasonable sense. Thus "My Belovéd is mine, and I am His, until the day breathe and the shadows be turned back" is right, provided that "until" be taken in an inclusive sense; for assuredly He will not cease to belong to His Bride in that Day, even though He may cease to feed among the lilies.

And that same word is used inclusively by Matthew when he says that Joseph knew not Mary until she had brought forth her firstborn son; for she remained a virgin after that. And in the verse "our eyes wait upon the

Lord our God, until He have mercy upon us," the psalmist does the same; for certainly he does not mean that we shall turn our eyes away, when God has once shown mercy. But if we take it that He "feeds among the lilies until the day breathe and the shadows be turned back," the word "until" must be understood in an exclusive sense, as indicating that His feeding thus will cease when that Day comes.

Are we to take "the Day" as meaning that of Resurrection? If so, it might seem strange at first sight that He should cease to feed among the lilies then, when His whole kingdom will be bright with them. But that is just the point. It is on sinners that He feeds, grinding them down by the sharp teeth of this life's discipline (if I may use the term) in order to incorporate them into Himself; and in that Day no sinners will remain. He will dwell among the lilies and take delight in them; but He will not feed. For, when perfection has been reached, nothing remains to be done. The will of God will henceforth be enjoyed and lived by, rather than laboriously carried out, even as it is enjoyed in heaven now.

But what if we take His feeding among the lilies as meaning that He takes delight in the purity of virtues? Virtues in that Day will indeed abound; but His enjoyment of them will be after another manner, more like drinking than eating. For the virtues then will be so wholly pure and unmixed with anything imperfect that He will not need to chew them as a solid, in order to get some little relish from them, but will drink them down with ease as well as pleasure. He tells us this Himself. "I will not drink henceforth of this fruit of the vine," He says, "until that Day when I drink it new with you in My Father's Kingdom"; and He makes no mention of eating. And this in fact agrees with the usual custom that drink should follow food.

OF THAT DAY'S "BREATHING"

Now let us think about the Day and the shadows which are mentioned here, and in what sense the Day breathes and by what power the shadows are turned back. The expression "until the Day breathe" occurs nowhere else but here, and it is strange. We speak of winds breathing, but not times; and men and animals breathe and live by doing so. The Holy Spirit also breathes, and is called Spirit for that reason. But why is this Day said to breathe, when it is neither wind nor animal nor spirit? And, what is more, not just to breathe but—literally—to breathe towards, aspire? No less unusual is the phrase "until the shadows be turned back"; for shadows are not turned back by the sun but are destroyed. Obviously we must look for a spiritual Day and spiritual shadows to explain these words.

The shadow beneath which Mary conceived was assuredly spiritual, and so was that of which the prophet says, "A spirit before our face is the Lord Christ; under His shadow shall we live among the nations." But I think the shadows here denote those hostile powers which the apostle describes as "the rulers of these darknesses," and that the term covers also those of our own race who cleave to them; for these will not be annihilated in that Day, but will have their power taken away.

That surely must soon come to pass, for these are the Last Days; the night is far spent, and the Day is at hand, the Day comes breathing in, the night breathes out. The night is the devil, and also Antichrist, whom the Lord, Who is the Day, shall slay with the breath of His mouth and destroy by the brightness of His coming.

There is doubtless also some significance in the fact that the day is said not to breathe merely but to breathe to or aspire. Perhaps we may interpret it like this. When God made man of the dust of the earth, He breathed into him the breath of life: That was man's day of *inspiration*. But when the woman, prompted by the serpent, ate of the forbidden fruit and gave it to her husband, that *conspiration* against God throttled their day of inspiration, so to speak, and substituted for it that of *expiration*—that is, of subjection to death. So we for our part must make haste to *respire*, to breathe free of that ancient conspiracy under which we were born, while yet there is time, and before the sighing *(suspirans)* horror of the night engulfs us.

A DAY OF NEW LIFE

We re-breathe thus; we come to life again, when the spirit begins to war against the flesh. And even the night of death will not prevail against this Day of revivification; the Day will shine all the brighter in that darkness, and the darkness will not swallow it up. The light of life will fail not, even when life departs; freed from the fetters of the body, the righteous soul will be free among the dead, sighted among the blind. It will be as when all Egypt lay in darkness, but "the children of Israel had light in all their dwellings"; the righteous will shine among the sons of darkness and see the more clearly because they have put off the shadows of the flesh. Thus will this Day be one of fuller *inspiration* than the first; and that, I think, is why the Holy Spirit has so spoken here.

Chapter Thirty-One

"Return! Be Thou, my Belovéd, like a roe or a fawn upon the mountains of Bethel!"

HOW CHRIST WILL COME TO JUDGMENT IN HIS HUMAN FORM

R*ETURN!"* WHAT? He has only this minute left you, and yet you call Him back? What can have happened in so short a time? Have you forgotten something? Yes, the Bride has forgotten everything that is not He, herself included. For Love is a force that overmasters every consideration of timidity or fitness. The Bridegroom has scarcely turned to go from her, when she implores Him to return, and to do so with speed.

You will not think this strange if you recall the hour when the Lord Jesus passed from this world to the Father, and the feelings of the Church, His newly-wedded Bride, when she saw herself thus forsaken by her only Hope. She loves Him and she needs Him; so she has a twofold reason for beseeching Him, since He must ascend up where He was before, at least to hasten His return. That is why she begs Him to be as those fleet-footed animals, the roe and the fawn; and that is what she asks for daily when she prays, "Thy Kingdom come!"

I think, however, that she has the weakness of these creatures in her mind, as well as their swiftness; for the roe is of the weaker sex and the fawn is weak by reason of its youth. It seems to me that she desires Him to come to Judgment with power indeed, and yet not in the form of God but in that human form in which He was not only born for us, but born a Child and of a woman only; that His own weakness may remind Him to have compassion in His day of wrath, and to put mercy before condemnation. For if He will be extreme to mark what is done amiss, who may abide it, even of the elect? The stars are not pure in His sight, and even in the angels He finds folly. Even the saints need pardon and must not trust in their own righteousness; for all have sinned and all need mercy. So, that He may remember mercy in His wrath, the Bride entreats Him to appear in the garb of mercy—that is to say, "in fashion as a Man."

OF THE NEED FOR THE JUDGE TO BE A MAN

It is necessary that this should be so. For "who shall stand when He appeareth?" Who shall face the transformation of appearances which the Judge's Coming will effect, even with this mitigation of His majesty and dread severity? And how much less could any man endure it, if He appeared without His Human Nature, as God alone, unapproachable in glory, unreachable in sublimity, incomprehensible in majesty? But now, when His wrath is kindled but a little, how welcome to the sons of grace, how strengthening to their faith and hope and confidence will be His Human Face!

Indeed the Father Himself has given the power of judgment to the Son, not because He is His own Son but because He is the Son of Man. How rightly is He called the Father of mercies, Who wills men to be judged by Man, so that amid all their fear and apprehension the elect may yet have confidence, because the Judge is their own flesh and blood! David foretold this too, in words that are part prayer, part prophecy. "Give the King Thy judgments, O God," he says, "and Thy righteousness unto the King's Son." The promise given by the angels is to the same effect. "This same Jesus, Who is taken up from you into heaven," they told the apostles, "shall so come in like manner as ye have seen Him going into heaven"—that is to say, in the same bodily form.

You will remember that, in an earlier discourse, we took the reference to His leaping as a fawn over and on the mountains as meaning that He passed over the wicked and chose only the good. The same interpretation holds good here, in reference to the Judgment; and is, I think, supported by the last words of the text, "Be Thou, my Belovéd, like a roe or a fawn *upon the mountains of Bethel.*" For Bethel means the House of God, and in that House there are no evil mountains, only good; and the Bridegroom, leaping as a fawn upon them, fulfills the prophecy, "The mountains and the hills shall break forth into singing."

OF THE COMINGS OF THE BRIDEGROOM
TO THE SOUL

Thus far, we have interpreted the words "Return! Be Thou, my Belovéd, like a roe or a fawn" as spoken by the universal Church. But the individual soul, that loves God tenderly, wisely and intensely, also is His Bride. Let me then try to tell you my own experience of the Bridegroom's comings. It will perhaps seem of little worth when you hear it; but I shall not mind that. For he who is spiritual will not despise me, and he who is not spiritual will just not understand.

"Return!" she says; and that is well. He went away, and now He is called back. Who will explain for me this mystery of change in God? How can the Word, Who fills all things, be said to go or to return? And how can He, Who is a Spirit, move from place to place? Or how can God be said to move in any sense, since He is utterly immutable?

Let us leave these things for such as can understand them. For, in expounding this sacred and mystical discourse, we must remember that the Scriptures are wont to present the unknown and invisible things of God to us by means of figures drawn from things we know—thus offering us, so to speak, a rare wine in a common cup. And, following this principle, it is natural that the soul aware of grace should recognise the presence of the Word; and, when the awareness goes, that she should mourn His absence and beg Him to return, saying with the prophet, "My face hath sought Thee: Thy Face, Lord, will I seek." For it is by this yearning of the soul that has once known His sweetness that the Word is recalled; and, when He goes, what can she do but cry unceasingly, "Return, return, return!"?

OF THE BRIDEGROOM'S COMING AND GOING

"Return!" The very word shows that she deserved His presence, even though not the plentitude of grace. And it may be that He withdrew Himself, in order that she might more eagerly entreat Him to return and hold Him tighter when He did so. He "made as though He would go further" once, not because He wanted to do so, but in order that He might hear those two men say, "Abide with us, O Lord!" And on the sea that time, when the apostles were toiling at their oars, He made as though He would have passed them by, only to prove their faith and have them ask Him in.

So is it with His dealings with the soul. When He is passing on, He wills us to detain Him; when He departs, He wills to be recalled. For He is no irrevocable Word; He goes and He returns, after His own good pleasure, visiting the soul as it were at break of day and proving it suddenly. His departure is always part of His deliberate dealing with the soul; and His return likewise is of His own will. And both are infinitely wise, though He alone knows the reason why He goes or comes.

It is clear, then, that the going and returning of the Word are for the soul just those vicissitudes of which He tells us in another place, "A little while and ye shall not see Me; and again a little while and ye shall see Me!" O little while and little while, O lengthy little while! Good Lord, dost Thou call that a little while in which we do not see Thee? With all good respect to Thy word, my Lord, I must confess that it is long to me—yes, much too long. Yet it is right to call that time both short and long, for it is short compared with our deserts, and very long indeed to our desires.

BERNARD SPEAKS OF HIS EXPERIENCE

But now let me try to tell you of my own experience, as I set out to do. I speak as a fool; and yet I must admit that the Word has come even to me, and that many times. But never, when He has thus entered into me, have I perceived the actual moment of His coming. I have felt that He was present; I remember afterwards that He was then with me; and sometimes I have sensed His coming in advance. But never have I been aware of the particular moment when He came or went. Whence He came from into my soul, whither He goes on leaving me, or by what road He enters or departs, I know not even now. "His footsteps are not known," as it is written.

Certainly it was not by my eyes that He entered, for He has no colour; nor was it by my ears, for He made not a sound. Neither was it my nostrils that discerned His presence, for His sweetness mingles with the mind, not with the air. The sense of taste did not detect Him either, for He is nothing that one eats or drinks; and touch was likewise powerless to apprehend Him, for He is utterly intangible.

How, then, did He come in? Or did He *not* come in, perhaps, because He never was outside? For He is not one of the things that exist exteriorly to us. And yet how can I say that He comes from within me, when I know that in me there is nothing that is good? I have ascended to the highest in myself, and lo! the Word was towering far above it. My curiosity has led me to explore my lowest depths as well, only to find that He went deeper yet. If I looked out from myself, I saw Him stretching farther than the farthest I could see; and, if I looked within, He was more inward still. So I recognized the truth of the apostle's words, "In Him we live and move and are." But blesséd is he in whom He is, who lives for Him and is moved by Him.

HOW BERNARD DETECTED THE WORD'S PRESENCE

You ask, then, how I knew that He was present, since His ways are past finding out? Because the Word is living and effective, and as soon as ever He has entered into me, He has aroused my sleeping soul, and stirred and softened and pricked my heart, that hitherto was sick and hard as stone. He had begun to pluck up and destroy, to build and plant, to water the dry places and shed light upon the dark, to open what was shut, to warm the chill, to make the crooked straight and the rough places plain; so that my soul has blessed the Lord and all that is within me praised His holy Name.

Thus has the Bridegroom entered into me; my senses told me nothing of His coming; I knew that He was present only by the movement of my heart; I perceived His power, because it put my sins to flight and exercised a strong control on all my impulses. I have been moved to wonder at His wisdom too, uncovering my secret faults and teaching me to see their sinfulness; and I have experienced His gentleness and kindness in such small measure of amendment as I have achieved; and, in the renewal and remaking of the spirit of my mind—that is, my inmost being, I have beheld to some degree the beauty of His glory and have been filled with awe as I gazed at His manifold greatness.

BERNARD'S RESPONSE WHEN THE WORD DEPARTED FROM HIM

But when the Word withdraws Himself from me, it is as when a fire is taken from beneath a boiling pot; my fervour and devotion languish and grow cold, and that is how I know that He has gone. My soul is then inevitably sad, till He return and my heart kindle in me once again. And, having known the blessedness of His indwelling once, how can I otherwise than cry "Return!" as does the Bride? As long as I live, that word of recall shall be mine.

As often as He leaves me, even so often will I call Him back, and I will pray Him to return, not empty-handed but "full of grace and truth," as He is wont to do, as He did yesterday, and the day before. And herein lies, I think, His likeness to a roe and to a fawn, for grace has the fawn's gaiety and truth the roe's keen eyes. And verily I need both truth and grace: truth, that I may be unable to conceal myself from Him, and grace that I may not desire to do so. For "grace and truth came by Jesus Christ," as John [the] Baptist says; and if the Lord, the Word, the Bridegroom of the soul, knocks at the door of mine with only one of these, He will make His entrance not as Bridegroom but as Judge. God grant that that may never be the case with me!

May He not enter into judgment

with His servant; but let Him rather come with peace and gaiety and gladness, yet with all seriousness, nonetheless, that His piercing Look may show myself to me and so restrain my forwardness and purge my joy. May He enter as the leaping fawn, mercifully passing over my offenses; may He enter as from the mountains of Bethel, gladsome and radiant, proceeding from the Father, sweet and gentle—He Who disdains not to be called and to become the Bridegroom of the soul that seeks for Him!

Chapter Thirty-Two

"Nightlong on my little bed I sought Him Whom my soul loveth. I will arise and go about the city; through the streets and squares I will seek Him Whom my soul loveth. I sought Him, and I found Him not. The watchmen who guard the city found me. Have you seen Him Whom my soul loveth? A little while after I had passed beyond them, I found Him Whom my soul loveth. I held Him, and I will not let Him go, till I have brought Him into my mother's house, into the chamber of her that bore me"

OF THE TIME, THE MANNER, AND THE PLACE IN WHICH GOD MUST BE SOUGHT

NIGHTLONG ON my little bed I sought Him Whom my soul loveth." The Bride has called the Bridegroom back, but He has not returned. Why so? In order that her love may be still further proved and exercised. He is not angry with her; He lets Himself appear unwilling to return when called, only to make her come and look for Him with even greater longing than before. So first she seeks Him on her little bed, but does not find Him there. Then she gets up and goes about the city, hither and thither through the streets and squares; but still she does not meet or even see Him.

She asks those whom she comes across, but they can give no certain news of Him. And so night after night. How ardent must her longing for Him be, to make her rise at night like this without a blush, and go through all the public places seeking Him, and asking everyone she meets if they have seen Him anywhere, undaunted in her quest by any obstacle and undeterred either by her natural desire for repose,

or by a bride's instinctive modesty, or by the terrors of the night! Yet she remains defrauded of her hope.

Why does the Spouse subject her to this persistent, unremitting disappointment, which induces weariness, kindles suspicions, fosters impatience, and is a cruel stepmother to love and an actual mother to despair? If He is still only feigning unwillingness to come to her, His pretence has become too trying altogether.

OF SEEKING FOR THE BRIDEGROOM AT THE WRONG TIME

The analogy of an earthly bride and bridegroom does not help us here. We have to seek for purely spiritual reasons why He Who says "Seek, and ye shall find" and "He that seeketh findeth" yet cannot be found. There are, I think, three reasons which at times render our seeking vain: we seek Him either not at the right time, or not in the right way, or not in the right place. The right time for seeking God is always *now*. "Now is the acceptable time, now is the day of salvation," and He promises "Before they call upon Me, I will say, Lo, I am here!" And if it is by good works that we seek God, "while we have time, let us do good unto all men"; and that all the more because the Lord Himself expressly warns us that "the night cometh, wherein no man can work."

Do you expect to find some future time in which to seek God and do good, other than this present day of mercy? Go, then, and wait in hell for the salvation that has been wrought upon earth! No Victim will remain for you, when you are dead in sin; the Son of God will not be crucified a second time; He died once and He does not die again; the Blood outpoured on earth does not go down to hell. All the sinners of the earth shall indeed drink thereof, but it avails not to quench the flames for devils, nor for men who have allied themselves with them.

OF SEEKING FOR THE BRIDEGROOM IN THE WRONG PLACES

You see, then, that one reason why our quest for God is unsuccessful is that we do not make it at the proper time. But the Bride does look for Him at the right time; so that is not what hinders her from finding Him. Nor is the manner of her seeking faulty either; for she is not halfhearted or lukewarm in her search, but tireless and full of ardour, as she ought to be. Let us consider, therefore, whether perhaps she looks for Him in the wrong place. "On my little bed," she says, "I sought Him Whom my soul loveth." But perhaps she should have looked for Him, for Whom the whole world is too strait, on a great bed, not on a little one! But I do not take exception to the "little bed" myself, for I remember that He was Himself born as a Little One for us. Yet the same prophet says,

"Rejoice and praise, O inhabitant of Sion, for great is the Holy One of Israel in the midst of thee!" The same Lord Who is great in Sion is little and weak among us, and needs to lie down in a little bed. Was not the sepulchre a little bed? Was not the manger one? Was not the Virgin's womb another? But the Bosom of the Father, whence He was begotten, was a great bed, not a little one, and more aptly compared to a royal throne than to a bed at all.

For the Son, abiding in the Father, is the joint Ruler with Him of everything that is; and we are told expressly that He *sits* at God's right Hand, and that the heavens are His throne. So the Bride is right to say, *"my* little bed"; for obviously whatever of weakness there is in God belongs not to His Nature but to ours. He took from us the birth, the feeding at His Mother's breast, the death and burial that He bore for us. The newborn babe's mortality, the little child's infirmity, the dying of the Crucified, the slumber of the corpse, all these belong to me. But now the former things are passed away, and all things are made new.

"Nightlong upon my little bed I sought Him Whom my soul loveth." What? You were looking for Him on *your* bed, when He had already returned to His own? Did you not see the Son of Man ascending where He was before? He has exchanged the stable and the grave for heaven now, and you still seek Him on your little bed? He is risen; He is not here! Why seek you the Strong in the bed of the weak, the Great One in the cot, the Glorified One in the cattle-shed? He has entered into the powers of the Lord, He has put on honour and might, and lo! He sits above the cherubim, Who lay beneath the stone! He will lie down no more; He sits. Or perhaps I should say He sits to judge and stands to succour us.

OF SEEKING THE BRIDEGROOM THROUGH THE NIGHTS

Ever since the Resurrection, then, the Church, though she had known Him hitherto according to the flesh, has known Him thus no longer. And you notice that the Bride says very beautifully, not "Him Whom I love," but "Him Whom my soul loves," showing that hers is a spiritual, not a carnal love. She is right, too, in saying that she sought Him nightlong—that is, through the nights. It is night always when we look for Him; for, were it day, He would reveal Himself and we should have no need to seek.

But she says "through the nights"; and, if you have no better explanation, I suggest that the plural denotes the nights of which this world has not a few—the night of Jewish unbelief, for instance, the night of heathen ignorance, the multifold night of heretical perversity, and the night of the carnal and degraded life of Catholics. You seek in vain through these nights for the Sun of Righteousness and the Light of Truth, which is the Bridegroom's Self, for Light has no fellowship with darkness.

And if someone objects that the Bride is not so foolish as to look for her Belovéd among those who have no knowledge of Him or who do not love Him, I would point out that what she says is, not that she *is* seeking Him through these nights, but that she did so once. She means that, when she was

a child, she understood and thought accordingly; so, seeking for the Truth where He was not, she failed to find Him, going astray like a sheep that is lost, as says the psalm.

The words "upon my little bed" will then refer, not to where she looked for Him but to where she herself reclined, by reason of her weakness and her youth; and this is borne out by the fact that she says next, "I will arise." That is completely right. How should she not arise, when once she knows that her Belovéd has arisen? But, O thou blesséd one, if thou be risen with Christ, it behooves thee to seek the things that are above, and to seek Him also where now He sits at God's right Hand, not down here below.

OF THE BRIDEGROOM'S GLORY AT THE RIGHT HAND OF GOD

"Through the streets and squares I will seek Him Whom my soul loveth." The Bride, still thinking as a child, imagined that, as soon as He was risen, He would resume His public ministry of teaching and of healing, and so reveal His glory to Israel, that those who had promised to accept Him, if He would come down from the cross, might perhaps actually do so, if they beheld Him risen from the dead. But she was wrong. He had finished the work which His Father had given Him to do; as she ought to have known from His own dying words, "It has been consummated." He was hastening back to His Father, Whom would say to Him, "Sit Thou at My Right Hand." And lifted up in that way from earth, He would draw all men to Himself, both more divinely and with greater power.

But she, longing to enjoy Him and not understanding the mystery, is once more disappointed of her hope and has to say, "I sought Him, and I found Him not"; so that His own words might be fulfilled, "Because I go to the Father, ye shall see Me no more." It must be so; because faith comes by hearing, not by sight, and must not be defrauded of its merit. The time for the open showing of His Resurrection glory is not yet; and, in the meantime, it is more concordant with supernal justice that the holy be not given to dogs, nor pearls to swine.

OF THE MUTUAL GLORIFICATION OF THE FATHER AND THE SON

And let the heaven and the heaven of heavens languish with longing and be thwarted of their hope, rather than that Almighty God Himself should be kept waiting any longer for the fulfilment of His Heart's desire, or the Only-Begotten be hindered another moment from entering into His glory! What glory can we mortals offer Him, worthy to hold Him back even for an instant from that which the Father has prepared for Him from all eternity? Nor is it fitting that the fulfilment of His own petition, "Father, glorify Thy Son," should be deferred. And yet I think those words are more a prophecy than a prayer; for the Son glorifies the Father (as He goes on to say) no less than the Father the Son; their glory is co-eternal and co-equal, and for the Son to say "Father, glorify Thy Son" is the same as to say "Glorify Thy Name"—that is, Thyself. Such mutual glorification had already taken place at the Lord's Baptism and Transfiguration; and now the Father must glorify His Name again, according to His promise.

But where? Not in the streets and squares, as the Bride supposes, unless they be those of which it is written "Thy streets, O Jerusalem, shall be paved with pure gold, and Alleluia shall be sung in all thy public places."

In those, the Son has indeed received glory from His Father, the like of which cannot be found elsewhere, even among the citizens of heaven. "For to which of the angels said He at any time, Sit thou on My right hand?" Thrones, Dominations, Principalities, and Powers desire to behold His glory; but none of them presumes to think he shares it. It is to my Lord only that the Lord has said these words; to Him alone, Who is co-equal with Him in glory, consubstantial in being, identical in nature, alike in majesty, and co-eval in eternity, has He granted to sit at His Right Hand. And there, there he who seeks the Lord will find Him and will see His glory—not the glory as of one among many, but the unique glory of the Sole-Begotten Son.

OF EARNESTLY SEEKING THE LORD

What then, O Bride, will you do? Do you think you can follow Him there? Can you or dare you penetrate to that holiest of holies, and behold the Son in the Father, the Father in the Son? No, no! Where He is, you cannot follow now, but you shall hereafter. But keep on following and seeking Him. Let not that unapproachable glory and sublimity deter you or make you give up hope of finding Him. All things are possible to the believer, if you can only believe. And "the Word is nigh thee, even in thy mouth and in thy heart."

Believe, and you have found Him; for finding and believing are the same. Believers know that Christ dwells in their hearts by faith; and what is nearer than a man's own heart?

Seek Him then, confidently and earnestly. "The Lord is good to the soul that seeks for Him." Seek Him by devout intention, follow Him by action, find Him by faith. What will faith not find? It reaches the unreachable, discovers the unknown, grasps the immeasurable, lays hold on things to come and, in a way, encompasses eternity itself. I dare even to say that I believe the Blesséd and Eternal Trinity, which I do not understand, and that I hold fast by faith that which I cannot take in by my intellect.

OF THE QUALITIES REQUIRED BY SHEPHERDS OF THE FLOCK

But someone says, "How shall the Bride believe without a preacher, since faith comes by hearing?" God will provide for this: Those who are to fulfil this office for her and prepare her for her marriage to the heavenly Bridegroom are already on the spot. For hear what she says next. "The watchmen who guard the city found me." Who are these watchmen? Surely those servants of whom the Savior said, "Blesséd are they whom the Lord, when He cometh, shall find watching." What good watchmen they are, who keep watch while we sleep, that they may give account for our souls! What good guardians are they who are wakeful in spirit and pass the night in prayer, who wisely expose the tricks of the enemy, forestall the plots of the ill-disposed, discover their wiles, break their snares, rend their nets, and foil their machinations!

These are lovers of the brethren and of the Christian people, who pray much for the brethren and the Holy City. These are they who, in their tender care for the sheep of the Lord committed to their charge, give their heart to resort early to the Lord Who made them, and pray before the Most High. They keep watch, and they pray at the same time, knowing their own insufficiency and that "except the Lord keep the city, the watchman waketh but in vain."

OF THE LORD'S TWOFOLD COMMAND

The fact that the Lord Himself gave the command to watch and pray, lest we enter into temptation, shows that, without this twofold activity on the part both of the faithful and of those who guard them, neither the City nor the Bride nor the Flock can continue in safety. Do you ask what difference there is between these three? They are all one: The City is so called, because it is a unity of many souls; the Bride, because she is beloved; the Flock, by reason of the tender handling it requires. Take not of this, you friends of the Bridegroom, if such indeed you are! It was not for nothing that the Lord said three times to Peter, "Lovest thou Me?" when confiding His sheep to His care. It was as if He said, "Unless your conscience bears you witness that you love Me perfectly and wholly, more than your own interests, more than your own family, more even than yourself, you must on no account take up this charge or have any dealings whatsoever with the sheep for whom I shed My Blood."

OF CARE FOR THE CITY, BRIDE, AND FLOCK

Give heed, then, you who have been called to the ministry; give heed to yourselves, and to the precious charge committed to your care. It is a City; watch, therefore, to keep it in safety and in concord. It is a Bride; see to her adornment. It is a Flock; be sure that it is given proper pasture. Perhaps the Lord's threefold question covers this threefold care, as well as the three loves I spoke about just now. And every part of this care is threefold in itself; for the City must be protected from tyrants, heretics, and evil spirits; the Bride must be adorned with good works, good habits, and good institutions; and the Flock must be fed on the Holy Scriptures according to their needs—the coarse grass of plain commandments for hard and stubborn souls, more tender herbage in the way of dispensations for the weak and fearful, and the good, strong, solid pasture of the counsels, discreetly set before healthy souls whose faculties have been trained to discern good and evil.

OF THE SHEPHERD'S OWN GOOD EXAMPLE

And, as for children, these must be fed, like little lambs, with the milk of exhortation, not with solid food at all. Besides which, good shepherds will never cease to fatten the flock with good and glad examples, and that from their own lives rather than from those of other people. I myself, for instance, shall carry little weight with you if I set before you the meekness of Moses, the patience of Job, the mercy of Samuel, the holiness of David and so forth, and show myself ungentle and impatient, unmerciful and anything but holy! I can only leave this to God's goodness, that He may supply to you that which I fail to give you and correct whatever I put wrong. But the good Shepherd of souls will always take care to have salt in Himself, as the Gospel says.

I want to expand a little what I have just said, for the benefit of those who, in their too great desire for position, assume burdens too heavy for their strength and so incur great danger. If I am not mistaken, a man needs to be at one and the same time strong, and spiritually minded, and faithful, merely to guard the City; for strength is needful that he may repel the enemy's attacks, spiritual-mindedness that he may discern their ambushes, and faithfulness, that he may not seek his own advantage.

But for the Bride's adornment—that is, for all that pertains to the purifying and correction of souls, who can doubt the further absolute necessity both of a sound moral judgment and of great diligence? Everyone appointed to this work should be as zealous for the Bride's glory as Paul was jealous over her with godly jealousy, that he might present her as a chaste virgin to Christ.

And, finally, how can an ignorant shepherd lead forth the flocks of the Lord with safety into the pastures of God's Word? But if he be learned but not virtuous, it is to be feared that, instead of feeding them by his fertile teaching, he will harm them by his barren life. It is, then, sheer temerity for anyone to undertake the burden of this office, unless he both possesses knowledge and lives a worthy life.

OF THE WATCHMEN, AND HOW THEY FIND THE BRIDE

The Bride, you will observe, says that the watchmen found her, not that she found them. Two questions thus arise. First, who are these watchmen? And then, in what sense do they find the Bride?

The watchmen surely are the apostles and apostolic men. For they it is who guard the City, that is to say, the Church that they have found; and they do this with the greater vigilance as they see her exposed to danger from within, as she is at this present time. For surely they have not withdrawn their protection now from her, on whose behalf they shed their blood, but guard and keep her day and night—that is, not only in their life but also in their death. And if you object that I am saying this as though I had seen the saints defending the Church with my own eyes, whereas in point of fact the matter is beyond human ken, my answer is that God's witness is greater than that of your own eyes and He declares, "I have set watchmen on thy walls, O Jerusalem, which shall never hold their peace, neither by day nor night."

"Oh, but that means the angels," you reply. The angels are included, that I do not deny; for they are all ministering spirits. But why should I not think the same of those who are the angels' equals in respect of power, and at the same time are all the more disposed to take a sympathetic interest in us, by reason of their kinship with us and the fact that they themselves have borne the same afflictions that we are suffering now? Theirs is the voice that says, "We went through fire and water, and Thou broughtest us out into a wealthy place." What? They have come safely through, and would leave us, their children, in the thick of the flames and the waves, without so much as stretching out a helping hand to us? Indeed it is not so.

OF THE KEEPERS OF THE CHURCH

It is well with thee, O Mother Church, it is well with thee in this place of thy pilgrimage, for thy help cometh both from heaven and from earth. Those who keep thee slumber not nor sleep. Thy keepers are the holy angels; the spirits and souls of the righteous are the watchmen on thy walls. Both alike have found thee; both alike protect thee, the saints with special care because without thee they will not themselves be perfected, the angels with a like solicitude because the wholeness of their number cannot be restored except through thee.

So much for the identity of the watchmen. We come now to the second question: In what sense did they find the Bride? I think it was their special task to find her, for thereto were they sent, as it is written, "How shall they preach, except they be sent?" The Bride was looking for her Spouse, and that He knew; for He Himself had urged her on to seek Him and to give herself to keep His laws. He, therefore, sent out gardeners (so to speak) to plant the truth in her and water it—in other words, to meet her on her way and give her certain news of her Belovéd, Who is Himself the Truth.

OF FINDING THE BRIDE

You notice also that she did not find Him Whom she sought, but was herself found by those for whom she was not seeking. There is a warning here for those who are not afraid to enter on the ways of life without a guide, thinking themselves to be as much masters as learners in the art of the spirit! Nor do they stop there. They collect disciples round them and become blind leaders of the blind. How many have fallen into dangerous error in this way! For, being ignorant of Satan's tricks, those who began in the spirit have ended up in the flesh and, by being shamefully deceived, have fallen into culpable disorder. Let any of you who are inclined that way take warning by the Bride, who failed to find Him Whom she sought until the watchmen met her and she availed herself of their instruction. He who does not open his heart without reserve to his director is opening the door of his soul to the seducer. And he who sends the sheep to pasture without a keeper is a herdsman not of sheep but of wolves.

OF THE WORK OF GOD, ANGELS, AND MEN

Let us consider further this finding of the Bride, for the word "found" seems to be used here in an unusual sense. In the great mystery of the chaste and holy union between Christ and the Church, three agents work together—God, the angelic host, and man. God could have wrought this work alone, without the smallest aid; His creatures, on the other hand, could have effected nothing by themselves; He admitted them to a share in the work solely for their own good. For He has made work to be a source of merit for man; and He allows the an-

gels to help in man's salvation, in order that they may be loved by men. It is indeed most fitting that this should be so; for men are obviously loved by angels, because it is they who must eventually repair the ancient losses in the angelic commonwealth, and it would not be right for the Kingdom of Charity, in which the human and the angel races are to reign together, to be governed by any other laws than those of mutual love between men and angels and between both and God.

There is, however, a great difference between the mode of operation in these three. God effects what He wills by willing only, without stir or motion, and without dependence on any place or time or cause or person. For He is the Lord of Hosts, Who judges all things in tranquillity; and He is Wisdom; Who sweetly orders all things. The angels likewise work without stir or fret, although their operation is accompanied by motion, both in time and in space. But man's activity is never free either from mental disturbance or from physical movement; for he is bidden to work out his own salvation in fear and trembling, and to eat his bread in the sweat of his brow.

OF PREDESTINATION, CREATION, AND INSPIRATION

Consider, next, that there are three steps in this work of our salvation which God reserves to Himself, and in which He is beforehand with all His fellow-workers. The three are these: Predestination, Creation, and Inspiration. Of these, Predestination began neither with the Church itself nor with the world; it is before all time. Creation began with time; and Inspiration takes place in time, when and where God wills. With God, therefore, the Church of the Elect has always existed; moreover, she has always been acceptable to Him and He has always loved her. But no one even of the blessèd spirits could have found the Church hidden away in that deep bosom of eternity, unless God to Whom eternity belongs had chosen to reveal her.

But when, at the Creator's nod, the Church at last appeared and could be seen, she was not found immediately either by men or angels; for she was hard to recognize, so shadowed was she by the earthly form of man and by the gloom of death. And never a one of the sons of men has entered this life without this shroud of disorder, save only He Who enters it without a stain. He is Immanuel—God-with-Us—Who, though He is one of us and for our sakes has taken the likeness of our curse and of our sin, yet has not taken their reality.

Of the rest, all have come into the world in the same condition, whether they be elect or reprobate. There is no distinction anywhere: all have sinned, all wear the token of their shame. So the Church could not be found by any creature, even when she was herself created; for she was hidden, for the time being, both within the blessèd bosom of Predestination and in the accursèd lump of our humanity.

But she who was thus hidden both by the Wisdom that predestined her and by the Power that created her, was made known in due time by Grace, according to the mode of working on which I have bestowed the name of Inspiration, because it consists in an inbreathing of the Bridegroom's Spirit into predestined human souls, in order to prepare in them a way for the Lord and the Gospel of His glory.

Without this prevenient grace, the watchmen would have toiled in vain at their preaching. But when they say the Word thus running very swiftly, the nations turning to the Lord so readily, all the tribes and languages united in the Faith, and all the ends of the earth gathered up into the bosom of the One Catholic and Apostolic Church that is the Mother of us all, then they recognised the riches of God's grace which had been hidden through the ages, and rejoiced that they had found her whom the Lord had chosen for His Bride before time was.

OF BEING FOUND BY THE WATCHMEN

I think, then, that when the Bride says that the watchmen found her, she means that she was gathered in by them and that they, so to speak, found out about her; but her preelection and her subsequent conversion she ascribes to Him, to Whom alone each soul must say, "Turn us, O God of our salvation!" He Who knows them that are His, Who knows whom He has chosen, foreknew the Bride from all eternity; we cannot therefore say that she was found by Him. But we may safely say that He prepared her to be found; for one of the watchmen themselves tells us, "I, John, saw the Holy City, New Jerusalem, coming down from God out of heaven, prepared as a Bride adorned for her husband." And hear the Preparer of the Church Himself pointing her out to the watchmen under another figure, when He says, "Lift up your eyes and look on the fields, that they are white"—that is to say, prepared—"already unto harvest."

The Head of the Household invites others to help Him in His work from the time when He knows that all things are now ready; so that, without much labour on their own part, they may be able to rejoice in their success and to share Paul's proud boast of being "fellow-labourers with God." For what is their work? It is to look for the Bride and, when they have found her, to give her news of her Belovéd. They are the Bridegroom's friends; therefore they seek His glory, not their own. And they will have no very heavy task with her; for she is here already, and already seeking Him with her whole heart, because her will has been made ready by the Lord.

And now she, whom Grace forestalled, herself forestalls her teachers and inquires, "Have you seen Him Whom my soul loveth?" This shows how right she was to say that they had found her—found her, that is, as already foreknown and forestalled by the Lord of the City. So was Cornelius found by Peter, and Paul by Ananias; the Lord prevented and prepared them both. And Philip found Nathanael, but the Lord had seen him first beneath the fig-tree and had prepared him to be found. In the same way Andrew found his brother Simon; but the Lord had foreseen Simon too, and foreknew that He would call him Cephas, because of his rock-like faith.

We read of Mary also that she was found with child by the Holy Ghost. And I think that the Bride of the Lord resembles His Mother in this; for, if she herself had not been full of the fruit of the Spirit, she would not have questioned the watchmen so familiarly. She did not wait for them to speak and say why they had come, but spoke to them herself, asking them out of the fullness of her heart, "Have you seen Him Whom my soul loveth?" For she knows how blesséd are the eyes that have seen, and asks them wonderingly, "Are you the people to whom it has been given to see Him Whom so many prophets and kings desired in vain to see? Are you the men who were found worthy to behold Wisdom in the flesh, Truth in the body, God in man? There are many who tell me, 'Lo, here He is!' or 'There!' But I deem it safer to be guided by you, who ate and drank with Him after He rose from death."

OF THE TENACITY WITH WHICH THE LOVING SOUL CLINGS TO HER LORD

"Have you seen Him Whom my soul loveth?" O headlong, eager, fiery, reckless love, which sufferest not the mind to entertain a thought except of thee, which spurnest and despisest all things else, and art contented only with thyself! Subverting order, disregarding custom, ignoring moderation, by thine unaided might thou overmasterest all considerations of fitness, reason, reticence, prudence, and discretion, and makest them subservient to thyself! Thus everything that this Bride says savours and speaks of thee and of nought else, so wholly hast thou claimed her as thine own, alike in heart and tongue. "Have you seen Him Whom my soul loveth?" she says—not naming Him, so certain is she that they know her thoughts.

OF THE NEED FOR LOVE TO UNDERSTAND THIS SONG

Strange language, truly—quite unlike the rest of Scripture but very characteristic of this marriage-song, in which it is the holy love behind the words that has to be considered, more than the words themselves. For Love speaks in it everywhere; if anyone would understand the things he reads in it, then let him love! For he who does not love will hear and read this Song in vain; the cold heart cannot grasp its burning eloquence. It is with love as with a language, such as Greek or Latin; just as, unless you know the tongue yourself, you will not understand it when you hear it spoken, so to the man who loves not, love's language appears crude, and will be only sounding brass and tinkling cymbal in his ears. But these watchmen have themselves received the power of loving from the Holy Spirit; they therefore understand the Spirit's words, and can reply forthwith in the same speech—that is to say, with loving acts of service.

They do indeed give her such pertinent instruction that she can shortly say, "A little while after I had passed beyond them, I found Him Whom my soul loves." She says "a little while," for their reply was brief; they handed her the Creed. She had to pass or come across them; for it was through them that she must learn the truth. But it was necessary also that she should pass beyond them, or she would not have found Him Whom she sought.

The watchmen were themselves aware of this; for they preached not themselves but the Lord Jesus, Who is undoubtedly both beyond them and

above. She had to pass beyond them for another reason too—because He in Whose steps she follows did the same. He did not only pass from death to life, He passed beyond to glory. Must she not do likewise? For she can never reach Him, unless she follows in His footsteps, whithersoever He goes. So you may say that to believe in the Resurrection is to pass; but to believe in the Ascension is to pass beyond. Christ is the Firstfruits of them that sleep; He has passed beyond and our faith follows Him. If He ascends to heaven, it is there; if He goes down to hell, it is there also. If He takes wings at dawn and dwells in the uttermost parts of the sea, there, says Faith, "Thy Hand shall lead me, and Thy right Hand shall hold me fast." For is it not our faith that the Bridegroom's All-good, Almighty Father has raised us up and made us sit along with Him at His right Hand in heaven?

OF THE CHURCH'S STEADFASTNESS

We come to the next words, "I held Him, and I will not let Him go, till I have brought Him into my mother's house, into the chamber of her that bore me." So indeed it has proved. Since the Ascension, the Christian family, the Church's faith and charity have never failed. Floods have come and winds have blown and beaten against her, but she has not fallen, for she is founded on a rock—the Rock of Christ. Neither the wordiness of the philosophers nor the jeers of the heretics nor the swords of the persecutors have been able to separate her from the love of God which is in Christ Jesus, so firmly does she cling to Him Whom her soul loves, so certain is she that it is good for her to hold her fast by God.

"It is good for glueing," says Isaiah. What stronger glue is there than this, which water cannot wash away nor winds break up nor swords cut through? "Many waters cannot quench love," as we read further on in this same Song. "I hold Him, and I will not let Him go." The holy patriarch said, "I will not let Thee go, except Thou bless me." But she will not release Him even then, "It is Thou Whom I want," she says, "not just Thy blessing. For whom have I in heaven but Thee? And there is none upon earth that I desire in comparison of Thee."

"I held Him, and I will not let Him go," she says. But perhaps He is as ready to be held as she to hold; for His delights are with the sons of men, and He has promised, "Lo, I am with you all the days, even unto the end of the age." What could be stronger than this bond, compassed by the one intense desire of two wills? She says, "I held Him." But at the same time she herself is held by Him, as she says in another place, "Thy right Hand hath held me." How can she fall, who both holds and is held? She holds Him by her strong faith and her tender love; but she would not long maintain her hold, if He did not hold her. It is the power and the mercy of the Lord that hold her fast.

OF THE ULTIMATE SALVATION OF THE JEWS

"I held Him, and I will not let Him go, till I have brought Him into my mother's house, into the chamber of her that bore me." Great is the Church's charity, for she does not grudge a share in her delights even to the Synagogue her rival! What could be kinder than to want to share Him Whom her soul loves with an enemy? And yet, "salvation is of the Jews"; it is not surprising really that this should be so. Let the Saviour return to the place whence He departed, that the remnant of Israel may be saved! Let not the branches be ungrateful to the root, nor the sons to their mother. Let not the branches grudge the root the sap that they took from it, nor the sons grudge their mother the milk drawn from her breasts.

Let the Church hold fast to the salvation which the Jews have lost; she holds it till the fullness of the nations shall come in and all Israel be saved. Let her desire the common salvation to be common property, since everyone can have it without anybody having any less! She does indeed do this; and she does more. She desires for her rival more even than salvation; she desires for her also the name and grace of Bride.

OF THE BRIDEGROOM'S ENTRY INTO THE HOUSE

Such charity would be incredible, did not the Bride's own words compel us to believe it. For she says, you notice, that she intends to bring Him to Whom she clings, not only into her mother's house but into her chamber, and that implies an unique prerogative. It would suffice for her mother's salvation if the Bridegroom entered her house, as He did that of Zacchaeus; but His entrance into the privacy of the chamber denotes a special grace, a secret shared between Him and her whose private room it is.

Salvation is for the house in general; the bridal chamber has its own delights. "I will bring Him into my mother's house," she says. What house is this, save that concerning which He warned the Jews, "Behold, your house shall be left unto you desolate"? He forsook His house; He left His heritage, as by the prophet's mouth He had foretold; and now the Bride is promising to bring Him back to it, and to restore its lost salvation to her mother's house! And, as if that were not enough, she adds that she will bring Him also into her mother's chamber. It is as Bridegroom that He enters there! O mighty power of love!

The Saviour had gone forth in anger from His house and His inheritance; and now He has so far relented and laid by His wrath towards her that He returns, not only as her Saviour but also as her Spouse! Blesséd art thou from the Lord, O daughter, who hast thus curbed the anger and restored the heritage! Blesséd art thou of thy mother, for whose sake wrath is turned away and Salvation returns in person!

"I am thy Salvation," He tells her, and He goes on to say, "I will espouse thee to Me in faith, I will espouse thee to Me in judgment and in righteousness, in mercy and in lovingkindnesses." But remember that she who effects this reconciliation is the Bride. You must not think, however, that she renounces her own rights in bringing her Mother and her Spouse together. Good daughter that she is, she wants to share Him with her Mother, but that does not mean that she herself will give Him up. He is enough for both of them; for they are one in Him. He is our Peace, Who hath made both one, that there may be one Bride and One Bridegroom, Jesus Christ our Lord, Who is God above all, blesséd for ever. Amen.

Chapter Thirty-Three

On the same passage as Chapter Thirty-Two

OF THE IMAGE AND LIKENESS OF GOD, IN WHICH THE SOUL IS MADE

THUS FAR, we have interpreted this passage as referring to the Word and the Church. Let us now consider it with reference to the Word and the soul.

Somebody says, "How can you couple the Word and the soul like that? What have they in common?" Much every way. The Word is the Image of God; the soul is *made* in the Image, and also in the Likeness. Take the Image first. The Word is Truth and Wisdom and Righteousness, and those constitute the Image; for the Word is Truth of Truth and Wisdom of Wisdom and Righteousness of Righteousness, in the same way that He is Light of Light and God of God.

The soul is none of these things, but she is capable of them and desires them; and perhaps that is why she is said to be made in the Image. She is a lofty creature, great in capacity for majesty and upright in her longing for it. But there is, none the less, a vast difference between her and the Word; for the Word's greatness and righteousness are according to His equality with the Father, and by generation; whereas the soul has these qualities by measure only, and by the gracious gift of God in her creation. In the Word, moreover, not only are His greatness and His uprightness one thing, but they are *one with Him;* whereas in the soul these things are distinct both from each other and from the soul itself. For though the soul is great because of her capacity for heavenly things, she is by no means upright but is bent. And even her greatness is not the same thing as herself; for the angels also possess a like capacity.

OF THE SOUL'S LIKENESS TO GOD

We said that the affinity between the Word and the soul resulted from the fact that the soul is made both in the Image of God and in His Likeness. Let us consider now the meaning of the latter; for the more we understand our noble origin, the more we shall blush for our unworthy life and try so to reform ourselves, God helping us, that we may approach with confidence to the embraces of the Word. The soul derives from this original Likeness to God three things: firstly, a natural Simplicity of being; secondly, Immortality; and thirdly, Freedom. By her natural Simplicity, to exist is for her the same thing as to live; but it is not the same thing as to live well and blessedly, though it serves as the starting-point whence she may proceed to both these things. Her Simplicity thus constitutes only a partial likeness to God; since with God existence and good and blessèd life are the same thing. In respect of her immortality also the soul is like the Word, but not equal to Him; for the Divine Immortality is incapable of any change, not only of the change of death. And the Freedom of the soul, which included both the power of discerning good and evil and the power of choice, is perhaps an even more obvious element in her likeness to the Word.

OF SIMPLICITY, IMMORTALITY, AND FREEDOM

These three qualities of Simplicity, Immortality, and Freedom are, then, in God; and they are also in the soul, essentially and always. For the plain teaching of Scripture in regard to the unlikeness to God which has been brought about by sin is not that the original God-likeness in the soul has been effaced, but that another likeness has been superimposed upon it. The soul has not put off her native form; she has put on a strange form over it. The latter is added and it hides the first; but the first is not lost and cannot be destroyed. Thus the apostle says, "Their foolish heart was darkened," or as the prophet puts it, "How is the gold become dim, the finest colour changed!" The gold bewails its tarnished state; but it is still gold. The perfect colour may be changed; but the base on which it is made up remains the same.

The soul's essential simplicity is unshaken; but it is hidden out of sight beneath a thick cloak of duplicity—that is to say, of human fraud, hypocrisy, and sham. By fraud the serpent tempted Eve, pretending that he was her friend; by fraud she and Adam, after their seduction, tried to hide their nakedness and shame. And the same poison of deceit has infected the whole of their posterity; for which of the sons of Adam can really bear to be known for what he is?

Nevertheless, in every soul the innate simplicity co-exists with this inherited duplicity, thereby increasing its confusion. And its immortality also continues, though shadowed and blackened by bodily death and attachment to mortal and transitory things. Freedom likewise persists; but it is perpetually opposed and enslaved by the law of sin warring in the members of the body.

OF THE BRIDE'S DISGUST FOR EVIL

When the soul perceives this contradiction in herself, what can she do but cry, "Lord, who is like unto Thee?" For the evil in her leads her to despair, but the great good in her recalls her towards hope. The more she is disgusted with the evil in herself, the more she yearns to realize the good, which also she sees, and to become what she was made, simple and upright, fearing God and departing from evil. Why should she not be able to depart from that which she was able to approach? Why should she not approach what she departed from?

Yet she must depend on grace for either movement; for it is wisdom that conquers vice, not nature or our own activity. But she has ground for confidence, because it is the Word to Whom she turns. He is not unmindful of the kinship and the persistent likeness between Himself and her, but graciously admits her who resembles Him in nature into the fellowship of the Holy Spirit. Like seeks like, even on the natural plane; and the Word seeks the soul crying, "Return, O Shulamite, return, that we may look upon thee!" He would not look at her when she was unlike Him; but, when His Likeness is restored, He will behold her gladly, and will admit her also to behold Himself. "For we know that, when He shall appear, we shall behold Him as He is."

OF THE RESTORATION OF OUR LIKENESS TO THE WORD

The cry "Lord, who is like unto Thee?" means, therefore, that though the restoration of our likeness to the Word is very difficult, it must not be regarded as impossible. Or, if you like, you may take it as a cry of wonder. For the Likeness which accompanies the vision of God and is itself the vision is assuredly most wonderful and worthy to be praised. Who does not stand amazed before the love of God, recalling her who spurned Him? And when the evil, which partly constitutes the soul's unlikeness to Him, is at long last removed out of the midst of her, there will be between them oneness of spirit, mutual beholding and mutual love.

"When that which is perfect is come, then that which is in part shall be done away," and there shall be between God and the soul love pure and perfected, full knowledge, open vision, indissoluble union, inseparable fellowship, and perfect likeness. Then the soul will know, even as she is known; she will love, even as she is loved; and the Bridegroom, Who is Jesus Christ our Lord, God above all, blessèd for ever, will rejoice over the Bride, knowing and known, loving and beloved.

ON RECOVERING THE LIKENESS THROUGH LOVE

We have seen that every soul, however burdened by sin and enmeshed in vices she may be, and in spite of the fact that she is an exile on earth and a prisoner in the body—we have seen, I say, that every soul, although she be thus damned and desperate, has none the less ground in herself not only for hoping for forgiveness but also for daring to aspire to the nuptials of the Word. Why should she fear to be allied in covenant relationship with God, and to bear love's sweet yoke together with the King of angels, what indeed should she hesitate to do with Him, by Whose Image and Likeness she knows herself to be still honoured and ennobled? Why should she tremble even at His Majesty, when her own origin is what it is? All that she has to do is to maintain her innate nobility by integrity of life, or rather to adorn the heavenly image stamped upon her with worthy deeds and dispositions, as with fitting colours.

Why, then, does she not get to work? The faculty of making effort is a great natural gift; but if it be not used, our other endowments will just go to waste, and that will be an outrage to the Giver. God has left us this witness to our Divine origin in our own hearts, in order that we may be continually spurred on by our likeness to the Word, to stay with Him or to return to Him, if we have left Him; which last of course we do, not by movement in space but by any spiritual motion away from His Likeness and so from our true self.

This unlikeness (as I said before) vitiates the soul's nature but does not destroy it. And her return is her conversion or turning to the Word, that she may be reformed by and conformed to Him. By what means is this change to be effected? By love. For it is written, "Be ye followers of God, as most dear children; and walk in love even as Christ loved you."

OF CONFORMITY BETWEEN
THE SOUL AND THE WORD

It is this conformity which makes the marriage between the soul and the Word, when she who is like Him by nature shows herself like Him in will also, loving as she is beloved. So, when she loves perfectly, this marriage is completed. What could be lovelier than this conformity? What more to be desired than this charity, which makes the soul, content no longer with a human master, boldly approach the Word Himself, cleave to Him and consult Him about everything with a quickness of perception proportionate to the intensity of her desire? This is a true bond of holy, spiritual marriage; and indeed, when conformity of will makes of the two one spirit, it is more than a bond; it is an embrace.

Nor is this conformity of will in the least impaired by the inequality of the partners; for love knows no respect of persons. Honour and fear are swallowed up in love; love is sufficient for itself and overpowers all other feelings, making them part of itself, so that the soul that loves just loves and ignores everything else. He Who deserves to be honoured and held in awe loves rather to be loved. He and the soul are Bridegroom and Bride; and He, the Bridegroom, is not only loving, He is Love.

OF GOD'S DEMAND FOR OUR LOVE

God demands fear, as Lord; honour, as Father; but as the Bridegroom He demands our love. Love is the highest of these three; without it fear has torment and honour is graceless. Fear is servile, unless love makes it free; and honour which does not proceed from love is adulation. Honour and fear are due to God alone; but He will accept neither, unless love's honey sweeten it. Love alone is enough by itself and of itself. It is at once a merit and its own reward. It seeks neither cause nor consequence beyond itself: it is its own fruit and its own object.

I love, because I love; I love, that I may love. A great thing is love, provided only that it returns always to the Fountain whence it springs and draws its ever-flowing waters from their Source. Love is the only faculty or power by which the creature renders the Creator the same good as that which it receives from Him. If God is angry with me, for instance, I am not angry with Him in return, but must abase myself and beg for pardon. If He accuses me, I do not fling an answering accusation back but must admit His justice. Nor if He judges me, will I judge Him, but rather worship Him. And, when He saves me, He does not ask me to save Him; nor does He Who sets all free Himself require to be freed by us. If He exercises His authority, my part is to serve Him; if He commands, my part is to obey; and it is not for me to require from Him either obedience or service in return. But now you see how different it is with love. When God loves us, He would have us love Him back, and nothing else. For He loves us, in order that He may be loved; because He knows that those who love Him are blessed in their loving.

OF THE NATURE OF PURE LOVE

Love is a great thing; but it has degrees, and the Bride's is the highest of all. Children love their father, but often their eyes are on the inheritance they hope to get from him, and they respect him more than they love him, for fear of losing it. Love which is motived by hope of getting something looks suspect to me. It is weak, for it will fail altogether if the hope be withdrawn; and it is impure, because it seeks for something other than itself.

Pure love is not mercenary, nor does it derive its strength from hope, nor suffer the anguish of distrust. This is the love of the Bride; it is itself her being and her hope; she is full of it and the Bridegroom is content with it. He requires nothing else from her, for she has nothing else to give. It is this which makes them Bridegroom and Bride; for it is the love perculiar to those joined in wedlock, and nobody else, not even a child, can share it.

Rightly, then, does the Bride renounce all other affections and devote herself wholly to love and love alone, since love is the one thing she can reciprocate. But when she has poured out her whole being in love, what does it amount to, beside that inexhaustible and ever-flowing Fount? The stream of Love Himself, of the Word Who is the Bridegroom, and the stream of her who loves Him, the soul who is the Bride, flow not with equal volume; you might as well compare a thirsty man to the spring at which he drinks!

What then? Are her hope of perfect union, her yearning and her longing, her confidence and ardour, to perish and fail of their purpose because she cannot keep up with the Giant Who runs apace, or equal the Honey in His sweetness, the Lamb in His meekness, the Lily in His dazzling purity, the Sun in His splendour and Love's own Self in love? No! For though she loves less than the Word, because she is a creature and is less, yet, if she loves with her whole being, nothing is lacking, for the whole is there. And to love like that is, as I said, to wed; for it is not possible for a soul to love thus and not to be beloved, and it is this reciprocity of love between the two that constitutes complete and perfect marriage.

THAT GOD ANTICIPATES THE SOUL IN HER QUEST FOR HIM

"Nightlong on my little bed I sought Him Whom my soul loveth." It is a great good to seek God; I think myself it is the greatest good the soul can have. It is at once the first of God's good gifts to her, and the highest stage of her progress. No virtue comes before it, for none is found in those who seek not God. Neither does any virtye follow it, for what end is there to the quest for God? "Seek His Face evermore," the psalmist says.

I think we shall not cease from seeking Him, even when we have found Him; for He is sought by longing, not by locomotion; and when the soul achieves the bliss of finding Him, her longing is not quenched but kindled, as fire flames the more when oil is poured upon it. That is how it is. Joy will be filled to the brim; but the desire and the ensuing quest will not come to an end. Try to imagine what this quest will be, that never fails of its Object, for He is always present; and what the longing that is unaccompanied by any anxious fear, because it always has His Fullness in possession.

OF BEING SOUGHT BY GOD

I have made these preliminary remarks, because it is so important for every soul among you who is seeking God to realize that He was first in the field, and was seeking you, or ever you began to search for Him. For, if you do not acknowledge this, the great good may become the greatest evil; for there is no worse crime than to take to oneself the credit for even a little of the grace one has received. You could not have sought the Word, when once you had gone forth or been cast out from Him, if He had not sought you. Left to itself, our soul is as a spirit that goeth and cometh not again, "I have gone astray," the wanderer says, "like a sheep that is lost. O seek Thy servant!" O man, you would return, then? But if you have the power to carry out your will, why do you ask for help? Why do you beg from another what you yourself already have in plenty? Clearly he has the will, but not the power. But whence has he the will? Assuredly, from the Word's visitation, the Word's search for the soul. And this search had not been without effect, for it has worked the willingness, without which no return is possible.

But the soul is so feeble, and the way back so beset with obstacles, that it is not enough for Him to seek her only once. However willing she is to return, the will alone is not enough; power to implement the will is needed too. "To will is present with me," the apostle says, "but how to perform that which is good I find not." So, in the verse I quoted before, the psalmist seeks for nothing save that he may be sought; he would not seek thus to be sought, if he had not been sought before; nor would he seek to be sought again, had he been sought enough.

I do not think, however, that our present text applies to the soul which has not yet received the grace of this second seeking—the soul, that is, which has not begun to return. For how could she go on to say that she will arise and go about the city and seek her Belovéd through the streets and squares, if she herself still needed to be sought? Let her seek Him as she can, provided she remembers always that He both sought her and loved her, before she either loved or looked for Him. And let us pray, dearly belovéd, that these same mercies may speedily prevent us too; for we stand in extreme need of them.

I do not say this of you all; many, I know, are walking in the love wherewith Christ loved us and are seeking Him in simplicity of heart. But there are others, I regret to say, who have as yet shown no indication of the prevenient grace, and therefore no sign of salvation. They are men who love themselves, not the Lord, and seek their own ends, not His.

OF SEEKING GOD

"I sought Him Whom my soul loveth." You have been incited to this quest by the kindness of Him Who both sought and loved you, before you loved or sought for Him; and you could neither seek nor love Him at all, had you not been anticipated by this twofold blessing of His love and quest for you. The love is the ground of the seeking, the seeking the fruit of the love and also its clear proof. You have been loved, so that you should not think that He is seeking you to punish you. You have been sought, so that you should not complain that you had been loved to no purpose. The love and the seeking combine to give you courage to dispel your diffidence, to urge you to return, to stir your affections. Hence come the zeal and ardour with which you seek Him Whom your soul loves; for just as you could not seek Him till you had been sought, so—now that He has sought you—you cannot but seek Him.

Those who do not love Him are afraid of Him and dare not return for fear of what may happen. But I, because I love, am not afraid. Because I love, I can no more doubt His love for me than mine for Him. If I reciprocate His love, why should I not reciprocate His search? He forgave me when I spurned Him; so why should He be angry when I seek Him? Kind is the Spirit of the Word, and kind the things He tells me; the Word desires and longs for me, He says; for He, Who searches the deep things of God and knows His thoughts of peace towards us, is in this secret between the Word and me. How can I fail to be inspirited to seek Him, when I have such experience of His mercy, and such assurance of the peace between us?

THE NEEDS OF THE SOUL, ON ACCOUNT OF WHICH SHE SEEKS THE WORD

"Nightly on my little bed I sought Him Whom my soul loveth." Our spiritual needs are doubtless as many as are our infidelities. Nevertheless we may say briefly that the soul seeks the Word in order to obtain from Him these seven things: Correction, Enlightenment, Virtue or Strength, Wisdom, Beauty, Fruitfulness, and lastly the blissful Enjoyment of Himself.

OF CORRECTION

First comes Correction. The Word says in the Gospel, "Agree with thine adversary quickly, whiles thou art in the way with him." What better counsel could He give, Who is Himself the Adversary to our carnal desires? But you cannot agree with Him, unless you disagree with yourself and become your own adversary in the long struggle with inveterate habits and inborn inclinations. You can no more win this battle by yourself than you can stop a rushing torrent with your finger or make Jordan flow backwards. You must seek the Word and agree with Him Who gives you the power so to do. You must flee for help to Him Who ranges Himself against you; so that He may oppose and threaten you no longer, but may approve of you and change you by His inpoured grace much more effectively than by His wrath.

OF ENLIGHTENMENT

The next need is Enlightenment, that we may know wherein His Will consists. Happy are you, if you can say with the psalmist, "Thy Word is a lantern unto my feet, and a light unto my paths." You have made no small progress if you have learned both to desire and to recognise the good. For the one gift is life and the other vision;

whereas formerly your soul was dead, in that you willed the evil, and blind, in that you did not know the good.

OF VIRTUE OR STRENGTH

Your soul, then, lives and sees, thanks to the help and working of the Word. He has set you on your two feet of Devotion and Knowledge; but "let him that thinketh he standeth take heed lest he fall." So you need Virtue, which means Strength, from Him against three enemies, the devil, the world, and yourself; and you must lean on Him, if you would keep upright, remembering His warning, "Without Me ye can do nothing."

OF WISDOM

In the Word Himself Virtue and Wisdom are perhaps one thing. But in the soul they have not the same action; and Wisdom, therefore, is the next thing we must seek from Him. I think you will not be far wrong if you define Wisdom as the *love* of Virtue; for where love is, toil becomes a pleasure. The foolishness of the first woman depraved the palate of our race right at the outset. But lo! Wisdom has again possessed Himself of the body and heart of a woman, in order that we, who by the one had been deformed unto foolishness, might be reformed unto wisdom by the other. And now Wisdom is for ever prevailing over evil in the hearts which it has entered, cleansing the vitiated palate of the soul and correcting the perverted taste.

How many good actions are performed without any enjoyment on the part of the doers, because they are actuated by some logical motive, or by circumstances, or even by necessity, and not by any relish for the good, as such! And, on the contrary, how many do wrong things, not because they like doing them, but because they are driven to do them by fear or the desire for something else! But those who really act from preference are either wise, delighting in the good for its own sake, or ill-disposed, delighting in the evil. To be reformed unto wisdom means, therefore, to have this happy experience of Wisdom's victory in one's own soul. And, as we look to Virtue to enable us to endure tribulations, so do we look to Wisdom to make us rejoice in them.

OF BEAUTY

The soul which has received Correction, Enlightenment, Virtue, and Wisdom has thereby recovered life, health, stability, and maturity; and she needs next the gift of Beauty. "The King shall desire thy beauty," says the prophet; and, in another place, "The Lord hath reigned, He is clothed with beauty." Of course He desires her, His Image and His Bride, to be clothed as Himself! And the closer the likeness, the dearer she will be. I think the beauty of the soul consists in what we call nobility or honesty. For nobility appears in the outward behaviour, but its dwelling and its root are in the conscience. And there is no brighter light and no more glorious witness than that which shines out when the Truth shines in the inmost heart and the heart has therefore a truthful vision of itself.

What is she really like, this noble, honest soul? She is chaste, modest, careful, circumspect, avoiding everything that might tarnish her conscience, which indeed is clear of any cause for shame or for averting her eyes from God's light. That is the beauty in which He takes pleasure and which we have named nobility or honesty. And when this beauty wholly fills the soul, it makes the body a mirror of itself; so that its loveliness shines out in a man's every action—his words, his looks, his movements, and even in his mirth. Blesséd is the soul that has thus put on the beauty of holiness and spotless innocence, sure proof of her conformity, not to the world but to the Word, Who is the Brightness of eternal life.

OF FRUITFULNESS

The soul which has progressed thus far dares to aspire to union with the Word. And why should she not do so, since she knows herself to be like Him, and therefore ripe for marriage? So, when you see a soul that has left all else and cleaves to the Word alone, who lives for the Word, rules herself by the Word and conceives by the Word what she brings forth by Him, a soul who can truthfully say, "To me to live is Christ, to die is gain"—when you see such a soul, I say, you must regard her as truly wedded to the Word. The heart of her Husband can safely trust in such a one; He knows that she is faithful, because she has accounted all things else as dross, in order to gain Him.

Souls are, however, rendered fruitful in two ways. Some holy mothers bring forth souls by preaching, as did Paul who says, "My little children, of whom I travail in birth again, til Christ be formed in you." Others bring forth deep insights into spiritual things by meditation. And, in this second sort of travail, the soul sometimes goes forth from herself and out of her bodily senses; so that, although aware of the Word, she is not aware of herself. It is when the soul is ravished by the Word's unutterable sweetness that she is thus stolen by Him from herself, as it were, in order that she may enjoy Him. But when she is bearing Him the fruit of souls she is otherwise affected; her thought is then all for her neighbour and his needs.

OF ENJOYMENT OF THE BRIDEGROOM

And truly the mother is happy in her offspring; but the Bride in the arms of her Spouse is happier still. Dear indeed are the children, the pledges of His love; but she prefers His kisses. It is good to save souls; but it is far more pleasant to depart and be with the Word. But when does that happen and how long does it last? Sweet intercourse it is, but brief and rare. And this—that we may blissfully enjoy Him—is the last need of which I spoke, for which we seek the Word.

IN PRAISE OF MODESTY

"Nightlong on my little bed I sought Him——" There is one more thing I should like to point out to you about this verse; and that is the modesty which the Bride shows in it. I do not think that there is any virtue lovelier than modesty; and I should like to take it in my hands like a beautiful flower, and present it to each of our young brethren here. Not that we elders do not need it too; but it is a jewel specially befitting both the life and the demeanour of the young; it is the sister of self-control, a certain index of good character, and a sure token of greater holiness to come.

The Wise Man says, "There is a shame that bringeth sin, and there is a shame that bringeth glory." That the Bride's shamefastness is of the latter kind is indicated by the time and place of her quest for the Word—"nightlong on my little bed." Nothing is so congenial to a modest mind as privacy; and this the night-time and the couch ensure. For we are bidden to enter our chamber when we want to pray, doubtless for the sake of privacy. And though this is enjoined partly as a measure of precaution, lest if men see us praying their praise may hinder our prayer's effect and rob us of its fruit, there is a lesson of modesty in the injunction too.

For nothing is more integral to modesty than its avoidance of praise and display; and nothing is more unfitting than ostentatious piety, especially in the young. For youth is the time to lay the foundations of religious life, as Jeremiah says, "It is good for a man that he bear the yoke in his youth." In the prayers we are about to offer, we shall use the words, "I am small"—literally, very young—"and of no reputation; yet do I not forget Thy commandments." These words will be a worthy act of praise on your part, if they express your genuine modesty.

OF THE TIME AND PLACE FOR PRAYER

He who would pray must choose the best time to do so, as well as the best place. A time of leisure is the fittest and most suitable, especially the silence of the night; for prayer is freer in the night, and purer too. How confidently then does prayer mount up, unknown to any except God and the holy angel who receives it on the heavenly altar! How acceptable and clear it is in its modesty then, how peaceful and serene with no noise or interruption to disturb it! And how pure and sincere it is, too, unsoiled by the dust of earthly care or desire for approbation!

How right and wise was the Bride to choose the night-time and her couch wherein to pray—that is, to seek the Word! For those two things are one; and you do not pray aright if in your prayer you seek for anything except the Word Himself, and that which you need for His sake; for all things are in Him. In Him is healing for your wounds, relief for your necessities, mending for your faults, and grace for further progress—everything, in fact, that it is good for a man to have.

It is unreasonable, therefore, to ask the Word for anything except Himself, when He is everything. For though we do sometimes seem to ask for the supply of our temporal needs, if it is for His service that we ask for them—as it ought to be—it is really for Himself that we are asking, even then. Those whose habit it is to use all to His glory know well what I mean.

OF THE COUCH AND NIGHT-TIME

There is a further spiritual meaning in the privacy of the couch and the night-time, which will repay investigation. For if we take the bed as signifying the weakness of our nature, and the night as denoting its ignorance, we shall see that the Bride has good reason for seeking the Word so earnestly. For He is the Power and the Wisdom of God, and He alone can meet her weakness with His Might, her darkness with His Light. If anyone questions this interpretation, let him remember what the prophet says, "May the Lord help him on his bed of sorrow. Thou hast turned all his couch in his weakness." So much for the bed.

And, as regards the night of ignorance, what could be plainer than that other psalm, which says, "They know not, neither will they understand, but walk on still in darkness." Does not that exactly express the ignorance into which all the human race are born? And Paul, knowing himself thus born in ignorance, gives thanks to the Father "Who hath delivered us from the power of darkness," and tells all the elect that they, therefore, "are not children of the night, nor of the darkness," but must "walk as children of light."

Revelations of Divine Love

Julian of Norwich

Introduction

IT WOULD BE DIFFICULT to decide which century in the history of western civilization was more calamitous, the twentieth or the fourteenth. In both, it seemed, everything that could go wrong did go wrong. Both centuries saw disasters, wars, pestilence, famine, and the rise and fall of great institutions. In both, people talked about the end of the world and speculated about the death or, at least, the silence of God. Both centuries had hope in short supply.

Most people alive today know little about those times. But to people alive in the 1300s, there was an unavoidable sense that everything was falling apart. According to church historian Justo Gonzalez, "The thirteenth century was the high point of medieval civilization." The fourteenth he simply called "The Collapse."[1]

Throughout that incredible period, the Church careened from one crisis to another. The century started with the heated dispute between Pope Boniface VIII and King Philip IV of France that ended with an attempt by some of the king's men to kidnap the pope, who died shortly thereafter of the shock. The popes soon fell under French control. In 1309 the papacy relocated from Rome to Avignon, a city not far from the French border. For the next seventy years, a series of French popes reigned in Avignon, while Catholics in the rest of Europe complained that the papacy was now merely an extension of French foreign policy.

This "Babylonian Captivity of the Church," as the years in Avignon have been called, was followed by another crisis, the "Great Papal Schism." The last Avignon pope, Gregory XI, died in 1378, shortly after he moved the papacy back to Rome. When his Italian successor proved to be highly uncooperative and unstable, French cardinals deposed him and elected another Pope in his place. But Urban VI refused to capitulate, which left the Church with two popes, one in Rome and the other in Avignon, both claiming all the rights and privileges that came with sitting on Peter's throne. This scandalous state of affairs (eventually the number of popes rose to *three*) lasted for over thirty years.

Needless to say, Christians complained bitterly about these and other matters. Many criticized priests who had taken vows of celibacy but openly flaunted their mistresses, or monastics who had taken vows of poverty but openly lived in the lap of luxury. Some Catholics, such as the English scholar John Wycliffe, challenged the papacy itself by suggesting that even popes must submit to the final authority of the Bible.

Nature also seemed to conspire to make people miserable. The fourteenth century marked the beginning of what geologists call the "Little Ice Age." The Baltic Sea froze over in 1303, then again in the winter of 1306–1307. Farmers all over Europe complained about the cold weather and a much shorter growing season. Continuing cold and heavy rains caused massive crop failures in 1315—and then widespread famine in 1316.

Not even mass starvation, however, could compare to the horror of the Black Death, which broke out in 1347–1348. By 1350, when the first wave of bubonic plague had passed, up to one-third of the people who lived between India and Iceland were dead. No one had ever seen anything like it: One version of the plague killed its victims in twenty-four hours, another took up to five days. According to eye witness accounts, some people went to bed healthy but were dead by dawn.

Highly contagious, the Black Death moved ahead like a huge flood: The plague arrived suddenly, took months to recede, then came back again. There were four major outbreaks of the plague during the century. Historians estimate that maybe 20 million people died from the Black Death, which meant that within a hundred years, Europe's population declined by about 50 percent. It is said that in Avignon 400 died every day until half of the city's population was gone. In Vienna 600 a day died; in Paris, the daily count was 800. In such places home after home stood vacant because entire families were lost. In many convents and monasteries, where people lived in such close proximity, everybody died.

If one escaped the plague, the chances were good one might die as a victim of violence or in one of the wars that raged throughout the fourteenth century. France and England started the Hundred Years' War in 1337; and the nobility throughout Europe fi-

nanced smaller wars by hiring knights to settle local disputes. Violence seemed to be commonplace; and innocent civilians suffered horribly. Life was cheap; and death was everywhere. In fact, the fourteenth century seemed obsessed with death. People fashioned grotesque death masks and speculated about the putrefaction of corpses and the torments of hell. Not surprisingly, a leading historian of the period has characterized the times as "ghoulish."[2] With obvious understatement, another historian called the century "a bad time for humanity" and "a period of anguish when there is no sense of an assured future."[3]

Nevertheless, faith survived in such times. And no one better symbolized the victory of hope over despair more than Julian of Norwich, one of the most important English mystics. Her work is still read and valued in the twentieth century.

JULIAN OF NORWICH (1342–1416?)

For all her fame, it is surprising how little we know about her. In fact, we do not even know her real name: It is believed that she was called Julian after the Church of St. Julian in Norwich, England, where she lived as an anchoress or recluse. Contemporary references to her are few. The famous English mystic Margery Kempe wrote about her visit to Norwich to seek Julian's spiritual guidance;[4] and Julian's name appeared as a beneficiary in four wills that date from 1403 to 1416. Other than those brief mentions, all we know about her comes from her writings.

On May 8, 1373, Julian was thirty years old and near death in her mother's home. She had been sick for about a week. When the end seemed imminent, the parish priest was called to administer Last Rites. Before leaving, he held a crucifix before her eyes and told her to comfort herself in her last moments by concentrating on the face of her Lord. As she did so, she fell into a trance and received sixteen "showings" or revelations. Much to everyone's surprise, she rapidly recovered, then spent the rest of her life trying to understand what had happened to her and what the revelations meant.

As she looked back, she remembered that she had asked God for a threefold favor some years before. She wanted an understanding of Christ's passion; some serious bodily sickness through which her faith could be tried and strengthened; and, as an expression of God's grace, three wounds, which she identified as contrition, compassion, and a longing for God.[5] In May of 1373, she got everything she asked for.

Sometime after her brush with death, most historians believe, she decided to become a recluse. The Middle Ages offered many options for Christian living. While most Christians continued to "live in the world," a minority felt called to church vocations—the priesthood, living as a monk or nun in a religious community, or living alone. Those who chose the solitary life were called recluses, or hermits or anchorites if they were men, and anchoresses if they were women.

Living accommodations for recluses varied. Some lived in the wilderness, in caves or stone huts, far removed from everyone else; while others set up their "anchorages" in towns, whose citizens valued having someone holy live nearby. Some anchorages were accurately called "cells" because of their tiny interiors; but others consisted of a number of rooms surrounded by a garden and high walls. Some anchorites or anchoresses lived totally by themselves; while others had servants to take care of their needs. In some cases recluses even had regular contact with outsiders, children who came to them for instruction or adults who came for spiritual advice. Some anchorages had a window that opened to the outside, which allowed the recluses to interact with the world without having to enter it.

Julian passed the last three or four decades of her life in an anchorage built into the wall of the St. Julian's Church at Norwich. She spent her time praying, reflecting on the "showings" that God had given her, and advising others (such as Margery Kempe) on spiritual matters. Though a recluse, Julian still lived in a suffering and dangerous world. The Black Death struck Norwich three times during her life-time and killed over half of the population; and a short and bloody Peasant Revolt broke out in England in 1381. But while others succumbed to hopelessness, Julian delivered a message of hope and optimism.

Modern readers might be surprised by the ability of medieval women to teach and influence the church. While it is true that women were not ordained as priests, they did have spiritual opportunities. As odd as it may sound to modern people, taking monastic vows gave medieval women *more*, not fewer options. Female monastics organized and ran their own communities, where they prayed, worked, studied, and taught; and female recluses could impact people outside their achorage walls. Some women thus became accomplished biblical scholars and theologians, which never would have happened had they pursued more usual lifestyles. Others were renowned for their spirituality and became sought-after advisors to bishops and popes and spiritual directors for both men and women. Some abbesses (female leaders of monastic communities) actually oversaw male monasteries as well as female convents. No view of the Middle Ages would be complete without considering the profound impact of women like Hildegard of Bingen, Mechtild of Magdeburg, Bridget of Sweden, and Gertrude. St. Teresa of Avila and St. Catherine of Siena have been officially designated as "Doctors of the Church" for their prodigious influence. Such women made up in piety and spiritual power what they lacked in official standing or institutional clout.[6]

REVELATIONS OF DIVINE LOVE

The *Revelations*, or *Showings*, as Julian preferred to call them, were published in two versions. The short text was probably written shortly after Julian's experience and contained twenty-five brief chapters which describe, with little comment, her sixteen showings. The long text was written about twenty years later and include her mature reflections on the meaning of her revelations in eighty-six chapters. About six times larger than the short text, the long text is reprinted in this volume.

The revelations covered a variety of topics, but they all focused in some way on the love of God. The first twelve revelations (chapters 4–26) showed how God's love was supremely demonstrated in the cross and passion of Christ. Nowhere else is the divine love seen so clearly. Like most mystics of her time, Julian goes into graphic detail about the suffering of Jesus: "After this I saw in my beholding His body bleeding freely in the furrows of the scourging. The fair skin was broken and beaten deep into the tender flesh with the sharp smittings. All about His sweet body the warm blood ran out so freely that there was seen neither skin nor wound, but as it were all blood."[7]

Revelation 13 (chapters 27–40) described love's triumph over all sin and suffering. "Thus our good Lord answered all the questions and doubts that I could bring up, saying for full comfort: 'I may make all things well: and I can make all things well: and I shall make all things well: and I will make all things well: and thou shalt see thyself that all manner of things shall be well.'"[8]

Revelation 14 (chapters 41–63) explored how the soul became united to God. Much of this unity came through prayer, which is grounded in the person of Christ himself. But ultimately, the soul is united with God because of God's eagerness to forgive sins. The Parable of the Lord and the Servant helped Julian understand God's intense desire to forgive. In the story, the servant turned away from the lord who had done nothing but love and provide for him. The servant's rebellion led to suffering, which the lord allowed for a while. Then the lord intervened: He forgave and restored the servant to his former place. God always cared more for restoring sinners than punishing them for their wrongdoing.

Revelation 15 (chapters 64–65) contrasted the pain of this life with the joy to come in heaven. As bad as life in the world can be, present suffering is nothing compared to the bliss that is up ahead. "For it is His will that we know that all the might of our enemy is locked in our Friend's hands. And therefore the soul that knoweth this surely, she shall dread only Him whom she loveth. . . . God willeth us to know that if we know Him and love Him and reverently dread Him, we shall have peace and be in great rest; and all that He doeth shall be great liking to us."⁹ Thus she saw all suffering and sickness in redemptive terms.

The night after she received the first fifteen revelations, Julian was given Revelation 16 (chapters 66–70), which confirmed the rest. Between Revelation 15 and 16, Julian had a spiritual relapse. Her pain returned and she doubted the reality of her previous experience. When she fell asleep, she had a terrible nightmare about being choked by the Devil. But God showed her that her soul was like a great city in which God is pleased to dwell. Not even another brief bout with despair could then shake her confidence and joy.

In the rest of *Revelations of Divine Love* (chapters 71–86), Julian reflected on a number of spiritual topics. Her conclusion is often quoted because it summarized so well her mystical experience of God: "Thus was I learned that love is our Lord's meaning. And I saw full surely in this, and in all, that before God made us, He loved us. Which love was never slaked, nor ever shall be. And in this love He hath done all His works. And in this love He hath made all things profitable to us. And in this love our life is everlasting."

To this day, Julian of Norwich remains somewhat controversial. Despite the fact that Christianity has a long and honored mystical tradition, many modern Christians are skeptical about such experiences. They ask: How do we know if such experiences came from God; what do we make of the extravagant and sometimes eccentric language that is common in mystical works; and how should we understand such material—in theological or devotional terms? Naturally, how one answers those questions depends to a large extent on what one thinks about the nature of religious experience and its relationship to other kinds of religious authority, including the Bible.

Julian never thought that the experience or content of her revelations were all that unusual. She saw herself as a loyal and orthodox daughter of the Church. "Yet in all things I believe as Holy Church preacheth and teacheth. For the faith of Holy Church, of which I had understanding beforehand and which, I hope by the grace of God, I will fully keep in use and in custom, stood continually in my sight. It was my will and meaning never to accept anything that could be contrary thereto."[10]

Nevertheless, her work held some surprises. None was more striking than her teaching on the Motherhood of God (see especially chapters 58–64). Other theologians and mystics before her had reflected on the feminine imagery for God in the Bible: for example, Augustine, Anselm, Bridget of Sweden, and Catherine of Siena. Bernard of Clairvaux and the Cistercians of the twelfth century were especially interested in exploring some of those themes. But Julian gave more attention to God's motherhood than anyone else in her time.

Julian was a thoroughgoing trinitarian who had no problem affirming God the Son or the maleness of Jesus. But she insisted that in Jesus Christ is found the Motherhood of God. "God Almighty is our kingly Father: and God All-wisdom is our kingly Mother: with the love and goodness of the Holy Ghost; which is all one God, one Lord." In the Trinity she saw "the property of the Fatherhood, and the property of the Motherhood, and the property of the Lordship—in one God." She called Jesus "our Mother, Brother, and Saviour." In him, God nurtures, holds, and feeds us. Just as a mother lovingly feeds her child, "our precious Mother Jesus, He can feed us with Himself; and doth, full courteously and tenderly, with the Blessed Sacrament, that is the precious food of true life."

For Julian, Jesus was not like a mother; all mothers are like Jesus. His love and care for his children defined what real motherhood is. According to one of Julian's modern interpreters, "Motherhood, Julian would say, is not a characteristic of womankind that Christ shares, but a characteristic of Christ which women share!"[11] It would be a serious mistake to read some modern feminist agenda back into Julian's words. She was not making a point about sex or the gender of God in her teaching about Mother Jesus. Rather she was trying to say something about the complexity of God's relationship with humanity. Julian believed that in the Triune God one found both fatherly and motherly characteristics and what we know as fatherhood and motherhood is rooted in who God is. Still, it is startling how modern Julian sounds.

Similarly, her views on sin and the complete absence of divine wrath (chapters 27–40) still raise a few eyebrows. Julian was bothered by sin, in herself and in others. But in Revelation 13, Jesus told her: "Sin must needs be, but all shall be well. All shall be well; and all manner of things shall be well." Still she wondered, how could all be well when sin's effects are so disastrous, when so many will be damned because of it? As she struggled with these issues, she came to conclusions that put her at odds with standard Catholic teaching. She said that deep down in all souls destined for heaven there is a godly will that never assented to sin and never could and that because God is love, God could not be wrathful (chapters 13, 37). In order to come to these conclusions, it seems, Julian had to soft-peddle the pervasiveness of sin and make a distinction between the wrathful God of the Old Testament and the loving God of the New. According to standard Catholic teaching, based on ample biblical evidence, God is both righteousness and love and even the wills of the saints have been affected by sin. But, as she reflected on the meaning of her revelations, Julian came to different conclusions.

The most striking thing about *Revelations of Divine Love* is its unfailing optimism. In light of the times in which she lived, her confidence in the future and in the "all will be well" of God is totally unexpected. Instead of seeing the Day of Doom and Judgment just around the corner, she looked beyond the horrors of her own time to the Last Day when the great love of God will stretch from one end of the universe to the other for all to see. She was no Pollyanna. She never tried to put the best face on a bad situation. She was just very sure of God,[12] totally confident that in the End the love of God will have the last word and that all of God's faithful ones will share in the Victory.

That kind of optimism is as welcome in the twentieth century as it was in the fourteenth. In a world torn by tribal warfare and religious intolerance, economic hardship and the plague of AIDS, ethnic cleansing and the seemingly unsolvable problems of our cities, declining resources and sagging hope, many people long to hear that "all will be well." And many people still find in *Revelations of Divine Love* a reason to hope in God.

THIS IS A REVELATION OF LOVE
THAT JESUS CHRIST, OUR ENDLESS BLISS,
MADE IN SIXTEEN SHEWINGS

THE FIRST is of His precious crowning of thorns; and therein was contained and made manifest the Blessed Trinity with the Incarnation and the unity between God and man's soul, with many fair shewings and teachings of endless wisdom and love; in which the shewings that follow are grounded and oned.

The second is of the discolouring of His fair face, which betokened His most dear passion.

The third is that God our Lord almighty, all wisdom, all love, as truly as He hath made all things that are, even thus He doeth and worketh all things that are done.

The fourth is the scourging of His tender body, with the plenteous shedding of His precious blood.

The fifth is that the fiend is overcome by the precious passion of Christ.

The sixth is the worshipful thanking of our Lord God, by which He rewardeth all His blessed servants in heaven.

The seventh is our oftentimes experiencing weal and woe; the experience of weal is a gracious touching and enlightening, with true sureness of endless joy: the experience of woe cometh from temptation, in heaviness and weariness of our mortal life, with a ghostly understanding that we are kept as truly in woe as in weal by the goodness of God.

The eighth is the last pains of Christ, and His cruel dying.

The ninth is of the liking which is in the Blessed Trinity for the hard passion of Christ and His pitiful dying. In which joy and liking He willeth that we be in solace and mirth with Him, until we come to the glory in heaven.

The tenth is, our Lord Jesus sheweth, in love, His blessed heart cloven in two.

The eleventh is a high ghostly shewing of His most dear Mother.

The twelfth is that our Lord is all-sovereign being.

The thirteenth is, that our Lord God willeth that we pay great regard to all the deeds which He hath done: to the great nobility of making all things: and to the excellence of man's making, which is above all His works: and to the precious amends He hath made for man's sin, turning all our blame into endless worship. He meaneth thus: "Behold and see! By the same might, wisdom and goodness that I have done all this, by this same might, wisdom and goodness I shall make all well that is not well; and thou shalt see it." And in this He willeth that we keep us in the faith and truth of Holy Church, not wishing to know His secrets, except in so far as this belongeth to us, in this life.

The fourteenth is that our Lord is the ground of our beseeching. Herein were seen two fair properties: One is rightful prayer; the other is true trust; both of which He willeth should be alike large. It is thus that our prayer pleaseth Him, and that He with His goodness filleth it full.

The fifteenth is that we shall be taken suddenly from all our pain and from all our woe; and by His goodness we shall come up above, where we shall have our Lord Jesus for our meed, and be filled full of joy and bliss in heaven.

The sixteenth is that the Blessed Trinity our Maker, in Christ Jesus our Saviour, endlessly dwelleth in our soul, worshipfully ruling and governing all things, us mightily and wisely saving and keeping, for love. And we shall not be overcome by our enemy.

THE SECOND CHAPTER
OF THE TIME OF THESE REVELATIONS; AND HOW SHE ASKED THREE PETITIONS

THESE revelations were shewed to a simple unlearned creature living in this mortal flesh, in the year of our Lord one thousand three hundred and seventy-three, on the thirteenth day of May.

OF HER DESIRE TO EXPERIENCE THE PASSION OF CHRIST

Before this, the creature desired three gifts of God's grace. The first was mind of the Passion; the second was bodily sickness; the third was to have of God's gift, three wounds. As for the first, I believed that I had experience, to some degree, of the passion of Christ; but I desired to have still more, by the grace of God. I would I had been, that time, with Magdalene and with the others that were Christ's lovers, that I might have seen, bodily, the passion that our Lord suffered for me—that I might have suffered with Him as did those others that loved Him.

And therefore I desired a bodily sight, that I might have more knowledge of the bodily pains of our Saviour, and of the compassion of our Lady and of all His true lovers that were living at that time and saw His pains. I would I had been one of them and had suffered with them. Other sight or shewing of God desired I never none until the soul should be separated from the body—(I believed I would be saved, by God's mercy). And this was my intention—that I should afterwards, because of that shewing, have more true mind of the passion of Christ.

OF HER DESIRE FOR BODILY SICKNESS

As for the second gift, there came to my mind, without any seeking, an earnest desire to have of God's gift a bodily sickness. I desired this sickness to be grievous even unto death (as long as, in that sickness, I might receive all the rites of Holy Church); I myself believing that I was going to die, and all creatures that saw me supposing the same. I wanted no manner of comfort either of the flesh or worldly life in that sickness; but I desired to have all the pains, bodily and ghostly, that I should have if I were about to die—all the dreads, temptations of fiends, and all manner of pains except the departing of the soul. Such was my meaning; for I desired, by the mercy of God, to be purified; so as afterwards to live more according to the worship of God because of that sickness. I hoped that this would stand to my credit when I should come to die (for I desired to be with my God and Maker soon).

OF HER DESIRE FOR THREE WOUNDS

These two desires, of the passion and of the sickness, I desired of Him with a condition; for I believed that mine was not the ordinary use of prayer. Therefore I said: "Lord, Thou knowest what I will—but only if it be Thy will that I have it. If it be not Thy will, good Lord, be not displeased; for I will only as Thou wilt." This sickness I desired in my youth—to have it when I was thirty years old.

As for the third gift, by the grace of God and the teaching of Holy Church, I conceived a mighty desire to receive three wounds in my life; that is to say, the wound of true contrition, the wound of kind compassion, and the wound of earnest longing for God. And just as I asked for the other two with a condition, so I asked for the third mightily and without any condition. The two desires of aforesaid passed from my mind; but the third dwelt there continually.

THE THIRD CHAPTER
OF THE SICKNESS OBTAINED
OF GOD BY PETITION

AND when I was thirty years and a half, God sent me a bodily sickness; in which I lay three days and three nights. And on the fourth night I received all the rites of Holy Church, and thought not to have lived till day. And after this I lay two days and two nights more. And on the third night, I thought oftentimes that I would pass away; and so thought they that were with me.

And yet in this time I felt a great loathsomeness to die—not for anything on earth that I wished to live for, nor for any pain that I was afraid of (for I trusted in God and His mercy), but for this: I wished to live in order to love God better and for a longer time, that I might, by the grace of that living, have more knowing and loving of God in the bliss of heaven. (For I considered all the time that I had lived here to be so little and short in the sight of that endless bliss.) Then I thought: "Good Lord, perhaps my living any longer may not be to Thy worship?" And I understood in my reason, and by the pains I felt, that I was going to die. And I assented fully with all the will of my heart to be at God's disposal.

OF HER NEAR DEATH EXPERIENCE

Thus I endured until day; and by then my body, as regards feeling, was dead from the middle downwards. Then I was helped up into a sitting position—and propped up, to give a greater freedom to my heart: that I might be at God's disposal, thinking on Him while my life should last. My curate was sent for to be present at my end. Before he came, my eyes were fixed upwards, and I could not speak. He set the cross before my face, and said: "I have brought the image of thy Saviour; look thereupon, and comfort thee therewith." But I believed I was well enough; for my eyes were set upwards into heaven whither I trusted to come by the mercy of God. Nevertheless, I consented to turn my eyes to confront the crucifix, if I could. And so I did. For I believed that I could endure longer looking straight forward than upwards. After this, my sight began to fail; and the chamber around me grew as dark as if it had been night, except about the image of the cross where the daylight remained (I knew not how). All the place by the cross was ugly and fearful to me, as though it were occupied by many fiends.

OF HER RESTORATION TO HEALTH

After this, the upper part of my body began to die—so much so that I had scarcely any feeling at all. My greatest pain was shortness of breath and the failing of life. And I thought truly that I would die. But then, suddenly, all my pain was taken from me and I was as right, especially in the upper part of my body, as ever I was before. I marvelled at this sudden change—it seemed to be a secret working of God, and not of kind. And yet I did not any the more believe that I should live because of feeling easier; and the feeling of this ease was no full ease to me. "No," I thought, "I would rather be freed from this world"—my heart was earnestly set thereupon.

Then it came suddenly to my mind that I should desire the second wound, that of our Lord's gift and of His grace I might be filled full, in body and in mind, with experience of His blessed passion, as I had prayed before. For I would that His pains were my pains, with compassion, and afterwards with longing unto God. Thus, I believed, I might with His grace obtain the wounds that I had desired before. But in all this I desired never any bodily sight, nor any manner of shewing of God: but only compassion—such as I believed a kindred soul might have with our Lord Jesus, who, for love, willed to become a mortal man. With Him I desired to suffer whilst I lived in this mortal body, according as God would give me the grace.

THE FOURTH CHAPTER
HERE BEGINNETH THE FIRST REVELATION, OF THE PRECIOUS CROWNING OF CHRIST

AND in this time, suddenly I saw the red blood running down from under the garland, hot and fresh, plenteous and life-like, just as it was in the time that the garland of thorns was pressed down on His blessed head. Even so I conceived truly that it was Himself, God and man, the same that suffered for me, who shewed it to me—without any intermediary.

OF THE BELIEVER'S JOY

In the same shewing, suddenly the Trinity filled full my heart with the utmost joy (thus I understood it shall be in heaven without end unto all that come thither). For the Trinity is God, and God is the Trinity. The Trinity is our Maker. The Trinity is our Keeper. The Trinity is our everlasting Lover. The Trinity is our endless Joy and our Bliss, by our Lord Jesus Christ and in our Lord Jesus Christ. And this was shewed in the first sight and in them all. For where Jesus appeareth, the Blessed Trinity is understood, as I see it.

OF CHRIST'S SUFFICIENCY

And I said: "Lord, bless us!" This I said with reverence for my meaning, in a mighty voice. For I was truly astounded by the wonder and the marvel, that He who is so reverend and dreadful should be so homely with a sinful creature still living in this wretched flesh. I took it that in this time our Lord Jesus, of His courteous love, wished to shew me comfort before the time of my temptation. For (I thought) it might well be that, by the permission of God and with His keeping, I should be tempted by fiends before I died. With this sight of His blessed passion, and with the Godhead that I saw in my understanding, I knew well that there was strength enough for me (and indeed for all living creatures that shall be saved) against all the fiends of hell, and against all ghostly enemies.

OF THE GREAT EXCELLENCE AND MEEKNESS OF THE BLESSED VIRGIN MARY

In this time He brought our Lady, Saint Mary, to my understanding. I saw her ghostly, in bodily likeness; a simple maiden and a meek: young of age, little more than a child—in the same stature as she was when she conceived. God also shewed me, in part, the wisdom and the truth of her soul. Wherein I understood the reverent beholding with which she beheld her God, who is her Maker; she marvelled, with great reverence, that He willed to be born of her that was a simple creature of His making.

For this was her marvelling—that He who was her Maker, willed to be born of her who was made. And this wisdom and truth—this knowing of the greatness of her Maker, and the littleness of herself that is made, made her to say full meekly to Gabriel, "Lo me here, God's handmaiden!" In this sight I understood truly that she is more in worthiness and in fullness of grace than all that God made beneath her. For nothing that is made is above

her except the blessed manhood of Christ, as I see it.

THE FIFTH CHAPTER
HOW GOD IS TO US EVERYTHING THAT IS GOOD, TENDERLY WRAPPING US ROUND

IN the same time that I saw this sight of His head bleeding, our good Lord shewed a ghostly sight of His homely loving. I saw that He is to us everything that is good and strengthening for our help. He is our clothing that, for love, wrappeth us up and windeth us about; embraceth us, all becloseth us and hangeth about us, for tender love; so that He can never leave us. And so, in this sight, I saw that He is to us everything that is good, as I understand it.

Also in this He shewed a little thing, the size of a hazelnut, which seemed to lie in the palm of my hand; and it was as round as any ball. I looked upon it with the eye of my understanding, and thought, "What may this be?" I was answered in a general way, thus: "It is all that is made." I wondered how long it could last; for it seemed as though it might suddenly fade away to nothing, it was so small. And I was answered in my understanding: "It lasts, and ever shall last; for God loveth it. And even so hath everything being—by the love of God."

OF THE NEED FOR SEEING ONESELF AS NOTHING

In this little thing I saw three properties. The first is that God made it; the second, that God loveth it; the third, that God keepeth it. And what beheld I in this? Truly, the Maker, the Lover and the Keeper. And until I am substantially oned to Him, I can never have full rest nor true bliss; that is to say, until I am so fastened to Him that there is no created thing at all between my God and me. And this little thing that is made—it seemed as though it would fade away to nothing, it was so small. We need to have knowledge of this—that we should reckon as naught everything that is made, to love and have God who is unmade.

For this is the reason why we are not all in ease of heart and of soul: That we seek here rest in this thing that is so little and where no rest is in; we know not our God that is almighty, all-wise and all-good. For He is very rest. It is His will to be known and it is His pleasure that we rest us in Him. All that is beneath Him sufficeth not to us. And this is the reason why no soul can be in rest until it is naughted of everything that is made. When the soul is willingly naughted, for love, so as to have Him who is All, then is she able to receive ghostly rest.

OF GOD'S GREATEST PLEASURE

And also our good Lord shewed that it is the greatest pleasure to Him that a simple soul come to Him nakedly, plainly and homely. This is the kind yearning of the soul, through the touching of the Holy Ghost, as I am given to understand by this shewing:

God, of Thy goodness, give me Thyself; for Thou art enough to me, and I can nothing ask that is less that would be full worship of Thee. And if I ask anything that is less, ever me wanteth; for in Thee only have I all.

These words, through the goodness of God, are full lovesome to the soul, and full near touch the will of our Lord. For His goodness fulfilleth all His creatures and all His blessed works, without end. For He is the endlessness, and He made us only for Himself; and He restored us by His blessed passion, and ever keepeth us in His blessed love. And all this is of His goodness.

THE SIXTH CHAPTER
HOW WE SHOULD PRAY

THIS shewing was given, as I understand it, to teach our soul wisely to cleave to the goodness of God. And in that same time our customary manner of praying was brought to my mind—how, because of unknowing of love, we employ many means. Then I saw truly that it is greater worship to God, and truly more delightful to Him, if we pray to Himself and of His goodness, and cleave thereunto, by His grace, with true understanding and steadfast belief, than if we used all the means that heart can think. For to use all these is too little, and not full worship to God. For in His goodness is all the whole, and therein faileth nothing at all.

There came into my mind at this same time these things, as I shall say. We pray to God by His holy flesh, by His precious blood, His holy passion, His most dear death and worshipful wounds. But all the blessed kindness and the endless life that we have because of all this—it is of the goodness of God. And we pray Him by the sweet love of the Mother that bore Him; but all the help that we have because of her—it is of His goodness. And we pray by His holy cross on which He died; but all the help and all the power that we have because of that cross—it is of His goodness.

And in the same wise, all the help that we have of special saints, and of all the blessed company of heaven, the very dear love and holy endless friendship that we have of them—it is of His goodness. The means that the goodness of God hath ordained to help us are full fair and many; of which the chief and most eminent means is the blessed kind which He took of the Maiden, along with all the means, belonging to our redemption and to our endless salvation, which went before and come after.

OF THE GREAT TENDER LOVE THAT OUR LORD HATH TO MAN'S SOUL

Wherefore it pleaseth Him that we seek Him and worship Him by these means, but understanding and knowing that He is the goodness of them all. For the highest prayer is to the goodness of God which cometh down to us, to the lowest part of our need. It quickeneth our soul, and maketh it to live; it maketh it to grow in grace and in virtue; it is nearest it in kind, and readiest to it in grace; it is, indeed, the very grace for which the soul seeketh and ever shall, until we know our God truly—He that hath us all beclosed in Himself.

Man goeth upright; his food is taken and hidden in his body as in a very fine purse. And in the time of his necessity the purse is opened, and then it is shut again—all in seemly fashion. That it is God that worketh this, is shewed there where it is said: "He cometh down to us, to the lowest part of our need." For He despiseth nothing of what He hath made. And He disdaineth not to serve us in the simplest offices that belong, in kind, to our body, for love of the soul that is made to His own likeness. For as the body is clad in clothes, and the flesh in skin, and the bones in flesh, and the heart in the breast; so are we, soul and body, clad and enclosed in the goodness of God. Yea, and more homely; for they all vanish, wasting away. But the goodness of God is ever whole and most near to us, without any comparison.

OF GOD'S WISH FOR US TO BE OCCUPIED WITH KNOWING AND LOVING HIM

Truly our Lover desireth that the soul cleave to Him with all its might; so that we are clinging, ever more and more, to His goodness. For of all things that heart can conceive, this most pleaseth God and soonest bringeth profit. Our soul is so preciously loved by Him that is highest that it passeth beyond the knowing of all creatures. That is to say, there is no creature made that can know how much and how sweetly and how tenderly our Maker loveth us. Therefore we may, with His grace and His help, stand in ghostly beholding with everlasting marvelling in this high, overpassing, immeasurable love that our Lord hath towards us, of His goodness.

And therefore we may ask of our Lover all that we will; for our kindly will is to have God, and the good will of God is to have us. Nor may we ever cease willing or loving, until we have Him in fullness of joy. And then we may no more will. It is His will that we be occupied in knowing and loving until the time come that we be fulfilled in heaven; therefore was this lesson of love shewed, as ye shall see. For the strength and ground of all was shewed in the first sight. For above all things, the beholding and the loving of the Maker maketh the soul to seem least in its own sight, and most filleth it with reverent dread and true meekness, and with plenty of charity towards its even-christians.

THE SEVENTH CHAPTER

HOW OUR LADY, BEHOLDING THE GREATNESS OF HER MAKER, THOUGHT HERSELF THE LEAST

AND to teach us thus, as I understand it, our good Lord shewed our Lady Saint Mary in that same time; that is, the high wisdom and truth that she had in the beholding of her Maker. This wisdom and truth made her to behold her God as so great, so high, so mighty, and so good that the greatness and nobleness of this beholding her God filled her full of reverent dread. And with this, she saw herself as so little and so low, so simple and so poor in regard of her God, that this reverent dread filled her full of meekness. Thus—in this ground—she was filled full of grace and of all manner of virtues, and surpasseth all creatures.

OF THE GREAT DROPS OF BLOOD RUNNING FROM UNDER THE GARLAND

And in all the time that He shewed this, that I have just told you, in ghostly sight, I saw continually the bodily sight of the head bleeding freely. The great drops of blood fell down from under the garland like pellets; they seemed to come straight out of the veins. As they came out they were a reddish brown, and the blood was very thick; but in their spreading forth they were bright red. And when they came to the eye-brows, there they vanished.

And though the bleeding continued until many things were seen and understood, nevertheless, the beauty and the life-like quality were there continually. And the plentifulness of the blood was like to the drops of water that fall from the eaves of a house after a great shower of rain—when they fall so thick that no man, by his ordinary senses, can count them. In their roundness as they spread over the forehead, they were like to the scale of the herring. These three comparisons came into my mind at the time: pellets, for the roundness of the drops, as they came forth; the scale of the herring, for their roundness as they spread; rain-drops from the eaves of a house, for the plentifulness innumerable.

This shewing was vivid and life-like, hideous and dreadful, sweet and lovely. But of all the sights that I saw, this was the greatest comfort to me: That our good Lord who is so reverend and dreadful is also so homely and so courteous. And this most filled me full of liking, and sureness of soul.

OF THE EXAMPLE SHEWED TO HER

For the understanding of this, He shewed me this simple example. The greatest worship that a mighty being or a great lord can do to a poor servant, if he wills to be homely with him, is to shew himself, as he truly is, both in private and publicly, with a glad countenance. Then thinketh the poor creature thus: "Lo! What more could this noble lord do, that is more worship and joy to me, than to shew this marvellous homeliness to me who am so little? In truth, this is greater joy and liking to me than if he gave me great gifts and remained himself a stranger to me."

This example, though it was shewed bodily, was so profound that a man's heart might be so carried away that he could almost forget himself in the joy of this great homeliness. And so it cometh to pass in respect of our Lord Jesus and ourselves. For truly, it is the greatest joy that could be, as I see it, that He who is highest and mightiest, noblest and worthiest, is the lowest and meekest, homeliest and most courteous. In deed and in truth, this marvellous joy shall He shew to us all, when we see Him.

And this is our Lord's will, that we have belief and trust, joy and liking, comfort and great solace in so far as we may, with His grace and with His help, unto the time that we see it truly. For the perfect fullness of joy that we shall have, as I see it, is this marvellous courtesy and homeliness from our Father, who is our Maker in our Lord Jesus Christ—who is our Brother and our Saviour.

Yet no man, in this life, can know this marvellous homeliness, except he have it by special shewing of our Lord, or by great plenty of grace, inwardly given by the Holy Ghost. But faith and belief, with charity, deserve this gift; and so it is received by grace. For in faith, together with hope and charity, our life is grounded. And the shewing, which is made to whomsoever God willeth, plainly teacheth the same, but openly, and setting forth many secret things that belong to our faith and belief, which it is worshipful to know. When the shewing, which is given for a time, is passed and vanished, then faith keepeth it, by the grace of the Holy Ghost, until our life's end.

Thus, in the shewing is seen none other than the faith, neither less nor more, as may be seen by our Lord's meaning in the same matter.

THE EIGHTH CHAPTER
A RECAPITULATION OF WHAT IS SAID

As long as I saw this sight of the plenteous bleeding of the head, I could not stint of these words—"Lord, bless us." And in this shewing I understood six things: The first is the tokens of His blessed passion; the second is the Maiden that is His most dear Mother; the third is the blessed Godhead that ever was and is and shall be—all-might, all-wisdom and all-love; the fourth is everything that He hath made—for well I know that heaven and earth and all that is made is great and large and fair and good; but the reason why it shewed so little to my sight was that I saw it in the presence of Him that is the Maker. For to a soul that seeth the Maker of all things, all that is made seemeth full little; the fifth is that He that made all that is made, made it for love—and by the same love it is kept, and shall be, without end, as it is before said; the sixth is that God is all that is good, as I see it—and the goodness that all things have, it is He.

WHAT WAS SHEWED TO HER WAS FOR ALL

All this our Lord shewed in the first sight, and gave me space and time to behold it. Then the bodily sight stinted; but the ghostly sight lived on in my understanding. And I abode with reverent dread, rejoicing in what I saw, and desiring, as much as I durst, to see more if it were His will, or the same sight for longer time. In all this I was much affected in charity towards my even-christians—that they might all see and know the same that I saw; for I would that it were a comfort to them. For all this sight was shewed to all, in general.

Then said I to them that were with me: "This day is doomsday for me." This I said because I thought I would die; for on that day that a man or woman dieth, he is judged, particularly: and so he shall be, without end, as I see it. This I said; for I desired them to love God the better, and to make them have mind that this life is short and to see an example of it. In all this time, I thought I would die; and that was, in a way, wonder and marvel to me; because, it seemed, this vision was shewed for them that should live.

All that I say of myself, this I mean to say of the person of all my even-christians. For I am taught in the shewing of our Lord God that such is His meaning. And therefore I pray you all, for God's sake, and counsel you for your own profit, that you cease to notice the wretch that it was shewed to, and mightily, wisely, and meekly behold into God; who, of His courteous love and endless goodness willed to shew it generally, unto the comfort of us all. For it is God's will that you receive it with as great a joy and liking as though Jesus had shewed it to you.

THE NINTH CHAPTER
OF THE MEEKNESS OF THIS WOMAN

I AM not good because of the shewing, but only if I love God the better. And in as much as you love God the better, it is more profit to you than to me. (I say this, not to them that are wise, for they know it well, but to you that are simple, for your ease and comfort; for we are all one in love.) For truly it was not shewed to me that God loveth me better than the least soul that is in grace.

And I am sure that there are many that never have shewing nor sight except of the common teaching of Holy Church, who love God better than I. For if I look at myself, as a single person, I am right naught. But if I look to the whole—then I am, in hope, in onehead of charity with all my even-christians. For in this onehead standeth the life of all mankind that shall be saved.

HOW HE THAT LOVETH HIS EVEN-CHRISTIAN FOR GOD LOVETH ALL THINGS

God is all that is good, as I see it. And God hath made all that is made; and God loveth all that He hath made. Thus He that loveth the whole—all His even-christians—for God, loveth all that is. (For in mankind that shall be saved is comprehended all, that is to say, all that is made, and the Maker of all. For in man is God, and in God is all.) He that loveth thus, loveth all. I am hopeful by the grace of God that he who beholdeth it thus shall be truly taught and mightily comforted when he needeth comfort. (I speak of them that shall be saved. For in this time God shewed me no other.)

Yet in all things I believe as Holy Church preacheth and teacheth. For the faith of Holy Church, of which I had understanding beforehand and which, I hope by the grace of God, I will fully keep in use and in custom, stood continually in my sight. It was my will and meaning never to accept anything that could be contrary thereto. With this intent and with this meaning I beheld the shewing with all my diligence. For in all this blessed shewing I beheld it [sc. the sight and the faith] as one in God's meaning.

The whole sight was shewed in three parts: by bodily sight, by words formed in my understanding, and by ghostly sight. But the ghostly sight I cannot or may not shew it as clearly and as fully as I would. Yet I trust in our Lord God almighty that He will, of His goodness and for your love, make you receive it more ghostly and more sweetly than I can or may tell it.

THE TENTH CHAPTER
THE SECOND REVELATION IS
OF HIS DISCOLORING

AND after this I saw, with bodily sight, in the face of the crucifix that hung before me, and upon which I gazed continually, a part of His passion: the contumely, the spitting, the soiling and the buffeting, and many distressful pains—more than I can tell; with a frequent changing of colour. At one time I saw how half the face, beginning from the ear, was cov-ered over with dried blood, ending in the middle of the face; and after that, the other half, in the same way; and between-whiles, the sight of the one side vanished as quickly as it came. This I saw bodily, but with difficulty and obscurely. I desired more bodily light so as to have seen more clearly. And I was answered in my reason: "If God willeth to shew thee more, He shall be thy light; thou needest none but Him." For I saw Him and sought Him.

We are, here, so blind and so unwise that we can never seek God until the time that He of His goodness sheweth Himself to us. And when we see some-thing of Him, graciously, then are we moved, by this same grace, to seek with a great desire to see Him more blissfully. And thus I saw Him and I sought Him; I had Him and I wanted Him. This is, and should be, our ordi-nary working in this life, as I see it.

And now in my understanding I was let down on to the sea-bed. And there I saw hills and dales, green, as though there were moss agrowing amongst the wrack and gravel. Then I under-stood that even were a man or a woman there under the broad water, if he could have sight of God, even as God is—with a man continually—he would be safe in soul and body, and take no harm. And above and beyond this, he would have more solace and comfort than all this world can or may tell. It is His will that we believe that we see Him continually, though it seemeth to us that the sight is but lit-tle. And in this belief, He maketh us to get ever more grace. For He will be seen, and He will be sought; He will be waited on and He will be trusted.

OF OUR REDEMPTION AND THE DISCOLORING OF THE VERNICLE

This second shewing was so low, so little, and so simple that my spirits were in great travail as I beheld in mourning, full of dread and longing. I was for some time in a fear, wondering whether it was a shewing or not. And then, on different occasions our Lord gave me clearer sight whereby I understood truly that it *was* a shewing; that it was a figure and a likeness of our unclean mortal slough, which our fair bright blessed Lord wore for our sins. With its many changes of color—brown and black, its pitiful and drawn look, it made me think of the holy vernicle of Rome, upon which He imprinted His own blessed face, when He was in His hard passion and going willingly to His death. Of this image many wondered how it could be so, since that He imprinted it with that blessed face which is the fairest in heaven, the flower of the earth and the fruit of the maiden's womb—how could this image be so discolored and so far from fairness? I desire to say as I have understood it by the grace of God:

We know in our faith and in our belief through the teaching and the preaching of Holy Church that the blissful Trinity made man's kind to His image and likeness. In the same manner, we know that when man fell so deep and so wretchedly by sin, there was no other help to restore man than through Him that made man. And He that made man for love, by this same love willed to restore man to the same bliss, and even more. For right as we were made like to the Trinity in our first making, our Maker willed that we should be like to Jesus Christ our Saviour, in heaven without end, by virtue of our again-making. Then between these two makings He willed, for love and for worship of man, to make Himself as like to man in this mortal life—in our foulness and in our wretchedness—as a man could be without guilt.

Hence the meaning is, as is beforesaid, that it was the image and likeness of our unclean mortal flesh, wherein our fair bright blessed Lord hid His Godhead. Though indeed I dare say, and we ought to believe, that so fair a man was never none but He, until the time that His fair colour was changed with travail and sorrow, passion and dying. Of this it is spoken in the eighth revelation, where it treateth more of the same likeness; the same is said of the vernicle of Rome—that it is alive in its many changes of colour, and its look is sometimes more comfortable and life-like, and sometimes more pitiful and death-like: as may be seen in the eighth revelation.

HOW IT PLEASETH GOD THAT WE SEEK HIM EARNESTLY

This vision was a lesson to my understanding, that the continual seeking of the soul pleaseth God much. For it can do no more than seek, suffer, and trust; and this is wrought, in every soul that hath it, by the Holy Ghost. But the clearness of the finding—that is of His special grace, whenever it is His will. The seeking with faith, hope and charity pleaseth our Lord; the finding pleaseth the soul and fulfilleth it with joy. Thus was my understanding taught that seeking is as good as beholding during the time that he willeth to suffer the soul to be in travail.

It is God's will that we seek unto the beholding of Him; for by that shall He shew us Himself, of His special grace whenever He will. And how a soul is to keep herself in the beholding of Him, that He shall teach, Himself—which is the most worship to Him and most profit to the soul, and most cometh of meekness and the virtues, with the grace and the leading of the Holy Ghost. For a soul that simply fasteneth himself to God with true trust, either in seeking or beholding—there is the most worship that he can do, as I see it.

OF SEEKING AND BEHOLDING GOD

There are two workings that can be seen in this vision: The one is seeking, the other is beholding. The seeking is common—every soul can have that, of His grace, and ought to have it: spiritual discernment and the teaching of Holy Church. It is God's will that we have three things in our seeking, of His gift. The first is that we seek as earnestly and willingly, without sloth, as may be with His grace; and gladly and merrily, without unreasonable heaviness or vain sorrow. The second is that we wait on Him steadfastly, for His love, without grudging or striving against Him, unto our life's end; for it shall last but a while. The third is that we trust in Him mightily, with full and true faith. For it is His will that we know that He shall appear suddenly and blissfully to all His lovers. For His working is secret; but He willeth to be perceived, and His appearing shall be right sudden. He will be trusted, because He is full courteous and homely. Blessed may He be!

THE ELEVENTH CHAPTER
THE THIRD REVELATION SHEWETH HOW GOD DOETH ALL THINGS EXCEPT SIN

AFTER this, I saw God in a point: The sight, I say, was in my understanding, by which I saw that He is in all things. I beheld with attention, seeing and knowing in it, that He doeth all that is done. (As I saw, I marvelled softly and with dread, and thought: "What is sin?") I saw truly that God doeth all things be they never so little. And I saw truly that nothing is done by hap or by chance, but all by the foreseeing wisdom of God. If a thing be hap or chance according to man's judgment, the cause is our blindness and lack of foreknowledge.

For those things that are in the foreseeing wisdom of God from without-beginning, which He rightfully and worshipfully and continually bringeth to their best end, in their coming-about they fall to our notice suddenly and without our knowledge. And thus, because of our blindness and lack of foreknowledge, we say that these things are by hap and by chance. So I understood in this shewing of love, and know well, that in the sight of our Lord God there is neither hap nor chance. Wherefore I needs must grant that all that is done is well done, since our Lord God doeth all.

In this time the working of creatures was not shewed, but only of our Lord God in creatures. For He is in the mid-point of all things, and He doeth all; but I was sure that He doeth no sin. Hence I saw truly that sin is no-deed; for in all this sin was not shewed. Nor would I any longer wonder over this, but simply beheld our Lord and what He willed to shew me. Thus as far as it could be for the time, the rightfulness of God's working was shewed to my soul. Rightfulness hath two fair properties: It is right, and it is full. Even so are all the works of our Lord, they need the working neither of mercy nor of grace; for where nothing faileth all things are rightful. (It was at another time that His shewing concerned the beholding of sin nakedly, and how then He useth the working of mercy and grace, as I shall tell you.)

HOW GOD NEVER CHANGES HIS PURPOSE

This vision, then, was shewed to my understanding because it is our Lord's will to have the soul truly turned into the beholding of Him, and of all His works as well; for they are full good. All His judgments are easy and sweet, and they bring to great ease the soul that is turned from the beholding of the blind judgment of man into the fair sweet judgment of our Lord God. For man beholdeth some deeds as well done, and some deeds as evil: but our Lord beholdeth them not so. For as all that hath being, in kind, is of God's making, so everything that is done is so in virtue of God's doing. It is easy to understand that the best deed is well done; and just so well done as is the best deed and the highest, even so well done is the least deed; and all according to His attributes, and in the order that our Lord hath ordained it to, from without-beginning: For there is no doer but He.

HOW GOD DOETH ALL THINGS IN THE FULLNESS OF HIS GOODNESS

I saw full truly that He changeth never His purpose in any manner of thing, nor ever shall, without end. For there was nothing unknown to Him in the rightness of His decrees, from without-beginning. And therefore all things were set in order, ere any thing was made, as they were to stand without end. And no manner thing shall fail in that point; for He hath made all things in the fullness of His goodness.

And therefore the blessed Trinity is ever fully pleased in all His works. All this He shewed me full blissfully, meaning it thus:

See, I am God; see, I am in all things; see, I do all things; see, I never lift My hands off My works, nor ever shall, without end; see, I lead all things to the end that I ordain it to, from without-beginning, by the same might, wisdom, and love that I made it with. How should anything be amiss?

Thus mightily, wisely, and lovingly was my soul questioned in this vision; and I saw truly that I needs must assent with great reverence, and have joy in God.

THE TWELFTH CHAPTER
THE FOURTH REVELATION SHEWETH HOW IT PLEASETH GOD RATHER AND BETTER THAT WE SHOULD WASH IN HIS BLOOD

AFTER this I saw in my beholding His body bleeding freely in the furrows of the scourging. The fair skin was broken and beaten deep into the tender flesh with the sharp smitings. All about His sweet body the warm blood ran out so freely that there was seen neither skin nor wound, but as it were all blood. And when it came to the point where it should have fallen to the ground, it vanished. Notwithstanding this, the bleeding continued for a while so that it could be seen without doubt; and it was so plenteous, in my sight, that had it really been blood, in kind and in substance, at that time, it would have saturated all the bed, and have spread all about—so it seemed to me.

Then it came to my mind that God hath made the waters of earth plenteous for our service and bodily refreshment, of the tender love that He hath to us. But yet it pleaseth Him better that we should use, full homely, His blessed blood to wash us clean from sin. For there is no liquor made, which it pleaseth Him so well to give us. For as it is most plenteous, so it is most precious; and that by the power of the blessed Godhead. It is of our own kind, and all blissfully floweth over us by the power of His precious love. This very dear blood of our Lord Jesus Christ, as truly as it is most precious, so truly it is most plenteous.

OF THE POWER OF HIS BLOOD

Behold and see the power of this precious plenty of His most dear blood. It descended down into hell, and delivered all those there that belong to the court of heaven, breaking their bonds. The precious plenty of His most dear blood floweth over all the earth, and is at hand to wash clean from sin all creatures of good will, who are, have been, and shall be. The precious plenty of His most dear blood ascendeth up into heaven, in the blessed body of our Lord Jesus Christ. It is flowing in Him, praying for us to the Father; and so it is and shall be, as long as we have need. And ever more it floweth in all heaven, rejoicing in the salvation of all man's kind that are there and shall be, unto the fulfilment of the number that is wanting.

THE THIRTEENTH CHAPTER
THE FIFTH REVELATION SHEWETH THAT
THE TEMPTATION OF THE FIEND IS
OVERCOME BY THE PASSION OF CHRIST

AFTERWARDS, before God shewed any words, He permitted me to behold in Him, for a suitable time, all that I had seen and all the understanding that was therein, so far as the simpleness of my soul could take it. Then, without voice or opening of lips, He formed in my soul these words: "Herewith is the fiend overcome." This word our Lord said, meaning His blessed passion which He had just shewed.

OF THE INCREASE OF OUR JOY

In this our Lord shewed a part of the fiend's malice and the fullness of his unmight. For He shewed that His passion is the overcoming of the fiend. God shewed that the fiend hath now the same malice that he had before the incarnation. And as sorely as he travaileth, even so continually he seeth that all souls belonging to salvation escape him, worshipfully, by the power of His precious passion. That is his sorrow; and most evilly is he afflicted. For all that God suffereth him to do turneth to our joy, and to his shame and pain. And he hath as much sorrow when God giveth him leave to work as when he worketh not; and that is because he can never do the ill that he would. For his might is all locked in God's hand. And though in God there can be no wrath, as I see it, yet our good Lord, having endless regard to His own worship and to the profit of all them that shall be saved, with might and right withstandeth the reprobate, who in their malice and frowardness busy themselves to be contrary, and act against God's will.

OF THE FIEND'S DEFEAT

Also I saw our Lord scorning his malice and bringing to naught his might; and He wills that we do likewise. At this sight I laughed mightily—which made them laugh that were about me. And their laughter was a liking to me; and I thought, "Would that all my even-christians had seen as I saw; then would they all have laughed with me." But I saw not Christ laughing—it was the sight that He shewed me, I well know, that made me to laugh. Yet I understood that we may laugh both for comfort of ourselves and in our rejoicing in God. For the fiend is overcome.

(This sight, where I saw Him scorn the fiend's malice, was by the fastening of my understanding inwardly to our Lord; that is to say, an inward shewing of His truth, in His unchanging expression. This, as I see it, is a worshipful attribute of His—to be immutable.)

Then I fell into more serious mood, and said to myself: "I see three things, game, scorn, and earnest. I see a game in which the fiend is overcome; I see scorn, in that God scorneth him, and he shall be scorned; and I see an earnest, in that he is overcome by the blissful passion and death of our Lord Jesus Christ, which was done in full great earnest."

And where I said "he is scorned," I meant that God scorneth him; that is to say, He seeth him now as He shall do without-end. For in this God shewed that the fiend is damned—which I meant when I said that he should be scorned. For I saw that he shall be scorned at doomsday, generally, by all that shall be saved—those of whose salvation he hath had great envy. For then he shall see that all the woe and tribulation he hath done shall be turned into increase of their joy without end. And all the pain and the sorrow he would have brought them to shall go with him to hell, for ever.

THE FOURTEENTH CHAPTER
THE SIXTH REVELATION IS OF THE WORSHIPFUL THANKS WITH WHICH HE REWARDETH HIS SERVANTS

AFTER this, our Lord said: "I thank thee for thy service, and for the travail of thy youth." And in this my understanding was lifted up into heaven, where I saw our Lord God as a Lord in His own house—a Lord who hath called all His most dear friends to a solemn feast. Then I saw the Lord taking no seat in His own house; but I saw Him royally reigning in his house, filling it all full with joy and mirth, Himself, endlessly; to bring gladness and solace to His most dear friends, full homely and full courteously, with a marvellous melody of endless love in His own fair blissful countenance: For the shining countenance of the Godhead filleth all heaven full of joy and bliss.

OF THREE DEGREES OF BLISS

God shewed three degrees of bliss that each soul shall have in heaven that hath willingly served God in any degree in earth. The first is the worshipful thanks of our Lord God that He shall receive when He is delivered out of pain. This thanks is so high and so worshipful that it seemeth that it would fill Him even if He received no more. For, methought, all the pain and travail that all living men might suffer could not have deserved the worshipful thanks that one man shall have who willingly shall have served God.

The second is that all the blessed creatures that are in heaven shall see this worshipful thanking—He maketh the service of Him known to all that are in heaven. When a king thanketh his subjects it is great worship to them; but if he maketh it known to all the realm, then their worship is much increased.

The third is that as new and as pleasing as the thanks is when it is first received, even so shall it last without end. And I saw how homely and sweetly was this shewed—that the age of every man shall be known in heaven, and he shall be rewarded for the time of his willing service. And especially the age of them that willingly and freely offer their youth is surpassingly rewarded and wonderfully thanked.

But I saw that whenever or what time a man or woman be truly turned to God for one day's service according to His endless will, they shall have all these three degrees of bliss. And the more that the loving soul seeth this courtesy of God, the more eager she is to serve Him all her life.

THE FIFTEENTH CHAPTER
THE SEVENTH REVELATION IS OF OUR OFTENTIMES FEELING WEAL AND WOE

AFTER this He shewed a sovereign ghostly liking in my soul. In this liking I was filled full of everlasting sureness, mightily fastened in me, with absence of all painful dread. This was so glad and so ghostly a feeling that I was all in peace, in ease, and in rest, so that there was nothing in earth that might have grieved me. Yet it lasted only for a while; and then I was left to myself, feeling the heaviness and weariness of life, and irksomeness of myself; so that I scarcely had patience to live. There was neither comfort nor ease as far as feelings go; only faith, hope, and charity—and in truth I had these but little in feeling.

But soon enough after this, our Lord gave me again the comfort and rest of soul, the liking and the sureness, so blissfully and so mightily that no dread nor any sorrow, nor pain bodily or ghostly that I might possibly experience, could have diseased me. And then I experienced again the pain; and then the liking; and now the one, and now the other, divers times—I suppose about twenty times. In the time of the joy I could have said with Saint Paul: "Nothing shall part me from the charity of Christ." And in the pain, I could have said with Saint Peter: "Lord, save me, I perish."

OF THE NEED FOR MAN
TO BE WITHOUT COMFORT

This vision was shewed to my understanding to teach me that it is expedient to some souls to have experience in this wise—sometimes to be in comfort, and sometimes to lack comfort and to be left to themselves. It is God's will that we know that He keepeth us surely, ever the same, in woe and in weal; and that for profit of his soul a man is sometimes left to himself, without his sin always being the cause. For in this time I had not sinned so as to be left to myself; also it was all so sudden. I did not deserve, either, to have the blessed feelings. Our Lord giveth them freely, when so He will; and sometimes suffereth us to be in woe. And both are the one love.

It is God's will that we keep us in comfort with all our might. For bliss is lasting without end; whilst pain is passing, and shall be brought to naught in them that shall be saved. Therefore it is not God's will that we keep step with our feeling of pains, by sorrowing and mourning for them; but rather at once pass them over, and keep ourselves in the endless liking which is God.

THE SIXTEENTH CHAPTER
THE EIGHTH REVELATION IS
OF THE LAST PITEOUS PAINS
OF CHRIST'S DYING

AFTER this Christ shewed me the part of His passion near His death. I saw His sweet face as it was then, dry and bloodless with the pallor of a dying man: deathly pale with the anguish. The pallor became more deathlike, first taking a bluish tinge; and then, as death affected the flesh more deeply, a brownish blue. His passion was shewed to me essentially in His blessed face—wherein I saw these four colours—and particularly in His lips, which were before a fresh and vivid red, pleasing to the sight. This changing colour in His dying was pitiful to see.

And also, as I gazed, His nostrils were clogged and dried, and His sweet body became brown and then black—the fair, fresh, and lively colour of Him changed and turned by the fever into this dying dryness. For in that time that our Saviour died upon the Rood, there was a sharp dry wind—I saw it—dreadfully cold. And when all the precious blood that could flow from His blessed body was bled out, there yet remained a moisture in the sweet flesh of Christ. But the loss of blood and the pain within, and the blowing of the wind and the cold from without, met together in the sweet body of Christ; these four dried up the flesh of Christ as time went on.

OF THE DISCOLOURING OF HIS FACE
AND THE DRYING OF HIS FLESH

The pain, sharp and bitter as it was, was yet long-lasting—I saw it. And the pain dried up all the lively quality of Christ's flesh. So I saw the sweet flesh dry before my eyes, part by part, and with marvellous pain. As long as there was spirit and life in Christ's flesh, so long suffered He. This pain seemed to last as long as if He had been seven nights in death, dying all the time, at the very point of passing away, and suffering always this great pain. Where I say "it seemed . . . as if He had been seven nights in death," this specifieth that His sweet body was so discoloured, so dry, so shrunken, so death-like and so piteous as though He had been seven nights in death, dying all the time. And methought that the drying of Christ's flesh was the greatest pain, and the last, of His passion.

THE SEVENTEENTH CHAPTER
OF THE FOURFOLD CAUSE OF THE GRIEVOUS BODILY THIRST OF CHRIST

IN this drying there was brought to my mind the word that Christ said: "I thirst." I saw in Christ a double thirst; the one, bodily, the other, ghostly. This was shewed me for the bodily thirst; what was shewed me for the ghostly thirst, I shall tell afterwards.

By the bodily thirst I understood that the moisture in the body failed; for the blessed flesh and bones were left all alone without blood or moisture. The body was drying up an exceeding long time, through the wounds caused by the nails and the weight of the body. For I perceived that because of the tenderness of His sweet hands and feet, and the size and grievous hardness of the nails, the wounds grew wider as the body constantly sagged by its weight in the long hanging.

OF HIS PITEOUS CROWNING

And in the beginning, whilst the flesh was still fresh and bleeding, the continual pressure of the thorns widened the wounds, caused by the piercing and tearing of the head in the binding-in of the crown (I saw it all baked with dry blood, with the sweet hair tangling the dry flesh amongst the thorns, and the thorns amidst the flesh as it dried). I saw further that the sweet skin and the tender flesh, mingled with hair and blood, had been prised loose from the bone by the thorns, and broken in many pieces; which were hanging down, and would

have fallen away had there still been natural moisture. (I saw not how this came about, but I understood that it was because of the sharp thorns.) The rough and grievous binding-on of the garland, unsparing and pitiless, had broken all the sweet skin and flesh—yea, and loosened it from the bone; it was torn in strips like a cloth, hanging down, and with its looseness and weight like to have fallen. This was great sorrow and fear to me; for methought I would not for my life have seen it fall.

This sight continued a while; then it began to change. I looked, and wondered—was it possible? Then I saw it was; for it began to dry and lose a part of the weight. The garland of thorns was dyed with the blood that was round about the garland—so that it was covered all round, like one garland on another. And this second garland [of blood] and the head were all one colour, the colour of clotted blood when it drieth. The skin of the flesh of His face and body that shewed was a little wrinkled, and of a tawny colour—the colour of dry board when it is old; and the face was browner than the body.

OF THE DRYING OF CHRIST'S BODY

I saw four reasons for the drying. The first was the loss of blood; the second, the pain which accompanied it; the third is that He was hanging up in the air as men hang out a cloth to dry; the fourth, that His bodily kind demanded drink, and there was no manner of comfort ministered to Him. Hard and grievous was that pain. But much harder and more grievous it was when the moisture failed, and all the flesh began to dry and shrink.

These were two pains that shewed in the blessed head. The first (the loss of blood) worked the drying whilst the flesh was moist. The second was a drawn-out pain, with the shrinking and the drying through the blowing of the wind from without; this dried Him more and pained Him with more than my heart can think, more than all His other pains: Concerning which, I saw that all that I can say is too little; they cannot be told.

OF THE TRUE LOVER'S GREATEST PAIN

The shewing of Christ's pains filled me full of pain. For though I knew well that He had suffered just the once; yet He wished to shew me His pain and fill me with mind of it, as I had before desired of Him. In all this time of Christ's presence, I felt no pain except for Christ's pain. Then it seemed I knew but little what His pain was that I had asked for; and like a wretch I repented me—thinking that had I known what it was like, I would have been loath to pray for it. For my pain seemed to pass beyond any bodily death; and I thought: "Is any pain in hell like this?" And I was answered in my reason: "Hell is a different pain, for there is despair." Of all the pains that lead to salvation, this is the greatest—to see the Lover suffer. How could any pain be greater than to see Him, that is all my life, all my bliss, and all my joy, suffer? Here felt I steadfastly that I loved Christ so much above myself that there was no pain that could be suffered like to the sorrow I had, to see Him in pain.

THE EIGHTEENTH CHAPTER
OF THE SPIRITUAL MARTYRDOM OF OUR LADY AND OTHER LOVERS OF CHRIST

HERE I saw, in part, the compassion of our blessed Lady Saint Mary, for Christ. She was so oned to Him in love, that the greatness of her love was cause of the greatness of her pain. In this I saw the substance of the kind of love His creatures have to Him, continued by grace. Which kind love was most abundantly shewed in His sweet Mother—an over-passing love. For as much as she loved Him more than any other, even so her pain surpassed all others. For ever the higher, the mightier, and the sweeter that the love is, the more sorrow it is to the lover to see that body that he loves, in pain. And so all His disciples and all His true lovers suffered more pain than in their own bodily dying. For I am sure, in my own feeling, that the least of them loved Him so far above themselves that it passeth all that I can say.

HOW ALL THINGS SUFFERED WITH CHRIST

Here I saw, in my understanding, a great oneing between Christ and us. For when He was in pain, we were in pain; and all creatures that could suffer pain, suffered with Him; that is to say, all creatures that God hath made for our service. Heaven and earth failed in their kind for sorrow at Christ's dying. For it belongeth to their kindly property to recognize as their Lord, Him in whom all their virtue standeth. And when He failed, then needs must they, for kindness, fail with Him in as much as they could, in sorrow for His pains. Thus those that were His friends suffered pain, for love; and all in general suffered. That is to say: They that knew Him not, suffered in the failing of every manner of comfort except in the mighty secret keeping of God.

I speak of two sorts of people that knew Him not—as may be understood by these two persons; one, Pilate; the other Saint Denis of France, who was at that time a pagan. For when he saw the wonders and marvels, the sorrows and dreads that befell in that time, he said: "Either the world is now at an end, or else he that is Maker of Kind is suffering." Wherefore he wrote on an altar: "This is the altar of the unknown God." It is God, of His goodness, that maketh the planets and the elements to work in their kind for both the blessed and the cursed; in that time this working was withdrawn from both. Wherefore it was that they who knew Him not were in sorrow in that time.

Thus was our Lord Jesus pained for us; and we all stand in this way of pain, with Him, and shall do until we come to His bliss; as I shall say hereafter.

The Nineteenth Chapter
OF THE COMFORTABLE BEHOLDING
OF THE CRUCIFIX

IN this time I would have looked away from the cross; yet I durst not. For I knew well that whilst I beheld the cross I was sure and safe; therefore I would not consent to put my soul in peril. For apart from the cross was no surety against the fears of fiends.

Then I had an offer in my reason; it was said to me, as though by a friend: "Look up to heaven to His Father." Then through the faith that I felt I saw well that there was nothing between

the cross and heaven that could have dis-eased me. Here then I must needs look up, or else answer. So I answered inwardly, with all the might of my soul, and said: "Nay, I cannot, for Thou art my heaven." This I said because I would not. For I would rather have been in that pain till doomsday than have come to heaven otherwise than by Him. For I knew well that He who had bound me so sore, would unbind me when He would.

THE FLESH MUST BE IN PAIN
UNTIL IT IS ONE WITH CHRIST

Thus was I taught to choose Jesus for my heaven, whom I saw at that time only in pain. No other heaven pleased me than Jesus, who shall be my bliss when I come there. And this hath ever been a comfort to me, that I chose Jesus, by His grace, to be my heaven in all this time of passion and sorrow. And that hath been a lesson to me that I should evermore do so— choose only Jesus to be my heaven, in weal and in woe. And though, as I said before, like a wretch I felt regret—if I had known what the pain was to be, I would have been loath to pray for it; yet here I saw truly that this was merely the grumbling and frailty of the flesh without the consent of the soul, to which God assigneth no blame.

Feeling of regret and wilful choice are two contraries both of which I had at that time; they are two parts, an outward and an inward. The outward part is our mortal flesh which is now in pain and woe, and shall be, in this life; of which I felt much in this time. The inward part is a high and a blessed life which is all in peace and in love; and this is more secretly felt. It was in this part that mightily, wisely, and willingly I chose Jesus to be my heaven.

In this I saw truly that the inward part is the master and sovereign of the outward, neither censuring nor taking heed of its desire; but all the intent of the will is set endlessly to be oned to our Lord Jesus. That the outward part could draw the inward to its own assent—this was not shewed to me; but that the inward part, by grace, draweth the outward part, and both shall be oned in bliss without end by the power of Christ—this was shewed.

THE TWENTIETH CHAPTER
OF THE INEFFABLE PASSION OF CHRIST

THUS I saw our Lord Jesus languishing a long time: For the oneing with the Godhead gave strength to the manhood to suffer, for love, more than all the rest of men might suffer. I mean not only more pain than all men might suffer, but also that He suffered more pain than all men of salvation that ever were from the first beginning unto the last day could tell of or fully reckon; having regard to the worthiness of this highest worshipful King and His shameful ignominious death. For He that is highest and worthiest was most foully condemned and utterly despised. For the highest point to be seen in His passion is to consider and to know that it is God that suffered; seeing, after this, two points which are lower. One is, what He suffered: and the other, for whom He suffered.

In this He brought to my mind, in part, the high nobility of the glorious Godhead, and therewith the preciousness and the tender nature of His blessed body—which are oned together; and also the loathfulness that there is in our kind to suffer pain. For as He was most sensitively and perfectly formed, right so He was most strong and mighty to suffer. And for the sins of every man that shall be saved He suffered; and He saw and endured every man's sorrow, desolation and anguish, in His kindness and love. For in as much as our Lady sorrowed for His pains, as much suffered He sorrow for her sorrows—and more; as much more as His sweet manhood is worthier in kind. As long as He was passible, He suffered for us. And now He is uprisen and no more passible, yet still He suffereth with us, as I shall say afterwards.

OF THREE THINGS
TO BE REMEMBERED

I, beholding all this by His grace, saw that the love which He hath to our soul was so strong in Him that wilfully He chose His passion with great desire; and meekly He suffered it with great joy. The soul that beholdeth this when touched by His grace shall truly see that these pains of Christ's passion pass all other pains; and that all these other pains shall be turned into everlasting joy by the power of Christ's passion. It is God's will, as I understand it, that we have three manners of beholding of His blessed passion; the first of which is the severe pain that He suffered, with contrition and compassion. That shewed our Lord in this time, and gave me the power and the grace to see it.

THE TWENTY-FIRST CHAPTER
HOW WE ARE NOW DYING
ON THE CROSS WITH CHRIST

I LOOKED for the going forth of the soul with all my might, and thought to have seen His body wholly dead. But I saw Him not so. For just at the time that it seemed to me His life could no longer last, and that the shewing of His end must needs be nigh, suddenly (I still beheld the cross) His blessed face changed. This change in Him changed me, and I was as glad and merry as it is possible to be.

Then our Lord brought to my mind these joyful words: "Where now is any trace of thy pain or of thy anguish?" And I was full of joy. I understood that in this life, as our Lord sees it, we are on His cross, dying with Him in our pains and our passion. Then suddenly His countenance shall be changed upon us, and we shall be with Him in heaven. Between this disposition and the other there shall be no break in time—and then we shall all be brought into joy. (Thus meant He in shewing these words: "Where now is any trace of thy pain or of thy grief?") And we shall be full of bliss.

HOW WE BECOME HEIRS
THROUGH HIS SUFFERING

Here saw I truly that if He shewed now to us His blessed face, there is no pain in earth nor in any other place that could trouble us, but all things would be to us joy and bliss. But because He sheweth us the dispositions of His passion which He bore in this life—His cross, therefore we are in dis-ease and travail with Him, as our kind demandeth. And the reason why He suffereth is that He willeth, of His goodness, to make us heirs with Him in His bliss. And in return for this little pain that we suffer here, we shall have an endless high knowing in God, which we could never have without it. And the more severe our pains shall have been with Him in His cross, the greater shall our worship be with Him in His kingdom.

THE TWENTY-SECOND CHAPTER
THE NINTH REVELATION SHEWETH
THREE HEAVENS

THEN said our good Lord, asking: "Art thou well paid that I suffered for thee?" I said: "Yea, good Lord, by Thy mercy: yea, good Lord, blessed mayest Thou be." Then said Jesus, our good Lord: "If thou art paid, I am paid. It is a joy, a bliss, and an endless liking to Me that ever I suffered passion for thee. And if I could suffer more, I would suffer more."

Whilst I experienced this, my understanding was lifted up into heaven; and there I saw three heavens. At this sight I greatly marvelled, and thought: "I see three heavens, and all are of the blessed manhood of Christ; and no one of them is greater, no one is less; no one is higher, no one is lower; but all are equal in blessedness."

OF THE FIRST HEAVEN

As for the first heaven, Christ shewed me His Father—not in bodily likeness, but in His Fatherhood and in His working: That is to say, I saw in Christ what the Father is. The working of the Father is this:—that He giveth a prize to His Son, Jesus Christ. This gift, this prize is so blissful to Jesus, that His Father could not have given Him a prize that would have pleased

Him better. The first heaven is His pleasing of the Father (it was shewed me as a heaven, for it was full of blessedness). For the Father is well pleased with all the deeds that Jesus has done concerning our salvation. Wherefore we are not only His by His buying, but also, by the courteous gift of His Father, we are His bliss, we are His prize, we are His worship, we are His crown.

This was a singular source of wonder, and a beholding full of delight—that we should be His crown. It is, as I say, so great a bliss to Jesus that He setteth at naught His travail and His passion and His cruel and shameful death.

OF THE INFINITE LOVE
OF CHRIST FOR US

In these words, "If I could suffer more I would suffer more," I saw truly that as often as He could die, so often He would: and love would never let Him have rest until He had done it. And I looked with great diligence to see how often He would die if He could. And truly, the number so far surpassed my understanding and my wits, that my reason might not or could not comprehend it or take it in. And suppose He had thus often died or were to die, even then He would set it at naught, for love. For though the sweet manhood of Christ could suffer but once, the goodness of Him can never cease to repeat the offer: Every day, He is ready for the same, if it were possible.

If He had said that He would, for my love, make new heavens and new earths, that were of little account—He could do this every day, if He would, without any travail; but to die for my love, so often that the number sur-passes a creature's reason—that is the highest offer that our Lord God could make to man's soul, as I see it. His meaning then is this:

How could it be, then, that I would not do, for thy love, all the things in My power which trouble Me not to do; seeing that I would wish, for thy love, to die so often—having no regard for My hard pains.

OF THE SECOND HEAVEN

And here saw I concerning the second heaven, as I beheld His blessed passion: The love that made Him to suffer passeth so far above all His pain as heaven is above earth. For the pain was a noble, precious, and worshipful deed done in time, by the working of love. But the love was without beginning, is, and shall be without end. In this love He said most sweetly this word, "if I could suffer more, I would suffer more." He said not "if it were needful to suffer more," but "if I could suffer more." For even though it were not needful, if He could suffer more, He would.

This deed and this work concerning our salvation was ordained as well as God could ordain it. It was done as worshipfully as Christ could do it. Herein I saw fullness of bliss in Christ; for His bliss would not have been full, if it could any better have been done than it was done.

THE TWENTY-THIRD CHAPTER
HOW CHRIST WILLETH THAT WE REJOICE WITH HIM GREATLY IN OUR REDEMPTION

IN these three words, "It is a joy, a bliss, and an endless liking to me," were shewed three heavens—thus, for the joy, I understood the good pleasure of the Father; for the bliss, the worship of the Son: and for the endless liking, the Holy Ghost. The Father is pleased, the Son is worshipped, the Holy Ghost liketh.

And here saw I concerning the third heaven as I beheld His blessed passion; that is to say, the joy and the bliss that maketh Him to like it. For our courteous Lord shewed His passion to me in five manners; of which the first is the bleeding of the head; the second is the discolouring of His blessed face; the third is the plenteous bleeding of the body as it was in the scourging; the fourth is the deep drying. These four, as hath been said before, were shewed as the pains of the passion.

The fifth is this that was shewed as the joy and bliss of the passion. For it is God's will that we have true liking, with Him, of our salvation; and He willeth that we be mightily comforted and strengthened therein; and He willeth that our soul be thus happily occupied, with His grace. For we are His bliss, and in us He hath liking without end; and so shall we have in Him, with His grace. All that He doeth for us, and has done and ever shall do, was never cost nor expense to Him, except when He died in our manhood. Beginning at the sweet incarnation, and lasting till the blessed uprising on Easter morrow—just so long endured the cost and the expense of the deed of our redemption. In this deed He ever rejoiceth, endlessly, as is before said.

Jesus willeth that we take heed of this bliss that is in the blessed Trinity concerning our salvation; and that we desire to have the same ghostly liking, as is before said. That is to say, our liking in our salvation should be like to the joy that Christ hath in our salvation, as much as may be whilst we are here. All the Trinity worked in the passion of Christ, ministering an abundance of power and plenty of grace to us by Him. But only the Maiden's Son suffered. Whereof all the blessed Trinity rejoiceth. This was shewed in the word, "Art thou well paid," and in the other word that Christ said, "If thou art well paid, I am well paid;" as if He had said: "It is joy and liking enough to Me, and I ask naught else from thee for My travail but that I might pay thee well."

OF THE PROPER QUALITY OF A GLAD GIVER

In this He brought to my mind the proper quality of a glad giver. A glad giver ever taketh but little heed of the thing that he giveth; all his desire and all his intent is to please and to solace him to whom he giveth it. And if the receiver take the gift gladly and thankfully, then the courteous giver setteth at naught all his cost and all his labor, in return for the joy and delight that he hath; for he hath pleased and solaced him that he loveth. Plenteously and fully was this shewed.

Think also wisely of the greatness of this word *ever*. For in it was shewed a high knowing of the love that Christ hath of our salvation, with the manifold joys that follow out of His passion. One is, He rejoiceth that He hath done it in deed, and shall no more suffer. Another is that He hath therewith bought us from the endless pains of hell. Another is that He hath brought us up into heaven, and hath made us to be His crown and His endless bliss.

THE TWENTY-FOURTH CHAPTER
THE TENTH REVELATION IS OUR LORD JESUS SHEWING IN LOVE HIS BLESSED HEART CLOVEN IN TWO, REJOICING

WITH a glad countenance our good Lord looked into His side, and beheld with joy. And with His sweet looking He led forth the understanding of His creature through this same wound into His side. And there, within, He shewed a fair and delightful place, large enough for all mankind that shall be saved to rest there, in peace and in love. Therewith He brought to my mind the most dear blood and precious water which He let pour out for love.

In His sweet beholding He shewed His blessed heart cloven in two; and in His sweet enjoying He shewed to my understanding, in part, the blissful Godhead—as far forth as He would at that time, and strengthening the poor soul to understand, so to say, the endless love that was without beginning and is and shall be ever. For with this our good Lord said, most blissfully, "Lo, how I love thee." As if He had said: "My darling, behold and see thy Lord, thy God, that is thy Maker and thine endless joy; see thine own Brother, thy Saviour; My child, behold and see what liking and what bliss I have in thy salvation; and for love of me, rejoice with me." To still more understanding was said this blessed word, "Lo, how I love thee." As if He had said:

Behold and see that I loved thee so much (before ever I died for thee) that I would die for thee. And now

I have died for thee, and have suffered as willingly as I may. And now is all My bitter pain and all My hard travail turned to My everlasting joy and bliss. And as to thee, how should it now be that thou shouldst anything pray Me that pleaseth Me, and that I should not full gladly grant it thee? For My pleasure is thy holiness and thine endless joy and bliss with Me.

This is the understanding that I had, said as simply as I can, of this blessed word, "Lo, how I loved thee." This shewed our good Lord to make us glad and merry.

THE TWENTY-FIFTH CHAPTER
THE ELEVENTH REVELATION IS A HIGH GHOSTLY SHEWING OF HIS MOTHER

HIS countenance full of this mirth and joy, our Lord looked down on the right side and brought to my mind our Lady, and where she stood during the time of His passion; and said, "Wilt thou see her?" In this sweet word it was as if He had said:

I know well that thou wilt see My blessed Mother; for after Myself she is the highest joy that I might shew thee; she is the most liking and worship to Me, and of all My blessed creatures sight of her is most desired.

Out of the marvellous high and special love that He hath for this sweet maiden His blessed Mother, our Lady Saint Mary, He sheweth her bliss and joy—such is the meaning of this sweet word. It was as if He said, "Wilt thou see how I love her so that thou mightest joy with Me in the love that I have in her, and she in Me?"

This sweet word our good Lord speaketh in love to all mankind that shall be saved (for our greater understanding) as it were to one person. It is as if He said: "Wilt thou see in her how thou art loved? For thy love I have made her so high, so noble, and so worthy. This liketh Me, and so will I that it do thee."

After Himself, she is the most blissful sight. Yet because of this I am not taught to long to see her bodily presence whilst I am here, but only the virtues of her blessed soul, her truth, her wisdom, her charity; whereby I am taught to know myself and reverently to dread my God.

OF THE THREE TIMES SHE SAW MARY

When our good Lord had shewed this, and said this word, "Wilt thou see her?" I answered and said, "Yea, good Lord, by Thy mercy; yea, good Lord, if it be Thy will." Oftentimes I prayed for this; and I thought I might see her in bodily likeness; but I saw her not so. For Jesus in that word shewed me a ghostly sight of her. And just as before I had seen her little and simple, now He shewed her high and noble and glorious, and pleasing to Him above all creatures.

Even so He willeth it to be known that all those who have liking in Him should have liking in her—in the same liking that He hath in her and she in Him. It was for greater understanding of this that He shewed this example: If a man love one creature especially and above all creatures, He will make all other creatures to love and to like that creature that He loveth so much. This

word that Jesus said "Wilt thou see her?" seemed to me the most liking word that He could give me of her—together with the ghostly shewing that He gave me of her. Our Lord shewed me no individual person except our Lady Saint Mary; but her He shewed three times: The first, as she was when she conceived; the second, as she was in her sorrow under the Cross; the third, as she is now, in liking, worship, and joy.

THE TWENTY-SIXTH CHAPTER
THE TWELFTH REVELATION IS THAT OUR LORD GOD IS SOVEREIGN BEING

AFTER this our Lord shewed Himself more glorified (if I saw aright) than I had seen Him before. Wherein I was taught that our soul shall never have rest till it come into Him, knowing that He is fullness of joy, homely, courteous, and blissful: True life. Oftentimes our Lord said:

I it am, I it am; I it am that is highest; I it am that thou lovest; I it am that thou likest; I it am that thou servest; I it am that thou longest; I it am that thou desirest; I it am that thou meanest; I it am that is all; I it am that Holy Church preacheth and teacheth thee; I it am that shewed Myself to thee here.

The number of His words passeth beyond my wits, and all my understanding, and all my powers; and they are the highest, as I see it. For therein is comprehended—I cannot tell what, except that the joy that I saw in the shewing of them passeth all that heart can think or soul could desire. Therefore these words are written here only that every man may receive them in our Lord's meaning, according to the grace of understanding and loving that God giveth Him.

THE TWENTY-SEVENTH CHAPTER
THE THIRTEENTH REVELATION IS THAT OUR LORD GOD WILLETH THAT WE HAVE GREAT REGARD TO ALL THE DEEDS THAT HE HATH DONE

AFTER this our Lord brought to my mind the great longing that I had for Him before. And I saw that nothing hindered me but sin; I beheld the same in us all in general. And it occurred to me that if sin had never been, we should all be clean and as like to our Lord as when He made us. Thus in my folly, even before this time, I often wondered why the beginning of sin was not prevented by the great foreseeing wisdom of God; for then—or so it seemed to me—all would have been well. Such a thought was much to be forsaken; yet nevertheless mourning and sorrow I made on this account, without any understanding or spiritual discernment. But Jesus, who in this vision informed me of all that I needed, answered with this word saying: "Sin must needs be, but all shall be well. All shall be well; and all manner thing shall be well."

OF THE GREAT AND ALL-SURPASSING PAIN CHRIST SUFFERED

In this naked word *sin* our Lord brought to my mind, in a general way, all that is not good: the shameful despising and the uttermost tribulation that He bore for us in this life, His dying and all His pains; and the suffering, bodily and ghostly, of all His creatures—for we are all partly brought to naught, and shall be so, following our Master Jesus, until we are fully purged (that is to say, until we are fully brought to naught) in regard of our mortal flesh, and of all those inward affections of ours which are not very good. I beheld this, with all the pains that ever were or ever shall be. (And with all this I understood that the passion of Christ was the greatest and all-surpassing pain.) All this was shewed in a moment; and it quickly changed over to comforting. For our good Lord would not that the soul be afraid of this ugly sight.

And yet I saw not sin. For I believe it hath no manner of substance nor particle of being. It cannot be known except by the pain that is caused thereby. This pain is some thing, if I see it aright, existing for a time. For it purgeth us, and maketh us to know ourselves and ask mercy; for the passion of our Lord is our comfort against all this—and such is His blessed will.

And for the tender love that our good Lord hath to all that shall be saved, He comforteth them swiftly and sweetly, meaning thus: "It is true that sin is the cause of all this pain. But all shall be well and all shall be well, and all manner thing shall be well." These words were said most tenderly; they shewed no manner of blame either to me or to any that shall be. Hence it would be a great unkindness in me to blame or to wonder at God because of my sin, since He blameth not me for sin.

In these same words I saw a high marvellous secret hid in God—a secret which He shall openly make known to us in heaven. In this knowing we shall truly see the cause why He permitted sin to come. And in this sight we shall endlessly have joy.

THE TWENTY-EIGHTH CHAPTER
HOW THE CHILDREN OF SALVATION
SHALL BE SHAKEN IN SORROWS;
BUT CHRIST REJOICETH THEREIN
WITH COMPASSION

THUS I saw how Christ hath compassion on us because of sin. And just as I was before, in the passion of Christ, filled full of pain and compassion, so in this I was, in part, filled with compassion for all my even-christians. (For full well He loveth the people that shall be saved—that is to say, God's servants.) Holy Church shall be shaken with sorrow and anguish and tribulation in this world, as men shake a cloth in the wind. But to this our Lord answered in this manner: "A great thing I shall make of this in heaven—a thing of endless worship and of everlasting joy"; so much so that our Lord, as I saw, rejoiceth in the tribulations of His servants, but with pity and compassion.

On every person that He loveth, in order to bring them to His bliss, He layeth something, which, though it is of no offence in His sight, is a reason why they are humbled and despised in this world, scorned and mocked and cast out. This He doeth to prevent their taking harm of the pomp and of the pride and of the vainglory of this wretched life, and to make ready the way for them to come to heaven in bliss that shall last without end. For He says: "I shall wholly break you of your vain affections and your vicious pride; and after that I shall gather you and make you meek and mild, clean and holy by oneing you to Me." And then I saw that all the kind compassion that a man hath for his even-christians, with charity—this is Christ in him.

OF THE BLISS CHRISTIANS ENJOY

The same being brought to naught that He shewed in His passion—it was shewed again here, in this compassion; wherein were two manners of understanding according to our Lord's meaning. One was of the bliss to which we are brought, wherein He willeth that we have joy; the other is, of the comfort in our pain—that we may know that it all shall turn to our worship and our profit by virtue of His passion; and that we may know that we suffered right naught alone, but with Him; that we may see Him, our ground; and that we may see that His sins and His tribulation so far surpass all that we might suffer, that it cannot be fully comprehended.

The beholding of this will save us from complaint and despair in feeling our pains. And though we see truly that our sins deserve them, yet His love excuseth us. Of His great courtesy He doeth away with all our blame, and beholdeth us with compassion and pity, as children innocent and lovable.

THE TWENTY-NINTH CHAPTER
ADAM'S SIN WAS THE GREATEST;
BUT THE SATISFACTION FOR IT
IS MORE PLEASING TO GOD THAN
EVER THE SIN WAS HARMFUL

BUT meanwhile I still remained, as I beheld, in sorrow and mourning, saying thus to our Lord—but meaning it with very great dread: "Ah, good Lord, but how can all be well in face of the great harm that is come by sin to Thy creatures?" Here I desired, as much as I durst, to have some more open declaring, wherewith I could be eased in this perplexity.

And to this our blessed Lord answered most meekly and with a lovely look. He shewed that Adam's sin was the greatest harm that ever was done or ever shall be, unto the world's end. And also He shewed that this is clearly known in all Holy Church on earth. Furthermore He taught me that I should behold the glorious remedy. For this making amends is more pleasing to God and worshipful unto man's salvation, without comparison, than ever was the sin of Adam harmful. Hence our blessed Lord meaneth this—and in His teaching we must take heed of it: "Seeing that I have made well the greatest harm, it is My will that thou shouldst know thereby that I shall make well all that is less."

THE THIRTIETH CHAPTER
HOW WE SHOULD HAVE JOY AND TRUST IN OUR SAVIOR

HE gave understanding of two parts of His truth. One part is our Saviour and our Salvation. This blessed part is open, clear and fair, and light and plenteous. For all mankind that are and shall be of good will are comprehended in this part. Herein we are bound and drawn to God, and counselled and taught, inwardly by the Holy Ghost and outwardly by Holy Church through the same grace. In this our Lord willeth that we should be occupied—having joy in Him: For He hath joy in us. The more plenteously we accept this joy, with reverence and meekness, the more thanks we deserve of Him, and the more progress we ourselves make. Thus we may see and enjoy.

HOW WE SHOULD NOT PRESUME TO KNOW HIS SECRET COUNSELS

This our part is our Lord. The other is hidden and closed to us—that is, all that belongeth not to our salvation. For that is our Lord's secret counsel. It belongeth to the royal Lordship of God to hold His secret counsels in peace. And it belongeth to His servants, out of obedience and reverence, not to wish to know His counsels. Yet our Lord hath pity and compassion on us in that some creatures make themselves so busy therein. And I am sure that if we knew how greatly we would please Him, and ease ourselves by leaving it alone, we would do so.

The saints in heaven refuse to know anything but what our Lord willeth to shew them. And also their charity and their desires are ruled according to the will of our Lord. And thus ought we to will—that our will be like to theirs. Then should we nothing will, nothing desire but the will of our Lord—just as they do. (For we are all one in God's meaning.) Here was I taught that we should have joy only in our blessed Saviour Jesus, and trust in Him for all things.

THE THIRTY-FIRST CHAPTER
OF THE LONGING AND THE SPIRITUAL THIRST OF CHRIST

THUS our good Lord answered all the questions and doubts that I could bring up, saying for full comfort: "I may make all things well; and I can make all things well; and I shall make all things well; and I will make all things well; and thou shalt see thyself that all manner of things shall be well." Where He saith "I may," I understand that the Father is meant; where

He saith "I can," the Son; where He saith "I will," the Holy Ghost; where He saith "I shall," the unity of the blessed Trinity—three Persons and one Truth. And where He saith "thou shalt see thyself," I understand the oneing of all mankind that shall be saved with the blissful Trinity.

In these five words God sheweth His will that we should be enclosed in rest and in peace. Thus shall the ghostly thirst of Christ be ended. For this is the ghostly thirst of Christ—the love-longing that lasteth and ever shall, till we see that sight at doomsday. We that are to be safe, and to be Christ's joy and His bliss, some of us are still here, and others are yet to come; and some shall be here in that day. Therefore this is His thirst and His love-longing for us here: to gather us all in Him unto our endless bliss (if I see it aright). For we are not yet as fully whole in Him as we shall be then.

We know in our faith—and it was also shewed in all the Revelations—that Christ Jesus is both God and man. In respect of His Godhead He is Himself highest bliss, and was so from without-beginning and so shall be without end—the self-same endless bliss, which can never be increased or diminished. This was plenteously seen in every shewing; and particularly in the twelfth, where He saith: "I it am that is Highest." In respect of His manhood (this too is known in our faith and was also shewed), Christ having the power of the Godhead suffered pains and passion and died, for love, in order to bring us to His bliss. These are the works of Christ's manhood wherein He hath His joy. This He shewed in the ninth Revelation, where He saith: "It is a joy, a bliss, and an endless liking that ever I suffered passion for thee." This is the bliss of Christ in His works; and this is His meaning when He saith in the same shewing that we are His bliss, we are His prize, we are His worship, we are His crown.

BY REASON OF HIS BODY, HE IS NOT YET FULLY GLORIFIED, NOR ALL IMPASSIBLE

In respect of His being our Head, Christ is glorified and impassible. But in respect of His body—in which all His members are knit—He is not yet fully glorified nor entirely impassible. The same thirst and longing that He had upon the rood-tree—that same desire, longing, and thirst (if I see it aright) was in Him from without-beginning; He hath the same now, and shall have, unto the time that the last soul to be saved shall have come up to His bliss. For as truly as there is in God the quality of compassion and pity, thus truly there is in God the quality of thirst and longing. And in virtue of this longing in Christ, we have to long, in our turn, for Him; and without it no soul can come to heaven.

This quality of longing and thirst cometh of the endless goodness of God, just as the quality of pity cometh of the same endless goodness (though, if I see it aright, longing and pity are separate qualities). In this goodness is the essence of the ghostly thirst, which is lasting in Him as long as we are in need, drawing us up to His bliss. All this was seen in the shewing of His compassion; and that too shall cease at doomsday. Thus He hath compassion and pity on us, and He hath longing to have us. But His wisdom and love permit not the end to come, until the best time.

THE THIRTY-SECOND CHAPTER
HOW ALL THINGS SHALL BE WELL AND SCRIPTURE FULFILLED

AT one time our good Lord said: "All things shall be well"; and at another He said: "Thou shalt see thyself that all manner of things shall be well." In these two sayings the soul received various manners of understanding. One was this: He wills we know that He taketh heed not only of noble things and great, but also of little and small, low and simple—of both the one and the other. This is His meaning when He saith "all manner thing shall be well"; for He wills we know that the least thing shall not be forgotten.

Another understanding was this: There are many evil deeds done in our sight, and such great harm taken that it seemeth to us impossible that things should ever come to a good end. As we look upon these, we sorrow and mourn for them, so that we cannot rest in the blissful beholding of God— as we ought to do. The cause is that in the use of our reason we are now so blind, so lowly, and so simple that we cannot know the high marvellous wisdom, the power and the goodness of the blissful Trinity. This is His meaning when He saith, "Thou shalt see thyself that all manner thing shall be well"; as if He said: "Accept it now faithfully and trustingly, and at the last end thou shalt see in truth and in fullness of joy."

So in the same five words beforesaid, "I may make all things well," I understand a mighty comfort in all the works of our Lord God that are to come. There is a deed which the blissful Trinity shall do in the last day (if I see it aright); but what that deed shall be, and how it shall be done, is unknown to all creatures which are beneath Christ, and shall be so until the time when it shall be done. The goodness and the love of our Lord God will us to know that it shall be done. But His might and wisdom by the same love will to hide and conceal from us what it shall be, and how it shall be done. The reason why He willeth us to know it just so is because He willeth us to be easier in our souls and peaceable in loving, leaving aside the beholding of all troubles that could hinder our having true joy in Him.

This is the great deed ordained by our Lord from without-beginning, treasured and hid in His blessed breast, known only to Himself, by which He shall make all things well. For just as the blessed Trinity made all things from naught, right so the same blessed Trinity shall make all well that is not well.

WE MUST STEADFASTLY HOLD THE FAITH OF HOLY CHURCH, AS IS CHRIST'S WILL

In this sight I marvelled greatly and beheld our faith. I mean this: Our faith is grounded in God's Word; and it belongeth to our faith to believe that God's Word shall stand in all points. One point of our faith is that many creatures shall be damned—for instance the angels who fell from heaven because of their pride, and are now fiends; and man on earth that dieth out of the faith of Holy Church, that is to say, those who are heathens; and also man that hath received christening but liveth an unchristian life and so dieth out of charity—all these shall be damned to hell without end, as Holy Church teacheth me to believe.

In view of all this it seemed to me impossible that all manner of things should be well according as our Lord shewed in this time. But I had no other answer to the difficulty in this shewing of our Lord's, except this: "What is impossible to thee is not impossible to Me; I shall save My word in all things—I shall make all things well."

Here I was taught by the grace of God that I should steadfastly keep me in the faith as I had understood it before, and that at the same time I should take my stand on and earnestly believe in what our Lord shewed in this time—that "all manner thing shall be well." For this is the great deed that our Lord shall do, in which He shall save His word in all things— He shall make well all that is not well. But what the deed shall be and how it shall be done there is no creature beneath Christ that knoweth it or shall know it until it is done—such was the understanding that I had of our Lord's meaning in this time.

THE THIRTY-THIRD CHAPTER
ALL DAMNED SOULS ARE DESPISED IN THE SIGHT OF GOD AS THE DEVIL IS

AND yet in this I desired, as much as I durst, to have had some sight of hell and of purgatory—though it was not my meaning to put to the proof anything that belongeth to our faith. (For I believed firmly and truly that hell and purgatory have the same purpose that Holy Church teaches them to have.) Rather my meaning was that I might have seen, for my instruction, in

all things that belong to my faith, how I might live the more perfectly unto God's worship and my soul's progress.

But for aught that I might desire I could see nothing at all of this, except (as is said before) in the fifth shewing, where I saw that the Devil is reproved by God and endlessly damned. By this sight I understood that of all creatures who are of the Devil's sort in this life and thus make their ending, there is no more mention made of them before God and His holy ones than there is of the Devil—notwithstanding that they are of man's kind, or whether they are christened or not.

THESE REVELATIONS DO NOT TAKE AWAY THE FAITH OF HOLY CHURCH, BUT STRENGTHEN IT

For though the Revelation that was shewed was of goodness, and in it was made but little mention of evil, yet I was not drawn thereby from any point of faith that Holy Church teacheth me to believe. Hence, though in the sight I had of the passion of Christ in different shewings (in the first and the second, and in the fourth and the eighth wherein I had, in part, experience of the sorrow of our Lady and of the true friends of His that saw His pains—as it is before said), I did not see specified particularly the Jews that did Him to death; yet notwithstanding this, I knew in my faith that they were accursed and damned without end, save those that were converted by grace. So was I strengthened and generally instructed to keep me in the faith, in each and every point, as I had understood it before, in the hope that I was therein by God's grace and mercy, and with the desire and prayer (such was my meaning) that I might continue therein unto my life's end.

THE MORE WE SEEK TO KNOW GOD'S SECRETS, THE LESS WE KNOW

It is God's will that we have great regard to all the deeds that He hath done. For He willeth by this regard that we know, trust, and believe all that He shall do; but it evermore behoveth us to leave off considering what that deed shall be. So let us desire to be like our brethren the saints in heaven who have no will at all except God's will. Then only shall we have joy in God, and be well satisfied both with the hiding and the shewing. For in our Lord's meaning I saw truly that the more we busy ourselves about knowing His secrets in that or in any other thing, the farther off we shall be from the knowing.

THE THIRTY-FOURTH CHAPTER
GOD SHEWETH THE SECRETS NECESSARY TO HIS LOVERS

OUR Lord shewed two manners of secrets. One is this great secret with all the secret points that belong thereto. And these secrets He willeth we know as hid until the time that He will clearly shew them to us. The others are the secrets which He Himself shewed openly in this Revelation. These are secrets which He willeth to make open and known to us; and He willeth us to know that it is His will for us to know them. They are secrets to us, not only because He wisheth them to be secrets to us, but on account of our blindness and our unknowing, for which He has great pity. Therefore He willeth to make them open to us Himself, so that we may know Him and love Him, and cleave to Him. For all that is expedient for us to wit and to know, with great courtesy our good Lord willeth to shew us what it is, along with all the preaching and teaching of Holy Church.

HOW THEY PLEASE GOD WHO RECEIVE DILIGENTLY THE PREACHING OF HOLY CHURCH

God shewed the very great pleasure that He taketh in all men and women who mightily and wisely receive the preaching and teaching of Holy Church. For He is Holy Church. He is its ground. He is its substance. He is its teaching. He is its teacher. He is the end and the reward towards which every kind soul travelleth. This is known, and shall be known to every soul to whom the Holy Ghost declareth it. And indeed I hope that all those who so seek shall speed; for they seek God. In the third shewing, then, where I saw that God does all that is done, I saw not sin; it was then I saw that all is well. But when God shewed me sin, then He said, "All shall be well."

THE THIRTY-FIFTH CHAPTER
HOW GOD DOETH ALL THAT IS GOOD

AFTER God had shewed so plenteously and fully of His mercy, I desired to know concerning a certain creature that I loved, whether that creature would continue in the good life which I hoped was begun in the grace of God. By expressing this desire concerning an individual, it seemed that I hindered myself, because in that moment I received no teaching. Then I was answered in my reason as though by a friendly mediator: "Take what your

Lord God shewed to you as spoken generally, beholding His courtesy. For it is greater worship to God to behold Him in all things than in any particular thing." I consented, and there I learned that it is greater worship to God to know all things in general than to shew preference for any thing in particular. And if I would act wisely according to this teaching, I would not be moved to gladness by any one thing in particular, nor be greatly saddened by any thing at all. For "all shall be well"; and the fullness of joy is to behold God in all things.

For by the same blessed might, wisdom, and goodness that He made all things, unto the same, as their end, our good Lord continually leadeth them, and Himself shall bring them thereto. And when it is time, we shall see it. The reason of this was shewed in the first Revelation, and more clearly in the third, where it is said, "I saw God in a point."

HOW GOD WORSHIPFULLY PERMITTETH
ALL THAT SHALL CEASE TO BE WHEN
SIN IS NO MORE

All that our Lord doeth is rightful, and all that He suffereth is worshipful. In these two are comprehended good and evil. All that is good our Lord doeth, and all that is evil our Lord suffereth. I do not say that evil is worshipful, but I say that the sufferance of our Lord God is worshipful; for by it His goodness shall be known without end; and His meekness and mildness by His working of mercy and grace.

Rightfulness is a thing so good that it cannot be better than it is. For God Himself is very rightfulness, and all His works are done as rightfully as they are ordained from without-beginning, by His high might, His high wisdom, and His high goodness—just as He hath ordained them for the best, even so He worketh continually, and leadeth them to the best end. He is ever fully pleased with Himself and with all His works.

The beholding of this blessed harmony is most sweet to the soul that seeth it by grace. All the souls that shall be saved are made rightful in heaven without end, in the sight of God, and by His own goodness. In this rightfulness we are endlessly kept and marvellously, above all creatures.

Mercy is a working that cometh of the goodness of God. And the working shall last as long as sin is permitted to pursue rightful souls. And when sin hath no longer leave to pursue, then the working of mercy shall cease. And then shall all be brought into rightfulness and stand therein without end. By His sufferance we fall; and in His blessed love, with His high might and wisdom, we are kept; and by mercy and grace we are raised to more manifold joy. Thus in rightfulness and in mercy He wills to be known and loved now and without end. The soul that wisely beholdeth in grace, is well satisfied with both, and enjoyeth endlessly.

THE THIRTY-SIXTH CHAPTER
OF ANOTHER EXCELLENT DEED THAT
OUR LORD SHALL DO

OUR Lord God shewed that a deed shall be done, and that He Himself shall do it. It shall be worshipful and marvellous and plenteous; by Him it shall be done, and He Himself shall do it. And this is the highest joy that the soul understood—that God Himself shall do it. Though I shall do right naught but sin, my sin shall not hinder His goodness working.

I saw that the beholding of this is a heavenly joy in a God-fearing soul that evermore kindly, by grace, desireth God's will. This deed shall be begun here; it shall be worshipful to God and plenteously profitable to all His lovers on earth; and ever as we come to heaven we shall see it in marvellous joy. It shall last thus, in its working, until the last day; and the worship and the bliss of it shall last in heaven, before God and all His holy saints, without end. Thus was this deed seen, and understood in our Lord's meaning. And the reason why He shewed it is to make us have joy in Him and all His works.

When I saw that the shewing continued, I understood that there was meant a great thing that was to come—a thing (as God shewed) which He Himself should do, and which hath the qualities before said. This He shewed most blissfully, meaning me to receive it wisely, faithfully, and trustingly; but what the deed would be—that was kept a secret from me. In this I saw that it is not His will that we should fear to know the things He sheweth. He sheweth them because He willeth us to know them, and by the knowing He willeth us to love Him and have liking in Him and endlessly enjoy Him. Because of the great love that He hath for us, He sheweth us all that is worshipful and profitable for the time.

And even the things He willeth to keep hidden for now, of His great goodness He sheweth them as hid. And in this shewing His will is that we believe and understand that we shall see them truly in His endless bliss. Therefore it behoveth us to have our joy in Him, for all that He sheweth and for all that He hideth. And if we willingly and meekly do so, we shall find therein great ease of mind and we shall have His endless thanks for it.

OF THE MEANING OF
OUR LORD'S WORDS

Here is the understanding of His words: "It shall be worshipful, marvellous, and plenteous"—that is, to man in general or rather to all that shall be saved: "By Me it shall be done, and God himself shall do it"—this shall be the highest joy that can be seen in this deed: That God Himself shall do it, and man shall do right naught but sin. This then is our good Lord's meaning; it is as if He said:

Behold and see! Here hast thou matter for meekness, here hast thou matter for love, here hast thou matter for knowing thyself, here hast thou matter for joy in Me. In this beyond all things thou canst please Me most.

And as long as we are in this life, whenever in our folly we turn to behold the reproved, tenderly our Lord toucheth us and blissfully claspeth, saying in our soul: "Let be, My love, My most dear child, and attend to Me (for I am enough to thee), and take joy in thy Saviour and thy salvation." That this is our Lord's working in us, I am sure; and the soul that is pierced within by grace shall see it and feel it. For though it is true that this deed must be taken as referring to man in general, yet it does not exclude the individual. What our good Lord willeth to do concerning His poor creatures is now unknown to me. But this deed and the aforementioned are not both the same, but two different ones. This one shall be known sooner; that is, as soon as we each come to heaven; and also it can be known here, in part, by those to whom our Lord giveth it. But the great deed aforementioned shall be known neither in heaven nor in earth until it be done.

GOD STILL PERFORMS MIRACLES

Furthermore He gave me special understanding and teaching concerning the working and shewing of miracles, in this way: "It is known that I have worked miracles heretofore, many, most high, marvellous and worshipful and great. And as I have done, so I do now continually, and shall do in time to come." It is known that before miracles come sorrows and anguish and trouble. And the reason is that we might know our own feebleness and the mischief that we fall into by sin, and to make us meek and to make us cry to God for help and grace. Great miracles come after this, of the high might and wisdom and goodness of God—as He sheweth His power and the joys of heaven in as much as may be in this passing life, for the strengthening of our faith and increase of hope, in charity. Wherefore it pleaseth Him to be known and worshipped in His miracles. His meaning then is that He willeth that we be not too overborne by the sorrows and tempestings that befall us. For it hath ever been so before coming of miracles.

THE THIRTY-SEVENTH CHAPTER
GOD KEEPETH HIS CHOSEN FULL SURELY, ALTHOUGH THEY SIN

GOD brought to mind that I would sin. But because of the liking that I had in beholding Him, I did not attend promptly to that shewing. But our Lord in His great mercy abode, and gave me the grace to attend. This shewing I took for myself, individually; but by all the gracious comfort that followed, as you shall see, I was taught to take it for all my even-christians, in general and in no way individually. Here I conceived a gentle fear; but to it our Lord answered, "I keep thee full surely." This word was spoken with more love and assuredness of ghostly keeping than I can or may tell of. For just as it was first shewed to me that I would sin, for all my even-christians, right so was shewed the comfort, the sureness of keeping. (What could make me love more my even-christians than to see in God that He loveth all that shall be saved as one soul, as it were?)

FOR IN THEM IS A GODLY WILL THAT NEVER TASTED SIN

In every soul that shall be saved is a godly will that never assenteth to sin and never shall. Just as there is a beastly will in the lower part, which can will nothing good, so there is a godly will in the higher part—a will so good that it can never will evil but ever willeth the good. For this cause we are those whom He loveth, and endlessly we do what pleaseth Him. This our good Lord shewed in the wholeness of love in which we stand together in His sight; so that He loveth us now, whilst we are here, as well as He shall do when we are there before His blessed face. And all our travail is for failing of love on our side.

THE THIRTY-EIGHTH CHAPTER
THE SIN OF THE CHOSEN SHALL BE TURNED TO JOY AND WORSHIP

GOD shewed that sin shall be no shame but rather worship for man. For right as for every sin, in truth, there is an answering pain, even so for every sin there is given a bliss to the same soul, by love. Right as different sins are punished by different pains, according to their grievousness, even so shall they be rewarded in heaven with different joys according as the sin has been painful and sorrowful to the soul on earth. The soul that shall come to heaven is so precious to God, and the place itself is so worshipful, that the goodness of God never permitteth a soul that is to come thither to sin finally.

But what sinners they are that shall be so rewarded by overpassing worship is made known in Holy Church on earth, and also in heaven. For in this sight my understanding was lifted up into heaven, and God brought joyfully to my mind David, and with him others of the old law without number. And in the new law He brought to my mind first Magdalene, then Peter and Paul, Thomas and Jude, Saint John of Beverley and others also, without number; how that they are known in the Church on earth with their sins— that it is to them no shame, but all is turned to their worship. And our courteous Lord sheweth of them here in part, just as it is there in fullness, where the token of their sin is turned into worship.

THE EXAMPLE OF JOHN OF BEVERLEY

And Saint John of Beverley—our Lord shewed him in his exaltation for our comfort and out of homeliness; He brought to my mind that He is a kind neighbor and of our knowing. And He called him Saint John of Beverley, just as we do; and that with a look most happy and sweet, shewing that Saint John is a very great saint in His sight, and a blissful one. At the same time He mentioned that in his youth and tender years he was God's most dear servant, most God-loving and God-fearing.

And yet God permitted him to fall; but He kept him mercifully so that he did not perish nor lose any time. And afterwards God raised him to more manifold grace; for by the contrition and the meekness that he had in his living God hath given him in heaven manifold joys, far surpassing what he would have had if he had not sinned nor fallen. That this is true, God sheweth on earth by working plenteous miracles around His body constantly. All this shewing was to make us glad and merry.

THE THIRTY-NINTH CHAPTER
OF THE SHARPNESS OF SIN AND THE GOODNESS OF CONTRITION

SIN is the sharpest scourge that any chosen soul can be smitten with—a scourge which greatly afflicteth a man or woman, breaketh him in pieces and purgeth him of his self-love; to the extent that at times he thinketh himself fit for nothing but to sink into hell; until such time as, by the touching of the Holy Ghost, contrition overtaketh him and turneth his bitterness into hope in God's mercy. Then his wounds begin to heal and his soul to revive as he is converted to the life of Holy Church.

The Holy Ghost leadeth him to confession to reveal his sins willingly, nakedly, and truly; with great sorrow and with great shame for having so befouled the fair image of God. Then he undertaketh the penance for all his sins enjoined by his confessor, who is instructed in Holy Church by the teaching of the Holy Ghost. This is a meekness that greatly pleaseth God. He also meekly taketh bodily sickness that is of God's sending, and the sorrow and shame coming from without, of the reproof and despising of the world, with all manner of annoyance and temptation that may fall upon us, ghostly or bodily.

Most preciously our good Lord keepeth us when it seemeth to us that we are well nigh forsaken and cast away for our sins. And because we see that we have deserved it, and because of the meekness that we get thereby, we are raised high in God's sight, by His grace. Then also, when our Lord will, He visiteth us with His special grace, with such contrition and also with compassion and true longing to God that we are at once delivered of sins and pain, and lifted up to bliss, equal with the saints.

By contrition we are made clean; by compassion we are made ready; by true longing for God we are made worthy. These are the three means, so I understood, whereby all souls come to heaven (that is to say, those that have been sinners) and shall be saved. It is by these medicines that every sinful soul must be healed. And after he is healed, his wounds are still seen before God—yet not as wounds but as honourable scars. Contrariwise, then, to our being punished here with sorrow and with penance, in heaven we shall be rewarded by the courteous love of our God almighty, who desireth that none that come thither should lose any degree of their labour. For He seeth sin as sorrow and pain to His lovers; and to them He assigneth no blame, for love.

HOW OUR KIND LORD WILLED US NOT TO DESPAIR

The reward that we receive shall not be little; it shall be high, glorious, and worshipful. And so shall all shame be turned into worship and joy. Our courteous Lord willeth not His servants to despair for often falling or for grievous falling. For our falling preventeth Him not from loving us. Peace and love always exist and work in us, though we are not always in peace and in love. But He willeth that we take heed of this, that He is the ground of all our life in love; and furthermore that He is our everlasting Keeper, and mightily defendeth us against these enemies of ours who are full fell and full fierce upon us. (And our need is the greater the more we give them occasion, by our falling.)

THE FORTIETH CHAPTER
IT BEHOVETH US TO LONG IN LOVE WITH JESUS, ESCHEWING SIN FOR LOVE

THIS is the sovereign friendship of our courteous Lord, that He keepeth us so tenderly whilst we are in our sins. And furthermore He toucheth us secretly and sheweth us our sins, by the sweet light of mercy and grace. But when we see ourselves so foul, then we think that God must be wroth with us for our sins; thus we are moved by the Holy Ghost, by His contrition, to pray and desire the amending of ourselves with all our might, so as to slake the wrath of God, until we find rest in soul and quiet of conscience. Then we hope that God hath forgiven us our sins. And truly He hath.

Then our courteous Lord sheweth Himself to the soul cheerfully, with glad countenance, with a friendly welcome, as though the soul had been in pain and in prison, and speaketh so:

> My dear darling, I am glad thou art come to Me; in all thy woe I have ever been with thee. And now thou seest Me in My love, and we are oned in bliss.

Thus are sins forgiven by grace and mercy, and our soul worshipfully received in joy (just as it shall be when it comes to heaven), as often as we experience the grace-giving working of the Holy Ghost and the power of Christ's passion.

Here I fully understood that all manner of things are prepared for us by the great goodness of God; so that when at last we are ourselves in peace and in charity we shall be truly saved. But because we cannot have this in fullness whilst we are here, it is right for us ever to live in sweet praying and love-longing with our Lord Jesus; since He longeth ever to bring us to the fullness of joy—as was said before, when He shewed His ghostly thirst.

THE VILENESS OF SIN SURPASSETH ALL PAINS

But if now, because of all this comfort that I have mentioned, any man or woman is foolishly tempted to say or to think that if this is true, it must be good to sin in order to have a greater reward, or else to attach less weight to sinning—let them beware of this temptation. For truly, if it come, it is false, and from the enemy. For the same true love that toucheth us all by His blessed strengthening, this same blessed love teacheth us to hate sin alone, for love.

And I am certain by my own experience, that the more every kind soul seeth this, in the courteous love of our Lord, he is the more loth to sin; and the more is he ashamed of his sins. For if there were laid before us all the pains that are in hell and purgatory and earth, including death—all other pains than sin, we should choose all those pains rather than sin. Sin is so vile and so hateful that it cannot be likened to any pain that is not sin. And a kind soul hateth no pain other than sin; for all is good but sin, and nothing is evil but sin.

GOD DESIRES FOR US TO LOVE SINNERS AS HE LOVES US

When we give our minds, by the working of mercy and grace, to love and meekness, we are made all fair and clean. As mighty and as wise as God is to save man, even so willing is He. For Christ Himself is the ground of all the laws of Christian men; He it is who taught us to do good and not evil. Here we may see that He is Himself this Charity; and He doeth to us as He teacheth us to do to others. For

He willeth that we be like Him in wholeness of endless love to ourselves and to our even-christians. And as His love for us is never broken for our sins, even so it is His will that our love should not be broken either for ourselves or for our even-christians. But He wills that we should hate the sin in itself, and endlessly love the soul of the sinner, as God loveth it; then we would hate sin as God hateth it, and love the soul as God loveth it.

These words, then, that God spoke "I keep thee most surely," are an endless comfort.

THE FORTY-FIRST CHAPTER
IT IS IMPOSSIBLE THAT WE SHOULD PRAY FOR MERCY AND LACK IT

AFTER this, our Lord shewed me concerning prayer. In this shewing I saw two conditions for prayer—as our Lord understandeth it; one is rightfulness, the other is sure trust. For oftentimes our trust is not full; we are not sure that God heareth us, because (so we imagine) of our unworthiness, and the fact that we feel nothing at all—for we are as barren and as dry oftentimes after our prayers as we were before. Thus, in our feelings and in our folly is the cause of this weakness of ours; and this is my own experience.

All this our Lord brought to my mind at once, and shewed these words:

I am the ground of thy beseeching. First, it is My will that thou have it—and seeing that I make thee to desire it, and seeing that I make thee to beseech it and thou beseechest it, how could it then be

that thou shouldst not have thy beseeching?

Thus in the first reason, with the three that follow, our Lord shewed a mighty comfort, as may be seen in these same words. In the first reason, where He saith "and thou beseechest it," He there sheweth the exceeding pleasure and endless reward that He willeth to give us for our beseeching. And the sixth reason (where He says "How could it then be?") was given an impossibility. For nothing is more impossible than that we should seek mercy and grace, and not have it. For all the things that our good Lord Himself maketh us to beseech, these He hath ordained to us from withoutbeginning.

Here then may we see that His proper goodness and not our beseeching is the cause of the goodness and the grace that He doeth to us; and that shewed He truly in all these sweet words where He saith "I am the ground." Our good Lord willeth that this be known amongst His lovers on earth; and the more we know it the more shall we beseech, if we understand it wisely—and that is our Lord's intention.

GOD LONGS FOR US TO PRAY ALWAYS

Beseeching is a true and gracegiving, lasting will of the soul which is oned and fastened to the will of our Lord, by the sweet and secret working of the Holy Ghost. Our Lord Himself is the first receiver of our prayer—it is thus that I saw it; He receiveth it most thankfully and with great joy sendeth it up above and setteth it in the treasury, where it shall never perish. It is there before God and all His holy saints, received continually, ever speeding our needs. And when we come into our bliss, it shall be given us as a part of our joy, with His endless worshipful thanks.

Our Lord is full of mirth and gladness because of our prayer. For, with His grace, it maketh us as like to Him in condition, as we are in kind; and such is His blessed will. He speaketh thus:

> Pray inwardly; though there seemeth to be no relish in it, yet it is profitable enough. Though thou shouldst feel naught, pray inwardly. Pray inwardly, though thou feelest naught, though thou seest naught, yea though it seemeth thou canst not pray for dryness and barrenness. In sickness and in feebleness thy prayer is full pleasant to Me (though thou seemingly hast but little savour for it), and so is all thy living prayer in My sight.

Because of the reward and the endless thanks that He desireth to give us, He is covetous of having us pray continually in His sight. God accepteth the good will and the labour of His servants, no matter how we feel. Wherefore it pleaseth Him that we should work in prayer and in good living by His help and His grace, reasonably and with discretion keeping our faculties turned towards Him; until we have Him whom we seek, in fullness of joy—that is, Jesus. And that shewed He in the fifteenth Revelation, where He saith, "Thou shalt have Me for thy reward."

OF THANKSGIVING IN PRAYER

Also to prayer belongeth thanksgiving. Thanksgiving is a true inward knowing, a turning of ourselves with great reverence and loving dread and with all our power to the working which our Lord stirreth us to inwardly, with joy and thanksgiving. And sometimes the abundance of it breaketh out into speech, and we say, "Good Lord, be merciful, blessed may Thou be." And at other times when the heart is dry, and we feel nothing, or when tempted by our enemy, we are driven by reason and by grace to cry out loud on our Lord, rehearsing His blessed passion and His great goodness. And so the power of our Lord's word pierceth the soul and quickeneth the heart, and bringeth it by His grace into true working, maketh it to pray most blissfully and have true joy in our Lord. This is a most lovely thanksgiving in His sight.

THE FORTY-SECOND CHAPTER
OF THREE THINGS THAT BELONG TO PRAYER

OUR Lord willeth us to have true understanding in what belongeth to our prayer, especially in three things. The first is to know by whom and how our prayer beginneth. By whom, he sheweth when He says "I am the ground"; and how, by His goodness, for He saith, "First, it is My will." The second is to know in what manner and how we should use our time of prayer; this is, that our will be turned to the will of our Lord in joy. This is His meaning when He saith, "I make thee to will it." The third is to know the fruit and end of our prayer; which is to be oned and like to our Lord in everything. To this meaning and to this end was all this lovely lesson shewed. He will help us, and He shall bring it about, as He says Himself, blessed may He be!

For this is our Lord's will—that our prayer and our trust be alike, large. For if we do not trust as much as we pray, we fail in full worship to our Lord in our prayer; and also we hinder and hurt ourselves. The reason is that we do not know truly that our Lord is the ground from whom our prayer springeth; nor do we know that it is given us by His grace and His love. If we knew this, it would make us trust to have of our Lord's gift all that we desire. For I am sure that no man asketh mercy and grace with sincerity, without mercy and grace being given to Him first.

Sometimes it cometh to our mind that we have prayed long time, and yet, seemingly, we have not received an answer. We should not be grieved on this account, but—and I am sure of this in our Lord's meaning—we merely await a better time, a greater grace, or a better gift. He willeth us to have true knowing in Him—that He is all-being. In this knowing He willeth that our understanding be grounded, with all our power and all our intent and all our meaning. In this ground He willeth that we take up our station and our dwelling.

HOW TO PRAY

In His own grace-giving light He willeth that we have understanding of the three things that follow. The first is the nobility and the excellence of our creation; the second, our precious and most dear again-buying; the third,

that everything beneath us He hath made to serve us, and preserveth it for our love. This then is His meaning; it is as if He said: "Behold and see that I have done all this before thy prayer; and now thou art, and prayest to Me." He meaneth this also—that it is our part to know that the greatest deeds are done as Holy Church teacheth.

And as we behold this with thanksgiving, we ought to pray for the deed that is now a-doing: that is, that He rule us and guide us in this life, to His worship, and bring us to His bliss. It is for this that He hath done everything. His meaning also is that we should see that He doeth it, and pray for it as well. But the latter is not enough; for if we pray and yet do not see that He doeth it, this maketh us heavy-hearted and full of doubt—which is not to His worship. And if we see that He doeth it, and yet pray not, we do not pay our debt. (And may that never be so!—which is to say, it is not so in His beholding.) But to see that He doeth it, and to pray forthwith—it is thus that He is worshipped and we sped.

All things that our Lord hath ordained, it is His will that we pray for them, either for particular things or for all in general. The joy and the bliss that He hath, and the thanks and the worship that we shall have, for this— it surpasseth the understanding of all creatures in this life, if I see it aright. For prayer is a right understanding of that fullness of joy that is to come, along with true longing and absolute trust that we shall savour and see the bliss that we are ordained to; which kindly maketh us to long. True understanding and love, with sweet grace-giving mindfulness in our Saviour, maketh us to trust; and thus it belongeth to our kind to have longing, and it belongeth to grace, to trust.

In these two workings our Lord beholdeth us continually—for this is our duty, and His goodness cannot assign to us any lesser task than belongeth to our diligence to perform. And even when we do it, it shall seem to us as nothing. And true though this is, let us do what we can, and meekly ask for mercy and grace; and whatever is wanting in us, we shall find it in Him. This is His meaning when He saith, "I am the ground of thy beseeching." In these blissful words and in the shewing I saw that all our wickedness and all our doubtful dreads may be fully overcome.

THE FORTY-THIRD CHAPTER
WHAT PRAYER DOETH WHEN ORDAINED TO GOD'S WILL

PRAYER oneth the soul to God. For though the soul is ever like to God in kind, and like also in substance when restored by grace, it is often unlike to Him in its condition, because of sin on man's part. But prayer is a witness that the soul willeth as God willeth, it strengtheneth a man's conscious working, and enableth him to receive grace. And hence He teacheth us to pray and mightily to trust that we shall have it.

For He beholdeth us in love, and willeth to make us partakers of His good will and deed. Therefore He moveth us to pray for what it pleaseth Him to do; and He willeth to reward us, and give us endless payment for the prayer and the good will that we have received of His gift. This was shewed in His words "and thou beseechest it." By these words God shewed such great pleasure and liking—as though He were beholden to us for every good deed that we do; and yet it is He that doeth it all. In as much, then, as we beseech Him that we may do the thing that pleaseth Him (it is as though He had said: "What couldst thou do to please Me more than to beseech Me mightily, wisely, and willingly, that thou mayest do that which I will to have done?"); it is thus that the soul by its prayer is in accord with God.

WHEN OUR DESIRE IS SATISFIED

But when our courteous Lord, of His special grace, sheweth Himself to our soul, then we have what we desire; and we do not see, in that time, any thing more to pray for. All our intent and all our might is set wholly upon this beholding of Him. And this is a high and ineffable prayer, as I see it. For all the reason why we pray is oned into the sight and the beholding of Him to whom we pray, with marvellous enjoyment and reverent dread, and such great sweetness and delight in Him that we can pray not at all, or only as He moveth us to do at the time.

I know well that the more the soul seeth of God, the more she desireth Him, by grace. But when we see Him not so, then feel we need and cause to pray, because of our weakness and the unreadiness of ourselves to receive Jesus. For when a soul is tempested, troubled, and left to herself because of her unrest, then it is time to pray, that she may make herself supple and docile, so as to receive God. (For by no manner of prayer can she make God supple to receive her: He is ever one and the same in His love.)

Thus I saw that whenever we see the need for prayer, then our Lord is with us, helping our desire. But when, of His special grace, we behold Him plainly and see no further need of prayer, then we are with Him; for He draweth us to Him by love. I saw and felt that His marvellous and super-abundant goodness filleth full all our powers; and saw also that His continual working in all manner of things is done so well, so wisely, and so mightily that it surpasseth all our imagining—beyond all that we can explain or even conceive. Then we can do no more but behold Him and enjoy, with a high and powerful desire to be entirely oned in Him, to be received into His dwelling, to enjoy in His loving, to delight in His goodness.

It is thus that we may, with His sweet grace in our own meek, continual prayer, come into Him now, in this life, by many secret touchings and sweet ghostly sights and feelings, measured out to us according as our simpleness can support it. This is wrought, and shall be, by the grace of the Holy Ghost until we die in longing for love. Then shall we all come into our Lord—ourselves clearly knowing, God abundantly having—until we are all endlessly hid in God—Him truly seeing and abundantly feeling, Him ghostly hearing and delectably smelling, Him all sweetly swallowing.

And there shall we see God face to face. Homely and all-abundantly the creature that is made shall see and endlessly behold God who is the Maker. For no man may see God and live after, that is, in this mortal life. But when He will shew Himself here, of His special grace, He strengtheneth the creature above the self, and measureth the shewing, according as this is His will and is profitable for the time.

THE FORTY-FOURTH CHAPTER
OF THE PROPERTIES OF THE TRINITY

GOD shewed, in all the Revelations, oftentimes, that man evermore worketh His will and His worship, lastingly and without stinting. What this working is was shewn in the first Revelation, and that in a marvellous setting; for it was shewn in the working of the soul of our blissful Lady, Saint Mary, in her truth and wisdom. And how it was shewn, I hope, by the grace of the Holy Ghost, I shall tell as I saw.

Truth seeth God, and Wisdom beholdeth God; and of these two cometh the third; that is, a holy marvellous delight in God, which is love. Where truth and wisdom are verily there is love, which cometh of them both—and all of God's making. For God is endless sovereign Truth, endless sovereign Wisdom, endless sovereign Love, unmade; and man's soul is a creature in God, having the same properties, but made. Evermore it doeth that which it was made for—it seeth God, it beholdeth God, it loveth God. Wherefore God rejoiceth in the creature, the creature with endless marvelling, in God.

With marvelling the creature seeth his God, his Lord and his Maker, how He is so high, so great, and so good in comparison with him that is made, that the creature seemeth as naught to himself. And yet the brightness and the clearness of truth and wisdom maketh him to see and to know that he is made for love; in which love God endlessly keepeth him.

THE FORTY-FIFTH CHAPTER
OF THE FIRM DEEP JUDGMENT OF GOD,
AND THE VARIABLE JUDGMENT OF MAN

GOD judgeth us upon our kind substance, which is ever kept whole and safe, one in Him; and this judgment is of His righteousness. Man judgeth us upon our changeable sensuality, which seemeth, now one thing, now another, according as it is dominated by the parts, and sheweth outwards. Thus this judgment is variable: Sometimes it is good and light, sometimes hard and heavy. In as much as it is good and light it belongeth to God's righteousness. But in as much as it is hard and heavy, our good Lord Jesus reformeth it by mercy and grace through the power of His blessed passion; and so He bringeth it into His righteousness. And though these two be thus accorded and oned, they shall be known separately in heaven, without end.

The first doom, which cometh of God's righteousness—that is, of His high endless life—is that fair sweet doom which was shewn throughout the fair Revelation, in which I saw Him assign to us no kind of blame. And yet, though this was sweet and delightful in the beholding of it, I could not fully rest at ease, because of the judgment of Holy Church—as I had first understood it, and which was continually before my mind. For according to this judgment, methought I needs must acknowledge myself a sinner; and, by the same judgment, I understood that sinners are sometimes worthy of blame and wrath. But these two I could not see in God; and therefore my attention and desire were more than I can or may tell. For the higher judgment God Himself shewed in this same time: Hence I needs must accept it; whilst the lower judgment was taught me before this, in Holy Church: So that I might not, by any means, leave go the lower judgment.

OF THE JUDGMENT OF HOLY CHURCH

This, then, was my desire: that I might see in God in what manner the judgment of Holy Church here on earth is true in His sight, and how it belongeth to me truly to acknowledge it; so that both judgments might be justified if this might be worshipful to God and the right way for me. To all this I had no other answer except a marvellous parable of a Lord and of a servant, as I shall say afterwards, and that full mistily shewn. Yet I stood in desire, and will so stand until my life's end, that I might understand by grace these two judgments, in so far as it belongeth to me to know. For all heavenly things and all earthly things that belong to heaven, are gathered up in these two judgments; and the more knowing and understanding, by the gracious leading of the Holy Ghost, that we have of these two judgments, the more we shall see and recognize our failings. And ever the more that we see them, the more naturally, by the help of grace, we shall long to be filled full of endless joy and bliss. For we are made thereto, and our substance is blessedly in God, and hath been after that it was made, and shall be without end.

THE FORTY-SIXTH CHAPTER

WE CANNOT KNOW OURSELVES IN THIS LIFE EXCEPT BY FAITH AND GRACE

THIS passing life that we lead here, in our sensuality, is not aware of what our true self is, except in faith. When we come to know and see truly and clearly what our self is, then shall we, truly and clearly, see and know our Lord God in fullness of joy. And therefore it needs must be that the nearer we are to our bliss, the more we shall long for it, and that both by nature and by grace. We can have knowing of our self in this life by the constant help and power of our high kind. In this knowledge we can increase and grow by the furthering and the speeding of mercy and grace; but we may never fully know our self up to our last moment—when this passing life, and all manner of woe and pain, shall have an end.

And therefore it properly belongeth to us, both by nature and by grace, to long and desire, with all our might, to know our self. For in this fullness of knowledge we shall truly and clearly know our God, in fullness of endless joy.

OF TWO KINDS OF BEHOLDING

Yet in all this time, from beginning to end, I had two kinds of beholding. One was in endless and constant love, with sureness of his keeping and of my blissful safety. The other was in the ordinary teaching of Holy Church, in which I was, from the first, formed and grounded; which it was my will to have in use and in understanding. And the beholding of this never left me. For by the shewing I was never moved nor led therefrom in one single point; rather had I therein teaching to love it and like it; for in it I could, with the help of our Lord and His grace, have increase of and be lifted up to more heavenly knowing and higher loving.

In all this beholding, then, methought I must needs see and know that we are sinners and do many evil things that we ought to avoid; and leave many good deeds undone that we ought to perform. Wherefore we deserve pain and blame and wrath. Yet notwithstanding all this, I saw truly that our Lord was never wroth nor shall He ever be. For He is God; He is Good; He is Truth; He is Love; He is Peace. His Might, His Wisdom, His Charity, and His Unity suffer Him not to be wroth. For I saw truly that it is against the property of His Wisdom, and against the property of His Goodness.

God is the goodness which may not be wroth; for God is naught but Goodness. Our soul is oned to Him, the unchangeable Goodness; and between God and our soul is neither wrath nor forgiveness, in His sight. For our soul is so completely oned to God, through His own Goodness, that between God and our soul there can be nothing.

To the understanding of this was the soul led by love and drawn by might in every shewing. That it is thus, our good Lord shewed, and how it is thus, truly of His great goodness He will have us desire to learn, that is to say, in as much as it is proper for His creature to know it. For everything that this simple soul understood, God willeth should be shewn and known. But those things He will have secret, mightily and wisely He Himself hideth, for love. For I saw in the same shewing that many a secret thing is hid, until the time that God of His goodness hath made us worthy to see it. Therewith I am well satisfied, abiding our Lord's will in these high marvels. And now I submit myself to my Mother, Holy Church, as a simple child should.

THE FORTY-SEVENTH CHAPTER
WE MUST REVERENTLY MARVEL,
AND MEEKLY YIELD OURSELVES,
EVER ENJOYING GOD

On two counts our soul must pay a debt; one is that we reverently marvel; the other is that we meekly endure, ever rejoicing in God. For He willeth us to know that in a short time we shall see clearly in Him all that we desire. Notwithstanding all this, I beheld, and wondered greatly: "What is the mercy and forgiveness of God?" For by the teaching that I had before, I understood that the mercy of God means the forgiveness of His wrath, after the time that we have sinned. For methought that, to a soul whose intent and desire is to love, the wrath of God were harder than any other pain; and therefore I took it that the forgiveness of His wrath should be one of the principal points of His mercy. But for aught that I might behold or desire to behold in all the shewings, I could not see this point.

But how I saw and understood the working of mercy, I shall say something of this, as God will give me grace. I understood it thus: Man is changeable in this life; and through frailty and ignorance he falleth into sin. He is unmighty and unwise of himself: And also his will is overlaid whenever he is in tempest and in sor-

row and woe. The cause of this is blindness: He seeth not God. For if he saw God continually, he would have no mischievous feeling nor any kind of stirring or sorrowing, which minister to sin. Such was my sight and experience at that time; and methought that the sight and the experience was high and plenteous and full of grace, concerning this our common feeling, in this life. Yet methought that it was but little and small compared with the great desire that the soul hath to see God.

OF FIVE AFFECTIONS
WITHIN THE BELIEVER

Now I felt within me five affections working: They are rejoicing, mourning, desire, dread, and true hope. Rejoicing: For God gave me knowing and understanding that it was Himself that I saw. Mourning: Because of my failing. Desire: That I might see Him ever more and more, yet understanding and knowing that we shall never have full rest until we see Him clearly and truly, in heaven. Dread: For that it appeared, in all that time, that the sight should fail and I should be left to myself. True hope: Because I saw that I should be kept in endless love by His mercy, and brought to His bliss.

The joy in this sight, with this true hope of His merciful keeping, made me to have feelings of comfort, so that the mourning and dread were not greatly painful. At the same time I beheld, in this shewing of God, that this kind of sight could not be continual in this life, both for the sake of His own worship, and for the increase of our endless joy. For this reason we fail oftentimes of the sight of Him; and straightway we fall back into our self. Then find we this feeling—the contrariness which is in our self—springing from that old root of our first sin, along with all that cometh of our own furthering of it. And in this we are travailed and tempted with the feeling of sin and of pain in many diverse ways, ghostly and bodily; such is our experience in this life.

THE FORTY-EIGHTH CHAPTER
OF MERCY AND GRACE

OUR good Lord the Holy Ghost, who is endless life dwelling in our soul full truly, keepeth it and worketh therein a peace, and bringeth it to ease by grace, and maketh it docile to God, and in accord with Him. This is the way of mercy in which our good Lord continually leadeth us as long as we are in this changeable life. For I saw no wrath except on man's part, and that forgiveth He in us.

Wrath is naught else but a frowardness and a contrariness to peace and love, which cometh of failing of might, or of wisdom, or of goodness; which failing is not in God, but on our part. For we, by sin and wretchedness, have in us a wrath and a continual contrariness to peace and to love. This shewed He full often in His lovely look of compassion and pity. For the ground of mercy is in love, and the working of mercy is our being kept in love.

This was shewed in such a manner that I was unable to perceive of the property of mercy except as it were all love, in love. I mean, this is what I saw: Mercy is a sweet gracious working, in love, mingled with plenteous pity. Mercy worketh in the keeping of us. Mercy worketh in turning all things to good in us. Mercy, for love, suffereth us to fail in a measure. In as much as we fail, in so much we fall; and in as much as we fall, in so much we die. For we must needs die in as much as we fail of the sight and the awareness of God who is our life. Our failing is dreadful, our falling is shameful, and our dying is sorrowful.

THE PROPERTIES OF MERCY AND GRACE

But yet in all this the sweet eye of pity and of love departeth never from us, and the working of mercy ceaseth not. For I beheld the property of mercy, and I beheld the property of grace—two ways of working in the one love. Mercy is a property full of pity; it belongeth to the Motherhood of tender love. Grace is a worshipful property; it belongeth to the royal Lordship of the same love. Mercy worketh by preserving, permitting, quickening, and healing: and all in tenderness of love. Grace worketh with mercy, by lifting up, rewarding, endlessly surpassing all that our loving and our travail deserveth, spreading abroad and making plain the high abundance and largesse of God's royal Lordship in His marvellous courtesy. All this cometh of the abundance of love. For grace worketh our dreadful failing into plenteous and endless solace. Grace worketh our shameful falling into high worshipful rising. Grace worketh our sorrowful dying into holy blessed life.

HOW WE SHALL REJOICE THAT WE SUFFERED WOE PATIENTLY

For I saw full truly that ever as our contrariness worketh unto us, here on earth, pain, shame and sorrow: Right so, and contrariwise, grace worketh unto us, in heaven, solace, worship, bliss, to overflowing; so far forth, that when we shall go up and receive that sweet reward which grace hath wrought, there we shall thank and bless our Lord endlessly, rejoicing that ever we suffered woe. This property of blessed love we shall know in God, which we might never have known, had not woe gone before. When I saw all this, I needs must grant that the mercy of God and the forgiveness slaketh and wasteth our wrath.

THE FORTY-NINTH CHAPTER
OUR LIFE IS GROUNDED IN LOVE; WITHOUT THE WHICH WE PERISH

HERE was a high marvel, shewn continually in all the Revelations to the soul, and beheld with great diligence; that our Lord, in Himself, may not forgive because He may not be wroth; it were impossible. This was shewed: That our life is all grounded and rooted in love. Hence to the soul that seeth so far forth into the high marvellous goodness of God as to see that we are endlessly oned to Him in love, nothing could be more impossible than that God should be wroth. For wrath and friendship are two contraries. He that layeth and destroyeth our wrath, and maketh us meek and mild—we must needs believe that He is ever, in the same love, meek and mild; which is contrary to wrath.

GOD IS NEVER WROTH

For I saw full truly that where our Lord appeareth, peace is established and wrath hath no place. I saw no manner of wrath in God, neither for a short time, nor for long. For truly, as I see it, if God could be wroth a while, we should have neither life, nor place, nor being. As truly as we have our being of the endless might of God, and of the endless wisdom, and of endless goodness; so also we have our keeping in the endless might of God, in the endless wisdom, and in the endless goodness. For though we feel in our self wrath, conflict, and strife, yet we are all mercifully beclosed in the mildness of God and in His meekness, in His benignity, and in His kindliness.

I saw full truly that all our endless friendship, our station, our life, and our being, is in God. The same endless goodness which keepeth us, when we sin, so that we perish not, that same endless goodness continually treateth with us unto a peace, against our wrath and our contrarious falling. It maketh us to see our need, and, with a true dread, mightily to seek unto God to have forgiveness, with a gracious desire of our salvation. For we cannot be blessedly saved until we be truly in peace and in love, which itself is our salvation. And though, by the wrath and the contrariness that is in us, we are now in tribulation, distress, and woe through falling into blindness and helplessness, yet are we sure and safe by the merciful keeping of God which preventeth our perishing.

OF THE SOUL AT PEACE

Yet we shall not be blessedly secure in the possession of our endless joy, until we be wholly in peace and in love: that is to say, full pleased with God, and with all His works and with all His judgments; and loving and at peace with our self, and with our even-christian, and with all that God loveth;

as Love liketh. This is what God's goodness doeth in us. Thus I saw that God is our very peace, and our sure Keeper when we be, ourselves, at unpeace. He continually worketh to bring us unto endless peace.

And when, by the working of mercy and grace, we are made meek and mild, then are we full safe; suddenly is the soul oned to God, when it is truly peaced in the self; for in Him is found no wrath. Thus I saw that when we are wholly in peace and in love, we find no contrariness, no manner of hindering. Whilst the contrariness which is now in us—our Lord God, of His goodness, maketh it to us full profitable. For though contrariness is the cause of all our tribulation and all our woe, our Lord Jesus taketh these and sendeth them up to heaven; where they are made more sweet and delectable than heart may think or tongue can tell. And when we come thither we shall find them, already turned into true fairness and endless worship. God, then, is our steadfast ground, and shall be our full bliss; He shall make us unchangeable even as He is, when we shall be there.

THE FIFTIETH CHAPTER
HOW THE CHOSEN SOUL WAS NEVER DEAD IN THE SIGHT OF GOD

In this mortal life mercy and forgiveness is our way, that ever more leadeth us to grace. Through the tempest and the sorrow that we fall into, on our side, we be often dead—according to man's judgment on earth. But in the sight of God, the soul that shall be safe was never dead nor shall ever be. Yet in this I wondered and pondered with all the diligence of my soul, after

this fashion: "Good Lord, I see Thee—that Thou art very truth; and I know truly that we sin grievously all day, and are most blameworthy. I cannot evade the knowing of this truth, yet I see not Thee shewing to us any manner of blame. How may this be?"

I knew by the common teaching of Holy Church, and by my own consciousness, that the blame of our sins continually hangeth upon us, from the first sin unto the time that we come up into heaven. Herein was my wonderment—that I saw our Lord God shewing to us no more blame than if we were as clean and holy as the angels are in heaven. Between these two opposites my reason was greatly travailed, because of my blindness, and could find no rest for fear that His blessed presence should pass from my sight, and I be left in unknowing as to how He beholdeth us in our sin. For either I must needs see in God that sin were all done away; or else I must needs see in God how He seeth it, whereby I might truly know how it belongeth to me to see sin, and the manner of our blame.

HOW THREE THINGS EMBOLDENED HER TO ASK OF GOD THE UNDERSTANDING OF THIS

My longing endured, in my continual beholding of Him; yet I could have no patience in my great fear and perplexity, whilst I thought: "If I take it thus, that we are not sinners nor blameworthy, then it seemeth as though I should err in failing to acknowledge the truth. But granted this truth—that we are sinners and blameworthy, good Lord, how may it then be that I cannot see this truth in Thee, who art my God and my Maker, in whom I desire to see all truth?

"Three reasons make me bold to ask this question. The first is that it is so low a thing—for if it were a high, I should be afraid to ask it. The second is that it is so common a thing—for if it were special and secret, also I should be afraid to ask it. The third is that I need to know, as it seemeth to me, if I am to go on living here, for the knowing of good and evil: How I may, by reason and by grace, part them asunder, and love goodness and hate evil, as Holy Church teacheth." So I cried, inwardly, with all my might, seeking unto God for help, on this fashion: "O Lord Jesus, King of bliss, how shall I find ease? Who shall tell me and teach me what it needeth me to know, if I cannot, at this time, see it in Thee?"

THE FIFTY-FIRST CHAPTER
A MARVELLOUS PARABLE OF A LORD AND A SERVANT

THEN our courteous Lord answered in shewing full mistily a wonderful parable of a lord that hath a servant; and gave me a sight for the understanding of both. This sight was shewed double in regard of the lord; and it was shewed double in regard of the servant. The first part was shewed ghostly in bodily likeness; the second part was shewed more ghostly without bodily likeness. As for the first part, I saw thus: two persons in bodily likeness—that is to say, a lord and a servant. And with this sight God gave me ghostly understanding: The lord sitteth in solemn state, in rest and in peace. The servant standeth before his lord reverently, ready to do his lord's will. The lord turneth upon his servant a look full of love, sweet and meek. He sendeth him into a certain place, to do his will. The servant not only goeth, but starteth out suddenly, and runneth in great haste, for love, to do his lord's will. But straightway he falleth down into a ravine, and taketh full great hurt; and then he groaneth and moaneth, waileth and turneth about, but he cannot rise or help himself in any manner.

OF THE SERVANT'S SEVEN GREAT PAINS

In all this, the most misfortune that I saw him in was failing of comfort; for he could not turn his face to look upon his loving lord, in whom is full comfort; though he was very close to him. But, as a man that was full feeble and unwise for the time, he attended only to his lasting feeling of woe. In this he suffered seven great pains. The first was the sore bruising that he had taken in his fall, which was to him great pain. The second was the heaviness of his body. The third was the feebleness following on these two. The fourth was that he was blinded in his reason and stunned in his mind; so much so that he had almost forgotten all care for himself. The fifth was that he could not rise. The sixth pain was to me the most marvellous, and this was that he lay all alone. I looked all about and beheld: But far or near, high or low, I saw no help for him. The seventh was that the place which he lay in was lonely, hard, and grievous. I marvelled how this servant could thus meekly suffer all this woe.

And I beheld with deliberation to discover if I could perceive in him any fault; or whether the lord would assign to him any kind of blame. And truly there was none seen; for his good will and his great desire were the only cause of his falling. He was as lovable and as good inwardly as he was when he stood before his lord, ready to do his will. Right thus, continually, his loving lord full tenderly beholdeth him; and now with a double regarding; one outward, full meekly and mildly, with great compassion and pity—and this was seen in the first shewing; another inward, more ghostly, which was shewed with a leading of my understanding into the Lord. In this sight I saw Him highly rejoicing for the worshipful rest and the high honour that He will, and shall, bring His servant to by His plenteous grace. And this was part of that second shewing.

Then was my understanding led again into the first shewing—both remaining in my mind; it was as though the courteous lord said: "Lo, my beloved servant! What harm and evil he hath had and endured in my service, for love of me, yea, and because of his good will! Is it not right that I should reward him, considering his fear and his dread, his hurt and his maiming, and all his woe? And besides all this, falleth it not to me to give him a gift that is better and more worshipful to him than his own wholeness should have been? Else, me thinketh I would give him no thanks."

Here an inward ghostly shewing of the Lord's meaning descended into my soul; in which I saw that it must needs be in accord with His great goodness and His own worship that His very dear servant, whom He loved so much, should be highly and blissfully rewarded without end; above what he

should have been if he had not fallen. Yea, and so far forth that his falling, and all the woe that he hath suffered thereby, shall be turned into high over-passing worship, and endless bliss.

THE SHEWING OF
THE PARABLE VANISHED

At this point the shewing of the parable vanished: and our good Lord led forth my understanding unto sight and shewing of the Revelation, to the end. But notwithstanding all this forthleading, my wonderment at the parable never went from me. For methought that it was given to me as an answer to my desire; and yet I could not have therein full understanding unto peace of mind, in that time. For in the servant (who, as I shall say, was shewed for Adam) I saw many diverse properties that could in no way be ascribed to the single Adam. And thus, in that time, I took my stand especially on three knowings, for the full understanding of this marvellous parable was not given me at that time. In this dark parable the secrets of the whole Revelation were yet much hid. (But this notwithstanding, I saw and understood that every shewing is full of secrets.)

Now, therefore, I must tell of these three properties in which I have found some relief. The first is the beginning of teaching which I understood therein, at the time. The second is the inward learning I have received therein since then. The third is the whole Revelation from beginning to end, which our Lord God of His goodness bringeth often and liberally to the sight of my understanding. These three are so oned in my understanding of them that I cannot nor may not separate them; and by these three, as one, I have teaching whereby I ought to believe and trust in our Lord God, that of the same goodness whereof He shewed it, and for the same end: Right so, of the same goodness and for the same end, He shall make it clear to us when it shall be His will!

AFTER NEARLY TWENTY YEARS SHE FULLY UNDERSTOOD THIS PARABLE

Twenty years after the time of the shewing, save three months, I had teaching inwardly, as I shall say: "It belongeth to thee to take heed of all the properties and conditions that were shewed in the parable, though it seemeth that this be misty and unyielding to thy regarding." I assented willingly and with great desire; examining inwardly and with deliberation all the points and properties that were shewed, in that same time, as far forth as my wits and my understanding would serve me, beginning at the lord and the servant; the manner of the sitting of the lord, and the place he sat on; the color of his clothing; his form; his outward appearance and nobility; his inward goodness; the manner of the servant's standing, and the place; its where and how; the manner of his clothing, its color and form; his outward behavior, and his inward goodness—his attractiveness.

OF THE SERVANT IN THE PARABLE

The lord that sat in solemn state, in rest and in peace, I understood that he is God. The servant that stood before him, I understood that he was shewed for Adam: That is to say, one man was shewed, in the time of his falling, to make thereby to be understood how God beholdeth every man and his falling. For in the sight of God every man is one man, and one man is every-man.

This man was hurt in his powers, and made full feeble; and he was stunned in his understanding, in that he was turned from the beholding of his Lord. But his will was preserved in God's sight; for his will I saw our Lord commend and approve. But he himself was hindered and blinded in the knowing of this true will; which is the cause to him of great sorrow and grievous distress. For he neither seeth clearly his loving Lord, who is full meek and mild towards him; nor seeth he truly how he himself is in the sight of his loving Lord. And well I knew, when these two be wisely and truly seen, we shall get rest and peace, in part here, and their fullness in bliss, in heaven by His plenteous grace.

This was a beginning of teaching which I saw in the same time, whereby I might come to know in what manner He beholdeth us in our sin. Next I saw that only pain blameth and punisheth, but our courteous Lord comforteth and succoureth. Ever He is of glad countenance to the soul, loving us, and longing to bring us to His bliss.

OF THE LORD IN THE PARABLE

The place that the Lord sat on was unadorned—the earth, a barren desert, a solitary wilderness. His clothing was ample and flowing, full seemly as befitteth a lord. The colour of it was blue as the sky, fair but not gaudy. His mien was merciful; and the colour of his face was a fair brown-white, the features well-proportioned; his eyes were dark and very beautiful, full of a lovely pity; and within Him a high world, long and broad, all full of endless heavenliness. The loving look that He turned upon His servant continually and especially in his falling—methought it might melt our hearts for love, and break them in two for joy.

This fair looking shewed itself as a seemly mingling which was marvellous to behold. One part was compassion and pity, the other joy and bliss. The joy and bliss overpass the compassion and pity as far as heaven is above earth; the pity was earthly, and the bliss heavenly. The compassion and pity of the Father was for the falling of Adam, who is His most beloved creature. The joy and the bliss was for the falling of His most dear Son, who is equal with the Father. The merciful beholding of His lovely face filled full all the earth, and descended down with Adam unto hell; and by this continual pity Adam was kept from endless death. This mercy and pity dwell with mankind unto the time that we come up into heaven.

But man is blinded in this life; and therefore we may not see our Father, God, as He is. But what time He, of His goodness, will shew Himself to man, He sheweth Himself in homely fashion, as man. Notwithstanding that sight, I saw verily that we ought to know and believe that the Father is not man; rather, this sitting on the earth, barren and desert, must be taken to mean that He made man's soul to be His own city and His dwelling place; which is most pleasing to Him of all His works. But what time man was fallen into sorrow and pain, He was not in fit state to fulfil that noble office. Therefore our gracious Father would prepare Himself no other place, but would sit upon the earth abiding mankind—which is mingled with earth—till what time, by His grace, His well-beloved Son had brought back His city into its noble fairness, with His hard travail.

The blueness of the clothing betokeneth His steadfastness; the brown colour of His fair face, with the lovely dark hue of the eyes, was most fit to shew His holy seriousness of purpose. The ample nature of His clothing which was shining fair about Him, betokeneth that in Him are enclosed all heavens and all endless joy and bliss. All this was shewed in a moment, where I say that "mine understanding was led into the Lord." In this moment, I saw Him highly rejoice for the worshipful restoring that He will and shall bring His servant to, by His plenteous grace.

THE SERVANT'S LOVE FOR THE LORD

And still I marvelled, beholding the Lord and the servant aforesaid. I saw the Lord sitting solemnly; and the servant standing reverently before his Lord. In this servant there is a double understanding; one outward, the other inward. Outwardly, he was clad simply, as a labourer who is ready for his work. He stood very near to the Lord, not straight in front of him, but a little to one side—on the left. His clothing was a white kirtle, single, old, and all bestained; dyed with the sweat of his body, close-fitting and short, about a hand's breadth below the knee, threadbare, as though it would soon be worn out, ready to be ragged and rent. And in this I marvelled greatly, thinking: "Now this is un-seemly clothing for the servant that is so highly bred to stand in, before so worshipful a Lord!"

But inwardly, in him was shewed a ground of love—the love which he had to the Lord; it was equal to the love which the Lord had to him. The ser-vant, of his wisdom, saw inwardly that there was but one thing to do that should be to the worship of the Lord. And the servant, for love, having no regard to himself nor to anything that might befall him, hastily did start and run, at the sending of his Lord, to do that which was His will and His wor-ship. It seemed, by his outward cloth-ing, as though he had been in continual labour, and a hard worker for a long time. But by the inward sight that I had, both of the Lord and of the servant, it seemed that he was a new servant: That is to say, now beginning his work—a servant who was never sent out before.

THE SERVANT'S LABOR FOR THE LORD

There was a treasure in the earth, which the Lord loved. I marvelled and thought what it might be. And I was answered in my understanding: "It is a food which is lovesome and pleasant to the Lord." For I saw the Lord sit, as a man, and I saw neither food nor drink wherewith to serve Him. This was one marvel. Another marvel was that this worthy Lord had no servant but one, and him He sent out. I beheld, thinking what manner of labour it might be that the servant would do. And then I understood that he would do the greatest labor and the hardest travail that there is: He would be a gardener, delving and dyking and sweating, and turning the earth up and down; he would seek the depths, and water the plants in season; and in this he would continue his travail, and make sweet floods to run, and noble plenteous fruit to spring forth.

This fruit he would bring before the Lord, and serve Him therewith to His liking; he would never return until he had made this food all ready, as he knew it would please his Lord; then he would take this food, with the drink, and bear it full worshipfully before the Lord. And all this time the Lord would sit, right in the same place, abiding the servant whom He sent out. Still I marvelled whence the servant came. For I saw in the Lord that He hath within Himself endless life and all manner of goodness, save the trea-sure that was in the earth. And that, too, was grounded in the Lord, in mar-vellous deepness of endless love; but it was not all to His worship until His servant should have thus nobly pre-pared it, and brought it before Him, presenting it in Himself. Outside the Lord was right naught but wilderness.

FURTHER REVELATION OF THE PARABLE'S MEANING

I understood not all what this para-ble meant; and therefore I marvelled whence the servant came.

In the servant is comprehended the second person of the Trinity. And in the servant is comprehended Adam; that is to say, every-man. Thus, when I say "the son," this meaneth the God-head which is equal to the Father's; and when I say "the servant," it meaneth Christ's manhood which is the true Adam. By the nearness of the servant is understood the Son; and by the stand-ing at the left side is understood Adam.

The Lord is God the Father; the servant is the Son Jesus Christ. The Holy Ghost is the equal love which is in Them both. When Adam fell, God's son fell; because of the true oneing which was made in heaven, God's Son could not be separated from Adam. (By Adam I understand every-man.) Adam fell from life to death unto the deeps of this wretched world, and after that into hell. God's Son fell, with Adam, into the deeps of the Maiden's womb, who was the fairest daughter of Adam; and that, for to excuse Adam from blame in heaven and earth; and mightily He fetched him out of hell.

By the wisdom and the goodness that was in the servant is understood God's Son; by the poor clothing of the labourer, standing near the left side, is understood the manhood of Adam, with all the mischief and feebleness that followeth. For in all this our good Lord shewed His own Son and Adam as one man. The power and the goodness that we have is of Jesus Christ; the feebleness and blindness that we have is of Adam, which two were shewed in the servant. Thus hath our good Lord Jesus taken upon Him all our blame. And therefore our Father nor may nor will any more blame assign to us than to His own well-beloved Son Jesus Christ.

Thus was He the servant, before His coming into earth, standing ready before the Father in purpose, till what time He would send Him to do the worshipful deed by which mankind was brought again into heaven. That is to say: notwithstanding that He is God, equal with the Father in respect of the Godhead; in His foreseeing purpose He would be man, to save man, in the fulfilling of the will of His Father.

OF THE SERVANT JESUS CHRIST

So He stood before His Father as a servant, willingly taking upon Himself all our charge. Then He set forth, full readily, at the Father's will. And straightway He fell, full low into the Maiden's womb; having no regard to Himself, nor to His hard lot. The white kirtle is His flesh; its singleness, that there was right naught between the Godhead and the manhood; its straitness is poverty; its age of Adam's wearing; its stains, the sweat of Adam's travailing; its shortness sheweth the servant as labourer. And thus I saw the Servant, as it were saying: "Lo, My dear Father, I stand before Thee in Adam's kirtle, all ready to set out, and to run. I would be on the earth, to Thy worship, whenever it is Thy will to send Me. How long must I desire it?" Full truly the Son knew when it would be the Father's will, and how long He must desire—that is to say, in respect of the Godhead; for He is the Wisdom of the Father. Wherefore this saying was shewed in the understanding of the manhood of Christ. For all mankind that shall be saved by the sweet incarnation and the passion of Christ, all is the manhood of Christ. He is the head and we are His members.

To the members, the day and the time is unknown, when every passing woe and sorrow shall have an end, and the everlasting joy and bliss shall be fulfilled. To see this day and time, all the company of heaven longeth or desireth. And all those under heaven who shall come thither—their way is by longing and desiring; which longing and desiring was shewed in the servant's standing before the Lord; or else in the Son's standing before the Father in Adam's kirtle. For the longing and desiring of all mankind that shall be saved appeared in Jesus. Jesus is all that shall be saved, and all that shall be saved is Jesus; and all this of the charity of God, with the obedience, meekness and patience, and the virtues that belong to us.

ON THE INCARNATION

Further, in this marvellous parable, I have teaching within me, as it were the beginning of an ABC, whereby I may have some understanding of our Lord's meaning. For all the privities of the whole Revelation are hid therein; notwithstanding that all the shewings are full of privities. The sitting of the Father betokeneth the Godhead; that is to say, it sheweth rest and peace; for in the Godhead there can be no travail. And that He sheweth Himself as Lord betokeneth our manhood. The standing of the servant betokeneth travail; on the left side, that He was not full worthy to stand straight in front of the Lord. His starting was the Godhead, and the running was the manhood. For the Godhead starteth from the Father, into the Maiden's womb, falling down into the taking of our nature. And in this falling He took great sore. The sore that He took was our flesh; in which, from the first, He had experience of mortal pains.

The fact that He stood in awe before the Lord, and not straight in front of Him, betokeneth that His clothing was not suited to the standing straight in front of the Lord; that could not, nor should not be His place as long as He

was a labourer. Nor might He sit with the Lord in rest and peace till He had won His peace, rightfully, with His hard travail. And by the left side is meant that the Father allowed His own Son, willingly, in the manhood, to suffer all man's pain, without sparing Him.

That His kirtle should be almost in rags and tatters is understood to mean the rods and scourges, the thorns and the nails, the drawing and the dragging, His tender flesh rending (as I saw in some measure: The flesh was torn from the skull, hanging in little pieces, until the bleeding stopped, and it began to dry and cling again to the bone). And by the wallowing and the writhing, the groaning and mourning, is understood that He could never rise again almightily (from the time that He was fallen into the Maiden's womb), until His body was slain and dead, and He yielded His soul into the Father's hand along with all mankind for whom He was sent.

At this point He began first to shew His might. For then He went into hell; and when He was there, then He raised up the great host out of the deep abyss, which had been truly knit to Him in high heaven. His body lay in the grave until Easter morrow; but from that time He lay never more. For there was truly and rightly ended the wallowing and the writhing, the groaning and the mourning.

Our foul mortal flesh that God's Son took upon Himself, which was Adam's old kirtle, strait, threadbare and short, then by our Saviour was made fair, new, white and bright, of endless cleanness, large and ample; fairer and richer than was the clothing which I saw on the Father. For that clothing was blue; but Christ's clothing is now of a fair, seemly blending of colours which is so marvellous that I cannot describe it, for it is all of very worship.

OF THE FATHER AND SON'S PRESENT STATE

Now sitteth not the Lord on the earth in the wilderness; but He sitteth on His rich and noble seat which He made in heaven, most to His liking. Now standeth not the Son before the Father, as a servant before the Lord in awe, and half-naked; but He standeth before the Father on an equality, richly clothed in blissful fullness, with a crown upon His head of precious richness. For it was shewed that we are His crown—the crown which is the Father's joy, the Son's worship, the Holy Ghost's liking, and endless marvellous bliss to all that are in heaven.

Now standeth not the Son before the Father on the left side, as a laborer; but He sitteth on the Father's right hand in endless rest and peace. (By this is not meant that the Son sitteth on the right hand beside His Father, as one man sitteth by another, in this life. For there is no such sitting, as I understand it, in the Trinity. But He sitteth on the Father's right hand; that is to say, right in the highest nobility of the Father's joy.)

Now is the spouse, God's Son, in peace, with His beloved wife, who is the fair maiden of endless joy. Now sitteth the Son, very God and very man, in His city in rest and in peace: the city which His Father hath allotted to Him in His endless purpose; and the Father in the Son, and the Holy Ghost in the Father and in the Son.

THE FIFTY-SECOND CHAPTER

GOD REJOICETH THAT HE IS OUR FATHER, BROTHER, AND SPOUSE

AND then I saw that God rejoiceth that He is our Father; and God rejoiceth that He is our Mother; and God rejoiceth that He is our true Spouse, and our soul His beloved wife. And Christ rejoiceth that He is our Brother; and Jesus rejoiceth that He is our Saviour.

These are five high joys, as I understand, in which He willeth that we rejoice, Him praising, Him thanking, Him loving, Him endlessly blessing—all those that shall be saved. During the time of this life, we have in us a marvellous mingling both of weal and of woe. We have in us our Lord Jesus Christ, uprisen; and we have in us the wretchedness and mischief of Adam's falling. Dying, by Christ we are steadfastly kept; and by touching of His grace, we are raised into sure trust of salvation. But by Adam's falling, we are so broken in our feelings, in various ways, by sins and by sundry pains, in which we are made dark and so blind that we can find scarcely any comfort.

But in our intentions we abide God, and faithfully trust to have mercy and grace; and this is His own working in us. He, of His goodness, openeth the eye of our understanding; by which we have sight; sometimes more and sometimes less, according as God giveth us the ability to receive it. At one time we are lifted up into the first, at another we are suffered to fall into the other. Thus this mingling is so perplexing in us, that we scarcely know, either concerning ourselves, or our fellow-christians in what way we stand; such is the marvellous nature of these various feelings. But yet, in each holy assent that we give to God when we experience Him truly, willing to be with Him with all our heart and with all our soul and with all our might, then indeed we hate and despise our evil stirrings, and all that might be an occasion of sin, ghostly or bodily.

GOD IS WITH US IN THREE WAYS

But again, when this sweetness is hid, we fall again into blindness, and so into woe and tribulation, in various ways; and then this is our comfort— that we know in our faith that by the power of Christ who is our Keeper, we assent never thereto. Rather we strive there against, and endure, in pain and in woe, praying, unto the time that He sheweth Himself again to us. Thus we stand in this mingling all the days of our life. But it is His will that we trust that He is lastingly with us; and this in three ways. He is with us in heaven, true man, us updrawing into His own person; this was shewed in the ghostly thirst. He is with us on earth, us leading; this was shewed in the third Revelation, where I saw God in a point. And He is with us in our soul, endlessly dwelling, ruling and guiding us; this was shewed in the sixteenth Revelation, as I shall say.

In the servant, then, was shewed the blindness and the mischief of Adam's falling; and in the servant was shewed the wisdom and goodness of God's Son. In the Lord was shewed the compassion and pity for Adam's woe; and in the Lord was shewed the high nobility and endless worship that mankind is come to by the power of the passion and the death of His well-beloved Son. Wherefore He mightily rejoiceth in His falling, for the high raising and fullness of bliss that mankind is come into, overpassing what we should have had, if He had not fallen. It was to see this overpassing nobility that my understanding was led unto God, in the same time that I saw the servant fall.

So we have now matter for mourning, because our sin is the cause of Christ's pains; and we have, lastingly, matter for joy, because endless love made Him to suffer. And therefore the creature that seeth and feeleth the working of love, by grace, hateth naught except sin. (Of all things, in my sight, love and hate are the hardest and most immeasurable contraries.)

WE NEVER ESCAPE SIN IN THIS LIFE

But notwithstanding all this, I saw and understood in our Lord's meaning, that we cannot, in this life, keep ourselves from sin all holy and in full cleanness, as we shall be in heaven. But we may well, by grace, keep ourselves from the sins which would lead us to endless pain, as Holy Church teacheth us; and eschew venial sins, reasonably, with all our might. And if we, by our blindness and our wretchedness, at any time fall, we should readily rise, conscious of the sweet touching of grace; and wilfully amend us, in the teaching of the Holy Church, according as the sin is grievous, and go forth with God, in love.

Neither should we, on one side, fall over low, turning to despair; nor, on the other, be over-reckless, as if we gave it no consideration. But meekly we should recognize our feebleness, realizing that we could not stand for the twinkling of an eye except by keeping of grace; and reverently cling to God, in Him only trusting. For on one wise is the beholding of God, and other wise is the beholding of man. It belongeth to man meekly to accuse himself; and it belongeth to the proper goodness of our Lord God courteously to excuse man.

OF THE TWOFOLD REGARD WITH WHICH THE LORD BEHELD THE FALLING OF HIS SERVANT

These are the two parts that were shewed in the twofold regard with which the Lord beheld the falling of His beloved servant. The one was shewed outward, full meekly and mildly, with great compassion and pity; the other inward, of endless love. And right thus, our Lord willeth that we accuse ourselves willingly and truthfully, seeing and knowing our falling, and all the harm that comes thereof; seeing and realizing that we can never restore it; and therewith that we willingly and truly see and know the everlasting love which He hath for us, and His plenteous mercy. To see and know both parts together, thus graciously, is the meek accusing that our good Lord asketh of us. He himself worketh it, where it is—in the lower part of man's life. This was shewed in His outward regard; in which shewing I saw two elements: One is the rueful falling of man; the other is the worshipful redemption that our Lord hath made for man.

The other regard, that was shewed inwardly, was of a much higher kind, and all a unity. For the life and the power that we have in our lower part is from the higher; and it cometh down to us by grace, by way of the kind love of the self. Between the one regard and the other there is no barrier, because it is all one love. This one blessed love now hath in us a double working. For in our lower part there are pains and passions, compassions and pities, mercies and forgivenesses, and other such, that are profitable. In our higher part are none of these, but all one high love and marvellous joy; in which marvellous joy, all pains are highly restored. And in this our good Lord shewed not only our excusing, but also the worshipful nobility that He shall bring us to; turning all our blame into endless worship.

THE FIFTY-THIRD CHAPTER
THE KINDNESS OF GOD ASSIGNETH NO BLAME TO THE CHOSEN

THUS I saw that it is His will for us to realize that He taketh no harder the falling of any creature that shall be saved than He took the falling of Adam; who, we know, was endlessly loved and surely kept in the time of all his need; and now is blissfully restored in high over-passing joy. For our Lord God is so good, so gentle, and so courteous that He can never assign failure to those in whom He shall be ever blessed and praised.

In all this that I have now told, my desire was answered in part, and my great fear somewhat eased, by the lovely gracious shewing of our Lord God; in which I saw and understood full surely that in every soul which shall be saved there is a godly will that never assented to sin, nor ever shall. This will is so good that it may never will evil, but evermore, continually, it willeth good and worketh good in the sight of God. Our Lord willeth that we know this in faith and belief; and especially, that in truth we have all this blessed will whole and safe in our Lord Jesus Christ.

For this same kind, with which heaven shall be filled, must needs be according to God's righteousness, so knit and oned in Him, that in it must be preserved a substance which never could nor should be separated from Him. And all this through His own good will and His endless foreseeing purpose. But notwithstanding this rightful knitting and this endless oneing, the redemption and the again-buying of mankind is needful and speedful in everything, in that it is done for the same purpose and the same end. This Holy Church, in our faith, teacheth us.

GOD HAS ALWAYS LOVED MAN

For I saw that God never began to love mankind; but right as mankind shall be in endless bliss, bringing to fulfilment the joy of God relative to His works; right so the same mankind hath been, in the foreknowledge of God, known and loved from without-beginning, according to His righteous plan. And by the endless purpose and decision and the full accord of the Trinity, the second Person was to be the ground and head of this fair human kind; of Him we are all sprung, in Him we are all enclosed, to Him we shall all go; finding in Him our full heaven in everlasting joy; according to the foreseeing purpose of all the blessed Trinity from without-beginning. For ere that He made us, He loved us; and when we were made we loved Him.

This is a love made of the divine sub-

stantial love of the Holy Ghost, mighty by reason of the Power of the Father, wise in the consciousness of the Wisdom of the Son. Thus is man's soul made by God, and in the same moment knit to God. I understand that man's soul is made of naught; that is to say, it is made, but not from anything that is made—as when God would make man's body He took the slime of the earth, which is a material mingled and blended, out of all bodily things: Thereof He made man's body. But for the making of man's soul, He would use naught at all: He simply made it. And thus is made-kind rightfully oned to the Maker, who is substantial unmade-kind, that is, God. Whence it is that there nor may be nor shall be anything at all between God and man's soul.

MAN IS GOD'S NOBLEST CREATION

In this endless love, man's soul is kept whole; as all the matter of the Revelations meaneth and sheweth; in which endless love we are led and preserved by God, and never shall be lost. For He willeth that we know that our soul is a life; which life, by His goodness and His grace, shall last in heaven without end; Him loving, Him thanking, Him praising. And right the same as we are to be without end, right so we were treasured in God, and hid: known and loved from without-beginning.

Therefore He willeth us to know that the noblest thing that ever He made is mankind; and the fullest substance and the highest power is the blessed soul of Christ. Furthermore He meaneth us to know that this best beloved soul was preciously knit to

Him in the making of it; and the knot is so subtle and so strong that this soul is oned unto God; in which oneing it is made endlessly holy. Furthermore He meaneth us to know that all the souls that shall be saved in heaven without end, are knit in this knot and oned in this oneing, and made holy in this holiness.

THE FIFTY-FOURTH CHAPTER
WE OUGHT TO REJOICE THAT GOD
DWELLETH IN OUR SOUL,
AND OUR SOUL IN GOD

AND through the great endless love that God hath to all mankind, He maketh no division, in love, between the blessed soul of Christ and the least soul that shall be saved. For it is full easy to believe and trust that the dwelling of the blessed soul of Christ is full high in the glorious Godhead. And truly, as I understood in our Lord's meaning, where the blessed soul of Christ is, there is the substance of all the souls that shall be saved by Christ.

Highly ought we to rejoice that God dwelleth in our soul; and much more highly ought we to rejoice that our soul dwelleth in God. Our soul is made to be God's dwelling-place; and the dwelling of our soul is God, which is unmade. A high understanding it is inwardly, to see and to know that God, who is our Maker, dwelleth in our soul. And a higher understanding it is, and more inwardly, to see and to know that our soul, that is made, dwelleth in God in substance. Of which substance, by God, we are what we are. And I saw no difference between God and our substance; but as it were all God. And yet my understanding took it that our substance is in God; that is to say, that God is God, and our substance is a creature in God.

For the almighty Truth of the Trinity, He is our Father; for He made us and keepeth us in Him. And the deep Wisdom of the Trinity is our Mother, in whom we are enclosed. And the high Goodness of the Trinity is our Lord; and in Him we are enclosed, and He in us. We are enclosed in the Father; and we are enclosed in the Son; and we are enclosed in the Holy Ghost. And the Father is enclosed in us, and the Son is enclosed in us, and the Holy Ghost is enclosed in us: all-mightiness, all-wisdom, and all-goodness—one God, one Lord.

And our faith is a power that cometh from our kind substance into our sensual soul, by the Holy Ghost. In which power, all our virtues come to us; for without that, no man may receive virtues. For it is naught else but a right understanding, with true belief and sure trust, of our being: That we are in God and He in us—which we see not. And this power, with all other that God hath ordained to us coming therein, worketh in us great things. For Christ is mercifully working in us, and we are graciously disposed to Him, through the gift and power of the Holy Ghost. This working maketh that we are Christ's children, and Christian in living.

THE FIFTY-FIFTH CHAPTER
CHRIST IS OUR WAY, LEADING AND
PRESENTING US TO THE FATHER

AND thus Christ is our way; us surely leading in His laws. And Christ, in His body, mightily beareth us up into heaven. For I saw that Christ, us all having in Him—that shall be saved by Him—worshipfully presenteth His Father in heaven with us. Which present with full thanks His Father receiveth, and courteously giveth it unto His Son, Jesus Christ. Which gift and working is joy to the Father, bliss to the Son, and liking to the Holy Ghost. And of all things that belong to us, it is most liking to our Lord that we rejoice in this joy which is in the blessed Trinity because of our salvation.

And this was seen in the ninth shewing, where it speaketh more of this matter. And notwithstanding àll our feeling—woe or weal—God willeth that we understand and believe that we are more verily in heaven than in earth. Our faith cometh from the kind love of our soul, and from the clear light of our reason, and from the steadfast mind which we have of God, in our first making. And what time our soul is breathed into our body—in which we are made sensual, at once mercy and grace begin to work, having of us care and keeping with pity and love. In which working, the Holy Ghost formeth, in our faith, hope that we shall come again to our substance up above, having increase and filled full of the power of Christ, through the Holy Ghost.

Thus I understood that the sensuality is grounded in kind, in mercy, and in grace. Which ground enableth us to receive gifts that lead us to endless life. For I saw full surely that our substance is in God; and I also saw that in our sensuality God is. For in the point where our soul is made sensual, there in the same point is the city of God, ordained for Him from without-beginning. Into which city He cometh, and never shall remove from it. For God is never out of the soul, in which He shall dwell blessedly without end. And this was seen in the sixteenth shewing, where it saith: "The place that Jesus taketh in the soul, He shall never remove from it."

And all the gifts that God may give to the creature, He hath given to His Son, Jesus, for us. Which gifts He, dwelling in us, hath enclosed in Him, unto the time that we shall be full grown; our soul with our body, and our body with our soul—each of them taking help of the other, until we are brought up to our full stature, according to the workings of Kind. And then, in this ground of Kind, the Holy Ghost, with working of mercy, graciously breatheth into us gifts leading to endless life.

THE SOUL IS A TRINITY

And thus was my understanding led, of God, to see in Him and to realize, to understand and to know, that our soul is a made trinity, like to the unmade blessed Trinity, known and loved from without-beginning; and in the making, oned to the Maker, as it is beforesaid. This sight was full sweet and marvellous to behold, peaceful and restful, secure and delightful. And because of the worshipful oneing that was thus made, of God, between the soul and the body, it must needs be that man's kind should be restored from a double death. Which restoring might never be, until the time that the second Person in the Trinity had taken the lower part of man's kind, to whom that higher part was oned, in the first making. And these two parts were in Christ—the higher and the lower; which is but one soul. The higher part was ever in peace with God, in full joy and bliss; the lower part, which is sensuality, suffered for the salvation of mankind.

And these two parts were seen and felt in the eighth shewing; in which my mind was filled full of feeling and mind of Christ's passion and His dying. And furthermore with this was a subtle feeling and a secret inward sight of the high part. And that was shewed in the same time in which I could not, in spite of the friendly offer, look up into heaven. And that was because of that same mighty beholding of the inward life. Which inward life is that high substance, that precious soul which is endlessly in joy of the Godhead.

THE FIFTY-SIXTH CHAPTER
IT IS EASIER TO KNOW GOD THAN OUR SOUL

AND thus I saw full surely that it is readier to us and more easy, to come to the knowing of God than to know our own soul. For our soul is so deep-grounded in God and so endlessly treasured, that we may not come to the knowing thereof until we have, first, knowing of God, who is the Maker; to whom it is oned. But notwithstanding I saw that we have, of our fullness, the desire wisely and truly to know our own soul; whereby we are learned to seek it where it is: and that is, in God. And thus, by the gracious leading of the Holy Ghost, we shall know them both in one. Whether we are stirred to know God or our own soul, both stirrings are good and true.

GOD IS NEARER THAN OUR OWN SOUL

God is nearer to us than our own soul. For He is the ground in whom our soul standeth; and He is the mean that keepeth the substance and sensuality together, so that they shall never part. For our soul sitteth in God in very rest; and our soul standeth in God in sure strength; and our soul is kindly rooted in God in endless love. And therefore, if we will to have knowing of our soul, and communing and dalliance therewith, it behoveth to seek into our Lord God, in whom it is enclosed. And of this enclosing I saw and understood more in the sixteenth shewing, as I shall say.

And as regards our substance, it may rightly be called our soul. And as regards our sensuality, it may rightly be called our soul. And that is, by the oneing that it hath in God. That worshipful city that our Lord Jesus sitteth in, it is our sensuality, in which He is enclosed. And our kindly substance is enclosed in Jesus; sitting, with the blessed soul of Christ, in rest in the Godhead. And I saw full surely that it must needs be that we should be in longing and in penance, until the time that we be led so deep into God, that we verily and truly know our own soul.

And soothly I saw that into this high deepness our good Lord Himself leadeth us, in the same love wherewith He made us, and in the same love wherewith He bought us, by mercy and grace, through the power of His blessed passion. And notwithstanding all this, we may never come to the full knowing of God, until we know, first, clearly, our own soul. For until the time that it is in the fullness of its powers we cannot be all holy; and that is, until our sensuality, by virtue of Christ's passion, be brought up into the substance, with all the profits of our tribulation that our Lord shall make us to get, by mercy and grace.

GOD WILLS FOR US TO DESIRE KNOWLEDGE OF KIND, MERCY, AND GRACE

I had, in part, touching: and it is grounded in kind. That is to say, our reason is grounded in God, who is substantial kindhood. Of this substantial kindhood, mercy and grace spring, and spread into us; working all things in fulfilling of our joy. These are our ground, in which we have our being, our increase and our fulfilling. For in kind we have our life and our being; and in mercy and grace we have our increase and our fulfilling. Here are three properties in one goodness; and wherever one worketh, all work, in the things which now belong to us. God willeth that we understand, desiring with all our heart and all our strength to have knowing of them, ever more and more unto the time that we shall be fulfilled.

For fully to know them and clearly to see them is naught else but the endless joy and bliss that we shall have in heaven; which God willeth that we begin here, in the knowing of His love. For by our reason alone we cannot profit, unless we have, equally therewith, mind and love. Nor can we be saved merely in that we have our kindly ground in God; unless we have, coming of the same ground, mercy and grace. For of these three workings, all together, we receive all our goods. Of which the first is goods of kind. For in our first making God gave us much good; and also greater goods, such as we could receive only in our spirit. But His foreseeing purpose, in His endless wisdom, willed that we should be double.

THE FIFTY-SEVENTH CHAPTER
IN OUR SUBSTANCE WE ARE FULL: IN OUR SENSUALITY WE FAIL

AND in respect of our substance, He made us so noble and so rich that ever more we work His will and His worship. (Where I say "we," it meaneth "man that shall be saved.") For truly I saw that we are whom He loveth and do what Him liketh, lastingly and without any stint. And of this great richness and of this high nobility, virtues, according to measure, come to our soul, what time it is knit to our body. In which knitting we are made sensual. And thus in our substance we are full, and in our sensuality we fail. Which failing God willeth to restore and fulfil by the working of mercy and grace, plenteously flowing into us from His own kind goodness. And thus this kind goodness ensureth that mercy and grace worketh in us. And the kind goodness that we have of Him enableth us to receive the working of mercy and grace.

I saw that our kind is in God, wholly; in which He maketh diversities, flowing out of Him, to work His will. Whomso kind keepeth, and mercy and grace restore and fulfil, of these none shall perish. For our kind which is the higher part is knit to God in the making; and God is knit to our kind which is the lower part, in taking of our flesh. And thus in Christ our two kinds are oned; for Christ is comprehended in the Trinity, in whom our higher part is grounded and rooted; and our lower part the second Person hath taken—which kind was first prepared for Him. For I saw full truly that all the works that God hath done, or ever shall, were full known to Him and beforeseen, from without-beginning. And for love He made mankind; and for the same love, Himself would become man.

OF BIDDINGS AND FORBIDDINGS

The next good that we receive is our faith; in which our profiting beginneth. And it cometh, this high largesse, of our kind substance, into our sensual soul. And it is grounded in us, and we in it, through the kind goodness of God, by the working of mercy and grace. Of this working come all our goods whereby we are directed and brought to salvation.

For the commandments of God come therein; concerning which we ought to have a two-fold understanding. One is, that we should understand and know what His biddings are, and how to love them and keep them. The other is that we should know His forbiddings—how to hate them and refuse them. For in these two is all our working comprehended.

Also in our faith come the seven sacraments, each following other in the order in which God hath instituted them for us, and every sort of virtue. For the same virtues that we have received of our substance, as given to us in kind, out of the goodness of God—these same virtues are given to us by the working of mercy, renewed in grace through the Holy Ghost. Which virtues and gifts become our treasure in Jesus Christ. For in that same time that God knit Himself to our body in the maiden's womb, He took our sensual soul. In taking which, having enclosed us all in Himself, He oned it to our substance. In this oneing He was perfect man; for Christ, having knit in Himself every man that shall be saved, is perfect man.

MARY IS OUR MOTHER

Thus our Lady is our Mother in whom we are all enclosed; and, of her, born in Christ. For she that is Mother of our Saviour is Mother of all that are saved in our Saviour. And our Saviour is our true Mother, in whom we are endlessly borne; and we shall never come out of Him.

Plenteously, fully and sweetly was this shewed. And it is spoken of in the first shewing, where it said: "We are all in Him enclosed, and He is enclosed in us." And it is spoken of in the sixteenth shewing, where it saith He sitteth in the soul. For it is His liking to reign in our understanding blissfully, and to sit in our soul restfully, and to dwell in our soul endlessly, working us all into Him. In which working He willeth that we be His helpers, giving to Him all our mind; learning His laws, keeping His counsels, desiring that all be done that He doeth, truly trusting in Him. For verily I saw that our substance is in God.

THE FIFTY-EIGHTH CHAPTER
GOD WAS NEVER DISPLEASED
WITH HIS CHOSEN WIFE

GOD the blissful Trinity—which is everlasting Being, right as He is endless from without-beginning, (right so it was in His endless purpose to make man's kind). Which fair kind was first prepared for his own Son, the second Person. And whenso He would, by full accord of all the Trinity, He made all of us at once. And in our making He knit us and oned us to Himself. By which oneing we are kept as clean and as noble as we were made. By virtue of that same precious oneing, we love our Maker and like Him, praise Him and thank Him and endlessly rejoice in Him. And this is the working which is wrought continually in every soul that shall be saved—the aforesaid godly will.

And thus, in our making, God almighty is our kindly Father; and God all-wisdom is our kindly Mother, with the love and goodness of the Holy Ghost; which is all one God, one Lord. And in the knitting and the oneing He is our very true Spouse, and we His loved wife and His fair maiden. With which wife He was never displeased; for He saith: "I love thee, and thou lovest me, and our love shall never be parted in two."

OF THREE PROPERTIES IN THE TRINITY

I beheld the working of all the blessed Trinity. In which beholding I saw and understood these three properties: the property of the Fatherhood, and the property of the Motherhood, and the property of the Lordship—in one God. In our Father almighty we have our keeping and our bliss, in respect of our kindly substance (which is applied to us by our creation), from without-beginning. And in the second Person, in understanding and wisdom, we have our keeping in respect of our sensuality, our restoring and our saving. (For He is our Mother, Brother and Saviour.) And in our good Lord the Holy Ghost we have our rewarding and our enrichment for our living and our travail, which, of His high plenteous grace, and in His marvellous courtesy, endlessly surpasseth all that we desire.

For all our life is in three. In the first we have our being: and in the second we have our increasing: and in the third we have our fulfilling. The first is kind; the second is mercy; the third is grace. For the first, I saw and understood that the high might of the Trinity is our Father, and the deep wisdom of the Trinity is our Mother, and the great love of the Trinity of our Lord. And all these we have in kind and in our substantial making.

OF OUR MOTHER

And furthermore, I saw that the second Person, who is our Mother substantially—the same very dear Person is now become our Mother sensually. For of God's making we are double, that is to say, substantial and sensual. Our substance is that higher part which we have in our Father, God almighty. And the second Person of the Trinity is our Mother in kind, in our substantial making—in whom we are grounded and rooted; and He is our Mother of mercy, in taking our sensuality. And thus "our Mother" meaneth for us different manners of His working, in whom our parts are kept unseparated. For in our Mother Christ, we have profit and increase; and in mercy He re-formeth and restoreth us; and by the power of His passion, His death and His uprising, oned us to our substance. Thus worketh our Mother in mercy to all His beloved children who are docile and obedient to Him.

And grace worketh with mercy; and especially in two properties, as it was shewed. Which working belongeth to the third Person, the Holy Ghost; He worketh by rewarding and giving. Rewarding is a gift—fulfilment of a pledge—that the Lord maketh to them that have laboured; and giving is a courteous working, of grace, fulfilling and surpassing all that is deserved by creatures.

OUR SENSUALITY IS IN CHRIST ALONE

Thus in our Father, God almighty, we have our being. And in our Mother of mercy we have our reforming and our restoring; in whom our parts are oned, and all made perfect; and by the enriching and giving, in grace, of the Holy Ghost, we are fulfilled. And our substance is in our Father, God almighty; and our substance is in our Mother, God all-wisdom; and our substance is in our Lord God the Holy Ghost, all-goodness. For our substance is whole in each Person of the Trinity, which is one God. But our sensuality is only in the second Person, Christ Jesus, in whom is the Father and the Holy Ghost. And in Him and by Him we are mightily taken out of hell, and out of the wretchedness in earth, and worshipfully brought up into heaven; and blissfully oned to our substance, increased in richness and nobility, by the power of Christ and by the grace and working of the Holy Ghost.

THE FIFTY-NINTH CHAPTER
WICKEDNESS IS TURNED TO BLISS IN THE CHOSEN BY MERCY AND GRACE

AND all this bliss we have by mercy and grace; which sort of bliss we might never have had nor known, if that property of goodness which is in God (whereby we have this bliss) had been cancelled out. For wickedness hath been permitted to rise up contrary to the goodness. But the goodness of mercy and grace stood contrary against that wickedness, and turned all to goodness and worship—unto all that shall be saved. For it is the property in God which doeth good against evil.

GOD IS OUR FATHER AND MOTHER

Thus Jesus Christ, who doeth good against evil, is our very Mother. We have our being of Him, there, where the ground of Motherhood beginneth; with all the sweet keeping of love that endlessly followeth. As truly as God is our Father, so truly is God our Mother. And that shewed He in all, and especially in these sweet words where He saith, "I it am." That is to say:

I it am: the might and the goodness of the Fatherhood. I it am: the wisdom and the kindness of Motherhood. I it am: the light and the grace that is all blessed love. I it am, the Trinity. I it am, the Unity. I it am the high sovereign Goodness of all manner thing. I it am that maketh thee to love. I it am that maketh thee to long. I it am, the endless fulfilling of all true desires.

For where the soul is highest, noblest, and most worshipful, there it is lowest, meekest, and mildest. And of this substantial ground we have all our virtues, in our sensuality, by gift of kind, and by helping and speeding of mercy and grace—without which we cannot profit. Our high Father almighty God, who is Being, He knew us and loved us from before-any-time. Of which knowing, in His full marvellous deep Charity, by the foreseeing endless counsel of all the blessed Trinity,

He willed that the second Person should become our Mother, our Brother, and our Savior. Whereof it followeth that as truly as God is our Father, so truly is God our Mother. Our Father willeth, our Mother worketh, our good Lord the Holy Ghost confirmeth.

And therefore it belongeth to us to love our God, in whom we have our being; Him reverently thanking and praising for our making; mightily praying to our Mother for mercy and pity, and to our Lord the Holy Ghost for help and grace. For in these three is all our life—kind, mercy, and grace; whereof we have mildness, patience, and pity, and hating of sin and wickedness. For it belongeth properly to the virtues to hate sin and wickedness.

OF MOTHERHOOD

And thus is Jesus our true Mother in kind, of our first making; and He is our true Mother in grace by His taking of our made kind. All the fair working and all the sweet kindly offices of most dear Motherhood are appropriated to the second Person. For in Him we have this godly will whole and secure without end, both in kind and in grace, of His own proper goodness. I understand three types of beholding of Motherhood in God. The first is the ground of making of our kind. The second is the taking of our kind—and there beginneth the Motherhood of grace. The third is Motherhood in working. And therein is a forthspreading, by the same grace, of a length and breadth, of a height and a deepness without end. And all is one love.

THE SIXTIETH CHAPTER
BUT JESUS IS OUR TRUE MOTHER, FEEDING US NOT WITH MILK, BUT WITH HIMSELF

BUT now it behoveth me to say a little more of this forthspreading, as I understand it in the meaning of our Lord: How that we are brought again by the Motherhood of mercy and grace into the kindly state, wherein we were made, by the Motherhood of kind love; which kind love never leaveth us.

Our kind Mother, our gracious Mother—for He would all wholly become our Mother in all things—He made the ground of His work to be full low and full mildly in the Maiden's womb. And that shewed He in the first shewing, where He brought that meek maiden before the eye of my understanding, in the simple stature, as she was when she conceived. That is to say: Our high God, the sovereign Wisdom of all, in this lowly place He arrayed Him and made Him all ready; in our poor flesh, Himself to do the service and office of Motherhood, in all things.

PROPERTIES OF MOTHERHOOD

The mother's service is nearest, readiest and surest; nearest, for it is most of kind; readiest, for it is most of love; surest, for it is most of truth. This office no one might nor could ever do to the full, except He alone. We know that all our mothers bear us to pain and to dying; a strange thing, that! But our true Mother Jesus, He alone beareth us to joy and to endless living; blessed may He be! Thus He sustaineth us within Him, in love and in travail unto the full time in which He willed to suffer the sharpest throes and most grievous pains that ever were, or ever shall be; and He died at the last. Yet all this might not fully satisfy His marvellous love. And that shewed He in these high overpassing words of love: "If I could suffer more, I would suffer more." He could no more die, but He would not cease working.

Wherefore it behoveth Him to feed us; for the very dear love of motherhood hath made Him our debtor. The mother can give her child to suck of her milk. But our precious Mother Jesus, He can feed us with Himself; and doth, full courteously and tenderly, with the Blessed Sacrament, that is the precious food of true life. And with all the sweet sacraments He sustaineth us full mercifully and graciously. And this was His meaning in those blessed words, where He said: "I it am that Holy Church preacheth to thee and teacheth thee"; that is to say, all the health and the life of the sacraments. "All the power and the grace of My word, all the goodness that is ordained to thee in Holy Church, I it am."

A MOTHER'S LOVE

The mother can lay her child tenderly to her breast. But our tender Mother Jesus can lead us, homely, into His blessed breast, by His sweet open side; and shew us there, in part, the Godhead and the joys of heaven, with a ghostly sureness of endless bliss. And that shewed He in the ninth Revelation, giving the same understanding in the sweet words where He saith: "Lo, how I love thee"—looking into His blessed side, rejoicing.

This fair lovely word *Mother*, it is so sweet and so kind in itself, that it cannot truly be said to any nor of any,

but to Him and of Him who is very Mother of life and of all. To the property of Motherhood belongeth kind love, wisdom, and knowing; and it is God. For though it is true that our bodily forthbringing is but little, lowly, and simple in comparison with our ghostly forthbringing; yet it is He that doeth the first in the creatures by whom it is done. The kind loving mother understandeth and knoweth the need of her child. She keepeth it full tenderly, as the kind and condition of motherhood will. And ever as it waxeth in age and in stature, she changeth her way of working, but not her love. And when it is come to a more advanced age, she suffereth it to be chastised, for the breaking down of vices, and to make the child receive virtues and grace. This work, with all that is fair and good, our Lord doeth it, in those by whom it is done.

Thus He is our Mother in kind by the working of grace in the lower part, for the sake of the higher. And He willeth that we know it. For He willeth to have all our love fastened to Him. And in this I saw that all the debts that we owe, by God's bidding, to fatherhood and motherhood is fulfilled in true loving of God. Which blessed love Christ worketh in us. And this was shewed in everything; but especially in the high plenteous words, where He saith: "I it am that thou lovest."

THE SIXTY-FIRST CHAPTER
JESUS USETH GREAT TENDERNESS WITH HIS CHILDREN

AND in our ghostly forthbringing He useth more tenderness (without any comparison) by as much as our soul is of more price in His sight. He kindleth our understanding, He prepareth our ways, He comforteth our soul, He enlighteneth our heart; and giveth us, in part, a knowing and loving in His blissful Godhead, with gracious mind of His sweet manhood and His blessed passion, with courteous marvelling at His high surpassing goodness. And He maketh us to love all that He loveth, for His love; and to be well satisfied with Him, and with all His works.

WHY GOD ALLOWS MEN TO FALL

And when we fall, hastily He raiseth us by the clasping of His love and the touching of His grace. And when we are strengthened by His sweet working, then we deliberately choose Him, by His grace, to be His servants and His lovers, lastingly without end. And yet, after this, He suffereth some of us to fall more hard and more grievously than ever we did before—or so it would seem. And then we think (for we are not all wise) that all we have begun is brought to naught. But it is not so. For we needs must fall; and we needs must see it.

For if we fell not, we should never know how feeble and how wretched we are, of ourselves. Nor should we know so fully the marvellous love of our Maker. For we shall truly see in heaven, without end, that we have grievously sinned in this life. Yet notwithstanding this, we shall truly see that we were never hurt in His love; nor were any the less precious in His sight. By the experience of this falling we shall have a high and a marvellous knowing of love in God, without end. For staunch and marvellous is that love which cannot or will not be broken because of trespass.

AN ADDITIONAL INSIGHT INTO FALLING

This was one understanding that was profitable. Another is the lowliness and meekness what we shall get by the sight of our falling. For thereby we shall highly be raised in heaven—to which we could never come without that meekness. And therefore we need to see it. For if we see it not, even though we fell, it would not profit us. Ordinarily, first we fall, and then we see it. And both are of the mercy of God. The mother may suffer her child to fall sometimes, and to be distressed in different ways, for its own profit. But she can never permit that any manner of peril come to her child, because of her love. And though, possibly, an earthly mother may suffer her child to perish, our heavenly Mother Jesus can never suffer us who are His children to perish. For He is almighty, all-wisdom and all-love: and so is none but He. Blessed may He be!

THE PROPER RESPONSE TO FALLING

But oftentimes, when our falling and our wretchedness is shewed to us, we are so sore adread, and so greatly ashamed of ourselves, that we scarcely know where to put ourselves. Yet even then our courteous Mother willeth not that we flee away: nothing could be more displeasing to Him. Rather, He willeth us to behave as a child. For when it is distressed and afraid, it runneth hastily to the mother. And if it can do naught else, it cryeth to the mother for help, with all its might. So will He have us behave as the meek child, saying thus: "My kind Mother, my gracious Mother, my most dear Mother, have mercy on me. I have made myself foul and unlike to Thee; and I cannot or may not amend it but with Thine help and grace." And if we do not feel eased at once, then we may be sure that He useth the way of a wise mother. For if He see that it is for our profit to mourn and to weep, He suffereth that, with compassion and pity—until the right time, out of love.

It is His will, then, that we behave as a child, who ever more kindly trusteth to the love of the mother, in weal and in woe. And He willeth that we betake us, mightily, to the faith of Holy Church; and find in her our most dear Mother, in solace and true understanding, with all the Communion of Saints. For a single person may often be broken—or so it seemeth to the self. But the whole Body of the Church was never broken, nor ever shall be, without end. And therefore a sure thing it is, a good and a gracious, to will, meekly and mightily, to be fastened and oned to our Mother Holy Church; that is, Christ Jesus. For the flood of mercy that is His most dear blood and precious water is plenteous to make us fair and clean. The blessed wounds of our Saviour are open, and rejoice to heal us. The sweet gracious hands of our Mother are ready and diligent about us.

For He, in all this working, fulfilleth the office of a kind nurse that hath naught else to do but to attend to the well-being of her child. It is His office to save us; it is His worship to do it, and it is his will that we know it. For He willeth that we love Him sweetly, and trust in Him meekly and mightily. And this shewed He in these gracious words, "I keep thee full surely."

THE SIXTY-SECOND CHAPTER
THE LOVE OF GOD SUFFERETH NEVER HIS CHOSEN TO LOSE TIME: FOR ALL THEIR TROUBLE IS TURNED INTO ENDLESS JOY

IN that time He shewed our frailty and our falling, our being broken and despoiled, our being crossed and accused: and all our woe, as far forth as methought could ever befall us in this life. But with it He shewed His blessed might, His blessed wisdom, His blessed love—that He keepeth us, in this time, as tenderly and as sweetly (for His worship) and as surely unto our salvation, as He doth when we are most in solace and comfort. And with that He raiseth us ghostly and highly in heaven; and turneth all to His worship and to our joy, without end.

For His precious love never suffereth us to lose time; and all this is of the kind goodness of God, by the working of grace. God is kind in His Being. That is to say: The Goodness which is Kind, is God. He is the Ground; He is the Substance; He is the very thing called Kindness. And He is the very Father and the very Mother of kinds. And all kinds that He hath made to flow out of Him to work His will, they must be restored and brought again into Him, by the salvation of man, through the working of grace. For of all the kinds that He hath set in various creatures separately, only in man is all the whole—in fullness and in power, in beauty and in goodness, in royalty and nobility, in all manner of eminence, of preciousness and honour.

OF OUR INDEBTEDNESS TO GOD

Here may we see that we are all indebted to God for kind, and we are indebted to God for grace. Here may we see that we need not go very far out of our way to get to know various kinds, but merely to Holy Church, into our Mother's breast; that is to say, into our own soul, where our Lord dwelleth. And there shall we find all; now in faith and in understanding, and afterwards truly in Himself, clearly, in bliss. But let no man nor woman understand this of himself, individually; for it is not so. This fair kind, it is general; it is our precious Mother, Christ. For Him was this fair kind prepared: For the worship and nobility of man's making and for the joy and the bliss of man's salvation; just as He saw, understood and knew it, from without-beginning.

THE SIXTY-THIRD CHAPTER
SIN IS MORE PAINFUL THAN HELL: AND VILE AND HARMFUL TO KIND; BUT GRACE SAVETH KIND AND DESTROYETH SIN

HERE may we see that it truly belongeth to us, of kind, to hate sin. For kind is all good and fair in itself. And grace was sent out to save kind and keep kind; and destroy sin and bring again fair kind into the blessed place whence it came (that is, God), with more nobleness and worship, by the virtuous working of grace. For it shall be seen before God, by all His Holy Ones, in joy without end.

Yet kind hath been tried in the fire of tribulation, and in it was found no lack nor defect. Thus are kind and grace one accord. For grace is God, and unmade Kind is God. He is two, in manner of working (but one in love): and neither of them worketh without the other—they may not be parted.

And when we, by the mercy of God and with His help, accord ourselves to kind and to grace, we shall see truly that sin is worse, more vile, and more painful than hell—there is no comparison; it is contrary to our fair kind. For as truly as sin is unclean, as truly sin is unkind. All this is a horrible thing to see for the loving soul that would be all fair and shining in the sight of God, as kind and grace teach.

OUR LIFE IS GROUNDED IN JESUS

But let us not be adread of this, except in as much as dread may speed us; but meekly make we our moan to our most dear Mother. And He shall all besprinkle us in His precious blood, and make our soul full soft and full mild, and heal us to full fairness in the process of time—for thus it is most worship to Him, and joy to us without end.

And of this sweet fair working He shall never cease nor stint Himself until all His most dear children be born and brought forth. And that shewed He where He gave the understanding of the ghostly thirst, which is the love-longing that shall last till doomsday.

Thus in our true Mother Jesus our life is grounded, in the foreseeing wisdom of Himself from without-beginning, with the high might of the Father and the sovereign goodness of the Holy Ghost. And in the taking of our kind He quickened us; and in His blessed dying upon the cross He bore us to endless life. And from that time, and now, He feedeth us and furthereth us, and ever shall until doomsday: right as the high sovereign kindness of Motherhood willeth, and the kindly need of childhood demandeth.

Fair and sweet is our heavenly Mother in the sight of our soul; precious and lovely are the gracious children in the sight of our heavenly Mother, with mildness and meekness and all the fair virtues that belong, in kind, to children. For kindly the children despair not of the mother's love, kindly the child presumeth not of itself, kindly the child loveth the mother and each one of them the other. These are the fair virtues (with all others that are like to them) wherewith our heavenly Mother is served and pleased. And I understood that there is no higher stature in this life than childhood—in the feebleness and failing of might and understanding—until the time that our gracious Mother hath brought us up to our Father's bliss. And there shall truly be made known to us His meaning, in the sweet words where He saith: "All shall be well; and thou shalt see it thyself that all manner thing shall be well."

THE SIXTY-FOURTH CHAPTER
THE FIFTEENTH REVELATION

AND then shall the bliss of our Motherhood in Christ be begun anew in the joys of our Father, God. Which new beginning shall last without end. This new beginning I understood thus: That all His blessed children, who are come out of Him by kind, should be brought again into Him by grace.

THE ABSENCE OF GOD IN THIS LIFE IS GREAT PAIN TO US

Before this time, I had, of God's gift, great longing and desire to be delivered of this world and of this life. For oftentimes I beheld the woe that is here, and the weal and the blessed being that is there. And even if there had been no pain in this life, but the absence of our Lord, it seemed to me, sometimes, that it was more than I might bear. And this made me to mourn, and earnestly to long; and also because of my own wretchedness, sloth, and weariness—that it liked me not to live and to travail as it fell to me to do.

OF DELIVERANCE FROM PAIN

And to all this our Lord answered, for comfort and patience, and said these words:

Suddenly thou shalt be taken from all thy pain, from all thy sickness, from all thy distress and from all thy woe. And thou shalt come up above, and thou shalt have Me for thy meed, and thou shalt be filled full of joy and bliss. And thou shalt never more have any manner of pain, nor any manner of sickness, nor any manner of disliking, nor wanting of will; but ever joy and bliss without end. Why then should it grieve thee to suffer a while, since it is My will, and for My worship?

And in this word "suddenly thou shalt be taken," I saw that God rewardeth man for the patience that he hath in abiding in God's will and His time; and that man stretcheth his patience across the time of his living, through unknowing of the time of his passing. This is of great profit. For if man knew his time, he would not have patience over that time.

And also it is God's will, that while the soul is in the body, it should seem to it that it is ever on the point of being taken. For all this life and this longing that we have here is but a point. And when we be taken suddenly out of pain into bliss, then pain shall be naught.

A VISION OF THE CHANGE TO COME

And in this time I saw a body lying on the earth. Which body was a heavy, fearful sight, without shape or form—a bloated mass of stinking mud. And suddenly, out of this body sprang a full fair creature, a little child fully shapen and formed, swift and full of life and whiter than the lily; it quickly glided up into heaven. The bloated mass of the body betokeneth the great wretchedness of our mortal flesh; and the littleness of the child betokeneth the cleanness and the purity of our soul. And I thought: "With this body this child's fairness cannot remain; nor can any foulness of body dwell with this child."

It is full blissful for man to be taken from pain, more than for pain to be taken from man. For if pain be taken from us, it can come again. Therefore this is a sovereign comfort and a blissful beholding for a soul in longing, that we shall be taken from pain. For in this promise I saw the merciful compassion that our Lord hath in us, for our woe, and a courteous pledge of cleansing deliverance. For it is His will that we be comforted in overpassing joy. And that He shewed in these words: "And thou shalt come up above; and thou shalt have Me for thy meed; and thou shalt be filled full of joy and bliss."

A BLISSFUL CONTEMPLATION

It is God's will that we set the point of our thought in this blissful behold-ing as oftentimes as we may and for as long a time keep ourselves therein, with His grace. For this is a blissful contemplation for the soul that is led of God; and it is full much to His worship, for the time that it lasteth.

And when we fall again to ourselves, by heaviness and ghostly blindness and feeling of pains ghostly and bodily, by reason of our frailty, it is God's will that we know that He hath not forgotten us. And so meaneth He in these words, and saith for comfort: "And thou shalt never more have pain in any manner: nor any manner of sickness, nor any manner of disliking, nor wanting of will; but ever joy and bliss. Why should it then grieve thee to suffer awhile, since it is My will and to My worship?"

It is God's will that we take His promises and His comforting as fully and as mightily as we may. And also it is His will that we take our abidings and our distress as lightly as we may, and set them at naught. For the more lightly that we take them, and the less price that we set on them, for love, the less pain shall we have in feeling of them, and the more thanks and meed shall we have for them.

THE SIXTY-FIFTH CHAPTER
HE THAT CHOOSETH GOD

AND thus I understood that what man or woman deliberately chooseth God in this life, for love, may be sure that he is loved without end. Which endless love worketh in him that grace. For He willeth us to hold trustfully to this—that we be as sure, in hope, of the bliss of heaven whilst we are here, as we shall be, in certainty, when we are there. And ever the more liking and joy that we take in this sureness, with reverence and meekness, the better it liketh Him. For this reverence that I mean (as it was shewed) is a holy courteous dread of our Lord, to which meekness is knit; and that is, that a creature see the Lord marvellous great, and herself marvellous little.

These virtues are had endlessly by the beloved of God. And they may now be seen and felt, in a measure, by the gracious presence of our Lord, when it is given. Which presence is most desirable, in everything. For it worketh that marvellous sureness, in true faith and steadfast hope, by the greatness of charity, in dread that is sweet and delightful. It is God's will that I see myself as much bound to Him in love, as if all that He hath done He had done for me. And thus should every soul think in regard of his Lover. That is to say: The charity of God maketh in us such a unity, that, when it is truly seen, no man can part himself from another. And so each soul ought to think that God hath done for him all that He hath done.

IT IS GOD'S WILL THAT WE DREAD NOTHING BUT HIM

And this sheweth He to make us to love Him and like Him, and nothing dread but Him. For it is His will that we know that all the might of our enemy is locked in our Friend's hands. And therefore the soul that knoweth this surely, she shall dread only Him whom she loveth. All other dreads— she setteth them among passions, bodily sickness, and imaginations. And therefore, though we be in so much

pain, woe, and distress that it seemeth that we can think of naught but the state that we are in, or that we feel; as soon as we may, let us pass lightly over it, and set it at naught.

And why? Because God willeth us to know that if we know Him and love Him and reverently dread Him, we shall have peace and be in great rest; and all that He doeth shall be great liking to us. And this shewed our Lord in these words: "Why should it then grieve thee to suffer awhile, seeing it is My will and to My worship?"

OF THE TIME OF THE REVELATION

Now have I told you of fifteen shewings, as God vouchsafed to minister them to my mind: Renewed by lightings and touchings, I hope of the same Spirit that shewed them all. Of which fifteen shewings the first began early in the morning, about the hour of four. And they lasted, shewn in order full fair and surely, each following the other, until it was past three in the day.

THE SIXTY-SIXTH CHAPTER
THE SIXTEENTH REVELATION, THE CONCLUSION AND CONFIRMATION OF ALL FIFTEEN

AND after this, the good Lord shewed the sixteenth Revelation, on the night following, as I shall say afterwards. Which sixteenth was the conclusion and confirmation of all the fifteen.

But first I needs must tell you about my feebleness, wretchedness and blindness. I have said (at the beginning, where it saith: "And in this, suddenly all my pain was taken from me") that of pain I had no grief nor distress as long as the fifteen shewings lasted.

But at the end, all was hid again, and I saw no more. And then I felt that I would go on living; but then my sickness came again; first in my head, with a loud sound and a noise. And suddenly all my body was filled full of sickness, like as it was before. And I was as barren and as dry as if I had never had but the least comfort. And as a wretch I mourned grievously, in feeling my bodily pains, and for the failing of comfort, ghostly and bodily.

OF THE VISIT OF A PARSON

Then came a religious, a parson, to me; and asked me how I fared. And I said I had raved during the day. But he laughed loud and heartily. And I said that the cross that stood before my face—it seemed to me that it bled freely. With this word, the parson to whom I spake grew very serious, and was filled with wonder. And straightway I was sore ashamed and abashed at my recklessness. And I thought: "This man, that saw nothing thereof, taketh seriously the least word that I say." And when I saw that he took it so seriously and with such reverence, I grew greatly ashamed and desired to make confession!

But I could not tell the fault to a priest; "for," I thought, "how would a priest believe me, when I, by saying I raved, shewed myself not to believe our Lord God?" Notwithstanding this, I believed Him truly during the time that I saw Him, and at that time it was my will and meaning ever to do so, without end. But like a fool, I let this pass out of my mind. Alas, what a wretch I was! This was a great sin and a great unkindness, that out of folly, and for feeling of a little bodily pain, I

so unwisely left, for the time, the comfort of all this blessed shewing of our Lord God.

Here may you see what I am of myself. But herein our courteous Lord would not leave me. And I lay still until night, trusting in His mercy; and then I began to sleep.

THE SIXTY-SEVENTH CHAPTER
YET THE DEVIL, AFTER THAT, HAD GREAT POWER TO MOLEST HER, NIGH UNTO DEATH

AND in my sleep, at the beginning, it seemed as though the fiend set himself at my throat, thrusting his face close to mine—the face of a young man, long and incredibly lean: I never saw its like. Its colour was red, like the tile-stone fresh from the kiln, with black spots in it like freckles—dirtier than a tile-stone. His hair was red as rust, cut short in front, with side-locks hanging down his cheeks. He looked at me with a malignant grin, shewing his white teeth. And the more he grinned, the more ugly he seemed. Body or hands had he none, of true shape; but with his paws he held me by the throat, and would have stopped my breath and killed me; but he might not.

This ugly shewing alone was made whilst I slept: no other was shewn so. And in all this time, I trusted to be saved and kept by the mercy of God; and our courteous Lord gave me grace to wake.

HER REALIZATION OF THE FIEND'S PRESENCE

I scarcely had any life in me. But the persons that were with me looked at me and wet my temples; and my heart began to take comfort. Immediately, a little smoke came in at the door, with a great heat and a foul stench. And then said I, "God bless us! Is all the place on fire?" For I thought it was a bodily fire that would burn us all to death. I asked them that were with me if they smelt any stench. They said "Nay," they smelt nothing.

I said, "Blessed be God." For then I understood that it was only the fiend, come to tempt me. Then straightway I betook me to what our Lord had shewed me on the same day, with all the faith of Holy Church (for I beheld both these as in one); and fled thereto, as to my comfort. And immediately all vanished away; and I was brought to great rest and peace, without sickness of body or dread of conscience.

THE SIXTY-EIGHTH CHAPTER
OF THE WORSHIPFUL CITY OF THE SOUL

AND then our good Lord opened my ghostly eye, and shewed me my soul in the midst of my heart. I saw the soul, so large as it were an endless world, and also as it were a blessed kingdom. And by the appointments that I saw therein, I understood that it is a worshipful city. In the midst of that city is our Lord Jesus, true God and true man, comely of person and tall of stature, the greatest bishop, most aweful king, Lord of highest honour. And I saw Him arrayed in majesty and honour. He sitteth in the soul, established in peace and rest. And He ruleth and maintaineth heaven and earth and all that is. The manhood with the Godhead sitteth in rest; the Godhead ruleth and maintaineth without any instrument or labour. And the soul is all occupied with the blessed Godhead which is sovereign Might, sovereign Wisdom, sovereign Goodness.

The place that Jesus taketh in our soul—He shall never remove therefrom without end. For in us is His homeliest home, and His endless dwelling. And in this He shewed the liking that He hath in the making of a creature. For well as the Father might make a creature, and well as the Son might make a creature; just so well the Holy Ghost willed that man's soul should be made. And so it was done. And therefore the blissful Trinity rejoiceth without end in the making of man's soul. For He saw from without-beginning what would please Him without end.

All things that He hath made shew His Lordship; as understanding was given, in the same time, by the example of a creature who is brought to see the great nobility of the kingdoms belonging to a lord. And when the creature had seen all the nobility below, then, marvelling, it was moved to seek up above into that high place where the Lord dwelleth (knowing by its reason that His dwelling must be in the worthiest place).

THE SOUL CAN HAVE REST
IN NOTHING BUT GOD

And thus I understood truly that our soul may never have rest in anything that is beneath itself. And when it cometh above all creatures into itself, yet it cannot dwell in the beholding of itself; but all its beholding is blissfully set in God who is the Maker, dwelling therein; for in man's soul is His true dwelling. And the highest light and the brightest shining of the city is the glorious love of our Lord God, as to my sight. And what can make us more rejoice in God than to see in Him that He rejoiceth in us, the highest of all His works?

For I saw in the same shewing that if the blessed Trinity could have made man's soul any the better, any the fairer, any the nobler than it was made, He would not have been fully pleased with the making of man's soul. But because He made man's soul as fair, as good and as precious as He could make a creature, therefore the blessed Trinity is fully pleased without end in the making of man's soul. And it is His will that our hearts be mightily raised above the depths of the earth and all vain sorrows, and rejoice in Him.

This was a delightful sight and a restful shewing, that is without end. And the beholding of this, while we are here, is full pleasant to God and full great speed to us. And the soul that thus beholdeth—the sight maketh it like to Him that is beheld, and oneth it to Him in rest and in peace, by His grace. And this was a special joy and bliss to me—that I saw Him sitting. For the sureness of sitting shewed endless dwelling. And He gave me to know truly that it was He who had shewed me all before.

CONFIRMATION OF HER REVELATIONS

And when I had beheld this with close attention, then shewed our Lord words, full meekly without voice and without opening of lips, just as He had done before, and said full sweetly:

Know it now well that it was no raving that thou sawest today. But take it and believe it and keep thee therein, and comfort thee therewith, and trust thereto; and thou shalt not be overcome.

These last words were said for learning of full true sureness that it is our Lord Jesus that shewed me all. And just as in the first words that our Lord shewed, He said (meaning His blessed passion), "Herewith is the fiend overcome;" just so in the last words He said, with full true faithfulness (meaning us all), "Thou shalt not be overcome."

And all this teaching and this true comfort, it is given generally, to all my even-christians, as is before said. And such is God's will. This word, "Thou shalt not be overcome," was said full sharply and full mightily, for sureness and comfort against all tribulations that may come. He said not "Thou shalt not be troubled, thou shalt not be travailed, thou shalt not be distressed"; but He said "Thou shalt not be overcome."

It is God's will that we take heed to these words, and that we be ever mighty in faithful trust in weal and woe. For He loveth us and liketh us; and so willeth He that we love Him and like Him, and mightily trust in Him. And all shall be well. And then all was finished, and I saw no more.

THE SIXTY-NINTH CHAPTER
OF THE DEVIL'S SECOND LONG
TEMPTATION TO DESPAIR

AFTER this, the fiend came again with his heat and his stench, and made me full busy. The stench was so vile and so painful, and the bodily heat so dreadful and hard to bear! Also, I heard talking, bodily, as between two people; and both, to my thinking, talked at once (as though they were in parliament), with great earnestness; and all was soft whispering. And I understood not what they said.

All this, it appeared, was to move me to despair; it seemed as though they scornfully imitated the telling of the Beads when they are said with noise of words, with much failing of that devout attention and wise diligence which we owe to God in our prayer. But our good Lord gave me the grace mightily to trust in Him, and to comfort my soul with bodily speech—as I might have done for another person who was in distress.

Yet it seemed to me that all this could not be likened to any bodily business.

THE SEVENTIETH CHAPTER
THE DEPARTURE OF THE FIENDS

MY bodily eyes I fixed on the same cross (on which I had gazed for my comfort before this time); my tongue I occupied with speech of Christ's passion and with rehearsing the faith of Holy Church; and my heart I fastened on God with all my trust and might. And I thought to myself: "Thou hast now great earnestness about keeping thee in the faith, that thou shouldst not be taken by thine enemies. If now from this time thou shouldst ever more be as busy about keeping thee from sin, this would be a good and sovereign occupation." And I thought: "Truly, were I safe from sin, I would be full safe from all the fiends in hell, and all the enemies of my soul."

And thus the fiends occupied me all that night and in the morning, till it was about nine in the day. And then they were all gone and past, and there was left nothing but a stink, which lasted still a while. I scorned him; and thus was I delivered from him by the power of Christ's passion. For "therewith is the fiend overcome," as our Lord Jesus Christ said before.

BUT SHE TRUSTED MIGHTILY IN GOD AND IN THE FAITH OF HOLY CHURCH

In all this blessed shewing, our Lord gave me to understand that sight of it should pass. But the faith keepeth it, with His own good will and His grace. For though He left me with neither sign nor token whereby I might know it; yet He left me with His own blessed word in true understanding, bidding me full mightily that I should believe it. And so I do; blessed may He be! I believe that it is our Saviour that shewed it, and that what He shewed is in the faith. And therefore I love it, ever rejoicing in it; and thereto I am bound—with all the meaning that He gave, and with the next words that follow: "Keep thee therein and trust thereto." Thus I am bound to keep it in my faith.

Yet on the same day that it was shewed, when the sight of it was passed, as a wretch I forsook it, and openly said that I had raved. But our Lord Jesus, of His mercy, would not let it perish. He shewed it all again within my soul; and with more fullness— with the blessed light of His precious love, saying these words full mightily and full meekly: "Know it now well, that it was no raving that thou saw today." As if He had said: "Because the sight had passed from thee, thou losedst it, and couldst not or mightest not keep it. But know it now." That is to say "now thou seest it." This was said not only for this time, but also that I might set thereupon the ground of my faith—there where he saith in the words immediately following: "but take it and believe it, and keep thee therein and comfort thee therewith, and trust thereto: and thou shalt not be overcome."

THE SEVENTY-FIRST CHAPTER
IN ALL TRIBULATION WE MUST BE STEADFAST IN THE FAITH, TRUSTING MIGHTILY IN GOD

IN these six words that follow where He saith "Take it," His meaning is to fasten it faithfully in our heart. For He willeth that it dwell with us, in faith, unto our life's end: and afterwards, in fullness of joy. It is His will that we have ever faithful trust in His blessed promises, knowing His goodness. For our faith is contraried in diverse manners by our own blindness and our ghostly enemy, within and without. And therefore our precious Lover helpeth us with ghostly light and true teaching in diverse manners within and without; whereby we may know Him. And therefore in whatever manner He teacheth us, He willeth that we perceive Him wisely, receive Him sweetly, and keep us in Him faithfully.

Above the faith there is no goodness kept in this life, as to my sight. And beneath the faith there is no health of soul. But in the faith—there willeth our Lord that we keep us. For we are able, by His goodness and His own working, to keep us in the faith. By His sufferance, through ghostly enmity, we are tried in the faith and made mighty. For if our faith had not enmity, it would deserve no meed. Such is the understanding that I have of our Lord's meaning.

Glad and merry and sweet is the blissful lovely looking of our Lord into our souls. For He ever beholdeth us as we live in loving longing; and it is His will that our soul look gladly unto Him, to grant Him His meed. And thus I hope that He, with His grace, hath brought and shall bring even more, that outward regard into the inward; and make us all at one with Him and with each other, in that true lasting Joy which is Jesus.

OF THREE LOOKINGS

I have understanding of three lookings of our Lord. The first is the look which He shewed in His passion, whilst He was with us in this life, in His dying. And though this looking is mournful and sorrowful, yet it is glad and merry, because He is God. The second look is of pity and compassion. And this sheweth He to all His lovers who have need of His mercy, with sureness of keeping. The third is the blissful look, such as shall be without end. And this was oftenest shewed and continued longest.

And thus in the time of our pain and woe, He sheweth us the look that belongeth to His passion and His cross, helping us to bear it by His own blessed power. And in the time of our sinning, He sheweth us the look of compassion and pity, mightily keeping and defending us against all our enemies.

And these two are, commonly, the looks which He sheweth us in this life; with which He mingleth the third (resembling, in part, what it shall be in heaven), by the gracious touching and sweet enlightening of our ghostly life. By that look we are kept in true faith, hope and charity, with contrition and devotion; and also with contemplation and all manner of true joys and sweet comforts. The blissful look of our Lord God worketh all this in us by grace.

THE SEVENTY-SECOND CHAPTER
SIN IN CHOSEN SOULS IS DEADLY FOR A TIME: BUT THEY ARE NOT DEAD IN THE SIGHT OF GOD

BUT now I needs must tell you in what manner I saw deadly sin in those creatures who would not die because of sin, but would live without end in the joy of God. I saw that two contraries could not be together in one place. The greatest contraries that there are, are the highest bliss and the deepest pain. The highest bliss there is is to have God in clearness of endless light, Him truly seeing, Him sweetly feeling, Him all perfectly having, in fullness of joy.

Thus was this blissful look of our Lord God shewed, in part. In which shewing I saw that sin was its greatest contrary: So far forth that as long as we have anything to do with sin, we shall never see clearly this blissful look of God. And the more horrible and grievous our sins are, the deeper are we, for that time, out of this blessed sight. And therefore it seemeth to us, oftentimes, as though we were in peril of death and in a part of hell; because of the sorrow and pain that sin meaneth to us. And thus we are dead for the time—out of very sight of our blissful life.

But in all this, I saw, in faith, that we are not dead in the sight of God, and He passeth never away from us; though He shall never have His full

bliss in us till we have our full bliss in Him—truly seeing His fair, blissful look. For we ordained thereto by kind and brought thereto by grace. Thus I saw how, with regard to those blessed creatures of endless life, sin is deadly for a short time.

OF THE SOUL'S LONGING

Ever the more clearly the soul seeth this blissful look, by grace of loving, the more it longeth to see it in fullness; that is to say, in His own likeness. For notwithstanding that our Lord God dwelleth now in us, and claspeth us and encloseth us, out of tender love, so that He can never leave us and is nearer to us than tongue can tell or heart can think; yet can we never cease from mourning nor from weeping, nor from seeking nor from longing, until we see Him clearly with this blissful look of His. (For in that precious sight no woe may abide nor weal fail.)

And in this I saw matter for mirth, and matter for mourning: Matter for mirth—that our Lord our Maker is so near to us and in us and we in Him, by sureness of keeping, because of His great goodness; matter for mourning—because our ghostly eye is so blind, and we are so borne down by the weight of our mortal flesh and the darkness of sin, that we cannot see our Lord clearly with that blissful look of His.

No, and because of this darkness we can scarce believe or trust His great love, and our sureness of keeping. And therefore it is as I say: We can never leave off mourning or weeping. Weeping here meaneth not merely the pouring out of tears from our bodily eye; but also unto a more ghostly understanding. For the kindly desire of our soul is so great and so unmeasurable, that if all the nobility that God ever made in heaven and in earth were given to us for our joy and comfort, apart from the sight of this fair blissful look of His; yet we would never take leave of mourning or ghostly weeping (that is to say painful longing), until we saw verily this fair blissful look of our Maker. And if we were to suffer all the pain that heart can think or tongue can tell, and we could, in that time, see this blissful look; all that pain would not grieve us.

THE REASON FOR THESE SHEWINGS

Thus is that blissful sight the end of all manner of pain unto loving souls, and fulfilling of all manner of joy and bliss. And that shewed He in the high marvellous words where He saith: "I it am that is highest; I it am that thou lovest; I it am that is all." It belongeth to us to have three knowings. The first is that we know our Lord God. The second is that we know ourselves—what we are by Him, in kind and in grace. The third is that we know meekly what we are with regard to our sin and our feebleness. And for these three was made all this shewing, as I understand it.

THE SEVENTY-THIRD CHAPTER
THESE REVELATIONS WERE SHOWN TRIPLE-WISE; AND OF A DOUBLE GHOSTLY SURENESS

ALL this blessed teaching of our Lord God was shewed in three ways: that is to say, by bodily sight, and by words formed in my understanding, and by ghostly sight. Of the bodily sight I have told as I saw, as truly as I can. And as regards the words, I have told them just as our Lord shewed them to me. Of the ghostly sight, I have spoken somewhat, but I can never explain it fully. Therefore of this ghostly sight I am moved to say more, as far as God will give me grace.

God shewed two sorts of sickness that we have: The one is impatience or sloth, in that we bear our travail and our pain heavily; the other is despair or doubtful dread, as I shall say afterwards. Sin He shewed in general (in which all special sins are comprehended); but He shewed none but these two in particular. It is these two that most exercise and trouble us, as our Lord shewed me; of which it is His will that we be amended (I mean those men and women who, for God's love, hate sin, and dispose themselves to do God's will.)

WE SHOULD GLADLY BEAR OUR PAINS

By our ghostly blindness, then, and our bodily heaviness we are most inclined to these two. And therefore it is God's will that they be known; and then we should reject them, as we do other sins. And as help against them, our Lord shewed full meekly the patience that He had in His hard passion; and also the joy and the liking that He hath of that passion, for love. And this He shewed as an example, that we should gladly and lightly bear our pains; for that is most pleasing to Him, and of endless profit to us.

And the reason why we are exercised over these things is because of unknowing of love. (For though the three Persons of the blessed Trinity are co-equal, yet the soul had most understanding of Love.) Yea, and it is His will that we have our beholding and our enjoyment in Love. And yet concerning this knowing we are most blind. For some of us believe that God is almighty and may do all; and that He is all-wisdom and can do all; but that He is all-love, and will do all—there we fail.

SIN DESTROYS COMFORT

It is this unknowing that most hindereth God's lovers, as I see it. For even when we begin to hate sin, and to amend us by ordinance of Holy Church, there dwelleth in us a dread that is an hindrance to us, through the beholding of our selves and our sins committed in the past. Because of our sins of every day, because we (or some of us) hold not to our promise, nor keep to the cleanness that our Lord setteth us in, but fall oftentimes into so much wretchedness that it is shame to us to mention it—the beholding of this maketh us so sorrowful and so heavy that we can scarcely see any comfort.

This dread we mistake sometimes for meekness. But it is a foul blindness and a wickedness. And yet we cannot despise it as we do any other sin that we recognize, though it cometh through lack of judgment, and is against truth. It is God's will that, of all the properties of the blessed Trinity, we have the greatest sureness and liking in love. For love maketh might and wisdom full meek to us. For just as, by His courtesy, God forgetteth our sin after the time that we repent us, so it is His will that we forget our sin, in respect of our stupid heaviness, and our doubtful dread.

THE SEVENTY-FOURTH CHAPTER
FOUR SORTS OF DREAD

FOR I have understanding of four sorts of dread. One is that state of fear which cometh upon a man suddenly in his frailty. This dread doeth good, because it helpeth to purge a man, as doth sickness or any other pain that is not sin. All such pains help a man if they are patiently accepted. The second is the dread of pain, by which a man is stirred up and awakened from the sleep of sin. For the man that is hard asleep in sin is not able, at the time, to receive the soft strengthening of the Holy Ghost until he hath felt this fear of pain, of bodily death, and of ghostly enemies. This dread moveth us to seek comfort and mercy of God. And thus this dread helpeth us as giving us an entry, enabling us to come to contrition through the blissful touching of the Holy Ghost.

The third is doubtful dread. In as much as it leadeth to despair, God willeth to have it turned into love in us, by true knowing of love; that is to say, that the bitterness of doubt be turned into the sweetness of kind love, by grace. For it can never please our Lord that His servants doubt in His goodness.

The fourth is reverent dread. There is no dread in us that fully pleaseth God, but reverent dread. It is full soft; for the more it is had, the less it is felt, because of the sweetness of love. Love and dread are brethren; and they are rooted in us by the goodness of our Maker; they shall never be taken from us without end. It belongeth to us, of kind, to love; and of grace, to love; and of kind, to dread; and of grace, to dread.

It belongeth to the Lordship and to the Fatherhood to be dreaded, as it belongeth to the Goodness to be loved. And it belongeth to us that are His servants and His children to dread Him in His Lordship and Fatherhood, as it belongeth to us to love Him in Goodness. And though this reverent dread and love are not both-in-one, but two in property and in working, yet neither of them may be had without the other. And therefore I am sure that he who loveth, dreadeth—though he feels it but little.

ONLY REVERENT DREAD IS HOLY

All dreads, other than reverent dread, which are proffered to us are not truly holy, though they come to us under colour of holiness. And hereby they can be known separately. The dread that maketh us hastily to fly from all that is not good unto our Lord's breast, like the child into its mother's lap, with all our will and with all our mind; knowing our feebleness and our great need, knowing His everlasting goodness and His great love; seeking unto Him only for salvation, cleaving to Him with sure trust—the dread that bringeth us into this working, it is kind and gracious, good and true. And all that is contrary to it, it is either wrong, or is mingled with wrong. Then is this the remedy—to recognize them both, and reject the wrong.

For the kind property of dread, which we have in this life by the gracious working of the Holy Ghost, the same shall be, in heaven, before God, gentle, courteous, and full sweet. And thus we shall, in love, be homely and near to God, and in dread, gentle and courteous to God, both qualities united equally. Desire we then, of our Lord God, to dread Him reverently and love Him meekly and trust in Him mightily. For when we dread Him reverently and love Him meekly, our trust is never in vain.

For the more that we trust and the more mightily that we trust, the more we please and worship our Lord in whom we trust. And if we fail in this reverent dread and meek love (God forbid that we should!), our trust is at once misruled for that time. And therefore we greatly need to pray our Lord for grace, that we may have this reverent dread and meek love, of His gift, in heart and in work. For without this no man can please God.

THE SEVENTY-FIFTH CHAPTER
WE NEED LOVE, LONGING, AND PITY

I SAW that God can do all that we need. These three we need: love, longing, and pity. Pity and love keep us in the time of our need. And the longing in the same love draweth us unto heaven. For God thirsteth to have allman, generally, in Himself. In which thirst He hath drawn up all His holy souls that are now in bliss. And in gaining His living members, ever He draweth up and drinketh; and yet He still thirsteth and longeth.

OF THREE SORTS OF LONGING IN GOD

I saw three sorts of longing in God, all directed to one end. The first is that

He longeth to teach us to know Him and to love Him ever more and more, as is proper and expedient to us. The second is that He longeth to have us up into bliss, as souls are when they are taken out of pain into heaven. The third is, to fill us full of bliss; and that shall be fulfilled on the last day, to last for ever.

For I saw (even as it is known in our faith) that then, pain and sorrow shall be ended in all that shall be saved. And we shall receive not merely the same bliss that souls in heaven had before, but we shall also receive a new bliss, which shall flow plenteously out of God into us, and fill us full. These are the goods which He hath ordained to give us from without-beginning. These goods are treasured and hid in Himself. And unto that time the creature is not powerful or worthy enough to receive them.

A REVERENT DREAD TOWARD GOD

In this we shall see truly the cause of all the deeds that God hath done. And ever more we shall see the cause of all the things that He hath permitted. The bliss and the fulfilment shall be so deep and high that, for wonder and marvel, all creatures shall have towards God a reverent dread so greatly overpassing that which was seen and felt before, that the pillars of heaven shall tremble and quake.

But this manner of trembling and dread shall contain no manner of pain; for it belongeth to the worthy majesty of God thus to be beheld by His creatures, with aweful trembling and quaking—but much more for joy, endlessly marvelling at the greatness of the Maker, and at the least part of all that is made. For the beholding of this maketh the creature marvellously meek and mild.

Wherefore it is God's will, and also it belongeth to us both in kind and in grace, to understand and to know this, desiring this sight and this working. For it leadeth us in the right way, and keepeth us in true life, and oneth us to God. And as good as God is, even so great is He. And as much as it belongeth to His Godhead to be loved, so much it belongeth to His great highness to be dreaded. For this reverent dread is the fairest courtesy that is in heaven, before God's face. And as much as He shall be known and loved, overpassing what He is now; in so much He shall be dreaded, overpassing what He is now. Wherefore it needs must be that all heaven and all earth shall tremble and quake, when the pillars shall tremble and quake.

THE SEVENTY-SIXTH CHAPTER
A LOVING SOUL HATETH SIN FOR ITS VILENESS MORE THAN ALL THE PAIN OF HELL

I SPEAK but little of this reverent dread, for I hope it may be seen in the matter told before; but I am certain that our Lord shewed me no souls except those that dread Him. And well I know that the soul that truly taketh the teaching of the Holy Ghost hateth sin for its vileness and horribleness more than it doth all the pain that is in hell. For the soul that beholdeth the goodness of our Lord Jesus hateth no hell but sin, as I see it. And therefore it is God's will that we should know sin, and pray earnestly and labor willingly, and seek teaching meekly so that we fall not blindly therein.

OF COMPASSION FOR MEN'S SINS

The soul that will be at rest, when other men's sins come to mind, should flee from them as from the pains of hell. For the beholding of other men's sins maketh, as it were, a thick mist before the eye of the soul; so that we cannot, for the time, see the fairness of God—unless we behold them with contrition along with the sinner, with compassion on Him and with holy desire to God for Him. For without this they annoy and trouble and hinder the soul that beholdeth them. This is my understanding of the shewing of the compassion.

OF THE HIGHEST WISDOM AND MOST FOLLY

In this blissful shewing of our Lord, I have understanding of two contraries: One is, that highest wisdom that a man may achieve in this life; the other is, the most folly. The highest wisdom is for a creature to do according to the will and counsel of His highest sovereign Friend. This blessed Friend is Jesus; and it is His will and counsel that we hold us with Him, and fasten us, homely, to Him evermore—in what state so ever we be. For whether we be foul or clean, we are ever one in His loving. Neither for weal nor for woe is it His will that we ever flee from Him; but because of our changeability we fall often into sin.

Then are we affected by the promptings of our enemy, and by our own folly and blindness. For they say thus: "Thou knowest well thou art a wretch and a sinner, and also untrue, for thou keepest not thy covenant. Thou hast promised oftentimes our Lord that thou shalt do better. And immediately thou fallest again into the same sins—especially into sloth and the wasting of time." (For this is the beginning of sin, as I see it, particularly in creatures that have given themselves to serve our Lord by inward beholding of His blissful goodness.) And this maketh us adread to appear before our courteous Lord.

Then it is that our enemy will abash us with this false dread of our wretchedness and the pain that he threateneth us with. For it is his intent to make us so heavy and so mournful in this that we let pass out of mind the blissful beholding of our everlasting Friend.

THE SEVENTY-SEVENTH CHAPTER
OF THE ENMITY OF THE FIEND, WHO LOSETH MORE IN OUR UPRISING THAN HE WINNETH BY OUR FALLING

OUR good Lord shewed the enmity of the fiend; whereby I understood that all that is contrary to love and peace is of the fiend and his company. And it belongeth to our feebleness and our folly to fall; and it belongeth to the mercy and grace that we have of the Holy Ghost to rise to more joy. And if our enemy winneth aught from us by our falling (and that is his pleasure), he loseth many times more in our rising through charity and meekness.

This glorious rising is to him such great sorrow and pain (for the hatred that he hath to our souls) that he burneth continually in envy. And all this sorrow that he would make us have shall turn against himself. And for this reason it was that our Lord scorned him, and shewed that he shall be scorned; and this made me mightily to laugh.

OF THE REMEDY
FOR MAN'S PREDICAMENT

This then is the remedy—that we be aware of our wretchedness, and flee to our Lord. For ever the more needy that we be, the more speedful it is for us to touch Him. And let us say thus, in our meaning: "I know well that I have deserved pain. But our Lord is almighty, and may punish me mightily, and He is all-wisdom, and can punish me wisely; and He is all-goodness, and loveth me tenderly." And in this beholding it is speedful to us to abide.

For it is a full lovely meekness in a sinful soul, wrought by the mercy and grace of the Holy Ghost, when we are willing, willfully and gladly, to take the scourging and chastising that our Lord Himself will give us. And this shall be full tender and full easy, if only we hold us pleased with Him and with all His works.

But concerning the penance that a man should take upon Himself—this was not shewed me; that is to say, it was not shewed me specifically. But this other was shewed, specially and highly and with a look full of love— that we should meekly and patiently bear and suffer the penance that God giveth us, with mind of His blessed passion. For when we have mind of His blessed passion, with pity and love, then we suffer with Him like as did His friends that saw it.

And this was shewed in the thirteenth Revelation, near the beginning where it speaketh of pity. For He saith: "Accuse not thyself that thy tribulation and thy woe is all thy fault. For it is not My will that thou shouldst be heavy and sorrowful without discretion. For I tell thee: Howsoever thou doest, thou shalt have woe. And therefore it is My will that thou wisely know the penance which thou art in continually—that thou mayest meekly take it for thy penance. And then shalt thou truly see that all this thy living is profitable penance." This place is a prison; this life is a penance. And in the remedy for it, He willeth that we rejoice. The remedy is that our Lord is with us, keeping us, and leading us to fullness of joy.

THE LORD IS OUR BLISS

For this is endless joy to us, in our Lord's meaning, that He that shall be our bliss when we come there—He is our keeper while we are here, our way and our heaven in true love and faithful trust. And of this He gave understanding in all, and especially in the shewing of His passion, where He made me mightily to choose Him for my heaven. Flee we to our Lord, and we shall be comforted. Touch we Him, and we shall be made clean. Cling we to Him, and we shall be secure and safe from all manner of perils. For our courteous Lord willeth that we be as homely with Him as heart can think or soul can desire.

But we must beware lest we take this homeliness so recklessly as to forsake courtesy. Our Lord Himself is sovereign Homeliness. But as homely as He is, even so courteous He is; for He is very Courtesy. And the blessed creatures that shall be in heaven with Him without end—these He will have like unto Himself in all things. To be like our Lord perfectly, this is our very salvation and our full bliss. And if we know not now we shall bear ourselves, let us desire this of our Lord, and He shall teach us; for this is to His own liking and His worship. Blessed may He be!

THE SEVENTY-EIGHTH CHAPTER
OUR LORD WILLETH THAT WE KNOW OF FOUR MANNERS OF GOODNESS THAT HE DOETH TO US

OUR Lord of His mercy sheweth us our sin and our feebleness, by the sweet gracious light of Himself. For our sin is so foul and horrible that He, of His courtesy, willeth not to shew it us except by the light of His mercy. It is His will that we have knowing of four things: The first is that He is the ground, of whom we have all our life and our being; the second is that He keepeth us mightily and mercifully during the time that we are in our sin, amongst all the enemies that come full fiercely upon us (we are so much the more in peril because we give them occasion, and know not our own need); the third is how courteously He keepeth us, and maketh us to know that we go amiss; the fourth is how steadfastly He abideth us, and changeth not His regard.

For it is His will that we be converted and oned to Him in love, as He is to us. And thus, by His gracious knowing, we can see that our sin is profitable, without despairing. For truly we need to see it; and by the sight we should be made ashamed of ourselves, and broken down with regard to our pride and presumption. For it behoveth us truly to see that of ourselves we are right naught but sin and wretchedness.

GOD GRACIOUSLY REVEALS OUR SINS TO US

And thus, by the sight of the less which our Lord sheweth us, the greater, which we see not, is laid waste. For He, of His courtesy, tempereth the sight to us. For it is so foul and horrible that we could not endure to see it as it is. And thus, by this meek knowing, through sorrow and contrition, we shall be broken off from all things that are not our Lord. And then shall our blessed Saviour perfectly heal us and one us to Himself.

This breaking and this healing our Lord meaneth for men in general. For He that is highest and nearest to God, can see Himself as sinful and needy as I do. And I, that am the least and lowest of those that shall be saved, can be comforted along with Him that is highest. Even so hath our Lord oned us in charity. When He shewed me that I should sin, for the joy that I had in beholding Him, I did not attend readily to that shewing. But our courteous Lord let it rest there, and desired to teach me no further, until He gave me the grace and will to attend.

And here I was taught that though we be lifted high into contemplation by the special gift of our Lord, yet it behoveth us therewith to have knowing and sight of our sin and of our feebleness. For without this knowing we cannot be safe. And also I saw that we cannot have this knowing of ourselves, or of our ghostly enemies (for they do not wish us so much good; and if it depended on their will, we should never see it till our dying day). Thus we are much indebted to God that He desireth Himself, for love, to shew it us in the time of mercy and of grace.

THE SEVENTY-NINTH CHAPTER
WE ARE TAUGHT CONCERNING OUR OWN SIN AND NOT OUR NEIGHBORS'

ALSO in this I had more understanding of that shewing where He shewed me that I should sin. I had taken it simply as referring to my own single person; for I was not otherwise prompted in that time. But by the high gracious comfort of our Lord that followed after, I saw that His meaning was for man in general, that is to say all-man, which is sinful and shall be unto the last day. Of which man I am a member (as I hope) by the mercy of God. For the blessed comfort that I saw is large enough for all.

And there was I learned that I should look at my own sin and not other men's, except it be for comfort or help of my even-christians. And also, in the same shewing where I saw that I should sin, there was I learned to be full of dread for unsureness of myself. For I know not how I shall fall; and I know not the measure nor the greatness of my sin. For that would I have found out, full of dread; and thereto I had no answer.

THE ENDLESSNESS AND IMMUTABILITY OF GOD'S LOVE

Also our courteous Lord, in that same time, shewed full sweetly and full mightily the endlessness and immutability of His love; and also His great goodness and His gracious inward keeping—that the love of Him and of our souls shall never be separated unto without-end. And thus in the dread I have occasion for meekness, which saveth me from presumption; and in the blessed shewing of love I have matter of true comfort and of joy, which saveth me from despair.

All this homely shewing of our courteous Lord is a lovely lesson and a sweet gracious teaching from Himself, in the comforting of our soul. For it is His will that we know, by the sweetness of the homely love of Him, that all that we see or feel, within or without, which is contrary to this, that it is of the enemy and not of God. So that if we be prompted to be the more careless in our living or in the keeping of our heart because we have knowing of this plenteous love; then we need greatly to beware of this prompting. If it come, it is untrue, and greatly ought we to hate it; for it hath no resemblance to God's will.

GOD WILLS THAT WE HASTILY TURN UNTO HIM

And when we are fallen by frailty or blindness, then our courteous Lord toucheth us, prompteth us and keepeth us. And then willeth He that we see our wretchedness, and meekly acknowledge it. But it is not His will that we busy ourselves greatly about our accusing, nor that we be too full of wretchedness about ourselves. Rather He willeth that we hastily turn unto Him; for He standeth all alone and abideth us continually in our mourning and moaning, until we come. He hath haste to have us turn to Him; for we are His joy and His delight, and He is the health of our life. (Where I say "He standeth all alone," I speak not of the blessed company in heaven, but I speak of His office and working here in earth—according to the manner of the shewing.)

THE EIGHTIETH CHAPTER
BY THREE THINGS GOD IS WORSHIPPED AND WE SAVED

BY three things man standeth in this life; by which three God is worshipped, and we are sped, kept and saved. The first is use of man's kindly reason; the second is the common teaching of Holy Church; the third is the inward gracious working of the Holy Ghost—and these three are all of one God. God is the ground of our kindly reason; and God is the teaching of Holy Church; and God is the Holy Ghost. And all are sundry gifts, to which He willeth that we have great regard, attending thereto. For they work in us continually, all together; they are great things. Of which greatness He willeth that we have knowing here—the ABC of them, as it were. That is to say, that we may have a little knowing of that whose fullness we shall have in heaven, which is for our profit.

CHRIST DOETH ALL

We know in our faith that God alone took our kind, and none but He; and furthermore that Christ alone did all the great works that belong to our salvation, and none but He. And even so He alone doeth now, in the last end; that is to say, He dwelleth here in us, and ruleth us and guideth us in this life and bringeth us to His bliss. And thus shall He do, as long as any soul is in earth, that shall come to heaven; and so far forth, that if there were no such soul in earth but one, He would be with that one, all alone, until He had brought it up to His bliss.

I believe and understand the ministrations of Holy Angels, as theologians tell; but this was not shewed to me. For Himself is nearest and meekest, highest and lowest, and doeth all— and not only all—that we need; but also He doeth all that is worshipful to our joy in heaven. And where I say He abideth us in our mourning and moaning, this meaneth all the true feeling that we have in ourselves of contrition and of compassion, and all the mourning and moaning that we are not oned with our Lord. And in as much as it is profitable it is Christ in us. And though some of us feel it seldom, it passeth never from Christ, till what time He hath brought us out of all our woe. For love suffereth Him never to be without pity.

And what time that we fall into sin, and leave mind of Him and keeping of our own soul; then beareth Christ, alone, all the charge of us. And thus standeth He, mourning and moaning. Then it belongeth to us, for reverence and kindness, to turn us quickly to our Lord, and leave Him not alone. He is here alone with us all. That is to say, He is here only for us. And what time I am a stranger to Him by sin, despair or sloth, then I let my Lord stand alone, in as much as He is in me. And thus it fareth with all of us who are sinners. And though it be so—that oftentimes we do thus—yet His goodness suffereth us never to be alone; but lastingly He is with us, and tenderly He excuseth, and ever shieldeth us from blame in His sight.

THE EIGHTY-FIRST CHAPTER
THIS BLESSED WOMAN SAW GOD IN DIVERSE MANNERS

OUR good Lord shewed Himself to His creature in diverse manners, both in heaven and in earth. But I saw Him take no place but in man's soul. He shewed Himself in earth in the sweet incarnation and His blessed passion; and in another manner He shewed Himself in earth—where I saw God in a point; and in another manner He shewed himself in earth—thus as it were in pilgrimage. (That is to say, He is here with us, leading us, and shall be, until He hath brought us all to His bliss, in heaven.) He shewed Himself diverse times reigning, as it is aforesaid, but principally in man's soul. He hath taken there His resting-place and His worshipful city. Out of which worshipful see He shall never rise nor remove, without-end.

OF LIFE AS PENANCE

Marvellous and stately is the place where the Lord dwelleth. And therefore He willeth that we readily turn us to His gracious touching, having more joy in His all-love than sorrow in our frequent fallings. For of anything that we may do, it is most worship to Him that we live, in our penance, gladly and merrily for His love. For He beholdeth us to tenderly that He seeth all our living here to be a penance. For the kind longing in us for Him is a lasting penance in us. Which penance He worketh in us, and mercifully helpeth us to bear it.

For His love maketh Him to long; His wisdom and His truth, with His righteousness, maketh Him to suffer us here; and in this manner He willeth to see it in us. For this is our kindly penance, as to my sight. This penance never goeth from us till what time we be fulfilled, and have Him for our meed. And therefore He willeth that

we set our hearts in our out-passing; that is to say, from the pain that we feel into the bliss that we trust to have.

THE EIGHTY-SECOND CHAPTER
GOD BEHOLDETH THE MOANING OF THE SOUL WITH PITY AND NOT WITH BLAME

BUT here shewed our courteous Lord the mourning and the moaning of our soul, meaning thus: "I know well thou willest to live for My love alone, gladly suffering all the penance that may come to thee. But inasmuch as thou livest not without sin, therefore thou art heavy and sorrowful. And if thou couldst live without sin, thou wouldst suffer, for My love, all the woe that might come to thee. And this is sooth. But be not too much grieved with the sin that falleth to thee against thy will."

And here I understand how the Lord beheld the servant with pity and not with blame. For this passing life asketh not to live all without sin. He loveth us endlessly; and we sin habitually; and He sheweth it us full mildly; and then we sorrow and mourn with discretion, turning us into the beholding of His mercy, cleaving to His love and to His goodness; seeing that He is our medicine, realizing that we do naught but sin. And thus by the meekness that we get, in this sight of our sin, faithfully knowing His everlasting love, Him thanking and Him praising, we please Him. "I love thee and thou lovest Me, and our love shall never be parted in two."

WE ARE KEPT IN GOD'S LOVE

And all this was shewed in ghostly understanding, seeing this blessed word "I keep thee full surely." And by the great desire that I saw in our blessed Lord, that we should live in this manner—that is to say, in longing and in enjoying, as all this lesson of love sheweth, thereby I understood that all that is contrary to this is not of Him, but it is of enmity. And it is His will that we know it, by the sweet gracious light of His kind love.

If there is any living on earth such as is continually kept from falling, I know not of it; for it was not shewed me. But this was shewed: That in falling and in rising we are preciously kept in the same love. For in the beholding of God we fall not, and in the beholding of ourselves we stand not. And both these be truth, as I see it. But the beholding of our Lord God is the higher truth. Then are we much indebted to Him, that He willeth, in this life, to shew us this high truth.

It is full profitable to us that we see these both at once. For the higher beholding keepeth us in ghostly joy, and true enjoying in God. The other, that is, the lower beholding, keepeth us in dread, and maketh us ashamed of ourselves. But our good Lord willeth ever that we hold us much more in the beholding of the higher, and yet not leave the knowing of the lower, until the time that we be brought up above, where we shall have our Lord Jesus to our meed, and be filled full of joy and bliss without end.

THE EIGHTY-THIRD CHAPTER
OF THREE PROPERTIES IN GOD, LIFE, LOVE, AND LIGHT

I HAD, in a measure, touching, sight and feeling in three properties of God. In which the strength and the effect of all Revelation standeth. And they were seen in every shewing; and most directly in the twelfth, where it is said often: "I it am." The properties are these: life, love, and light. In life is marvellous homeliness; in love is gentle courtesy; and in light is endless kindhood. These three properties were seen in one goodness; into which goodness my reason would be oned—cleaving to it with all its might. I beheld with reverent dread, highly marvelling in the sight and in the feeling of the sweet accord—that our reason is in God, understanding that it is the highest gift that we have received, and it is grounded in Kind.

Our faith is a light, kindly coming from our endless Day that is our Father God. In which light our Mother Christ and our good Lord the Holy Ghost lead us, in this passing life. This light is measured discerningly, standing unto us, at need, in the night. The light is the cause of our life, the night is the cause of our pain and all our woe. For which woe we deserve endless meed and thanks from God. For we, with mercy and grace, willfully know and believe our light, going therein wisely and mightily. And at the end of woe, suddenly our eye shall be opened, and in clearness of sight our light shall be full. Which light is God, our Maker, Father, and Holy Ghost in Christ Jesus our Savior. Thus I saw and understood that our faith is our light in our night. Which light is God, our endless Day.

THE EIGHTY-FOURTH CHAPTER
CHARITY IS THIS LIGHT

THIS light is charity; and the measuring of this light is done to us profitably by the wisdom of God. For neither is the light so large that we can see clearly our blissful day, nor is it all shut out from us. But it is a light such as we may live in profitably with labour—deserving the worshipful thanks of God. And this was seen in the sixth shewing, where He saith: "I thank thee for thy service and for thy labour."

OF FAITH, HOPE, AND CHARITY

Thus charity keepeth us in faith and in hope. And faith and hope lead us into charity. And at the end, all shall be charity. I had three manners of understandings in this light of charity. The first is charity unmade; the second is charity made; the third is charity given. Charity unmade is God; charity made is our soul in God; charity given is the virtue. And that is a gracious gift, in the working of which we love God for himself and ourselves in God and all that God loveth, for God.

THE EIGHTY-FIFTH CHAPTER
GOD SUFFERETH HIS CHOSEN
TO BE HURT IN A WAY THAT THEIR
BLISS MIGHT BE LESSENED

AND in this sight I marvelled highly. For notwithstanding our simpleness and our blindness here, our Lord endlessly beholdeth us, rejoicing in this working. And we can please Him best of all by believing this truly, and rejoicing with Him and in Him. For as truly as we shall be in the bliss of God without end, Him praising and thanking; so truly we have been in the foreknowledge of God, loved and known in His endless purpose from withoutbeginning. In which unbegun love He made us, and in the same love He keep-

eth us, and never suffereth us to be hurt in a way that our bliss might be lessened.

And therefore, when judgment is given, and we are all brought up above, then shall we clearly see in God the secrets which now are hid from us. And then none of us shall be prompted to say of anything: "Lord, if it had been thus, it had been well"; but we shall all say with one voice: "Lord, blessed may Thou be! For it is thus, and it is well. Now we see truly that all thing is done as was Thine ordinance before anything was made."

THE EIGHTY-SIXTH CHAPTER
IT WAS ANSWERED THAT THE CAUSE OF
THIS SHEWING WAS LOVE: WHICH LOVE
MAY JESUS GRANT US

THIS book is begun by God's gift and His grace; but it is not yet performed, as I see it. For charity's sake, let us pray all together with God's working, thanking, trusting, enjoying. For it is thus that our good Lord willeth us to pray, according to the understanding that I took in all His meaning, and in the sweet words that He said full merrily, "I am ground of thy beseeching." For I saw truly and understood in our Lord's meaning that He shewed it because He will have it known more than it is. In which knowing He will give us grace to love Him and cleave to Him. For He beheld His heavenly treasure with so great love on earth, that He willeth to give more light and solace in heavenly joy, in drawing our hearts from the sorrow and darkness which we are in.

And from the time that it was shewed, I desired oftentimes to know what was our Lord's meaning in it.

And fifteen years after, and more, I was answered in ghostly understanding: "What, wouldst thou know thy Lord's meaning in this thing? Know it well. Love was His meaning. Who sheweth it thee? Love. Wherefore sheweth He it thee? For Love. Hold thee therein. Thou shalt know more in the same, but thou shalt never know other therein, without end."

OF GOD'S UNENDING LOVE

Thus was I learned that love is our Lord's meaning. And I saw full surely in this, and in all, that before God made us, He loved us. Which love was never slaked, nor ever shall be. And in this love He hath done all His works. And in this love He hath made all things profitable to us. And in this love our life is everlasting. In our making we had beginning, but the love wherein He made us was in Him from without-beginning. In which love we have our beginning. And all this shall we see in God without end.

Thanks be to God.

Here endeth the Book of Revelations of Julian, the Anchoress of Norwich. On whose soul may God have mercy.

COLOPHON

I PRAY almighty God that this book come only to the hands of them that will be His faithful lovers, and to them that will submit them to the faith of Holy Church, and obey the wholesome understanding and teaching of men that be of virtuous life, sober years and profound learning. For this Revelation is high divinity, and high wisdom; wherefore it cannot dwell with Him who is a thrall to sin and to the Devil.

And beware that thou take not one thing and leave another, according to thy affection and liking—for that is the way of an heretic; but take everything with other, truly understanding that all is according to Holy Scripture, and grounded in the same. This Jesus, our very love, light and truth, shall shew to all clean souls that, with meekness, ask perseveringly of Him this wisdom.

And thou to whom this book shall come, thank highly and heartily our Saviour Christ Jesus, that He made these shewings and revelations for thee and to thee, of His endless love, mercy and goodness, for thine and our safe guide and conduct to everlasting bliss. The which may Jesus grant us. Amen.

Here end the sublime and wonderful Revelations of the unutterable love of God in Jesus Christ, vouchsafed to a dear lover of His, and, in her, to all His dear friends and lovers; whose hearts, like hers, burn in the love of our dearest Jesus.

The
Imitation
of Christ

Thomas à Kempis

Introduction

BY THE LATE fourteenth century, nearly everyone noticed a crisis in piety. In many parts of Christian Europe, churches were open, but few people attended. Despite their deep spiritual longings, many believers found it difficult, if not impossible, to find God within the institutional expressions of Christendom. Religion and all its trappings did not satisfy.

There was plenty of blame to go around for this widespread spiritual lethargy. For nearly a hundred years, the church's hierarchy had been in shambles. During the "Babylonian Captivity of the Church" (1309–1377), the papacy resided in Avignon and was controlled by the French crown. Then, during the "Great Papal Schism" (1378–1417), the Church was faced with the spectacle of having to choose between two (or three) rival popes at a time. High church offices were available to the highest bidder: By paying off the right people, wealthy patrons could even get their teenaged sons or nephews appointed as bishops or cardinals. Laypeople complained about bishops who were more interested in fox hunting than faithful service and local priests who did not know enough Latin to say mass properly.

Even the church's formidable theological establishment showed signs of serious fracturing. The magnificent achievement of Thomas Aquinas (1225–1274), who synthesized theology and philosophy into the middle age's most impressive theological system, was openly challenged by other theologians (John Duns Scotus and William Occam, to name just two) who denied that revelation and reason were always reconcilable. The more the theologians disputed, the denser theology became, until finally the experts seemed paralyzed by their subtle distinctions and their technical vocabulary. Many people concluded that this kind of "scholastic" theology actually undercut authentic Christian piety, rather than supported it.

Under these circumstances, it is not surprising that by the fifteenth century, the cries for change were everywhere. While many reformers attempted to change the church's structure and doctrine, others sought a reformation of its piety. Probably the best example of the latter was the work of the Brethren of the Common Life, from which came Thomas à Kempis's *The Imitation of Christ.* Thanks to the new technology of the printing press, Thomas's book of piety became one of the world's first best sellers and without question, the most popular book of devotion in the history of the Catholic Church. Since it was first published in 1471, it has gone through over six thousand separate editions, in dozens of languages. Some have even claimed that in the last five hundred years, it has been the most widely read book in the world, with the exception of the Bible.

THOMAS À KEMPIS (1380–1471)

Thomas Hammerlein was born in 1380 in the small Dutch town of Kempen, which was located not far from Cologne. His parents were able to send him and his older brother, John, to a school in the nearby town of Deventer which was run by a reform-minded group of laymen called the Brethren of the Common Life.

The schools of the Brethren of the Common Life became famous as places where scholarship and devotion went together. But it is important to realize that the work of the Brethren followed a century of intense and varied reforming activity. For example, the "Conciliar Movement" tried to break the stalemate of the papal schism by returning to the much earlier practice of letting church councils have the final say in big disputes. Some "conciliarists" even hoped that regularly-called church councils might exercise permanent authority over the popes. Though a number of church councils were held (Pisa in 1409; Constance in 1414–1418; Pavia and Siena in 1423; Basel, Ferrara, and Florence in 1431–1445), the conciliar movement ultimately failed to achieve its goals; but it did prove that many people were ready for radical change in the way the church was run.

Similarly, outspoken reformers like John Wycliffe (1328?–1384) in England and John Huss (1369?–1415) in Bohemia challenged papal authority and claimed that if popes did not conform to the Bible in their teaching and behavior, they should not be obeyed. Though Wycliffe, Huss, and the conciliarists had much in common, there were limits beyond which even church councils would not go. For the most part, conciliarists wanted to stop the papacy's abuse of power and the clergy's misconduct, and they showed lit-

tle toleration of doctrinal deviation in other matters. Years before, when Wycliffe attacked the church's sacramental system, he lost support from those who had applauded his attacks on a corrupt papacy. Huss, who agreed with Wycliffe on most things, had also criticized the sale of indulgences and his own king's military alliance with the pope. In the end, politics and theology conspired at the Council of Constance, which condemned both men. Huss was burned at the stake in 1415; and because Wycliffe had already died in 1384, officials had to disinter his body to carry out the council's order. They burned his corpse and threw the ashes in the Swift River. Of course, burning heretics never puts a stop to heresy. In England the Lollards continued to preach Wycliffe's message; and in Bohemia, some of Huss's followers took up arms and actually held off invading papal armies for years.

No matter how hard some resisted, reform was in the wind; and nothing could stop it. In 1490 a fiery Dominican friar named Girolamo Savonarola began preaching reform in Florence, Italy. He challenged not only the abuses of the church's hierarchy, but the worldliness of the Florentines. Claiming the gift of prophecy, Savonarola gathered a huge popular following: When he urged the city to give up its "vanities," hundreds of citizens brought their jewelry, wigs, party dresses, and games of chance and tossed them on a huge bonfire in the city square. It was inevitable that Savonarola made many enemies. The pope excommunicated him in 1496; and the upper classes deeply resented his attacks on them and their financial interests. In 1498 a mob took him prisoner, beat him, and turned him over to the authorities who tortured him to get a confession of wrongdoing. A church court condemned him as a heretic. This time the bonfire was for him. Exercising an odd kind of mercy, the authorities hanged him before consigning his body to the flames.

Not all efforts at reform were so dangerous. A reforming spirit was evident in the "new learning," which has also been called the Renaissance ("new birth") of classical knowledge. Put off by the convolutions of scholastic theology, many scholars in the fourteenth and fifteenth centuries simply by-passed it and looked to ancient Greece and Rome for their inspiration. They were struck by the optimistic emphases on human dignity and potential in classical literature, art, and architecture and decided to emulate it. Because of this return to the study of what many called the "humanities," the new learning was often called "humanism." Though some humanists were eager to depart from the Christian tradition, others used humanism to deepen their Christian commitments. The farther north in Europe one went, the more Christian the humanism became.

For Christian humanists, then, the "classics" meant the writings of the church fathers and the Greek New Testament. When they compared the beliefs and practices of the early church and the teachings of the Bible to those of the church in their own day, the humanists found glaring differences. For example, early Christianity was doctrinally leaner, more committed to the simplicity and humility of Jesus, and less interested in wealth and temporal power. Many people were shocked to discover that a number of the most common practices of medieval Christianity (for example, the veneration of relics and the sale of indulgences) were not found in either the New Testament or the post-apostolic church.

Erasmus (1466?–1536), a Dutchman who taught at Oxford, is often called the "Prince of the Humanists." He used satire to criticize the church's extravagance and shortcomings (*The Praise of Folly*, 1511), published a critically acclaimed Greek New Testament (1516), and called for a return to the simple "philosophy of Christ," by which he meant the original teachings of Jesus, minus all later additions. In many ways, the humanists' catalog of complaints against the church looked very much like that of the Protestant Reformers, whose lives often overlapped with theirs. As one historian has observed, "Erasmus laid the egg; but Luther [who started the Protestant Reformation in Germany] hatched it!"

Erasmus was a product of one of the Brethren of the Common Life's schools, where scholarship and a mild form of mysticism went hand in hand. We have already seen how Bernard of Clairvaux and Julian of Norwich had life-changing mystical encounters with God. But they were not the only ones. In the fourteenth and fifteenth centuries, many Christians found in mysticism a more direct way to God than seemed possible in the thoroughly institutionalized system of the church.

The Brethren grew out of an earlier movement of German mystics called the Friends of God. Men like Meister Eckhart (1260–1327), Henry Suso

(1295?–1366), John Tauler (c.1300–1381), and John of Ruysbroeck (1293–1381) were extremely popular preachers who called for people to deny themselves, repent of their sins, and follow in Christ's footsteps by imitating his humility, love, and devotion to the Father. It was out of this circle of Friends that the *German Theology* was written. It served as an important textbook in the fourteenth and fifteenth centuries to spread the teachings of German mysticism and deepen piety among the devout.

John of Ruysbroeck carried German mysticism up the Rhine River into Holland. Though quite enthusiastic and emotional, his preaching had a practical side to it. Unlike some mystics, he recognized that not everyone was cut out for the kind of intense contemplation most mystics engaged in.

Ruysbroeck quickly attracted a following among the Dutch. One of his students, Gerhard Groote (1340–1384), followed his lead and developed a more practical form of mysticism that combined love for God with service to others. His approach came to be called the "new devotion." In 1384 Groote and a friend, Florentius Radewyn (1350–1400), founded the Brethren of the Common Life in Deventer, Holland. The Brethren was an informal lay organization, not a new monastic order, at least not at first. Instead of following a complicated monastic rule, Groote urged his followers to adopt a simple, apostolic life-style; dress alike in gray robes; live together in "brother houses"; and help each other to imitate Jesus as much as possible. Instead of supporting themselves by begging, the Brethren taught school and copied old manuscripts.

The movement spread rapidly, mainly through its schools. Their students came from all walks of life and went out to serve in both secular and religious vocations. Students were taught to think critically and to seek purity of life. It did not take long for the Brethren schools to become centers of piety, scholarship, and reform.

All kinds of people responded to the Brethren's insistence that a pure life was necessary for higher religious experience. They liked the emphasis on religion as voluntary and self-directed. Fearing such independence, the Bishop of Utrecht tried to stop the Brethren of the Common Life by forbidding Gerhard Groote to preach. Deeply disappointed by the church's opposition, Groote died of the plague shortly thereafter; but his movement could not be stopped.

Thomas à Kempis was, therefore, part of a long-standing reform tradition. He worked hard at the Brethren school in Deventer. Under the strict discipline of his teacher, he became a good Latin and Scripture scholar and an accomplished copyist. When he was about twenty, he entered the brother house at Mount St. Agnes near Zwolle, which had become quite monastic after the Brothers joined forces with some Augustinian Canons. After a six-year novitiate, he formally entered the order; then, after another eight years, he became a priest. He remained at Mount St. Agnes for the rest of his life. For over seventy years, he performed the duties of a member of the community. He cared for the sick, took years to make a single copy of the Scriptures, and for a while supervised the training of novices. After fulfilling a number of different responsibilities in the monastery, he died in 1471, at the age of ninety-one. Shortly after his death, the book was published that made him and the "new devotion" widely known.

Though Thomas's name has been identified with *The Imitation of Christ* since its publication in 1471, many scholars have questioned his authorship. A number of other possibilities have been suggested: Walter Hilton, the English author of *Scale of Perfection;* Bernard of Clairvaux; John Gerson of the University of Paris; and Gerhard Groote. Though it is certain that Thomas did not actually write all of the material in *The Imitation of Christ,* there is no compelling reason to doubt that he was responsible for the final work. Most likely, the book as we have it today is a combination of materials Thomas wrote himself and materials he collected from others (mainly Gerhard Groote?), though by now it is hard for modern readers to tell which is which.

The work is divided into four parts. The First Book includes preparatory instructions for living the spiritual life. Chapters I–XVI are written for all Christians; while chapters XVII–XXI are mainly for those in religious communities. Chapters XXII–XXV focus on human misery, the certainty of death, the coming judgment, and the "zealous amendment of our whole life."

The Second Book contains general admonitions on the devotional life, centered on the person of Christ. "Give, therefore, place to Christ and refuse entrance to all others. When thou hast Christ, thou art rich, and has sufficient. He shall be thy provider and faithful watchman in all things, so that thou hast no need to trust in men, for men soon change and swiftly pass away, but Christ remaineth for ever and standeth by us firmly even to the end."[1] Another important theme is the "Royal Way of the Holy Cross" (ch. XII), which emphasizes the importance of suffering in the Christian life.

In the Third Book, the main theme is "inward consolation." Thomas examines a number of issues, including the power of love (chs. V–VI), the importance of humility (chs. VII–VIII), the dangers of success (chs. XXXIX–XLV), what to do when others oppose you (ch. XLVI), and the supremacy of grace (chs. LV–LIX). "I had rather be poor for Thy sake, than rich without Thee. I choose rather to be a pilgrim upon the earth with Thee than without Thee to possess heaven. Where Thou art, there is heaven; and where Thou are not, behold there death and hell."[2]

The Fourth Book concentrates on Holy Communion and the importance of spiritual preparation for priests who serve it and laypeople who receive it. "And although I be unworthy to have all those feelings of devotion, yet do I offer Thee the whole affection of my heart, even as though I alone had all those most grateful inflamed desires. Yea, also, whatsoever things a pious mind is able to conceive and long for, all these with the deepest veneration and inward fervor do I offer and present unto Thee. I desire to reserve nothing unto myself, but freely and entirely to offer myself and all that I have unto Thee for a sacrifice."[3]

The Imitation of Christ, then, is a collection of spiritual sayings on a variety of themes. Thomas quoted the Bible most of all—mainly the Psalms, the words of Jesus, and the epistles of Paul—but he also used quotations from Augustine, Bernard of Clairvaux, and a number of the German mystics, including Eckhart, Tauler, Suso, and Ruysbroeck. Because of such a variety of sources, it is difficult to generalize about the book's content; but it is possible to detect a point of view. For Thomas à Kempis, the Christian life consisted chiefly in who we are, not just what we know or believe. While Thomas was not indifferent to theological orthodoxy, he clearly rejected the approach of the scholastic theologians. "What doth it profit thee to enter into deep discussion concerning the Holy Trinity, if thou lack humility, and be thus displeasing to the Trinity? For verily it is not deep words that make a man holy and upright; it is a good life which maketh a man dear to God. I had rather feel contrition than be skilful in the definition thereof. If thou knewest the whole Bible, and the sayings of all the philosophers, what should all this profit thee without the love and grace of God?"[4]

Faith is more likely to come to the simple believer than the well-trained scholar. "God walketh with the simple, revealeth Himself to the humble, giveth understanding to babes, openeth the sense to pure minds, and hideth grace from the curious and proud. Human reason is weak and may be deceived; but true faith cannot be deceived."[5]

Here, then, is an approach open to all, not just the experts. To experience the ultimate good in God, people need to deny themselves and recognize that by themselves they are powerless to please God. Following Augustine's lead, Thomas taught that human nature is fallen: "For being fallen through the first man Adam, and corrupted through sin, the punishment of this stain descended upon all men; so that Nature itself, which was framed good and right by Thee, is now used to express the vice and infirmity of corrupted Nature; because its motion left unto itself draweth men away to evil and to lower things. For the little power which remaineth is as it were one spark lying hid in the ashes."[6]

Thus God's grace is necessary for salvation; but imitators of Christ must strive with all their might to deny themselves and follow him. "My *Son*, thou canst not possess perfect liberty unless thou altogether deny thyself. All they are enslaved who are possessors of riches, they who love themselves, the selfish, the curious, the restless; those who ever seek after soft things, and not after the things of Jesus Christ; those who continually plan and devise that which will not stand. For whatsoever cometh not of God shall perish. Hold fast the short and complete saying, 'Renounce all things, and thou shalt find all things; give up thy lust, and thou shalt find rest'."[7]

The Imitation of Christ has been criticized for its individualistic approach to religion: Nowhere does Thomas point to Christ's teaching about serving others, feeding the hungry, or applying the gospel to problems outside the self. While this criticism is certainly true, one should remember that he wrote the book primarily to help novices and others who sought to examine their inner lives.

The book intended to promote self-examination, not a life of action.

Similarly, sometimes later Protestants have wished that Thomas could have given more attention to faith. Though he wrote often about God's grace and the necessity of faith for salvation, Thomas never quite put them together the way Protestants would later on: that we are saved by God's grace *through* faith in Christ alone, apart from works—even good religious works. But then, one must remember that Thomas à Kempis died in 1471, a dozen years before Martin Luther was born, and half a century before Luther published *The Freedom of the Christian*, which clearly articulated the doctrine of justification by faith.

Nevertheless, John Wesley, the founder of the Methodists and one of the leading Protestants of the eighteenth century, praised Thomas à Kempis's book and suggested that his followers meditate on it daily for the improvement of their immortal souls. In fact, he translated and abridged *The Imitation of Christ* so that the Methodists could do just that.[8]

The enduring value of this book is its unyielding message that the authentic Christian life seeks to follow Christ's example. In our time, as in Thomas's, that message is especially appealing to those who seek a more personal and less programmatic approach to the religious life. All human enterprises—even religious ones—will inevitably disappoint. But Jesus Christ never does. That was Thomas's basic insight, which accounts for the ongoing appeal of his book.

The First Book

ADMONITIONS PROFITABLE FOR THE SPIRITUAL LIFE

CHAPTER I

OF THE IMITATION OF CHRIST, AND OF CONTEMPT OF THE WORLD AND ALL ITS VANITIES

*H*E THAT FOLLOWETH me *shall not walk in darkness,* saith the Lord. These are the words of Christ; and they teach us how far we must imitate His life and character, if we seek true illumination, and deliverance from all blindness of heart. Let it be our most earnest study, therefore, to dwell upon the life of Jesus Christ.

His teaching surpasseth all teaching of holy men, and such as have His Spirit find therein *the hidden manna.* But there are many who, though they frequently hear the Gospel, yet feel but little longing after it, because they have not the mind of Christ. He, therefore, that will fully and with true wisdom understand the words of Christ, let him strive to conform his whole life to that mind of Christ.

What doth it profit thee to enter into deep discussion concerning the Holy Trinity, if thou lack humility, and be thus displeasing to the Trinity? For verily it is not deep words that make a man holy and upright; it is a good life which maketh a man dear to God.

I had rather feel contrition than be skilful in the definition thereof. If thou knewest the whole Bible, and the sayings of all the philosophers, what should all this profit thee without the love and grace of God? *Vanity of vanities, all is vanity,* save to love God, and Him only to serve. That is the highest wisdom, to cast the world behind us, and to reach forward to the heavenly kingdom.

THE DANGER OF WORLDLY THINGS

It is vanity then to seek after, and to trust in, the riches that shall perish. It is vanity, too, to covet honours, and to lift up ourselves on high. It is vanity to follow the desires of the flesh and be led by them, for this shall bring misery at the last.

It is vanity to desire a long life, and to have little care for a good life. It is vanity to take thought only for the life which now is, and not to look forward to the things which shall be hereafter. It is vanity to love that which quickly passeth away, and not to hasten where eternal joy abideth.

Be oftimes mindful of the saying, *The eye is not satisfied with seeing, nor the ear with hearing.* Strive, therefore, to turn away thy heart from the love of the things that are seen, and to set it upon the things that are not seen. For they who follow after their own fleshly lusts, defile the conscience, and destroy the grace of God.

CHAPTER II

OF THINKING HUMBLY OF ONESELF

*T*HERE is naturally in every man a desire to know, but what profiteth knowledge without the fear of God? Better of a surety is a lowly peasant who serveth God, than a proud philosopher who watcheth the stars and neglecteth the knowledge of himself. He who knoweth himself well is vile in his own sight; neither regardeth he the praises of men. If I knew all the things that are in the world, and were not in charity, what should it help me before God, who is to judge me according to my deeds?

Rest from inordinate desire of knowledge, for therein is found much distraction and deceit. Those who have knowledge desire to appear learned, and to be called wise. Many things there are to know which profiteth little or nothing to the soul. And foolish out of measure is he who attendeth upon other things rather than those which serve to his soul's health. Many words satisfy not the soul, but a good life refresheth the mind, and a pure conscience giveth great confidence towards God.

THE MOST PROFITABLE LESSON

The greater and more complete thy knowledge, the more severely shalt thou be judged, unless thou hast lived holily. Therefore be not lifted up by any skill or knowledge that thou hast; but rather fear concerning the knowledge which is given to thee. If it seemeth to thee that thou knowest many things, and understandest them well, know also that there are many more things which thou knowest not. *Be not high-minded,* but rather confess thine ignorance. Why desirest thou to lift thyself above another, when there are found many more learned and more skilled in the Scripture than thou? If thou wilt know and learn anything with profit, love to be thyself unknown and to be counted for nothing.

That is the highest and most profit-able lesson, when a man truly knoweth and judgeth lowly of himself. To account nothing of one's self, and to think always kindly and highly of others, this is great and perfect wisdom. Even shouldest thou see thy neighbour sin openly or grievously, yet thou oughtest not to reckon thyself better than he, for thou knowest not how long thou shalt keep thine integrity. All of us are weak and frail; hold thou no man more frail than thyself.

CHAPTER III

OF THE KNOWLEDGE OF TRUTH

HAPPY is the man whom Truth by itself doth teach, not by figures and transient words, but as it is in itself. Our own judgment and feelings often deceive us, and we discern but little of the truth. What doth it profit to argue about hidden and dark things, concerning which we shall not be even reproved in the judgment, because we knew them not? Oh, grievous folly, to neglect the things which are profitable and necessary, and to give our minds to things which are curious and hurtful! Having eyes, we see not.

And what have we to do with talk about genus and species! He to whom the Eternal Word speaketh is free from multiplied questionings. From this One Word are all things, and all things, speak of Him; and this is the Beginning which also speaketh unto us. No man without Him understandeth or rightly judgeth. The man to whom all things are one, who bringeth all things to one, who seeth all things in one, he is able to remain steadfast of spirit, and at rest in God.

O God, who art the Truth, make me one with Thee in everlasting love. It wearieth me oftentimes to read and listen to many things; in Thee is all that I wish for and desire. Let all the doctors hold their peace; let all creation keep silence before Thee: speak Thou alone to me.

UNITY AND SIMPLICITY INCREASE UNDERSTANDING

The more a man hath unity and simplicity in himself, the more things and the deeper things he understandeth; and that without labour, because he receiveth the light of understanding from above. The spirit which is pure, sincere, and steadfast, is not distracted though it hath many works to do, because it doth all things to the honour of God, and striveth to be free from all thoughts of self-seeking.

Who is so full of hindrance and annoyance to thee as thine own undisciplined heart? A man who is good and devout arrangeth beforehand within his own heart the works which he hath to do abroad; and so is not drawn away by the desires of his evil will, but subjecteth everything to the judgment of right reason. Who hath a harder battle to fight than he who striveth for self-mastery? And this should be our endeavour, even to master self, and thus daily to grow stronger than self, and go on unto perfection.

All perfection hath some imperfection joined to it in this life, and all our power of sight is not without some darkness. A lowly knowledge of thyself is a surer way to God than the deep searchings of a man's learning. Not that learning is to be blamed, nor the taking account of anything that is good; but a good conscience and a holy life is better than all. And because many seek knowledge rather than good living, therefore they go astray, and bear little or no fruit.

THE GLORY OF THE WORLD PASSETH AWAY

O if they would give that diligence to the rooting out of vice and the planting of virtue which they give unto vain questionings: There had not been so many evil doings and stumbling-blocks among the laity, nor such ill living among houses of religion. Of a surety, at the Day of Judgment it will be demanded of us, not what we have read, but what we have done; not how well we have spoken, but how holily we have lived.

Tell me, where now are all those masters and teachers, whom thou knewest well, whilst they were yet with you, and flourished in learning? Their stalls are now filled by others, who perhaps never have one thought concerning them. Whilst they lived they seemed to be somewhat, but now no one speaks of them.

Oh how quickly passeth the glory of the world away! Would that their life and knowledge had agreed together! For then would they have read and inquired unto good purpose. How many perish through empty learning in this world, who care little for serving God. And because they love to be great more than to be humble, therefore they *"have become vain in their imaginations."*

He only is truly great, who hath great charity. He is truly great who deemeth himself small, and counteth all height of honour as nothing. He is the truly wise man, who counteth all earthly things as dung that he may win Christ. And he is the truly learned man, who doeth the will of God, and forsaketh his own will.

CHAPTER IV
OF PRUDENCE IN ACTION

WE must not trust every word of others or feeling within ourselves, but cautiously and patiently try the matter, whether it be of God. Unhappily we are so weak that we find it easier to believe and speak evil of others, rather than good. But they that are perfect, do not give ready heed to every news-bearer, for they know man's weakness that it is prone to evil and unstable in words.

This is great wisdom, not to be hasty in action, or stubborn in our own opinions. A part of this wisdom also is not to believe every word we hear, nor to tell others all that we hear, even though we believe it. Take counsel with a man who is wise and of a good conscience; and seek to be instructed by one better than thyself, rather than to follow thine own inventions. A good life maketh a man wise toward God, and giveth him experience in many things. The more humble a man is in himself, and the more obedient towards God, the wiser will he be in all things, and the more shall his soul be at peace.

CHAPTER V
OF THE READING OF HOLY SCRIPTURES

IT is Truth which we must look for in Holy Writ, not cunning of words. All Scripture ought to be read in the spirit in which it was written. We must rather seek for what is profitable in Scripture, than for what ministereth to subtlety in discourse.

Therefore we ought to read books which are devotional and simple, as well as those which are deep and difficult. And let not the weight of the writer be a stumbling-block to thee, whether he be of little or much learning, but let the love of the pure Truth draw thee to read. Ask not, who hath said this or that, but look to what he says.

Men pass away, but the truth of the Lord endureth for ever. Without respect of persons God speaketh to us in divers manners. Our own curiosity often hindereth us in the reading of holy writings, when we seek to understand and discuss, where we should pass simply on.

It thou wouldst profit by thy reading, read humbly, simply, honestly, and not desiring to win a character for learning. Ask freely, and hear in silence the words of holy men; nor be displeased at the hard sayings of older men than thou, for they are not uttered without cause.

CHAPTER VI
OF INORDINATE AFFECTIONS

WHENSOEVER a man desireth aught above measure, immediately he becometh restless. The proud and the avaricious man are never at rest; while the poor and lowly of heart abide in the multitude of peace. The man who is not yet wholly dead to self, is soon tempted, and is overcome in small and trifling matters.

It is hard for him who is weak in spirit, and still in part carnal and inclined to the pleasures of sense, to withdraw himself altogether from earthly desires. And therefore, when he withdraweth himself from these, he is often sad, and easily angered too if any oppose his will.

But if, on the other hand, he yield to his inclination, immediately he is weighed down by the condemnation of his conscience; for that he hath followed his own desire, and yet in no way attained the peace which he hoped for. For true peace of heart is to be found in resisting passion, not in yielding to it. And therefore there is no peace in the heart of a man who is carnal, nor in him who is given up to the things that are without him, but only in him who is fervent towards God and living the life of the Spirit.

CHAPTER VII
OF FLEEING FROM VAIN HOPE AND PRIDE

VAIN is the life of that man who putteth his trust in men or in any created Thing. Be not ashamed to be the servant of others for the love of Jesus Christ, and to be reckoned poor in this life. Rest not upon thyself, but build thy hope in God. Do what lieth in thy power, and God will help thy good intent. Trust not in thy learning, nor in the cleverness of any that lives, but rather trust in the favour of God, who resisteth the proud and giveth grace to the humble.

Boast not thyself in thy riches if thou hast them, nor in thy friends if they be powerful, but in God, who giveth all things, and in addition to all things desireth to give even Himself. Be not lifted up because of thy strength or beauty of body, for with only a slight sickness it will fail and wither away. Be not vain of thy skilfulness or ability, lest thou displease God, from whom cometh every good gift which we have.

HUMBLE THYSELF

Count not thyself better than others, lest perchance thou appear worse in the sight of God, who knoweth what is in man. Be not proud of thy good works, for God's judgments are of another sort than the judgments of man, and what pleaseth man is ofttimes displeasing to Him.

If thou hast any good, believe that others have more, and so thou mayest preserve thy humility. It is no harm to thee if thou place thyself below all others; but it is great harm if thou place thyself above even one. Peace is ever with the humble man, but in the heart of the proud there is envy and continual wrath.

CHAPTER VIII
OF THE DANGER OF TOO MUCH FAMILIARITY

OPEN not thine heart to every man, but deal with one who is wise and feareth God. Be seldom with the young and with strangers. Be not a flatterer of the rich; nor willingly seek the society of the great. Let thy company be the humble and the simple, the devout and the gentle, and let thy discourse be concerning things which edify. Be not familiar with any woman, but commend all good women alike unto God. Choose for thy companions God and His Angels only, and flee from the notice of men.

We must love all men, but not make close companions of all. It sometimes falleth out that one who is unknown to us is highly regarded through good report of him, whose actual person is nevertheless unpleasing to those who behold it. We sometimes think to please others by our intimacy, and forthwith displease them the more by the faultiness of character which they perceive in us.

CHAPTER IX
OF OBEDIENCE AND SUBJECTION

IT is verily a great thing to live in obedience, to be under authority, and not to be at our own disposal. Far safer is it to live in subjection than in a place of authority. Many are in obedience from necessity rather than from love; these take it amiss, and repine for small cause. Nor will they gain freedom of spirit, unless with all their heart they submit themselves for the love of God.

Though thou run hither and thither, thou wilt not find peace, save in humble subjection to the authority of him who is set over thee. Fancies about places and change of them have deceived many.

HEARKEN UNTO COUNSEL

True it is that every man willingly followeth his own bent, and is the more inclined to those who agree with him. But if Christ is amongst us, then it is necessary that we sometimes yield up our own opinion for the sake of peace. Who is so wise as to have perfect knowledge of all things? Therefore trust not too much to thine own opinion, but be ready also to hear the opinions of others. Though thine own opinion be good, yet if for the love of God thou foregoest it, and followest that of another, thou shalt the more profit thereby.

Ofttimes I have heard that it is safer to hearken and to receive counsel than to give it. It may also come to pass that each opinion may be good; but to refuse to hearken to others when reason or occasion requireth it, is a mark of pride or wilfulness.

CHAPTER X
OF THE DANGER OF SUPERFLUITY OF WORDS

AVOID as far as thou canst the tumult of men; for talk concerning worldly things, though it be innocently undertaken, is a hindrance, so quickly are we led captive and defiled by vanity. Many a time I wish that I had held my peace, and had not gone amongst men. But why do we talk and gossip so continually, seeing that we so rarely resume our silence without some hurt done to our conscience? We like talking so much because we hope by our conversations to gain some mutual comfort, and because we seek to refresh our wearied spirits by variety of thoughts. And we very willingly talk and think of those things which we love or desire, or else of those which we most dislike.

But alas! it is often to no purpose and in vain. For this outward consolation is no small hindrance to the inner comfort which cometh from God. Therefore must we watch and pray that time pass not idly away. If it be right and desirable for thee to speak, speak things which are to edification.

Evil custom and neglect of our real profit tend much to make us heedless of watching over our lips. Nevertheless, devout conversation on spiritual things helpeth not a little to spiritual progress, most of all where those of kindred mind and spirit find their ground of fellowship in God.

CHAPTER XI
OF SEEKING PEACE OF MIND AND OF SPIRITUAL PROGRESS

WE may enjoy abundance of peace if we refrain from busying ourselves with the sayings and doings of others, and things which concern not ourselves. How can he abide long time in peace who occupieth himself with other men's matters, and with things without himself, and meanwhile payeth little or rare heed to the self within? Blessed are the single-hearted, for they shall have abundance of peace.

How came it to pass that many of the saints were so perfect, so contemplative of Divine things? Because they steadfastly sought to mortify themselves from all worldly desires, and so were enabled to cling with their whole heart to God, and be free and at leisure for the thought of Him. We are too much occupied with our own affections, and too anxious about transitory things. Seldom, too, do we entirely conquer even a single fault, nor are we zealous for daily growth in grace. And so we remain lukewarm and unspiritual.

Were we fully watchful of ourselves, and not bound in spirit to outward things, then might we be wise unto salvation, and make progress in Divine contemplation. Our great and grievous stumbling-block is that, not being freed from our affections and desires, we strive not to enter into the perfect way of the saints. And when even a little trouble befalleth us, too quickly are we cast down, and fly to the world to give us comfort.

If we would quit ourselves like men, and strive to stand firm in the battle, then should we see the Lord helping us from Heaven. For He Himself is alway ready to help those who strive and who trust in Him; yea, He provideth for us occasions of striving, to the end that we may win the victory. If we look upon our progress in religion as a progress only in outward observances and forms, our devoutness will soon come to an end. But let us lay the axe to the very root of our life, that, being cleansed from affections, we may possess our souls in peace.

THE COST OF SPIRITUAL PROGRESS

If each year should see one fault rooted out from us, we should go quickly on to perfection. But on the contrary, we often feel that we were better and holier in the beginning of our conversion than after many years of profession. Zeal and progress ought to increase day by day; yet now it seemeth a great thing if one is able to retain some portion of his first ardour. If we would put some slight stress on ourselves at the beginning, then afterwards we should be able to do all things with ease and joy.

It is a hard thing to break through a habit, and a yet harder thing to go contrary to our own will. Yet if thou overcome not slight and easy obstacles, how shalt thou overcome greater ones? Withstand thy will at the beginning, and unlearn an evil habit, lest it lead thee little by little into worse difficulties. Oh, if thou knewest what peace to thyself thy holy life should bring to thyself, and what joy to others, methinketh thou wouldst be more zealous for spiritual profit.

CHAPTER XII
OF THE USES OF ADVERSITY

IT is good for us that we sometimes have sorrows and adversities, for they often make a man lay to heart that he is only a stranger and sojourner, and may not put his trust in any worldly thing. It is good that we sometimes endure contradictions, and are hardly and unfairly judged, when we do and mean what is good. For these things help us to be humble, and shield us from vain-glory. For then we seek the more earnestly the witness of God, when men speak evil of us falsely, and give us no credit for good.

Therefore ought a man to rest wholly upon God, so that he needeth not seek much comfort at the hand of men. When a man who feareth God is afflicted or tried or oppressed with evil thoughts, then he seeth that God is the most necessary unto him, since without God he can do no good thing. Then he is heavy of heart, he groaneth, he crieth out for the very disquietness of his heart. Then he groweth weary of life, and would fain depart and be with Christ. By all this he is taught that in the world there can be no perfect security or fulness of peace.

CHAPTER XIII
OF RESISTING TEMPTATION

So long as we live in the world, we cannot be without trouble and trial. Wherefore it is written in Job, *The life of man upon the earth is a trial.* And therefore ought each of us to give heed concerning trials and temptations, and watch unto prayer, lest the devil find occasion to deceive; for he never sleepeth, but goeth about seeking whom he may devour. No man is so perfect in holiness that he hath never temptations, nor can we ever be wholly free from them.

Yet, notwithstanding, temptations turn greatly unto our profit, even though they be great and hard to bear; for through them we are humbled, purified, instructed. All saints have passed through much tribulation and temptation, and have profited thereby. And they who endured not temptation became reprobate and fell away. There is no position so sacred, no place so secret, that it is without temptations and adversities.

ALL HAVE TEMPTATIONS

There is no man wholly free from temptations so long as he liveth, because we have the root of temptation within ourselves, in that we are born in concupiscence. One temptation or sorrow passeth, and another cometh; and always we shall have somewhat to suffer, for we have fallen from perfect happiness. Many who seek to fly from temptations fall yet more deeply into them. By flight alone we cannot overcome, but by endurance and true humility we are made stronger than all our enemies.

He who only resisteth outwardly and pulleth not up by the root, shall profit little; nay, rather temptations will return to him the more quickly, and will be the more terrible. Little by little, through patience and long-suffering, thou shalt conquer by the help of God, rather than by violence and thine own strength of will. In the midst of temptation often seek counsel; and deal not hardly with one who is tempted, but comfort and strengthen him as thou wouldest have done unto thyself.

RESIST TEMPTATIONS EARLY

The beginning of all temptations to evil is instability of temper and want of trust in God; for even as a ship without a helm is tossed about by the waves, so is a man who is careless and infirm of purpose tempted, now on this side, now on that. As fire testeth iron, so doth temptation the upright man.

Oftentimes we know not what strength we have; but temptation revealeth to us what we are. Nevertheless, we must watch, especially in the beginnings of temptation; for then is the foe the more easily mastered, when he is not suffered to enter within the mind, but is met outside the door as soon as he hath knocked. Wherefore one saith,

> Check the beginnnings;
>   once thou might'st
>   have cured,
> But now 'tis past thy
>   skill, too long hath it
>   endured.

For first cometh to the mind the simple suggestion, then the strong imagination, afterwards pleasure, evil affection, assent. And so little by little the enemy entereth in altogether, because he was not resisted at the beginning. And the longer a man delayeth his resistance, the weaker he groweth, and the stronger groweth the enemy against him.

Some men suffer their most grievous temptations in the beginning of their conversion, some at the end. Some are sorely tried their whole life long. Some there are who are tempted but lightly, according to the wisdom and justice of the ordering of God, who knoweth the character and circumstances of men, and ordereth all things for the welfare of His elect.

TEMPTATIONS AND TROUBLE PROVE A MAN

Therefore we ought not to despair when we are tempted, but the more fervently should cry unto God, that He will vouchsafe to help us in all our tribulation; and that He will, as St. Paul saith, *with the temptation make a way to escape that we may be able to bear it.* Let us therefore humble ourselves under the mighty hand of God in all temptation and trouble, for He will save and exalt such as are of an humble spirit.

In temptations and troubles a man is proved, what progress he hath made, and therein is his reward the greater, and his virtue doth the more appear. Nor is it a great thing if a man be devout and zealous so long as he suffereth no affliction; but if he behave himself patiently in the time of adversity, then is there hope of great progress. Some are kept safe from great temptations, but are overtaken in those which are little and common, that the humiliation may teach them not to trust to themselves in great things, being weak in small things.

CHAPTER XIV
ON AVOIDING RASH JUDGMENT

Look well unto thyself, and beware that thou judge not the doings of others. In judging others a man laboureth in vain; he often erreth, and easily falleth into sin; but in judging and examining himself he always laboureth to good purpose. According as a matter toucheth our fancy, so oftentimes do we judge of it; for easily do we fail of true judgment because of our own personal feeling. If God were always the sole object of our desire, we should the less easily be troubled by the erring judgment of our fancy.

But often some secret thought lurking within us, or even some outward circumstance, turneth us aside. Many are secretly seeking their own ends in what they do, yet know it not. They seem to live in good peace of mind so long as things go well with them, and according to their desires, but if their desires be frustrated and broken, immediately they are shaken and displeased. Diversity of feelings and opinions very often brings about dissensions between friends, between countrymen, between religious and godly men.

Established custom is not easily relinquished, and no man is very easily led to see with the eyes of another. If thou rest more upon thy own reason or experience than upon the power of Jesus Christ, thy light shall come slowly and hardly; for God willeth us to be perfectly subject unto Himself, and all our reason to be exalted by abundant love towards Him.

CHAPTER XV
OF WORKS OF CHARITY

FOR no worldly good whatsoever, and for the love of no man, must anything be done which is evil, but for the help of the suffering a good work must sometimes be postponed, or be changed for a better; for herein a good work is not destroyed, but improved. Without charity no work profiteth, but whatsoever is done in charity, however small and of no reputation it be, bringeth forth good fruit; for God verily considereth what a man is able to do, more than the greatness of what he doth.

He doth much who loveth much. He doth much who doth well. He doth well who ministereth to the public good rather than to his own. Oftentimes that seemeth to be charity which is rather carnality, because it springeth from natural inclination, self-will, hope of repayment, desire of gain.

THE FRUITS OF TRUE AND PERFECT CHARITY

He who hath true and perfect charity, in no wise seeketh his own good, but desireth that God alone be altogether glorified. He envieth none, because he longeth for no selfish joy; nor doth he desire to rejoice in himself, but longeth to be blessed in God as the highest good.

He ascribeth good to none save to God only, the Fountain whence all good proceedeth, and the End, the Peace, the joy of all saints. Oh, he who hath but a spark of true charity, hath verily learned that all worldly things are full of vanity.

CHAPTER XVI
OF BEARING WITH THE FAULTS OF OTHERS

THOSE things which a man cannot amend in himself or in others, he ought patiently to bear, until God shall otherwise ordain. Bethink thee that perhaps it is better for thy trial and patience, without which our merits are but little worth. Nevertheless thou oughtest, when thou findeth such impediments, to beseech God that He would vouchsafe to sustain thee, that thou be able to bear them with a good will.

If one who is once or twice admonished refuse to hearken, strive not with him, but commit all to God, that His will may be done and His honour be shown in His servants, for He knoweth well how to convert the evil unto good. Endeavour to be patient in bearing with other men's faults and infirmities whatsoever they be, for thou thyself also hast many things which have need to be borne with by others.

If thou canst not make thine own self what thou desireth, how shalt thou be able to fashion another to thine own liking. We are ready to see others made perfect, and yet we do not amend our own shortcomings.

CONSIDER ONE ANOTHER

We will that others be straitly corrected, but we will not be corrected ourselves. The freedom of others displeaseth us, but we are dissatisfied that our own wishes shall be denied us. We desire rules to be made restraining others, but by no means will we suffer ourselves to be restrained. Thus therefore doth it plainly appear how seldom we weigh our neighbour in the same balance with ourselves. If all men were perfect, what then should we have to suffer from others for God?

But now hath God thus ordained, that we may learn to bear one another's burdens, because none is without defect, none without a burden, none sufficient of himself, none wise enough of himself; but it behoveth us to bear with one another, to comfort one another, to help, instruct, admonish one another. How much strength each man hath is best proved by occasions of adversity: for such occasions do not make a man frail, but show of what temper he is.

CHAPTER XVII
OF A RELIGIOUS LIFE

IT behoveth thee to learn to mortify thyself in many things, if thou wilt live in amity and concord with other men. It is no small thing to dwell in a religious community or congregation, and to live there without complaint, and therein to remain faithful even unto death. Blessed is he who hath lived a good life in such a body, and brought it to a happy end.

If thou wilt stand fast and wilt profit as thou oughtest, hold thyself as an exile and a pilgrim upon the earth. Thou wilt have to be counted as a fool for Christ, if thou wilt lead a religious life.

The clothing and outward appearance are of small account; it is change of character and entire mortification of the affections which make a truly religious man. He who seeketh aught save God and the health of his soul, shall find only tribulation and sorrow. Nor can he stand long in peace, who striveth not to be least of all and servant of all.

Thou art called to endure and to labour, not to a life of ease and trifling talk. Here therefore are men tried as gold in the furnace. No man can stand, unless with all his heart he will humble himself for God's sake.

CHAPTER XVIII
OF THE EXAMPLE OF
THE HOLY FATHERS

CONSIDER now the lively examples of the holy fathers, in whom shone forth real perfectness and religion, and thou shalt see how little, even as nothing, is all that we do. Ah! What is our life when compared to theirs? They, saints and friends of Christ as they were, served the Lord in hunger and thirst, in cold and nakedness, in labour and weariness, in watchings and fastings, in prayer and holy meditations, in persecutions and much rebuke.

HOW THE HOLY FATHERS LIVED

O how many and grievous tribulations did the Apostles, Martyrs, Confessors, Virgins endure; and all others who would walk in the footsteps of Christ. For they hated their souls in this world that they might keep them unto life eternal.

O how strict and retired a life was that of the holy fathers who dwelt in the desert! what long and grievous temptations they did suffer! how often were they assaulted by the enemy! what frequent and fervid prayers did they offer unto God! what strict fasts did they endure! what fervent zeal and desire after spiritual profit did they manifest! how bravely did they fight that their vices might not gain the mastery! how entirely and steadfastly did they reach after God! By day they laboured, and at night they gave themselves ofttimes unto prayer; yea, even when they were labouring they ceased not from mental prayer.

They spent their whole time profitably; every hour seemed short for retirement with God; and through the great sweetness of contemplation, even the need of bodily refreshment was forgotten. They renounced all riches, dignities, honours, friends, kinsmen; they desired nothing from the world; they ate the bare necessaries of life; they were unwilling to minister to the body even in necessity. Thus were they poor in earthly things, but rich above measure in grace and virtue. Though poor to the outer eye, within they were filled with grace and heavenly benedictions.

THEIR FRUIT REMAINETH

They were strangers to the world, but unto God they were as kinsmen and friends. They seemed unto themselves as of no reputation, and in the world's eyes contemptible; but in the sight of God they were precious and beloved. They stood fast in true humility, they lived in simple obedience, they walked in love and patience; and thus they waxed strong in spirit, and obtained great favour before God. To all religious men they were given as an example, and they ought more to provoke us unto good livings than the number of the lukewarm tempteth to carelessness of life.

O how great was the love of all religious persons at the beginning of this sacred institution! O what devoutness of prayer! what rivalry in holiness! what strict discipline was observed! what reverence and obedience under the rule of the master showed they in all things!

The traces of them that remain until now testify that they were truly holy and perfect men, who fighting so bravely trod the world underfoot. Now a man is counted great if only he be not a trangressor, and if he can only endure with patience what he hath undertaken.

THE DANGER OF SLOTH

O the coldness and negligence of our times, that we so quickly decline from the former love, and it is become a weariness to live, because of sloth and lukewarmness. May progress in holiness not wholly fall asleep in thee, who many times hast seen so many examples of devout men!

CHAPTER XIX
OF THE EXERCISES OF A RELIGIOUS MAN

THE life of a Christian ought to be adorned with all virtues, that he may be inwardly what he outwardly appeareth unto men. And verily it should be yet better within than without, for God is a discerner of our heart, Whom we must reverence with all our hearts wheresoever we are, and walk pure in His presence as do the angels.

We ought daily to renew our vows, and to kindle our hearts to zeal, as if each day were the first day of our conversion, and to say, "Help me, O God, in my good resolutions, and in Thy holy service, and grant that this day I may make a good beginning, for hitherto I have done nothing!"

THE VALUE OF RESOLUTION

According to our resolution so is the rate of our progress, and much diligence is needful for him who would make good progress. For if he who resolveth bravely oftentimes falleth short, how shall it be with him who resolveth rarely or feebly? But manifold causes bring about abandonment of our resolution, yet a trivial omission of holy exercises can hardly be made without some loss to us.

The resolution of the righteous dependeth more upon the grace of God than upon their own wisdom; for in Him they always put their trust, whatsoever they take in hand. For man proposeth, but God disposeth; and *the way of a man is not in himself.*

If a holy exercise be sometimes omitted for the sake of some act of piety, or of some brotherly kindness, it can easily be taken up afterwards; but if it be neglected through distaste or slothfulness, then is it sinful, and the mischief will be felt. Strive as earnestly as we may, we shall still fall short in many things.

Always should some distinct resolution be made by us; and, most of all, we must strive against those sins which most easily beset us. Both our outer and inner life should be straitly examined and ruled by us, because both have to do with our progress.

If thou canst not be always examining thyself, thou canst at certain seasons, and at least twice in the day, at evening and at morning. In the morning make thy resolves, and in the evening inquire into thy life; how thou hast sped to-day in word, deed, and thought; for in these ways thou hast often perchance offended God and thy neighbour.

Gird up thy loins like a man against the assaults of the devil; bridle thine appetite, and thou wilt soon be able to bridle every inclination of the flesh. Be thou never without something to do; be reading, or writing, or praying, or meditating, or doing something that is useful to the community. Bodily exercises, however, must be undertaken with discretion, nor are they to be used by all alike.

SPIRITUAL EXERCISES

The duties which are not common to all must not be done openly, but are safest carried on in secret. But take heed that thou be not careless in the common duties, and more devout in the secret; but faithfully and honestly discharge the duties and commands which lie upon thee, then afterwards, if thou hast still leisure, give thyself to thyself as thy devotion leadeth thee.

All cannot have one exercise, but one suiteth better to this man and another to that. Even for the diversity of season different exercises are needed, some suit better for feasts, some for fasts. We need one kind in time of temptations and others in time of peace and quietness. Some are suitable to our times of sadness, and others when we are joyful in the Lord.

When we draw near the time of the great feasts, good exercises should be renewed, and the prayers of holy men more fervently besought. We ought to make our resolutions from one Feast to another, as if each were the period of our departure from this world, and of entering into the eternal feast. So ought we to prepare ourselves earnestly at solemn seasons, and the more solemnly to live, and to keep straightest watch upon each holy observance, as though we were soon to receive the reward of our labours at the hand of God.

And if this be deferred, let us believe ourselves to be as yet ill-prepared, and unworthy as yet of the glory which shall be revealed in us at the appointed season; and let us study to prepare ourselves the better for our end. *Blessed is that servant,* as the Evangelist Luke hath it, *whom, when the Lord cometh He shall find watching. Verily I say unto you He will make him ruler over all that He hath.*

CHAPTER XX
OF THE LOVE OF SOLITUDE AND SILENCE

SEEK a suitable time for thy meditation, and think frequently of the mercies of God to thee. Leave curious questions. Study such matters as bring thee sorrow for sin rather than amusement. If thou withdraw thyself from trifling conversation and idle goings about, as well as from novelties and gossip, thou shalt find thy time sufficient and apt for good meditation. The greatest saints used to avoid as far as they could the company of men, and chose to live in secret with God.

FORSAKE THE MULTITUDE

One hath said, "As oft as I have gone among men, so oft have I returned less a man." This is what we often experience when we have been long time in conversation. For it is easier to be altogether silent than it is not to exceed in word. It is easier to remain hidden at home than to keep sufficient guard upon thyself out of doors.

He, therefore, that seeketh to reach that which is hidden and spiritual, must go with Jesus "apart from the multitude." No man safely goeth abroad who loveth not to rest at home. No man safely talketh but he who loveth to hold his peace. No man safely ruleth but he who loveth to be subject. No man safely commandeth but he who loveth to obey.

No man safely rejoiceth but he who hath the testimony of a good conscience within himself. The boldness of the saints was always full of the fear of God. Nor were they the less earnest and humble in themselves, because they shone forth with great virtues and grace.

But the boldness of wicked men springeth from pride and presumption, and at the last turneth to their own confusion. Never promise thyself security in this life, howsoever good a monk or devout a solitary thou seemest.

THE VALUE OF TEMPTATION

Often those who stand highest in the esteem of men, fall the more grievously because of their over great confidence. Wherefore it is very profitable unto many that they should not be without inward temptation, but should be frequently assaulted, lest they be over confident, lest they be indeed lifted up into pride, or else lean too freely upon the consolations of the world. O how good a conscience should that man keep, who never sought a joy that passeth away, who never became entangled with the world! O how great peace and quiet should he possess, who would cast off all vain care, and think only of healthful and divine things, and build his whole hope upon God!

No man is worthy of heavenly consolation but he who hath diligently exercised himself in holy compunction. If thou wilt feel compunction within thy heart, enter into thy chamber and shut out the tumults of the world, as it is written, *Commune with your own heart in your own chamber and be still.* In retirement thou shalt find what often thou wilt lose abroad. Retirement, if thou continue therein, groweth sweet, but if thou keep not in it, begetteth weariness. If in the beginning of thy conversation thou dwell in it and keep it well, it shall afterwards be to thee a dear friend, and a most pleasant solace.

THE VALUE OF SOLITUDE

In silence and quiet the devout soul goeth forward and learneth the hidden things of the Scriptures. Therein findeth she a fountain of tears, wherein to wash and cleanse herself each night, that she may grow the more dear to her Maker as she dwelleth the further from all worldly distraction. To him who withdraweth himself from his acquaintance and friends God with His holy angels will draw nigh.

It is better to be unknown and take heed to oneself than to neglect oneself and work wonders. It is praiseworthy for a religious man to go seldom abroad, to fly from being seen, to have no desire to see men.

Why wouldest thou see what thou mayest not have? *The world passeth away and the lust thereof.* The desires of sensuality draw thee abroad, but when an hour is past, what dost thou bring home, but a weight upon thy conscience and distraction of heart? A merry going forth bringeth often a sorrowful return, and a merry evening maketh a sad morning.

So doth all carnal joy begin pleasantly, but in the end it gnaweth away and destroyeth. What canst thou see abroad which thou seest not at home? Behold the heaven and the earth and the elements, for out of these are all things made.

AVOID VAIN THINGS

What canst thou see anywhere which can continue long under the sun? Thou believest perchance that thou shalt be satisfied, but thou wilt never be able to attain unto this. If thou shouldest see all things before thee at once, what would it be but a vain vision? Lift up thine eyes to God on high, and pray that thy sins and negligences may be forgiven.

Leave vain things to vain men, and mind thou the things which God hath commanded thee. Shut thy door upon thee, and call unto thyself Jesus thy beloved. Remain with Him in thy chamber, for thou shalt not elsewhere find so great peace.

If thou hadst not gone forth nor listened to vain talk, thou hadst better kept thyself in good peace. But because it sometimes delighteth thee to hear new things, thou must therefore suffer trouble of heart.

Chapter XXI
OF COMPUNCTION OF HEART

IF thou wilt make any progress keep thyself in the fear of God, and long not to be too free, but restrain all thy senses under discipline and give not thyself up to senseless mirth. Give thyself to compunction of heart and thou shalt find devotion. Compunction openeth the way for many good things, which dissoluteness is wont quickly to lose. It is wonderful that any man can ever rejoice heartily in this life who considereth and weigheth his banishment, and the manifold dangers which beset his soul.

Through lightness of heart and neglect of our shortcomings we feel not the sorrows of our soul, but often vainly laugh when we have good cause to weep. There is no true liberty nor real joy, save in the fear of God with a good conscience. Happy is he who can cast away every cause of distraction and bring himself to the one purpose of holy compunction.

Happy is he who putteth away from him whatsoever may stain or burden his conscience. Strive manfully; custom is overcome by custom. If thou knowest how to let men alone, they will gladly let thee alone to do thine own works.

MIND THINE OWN BUSINESS

Busy not thyself with the affairs of others, nor entangle thyself with the business of great men. Keep always thine eye upon thyself first of all, and give advice to thyself specially before all thy dearest friends. If thou hast not the favour of men, be not thereby cast down, but let thy concern be that thou holdest not thyself so well and circumspectly, as becometh a servant of God and a devout monk.

It is often better and safer for a man not to have many comforts in this life, especially those which concern the flesh. But that we lack divine comforts or feel them rarely is to our own blame, because we seek not compunction of heart, nor utterly cast away those comforts which are vain and worldly.

Know thyself to be unworthy of divine consolation, and worthy rather of much tribulation. When a man hath perfect compunction, then all the world is burdensome and bitter to him. A good man will find sufficient cause for mourning and weeping; for whether he considereth himself, or pondereth concerning his neighbour, he knoweth that no man liveth here without tribulation, and the more thoroughly he considereth himself, the more thoroughly he grieveth. Grounds for just grief and inward compunction there are in our sins and vices, wherein we lie so entangled that we are but seldom able to contemplate heavenly things.

THE CAUSE OF INDIFFERENCE

If thou thoughtest upon thy death more often than how long thy life should be, thou wouldest doubtless strive more earnestly to improve. And if thou didst seriously consider the future pains of hell, I believe thou wouldest willingly endure toil or pain and fear not discipline. But because these things reach not the heart, and we still love pleasant things, therefore we remain cold and miserably indifferent.

Oftentimes it is from poverty of spirit that the wretched body is so easily led to complain. Pray therefore humbly unto the Lord that He will give thee the spirit of compunction and say in the language of the prophet, *Feed me, O Lord, with bread of tears, and give me plenteousness of tears to drink.*

CHAPTER XXII

ON THE CONTEMPLATION OF HUMAN MISERY

THOU art miserable wheresoever thou art, and whithersoever thou turnest, unless thou turn thee to God. Why art thou disquieted because it happeneth not to thee according to thy wishes and desires? Who is he that hath everything according to his will? Neither I, nor thou, nor any man upon the earth.

There is no man in the world free from trouble or anguish, though he were King or Pope. Who is he who hath the happiest lot? Even he who is strong to suffer somewhat for God.

There are many foolish and unstable men who say, "See what a prosperous life that man hath, how rich and how great he is, how powerful, how exalted." But lift up thine eyes to the good things of heaven, and thou shalt see that all these worldly things are nothing, they are utterly uncertain, yea, they are wearisome, because they are never possessed without care and fear. The happiness of man lieth not in the abundance of temporal things but a moderate portion sufficeth him. Our life upon earth is verily wretchedness.

The more a man desireth to be spiritual, the more bitter doth the present life become to him; because he the better understandeth and seeth the defects of human corruption. For to eat, to drink, to watch, to sleep, to rest, to labour, and to be subject to the other necessities of nature, is truly a great wretchedness and affliction to a devout man, who would fain be released and free from all sin.

SET THINE AFFECTION ON THINGS ABOVE

For the inner man is heavily burdened with the necessities of the body in this world. Wherefore the prophet devoutly prayeth to be freed from them, saying, *Deliver me from my necessities, O Lord.* But woe to those who know not their own misery, and yet greater woe to those who love this miserable and corruptible life. For to such a degree do some cling to it (even though by labouring or begging they scarce procure what is necessary for subsistence) that if they might live here always, they would care nothing for the Kingdom of God.

Oh foolish and faithless of heart, who lie buried so deep in worldly things, that they relish nothing save the things of the flesh! Miserable ones! they will too sadly find out at the last, how vile and worthless was that which they loved.

The saints of God and all loyal friends of Christ held as nothing the things which pleased the flesh, or those which flourished in this life, but their whole hope and affection aspired to the things which are above. Their whole desire was borne upwards to everlasting and invisible things, lest they should be drawn downwards by the love of things visible.

MAN'S TENDENCY TO EVIL

Lose not, brother, thy loyal desire of progress to things spiritual. There is yet time; the hour is not past. Why wilt thou put off thy resolution? Arise, begin this very moment, and say,

"Now is the time to do: Now is the time to fight, now is the proper time for amendment."

When thou art ill at ease and troubled, then is the time when thou art nearest unto blessing. Thou must *go through fire and water that God may bring thee into a wealthy place.* Unless thou put force upon thyself, thou wilt not conquer thy faults.

So long as we carry about with us this frail body, we cannot be without sin, we cannot live without weariness and trouble. Gladly would we have rest from all misery; but because through sin we have lost innocence, we have lost also the true happiness. Therefore must we be patient, and wait for the mercy of God, *until this tyranny be overpast,* and this *mortality be swallowed up of life.*

O how great is the frailty of man, which is ever prone to evil! To-day thou confessest thy sins, and to-morrow thou committest again the sins thou didst confess. Now dost thou resolve to avoid a fault, and within an hour thou behavest thyself as if thou hadst never resolved at all.

Good cause have we therefore to humble ourselves, and never to think highly of ourselves, seeing that we are so frail and unstable. And quickly may that be lost by our negligence, which by much labour was hardly attained through grace.

What shall become of us at the end, if at the beginning we are lukewarm and idle? Woe unto us, if we choose to rest, as though it were a time of peace and security, while as yet no sign appeareth in our life of true holiness. Rather had we need that we might begin yet afresh, like good novices, to be instructed unto good living, if haply there might be hope of some future amendment and greater spiritual increase.

CHAPTER XXIII
OF MEDITATION UPON DEATH

VERY quickly will there be an end of thee here; take heed therefore how it will be with thee in another world. To-day man is, and to-morrow he will be seen no more. And being removed out of sight, quickly also he is out of mind. O the dulness and hardness of man's heart, which thinketh only of the present, and looketh not forward to the future. Thou oughtest in every deed and thought so to order thyself, as if thou wert to die this day.

If thou hadst a good conscience thou wouldst not greatly fear death. It were better for thee to watch against sin, than to fly from death. If to-day thou art not ready, how shalt thou be ready to-morrow? To-morrow is an uncertain day; and how knowest thou that thou shalt have a to-morrow?

What doth it profit to live long, when we amend so little? Ah! long life doth not always amend, but often the more increaseth guilt. Oh that we might spend a single day in this world as it ought to be spent!

Many there are who reckon the years since they were converted, and yet oftentimes how little is the fruit thereof. If it is a fearful thing to die, it may be perchance a yet more fearful thing to live long. Happy is the man who hath the hour of his death always before his eyes, and daily prepareth himself to die. If thou hast ever seen one die, consider that thou also shalt pass away by the same road.

BE PREPARED TO DIE

When it is morning reflect that it may be thou shalt not see the evening, and at eventide dare not to boast thyself of the morrow. Always be thou prepared, and so live that death may never find thee unprepared. Many die suddenly and unexpectedly. For *at such an hour as ye think not, the Son of Man cometh.* When that last hour shall come, thou wilt begin to think very differently of thy whole life past, and wilt mourn bitterly that thou hast been so negligent and slothful.

Happy and wise is he who now striveth to be such in life as he would fain be found in death! For a perfect contempt of the world, a fervent desire to excel in virtue, the love of discipline, the painfulness of repentance, readiness to obey, denial of self, submission to any adversity for love of Christ; these are the things which shall give great confidence of a happy death.

Whilst thou art in health thou hast many opportunities of good works; but when thou art in sickness I know not how much thou wilt be able to do. Few are made better by infirmity: Even as they who wander much abroad seldom become holy.

Trust not thy friends and kinsfolk, nor put off the work of thy salvation to the future, for men will forget thee sooner than thou thinkest. It is better for thee now to provide in time, and to send some good before thee, than to trust to the help of others. If thou art not anxious for thyself now, who, thinkest thou, will be anxious for thee afterwards?

Now the time is most precious. *Now is the accepted time, now is the day of salvation.* But, alas! that thou spendest not well this time, wherein thou mightest lay up treasure which should profit thee everlastingly. The hour will come when thou shalt desire one day, yea, one hour, for amendment of life, and I know not whether thou shalt obtain.

Oh, dearly beloved, from what danger thou mightest free thyself, from what great fear, if only thou wouldst always live in fear, and in expectation of death! Strive now to live in such wise that in the hour of death thou mayest rather rejoice than fear. Learn now to die to the world, so shalt thou begin to live with Christ. Learn now to condemn all earthly things, and then mayest thou freely go unto Christ. Keep under thy body by penitence, and then shalt thou be able to have a sure confidence.

THE UNCERTAINTY OF LIFE

Ah, foolish one! why thinkest thou that thou shalt live long, when thou art not sure of a single day? How many have been deceived, and suddenly have been snatched away from the body! How many times hast thou heard how one was slain by the sword, another was drowned, another falling from on high broke his neck, another died at the table, another whilst at play! One died by fire, another by the sword, another by the pestilence, another by the robber. Thus cometh death to all, and the life of men swiftly passeth away like a shadow.

Who will remember thee after thy death? And who will entreat for thee? Work, work now, oh dearly beloved, work all that thou canst. For thou knowest not when thou shalt die, nor what shall happen unto thee after death.

While thou hast time, lay up for thyself undying riches. Think of nought but of thy salvation; care only for the things of God. *Make to thyself friends,* by venerating the saints of God and walking in their steps, *that when thou failest, thou mayest be received into everlasting habitations.*

Keep thyself as a stranger and a pilgrim upon the earth, to whom the things of the world appertain not. Keep thine heart free, and lifted up towards God, *for here have we no continuing city.* To Him direct thy daily prayers with crying and tears, that thy spirit may be found worthy to pass happily after death unto its Lord. Amen.

CHAPTER XXIV
OF THE JUDGMENT AND PUNISHMENT OF THE WICKED

IN all that thou doest, remember the end, and how thou wilt stand before a strict judge, from whom nothing is hid, who is not bribed with gifts, nor accepteth excuses, but will judge righteous judgment. O most miserable and foolish sinner who art sometimes in fear of the countenance of an angry man, what wilt thou answer to God, who knoweth all thy misdeeds?

Why dost thou not provide for thyself against the day of judgment, when no man shall be able to be excused or defended by means of another, but each one shall bear his burden himself alone? Now doth thy labour bring forth fruit, now is thy weeping acceptable, thy groaning heard, thy sorrow well pleasing to God, and cleansing to thy soul.

PURIFICATION OF THE SOUL

Even here on earth the patient man findeth great occasion of purifying his soul. When suffering injuries he grieveth more for the other's malice than for his own wrong; when he prayeth heartily for those that despitefully use him, and forgiveth them from his heart; when he is not slow to ask pardon from others; when he is swifter to pity than to anger; when he frequently denieth himself and striveth altogether to subdue the flesh to the spirit. Better is it now to purify the soul from sin, than to cling to sins from which we must be purged hereafter. Truly we deceive ourselves by the inordinate love which we bear towards the flesh.

What is it which that fire shall devour, save thy sins? The more thou sparest thyself and followest the flesh, the more heavy shall thy punishment be, and the more fuel art thou heaping up for the burning. For wherein a man hath sinned, therein shall he be the more heavily punished. There shall the slothful be pricked forward with burning goads, and the gluttons be tormented with intolerable hunger and thirst. There shall be the luxurious and the lovers of pleasure be plunged into burning pitch and stinking brimstone and the envious shall howl like mad dogs for very grief.

No sin will there be which shall not be visited with its own proper punishment. The proud shall be filled with utter confusion, and the covetous shall be pinched with miserable poverty. An hour's pain there shall be more grievous than a hundred years here of the bitterest penitence. No quiet shall be there, no comfort for the lost, though here sometimes there is respite from pain, and enjoyment of the solace of friends.

Be thou anxious now and sorrowful for thy sins, that in the day of judgment thou mayest have boldness with the blessed. For *then shall the righteous man stand in great boldness before the face of such as have afflicted him and made no account of his labours.* Then shall he stand up to judge, he who now submitteth himself in humility to the judgments of men. Then shall the poor and humble man have great confidence, while the proud is taken with fear on every side.

THE WISE MAN

Then shall it be seen that he was the wise man in this world who learned to be a fool and despised for Christ. Then shall all tribulation patiently borne delight us, while the mouth of the ungodly shall be stopped. Then shall every godly man rejoice, and every profane man shall mourn. Then the afflicted flesh shall more rejoice than if it had been alway nourished in delights.

Then the humble garment shall put on beauty, and the precious robe shall hide itself as vile. Then the little poor cottage shall be more commended than the gilded palace. Then enduring patience shall have more might than all the power of the world. Then simple obedience shall be more highly exalted than all wordly wisdom.

Then a pure and good conscience shall more rejoice than learned philosophy. Then contempt of riches shall have more weight than all the treasure of the children of this world. Then shalt thou find more comfort in having prayed devoutly than in having fared sumptuously. Then thou wilt rather rejoice in having kept silence than in having made long speech. Then holy deeds shall be far stronger than many fine words. Then a strict life and sincere penitence shall bring deeper pleasure than all earthly delight.

Learn now to suffer a little, that then thou mayest be enabled to escape heavier sufferings. Prove first here, what thou art able to endure hereafter. If now thou art able to bear so little, how wilt thou be able to endure eternal torments? If now a little suffering maketh thee so impatient, what shall hell-fire do then? Behold of a surety thou art not able to have two Paradises, to take thy fill or delight here in this world, and to reign with Christ hereafter.

LOVE GOD AND SERVE HIM ONLY

If even unto this day thou hadst ever lived in honours and pleasures, what would the whole profit thee if now death came to thee in an instant? All therefore is vanity, save to love God and to serve Him only. For he who loveth God with all his heart feareth not death, nor punishment, nor judgment, nor hell, because perfect love giveth sure access to God.

But he who still delighteth in sin, no marvel if he is afraid of death and judgment. Nevertheless it is a good thing, if love as yet cannot restrain thee from evil, that at least the fear of hell should hold thee back. But he who putteth aside the fear of God cannot long continue in good, but shall quickly fall into the snares of the devil.

CHAPTER XXV
OF THE ZEALOUS AMENDMENT
OF OUR WHOLE LIFE

BE thou watchful and diligent in God's service, and bethink thee often why thou hast renounced the world. Was it not that thou mightest live to God and become a spiritual man? Be zealous, therefore, for thy spiritual profit, for thou shalt receive shortly the reward of thy labours, and neither fear nor sorrow shall come any more into thy borders.

Now shalt thou labour a little, and thou shalt find great rest, yea everlasting joy. If thou shalt remain faithful and zealous in labour, doubt not that God shall be faithful and bountiful in rewarding thee. It is thy duty to have a good hope that thou wilt attain the victory, but thou must not fall into security lest thou become slothful or lifted up.

SEEK THE GOOD AND ACCEPTABLE WILL OF GOD

A certain man being in anxiety of mind, continually tossed about between hope and fear, and being on a certain day overwhelmed with grief, cast himself down in prayer before the altar in a church, and meditated within himself, saying, "Oh! if I but knew that I should still persevere," and presently heard within him a voice from God, "And if thou didst know it, what wouldst thou do? Do now what thou wouldst do then, and thou shalt be very secure."

And straightway being comforted and strengthened, he committed himself to the will of God and the perturbation of spirit ceased, neither had he a mind any more to search curiously to know what should befall him hereafter, but studied rather to inquire what was the good and acceptable will of God, for the beginning and perfecting of every good work.

Hope in the Lord and be doing good, saith the Prophet; *dwell in the land and thou shalt be fed* with its riches. One thing there is which holdeth back many from progress and fervent amendment, even the dread of difficulty, or the labour of the conflict. Nevertheless they advance above all others in virtue who strive manfully to conquer those things which are most grievous and contrary to them, for there a man profiteth most and meriteth greater grace where he most overcometh himself and mortifieth himself in spirit.

THE PROFIT OF GOOD EXAMPLES

But all men have not the same passions to conquer and to mortify, yet he who is diligent shall attain more profit, although he have stronger passions, than another who is more temperate of disposition, but is withal less fervent in the pursuit of virtue. Two things specially avail unto improvement in holiness, namely firmness to withdraw ourselves from the sin to which by nature we are most inclined, and earnest zeal for that good in which we are most lacking. And strive also very earnestly to guard against and subdue those faults which displease thee most frequently in others.

Gather some profit to thy soul wherever thou art, and wherever thou seest or hearest good examples, stir thyself to follow them, but where thou seest anything which is blameworthy, take heed that thou do not the same; or if at any time thou hast done it, strive quickly to amend thyself. As thine eye observeth others, so again are the eyes of others upon thee.

How sweet and pleasant is it to see zealous and godly brethren temperate and of good discipline; and how sad is it and grievous to see them walking disorderly, not practising the duties to which they are called. How hurtful a thing it is to neglect the purpose of their calling, and turn their inclinations to things which are none of their business.

LACK OF DISCIPLINE LEADS TO RUIN

Be mindful of the duties which thou hast undertaken, and set always before thee the remembrance of the Crucified. Truly oughtest thou to be ashamed as thou lookest upon the life of Jesus Christ, because thou hast not yet endeavoured to conform thyself more unto Him, though thou hast been a long time in the way of God. A religious man who exercises himself seriously and devoutly in the most holy life and passion of our Lord shall find there abundantly all things that are profitable and necessary for him, neither is there need that he shall seek anything better beyond Jesus. Oh! if Jesus crucified would come into our hearts, how quickly, and completely should we have learned all that we need to know!

He who is earnest receiveth and beareth well all things that are laid upon him. He who is careless and lukewarm hath trouble upon trouble, and suffereth anguish upon every side, because he is without inward consolation, and is forbidden to seek that which is outward. He who is living without discipline is exposed to grievous ruin. He who seeketh easier and lighter discipline shall always be in distress, because one thing or another will give him displeasure.

SPIRITUAL REFRESHMENTS OF THE SOUL

O! if no other duty lay upon us but to praise the Lord our God with our whole heart and voice! Oh! if thou never hadst need to eat or drink, or sleep, but wert always able to praise God, and to give thyself to spiritual exercises alone; then shouldst thou be far happier than now, when for so many necessities thou must serve the flesh. O! that these necessities were not, but only the spiritual refreshments of the soul, which alas we taste too seldom.

When a man hath come to this, that he seeketh comfort from no created thing, then doth he perfectly begin to enjoy God, then also will he be well contented with whatsoever shall happen unto him. Then will he neither rejoice for much nor be sorrowful for little, but he committeth himself altogether and with full trust unto God, who is all in all to him, to whom nothing perisheth nor dieth, but all things live to Him and obey His every word without delay.

BE DILIGENT

Remember always thine end, and how the time which is lost returneth not. Without care and diligence thou shalt never get virtue. If thou beginnest to grow cold, it shall begin to go ill with thee, but if thou givest thyself unto zeal thou shalt find much peace, and shalt find thy labour the lighter because of the grace of God and the love of virtue. A zealous and diligent man is ready for all things.

It is greater labour to resist sins and passions than to toil in bodily labours. He who shunneth not small faults falleth little by little into greater. At eventide thou shalt always be glad if thou spend the day profitably. Watch over thyself, stir thyself up, admonish thyself, and howsoever it be with others, neglect not thyself. The more violence thou dost unto thyself, the more thou shall profit. Amen.

The Second Book

ADMONITIONS CONCERNING THE INNER LIFE

CHAPTER I
OF THE INWARD LIFE

THE *KINGDOM OF GOD is within you,* saith the Lord. Turn thee with all thine heart to the Lord and forsake this miserable world, and thou shalt find rest unto thy soul. Learn to despise outward things and to give thyself to things inward, and thou shalt see the kingdom of God come within thee. For the kingdom of God is peace and joy in the Holy Ghost, and it is not given to the wicked.

Christ will come to thee, and show thee His consolation, if thou prepare a worthy mansion for Him within thee. All His glory and beauty is from within, and there it pleaseth Him to dwell. He often visiteth the inward man and holdeth with him sweet discourse, giving him soothing consolation, much peace, friendship exceeding wonderful.

Go to, faithful soul, prepare thy heart for this bridegroom that he may vouchsafe to come to thee and dwell within thee, for so He saith, *if any man loveth me he will keep my words: and my Father will love him, and we will come unto him and make our abode with him.* Give, therefore, place to Christ and refuse entrance to all others. When thou hast Christ, thou art rich, and hast sufficient. He shall be thy provider and faithful watchman in all things, so that thou hast no need to trust in men, for men soon change and swiftly pass away, but Christ re-maineth for ever and standeth by us firmly even to the end.

TRUST NOT MORTAL MAN

There is no great trust to be placed in a frail and mortal man, even though he be useful and dear to us, neither should much sorrow arise within us if sometimes he oppose and contradict us. They who are on thy side to-day, may to-morrow be against thee, and often are they turned round like the wind.

Put thy whole trust in God and let Him be thy fear and thy love, He will answer for thee Himself, and will do for thee what is best. *Here hast thou no continuing city,* and wheresoever thou art, thou art a stranger and a pilgrim, and thou shalt never have rest unless thou art closely united to Christ within thee.

Why dost thou cast thine eyes hither and thither, since this is not the place of thy rest? In heaven ought thy habitation to be, and all earthly things should be looked upon as it were in the passing by. All things pass away and thou equally with them. Look that thou cleave not to them lest thou be taken with them and perish.

Let thy contemplation be on the Most High, and let thy supplication be directed unto Christ without ceasing. If thou canst not behold high and heavenly things, rest thou in the passion of Christ and dwell willingly in His sacred wounds. For if thou devoutly fly to the wounds of Jesus, and the precious marks of the nails and the spear, thou shalt find great comfort in tribulation, nor will the slights of men trouble thee much, and thou wilt easily bear their unkind words.

AFFLICTION AWAITS THE BELIEVER

Christ also, when He was in the world, was despised and rejected of men, and in His greatest necessity was left by His acquaintance and friends to bear these reproaches. Christ was willing to suffer and be despised, and darest thou complain of any? Christ had adversaries and gainsayers, and dost thou wish to have all men thy friends and benefactors? Whence shall thy patience attain her crown if no adversity befall thee? If thou art unwilling to suffer any adversity, how shalt thou be the friend of Christ? Sustain thyself with Christ and for Christ if thou wilt reign with Christ.

If thou hadst once entered into the mind of Jesus, and hadst tasted yea even a little of his tender love, then wouldst thou care nought for thine own convenience or inconvenience, but wouldst rather rejoice at trouble brought upon thee, because the love of Jesus maketh a man to despise himself. He who loveth Jesus, and is inwardly true and free from inordinate affections, is able to turn himself readily unto God, and to rise above himself in spirit, and to enjoy fruitful peace.

OUTWARD THINGS DISTRACT US

He who knoweth things as they are and not as they are said or seem to be, he truly is wise, and is taught of God more than of men. He who knoweth how to walk from within, and to set little value upon outward things, requireth not places nor waiteth for seasons, for holding his intercourse with God. The inward man quickly recollecteth himself, because he is never entirely given up to outward things.

No outward labour and no necessary occupations stand in his way, but as events fall out, so doth he fit himself to them. He who is rightly disposed and ordered within careth not for the strange and perverse conduct of men. A man is hindered and distracted in so far as he is moved by outward things.

If it were well with thee, and thou wert purified from evil, all things would work together for thy good and profiting. For this cause do many things displease thee and often trouble thee, that thou art not yet perfectly dead to thyself nor separated from all earthly things. Nothing so defileth and entangleth the heart of man as impure love towards created things. If thou rejectest outward comfort thou wilt be able to contemplate heavenly things and frequently to be joyful inwardly.

CHAPTER II
OF LOWLY SUBMISSION

MAKE no great account who is for thee or against thee, but mind only the present duty and take care that God be with thee in whatsoever thou doest. Have a good conscience and God will defend thee, for he whom God will help no man's perverseness shall be able to hurt. If thou knowest how to hold thy peace and to suffer, without doubt thou shalt see the help of the Lord. He knoweth the time and the way to deliver thee, therefore must thou resign thyself to Him. To God it belongeth to help and to deliver from all confusion. Oftentimes it is very profitable for keeping us in greater humility, that others know and rebuke our faults.

When a man humbleth himself for his defects, he then easily pacifieth others and quickly satisfieth those that are angered against him. God protecteth and delivereth the humble man, He loveth and comforteth the humble man, to the humble man He inclineth Himself, on the humble He bestoweth great grace, and when he is cast down He raiseth him to glory: to the humble He revealeth His secrets, and sweetly draweth and inviteth him to Himself. The humble man having received reproach, is yet in sufficient peace, because he resteth on God and not on the world. Reckon not thyself to have profited in anywise unless thou feel thyself to be inferior to all.

CHAPTER III
OF THE GOOD, PEACEABLE MAN

FIRST keep thyself in peace, and then shalt thou be able to be a peacemaker towards others. A peaceable man doth more good than a well-learned. A passionate man turneth even good into evil and easily believeth evil; a good, peaceable man converteth all things into good. He who dwelleth in peace is suspicious of none, but he who is discontented and restless is tossed with many suspicions, and is neither quiet himself nor suffereth others to be quiet. He often saith what he ought not to say, and omitteth what it were more expedient for him to do. He considereth to what duties others are bound, and neglecteth those to which he is bound himself. Therefore be zealous first over thyself, and then mayest thou righteously be zealous concerning thy neighbour.

THE COST OF PEACE

Thou knowest well how to excuse and to colour thine own deeds, but thou wilt not accept the excuses of others. It would be more just to accuse thyself and excuse thy brother. If thou wilt that others bear with thee, bear thou with others. Behold how far thou art as yet from the true charity and humility which knows not how to be angry or indignant against any save self alone.

It is no great thing to mingle with the good and the meek, for this is naturally pleasing to all, and every one of us willingly enjoyeth peace and liketh best those who think with us: but to be able to live peaceably with the hard and perverse, or with the disorderly, or those who oppose us, this is a great grace and a thing much to be commended and most worthy of a man.

There are who keep themselves in peace and keep peace also with others, and there are who neither have peace nor suffer others to have peace; they are troublesome to others, but always more troublesome to themselves. And there are who hold themselves in peace, and study to bring others unto peace; nevertheless, all our peace in this sad life lieth in humble suffering rather than in not feeling adversities. He who best knoweth how to suffer shall possess the most peace; that man is conqueror of himself and lord of the world, the friend of Christ, and the inheritor of heaven.

CHAPTER IV
OF A PURE MIND AND
SIMPLE INTENTION

BY two wings is man lifted above earthly things, even by simplicity and purity. Simplicity ought to be in the intention, purity in the affection. Simplicity reacheth towards God, purity apprehendeth Him and tasteth Him. No good action will be distasteful to thee if thou be free within from inordinate affection.

If thou reachest after and seekest nothing but the will of God and the benefit of thy neighbour, thou wilt entirely enjoy inward liberty. If thine heart were right, then should every creature be a mirror of life and a book of holy doctrine. There is no creature so small and vile but that it showeth us the goodness of God.

JOY BELONGS TO THE PURE OF HEART

If thou wert good and pure within, then wouldst thou look upon all things without hurt and understand them aright. A pure heart seeth the very depths of heaven and hell. Such as each one is inwardly, so judgeth he outwardly.

If there is any joy in the world surely the man of pure heart possesseth it, and if there is anywhere tribulation and anguish, the evil conscience knoweth it best. As iron cast into the fire loseth rust and is made altogether glowing, so the man who turneth himself altogether unto God is freed from slothfulness and changed into a new man.

When a man beginneth to grow lukewarm, then he feareth a little labour, and willingly accepteth outward consolation; but when he beginneth perfectly to conquer himself and to walk manfully in the way of God, then he counteth as nothing those things which aforetime seemed to be so grievous unto him.

CHAPTER V
OF SELF-ESTEEM

WE cannot place too little confidence in ourselves, because grace and understanding are often lacking to us. Little light is there within us, and what we have we quickly lose by negligence. Oftentimes we perceive not how great is our inward blindness. We often do ill and excuse it worse.

Sometimes we are moved by passion and count it zeal; we blame little faults in others and pass over great faults in ourselves. Quickly enough we feel and reckon up what we bear at the hands of others, but we reflect not how much others are bearing from us. He who would weigh well and rightly his own doings would not be the man to judge severely of another.

THE SPIRITUALLY-MINDED MAN

The spiritually-minded man putteth care of himself before all cares; and he who diligently attendeth to himself easily keepeth silence concerning others. Thou wilt never be spiritually minded and godly unless thou art silent concerning other men's matters and take full heed to thyself. If thou think wholly upon thyself and upon God, what thou seest out of doors shall move thee little. Where art thou when thou art not present to thyself? and when thou hast overrun all things, what hath it profited thee, thyself being neglected? If thou wouldst have peace and true unity, thou must put aside all other things, and gaze only upon thyself.

Then thou shalt make great progress if thou keep thyself free from all temporal care. Thou shalt lamentably fall away if thou set a value upon any worldly thing. Let nothing be great, nothing high, nothing pleasing, nothing acceptable unto thee, save God Himself or the things of God.

Reckon as altogether vain whatsoever consolation comes to thee from a creature. The soul that loveth God looketh not to anything that is beneath God. God alone is eternal and incomprehensible, filling all things, the solace of the soul, and true joy of the heart.

CHAPTER VI
OF THE JOY OF A GOOD CONSCIENCE

THE testimony of a good conscience is the glory of a good man. Have a good conscience and thou shalt ever have joy. A good conscience is able to bear exceeding much, and is exceeding joyful in the midst of adversities; an evil conscience is ever fearful and unquiet. Thou shalt rest sweetly if thy heart condemn thee not. Never rejoice unless when thou hast done well.

The wicked have never true joy, nor feel internal peace, for *there is no peace, saith my God, to the wicked.* And if they say "we are in peace, there shall no harm happen unto us, and who shall dare to do us hurt?" believe them not, for suddenly shall the wrath of God rise up against them, and their deeds shall be brought to nought, and their thoughts shall perish.

To glory in tribulation is not grievous to him who loveth; for such glorying is glorying in the Cross of Christ. Brief is the glory which is given and received of men. Sadness always goeth hand in hand with the glory of the world. The glory of the good is in their conscience, and not in the report of men. The joy of the upright is from God and in God, and their joy is in the truth.

He who desireth true and eternal glory careth not for that which is temporal; and he who seeketh temporal glory, or who despiseth it from his heart, is proved to bear little love for that which is heavenly. He who careth for neither praises nor reproaches hath great tranquillity of heart.

THE SOURCE OF CONTENTMENT

He will easily be contented and filled with peace, whose conscience is pure. Thou art none the holier if thou art praised, nor the viler if thou art reproached. Thou art what thou art; and thou canst not be better than God pronounceth thee to be.

If thou considerest well what thou art inwardly, thou wilt not care what men will say to thee. *Man looketh on the outward appearance, but the Lord looketh on the heart:* Man looketh on the deed, but God considereth the intent. It is the token of a humble spirit always to do well, and to set little by oneself. Not to look for consolation from any created thing is a sign of great purity and inward faithfulness.

He that seeketh no outward witness on his own behalf, showeth plainly that he hath committed himself wholly to God. *For not he that commendeth himself is approved,* as St. Paul saith, *but whom the Lord commendeth.* To walk inwardly with God, and not to be held by any outer affections, is the state of a spiritual man.

CHAPTER VII
OF LOVING JESUS ABOVE ALL THINGS

BLESSED is he who understandeth what it is to love Jesus, and to despise himself for Jesus' sake. He must give up all that he loveth for his Beloved, for Jesus will be loved alone above all things. The love of created things is deceiving and unstable, but the love of Jesus is faithful and lasting.

He who cleaveth to created things will fall with their slipperiness; but he who embraceth Jesus will stand upright for ever. Love Him and hold Him for thy friend, for He will not forsake thee when all depart from thee, nor will He suffer thee to perish at the last. Thou must one day be separated from all, whether thou wilt or wilt not.

JESUS, OUR ONLY SOURCE OF HELP

Cleave thou to Jesus in life and death, and commit thyself unto His faithfulness, who, when all men fail thee, is alone able to help thee. Thy Beloved is such, by nature, that He will suffer no rival, but alone will possess thy heart, and as a king will sit upon His own throne. If thou wouldst learn to put away from thee every created thing, Jesus would freely take up His abode with thee. Thou wilt find all trust little better than lost which thou hast placed in men, and not in Jesus. Trust not nor lean upon a reed shaken with the wind, because *all flesh is grass, and the goodliness thereof falleth as the flower of the field.*

Thou wilt be quickly deceived if thou lookest only upon the outward appearance of men, for if thou seekest thy comfort and profit in others, thou shalt too often experience loss. If thou seekest Jesus in all things thou shalt verily find Jesus, but if thou seekest thyself thou shalt also find thyself, but to thine own hurt. For if a man seeketh not Jesus he is more hurtful to himself than all the world and all his adversaries.

CHAPTER VIII
OF THE INTIMATE LOVE OF JESUS

WHEN Jesus is present all is well and nothing seemeth hard, but when Jesus is not present everything is hard. When Jesus speaketh not within, our comfort is nothing worth, but if Jesus speaketh but a single word great is the comfort we experience. Did not Mary Magdalene rise up quickly from the place where she wept when Martha said to her, *The Master is come and calleth for thee?* Happy hour when Jesus calleth thee from tears to the joy of the spirit! How dry and hard art thou without Jesus! How senseless and vain if thou desirest aught beyond Jesus! Is not this greater loss than if thou shouldst lose the whole world?

What can the world profit thee without Jesus? To be without Jesus is the nethermost hell, and to be with Jesus is sweet Paradise. If Jesus were with thee no enemy could hurt thee. He who findeth Jesus findeth a good treasure, yea, good above all good; and he who loseth Jesus loseth exceeding much, yea, more than the whole world. Most poor is he who liveth without Jesus, and most rich is he who is much with Jesus.

HOW TO LIVE WITH JESUS

It is great skill to know how to live with Jesus, and to know how to hold Jesus is great wisdom. Be thou humble and peaceable and Jesus shall be with thee. Be godly and quiet, and Jesus will remain with thee. Thou canst quickly drive away Jesus and lose His favour if thou wilt turn away to the outer things. And if thou hast put Him to flight and lost Him, to whom wilt thou flee, and whom then wilt thou seek for a friend?

Without a friend thou canst not live long, and if Jesus be not thy friend above all thou shalt be very sad and desolate. Madly therefore doest thou if thou trusteth or findest joy in any other. It is preferable to have the whole world against thee, than Jesus offended with thee. Therefore of all that are dear to thee, let Jesus be specially loved.

Let all be loved for Jesus' sake, but Jesus for His own. Jesus Christ alone is to be specially loved, for He alone is found good and faithful above all friends. For His sake and in Him let both enemies and friends be dear to thee, and pray for them all that they may all know and love Him.

Never desire to be specially praised or loved, because this belongeth to God alone, who hath none like unto Himself. Nor wish thou that any one set his heart on thee, nor do thou give thyself up to the love of any, but let Jesus be in thee and in every good man.

AVOID ENTANGLEMENTS WITH CREATED THINGS

Be pure and free within thyself, and be not entangled by any created thing. Thou oughtest to bring a bare and clean heart to God, if thou desirest to be ready to see how gracious the Lord is. And in truth, unless thou be prevented and drawn on by His grace, thou wilt not attain to this, that having cast out and dismissed all else, thou alone art united to God.

For when the grace of God cometh to a man, then he becometh able to do all things, and when it departeth then he will be poor and weak and given up unto troubles. In these thou art not to be cast down nor to despair, but to rest with calm mind on the will of God, and to bear all things which come upon thee unto the praise of Jesus Christ; for after winter cometh summer, after night returneth day, after the tempest a great calm.

CHAPTER IX

OF THE LACK OF ALL COMFORT

It is no hard thing to despise human comfort when divine is present. It is a great thing, yea very great, to be able to bear the loss both of human and divine comfort; and for the love of God willingly to bear exile of heart, and in nought to seek oneself, nor to look to one's own merit.

What great matter is it, if thou be cheerful of heart and devout when favour cometh to thee? That is an hour wherein all rejoice. Pleasantly enough doth he ride whom the grace of God carrieth. And what marvel, if he feeleth no burden who is carried by the Almighty, and is led onwards by the Guide from on high?

We are willing to accept anything for comfort, and it is difficult for a man to be freed from himself. The holy martyr Laurence overcame the love of the world and even of his priestly master, because he despised everything in the world which seemed to be pleasant; and for the love of Christ he calmly suffered even God's chief priest, Sixtus, whom he dearly loved, to be taken from him. Thus by the love of the Creator he overcame the love of man, and instead of human comfort he chose rather God's good pleasure. So also learn thou to resign any near and beloved friend for the love of God. Nor take it amiss when thou hast been deserted by a friend, knowing that we must all be parted from one another at last.

Mightily and long must a man strive within himself before he learn altogether to overcome himself, and to draw his whole affection towards God. When a man resteth upon himself, he easily slippeth away unto human comforts. But a true lover of Christ, and a diligent seeker after virtue, falleth not back upon those comforts, nor seeketh such sweetnesses as may be tasted and handled, but desireth rather hard exercises, and to undertake severe labours for Christ.

EXPERIENCING GOD'S FAVOUR

When, therefore, spiritual comfort is given by God, receive it with giving of thanks, and know that it is the gift of God, not thy desert. Be not lifted up, rejoice not overmuch nor foolishly presume, but rather be more humble for the gift, more wary and more careful in all thy doings; for that hour will pass away, and temptation will follow.

When comfort is taken from thee, do not straightway despair, but wait for the heavenly visitation with humility and patience, for God is able to give thee back greater favour and consolation. This is not new nor strange to those who have made trial of the way of God, for with the great saints and the ancient prophets there was often this manner of change.

Wherefore one said when the favour of God was present with him, *I said in my prosperity I shall never be moved,* but he goeth on to say what he felt within himself when the favour departed: *Thou didst turn Thy face from me, and I was troubled.* In spite whereof he in no wise despaireth, but the more instantly entreateth God, and saith, *Unto Thee, O Lord, will I cry, and will pray unto my God;* and

then he receiveth the fruit of his prayer, and testifieth how he hath been heard, saying, *The Lord heard me and had mercy upon me, the Lord was my helper.* But wherein? *Thou hast turned my heaviness into joy, Thou hast put off my sackcloth and girded me with gladness.*

If it was thus with the great saints, we who are poor and needy ought not to despair if we are sometimes in the warmth and sometimes in the cold, for the Spirit cometh and goeth according to the good pleasure of His will. Wherefore holy Job saith, *Thou dost visit him in the morning, and suddenly Thou dost prove him.*

Whereupon then can I hope, or wherein may I trust, save only in the great mercy of God, and the hope of heavenly grace? For whether good men are with me, godly brethren or faithful friends, whether holy books or beautiful discourses, whether sweet hymns and songs, all these help but little, and have but little savour when I am deserted by God's favour and left to mine own poverty. There is no better remedy, then, than patience and denial of self, and an abiding in the will of God.

TEMPTATION, OUR COMMON LOT

I have never found any man so religious and godly, but that he felt sometimes a withdrawal of the divine favour, and lack of fervour. No saint was ever so filled with rapture, so enlightened, but that sooner or later he was tempted. For he is not worthy of the great vision of God, who, for God's sake, hath not been exercised by some temptation. For temptation is wont to go before as a sign of the comfort which shall follow, and heavenly comfort is promised to those who are proved by temptation. As it is written, *To him that overcometh I will give to eat of the tree of life.*

Divine comfort is given that a man may be stronger to bear adversities. And temptation followeth, lest he be lifted up because of the benefit. The devil sleepeth not; thy flesh is not yet dead; therefore, cease thou not to make thyself ready unto the battle, for enemies stand on thy right hand and on thy left, and they are never at rest.

CHAPTER X
OF GRATITUDE FOR THE GRACE OF GOD

WHY seekest thou rest when thou art born to labour? Prepare thyself for patience more than for comforts, and for bearing the cross more than for joy. For who among the men of this world would not gladly receive consolation and spiritual joy if he might always have it? For spiritual comforts exceed all the delights of the world, and all the pleasures of the flesh. For all worldly delights are either empty or unclean, whilst spiritual delights alone are pleasant and honourable, the offspring of virtue, and poured forth by God into pure minds. But no man can always enjoy these divine comforts at his own will, because the season of temptation ceaseth not for long.

Great is the difference between a visitation from above and false liberty of spirit and great confidence in self. God doeth well in giving us the grace of comfort, but man doeth ill in not immediately giving God thanks thereof. And thus the gifts of grace are not able to flow unto us, because we are ungrateful to the Author of them, and return them not wholly to the Fountain whence they flow. For grace ever becometh the portion of him who is grateful and that is taken away from the proud, which is wont to be given to the humble.

THE PLACE OF HUMILITY

I desire no consolation which taketh away from me compunction, I love no contemplation which leadeth to pride. For all that is high is not holy, nor is everything that is sweet good; every desire is not pure; nor is everything that is dear to us pleasing unto God. Willingly do I accept that grace whereby I am made humbler and more wary and more ready to renounce myself.

He who is made learned by the gift of grace and taught wisdom by the stroke of the withdrawal thereof, will not dare to claim any good thing for himself, but will rather confess that he is poor and needy. *Give unto God the thing which is God's*, and ascribe to thyself that which is thine; that is, give thanks unto God for His grace, but for thyself alone confess thy fault, and that thy punishment is deserved for thy fault.

Sit thou down always in the lowest room and thou shalt be given the highest place. For the highest cannot be without the lowest. For the highest saints of God are least in their own sight, and the more glorious they are, so much the lowlier are they in themselves; full of grace and heavenly glory, they are not desirous of vainglory; resting on God and strong in His might, they cannot be lifted up in any wise.

And they who ascribe unto God all the good which they have received, "seek not glory one of another, but the glory which cometh from God only," and they desire that God shall be praised in Himself and in all His saints above all things, and they are always striving for this very thing.

IN EVERYTHING GIVE THANKS

Be thankful, therefore, for the least benefit and thou shalt be worthy to receive greater. Let the least be unto thee even as the greatest, and let that which is of little account be unto thee as a special gift. If the majesty of the Giver be considered, nothing that is given shall seem small and of no worth, for that is not a small thing which is given by the Most High God.

Yea, though He gave punishment and stripes, we ought to be thankful, because He ever doth for our profit whatever He suffereth to come upon us. He who seeketh to retain the favour of God, let him be thankful for the favour which is given, and patient in respect of that which is taken away. Let him pray that it may return; let him be wary and humble that he lose it not.

CHAPTER XI
OF THE FEWNESS OF THOSE WHO LOVE THE CROSS OF JESUS

JESUS hath many lovers of His heavenly kingdom, but few bearers of His Cross. He hath many seekers of comfort, but few of tribulation. He findeth many companions of His table, but few of His fasting. All desire to rejoice with Him, few are willing to undergo anything for His sake. Many follow Jesus that they may eat of His loaves, but few that they may drink of the cup of His passion.

Many are astonished at His Miracles, few follow after the shame of His Cross. Many love Jesus so long as no adversities happen to them. Many praise Him and bless Him, so long as they receive any comforts from Him. But if Jesus hide Himself and withdraw from them a little while, they fall either into complaining or into too great dejection of mind.

But they who love Jesus for Jesus' sake, and not for any consolation of their own, bless Him in all tribulation and anguish of heart as in the highest consolation. And if He should never give them consolation, nevertheless they would always praise Him and always give Him thanks.

THE POWER OF PURE LOVE

Oh what power hath the pure love of Jesus, unmixed with any gain or love of self! Should not all they be called mercenary who are always seeking consolations? Do they not prove themselves lovers of self more than of Christ who are always seeking their own gain and advantage? Where shall be found one who is willing to serve God altogether for nought?

Rarely is any one found so spiritual as to be stripped of all selfish thoughts, for who shall find a man truly poor in spirit and free of all created things? "His value is from afar, yea from the ends of the earth." A man may give away all his goods, yet that is nothing; and if he do many deeds of penitence, yet that is a small thing; and though he understand all knowledge, yet that is afar off; and if he have great virtue and zealous devotion, yet much is lacking unto him, yea, one thing which is the most necessary to him of all.

What is it then? That having given up all things besides, he give up himself and go forth from himself utterly, and retain nothing of self-love; and having done all things which he knoweth to be his duty to do, that he feel that he hath done nothing. Let him not reckon that much which might be much esteemed, but let him pronounce himself to be in truth an uprofitable servant, and the Truth Himself saith, *When ye have done all things that are commanded you, say, we are unprofitable servants.* Then may he be truly poor and naked in spirit, and be able to say with the Prophet, *As for me, I am poor and needy.* Nevertheless, no man is richer than he, no man stronger, no man freer. For he knoweth both how to give up himself and all things, and how to be lowly in his own eyes.

CHAPTER XII
OF THE ROYAL WAY OF THE HOLY CROSS

THAT seemeth a hard saying to many, *If any man will come after Me, let him deny himself and take up his Cross and follow Me.* But it will be much harder to hear that last sentence, *Depart from me, ye wicked, into eternal fire.* For they who now willingly hear the word of the Cross and follow it, shall not then fear the hearing of eternal damnation. This sign of the Cross shall be in heaven when the Lord cometh to Judgment. Then all servants of the Cross, who in life have conformed themselves to the Crucified, shall draw nigh unto Christ the Judge with great boldness.

Why fearest thou then to take up the cross which leadeth to a kingdom? In the Cross is health, in the Cross is life, in the Cross is protection from enemies, in the Cross is heavenly sweetness, in the Cross strength of mind, in the Cross joy of the spirit, in the Cross the height of virtue, in the Cross perfection of holiness. There is no health of the soul, no hope of eternal life, save in the Cross.

Take up therefore, thy cross and follow Jesus and thou shalt go into eternal life. He went before thee bearing His Cross and died for thee upon the Cross, that thou also mayest bear thy cross and mayest love to be crucified upon it. For if thou be dead with Him, thou shalt also live with Him, and if thou be a partaker of His sufferings thou shalt be also of His glory.

THE CENTRALITY OF THE CROSS

Behold everything dependeth upon the Cross, and everything lieth in dying; and there is none other way unto life and to true inward peace, except the way of the Holy Cross and of daily mortification. Go where thou wilt, seek whatsoever thou wilt, and thou shalt find no higher way above nor safer way below, than the way of the Holy Cross. Dispose and order all things according to thine own will and judgment, and thou shalt ever find something to suffer either willingly or unwillingly, and thus thou shalt ever find thy cross. For thou shalt either feel pain of body, or tribulation of spirit within thy soul.

Sometimes thou wilt be forsaken of God, sometimes thou wilt be tried by thy neighbour, and which is more, thou wilt often be wearisome to thyself. And still thou canst not be delivered nor eased by any remedy or consolation, but must bear so long as God will. For God will have thee learn to suffer tribulation without consolation, and to submit thyself fully to it, and by tribulation be made more humble.

No man understandeth the Passion

of Christ in his heart so well as he who hath had somewhat of the like suffering himself. The Cross therefore is always ready, and every where waiteth for thee. Thou canst not flee from it whithersoever thou hurriest, for whithersoever thou comest, thou bearest thyself with thee, and shalt ever find thyself. Turn thee above, turn thee below, turn thee without, turn thee within, and in them all thou shalt find the Cross; and needful is it that thou everywhere possess patience if thou wilt have internal peace and gain the everlasting crown.

If thou willingly bear the Cross, it will bear thee, and will bring thee to the end which thou seekest, even where there shall be the end of suffering; though it shall not be here. If thou bear it unwillingly, thou makest a burden for thyself and greatly increaseth thy load, and yet thou must bear it. If thou cast away one cross, without doubt thou shalt find another and perchance a heavier.

NO SAINT IS WITHOUT A CROSS

Thinkest thou to escape what no mortal hath been able to avoid? Which of the saints in the world hath been without the cross and tribulation? For not even Jesus Christ our Lord was one hour without the anguish of His Passion, so long as He lived. *It behooved,* He said, *Christ to suffer and to rise from the dead, and so enter into His glory.* And how dost thou seek another way than this royal way, which is the way of the Holy Cross?

The whole life of Christ was a cross and martyrdom, and dost thou seek for thyself rest and joy? Thou art wrong, thou art wrong, if thou seekest aught but to suffer tribulations, for this whole mortal life is full of miseries, and set round with crosses. And the higher a man hath advanced in the spirit, the heavier crosses he will often find, because the sorrow of his banishment increaseth with the strength of his love.

But yet the man who is thus in so many wise afflicted, is not without refreshment of consolation, because he feeleth abundant fruit to be growing within him out of the bearing of his cross. For whilst he willingly submitteth himself to it, every burden of tribulation is turned into an assurance of divine comfort, and the more the flesh is wasted by affliction, the more is the spirit strengthened mightily by inward grace.

And ofttimes so greatly is he comforted by the desire for tribulation and adversity, through love of conformity to the Cross of Christ, that he would not be without sorrow and tribulation; for he believeth that he shall be the more acceptable to God, the more and the heavier burdens he is able to bear for His sake. This is not the virtue of man, but the grace of Christ which hath such power and energy in the weak flesh, that what it naturally hateth and fleeth from, this it draweth to and loveth through fervour of spirit.

NO MAN LOVES A CROSS

It is not in the nature of man to bear the cross, to love the cross, to keep under the body and to bring it into subjection, to fly from honours, to bear reproaches meekly, to despise self and desire to be despised, to bear all adversities and losses, and to desire no prosperity in this world. If thou lookest to thyself, thou wilt of thyself be able to do none of this; but if thou trustest in the Lord, endurance shall be given thee from heaven, and the world and the flesh shall be made subject to thy command. Yea, thou shalt not even fear thine adversary the devil, if thou be armed with faith and signed with the Cross of Christ.

Set thyself, therefore, like a good and faithful servant of Christ, to the manful bearing of the Cross of thy Lord, who out of love was crucified for thee. Prepare thyself for the bearing many adversities and manifold troubles in this wretched life; because so it shall be with thee wheresoever thou art, and so in very deed thou shalt find it, wherever thou hide thyself.

This it must be; and there is no means of escaping from tribulation and sorrow, except to bear them patiently. Drink thou lovingly thy Lord's cup if thou desirest to be His friend and to have thy lot with Him. Leave consolations to God; let Him do as seemeth best to Him concerning them. But do thou set thyself to endure tribulations, and reckon them the best consolations; for *the sufferings of this present time are not worthy to be compared with the glory which shall be revealed in us,* nor would they be even if thou wert to endure them all.

WHEN TRIBULATION IS SWEET

When thou hast come to this, that tribulation is sweet and pleasant to thee for Christ's sake, then reckon that it is well with thee, because thou hast found paradise on earth. So long as it is hard to thee to suffer and thou desirest to escape, so long it will not be well with thee, and tribulations will follow thee everywhere.

If thou settest thyself to that thou oughtest, namely, to suffer and to die,

it shall soon go better with thee, and thou shalt find peace. Though thou shouldest be caught up with Paul unto the third heaven, thou art not on that account secure from suffering evil. *I will show him,* saith Jesus, *what great things he must suffer for My Name's sake.* It remaineth, therefore, to thee to suffer, if thou wilt love Jesus and serve Him continually.

Oh that thou wert worthy to suffer something for the name of Jesus, how great glory should await thee, what rejoicing among all the saints of God, what bright example also to thy neighbour! For all men commend patience, although few be willing to practise it. Thou oughtest surely to suffer a little for Christ when many suffer heavier things for the world.

ON BEARING ADVERSITIES FOR CHRIST

Know thou of a surety that thou oughtest to lead the life of a dying man. And the more a man dieth to himself, the more he beginneth to live towards God. None is fit for the understanding of heavenly things, unless he hath submitted himself to bearing adversities for Christ.

Nothing more acceptable to God, nothing more healthful for thyself in this world, than to suffer willingly for Christ. And if it were thine to choose, thou oughtest rather to wish to suffer adversities for Christ, than to be refreshed with manifold consolations, for thou wouldest be more like Christ and more conformed to all saints. For our worthiness and growth in grace lieth not in many delights and consolations, but rather in bearing many troubles and adversities.

If indeed there had been anything

better and more profitable to the health of men than to suffer, Christ would surely have shown it by word and example. For both the disciples who followed Him, and all who desire to follow Him, He plainly exhorteth to bear their cross, and saith, *If any man will come after Me, let him deny himself and take up his cross, and follow Me.* So now that we have thoroughly read and studied all things, let us hear the conclusion of the whole matter. *We must through much tribulation enter into the kingdom of God.*

The Third Book

ON INWARD CONSOLATION

CHAPTER I
OF THE INWARD VOICE OF CHRIST
TO THE FAITHFUL SOUL

I WILL HEARKEN what the Lord God shall say within me. Blessed is the soul which heareth the Lord speaking within it, and receiveth the word of consolation from His mouth. Blessed are the ears which receive the echoes of the soft whisper of God, and turn not aside to the whisperings of this world. Blessed truly are the ears which listen not to the voice that soundeth without, but to that which teacheth truth inwardly. Blessed are the eyes which are closed to things without, but are fixed upon things within.

Blessed are they who search inward things and study to prepare themselves more and more by daily exercises for the receiving of heavenly mysteries. Blessed are they who long to have leisure for God, and free themselves from every hindrance of the world. Think on these things, O my soul, and shut the doors of thy carnal desires, so mayest thou hear what the Lord God will say within thee.

These things saith thy Beloved, "I am thy salvation, I am thy peace and thy life. Keep thee unto Me, and thou shalt find peace." Put away thee all transitory things, seek those things that are eternal. For what are all temporal things but deceits, and what shall all created things help thee if thou be forsaken by the Creator? Therefore put all things else away, and give thyself to the Creator, to be well pleasing and faithful to Him, that thou mayest be able to attain true blessedness.

CHAPTER II
WHAT THE TRUTH SAITH INWARDLY
WITHOUT NOISE OF WORDS

SPEAK, Lord, for thy servant heareth. I am Thy servant; O give me understanding that I may know Thy testimonies. Incline my heart unto the words of Thy mouth. Let thy speech distil as the dew. The children of Israel spake in old time to Moses, *Speak thou unto us and we will hear, but let not the Lord speak unto us lest we die.* Not thus, O Lord, not thus do I pray, but rather with Samuel the prophet, I beseech Thee humbly and earnestly, *Speak, Lord, for Thy servant heareth.* Let not Moses speak to me, nor any prophet, but rather speak Thou, O Lord, who didst inspire and illuminate all the prophets; for Thou alone without them canst perfectly fill me with knowledge, whilst they without Thee shall profit nothing.

SPEAK, LORD

They can indeed utter words, but they give not the spirit. They speak with exceeding beauty, but when Thou art silent they kindle not the heart. They give us scriptures, but Thou makest known the sense thereof. They bring us mysteries, but Thou revealest the things which are signified. They utter commandments, but Thou helpest to the fulfilling of them. They show the way, but Thou givest strength for the journey. They act only outwardly, but Thou dost instruct and enlighten the heart. They water, but Thou givest the increase. They cry with words, but Thou givest understanding to the hearer.

Therefore let not Moses speak to me, but Thou, O Lord my God, Eternal Truth; lest I die and bring forth no fruit, being outwardly admonished, but not enkindled within; lest the word heard but not followed, known but not loved, believed but not obeyed, rise up against me in the judgment. *Speak, Lord, for Thy servant heareth; Thou hast the words of eternal life.* Speak unto me for some consolation unto my soul, for the amendment of my whole life, and for the praise and glory and eternal honour of Thy Name.

CHAPTER III

HOW ALL THE WORDS OF GOD ARE TO BE HEARD WITH HUMILITY, AND HOW MANY CONSIDER THEM NOT

"My Son, hear My words, for My words are most sweet, surpassing all the knowledge of the philosophers and wise men of this world. *My words are spirit, and they are life*, and are not to be weighed by man's understanding. They are not to be drawn forth for vain approbation, but to be heard in silence, and to be received with all humility and with deep love."

And I said, *"Blessed is the man whom Thou teachest, O Lord, and instructest him in Thy law, that Thou mayest give him rest in time of adversity*, and that he be not desolate in the earth."

MISPLACED VALUES

"I," saith the Lord, "taught the prophets from the beginning, and even now cease I not to speak unto all; but many are deaf and hardened against My voice; many love to listen to the world rather than to God; they follow after the desires of the flesh more readily than after the good pleasure of God.

"The world promiseth things that are temporal and small, and it is served with great eagerness. I promise things that are great and eternal, and the hearts of mortals are slow to stir. Who serveth and obeyeth Me in all things, with such carefulness as he serveth the world and its rulers?

Be thou ashamed, O Sidon, saith
   the sea;
And if thou reason seekest, hear
   thou me.

For a little reward men make a long journey; for eternal life many will scarce lift a foot once from the ground. Mean reward is sought after; for a single piece of money sometimes there is shameful striving; for a thing which is vain and for a trifling promise, men shrink not from toiling day and night.

"But, O shame! for an unchangeable good, for an inestimable reward, for the highest honour and for a glory that fadeth not away, it is irksome to them to toil even a little. Be thou ashamed therefore, slothful and discontented servant, for they are found readier unto perdition than thou unto life. They rejoice more heartily in vanity than thou in the truth.

"Sometimes, indeed, they are disappointed of their hope, but My promise faileth no man, nor sendeth away empty him who trusteth in Me. What

I have promised I will give; what I have said I will fulfil; if only a man remain faithful in My love unto the end. Therefore am I the rewarder of all good men, and a strong approver of all who are godly.

GIVE HEED TO MY WORDS

"Write My words in thy heart and consider them diligently, for they shall be very needful to thee in time of temptation. What thou understandest not when thou readest, thou shalt know in the time of thy visitation. I am wont to visit Mine elect in twofold manner, even by temptation and by comfort, and I teach them two lessons day by day, the one in chiding their faults, the other in exhorting them to grow in grace. He who hath My words and rejecteth them, hath one who shall judge him at the last day."

A PRAYER FOR THE SPIRIT OF DEVOTION

O Lord my God, Thou art all my good, and who am I that I should dare to speak unto Thee? I am the very poorest of Thy servants, an abject worm, much poorer and more despicable than I know or dare to say. Nevertheless remember, O Lord, that I am nothing, I have nothing, and can do nothing.

Thou only art good, just and holy; Thou canst do all things, art over all things, fillest all things, leaving empty only the sinner. Call to mind Thy tender mercies, and fill my heart with Thy grace, Thou who wilt not that Thy work should return to Thee void.

How can I bear this miserable life unless Thy mercy and grace strengthen me? Turn not away Thy face from me, delay not Thy visitation. Withdraw not Thou Thy comfort from me, lest my soul "gasp after thee as a thirsty land." Lord, teach me to do Thy will; teach me to walk humbly and uprightly before Thee, for Thou art my wisdom, who knowest me in truth, and knewest me before the world was made and before I was born into the world.

CHAPTER IV
HOW WE MUST WALK IN TRUTH AND HUMILITY BEFORE GOD

"My Son! walk before Me in truth, and in the simplicity of thy heart seek Me continually. He who walketh before Me in the truth shall be safe from evil assaults, and the truth shall deliver him from the wiles and slanders of the wicked. If the truth shall make thee free, thou shalt be free indeed, and shalt not care for the vain words of men."

Lord, it is true as Thou sayest; let it, I pray Thee, be so with me; let Thy Truth teach me; let it keep me and preserve me safe unto the end. Let it free me from all evil and inordinate affection, and I will walk before Thee in great freedom of heart.

CONSIDER THY WEAKNESS

"I will teach thee," saith the Truth, "the things which are right and pleasing before Me. Think upon thy sins with great displeasure and sorrow, and never think thyself anything because of thy good works. Verily thou art a sinner, liable to many passions, yea, tied and bound with them. Of thyself thou always tendest unto nothing, thou wilt quickly fall, quickly be conquered, quickly disturbed, quickly undone. Thou hast nought whereof to glory, but many reasons why thou shouldst reckon thyself vile, for thou art far weaker than thou art able to comprehend.

"Let, therefore, nothing which thou doest seem to thee great; let nothing be grand, nothing of value or beauty, nothing worthy of honour, nothing lofty, nothing praiseworthy or desirable, save what is eternal. Let the eternal truth please thee above all things, let thine own great vileness diplease thee continually. Fear, denounce, flee nothing so much as thine own faults and sins, which ought to be more displeasing to thee than any loss whatsoever of goods.

"There are some who walk not sincerely before Me, but being led by curiosity and pride, they desire to know My secret things and to understand the deep things of God, whilst they neglect themselves and their salvation. These often fall into great temptations and sins because of their pride and curiosity, for I am against them.

NEGLECT THE WORLD

"Fear thou the judgments of God; fear greatly the wrath of the Almighty. Shrink from debating upon the works of the Most High, but search narrowly thine own iniquities into what great sins thou hast fallen, and how many good things thou hast neglected. There are some who carry their devotion only in books, some in pictures, some in outward signs and figures; some have Me in their mouths, but little in their hearts. Others there are who, being enlightened in their understanding and purged in their affections, continually long after eternal things, hear of earthly things with unwillingness, obey the necessities of nature with sorrow. And these understand what the Spirit of truth speaketh in them; for He teacheth them to despise earthly things and to love heavenly; to neglect the world and to desire heaven all the day and night."

Chapter V
OF THE WONDERFUL POWER
OF THE DIVINE LOVE

I BLESS Thee, O Heavenly Father, Father of my Lord Jesus Christ, for that Thou hast vouchsafed to think of me, poor that I am. *O, Father of Mercies and God of all comfort*, I give thanks unto Thee, who refreshest me sometimes with thine own comfort, when I am unworthy of any comfort. I bless and glorify Thee continually, with thine only begotten Son and the Holy Ghost, the Paraclete, for ever and ever. O Lord God, Holy lover of my soul, when Thou shalt come into my heart, all my inward parts shall rejoice. Thou art my glory and the joy of my heart. Thou art my hope and my refuge in the day of my trouble.

THE EFFECT OF LOVE

But because I am still weak in love and imperfect in virtue, I need to be strengthened and comforted by Thee; therefore visit Thou me often and instruct me with Thy holy ways of discipline. Deliver me from evil passions, and cleanse my heart from all inordinate affections, that, being healed and altogether cleansed within, I may be made ready to love, strong to suffer, steadfast to endure.

Love is a great thing, a good above all others, which alone maketh every heavy burden light, and equaliseth every inequality. For it beareth the burden and maketh it no burden, it maketh every bitter thing to be sweet and of good taste. The surpassing love of Jesus impelleth to great works, and exciteth to the continual desiring of greater perfection.

Love willeth to be raised up, and not to be held down by any mean thing. Love willeth to be free and aloof from all worldly affection, lest its inward power of vision be hindered, lest it be entangled by any worldly prosperity or overcome by adversity. Nothing is sweeter than love, nothing stronger, nothing loftier, nothing broader, nothing pleasanter, nothing fuller or better in heaven nor on earth, for love was born of God and cannot rest save in God above all created things.

ENLARGE ME IN LOVE

He who loveth flyeth, runneth, and is glad; he is free and not hindered. He giveth all things for all things, and hath all things in all things, because he resteth in One who is high above all, from whom every good floweth and proceedeth. He looketh not for gifts, but turneth himself to the Giver above all good things.

Love oftentimes knoweth no measure, but breaketh out above all measure; love feeleth no burden, reckoneth not labours, striveth after more than it is able to do, pleadeth not impossibility, because it judgeth all things which are lawful for it to be possible. It is strong therefore for all things, and it fulfilleth many things, and is successful where he who loveth not faileth and lieth down.

Love is watchful, and whilst sleeping still keepeth watch; though fatigued it is not weary; though pressed it is not forced; though alarmed it is not terrified, but like the living flame and the burning torch, it breaketh forth on high and securely triumpheth. If a man loveth, he knoweth what this voice crieth. For the ardent affection of the soul is a great clamour in the ears of God, and it saith: My God, my Beloved! Thou art all mine, and I am all Thine.

Enlarge Thou me in love, that I may learn to taste with the innermost mouth of my heart how sweet it is to love, to be dissolved, and to swim in love. Let me be holden by love, mounting above myself through exceeding fervour and admiration. Let me sing the song of love, let me follow Thee my Beloved on high, let my soul exhaust itself in Thy praise, exulting with love. Let me love Thee more than myself, not loving myself except for Thy sake, and all men in Thee who truly love Thee, as the law of love commandeth which shineth forth from Thee.

THE NATURE OF LOVE

Love is swift, sincere, pious, pleasant, gentle, strong, patient, faithful, prudent, long-suffering, manly, and never seeking her own; for wheresoever a man seeketh his own, there he falleth from love. Love is circumspect, humble, and upright; not weak, not fickle, nor intent on vain things; sober, chaste, steadfast, quiet, and guarded in all the senses. Love is subject and obedient to all that are in authority, vile and lowly in its own sight, devout and grateful towards God, faithful and always trusting in Him even when God hideth His face, for without sorrow we cannot live in love.

He who is not ready to suffer all things, and to conform to the will of the Beloved, is not worthy to be called a lover of God. It behoveth him who loveth to embrace willingly all hard and bitter things for the Beloved's sake, and not to be drawn away from Him because of any contrary accidents.

CHAPTER VI
OF THE PROVING OF THE TRUE LOVER

"MY Son, thou art not yet strong and prudent in thy love."

Wherefore, O my Lord?

"Because for a little opposition thou fallest away from thy undertakings, and too eagerly seekest after consolation. The strong lover standeth fast in temptations, and believeth not the evil persuasions of the enemy. As in prosperity I please him, so in adversity I do not displease.

"The prudent lover considereth not the gift of the lover so much as the love of the giver. He looketh for the affection more than the value, and setteth all gifts lower than the Beloved. The noble lover resteth not in the gift, but in Me above every gift.

GUARD THY THOUGHTS

"All is not lost, though thou sometimes think of Me or of My saints, less than thou shouldest desire. That good and sweet affection which thou sometimes perceivest is the effect of present grace and some foretaste of the heavenly country; but hereon thou must not too much depend, for it goeth and cometh. But to strive against the evil motions of the mind which come to us, and to resist the suggestions of the devil, is a token of virtue and great merit.

"Therefore let not strange fancies disturb thee, whencesoever they arise. Bravely observe thy purpose and thy upright intentions towards God. It is not an illusion when thou art sometimes suddenly carried away into rapture, and then suddenly art brought back to the wonted vanities of thy heart. For thou dost rather unwillingly undergo them than cause them; and so long as they displease thee and thou strivest against them, it is a merit and no loss.

RESIST THE EVIL ONE

"Know thou that thine old enemy altogether striveth to hinder thy pursuit after good, and to deter thee from every godly exercise, to wit, the contemplation of the saints, the pious remembrance of My passion, the profitable recollection of sin, the keeping of thy own heart, and the steadfast purpose to grow in virtue. He suggesteth to thee many evil thoughts, that he may work in thee weariness and terror, and so draw thee away from prayer and holy reading. Humble confession displeaseth him, and if he were able he would make thee to cease from Communion. Believe him not, nor heed him, though many a time he hath laid for thee the snares of deceit.

"Account it to be from him, when he suggesteth evil and unclean thoughts. Say unto him, 'Depart unclean spirit; put on shame, miserable one; horribly unclean art thou, who bringest such things to mine ears. Depart from me, detestable deceiver; thou shalt have no part in me; but Jesus shall be with me, as a strong warrior, and thou shalt stand confounded. Rather would I die and bear all suffering, than consent unto thee. Hold thy peace and be dumb; I will not hear thee more, though thou plottest more snares against me. *The Lord is my light and my salvation: whom then shall I fear? Though a host of men should rise up against me, yet shall not my heart be afraid. The Lord is my strength and my Redeemer.'*

BEWARE OF PRIDE

"Strive thou like a good soldier; and if sometimes thou fail through weakness, put on thy strength more bravely than before, trusting in My more abundant grace, and take thou much heed of vain confidence and pride. Because of it many are led into error, and sometimes fall into blindness wellnigh irremediable. Let this ruin of the proud, who foolishly lift themselves up, be to thee for a warning and a continual exhortation to humility."

CHAPTER VII
OF HIDING OUR GRACE UNDER THE GUARD OF HUMILITY

"MY Son, it is better and safer for thee to hide the grace of devotion, and not to lift thyself up on high, nor to speak much thereof, nor to value it greatly; but rather to despise thyself, and to fear as though this grace were given to one unworthy thereof. Nor must thou depend too much upon this feeling, for it can very quickly be turned into its opposite.

"Think when thou art in a state of grace how miserable and poor thou art wont to be without grace. Nor is there advance in spiritual life in this alone, that thou hast the grace of consolation, but that thou humbly and unselfishly and patiently takest the withdrawal thereof; so that thou cease not from the exercise of prayer, nor suffer thy other common duties to be in anywise neglected; rather do thy task more readily, as though thou hadst gained more strength and knowledge; and do not altogether neglect thyself because of the dearth and anxiety of spirit which thou feelest.

A WARNING AGAINST PRESUMPTION

"For there are many who, when things have not gone prosperous with them, become forthwith impatient or slothful. *For the way of a man is not in himself,* but it is God's to give and to console, when He will, and as much as He will, and whom He will, as it shall please Him, and no further. Some who were presumptuous because of the grace of devotion within them, have destroyed themselves, because they would do more than they were able, not considering the measure of their own littleness, but rather following the impulse of the heart than the judgment of the reason.

"And because they presumed beyond what was well-pleasing unto God, therefore they quickly lost grace. They became poor and were left vile, who had built for themselves their nest in heaven; so that being humbled and stricken with poverty, they might learn not to fly with their own wings, but to put their trust under My feathers. They who are as yet new and unskilled in the way of the Lord, unless they rule themselves after the counsel of the wise, may easily be deceived and led away.

"But if they wish to follow their own fancies rather than trust the experience of others, the result will be very dangerous to them if they still refuse to be drawn away from their own notion. Those who are wise in their own conceits, seldom patiently endure to be ruled by others. It is better to have a small portion of wisdom with humility, and a slender understanding, than great treasures of sciences with vain self-esteem.

"It is better for thee to have less than much of what may make thee proud. He doeth not very discreetly who giveth himself entirely to joy, forgetting his former helplessness and the chaste fear of the Lord, which feareth to lose the grace offered. Nor is he very wise, after a manly sort, who in time of adversity, or any trouble whatsoever, beareth himself too despairingly, and feeleth concerning Me less trustfully than he ought.

TRUE MERIT

"He who in time of peace willeth to be oversecure shall be often found in time of war overdispirited and full of fears. If thou knewest always how to continue humble and moderate in thyself, and to guide and rule thine own spirit well, thou wouldest not so quickly fall into danger and mischief.

"It is good counsel that when fervour of spirit is kindled, thou shouldest meditate how it will be with thee when the light is taken away. Which when it doth happen, remember that still the light may return again, which I have taken away for a time for a warning to thee, and also for mine own glory. Such a trial is often more useful than if thou hadst always things properous according to thine own will.

"For merits are not to be reckoned by this, that a man hath many visions or consolations, or that he is skilled in the Scriptures, or that he is placed in a high situation; but that he is grounded upon true humility and filled with divine charity, that he always purely and uprightly seeketh the honour of God, that he setteth not by himself, but un-

feignedly despiseth himself, and even rejoiceth to be despised and humbled by others more than to be honoured."

CHAPTER VIII
OF A LOW ESTIMATION OF SELF IN THE SIGHT OF GOD

I WILL speak unto my Lord who am but dust and ashes. If I count myself more, behold Thou standest against me, and my iniquities bear true testimony, and I cannot gainsay it. But if I abase myself, and bring myself to nought, and shrink from all self-esteem, and grind myself to dust, which I am, Thy grace will be favourable unto me, and Thy light will be near unto my heart; and all self-esteem, how little soever it be, shall be swallowed up in the depths of my nothingness, and shall perish for ever.

There Thou showest to me myself, what I am, what I was, and whither I have come: *so foolish was I and ignorant*. If I am left to myself, behold I am nothing; I am all weakness; but if suddenly Thou look upon me, immediately I am made strong, and filled with new joy. And it is great marvel that I am so suddenly lifted up, and so graciously embraced by Thee, since I am always being carried to the deep by my own weight.

GOD'S INFINITE GOODNESS

This is the doing of Thy love which freely goeth before me and succoureth me in so many necessities, which guardeth me also in great dangers and snatcheth me, as I may truly say, from innumerable evils. For verily, by loving myself amiss, I lost myself, and by seeking and sincerely loving Thee alone, I found both myself and Thee, and through love I have brought myself to yet deeper nothingness: Because Thou, O most sweet Lord, dealest with me beyond all merit, and above all which I dare ask or think.

Blessed be Thou, O my God, because though I be unworthy of all Thy benefits, Thy bountiful and infinite goodness never ceaseth to do good even to ingrates and to those who are turned far from Thee. Turn Thou us unto Thyself, that we may be grateful, humble, and godly, for Thou art our salvation, our courage, and our strength.

CHAPTER IX
THAT ALL THINGS ARE TO BE REFERRED TO GOD, AS THE FINAL END

"My Son, I must be thy Supreme and final end, if thou desirest to be truly happy. Out of such purpose thy affection shall be purified, which too often is sinfully bent upon itself and upon created things. For if thou seekest thyself in any matter, straightway thou wilt fail within thyself and grow barren. Therefore refer everything to Me first of all, for it is I who gave thee all. So look upon each blessing as flowing from the Supreme Good, and thus all things are to be attributed to Me as their source.

HOPE THOU IN GOD

"From Me the humble and great, the poor and the rich, draw water as from a living fountain, and those who serve Me with a free and faithful spirit shall receive grace for grace. But he who will glory apart from Me, or will be delighted with any good which lieth in himself, shall not be established in true joy, nor shall be enlarged in heart, but shall be greatly hindered and thrown into tribulation.

"Therefore thou must not ascribe any good to thyself, nor look upon virtue as belonging to any man, but ascribe it all unto God, without whom man hath nothing. I gave all, I will receive all again, and with great strictness require I the giving of thanks.

"This is the Truth, and by it the vanity of boasting is put to flight. And if heavenly grace and true charity shall enter into thee, there shall be no envy, nor straitening of the heart, nor shall any self-love take possession of thee. For divine charity conquereth all things, and enlargeth all powers of the soul. If thou art truly wise, thou wilt rejoice in Me alone, thou wilt hope in Me alone; for there is *none good but one, that is God*, Who is to be praised above all things, and in all things to receive blessing."

CHAPTER X
THAT IT IS SWEET TO DESPISE THE WORLD AND TO SERVE GOD

Now will I speak again, O my Lord, and hold not my peace; I will say in the ears of my God, my Lord, and my King, who is exalted above all, *Oh how plentiful is Thy goodness which Thou hast laid up for them that fear Thee!* But what art Thou to those who love Thee? What to those who serve Thee with their whole heart?

Truly unspeakable is the sweetness of the contemplation of Thee, which Thou bestowest upon those who love Thee. In this most of all Thou hast showed me the sweetness of Thy charity, that when I was not, Thou madest me, and when I wandered far from Thee, Thou broughtest me back that I might serve Thee, and commandedst me to love Thee.

GOD SERVES MAN

O Fountain of perpetual love, what shall I say concerning Thee? How shall I be unmindful of Thee, who didst vouchsafe to remember me, even after I pined away and perished? Thou hast had mercy beyond all hope upon Thy servant, and hast showed Thy grace and friendship beyond all deserving. What reward shall I render Thee for this Thy grace? For it is not given unto all to renounce this world and its affairs, and to take up a religious life.

For is it a great thing that I should serve Thee, whom every creature ought to serve? It ought not to seem a great thing to me to serve Thee; but rather this appeareth to me a great and wonderful thing, that Thou vouchsafest to receive as Thy servant one so poor and unworthy, and to join him unto Thy chosen servants.

Behold all things which I have are Thine, and with them I serve Thee. And yet verily it is Thou who servest me, rather than I Thee. Behold the heaven and the earth which Thou hast created for the service of men; they are at Thy bidding, and perform daily whatsoever Thou dost command. Yea, and this is little; for Thou hast even ordained the Angels for the service of man. But it surpasseth even all these things, that Thou Thyself didst vouchsafe to minister unto man, and didst promise that Thou wouldest give Thyself unto him.

SERVE THE LORD WITH GLADNESS

What shall I render unto Thee for all these Thy manifold mercies? Oh that I were able to serve Thee all the days of my life! Oh that even for one day I were enabled to do Thee service worthy of Thyself! For verily Thou art worthy of all service, all honour, and praise without end. Verily Thou art my God, and I am Thy poor servant, who am bound to serve Thee with all my strength, nor ought I ever to grow weary of Thy praise. This is my wish, this is my exceeding great desire, and whatsoever is lacking to me, vouchsafe Thou to supply.

It is great honour, great glory to serve Thee, and to despise all for Thy sake. For they shall have great grace who of their own will shall submit themselves to Thy most holy service. They who for Thy love have cast away every carnal delight shall find the sweetest consolation of the Holy Ghost. They who enter the narrow way of life for Thy Name's sake, and have put away all worldly cares, shall attain great liberty of spirit.

Oh grateful and delightsome service of God, whereby man is made truly free and holy! Oh sacred condition of the religious servant, which maketh man equal to the Angels, well-pleasing unto God, terrible to evil spirits, and acceptable to all faithful ones! Oh service to be embraced and ever desired, in which the highest good is promised, and joy is gained which shall remain for evermore!

CHAPTER XI

THAT THE DESIRES OF THE HEART ARE TO BE EXAMINED AND GOVERNED

"MY Son, thou hast still many things to learn, which thou hast not well learned yet."

What are they, Lord?

"To place thy desire altogether in subjection to My good pleasure, and not to be a lover of thyself, but an earnest seeker of My will. Thy desires often excite and urge thee forward; but consider with thyself whether thou art not more moved for thine own objects than for My honour. If it is Myself that thou seekest, thou shalt be well content with whatsoever I shall ordain; but if any pursuit of thine own lieth hidden within thee, behold it is this which hindereth and weigheth thee down.

TAKE COUNSEL OF ME

"Beware, therefore, lest thou strive too earnestly after some desire which thou hast conceived, without taking counsel of Me; lest haply it repent thee afterwards, and that displease thee which before pleased, and for which thou didst long as for a great good. For not every affection which seemeth good is to be forthwith followed; neither is every opposite affection to be immediately avoided. Sometimes it is expedient to use restraint even in good desires and wishes, lest through importunity thou fall into distraction of mind, lest through want of discipline thou become a stumbling-block to others, or lest by the resistance of others thou be suddenly disturbed and brought to confusion.

"Sometimes, indeed, it is needful to use violence, and manfully to strive against the sensual appetite, and not to consider what the flesh may or not will; but rather to strive after this, that it may become subject, however unwillingly, to the spirit. And for so long it ought to be chastised and compelled to undergo slavery, even until it be ready for all things, and learn to be contented with little, to be delighted with things simple, and never to murmur at any inconvenience."

CHAPTER XII
OF THE INWARD GROWTH OF PATIENCE, AND OF THE STRUGGLE AGAINST EVIL DESIRES

O LORD God, I see that patience is very necessary unto me; for many things in this life fall out contrary. For howsoever I may have contrived for my peace, my life cannot go on without strife and trouble.

"Thou speakest truly, My Son. For I will not that thou seek such a peace as is without trials, and knoweth no adversities; but rather that thou shouldest judge thyself to have found peace, when thou art tried with manifold tribulations, and proved by many adversities. If thou shalt say that thou art not able to bear much, how then wilt thou sustain the fire hereafter? Of two evils we should always choose the less. Therefore, that thou mayest escape eternal torments hereafter, strive on God's behalf to endure present evils bravely. Thinkest thou that the children of this world suffer nought, or but little? Thou wilt not find it so, even though thou find out the most prosperous.

THE END OF THE RICH

"'But,' thou wilt say, 'they have many delights, and they follow their own wills, and thus they bear lightly their tribulations.'

"Be it so, grant that they have what they list; but how long, thinkest thou, will it last? Behold, like the smoke those who are rich in this world will pass away, and no record shall remain of their past joys. Yea, even while they yet live, they rest not without bitterness and weariness and fear. For from the very same thing wherein they find delight, thence they oftentimes have the punishment of sorrow.

"Justly it befalleth them, that because out of measure they seek out and pursue pleasures, they enjoy them not without confusion and bitterness. Oh how short, how false, how inordinate and wicked are all these pleasures! Yet because of their sottishness and blindness men do not understand; but like brute beasts, for the sake of a little pleasure of this corruptible life, they incur death of the soul. *Thou therefore, my son, go not after thy lusts, but refrain thyself from thine appetites. Delight thou in the Lord, and He shall give thee thy heart's desire.*

HOW TO FIND TRUE DELIGHT

"For if thou wilt truly find delight, and be abundantly comforted of Me, behold in the contempt of all worldly things and in the avoidance of all worthless pleasures shall be thy blessing, and fulness of consolation shall be given thee. And the more thou withdrawest thyself from all solace of creatures, the more sweet and powerful consolations shalt thou find.

"But at the first thou shalt not attain to them, without some sorrow and hard striving. Long-accustomed habit will oppose, but it shall be overcome by better habit. The flesh will murmur again and again, but will be restrained by fervour of spirit. The old serpent will urge and embitter thee, but will be put to flight by prayer; moreover, by useful labour his entrance will be greatly obstructed."

CHAPTER XIII

OF THE OBEDIENCE OF ONE IN LOWLY SUBJECTION AFTER THE EXAMPLE OF JESUS CHRIST

"My Son, he who striveth to withdraw himself from obedience, withdraweth himself also from grace, and he who seeketh private advantages, loseth those which are common unto all. If a man submit not freely and willingly to one set over him, it is a sign that his flesh is not yet perfectly subject to himself, but often resisteth and murmureth. Learn therefore quickly to submit thyself to him who is over thee, if thou seekest to bring thine own flesh into subjection. For the outward enemy is very quickly overcome if the inner man have not been laid low.

"There is no more grievous and deadly enemy to the soul than thou art to thyself, if thou art not led by the Spirit. Thou must not altogether conceive contempt for thyself, if thou wilt prevail against flesh and blood. Because as yet thou inordinately lovest thyself, therefore thou shrinkest from yielding thyself to the will of others.

LEARN TO HUMBLE THYSELF

"But what great thing is it that thou, who art dust and nothingness, yieldest thyself to man for God's sake, when I, the Almighty and the Most High, who created all things out of nothing, subjected Myself to man for thy sake? I became the most humble and despised of men, that by My humility thou mightest overcome thy pride. Learn to obey, O dust! Learn to humble thyself, O earth and clay, and to bow thyself beneath the feet of all. Learn to crush thy passions, and to yield thyself in all subjection.

"Be zealous against thyself, nor suffer pride to live within thee, but so show thyself subject and of no reputation, that all may be able to walk over thee, and tread thee down as the clay in the streets. What hast thou, O foolish man, of which to complain? What,

O vile sinner, canst thou answer those who speak against thee, seeing thou hast so often offended God, and many a time hast deserved hell?

"But Mine eye hath spared thee, because thy soul was precious in My sight; that thou mightest know My love, and mightest be thankful for My benefits; and that thou mightest give thyself altogether to true subjection and humility, and patiently bear the contempt which thou meritest."

Chapter XIV

OF MEDITATION UPON THE HIDDEN JUDGMENTS OF GOD, THAT WE MAY NOT BE LIFTED UP BECAUSE OF OUR WELL-DOING

Thou sendest forth Thy judgments against me, O Lord, and shakest all my bones with fear and trembling, and my soul trembleth exceedingly. I stand astonished, and remember that *the heavens are not clean in thy sight*. If *Thou chargest Thine angels with folly, and didst spare them not*, how shall it be unto me? Stars have fallen from heaven, and what shall I dare who am but dust? They whose works seemed to be praiseworthy, fell into the lowest depths, and they who did eat Angels' food, them have I seen delighted with the husks that the swine do eat.

There is therefore no holiness, if Thou, O Lord, withdraw Thine hand. No wisdom profiteth, if Thou leave off to guide the helm. No strength availeth, if Thou cease to preserve. No purity is secure, if Thou protect it not. No self-keeping availeth, if Thy holy watching be not there. For when we are left alone we are swallowed up and perish, but when we are visited, we are raised up, and we live. For indeed we are unstable, but are made strong

through Thee; we grow cold, but are rekindled by Thee.

THE INSIGNIFICANCE OF MAN

Oh, how humbly and abjectly must I reckon of myself, how must I weigh it as nothing, if I seem to have nothing good! Oh, how profoundly ought I to submit myself to Thy unfathomable judgments, O Lord, when I find myself nothing else save nothing, and again nothing! Oh weight unmeasurable, oh ocean which cannot be crossed over, where I find nothing of myself save nothing altogether! Where, then, is the hiding-place of glory, where the confidence begotten of virtue? All vainglory is swallowed up in the depths of Thy judgments against me.

What is all flesh in Thy sight? *For how shall the clay boast against Him that fashioned it?* How can he be lifted up in vain speech whose heart is subjected in truth to God? The whole world shall not lift him up whom Truth hath subdued; nor shall he be moved by the mouth of all who praise him, who hath placed all his hope in God. For they themselves who speak, behold, they are all nothing; for they shall cease with the sound of their words, *but the truth of the Lord endureth for ever.*

Chapter XV

HOW WE MUST STAND AND SPEAK, IN EVERYTHING THAT WE DESIRE

"My Son, speak thou thus in every matter, 'Lord, if it please Thee, let this come to pass. Lord, if this shall be for Thine honour, let it be done in Thy Name. Lord, if thou see it good for me, and approve it as useful, then grant me to use it for Thy honour. But if Thou knowest that it shall be hurtful unto me, and not profitable for the health of my soul, take the desire away from me!'

"For not every desire is from the Holy Ghost, although it appear to a man right and good. It is difficult to judge with certainty whether a good or an evil spirit move thee to desire this or that, or whether thou art moved by thine own spirit. Many have been deceived at the last, who seemed at the beginning to be moved by a good spirit.

EXAMINE THY DESIRES

"Therefore, whatsoever seemeth to thee desirable, thou must always desire to seek after it with the fear of God and humility of heart, and most of all, must altogether resign thyself, and commit all unto Me and say, 'Lord, thou knowest what is best; let this or that be, according as Thou wilt. Give what Thou wilt, so much as Thou wilt, when Thou wilt. Do with me as Thou knowest best, and as best shall please Thee, and as shall be most to Thine honour. Place me where Thou wilt, and freely work Thy will with me in all things. I am in Thine hand, and turn me in my course. Behold, I am Thy servant, ready for all things; for I desire to live not to myself but to Thee. Oh, that I might live worthily and perfectly.'"

A PRAYER TO BE ENABLED TO DO GOD'S WILL PERFECTLY

Grant me Thy grace, most merciful Jesus, that it may be with me, and work in me, and persevere with me, even unto the end. Grant that I may ever desire and wish whatsoever is most pleasing and dear unto Thee. Let Thy will be mine, and let my will alway follow Thine, and entirely accord with it. May I choose and reject whatsoever Thou dost; yea, let it be impossible for me to choose or reject except according to Thy will.

Grant that I may die to all worldly things, and for Thy sake love to be despised and unknown in this world. Grant unto me, above all things that I can desire, to rest in Thee, and that in Thee my heart may be at peace. Thou art the true peace of the heart, Thou alone its rest; apart from Thee all things are hard and unquiet. In Thee alone, the supreme and eternal God, *I will lay me down in peace and take my rest*. Amen.

CHAPTER XVI

THAT TRUE SOLACE IS TO BE SOUGHT IN GOD ALONE

WHATSOEVER I am able to desire or to think of for my solace, I look for it not here, but hereafter. For if I alone had all the solaces of this world, and were able to enjoy all its delights, it is certain that they could not endure long. Wherefore, O my soul, thou canst be fully comforted and perfectly refreshed, only in God, the Comforter of the poor, and the lifter up of the humble. Wait but a little while, my soul, wait for the Divine promise, and thou shalt have abundance of all good things in heaven.

If thou longest too inordinately for the things which are now, thou shalt lose those which are eternal and heavenly. Let temporal things be in the use, eternal things in the desire. Thou canst not be satisfied with any temporal good, for thou wast not created for the enjoyment of these.

THERE IS NO HAPPINESS APART FROM GOD

Although thou hadst all the good things which ever were created, yet couldst not thou be happy and blessed; all thy blessedness and thy felicity lieth in God who created all things; not such felicity as seemeth good to the foolish lover of the world, but such as Christ's good and faithful servants wait for, and as the spiritual and pure in heart sometimes taste, whose *conversation is in heaven.*

All human solace is empty and short-lived; blessed and true is that solace which is felt inwardly, springing from the truth. The godly man everywhere beareth about with him his own Comforter, Jesus, and saith unto Him: "Be with me, Lord Jesus, always and everywhere. Let it be my comfort to be able to give up cheerfully all human comfort. And if Thy consolation fail me, let Thy will and righteous approval be alway with me for the highest comfort. *For Thou wilt not always be chiding, neither keepest Thou Thine anger for ever."*

CHAPTER XVII

THAT ALL CARE IS TO BE CAST UPON GOD

"My Son, suffer me to do with thee what I will; I know what is expedient for thee. Thou thinkest as a man, in many things thou judgest as human affection persuadeth thee."

Lord, what Thou sayest is true. Greater is Thy care for me than all the care which I am able to take for myself. For too insecurely doth he stand who casteth not all his care upon Thee. Lord, so long as my will standeth right and firm in Thee, do with me what Thou wilt, for whatsoever Thou shalt do with me cannot be aught but good.

Blessed be Thou if Thou wilt leave me in darkness: blessed also be Thou if Thou wilt leave me in light. Blessed be Thou if Thou vouchsafe to comfort me, and always blessed be Thou if Thou cause me to be troubled.

ACCORDING TO THY WILL, LORD

"My Son! even thus thou must stand if thou desirest to walk with Me. Thou must be ready alike for suffering or rejoicing. Thou must be poor and needy as willingly as full and rich."

Lord, I will willingly bear for Thee whatsoever Thou wilt have to come upon me. Without choice I will receive from thy hand good and evil, sweet and bitter, joy and sadness, and will give Thee thanks for all things which shall happen unto me.

Keep me from all sin, and I will not fear death nor hell. Only cast me not away for ever, nor blot me out of the book of life. Then no tribulation which shall come upon me shall do me hurt.

CHAPTER XVIII

THAT TEMPORAL MISERIES ARE TO BE BORNE PATIENTLY AFTER THE EXAMPLE OF CHRIST

"My Son! I came down from heaven for thy salvation; I took upon Me thy miseries not of necessity, but drawn by love that thou mightest learn patience and mightest bear temporal miseries without murmuring. For from the hour of My birth, until My death upon the Cross, I ceased not from bearing of sorrow; I had much lack of temporal things; I oftentimes heard many reproaches against Myself; I gently bore contradictions and hard words; I received ingratitude for benefits, blasphemies for My miracles, rebukes for My doctrine."

THE NEED FOR PATIENCE

Lord, because Thou wast patient in Thy life, herein most of all fulfilling the commandment of Thy Father, it is well that I, miserable sinner, should patiently bear myself according to Thy will, and as long as Thou wilt have it so, should bear about with me for my salvation, the burden of this corruptible life. For although the present life seemeth burdensome, it is nevertheless already made very full of merit through Thy grace, and to those who are weak it becometh easier and brighter through Thy example and the footsteps of Thy saints.

But it is also much more full of consolation than it was of old, under the old Testament, when the gate of heaven remained shut; and even the way to heaven seemed more obscure when so few cared to seek after the heavenly kingdom. But not even those who were then just and in the way of salvation were able, before Thy Passion and the ransom of Thy holy Death, to enter the kingdom of heaven.

Oh what great thanks am I bound to give Thee, who hast vouchsafed to show me and all faithful people the good and right way to Thine eternal kingdom, for Thy way is our way, and by holy patience we walk to Thee who art our Crown. If Thou hadst not gone before and taught us, who would care to follow? Oh, how far would they have gone backward if they had not beheld Thy glorious example! Behold we are still lukewarm, though we have heard of Thy many signs and discourses; what would become of us if we had not such a light to help us follow Thee?

CHAPTER XIX

OF BEARING INJURIES, AND WHO SHALL BE APPROVED AS TRULY PATIENT

"WHAT sayest thou, My Son? Cease to complain; consider My suffering and that of My saints. *Thou hast not yet resisted unto blood.* It is little which thou sufferest in comparison with those who have suffered so many things, have been so strongly tempted, so grievously troubled, so manywise proved and tried.

"Thou oughtest therefore to call to mind the more grievous sufferings of others that thou mightest bear thy lesser ones more easily, and if they seem not to thee little, see that it is not thy impatience which is the cause of this. But whether they be little or whether they be great, study to bear them all with patience.

"So far as thou settest thyself to bear patiently, so far thou dost wisely and art deserving of the more merit; thou shalt also bear the more easily if thy mind and habit are carefully trained hereunto. And say not 'I cannot bear these things from such a man, nor are things of this kind to be borne by me, for he hath done me grievous harm and imputeth to me what I had never thought: but from another I will suffer patiently, such things as I see I ought to suffer.' Foolish is such a thought as this, for it considereth not the virtue of patience, nor by whom that virtue is to be crowned, but it rather weigheth persons and offences against self.

THE TRULY PATIENT MAN

"He is not truly patient who will only suffer as far as seemeth right to himself and from whom he pleaseth. But the truly patient man considereth not by what man he is tried, whether by one above him, or by an equal or inferior, whether by a good and holy man, or a perverse and unworthy; but indifferently from every creature, whatsoever or how often soever adversity happeneth to him, he gratefully accepteth all from the hand of God and counteth it great gain: For with God nothing which is borne for His sake, however small, shall lose its reward.

"Be thou therefore ready for the fight if thou wilt have the victory. Without striving thou canst not win the crown of patience; if thou wilt not suffer thou refusest to be crowned. But if thou desirest to be crowned, strive manfully, endure patiently. Without labour thou drawest not near to rest, nor without fighting comest thou to victory."

A PRAYER FOR PATIENCE

Make possible to me, O Lord, by grace what seemeth impossible to me by nature. Thou knowest how little I am able to bear, and how quickly I am cast down when a like adversity riseth up against me. Whatsoever trial of tribulation may come to me, may it become unto me pleasing and acceptable, for to suffer and be vexed for Thy sake is exceeding healthful to the soul.

CHAPTER XX

OF CONFESSION OF OUR INFIRMITY AND OF THE MISERIES OF THIS LIFE

I WILL acknowledge my sin unto Thee; I will confess to Thee, Lord, my infirmity. It is often a small thing which castest me down and maketh me sad. I resolve that I will act bravely, but when a little temptation cometh, immediately I am in a great strait. Wonderfully small sometimes is the matter whence a grievous temptation cometh, and whilst I imagine myself safe for a little space; when I am not considering, I find myself often almost overcome by a little puff of wind.

THE NEED FOR HEAVENLY FORTITUDE

Behold, therefore, O Lord, my humility and my frailty, which is altogether known to Thee. Be merciful unto me, and *draw me out of the mire that I sink not,* lest I ever remain cast down.

This is what frequently throweth me backward and confoundeth me before Thee, that I am so liable to fall, so weak to resist my passions. And though their assault is not altogether according to my will, it is violent and grievous, and it altogether wearieth me to live thus daily in conflict. Herein is my infirmity made known to me, that hateful fancies always rush in far more easily than they depart.

Oh that Thou, most mighty God of Israel, Lover of all faithful souls, wouldst look upon the labour and sorrow of Thy servant, and give him help in all things whereunto he striveth. Strengthen me with heavenly fortitude, lest the old man, this miserable flesh, not being yet fully subdued to the spirit, prevail to rule over me; against which I ought to strive so long as I remain in this most miserable life.

Oh what a life is this, where tribulations and miseries cease not, where all things are full of snares and of enemies, for when one tribulation or temptation goeth, another cometh, yea, while the former conflict is yet raging others come more in number and unexpected.

THE LUSTS OF THE FLESH

And how can the life of man be loved, seeing that it hath so many bitter things, that it is subjected to so many calamities and miseries. How can it be even called life, when it produces so many deaths and plagues? The world is often reproached because it is deceitful and vain, yet notwithstanding it is not easily given up, because the lusts of the flesh have too much rule over it. Some draw us to love, some to hate. The lust of the flesh, the lust of the eyes, and the pride of life, these draw to love of the world; but the punishments and miseries which righteously follow these things, bring forth hatred of the world and weariness.

But, alas! an evil desire conquereth a mind given to the world, and thinketh it happiness to be under the nettles because it savoureth not nor perceiveth the sweetness of God nor the inward gracefulness of virtue. But they who perfectly despise the world and strive to live unto God in holy discipline, these are not ignorant of the divine sweetness promised to all who truly deny themselves and see clearly how grievously the world erreth, and in how many ways it is deceived.

CHAPTER XXI

THAT WE MUST REST IN GOD ABOVE ALL GOODS AND GIFTS

ABOVE all things and in all things thou shalt rest alway in the Lord, O my soul, for He Himself is the eternal rest of the saints. Grant me, most sweet and loving Jesus, to rest in Thee above every creature, above all health and beauty, above all glory and honour, above all power and dignity, above all knowledge and skilfulness, above all riches and arts, above all joy and exultation, above all fame and praise, above all sweetness and consolation, above all hope and promise, above all merit and desire, above all gifts and rewards which Thou canst give and pour forth, above all joy and jubilation which the mind is able to receive and feel; in a word, above Angels and Archangels and all the army of heaven, above all things visible and invisible, and above everything which Thou, O my God, art not.

THE HIGHEST GOOD

For Thou, O Lord, my God, art best above all things; Thou only art the Most High, Thou only the Almighty, Thou only the All-sufficient, and the Fulness of all things; Thou only the All-delightsome and the All-comforting; Thou alone the altogether lovely and altogether loving; Thou alone the Most Exalted and Most Glorious above all things; in Whom all things are, and were, and ever shall be, altogether and all-perfect.

And thus it falleth short and is insufficient whatsoever Thou givest to me without Thyself or whatsoever Thou revealest or dost promise concerning Thyself, whilst Thou art not seen or fully possessed: Since verily my heart cannot truly rest nor be entirely content, except it rest in Thee, and go beyond all gifts and every creature.

THE SOURCE OF TRUE LIBERTY

O my most beloved Spouse, Jesus Christ, most holy Lover of my soul, Ruler of this whole Creation, who shall give me the wings of true liberty, that I may flee to Thee and find rest? Oh when shall it be given me to be open to receive Thee to the full, and to see how sweet Thou art, O Lord my God? When shall I collect myself altogether in Thee, that because of Thy love I may not feel myself at all, but may know Thee only above every sense and measure, in measure not known to others.

But now I ofttimes groan, and bear my sad estate with sorrow; because many evils befall me in this vale of miseries which continually disturb and fill me with sorrow, and encloud me, continually hinder and fill me with care, allure and entangle me, that I cannot have free access to Thee, nor enjoy that sweet intercourse which is always near at hand to the blessed spirits. Let my deep sighing come before Thee, and my manifold desolation on the earth.

O Jesus, Light of Eternal Glory, solace of the wandering soul, before Thee my mouth is without speech, and my silence speaketh to Thee. How long will my Lord delay to come unto me? Let Him come unto me, His poor and humble one, and make me glad. Let Him put forth His hand, and deliver His holy one from every snare. Come, Oh come; for without Thee shall be no joyful day or hour, for Thou art my joy, and without Thee is my table empty. I am miserable, and in a manner imprisoned and loaded with fetters, until Thou refresh me by the light of Thy presence, and give me liberty, and show Thy loving countenance.

SEEK YE THE LORD

Let others seek some other thing instead of Thee, whatsoever it shall please them; but for my part nothing else pleaseth or shall please, save Thou, my God, my hope, my eternal salvation. I will not hold my peace, nor cease to implore, until Thy grace return, and until Thou speak to me within.

"Behold, here I am! Behold, I come to thee, for thou didst call Me. Thy tears and the longing of thy soul, thy humbleness and contrition of heart have inclined Me, and brought Me to thee."

And I said, Lord, I have called upon Thee, and I have longed to enjoy Thee, being ready to reject everything for Thy sake. For Thou didst first move me to seek Thee. Therefore, blessed be Thou, O Lord, who has wrought this good work upon Thy servant, according to the multitude of Thy mercy.

What then hath Thy servant to say in Thy presence, save to humble himself greatly before Thee, being alway mindful of his own iniquity and vileness. For there is none like unto Thee in all marvels of heaven and earth. Excellent are Thy works, true are Thy judgments, and by Thy Providence are all things governed. Therefore praise and glory be unto Thee, O Wisdom of the Father, let my mouth and my soul and all created things praise and bless Thee together.

CHAPTER XXII

OF THE RECOLLECTION OF GOD'S MANIFOLD BENEFITS

OPEN, O Lord, my heart in Thy law, and teach me to walk in the way of Thy commandments. Grant me to understand Thy will and to be mindful of Thy benefits, both general and special, with great reverence and diligent meditation, that thus I may be able worthily to give Thee thanks. Yet I know and confess that I cannot render Thee due praises for the least of Thy mercies. I am less than the least of all the good things which Thou gavest me; and when I consider Thy majesty, my spirit faileth because of the greatness thereof.

ALL GIFTS ARE FROM GOD

All things which we have in the soul and in the body, and whatsoever things we possess, whether outwardly or inwardly, naturally or supernaturally, are Thy good gifts, and prove Thee, from whom we have received them all, to be good, gentle, and kind. Although one receiveth many things, and another fewer, yet all are Thine, and without Thee not even the least thing can be possessed.

He who hath received greater cannot boast that it is of his own merit, nor lift himself up above others, nor condemn those beneath him; for he is the greater and the better who ascribeth least to himself, and in giving thanks is the humbler and more devout; and he who holdeth himself to be viler than all, and judgeth himself to be the more unworthy, is the apter for receiving greater things.

But he who hath received fewer gifts, ought not to be cast down, nor to take it amiss, nor to envy him who is richer; but rather ought he to look unto Thee, and to greatly extol Thy goodness, for Thou pourest forth Thy gifts so richly, so freely and largely, without respect of persons. All things come of Thee; therefore in all things shalt thou be praised. Thou knowest what is best to be given to each; and why this man hath less, and that more, is not for us but for Thee to understand, for unto Thee each man's deservings are fully known.

REJOICE IN THE GIVER NOT THE GIFT

Wherefore, O Lord God, I reckon it even a great benefit, not to have many things, whence praise and glory may appear outwardly, and after the thought of men. For so it is that he who considereth his own poverty and vileness, ought not only to draw therefrom no grief or sorrow, or sadness of spirit, but rather comfort and cheerfulness; because Thou, Lord, hast chosen the poor and humble, and those who are poor in this world, to be Thy friends and acquaintance. So give all Thine apostles witness whom Thou hast made princes in all lands. Yet they had their conversation in this world blameless, so humble and meek, without any malice or deceit, *that they even rejoiced to suffer rebukes for Thy Name's sake*, and what things the world hateth, they embraced with great joy.

Therefore ought nothing so much to rejoice him who loveth Thee and knoweth Thy benefits, as Thy will in him, and the good pleasure of Thine eternal Providence, wherewith he ought to be so contented and comforted, that he would as willingly be the least as any other would be the greatest, as peaceable and contented in the lowest as in the highest place, and as willingly held of small and low account and of no name or reputation as to be more honourable and greater in the world than others. For Thy will and the love of Thine honour ought to go before all things, and to please and comfort him more, than all benefits that are given or may be given to himself.

Chapter XXIII

OF FOUR THINGS WHICH BRING GREAT PEACE

"My Son, now will I teach thee the way of peace and of true liberty."

Do, O my Lord, as Thou sayest, for this is pleasing unto me to hear.

"Strive, My Son, to do another's will rather than thine own. Choose always to have less rather than more. Seek always after the lowest place, and to be subject to all. Wish always and pray that the will of God be fulfilled in thee. Behold, such a man as this entereth into the inheritance of peace and quietness."

O my Lord, this Thy short discourse hath in itself much of perfectness. It is short in words but full of meaning, and abundant in fruit. For if it were possible that I should fully keep it, disturbance would not so easily arise within me. For as often as I feel myself disquieted and weighed down, I find myself to have gone back from this teaching. But Thou, Who art Almighty, and always lovest progress in the soul, vouchsafe more grace, that I may be enabled to fulfil Thy exhortation, and work out my salvation.

A PRAYER AGAINST EVIL THOUGHTS

O Lord my God, be not Thou far from me, my God, haste Thee to help me, for many thoughts and great fears have risen up against me, afflicting my soul. How shall I pass through them unhurt? how shall I break through them?

"I," saith He, *"will go before thee, and make the crooked places straight. I will open the prison doors, and reveal to thee the secret places."*

Do, Lord, as Thou sayest; and let all evil thoughts fly away before Thy face.

This is my hope and my only comfort, to fly unto Thee in all tribulation, to hope in Thee, to call upon Thee from my heart and patiently wait for Thy loving kindness.

A PRAYER FOR ENLIGHTENMENT OF THE MIND

Enlighten me, Blessed Jesus, with the brightness of Thy inner light, and cast forth all darkness from the habitation of my heart. Restrain my many wandering thoughts, and carry away the temptations which strive to do me hurt. Fight Thou mightily for me, and drive forth the evil beasts, so call I alluring lusts, that *peace may be within Thy walls and plenteousness of praise within Thy palaces,* even in my pure conscience. Command Thou the winds and the storms, say unto the sea, "Be still"; say unto the stormy wind, "Hold thy peace," so shall there be a great calm.

Oh send forth Thy light and Thy truth, that they may shine upon the earth; for I am but earth without form and void until Thou give me light. Pour forth Thy grace from above; water my heart with the dew of heaven; give the waters of devotion to water the face of the earth, and cause it to bring forth good and perfect fruit.

Lift up my mind which is oppressed with the weight of sins, and raise my whole desire to heavenly things; that having tasted the sweetness of the happiness which is from above, it may take no pleasure in thinking of things of earth.

Draw me and deliver me from every unstable comfort of creatures, for no created thing is able to satisfy my desire and to give me comfort. Join me to Thyself by the inseparable bond of love, for Thou alone art sufficient to him that loveth Thee, and without Thee all things are vain toys.

CHAPTER XXIV
OF AVOIDING OF CURIOUS INQUIRY INTO THE LIFE OF ANOTHER

"My Son, be not curious, nor trouble thyself with vain cares. *What is that to thee? Follow thou Me.* For what is it to thee whether a man be this or that, or say or do thus or thus? Thou hast no need to answer for others, but thou must give an answer for thyself. Why therefore dost thou entangle thyself?

"Behold, I know all men, and I behold all things which are done under the sun; and I know how it standeth with each one, what he thinketh, what he willeth, and to what end his thoughts reach. All things therefore are to be committed to Me; watch thou thyself in godly peace, and leave him who is unquiet to be unquiet as he will. Whatsoever he shall do or say, shall come unto him, for he cannot deceive Me.

"Trouble not thyself about the shadow of a great name, nor about the friendship of many, nor about the love of men towards thee. For these things beget distraction and great sorrows of heart. My word should speak freely unto thee, and I would reveal secrets, if only thou didst diligently look for My appearing, and didst open unto Me the gates of thy heart. *Be sober and watch unto prayer,* and humble thyself in all things."

CHAPTER XXV
WHEREIN FIRM PEACE OF HEART AND TRUE PROFIT CONSIST

"My Son, I have said, *Peace I leave with you, My peace I give unto you, not as the world giveth give I unto you.* All men desire peace, but all do not care for the things which belong unto true peace. My peace is with the humble and lowly in heart. Thy peace shall be in much patience. If thou heardest Me, and didst follow My voice, thou shouldest enjoy much peace."

What then shall I do, Lord?

"In everything take heed to thyself what thou doest, and what thou sayest; and direct all thy purpose to this, that thou please Me alone, and desire or seek nothing apart from Me. But, moreover, judge nothing rashly concerning the words or deeds of others, nor meddle with matters which are not committed to thee; and it may be that thou shalt be disturbed little or rarely. Yet never to feel any disquiet, nor to suffer any pain of heart or body, this belongeth not to the present life, but is the state of eternal rest.

"Therefore count not thyself to have found true peace, if thou hast felt no grief; nor that then all is well if thou hast no adversary; nor that this is perfect if all things fall out according to thy desire. Nor then reckon thyself to be anything great, or think that thou art specially beloved, if thou art in a state of great fervour and sweetness of spirit; for not by these things is the true lover of virtue known, nor in them doth the profit and perfection of man consist."

ACCEPT PROSPERITY AND ADVERSITY ALIKE

In what then, Lord?

"In offering thyself with all thy heart to the Divine Will, in not seeking the things which are thine own, whether great or small, whether temporal or eternal; so that thou remain with the same steady countenance in giving of thanks between prosperity and adversity, weighing all things in an equal balance. If thou be so brave and long-suffering in hope that when inward comfort is taken from thee, thou even prepare thy heart for the more endurance, and justify not thyself, as though thou oughtest not to suffer these heavy things, but dost justify Me in all things that I appoint, and dost bless My Holy Name, then dost thou walk in the true and right way of peace, and shalt have a sure hope that thou shalt again behold My face with joy. For if thou come to an utter contempt of thyself, know that then thou shalt enjoy abundance of peace, as much as is possible where thou art but a wayfaring man."

Chapter XXVI

OF THE EXALTATION OF A FREE SPIRIT, WHICH HUMBLE PRAYER MORE DESERVETH THAN DOTH FREQUENT READING

LORD, this is the work of a perfect man, never to slacken his mind from attention to heavenly things, and among many cares to pass along as it were without care, not after the manner of one indifferent, but rather with the privilege of a free mind, cleaving to no creature with inordinate affection.

DELIVER ME FROM EVIL

I beseech Thee, my most merciful Lord God, preserve me from the cares of this life, lest I become too much entangled; from many necessities of the body, lest I be taken captive by pleasure; from all obstacles of the spirit, lest I be broken and cast down with cares. I say not from those things which the vanity of the world goeth about after with all eagerness, but from those miseries, which by the universal curse of mortality weigh down and hold back the soul of thy servant in punishment, that it cannot enter into liberty of spirit, so often as it would.

O my God, sweetness unspeakable, turn into bitterness all my fleshly consolation, which draweth me away from the love of eternal things, and wickedly allureth toward itself by setting before me some present delight. Let not, O my God, let not flesh and blood prevail over me; let not the world and its short glory deceive me; let not the devil and his craftiness supplant me.

Give me courage to resist, patience to endure, constancy to persevere. Grant, in place of all consolations of the world, the most sweet unction of Thy Spirit, and in place of carnal love, pour into me the love of Thy Name.

BE MODERATE IN ALL THINGS

Behold, food and drink and clothing, and all the other needs appertaining to the support of the body, are burdensome to the devout spirit. Grant that I may use such things with moderation, and that I be not entangled with inordinate affection for them. To cast away all these things is not lawful, because nature must be sustained, but to require superfluities and things which merely minister delight, the holy law forbiddeth; for otherwise the flesh would wax insolent against the spirit. In all these things, I beseech Thee, let Thy hand guide and teach me, that I in no way exceed.

Chapter XXVII

THAT PERSONAL LOVE GREATLY HINDERETH FROM THE HIGHEST GOOD

"MY Son, thou must give all for all, and be nothing of thine own. Know thou that the love of thyself is more hurtful to thee than anything in the world. According to the love and inclination which thou hast, everything more or less cleaveth to thee. If thy love be pure, sincere, well-regulated, thou shalt not be in captivity to anything. Do not covet what thou mayest not have; do not have what is able to hinder thee, and to rob thee of inward liberty. It is wonderful that thou committest not thyself to Me from the very bottom of thy heart, with all things which thou canst desire or have.

SUBTRACT THINGS; MULTIPLY JOY

"Why art thou consumed with vain sorrow? Why art thou wearied with superfluous cares? Stand thou by My good pleasure, and thou shalt suffer no loss. If thou seekest after this or that, and wilt be here or there, according to thine own advantage or the fulfilling of thine own pleasure, thou shalt never be in quiet, nor free from care, because in everything somewhat will be found lacking, and everywhere there will be somebody who opposeth thee.

"Therefore it is not gaining or multiplying of this thing or that which advantageth thee, but rather the despising it and cutting it by the root out of thy heart; which thou must not only understand of money and riches, but of the desire after honour and vain praise, things which all pass away with the world. The place availeth little if the spirit of devotion is wanting; nor shall that peace stand long which is sought from abroad, if the state of thy heart is without the true foundation, that is, if it abide not in Me. Thou mayest change, but thou canst not better thyself; for when occasion ariseth

and is accepted thou shalt find what thou didst fly from, yea more."

A PRAYER FOR CLEANSING OF THE HEART AND FOR HEAVENLY WISDOM

Strengthen me, O God, by the grace of Thy Holy Spirit. Give me virtue to be strengthened with might in the inner man, and to free my heart from all fruitless care and trouble, and that I be not drawn away by various desires after any things whatsoever, whether of little value or great, but that I may look upon all as passing away, and myself as passing away with them; because there is *no profit under the sun, and all is vanity* and *vexation of spirit.* Oh how wise is he that considereth thus!

Give me, O Lord, heavenly wisdom, that I may learn to seek Thee above all things and to find Thee; to relish Thee above all things and to love Thee; and to understand all other things, even as they are, according to the order of Thy wisdom. Grant me prudently to avoid the flatterer, and patiently to bear with him that opposeth me; for this is great wisdom, not to be carried by every wind of words, nor to give ear to the wicked flattering Siren; for thus do we go safely on in the way we have begun.

CHAPTER XXVIII
AGAINST THE TONGUES OF DETRACTORS

"MY Son, take it not sadly to heart, if any think ill of thee, and say of thee what thou art unwilling to hear. Thou oughtest to think worse of thyself, and to believe no man weaker than thyself. If thou walkest inwardly, thou wilt not weigh flying words above their value. It is no small prudence to keep silence in an evil time and to turn inwardly unto Me, and not to be troubled by human judgment.

"Let not thy peace depend upon the word of men; for whether they judge well or ill of thee, thou art not therefore any other man than thyself. Where is true peace or true glory? Is it not in Me? And he who seeketh not to please men, nor feareth to displease, shall enjoy abundant peace. From inordinate love and vain fear ariseth all disquietude of heart, and all distraction of the senses."

CHAPTER XXIX

HOW WHEN TRIBULATION COMETH WE MUST CALL UPON AND BLESS GOD

BLESSED be thy name, O Lord, for evermore, who hast willed this temptation and trouble to come upon me. I cannot escape it, but have need to flee unto Thee, that Thou mayest succour me and turn it unto me for good. Lord, now am I in tribulation, and it is not well within my heart, but I am sore vexed by the suffering which lieth upon me.

And now, O dear Father, what shall I say? I am taken among the snares. *Save me from this hour, but for this cause came I unto this hour,* that Thou mightest be glorified when I am deeply humbled and am delivered through Thee. *Let it be Thy pleasure to deliver me;* for what can I do who am poor, and without Thee whither shall I go? Give patience this time also. Help me, O Lord my God, and I will not fear how much soever I be weighed down.

THOU ART ABLE TO DELIVER ME

And now amid these things what shall I say? Lord, Thy will be done. I have well deserved to be troubled and weighed down. Therefore I ought to bear, would that it be with patience, until the tempest be overpast and comfort return. Yet is Thine omnipotent arm able also to take this temptation away from me, and to lessen its power that I fall not utterly under it, even as many a time past Thou has helped me, O God, my merciful God. And as much as this deliverance is difficult to me, so much is it easy to Thee, O right hand of the most Highest.

CHAPTER XXX

OF SEEKING DIVINE HELP, AND THE CONFIDENCE OF OBTAINING GRACE

"MY Son, I the Lord am *a stronghold in the day of trouble.* Come unto Me, when it is not well with thee.

"This it is which chiefly hindereth heavenly consolation, that thou too slowly betakest thyself unto prayer. For before thou earnestly seekest unto Me, thou dost first seek after many means of comfort, and refresheth thyself in outward things: so it cometh to pass that all things profit thee but little until thou learn that it is I who deliver those who trust in Me; neither beside Me is there any strong help, nor profitable counsel, not enduring remedy.

"But now, recovering courage after the tempest, grow thou strong in the light of My mercies, for I am nigh, saith the Lord, that I may restore all things not only as they were at the first, but also abundantly and one upon another.

DO NOT FEAR THE FUTURE

"For is anything too hard for Me, or shall I be like unto one who saith and doeth not? Where is thy faith? Stand fast and with perseverance. Be long-suffering and strong. Consolation will come unto thee in its due season. Wait for Me; yea, wait; I will come and heal thee. It is temptation which vexeth thee, and a vain fear which terrifieth thee.

"What doth care about future events bring thee, save sorrow upon sorrow? *Sufficient for the day is the evil thereof.* It is vain and useless to be disturbed or lifted up about future things which perhaps will never come.

"But it is the nature of man to be deceived by fancies of this sort, and it is a sign of a mind which is still weak to be so easily drawn away at the suggestion of the enemy. For he careth not whether he deceive and beguile by true means or false; whether he throw thee down by the love of the present or fear of the future. Therefore let not thy heart be troubled, neither let it be afraid. Believe in Me, and put thy trust in My mercy.

"When thou thinkest thyself far removed from Me, I am often the nearer. When thou reckonest that almost all is lost, then often is greater opportunity of gain at hand. All is not lost when something goeth contrary to thy wishes. Thou oughtest not to judge according to present feeling, nor so to take or give way to any grief which befalleth thee, as if all hope of escape were taken away.

GOD DOETH ALL THINGS WELL

"Think not thyself totally abandoned, although for the time I have sent to thee some tribulation, or have even withdrawn some cherished consolation; for this is the way to the Kingdom of Heaven. And without doubt it is better for thee and for all My other servants, that ye should be proved by adversities, than that ye should have all things as ye would.

"I know thy hidden thoughts: and that it is very needful for thy soul's health that sometimes thou be left without relish, lest perchance thou be lifted up by prosperity, and desirous to please thyself in that which thou art not. What I have given I am able to take away, and to restore again at My good pleasure.

"When I shall have given, it is Mine; when I shall have taken away, I have not taken what is thine; *for every good gift and every perfect gift* is from Me. If I shall have sent upon thee grief or any vexation, be not angry, nor let thy heart be sad; I am able quickly to lift thee up and to change every burden into joy. But I am just and greatly to be praised, when I do thus unto thee.

REJOICE IN ADVERSITY

"If thou rightly consider, and look upon it with truth, thou oughtest never to be so sadly cast down because of adversity, but rather shouldst rejoice and give thanks; yea, verily to count it to the highest joy that I afflict thee with sorrows and spare thee not. *As My Father hath loved Me, so love I you;* thus have I spoken unto My beloved disciples: whom I sent forth not unto worldly joys, but to great strivings; not unto honours, but unto contempt; not unto ease, but to labours; not unto rest, but to bring forth much fruit with patience. My son, remember these words."

CHAPTER XXXI

OF THE NEGLECT OF EVERY CREATURE, THAT THE CREATOR MAY BE FOUND

O LORD, I still need more grace, if I would arrive where neither man nor any other creature may hinder me. For so long as anything keepeth me back, I cannot freely fly unto Thee. He desired eagerly thus to fly, who cried, saying, *Oh that I had wings like a dove, for then would I flee away and be at rest.* What is more peaceful than the single eye? And what more free than he that desireth nothing upon earth?

Therefore must a man rise above every creature, and perfectly forsake himself, and with abstracted mind to stand and behold that Thou, the Creator of all things, hast among Thy creatures nothing like unto Thyself. And except a man be freed from all creatures, he will not be able to reach freely after Divine things. Therefore few are found who give themselves to contemplation, because few know how to separate themselves entirely from perishing and created things.

WHY GRACE IS NECESSARY

For this much grace is necessary, which may lift up the soul and raise it above itself. And except a man be lifted up in the spirit, and freed from all creatures, and altogether united to God, whatsoever he knoweth, whatsoever even he hath, it mattereth but little. He who esteemeth anything great save the one only incomprehensible, eternal, good, shall long time be little and lie low. For whatsoever is not God is nothing, and ought to be counted for nothing.

Great is the difference between a godly man, illuminated with wisdom, and a scholar learned in knowledge and given to books. Far nobler is that doctrine which floweth down from the divine fulness above, than that which is acquired laboriously by human study.

CONSIDER THY INWARD CONDITION

Many are found who desire contemplation, but they do not strive to practice those things which are required thereunto. It is also a great impediment, that much is made of symbols and external signs, and too little of thorough mortification. I know not how it is, and by what spirit we are led, and what we who would be deemed spiritual are aiming at, that we give so great labour and so eager solicitude for transitory and worthless things, and scarcely ever gather our senses together to think at all of our inward condition.

Ah, me! Forthwith after a little recollection we rush out of doors, and do not subject our actions to a strict examination. Where our affections are set we take no heed, and we weep not that all things belonging to us are so defiled. For because *all flesh had corrupted itself upon the earth*, the great deluge came. Since therefore our inmost affections are very corrupt, it followeth of necessity that our actions also are corrupt, being the index of a deficient inward strength. Out of a pure heart proceedeth the fruit of good living.

LOOK NOT ON OUTWARD APPEARANCE

We demand, how much a man hath done; but from how much virtue he acted, is not so narrowly considered. We ask if he be strong, rich, handsome, clever, whether he is a good writer, good singer, good workman; but how poor he may be in spirit, how patient and gentle, how devout and meditative, on these things many are silent. Nature looketh upon the outward appearance of a man; grace turneth its thought to the heart. The former frequently judgeth amiss; the latter trusteth in God, that it may not be deceived.

CHAPTER XXXII
OF SELF-DENIAL AND THE CASTING AWAY ALL SELFISHNESS

"MY *Son*, thou canst not possess perfect liberty unless thou altogether deny thyself. All they are enslaved who are possessors of riches, they who love themselves, the selfish, and curious, the restless; those who ever seek after soft things, and not after the things of Jesus Christ; those who continually plan and devise that which will not stand. For whatsoever cometh not of God shall perish. Hold fast the short and complete saying, 'Renounce all things, and thou shalt find all things; give up thy lust, and thou shalt find rest.' Dwell upon this in thy mind, and when thou art full of it, thou shalt understand all things."

O Lord, this is not the work of a day, nor children's play; verily in this short saying is enclosed all the perfection of the religious.

HEAVENLY WISDOM

"My son, thou oughtest not to be turned aside, nor immediately cast down, because thou hast heard the way of the perfect. Rather oughtest thou to be provoked to higher aims, and at the least to long after the desire thereof. Oh that it were so with thee, and that thou hadst come to this, that thou wert not a lover of thine own self, but wert ready always to My nod, and to his whom I have placed over thee as thy father. Then shouldest thou please Me exceedingly, and all thy life should go on in joy and peace.

"Thou hast still many things to re-nounce, which if thou resign not utterly to Me, thou shalt not gain what thou seekest. *I counsel thee to buy of Me gold tried in the fire, that thou mayest be rich*, that is heavenly wisdom, which despiseth all base things. Put away from thee earthly wisdom, and all pleasure, whether common to men, or thine own.

"I tell thee that thou must buy vile things with those which are costly and great in the esteem of men. For wonderfully vile and small, and almost given up to forgetfulness, doth true heavenly wisdom appear, which thinketh not high things of itself, nor seeketh to be magnified upon the earth; many honour it with their lips, but in heart are far from it; it is indeed the precious pearl, which is hidden from many."

CHAPTER XXXIII
OF INSTABILITY OF THE HEART, AND OF DIRECTING THE AIM TOWARDS GOD

"MY Son, trust not thy feeling, for that which is now will be quickly changed into somewhat else. As long as thou livest thou art subject to change, howsoever unwilling; so that thou art found now joyful, now sad; not at peace, now disquieted; now devout, now indevout; now studious, now careless; now sad, now cheerful.

"But the wise man, and he who is truly learned in spirit, standeth above these changeable things, attentive not to what he may feel in himself, or from what quarter the wind may blow, but that the whole intent of his mind may carry him on to the due and much-desired end. For thus will he be able to remain one and the same and unshaken, the single eye of his desire being steadfastly fixed, through the manifold changes of the world, upon Me.

THE EYE OF INTENTION

"But according as the eye of intention be the more pure, even so will a man make his way steadfastly through the manifold storms. But in many the eye of pure intention waxeth dim; for it quickly resteth itself upon anything pleasant which occurreth, and rarely is any man found altogether free from the blemish of self-seeking. So the Jews of old came to Bethany, to the house of Martha and Mary, that they might see not Jesus, but Lazarus, whom He had raised from the dead. Therefore must the eye of the intention be cleansed, that it may be single and right, and above all things which come in its way, may be directed unto Me."

CHAPTER XXXIV

THAT TO HIM WHO LOVETH GOD IS SWEET ABOVE ALL THINGS AND IN ALL THINGS

BEHOLD, God is mine, and all things are mine! What will I more, and what more happy thing can I desire? O delightsome and sweet world! that is, to him that loveth the Word, *not the world, neither the things that are in the world.* My God, my all! To him that understandeth, that word sufficeth, and to repeat it often is pleasing to him that loveth it. When Thou art present all things are pleasant; when Thou art absent, all things are wearisome.

Thou makest the heart to be at rest, givest it deep peace and festal joy. Thou makest it to think rightly in every matter, and in every matter to give Thee praise; neither can anything please long without Thee but if it would be pleasant and of sweet savour,

Thy grace must be there, and it is Thy wisdom which must give unto it a sweet savour.

FROM VANITY TO VERITY

To him who tasteth Thee, what can be distasteful? And to him who tasteth Thee not, what is there which can make him joyous? But the worldly wise, and they who enjoy the flesh, these fail in Thy wisdom; for in the wisdom of the world is found utter vanity, and to be carnally minded is death.

But they who follow after Thee through contempt of worldly things, and mortification of the flesh, are found to be the truly wise because they are carried from vanity to verity, from the flesh to the spirit. They taste that the Lord is good, and whatsoever good they find in creatures, they count it all unto the praise of the Creator. Unlike, yea, very unlike is the enjoyment of the Creator to enjoyment of the Creature, the enjoyment of eternity and of time, of light uncreated and of light reflected.

O Light everlasting, surpassing all created lights, dart down Thy ray from on high which shall pierce the inmost depths of my heart. Give purity, joy, clearness, life to my spirit that with all its powers it may cleave unto Thee with rapture passing man's understanding.

Oh when shall that blessed and longed-for time come when Thou shalt satisfy me with Thy presence, and be unto me all in all? So long as this is delayed, my joy shall not be full. Still, ah me! the old man liveth in me: He is not yet all crucified, not yet quite dead; still he lusteth fiercely against the spirit, wageth inward wars, nor suffereth the soul's kingdom to be in peace.

But *Thou who rulest the raging of*

the sea, and stillest the waves thereof when they arise, rise up and help me. *Scatter the people that delight in war.* Destroy them by Thy power. Show forth, I beseech Thee, Thy might, and let Thy right hand be glorified, for I have no hope, no refuge, save in Thee, O Lord my God.

CHAPTER XXXV

THAT THERE IS NO SECURITY AGAINST TEMPTATION IN THIS LIFE

"My Son, thou art never secure in this life, but thy spiritual armour will always be needful for thee as long as thou livest. Thou dwellest among foes, and art attacked on the right hand and on the left. If therefore thou use not on all sides the shield of patience, thou wilt not remain long unwounded.

"Above all, if thou keep not thy heart fixed upon Me with steadfast purpose to bear all things for My sake, thou shalt not be able to bear the fierceness of the attack, nor to attain to the victory of the blessed. Therefore must thou struggle bravely all thy life through, and put forth a strong hand against those things which oppose thee. For to him that overcometh is the hidden manna given, but great misery is reserved for the slothful.

BE FAITHFUL UNTO DEATH

"If thou seek rest in this life, how then wilt thou attain unto the rest which is eternal? Set not thyself to attain much rest, but much patience. Seek the true peace, not in earth but in heaven, not in man nor in any created thing, but in God alone.

"For the love of God thou must willingly undergo all things, whether labours in sorrows, temptations, vexations, anxieties, necessities, infirmities, injuries, gainsayings, rebukes, humiliations, confusions, corrections, despisings; these things help unto virtue; these things prove the scholar of Christ; these things fashion the heavenly crown. I will give thee an eternal reward for short labour, and infinite glory for transient shame.

"Thinkest thou that thou shalt always have spiritual consolations at thy will? My saints had never such, but instead thereof manifold griefs, and divers temptations, and heavy desolations. But patiently they bore themselves in all, and trusted in God more than in themselves, knowing that *the sufferings of this present time are not worthy to be compared with the glory which shall be revealed in us.*

"Wouldst thou have that immediately which many have hardly attained unto after many tears and hard labours? Wait for the Lord, quit thyself like a man and be strong; be not faint-hearted, nor go aside from Me, but constantly devote thy body and soul to the glory of God. I will reward thee plenteously, *I will be with thee in trouble."*

CHAPTER XXXVI

AGAINST VAIN JUDGMENTS OF MEN

"My Son, anchor thy soul firmly upon God, and fear not man's judgment, when conscience pronounceth thee pious and innocent. It is good and blessed thus to suffer; nor will it be grievous to the heart which is humble, and which trusteth in God more than in itself. Many men have many opinions, and therefore little trust is to be placed in them. But moreover it is impossible to please all. Although Paul studied to please all men in the Lord, and *to become all things to all men,* yet nevertheless *with him it was a very small thing that he should be judged by man's judgment."*

He laboured abundantly, as much as in him lay, for the building up and the salvation of others; but he could not avoid being sometimes judged and despised by others. Therefore he committed all to God, who knew all, and by patience and humility defended himself against evil speakers, or foolish and false thinkers, and those who accused him according to their pleasure. Nevertheless, from time to time he replied, lest his silence should become a stumbling-block to those who were weak.

DO NOT FEAR ANY MAN

"Who art thou, that thou shouldst be afraid of a man that shall die? To-day he is, and to-morrow his place is not found. Fear God and thou shalt not quail before the terrors of men. What can any man do against thee by words or deeds? He hurteth himself more than thee, nor shall he escape the judgment of God, whosoever he may be.

"Have thou God before thine eyes, and do not contend with fretful words. And if for the present thou seem to give way, and to suffer confusion which thou hast not deserved, be not angry at this, nor by impatience diminish thy reward; but rather look up to Me in heaven, for I am able to deliver thee from all confusion and hurt, and to render to every man according to his works."

CHAPTER XXXVII

OF PURE AND ENTIRE RESIGNATION OF SELF, FOR THE OBTAINING LIBERTY OF HEART

"MY Son, lose thyself and thou shalt find Me. Stand still without all choosing and all thought of self, and thou shalt ever be a gainer. For more grace shall be added to thee, as soon as thou resignest thyself, and so long as thou dost not turn back to take thyself again."

O Lord, how often shall I resign myself, and in what things shall I lose myself?

"Always; every hour: in that which is little, and in that which is great. I make no exception, but will that thou be found naked in all things. Otherwise how canst thou be Mine and I thine, unless thou be inwardly and outwardly free from every will of thine own? The sooner thou dost this, the better shall it be with thee; and the more fully and sincerely, the more thou shalt please Me, and the more abundantly shalt thou be rewarded.

THE SECRET OF INNER PEACE

"Some resign themselves, but with certain reservations, for they do not fully trust in God, therefore they think that they have some provision to make for themselves. Some again at first offer everything; but afterwards being pressed by temptation they return to their own devices, and thus make no progress in virtue.

"They will not attain to the true liberty of a pure heart, nor to the grace of My sweet companionship, unless they first entirely resign themselves and daily offer themselves up as a sacrifice; without this the union which bringeth forth fruit standeth not nor will stand.

"Many a time I have said unto thee, and now say again, Give thyself up, resign thyself, and thou shalt have great inward peace. Give all for all;

demand nothing, ask nothing in return; stand simply and with no hesitation in Me, and thou shalt possess Me. Thou shalt have liberty of heart, and the darkness shall not overwhelm thee.

"For this strive thou, pray for it, long after it, that thou mayest be delivered from all possession of thyself, and nakedly follow Jesus who was made naked for thee; mayest die unto thyself and live eternally to Me. Then shall all vain fancies disappear, all evil disturbings, and superfluous cares. Then also shall immoderate fear depart from thee, and inordinate love shall die."

Chapter XXXVIII
OF A GOOD GOVERNMENT IN EXTERNAL THINGS, AND OF HAVING RECOURSE TO GOD IN DANGERS

"My Son, for this thou must diligently make thy endeavour, that in every place and outward action or occupation thou mayest be free within, and have power over thyself; and that all things be under thee, not thou under them; that thou be master and ruler of thy actions, not a slave or hireling, but rather a free and true Hebrew, entering into the lot and the liberty of the children of God, who stand above the present and look upon the eternal, who with the left eye behold things transitory, and with the right things heavenly; whom temporal things draw not to cleave unto, but who rather draw temporal things to do them good service, even as they were ordained of God to do, and appointed by the Master Workman, who hath left nought in His creation without aim and end.

SEEK GOD'S COUNSEL

"And if in any chance of life thou stand not in outward appearances, nor judgest things which are seen and heard by the fleshy sense, but straightway in every cause enterest with Moses into the tabernacle to ask counsel of God; thou shalt hear a divine response and come forth instructed concerning many things that are and shall be. For always Moses had recourse to the tabernacle for the solving of all doubts and questionings; and fled to the help of prayer to be delivered from the dangers and evil deeds of men.

"Thus also oughtest thou to fly to the secret chamber of thy heart, and earnestly implore the divine succour. For this cause we read that Joshua and the children of Israel were deceived by the Gibeonites, that they *asked not counsel at the mouth of the Lord,* but being too ready to listen to fair speeches, were deceived by pretended piety."

Chapter XXXIX
THAT MAN MUST NOT BE IMMERSED IN BUSINESS

"My Son, always commit thy cause to Me; I will dispose it aright in due time. Wait for My arrangement of it, and then thou shalt find it for thy profit."

O Lord, right freely I commit all things to Thee; for my planning can profit but little. Oh that I did not dwell so much on future events, but could offer myself altogether to Thy pleasures without delay.

"My Son, a man often striveth vehemently after somewhat which he desireth; but when he hath obtained it he beginneth to be of another mind, because his affections towards it are not lasting, but rather rush on from one thing to another. Therefore it is not really a small thing, when in shall things we resist self."

The true progress of man lieth in self-denial, and a man who denieth himself is free and safe. But the old enemy, opposer of all good things, ceaseth not from temptation; but day and night setteth his wicked snares, if haply he may be able to entrap the unwary. *Watch and pray*, saith the Lord, *lest ye enter into temptation.*

CHAPTER XL
THAT MAN HATH NO GOOD IN HIMSELF, AND NOTHING WHEREOF TO GLORY

LORD, what is man that Thou art mindful of him, or the son of man that Thou visitest him? What hath man deserved, that Thou shouldest bestow thy favour upon him? Lord, what cause can I have of complaint, if Thou forsake me? Or what can I justly allege, if Thou refuse to hear my petition?

Of a truth, this I may truly think and say, Lord, I am nothing, I have nothing that is good of myself, but I fall short in all things, and ever tend unto nothing. And unless I am helped by Thee and inwardly supported, I become altogether lukewarm and reckless.

But Thou, O Lord, art always the same, and endurest for ever, always good, righteous, and holy; doing all things well, righteously, and holily, and disposing all in Thy wisdom. But I who am more ready to go forward than backward, never continue in one stay, because changes sevenfold pass over me. Yet it quickly becometh better when it so pleaseth Thee, and Thou puttest forth Thy hand to help me; be-

cause Thou alone canst aid without help of man, and canst so strengthen me that my countenance shall be no more changed, but my heart shall be turned to Thee, and rest in Thee alone.

THE DANGER OF VAINGLORY

Wherefore, if I but knew well how to reject all human consolations, whether for the sake of gaining devotion, or because of the necessity by which I was compelled to seek Thee, seeing there is no man who can comfort me; then could I worthily trust in Thy grace, and rejoice in the gift of new consolation.

Thanks be to Thee, from whom all cometh, whensoever it goeth well with me! But I am vanity and nothing in Thy sight, a man inconstant and weak. What then have I whereof to glory, or why do I long to be held in honour? Is it not for nought? This also is utterly vain.

Verily vainglory is an evil plague, the greatest of vanities, because it draweth us away from the true glory, and robbeth us of heavenly grace. For whilst a man pleaseth himself he displeaseth Thee; whilst he gapeth after the praises of man, he is deprived of true virtues.

SEEK GOD'S GLORY NOT THINE OWN

But true glory and holy rejoicing lieth in glorying in Thee and not in self; in rejoicing in Thy Name, not in our own virtue; in not taking delight in any creature, save only for Thy sake. Let thy Name, not mine be praised; let Thy work, not mine be magnified; let Thy holy Name be blessed, but to me let nought be given of the praises of men.

Thou art my glory, Thou art the joy

of my heart. In Thee will I make my boast and be glad all the day long, but for myself let me not glory *save only in my infirmities.*

Let the Jews seek *the honour which cometh from one another;* but I will ask for that which *cometh from God only.* Truly all human glory, all temporal honour, all worldly exultation, compared to Thy eternal glory, is but vanity and folly. O God my Truth and my Mercy, Blessed Trinity, to Thee alone be all praise, honour, power, and glory for ever and for ever. Amen.

CHAPTER XLI
OF CONTEMPT OF ALL TEMPORAL HONOUR

"MY SON, make it no matter of thine, if thou see others honoured and exalted, and thyself despised and humbled. Lift up thine heart to Me in heaven, and then the contempt of men upon earth will not make thee sad."

O Lord, we are in blindness, and are quickly seduced by vanity. If I look rightly within myself, never was injury done unto me by any creature, and therefore I have nought whereof to complain before Thee. But because I have many times and grievously sinned against Thee, all creatures do justly take arms against me.

Therefore to me confusion and contempt are justly due, but to Thee praise and honour and glory. And except I dispose myself for this, namely, to be willing that every creature should despise and desert me, and that I should be esteemed altogether as nothing, I cannot be inwardly filled with peace and strength, nor spiritually enlightened, nor fully united to Thee.

CHAPTER XLII
THAT OUR PEACE IS NOT TO BE PLACED IN MEN

"MY SON, if thou set thy peace on any person because thou hast high opinion of him, and art familiar with him, thou shalt be unstable and entangled. But if thou betake thyself to the everliving and abiding Truth, the desertion or death of a friend shall not make thee sad. In Me ought the love of thy friend to subsist, and for My sake is every one to be loved, whosoever he be, who appeareth to thee good, and is very dear to thee in this life. Without Me friendship hath no strength or endurance; neither is that love true and pure, which I unite not.

"Thou oughtest to be so dead to such affections of beloved friends, that as far as in thee lieth, thou wouldst rather choose to be without any companionship of men. The nearer a man approacheth to God, the further he recedeth from all earthly solace. The deeper also he descendeth into himself, and the viler he appeareth in his own eyes, the higher he ascendeth towards God.

DO NOT HINDER THE GRACE OF GOD

"But he who attributeth anything good to himself, hindereth the grace of God from coming to him, because the grace of the Holy Ghost ever seeketh the humble heart. If thou couldst make thyself utterly nothing, and empty thyself of the love of every creature, then should it be My part to overflow unto thee with great grace.

"When thou settest thine eyes upon creatures, the face of the Creator is withdrawn from thee. Learn in all things to conquer thyself for thy Creator's sake, then shalt thou be able to attain unto divine knowledge. How small soever anything be, if it be loved and regarded inordinately, it holdeth us back from the highest good, and corrupteth."

CHAPTER XLIII
AGAINST VAIN AND WORLDLY KNOWLEDGE

"My Son, let not the fair and subtle sayings of men move thee. *For the kingdom of God is not in word, but in power.* Give ear to My words, for they kindle the heart and enlighten the mind, they bring contrition, and they supply manifold consolations.

"Never read thou the word that thou mayest appear more learned or wise; but study for the mortification of thy sins, for this will be far more profitable for thee than the knowledge of many difficult questions.

"When thou hast read and learned many things, thou must always return to one first principle. I am *He that teacheth man knowledge*, and I give unto babes clearer knowledge than can be taught by man. He to whom I speak will be quickly wise and shall grow much in the spirit. Woe unto them who inquire into many curious questions from men, and take little heed concerning the way of My service.

"The time will come when Christ will appear, the Master of masters, the Lord of the Angels, to hear the lessons of all, that is to examine the consciences of each one. And then will He *search Jerusalem with candles*, and the *hidden things of darkness* shall be made manifest, and the arguings of tongues shall be silent.

THE MASTER TEACHER

"I am He who in an instant lift up the humble spirit, to learn more reasonings of the Eternal Truth, than if a man had studied ten years in the schools. I teach without noise of words, without confusion of opinions, without striving after honour, without clash of arguments.

"I am He who teach men to despise earthly things, to loathe things present, to seek things heavenly, to enjoy things eternal, to flee honours, to endure offences, to place all hope in Me, to desire nothing apart from Me, and above all things to love Me ardently.

"For there was one, who by loving Me from the bottom of his heart, learned divine things, and spake things that were wonderful; he profited more by forsaking all things than by studying subtleties. But to some I speak common things, to others special; to some I appear gently in signs and figures, and again to some I reveal mysteries in much light. The voice of books is one, but it informeth not all alike; because I inwardly am the Teacher of truth, the Searcher of the heart, the Discerner of the thoughts, the Mover of actions, distributing to each man, as I judge meet."

CHAPTER XLIV
OF NOT TROUBLING OURSELVES ABOUT OUTWARD THINGS

"My Son, in many things it behoveth thee to be ignorant, and to esteem thyself as one dead upon the earth, and as one to whom the whole world is crucified. Many things also thou must pass by with deaf ear, and must rather think upon those things which belong unto thy peace. It is more profitable to turn away thine eyes from those things that displease, and to leave each man to his own opinion, than to give thyself to discourses of strife. If thou stand well with God and hast His judgment in thy mind, thou wilt verily easily bear to be as one conquered."

O Lord, to what have we come? Behold a temporal loss is mourned over; for a trifling gain we labour and hurry; and spiritual loss passeth away into forgetfulness, and we rarely recover it. That which profiteth little or nothing is looked after, and that which is altogether necessary is negligently passed by; because the whole man slideth away to outward things, and unless he quickly recovereth himself in outward things he willingly lieth down.

CHAPTER XLV

THAT WE MUST NOT BELIEVE EVERYONE, AND THAT WE ARE PRONE TO FALL IN OUR WORDS

LORD, be thou my help in trouble, for vain is the help of man. How often have I failed to find faithfulness, where I thought I possessed it. How many times I have found it where I least expected. Vain therefore is hope in men, but the salvation of the just, O God, is in Thee. Blessed be thou, O Lord my God, in all things which happen unto us. We are weak and unstable; we are quickly deceived and quite changed.

TRUST GOD NOT MEN

Who is the man who is able to keep himself so warily and circumspectly as not sometimes to come into some snare of perplexity? But he who trusteth in Thee, O Lord, and seeketh Thee with an unfeigned heart, doth not so easily slip. And if he fall into any tribulation, howsoever he may be entangled, yet very quickly he shall be delivered through Thee, or by Thee shall be comforted, because Thou wilt not forsake him that trusteth in Thee unto the end.

A friend who continueth faithful in all the distresses of his friend is rare to be found. Thou, O Lord, Thou alone art most faithful in all things, and there is none other like unto Thee.

Oh, how truly wise was that holy soul which said, "My mind is steadfastly fixed, and it is grounded in Christ." If thus it were with me, the fear of man should not so easily tempt me, nor the arrows of words move me. Who is sufficient to foresee all things, who to guard beforehand against future ills? If even things which are foreseen sometimes hurt us, what can things which are not foreseen do, but grievously injure? But wherefore have I not better provided for myself, miserable that I am?

Why, too, have I given such heed to others? But we are men, nor are we other than frail men, even though by many we are reckoned and called angels. Whom shall I trust, O Lord, whom shall I trust but Thee? Thou art the Truth, and deceivest not, nor canst be deceived. And on the other hand, *Every man is a liar,* weak, unstable and frail, especially in his words, so that one ought scarcely ever to believe what seemeth to sound right on the face of it.

KEEP SILENT

With what wisdom hast thou warned us beforehand to *beware of men,* and that *a man's foes are they of his own household,* and that we must not believe if one say unto us *Lo here, or Lo there.* I have been taught by my loss, and O that I may prove more careful and not foolish hereby. "Be cautious," saith some one: "be cautious, keep unto thyself what I tell thee." And whilst I am silent and believe that it is hid with me, he himself cannot keep silence concerning it, but straightway betrayeth me and himself, and goeth his way.

Protect me, O Lord, from such mischief-making and reckless men; let me not fall into their hands, nor ever do such things myself. Put a true and steadfast word into my mouth, and remove a deceitful tongue far from me. What I would not suffer, I ought by all means to beware of doing.

Oh, how good and peacemaking a thing it is to be silent concerning others, and not carelessly to believe all reports, nor to hand them on further; how good also to lay one's self open to few, to seek ever to have Thee as the beholder of the heart; not to be carried about with every wind of words, but to desire that all things inward and outward be done according to the good pleasure of Thy will!

How safe for the preserving of heavenly grace to fly from human approval, and not to long after the things which seem to win admiration abroad, but to follow with all earnestness those things which bring amendment of life and heavenly fervour! How many have been injured by their virtue being made known and too hastily praised. How truly profitable hath been grace preserved in silence in this frail life, which, as we are told, is all temptation and warfare.

CHAPTER XLVI
OF HAVING CONFIDENCE IN GOD WHEN EVIL WORDS ARE CAST AT US

"MY Son, stand fast and believe in Me. For what are words but words? They fly through the air, but they bruise no stone. If thou are guilty, think how thou wouldst gladly amend thyself; if thou knowest nothing against thyself, consider that thou wilt gladly bear this for God's sake.

"It is little enough that thou sometimes hast to bear hard words, for thou art not yet able to bear hard blows. And wherefore do such trivial matters go to thine heart, except that thou art yet carnal, and regardest men more than thou oughtest? For because thou fearest to be despised, thou art unwilling to be reproved for thy faults, and seekest paltry shelters of excuses.

"But look better into thyself, and thou shalt know that the world is still alive in thee, and the vain love of pleasing men. For when thou fleest away from being abased and confounded for thy faults, it is plain that thou art neither truly humble nor truly dead to the world, and that the world is not crucified to thee.

"But hearken to My word, and thou shalt not care for ten thousand words of men. Behold, if all things could be said against thee which the utmost malice could invent, what should it hurt thee if thou wert altogether to let it go, and make no more account of it than of a mote? Could it pluck out a single hair of thy head?

GOD THE JUST JUDGE

"But he that hath no heart within him, and hath not God before his eyes, is easily moved by a word of reproach; but he who trusteth in Me, and seeketh not to abide by his own judgment, shall be free from the fear of men. For I am the Judge and the Discerner of all secrets; I know how the thing hath been done; I know both the injurer and the bearer. From Me went forth that word, by My permission this hath happened, *that the thoughts of many hearts may be revealed.* I shall judge the guilty and the innocent; but beforehand I have willed to try them both by a secret judgment.

"The testimony of men often deceiveth. My judgment is true; it will stand, and it shall not be overturned. It commonly lieth hid, and only to few in certain cases is it made known; yet it never erreth, nor can err, although it seem not right to the eyes of foolish men. To Me, therefore, must men have recourse in all judgment, and must not lean to their opinion.

"For *there shall no evil happen to the just,* whatsoever may be sent to him by God. Even though some unjust charge be brought against him, he will care little; nor, again, will he exult above measure, if through others he be clearly vindicated. For he considereth that I am *He who try the hearts and reins,* who judge not outwardly and according to human appearance; for often in Mine eyes that is found blameworthy which in the judgment of men is held worthy of praise."

THE NEED TO BEAR REBUKE MEEKLY

O Lord God, O Judge, just, strong, and patient, who knowest the frailty and sinfulness of men, be Thou my strength and my whole confidence; for my own conscience sufficeth me not. Thou knowest what I know not; and therefore ought I under all rebuke to humble myself, and to bear it meekly. Therefore mercifully forgive me as often as I have not done this, and grant me the next time the grace of greater endurance.

For better unto me is Thine abundant pity for the attainment of Thy pardon, than the righteousness which I believe myself to have for defence against my conscience, which lieth wait against me. Although *I know nothing against myself, yet am I not hereby justified,* because if Thy mercy were removed away, *in Thy sight should no man living be justified.*

CHAPTER XLVII
THAT ALL TROUBLES ARE TO BE ENDURED FOR THE SAKE OF ETERNAL LIFE

"MY Son, let not the labours which thou hast undertaken for Me break thee down, nor let tribulations cast thee down in any wise, but let My promise strengthen and comfort thee in every event. I am sufficient to reward thee above all measure and extent. Not long shalt thou labour here, nor always be weighed down with sorrows. Wait yet a little while, and thou shalt see a speedy end of thine evils. An hour shall come when all labour and confusion shall cease. Little and short is all that passeth away with time.

"Do earnestly what thou dost; labour faithfully in My vineyard; I will be thy reward. Write, read, sing, weep, be silent, pray, endure adversities manfully; eternal life is worthy of all these conflicts, yea, and of greater. Peace shall come *in one day which is known to the Lord; which shall be neither day nor night,* but light eternal, infinite clearness, steadfast peace, and undisturbed rest. Thou shalt not say then, *Who shall deliver me from the body of this death?* nor cry out, *Woe is me, for my sojourning is prolonged,* because death will be utterly destroyed, and there shall be salvation which can never fail, no more anxiety, happy delight, sweet and noble society.

OUR CROWN OF REJOICING

"Oh, if thou sawest the unfading crowns of the saints in heaven, and with what great glory they now rejoice, who aforetime were reckoned by this world contemptibly and as it were unworthy of life, truly thou wouldst immediately humble thyself even to the earth, and wouldst desire rather to be in subjection to all, than to have authority over one; nor wouldst thou long for pleasant days of this life, but wouldst more rejoice to be afflicted for God's sake, and wouldst esteem it gain to be counted for nought amongst men.

"Oh, if these things were sweet to thy taste, and moved thee to the bottom of thine heart, how shouldst thou dare even once to complain? Are not all laborious things to be endured for the sake of eternal life? It is no small thing, the losing or gaining the Kingdom of God. Lift up therefore thy face to heaven. Behold, I and all My saints with Me, who in this world had a hard conflict, now rejoice, are now comforted, are now secure, are now at peace, and shall remain with Me evermore in the Kingdom of My Father."

CHAPTER XLVIII

OF THE DAY OF ETERNITY AND OF THE STRAITNESSES OF THIS LIFE

OH most blessed mansion of the City which is above! Oh most clear day of eternity which the night obscureth not, but the Supreme Truth ever enlighteneth! Day always joyful, always secure and never changing its state into those which are contrary. Oh would that this day might shine forth, and that all these temporal things would come to an end. It shineth indeed upon the Saints, glowing with unending brightness, but only from afar and through a glass, upon those who are pilgrims on the earth.

The citizens of heaven know how glorious that day is; the exiled sons of Eve groan, because this is bitter and wearisome. The days of this life are few and evil, full of sorrows and straits, where man is defiled with many sins, ensnared with many passions, bound fast with many fears, wearied with many cares, distracted with many questionings, entangled with many vanities, compassed about with many errors, worn away with many labours, weighed down with temptations, enervated by pleasures, tormented by poverty.

LONGING FOR INTIMACY WITH GOD

Oh when shall there be an end of these evils? When shall I be delivered from the wretched slavery of my sins? When shall I be mindful, O Lord, of Thee alone? When shall I rejoice in Thee to the full? When shall I be in true liberty without any impediment, without any burden on mind or body? When shall there be solid peace, peace immovable and secure, peace within and without, peace firm on every side?

Blessed Jesus, when shall I stand to behold Thee? When shall I gaze upon the glory of Thy kingdom? When shalt Thou be to me all in all? Oh when shall I be with Thee in Thy Kingdom which Thou hast prepared from the foundation of the world for them that love Thee? I am left destitute, an exile in a hostile land, where are daily wars and grievous misfortunes.

Console my exile, mitigate my sorrow, for towards Thee all my desire longeth. For all is to me a burden, whatsoever this world offereth for consolation. I yearn to enjoy Thee intimately, but I cannot attain unto it. I long to cleave to heavenly things, but temporal things and unmortified passions press me down.

In my mind I would be above all things, but in my flesh I am unwillingly compelled to be beneath them. So, wretched man that I am, I fight with myself, and am made grievous even unto myself, while the spirit seeketh to be above and the flesh to be beneath.

TURN YOUR THOUGHTS TO GOD

Oh how I suffer inwardly, while with the mind I discourse on heavenly things, and presently a crowd of carnal things rusheth upon me whilst I pray. *My God, be not Thou far from me,* nor depart in wrath from Thy servant. *Cast forth Thy lightning and scatter them; send out Thine arrows,* and let all delusions of my enemy be confounded. Recall my senses unto Thyself, cause me to forget all worldly things; grant me quickly to cast away and despise the imaginations of sin. Succour me, O Eternal Truth, that no vanity may move me.

Come unto me, O Heavenly Sweetness, and let all impurity flee from before Thy face. Pardon me also, and of Thy mercy deal gently with me, whensoever in prayer I think on anything besides Thee; for truly I confess that I am wont to be continually distracted. For often and often, where in the body I stand or sit, there I myself am not; but rather am I there, whither I am borne by my thoughts. Where my thought is, there am I; and there commonly is my thought where that which

I love is. That readily occurreth to me, which naturally delighteth, or pleaseth through custom.

Wherefore Thou, who art the Truth, hast plainly said, *Where your treasure is, there will your heart be also.* If I love heaven, I gladly meditate on heavenly things. If I love the world, I rejoice in the delights of the world, and am made sorry by its adversities. If I love the flesh, I am continually imagining the things which belong to the flesh; if I love the spirit, I am delighted by meditating on spiritual things. For whatsoever things I love, on these I readily converse and listen, and carry home with me the images of them.

But blessed is that man who for Thy sake, O Lord, is willing to part from all creatures; who doth violence to his fleshly nature and crucifieth the lusts of the flesh by the fervour of his spirit, so that with serene conscience he may offer unto Thee a pure prayer, and be made worthy to enter into the angelic choirs, having shut out from himself, both outwardly and inwardly, all worldly things.

CHAPTER XLIX

OF THE DESIRE AFTER ETERNAL LIFE, AND HOW GREAT BLESSINGS ARE PROMISED TO THOSE WHO STRIVE

"My Son, when thou feelest the desire of eternal happiness to be poured into thee from above, and longest to depart from the tabernacle of this body, that thou mayest contemplate My glory without shadow of turning, enlarge thine heart, and take in this holy inspiration with all thy desire. Give most hearty thanks to the Supreme Goodness, who dealeth with thee so graciously, visiteth thee so lovingly, stirreth thee up so fervently, raiseth thee so powerfully, lest thou sink down through thine own weight, to earthly things.

"For not by thine own meditating or striving dost thou receive this gift, but by the soul gracious condescension of Supreme Grace and Divine regard; to the end that thou mayest make progress in virtue and in more humility, and prepare thyself for future conflicts, and cleave unto Me with all the affection of thy heart, and strive to serve Me with fervent will.

"My Son, often the fire burneth, but the flame ascendeth not without smoke. So also the desires of some men burn towards heavenly things, and yet they are not free from the temptation of carnal affection. Thus therefore they are not acting with an altogether simple desire for God's glory when they pray to Him so earnestly. Such too, is oftentimes thy desire, when thou hast imagined it to be so earnest. For that is not pure and perfect which is tainted with thine own self-seeking.

TRIALS PRECEDE TRIUMPH

"Seek thou not what is pleasant and advantageous to thyself, but what is acceptable and honourable unto Me; for if thou judgest rightly, thou must choose and follow after My appointment rather than thine own desire; yea, rather than anything that can be desired. I know thy desire, and I have heard thy many groanings. Already thou longest to be in the glorious liberty of the children of God; already the eternal home delighteth thee, and the heavenly country full of joy; but the hour is not yet come; there remaineth still another season, even a season of warfare, a season of labour

and probation. Thou desirest to be filled with the Chief Good, but thou canst not attain it immediately. I AM that Good; wait for Me, until the Kingdom of God shall come.

"Thou must still be tried upon earth, and be exercised in many things. Consolation shall from time to time be given thee, but abundant satisfying shall not be granted. Be strong therefore, and be thou brave both in working and in suffering things which are against thy nature. Thou must put on the new man, and be changed into another man. Thou must often do what thou wouldst not; and thou must leave undone what thou wouldst do.

"What pleaseth others shall have good success; what pleaseth thee shall have no prosperity. What others say shall be listened to; what thou sayest shall receive no heed. Others shall ask and receive; thou shalt ask and not obtain. Others shall be great in the report of men, but about thee shall nothing be spoken. To others this or that shall be entrusted; thou shalt be judged useful for nought.

THE GLORY TO COME

"For this cause nature shall sometimes be filled with sadness; and it is a great thing if thou bear it silently. In this and many like things the faithful servant of the Lord is wont to be tried, how far he is able to deny himself and bring himself into subjection in all things. Scarcely is there anything in which thou hast need to mortify thyself so much as in seeing things which are adverse to thy will; especially when things are commanded thee to be done which seem to thee inexpedient or of little use to thee. And because thou darest not resist a higher power, being under authority, therefore it seemeth hard for thee to shape thy course according to the nod of another, and to forego thine own opinion.

"But consider, My Son, the fruit of these labours, the swift end, and the reward exceeding great; and thou shalt find it no pain to bear them then, but rather the strongest solace of thy patience. For even in exchange for this trifling desire which thou hast readily forsaken, thou shalt always have thy will in Heaven. There verily thou shalt find all that thou wouldst, all that thou canst long for. There thou shalt have all good within thy power without the fear of losing it. There thy will, ever at one with Mine, shall desire nothing outward, nothing for itself.

"There no man shall withstand thee, none shall complain of thee, none shall hinder, nothing shall stand in thy path; but all things desired by thee shall be present together, and shall refresh thy whole affection, and fill it up even to the brim. There I will glory for the scorn suffered here, the garment of praise for sorrow, and for the lowest place a throne in the Kingdom, for ever. There shall appear the fruit of obedience, the labour of repentance shall rejoice, and humble subjection shall be crowned gloriously.

BY LIFE OR BY DEATH

"Now therefore bow thyself humbly under the hands of all men; nor let it trouble thee who said this or who ordered that; but take special heed that whether thy superior, thy inferior, or thy equal, require anything from thee, or even show a desire for it; take it all in good part, and study with a good will to fulfil the desire.

"Let one seek this, another that; let this man glory in this, and that man in that, and be praised a thousand thousand times, but rejoice thou only in the contempt of thyself, and in Mine own good pleasure and glory. This is what thou art to long for, even that whether *by life or by death God may be ever magnified in thee.*"

CHAPTER L

HOW A DESOLATE MAN OUGHT TO COMMIT HIMSELF INTO THE HANDS OF GOD

O LORD, Holy Father, be Thou blessed now and evermore; because as Thou wilt so it is done, and what Thou doest is good. Let Thy servant rejoice in Thee, not in himself, nor in any other; because thou alone art the true joy, Thou art my hope and my crown, Thou art my joy and my honour, O Lord.

What hath Thy servant, which he received not from Thee, even without merit of his own? Thine are all things which Thou hast given, and which Thou hast made. *I am poor and in misery even from my youth up,* and my soul is sorrowful unto tears; sometimes also it is disquieted within itself, because of the sufferings which are coming upon it.

I long after the joy of peace; for the peace of Thy children do I beseech, for in the light of Thy comfort they are fed by Thee. If Thou give peace, if Thou pour into me holy joy, the soul of Thy servant shall be full of melody, and devout in Thy praise. But if Thou withdraw Thyself as too often Thou art wont, he will not be able to run in the way of Thy commandments, but rather he will smite his breast and will bow his knees; because it is not with him as yesterday and the day before, *when Thy candle shined upon his head, and he walked under the shadow of Thy wings,* from the temptations which beset him.

THE TRYING OF OUR FAITH

O Father, righteous and ever to be praised, the hour cometh when Thy servant is to be proved. O beloved Father, it is well that in this hour Thy servant suffer somewhat for Thy sake. O Father, evermore to be adored, as the hour cometh which Thou foreknewest from everlasting, when for a little while Thy servant should outwardly bow down, but always live inwardly with Thee; when for a little while he should be little regarded, humbled, and fail in the eyes of men; should be wasted with sufferings and weaknesses, to rise again with Thee in the dawn of the new light, and be glorified in the heavenly places. O Holy Father, Thou hast ordained it so, and so hast willed it; and that is done which Thou Thyself hast commanded.

For this is Thy favour to Thy friend, that he should suffer and be troubled in the world for Thy love's sake, how often soever, and by whomsoever and whosoever Thou hast suffered it to be done. Without Thy counsel and providence, and without cause, nothing cometh to pass on the earth. *It is good for me, Lord, that I had been in trouble, that I may learn Thy statues,* and may cast away all pride of heart and presumption. It is profitable for me that confusion hath covered my face, that I may seek to Thee for consolation rather than unto men. By this also I have learned to dread Thine unsearchable judgment, who afflictest the just with the wicked, but not without equity and justice.

THE FATHER'S LOVING DISCIPLINE

Thanks be unto Thee, because Thou hast not spared my sins, but hast beaten me with stripes of love, inflicting pains, and sending troubles upon me without and within. There is none who can console me, of all things which are under heaven, but Thou only, O Lord my God, Thou heavenly Physician of souls, *who dost scourge and hast mercy, who leadest down to hell and bringest up again.* Thy discipline over me, and Thy rod itself shall teach me.

Behold, O beloved Father, I am in Thy hands, I bow myself under the rod of Thy correction. Smite my back and my neck that I may bend my crookedness to Thy will. Make me a pious and lowly disciple, as Thou wert wont to be kind, that I may walk according to every nod of Thine. To Thee I commend myself and all that I have for correction; better is it to be punished here than hereafter.

Thou knowest all things and each of them; and nothing remaineth hid from Thee in man's conscience. Before they are, thou knowest that they will be, and Thou needest not that any man teach Thee or admonish Thee concerning the things which are done upon the earth. Thou knowest what is expedient for my profit, and how greatly trouble serveth unto the scrubbing off the rust of sin. Do with me according to Thy desired good pleasure, and despise not my life which is full of sin, known to none so entirely and fully as to Thee alone.

THE NEED FOR DISCERNMENT

Grant me, O Lord, to know that which ought to be known; to love that which ought to be loved; to praise that which pleaseth Thee most, to esteem that which is precious in Thy sight, to blame that which is vile in Thine eyes. Suffer me not to judge according to the sight of bodily eyes, nor to give sentence according to the hearing of the ears of ignorant men; but to discern in true judgment between visible and spiritual things, and above all things to be ever seeking after the will of Thy good pleasure.

Oftentimes the senses of men are deceived in judging; the lovers of the world also are deceived in that they love only visible things. What is a man better because by man he is reckoned very great? The deceiver deceiveth the deceiver, the vain man the vain, the blind man the blind, the weak man the weak, when they exalt one another; and in truth they rather put to shame, while they foolishly praise. For as humble St. Francis saith, "What each one is in Thine eyes, so much he is, and no more."

CHAPTER LI

THAT WE MUST GIVE OURSELVES TO HUMBLE WORKS WHEN WE ARE UNEQUAL TO THOSE THAT ARE LOFTY

"MY Son, thou art not always able to continue in very fervent desire after virtues, nor to stand fast in the loftier region of contemplation; but thou must of necessity sometimes descend to lower things because of thine original corruption, and bear about the burden of corruptible life, though unwillingly and with weariness. So long as thou wearest a mortal body, thou shalt feel weariness and heaviness of heart. Therefore thou oughtest to groan often in the flesh because of the burden of the flesh, inasmuch as thou canst not give thyself to spiritual stud-

ies and divine contemplation unceasingly.

"At such a time it is expedient for thee to flee to humble and external works, and to renew thyself with good actions; to wait for My coming and heavenly visitation with sure confidence; to bear thy exile and drought of mind with patience, until thou be visited by Me again, and be freed from all anxieties. For I will cause thee to forget thy labours, and altogether to enjoy eternal peace.

"I will spread open before thee the pleasant pastures of the Scriptures, that with enlarged heart thou mayest begin to run in the way of My commandments. And thou shalt say, *The sufferings of this present time are not worthy to be compared with the glory which shall be revealed in us.'*

CHAPTER LII

THAT A MAN OUGHT NOT TO RECKON HIMSELF WORTHY OF CONSOLATION, BUT MORE WORTHY OF CHASTISEMENT

O LORD, I am not worthy of Thy consolation, nor of any spiritual visitation; and therefore Thou dealest justly with me, when Thou leavest me poor and desolate. For if I were able to pour forth tears like the sea, still should I not be worthy of Thy consolation. Therefore am I nothing worthy save to be scourged and punished, because I have grievously and many a time offended Thee, and in many things have greatly sinned. Therefore, true account being taken, I am not worthy even of the least of Thy consolations.

But Thou, gracious and merciful God, who willest not that Thy works should perish, to show forth the riches of Thy mercy upon the vessels of mercy, vouchsafest even beyond all his own deserving, to comfort Thy servant above the measure of mankind. For Thy consolations are not like unto the discoursings of men.

What have I done, O Lord, that Thou shouldst bestow any heavenly comfort upon me? I remember not that I have done any good, but have been ever prone to sin and slow to amendment. It is true and I cannot deny it. If I should say otherwise, Thou wouldst rise up against me, and there would be none to defend me.

What have I deserved for my sins but hell and everlasting fire? In very truth I confess that I am worthy of all scorn and contempt, nor is it fit that I should be remembered among Thy faithful servants. And although I be unwilling to hear this, nevertheless I will for the Truth's sake, accuse myself of my sins, that the more readily I may prevail to be accounted worthy of Thy mercy.

AN ACCEPTABLE SACRIFICE

What shall I say, guilty that I am and filled with confusion? I have no mouth to utter, unless it be this word alone, "I have sinned, Lord, I have sinned; have mercy upon me, forgive me." *Let me alone, that I may take comfort a little before I go whence I shall not return even to the land of darkness and the shadow of death.*

What dost thou so much require of a guilty and miserable sinner, as that he be contrite, and humble himself for his sins? In true contrition and humiliation of heart is begotten the hope of pardon, the troubled conscience is reconciled, lost grace is recovered, a man is preserved from the wrath to come, and God and the penitent soul hasten to meet each other with a holy kiss.

The humble contrition of sinners is an acceptable sacrifice unto Thee, O Lord, sending forth a smell sweeter far in Thy sight than the incense. This also is that pleasant ointment which Thou wouldst have poured upon Thy sacred feet, *for a broken and contrite heart Thou hast never despised.* There is the place of refuge from the wrathful countenance of the enemy. There is amended and washed away whatsoever evil hath elsewhere been contracted.

CHAPTER LIII
THAT THE GRACE OF GOD DOTH NOT JOIN ITSELF TO THOSE WHO MIND EARTHLY THINGS

"MY Son, precious is My grace, it suffereth not itself to be joined with outward things, nor with earthly consolations. Therefore thou oughtest to cast away all things which hinder grace, if thou longest to receive the inpouring thereof. Seek a secret place for thyself, love to dwell alone with thyself, desire the conversation of no one; but rather pour out thy devout prayer to God, that thou mayest possess a contrite mind and a pure conscience.

"Count the whole world as nought; seek to be alone with God before all outward things. For thou canst not be alone with Me, and at the same time be delighted with transitory things. Thou oughtest to be separated from thy acquaintances and dear friends, and keep thy mind free from all worldly comfort. So the blessed Apostle Peter beseecheth, that Christ's faithful ones bear themselves in this world as strangers and pilgrims.

THE CONQUEST OF SELF

"Oh how great a confidence shall there be to the dying man whom no affection to anything detaineth in the world? But to have a heart so separated from all things, a sickly soul doth not yet comprehend, nor doth the carnal man know the liberty of the spiritual man. But if indeed he desire to be spiritually minded, he must renounce both those who are far off, and those who are near, and to beware of no man more than himself.

"If thou perfectly conquer thyself, very easily shalt thou subdue all things besides. Perfect victory is the triumph over oneself. For whoso keepeth himself in subjection, in such manner that the sensual affections obey the reason, and the reason in all things obeyeth Me, he truly is conqueror of himself, and lord of the world.

"If thou desire to climb to this height, thou oughtest to start bravely, and to lay the axe to the root, to the end that thou mayest pull up and destroy the hidden inordinate inclination towards thyself, and towards all selfish and earthly good. From this sin, that a man loveth himself too inordinately, almost everything hangeth which needeth to be utterly overcome: when that evil is conquered and put under foot, there shall be great peace and tranquillity continually.

"But because few strive earnestly to die perfectly to themselves, and do not heartily go forth from themselves, therefore do they remain entangled in themselves, and cannot be raised in spirit above themselves. But he who desireth to walk at liberty with Me, must of necessity mortify all his evil and inordinate affections, and must cling to no creature with selfish love."

Chapter LIV

OF THE DIVERSE MOTIONS OF NATURE AND OF GRACE

"My Son, pay diligent heed to the motions of Nature and of Grace, because they move in a very contrary and subtle manner, and are hardly distinguished save by a spiritual and inwardly enlightened man. All men indeed seek good, and make pretence of something good in all that they say or do; and thus under the appearance of good many are deceived.

NATURE AND GRACE CONTRASTED

"Nature is deceitful and draweth away, ensnareth, and deceiveth many, and always hath self for her end; but Grace walketh in simplicity and turneth away from every appearance of evil, maketh no false pretences, and doeth all entirely for the sake of God, in whom also she finally resteth.

"Nature is very unwilling to die, and to be pressed down, and to be overcome, and to be in subjection, and to bear the yoke readily; but Grace studieth self-mortification, resisteth sensuality, seeketh to be subdued, longeth to be conquered, and willeth not to use her own liberty. She loveth to be held by discipline, and not to have authority over any, but always to live, to remain, to have her being under God, and for God's sake is ready to be humbly subject to every ordinance of man.

"Nature laboureth for her own advantage, and considereth what profit she may gain from another; but Grace considereth more, not what may be useful and convenient to self, but what may be profitable to the many.

"Nature willingly receiveth honour and reverence; but Grace faithfully ascribeth all honour and glory to God.

"Nature feareth confusion and contempt, and Grace rejoiceth to suffer shame for the name of Jesus.

"Nature loveth ease and bodily quiet; Grace cannot be unemployed, but gladly embraceth labour.

"Nature seeketh to possess things curious and attractive, and abhorreth those which are rough and cheap; Grace is delighted with things simple and humble, despiseth not those which are rough, nor refuseth to be clothed with old garments.

THE TEMPORAL VERSUS THE ETERNAL

"Nature hath regard to things temporal, rejoiceth in earthly lucre, is made sad by loss, vexed by any little injurious word; but Grace reacheth after things eternal, cleaveth not to those which are temporal, is not perturbed by losses, nor embittered by any hard words, because she hath placed her treasure and joy in heaven where nought perisheth.

"Nature is covetous, and receiveth more willingly than she giveth, loveth things that are personal and private to herself; while Grace is kind and generous, avoideth selfishness, is contented with a little, believeth that it is more blessed to give than to receive.

"Nature inclineth thee to created things, to thine own flesh, to vanities and dissipation; but Grace draweth to God and to virtues, renounceth creatures, fleeth from the world, hateth the desires of the flesh, restraineth vagaries, blusheth to be seen in public.

"Nature is glad to receive some outward solace in which the senses may have delight; but Grace seeketh to be comforted in God alone, and to have delight in the chief good above all visible things.

"Nature doeth everything for her own gain and profit, can do nothing as a free favour, but hopeth to attain something as good or better, or some praise or favour for her benefits; and she loveth that her own deeds and gifts should be highly valued; but Grace seeketh nothing temporal, nor requireth any other gift of reward than God alone; neither longeth she for more of temporal necessities than such as may suffice for the attaining of eternal life.

MAN'S PERSPECTIVE, GOD'S PERSPECTIVE

"Nature rejoiceth in many friends and kinsfolk, she boasteth of noble place and noble birth, she smileth on the powerful, flattereth the rich, applaudeth those who are like herself; but Grace loveth even her enemies, and is not lifted up by the multitude of friends, setteth no store upon high place or high birth, unless there be greater virtue therewith; favoureth the poor man more than the rich, hath more sympathy with the innocent than with the powerful; rejoiceth with the truthful, not with the liar; always exhorteth the good to strive after better gifts of grace, and to become by holiness like unto the Son of God.

"Nature quickly complaineth of poverty and of trouble; Grace beareth want with constancy.

"Nature looketh upon all things in reference to herself; striveth and argueth for self; but Grace bringeth back all things to God from whom they came at the beginning; ascribeth no good to herself nor arrogantly presumeth; is not contentious, nor preferreth her own opinion to others, but in every sense and understanding submitteth herself to the Eternal wisdom and the Divine judgment.

A SPECIAL GIFT OF GOD

"Nature is eager to know secrets and to hear new things; she loveth to appear abroad, and to make experience of many things through the senses; she desireth to be acknowledged and to do those things which win praise and admiration; but Grace careth not to gather up new or curious things, because all this springeth from the old corruption, whereas there is nothing new or lasting upon earth.

"So she teacheth to restrain the senses, to shun vain complacency and ostentation, to hide humbly those things which merit praise and real admiration, and from everything and in all knowledge to seek after useful fruit, and the praise and honour of God. She desireth not to receive praise for herself or her own, but longeth that God be blessed in all His gifts, who out of unmingled love bestoweth all things."

This Grace is a supernatural light, and a certain special gift of God, and the proper mark of the elect, and the pledge of eternal salvation; it exalteth a man from earthly things to love those that are heavenly; and it maketh the carnal man spiritual. So far therefore as Nature is utterly pressed down and overcome, so far is greater Grace bestowed and the inner man is daily created anew by fresh visitations, after the image of God.

CHAPTER LV

OF THE CORRUPTION OF NATURE AND THE EFFICACY OF DIVINE GRACE

O LORD my God, who hast created me after thine own image and simili-tude, grant me this grace, which Thou hast shown to be so great and so necessary for salvation, that I may conquer my wicked nature, which draweth me to sin and to perdition. For I feel in my flesh the law of sin, contradicting the law of my mind, and bringing me into captivity to the obedience of sensuality in many things; nor can I resist its passions, unless Thy most holy grace assist me, fervently poured into my heart.

THE NEED OF GRACE

There is need of Thy grace, yea, and of a great measure thereof, that my nature may be conquered, which hath alway been prone to evil from my youth. For being fallen through the first man Adam, and corrupted through sin, the punishment of this stain descended upon all men, so that *Nature* itself, which was framed good and right by Thee, is now used to express the vice and infirmity of corrupted Nature; because its motion left unto itself draweth men away to evil and to lower things.

For the little power which remaineth is as it were one spark lying hid in the ashes. This is Natural reason itself, encompassed with thick clouds, having yet a discernment of good and evil, a distinction of the true and the false, though it be powerless to fulfil all that it approveth, and possess not yet the full light of truth, nor healthfulness of its affections.

Hence it is, O my God, that *I delight in Thy law after the inward man*, knowing that Thy *commandment is holy and just and good;* reproving also all evil, and the sin that is to be avoided: yet *with the flesh I serve the law of sin,* whilst I obey sensuality rather than reason. Hence it is that *to will to do good is present with me, but how to perform it I find not.*

Hence I ofttimes purpose many good things; but because grace is lacking to help mine infirmities, I fall back before a little resistance and fail. Hence it cometh to pass that I recognize the way of perfectness, and see very clearly what things I ought to do; but pressed down by the weight of my own corruption, I rise not to the things which are more perfect.

Oh how entirely necessary is Thy grace to me, O Lord, for a good beginning, for progress, and for bringing to perfection. For without it I can do nothing, but *I can do all things through Thy grace which strengtheneth me.* O truly heavenly grace, without which our own merits are nought, and no gifts of Nature at all are to be esteemed. Arts, riches, beauty, strength, wit, eloquence, they all avail nothing before Thee, O Lord, without Thy grace.

For the gifts of Nature belong to good and evil alike; but the proper gift of the elect is grace—that is, love—and they who bear the mark thereof are held worthy of everlasting life. So mighty is this grace, that without it neither the gift of prophecy nor the working of miracles, nor any speculation, howsoever lofty, is of any value at all. But neither faith, nor hope, nor any other virtue is accepted with Thee without love and grace.

THE NATURE OF GRACE

O most blessed grace that makest the poor in spirit rich in virtues, and renderest him who is rich in many things humble in spirit, come Thou, descend upon me, fill me early with Thy consolation, lest my soul fail through weariness and drought of mind. I beseech thee, O Lord, that I may find grace in Thy sight, for *Thy grace is sufficient for me,* when I obtain not those things which Nature longeth for. If I be tempted and vexed with many tribulations, I will fear no evil, while Thy grace remaineth with me. This alone is my strength, this bringeth me counsel and help. It is more powerful than all enemies, and wiser than all the wise men in the world.

It is the mistress of truth, the teacher of discipline, the light of the heart, the solace of anxiety, the banisher of sorrow, the deliverer from fear, the nurse of devotion, the drawer forth of tears. What am I without it, save a dry tree, a useless branch, worthy to be cast away! "Let Thy grace, therefore, O Lord, always prevent and follow me, and make me continually given to all good works, through Jesus Christ, Thy Son. Amen."

CHAPTER LVI

THAT WE OUGHT TO DENY OURSELVES, AND TO IMITATE CHRIST BY MEANS OF THE CROSS

"MY Son, so far as thou art able to go out of thyself so far shalt thou be able to enter into Me. As to desire no outward thing worketh internal peace, so the forsaking of self inwardly joineth unto God. I will that thou learn perfect self-denial, living in My will without contradiction or complaint. Follow Me: *I am the way, the truth, and the life.* Without the way thou canst not go, without the truth thou canst not know, without the life thou canst not live.

"I am the Way which thou oughtest to follow; the Truth which thou oughtest to believe; the Life which thou oughtest to hope for. I am the Way unchangeable; the Truth infallible; the Life everlasting. I am the Way altogether straight, the Truth supreme, and true Life, the blessed Life, the uncreated Life. If thou remain in My way thou shalt know the Truth, *and the truth shall make thee free.* and thou shalt lay hold on eternal life.

ON KEEPING GOD'S COMMANDMENTS

"If thou wilt enter into life, keep the commandments. If thou wilt know the truth, believe in Me. *If thou wilt be perfect, sell all that thou hast.* If thou wilt be My disciple, deny thyself. If thou wouldst possess the blessed life, despise the life which now is. If thou wilt be exalted in heaven, humble thyself in the world. If thou wilt reign with Me, bear the cross with Me; for only the servants of the cross find the way of blessedness and of true light."

O Lord Jesu, forasmuch as Thy life was straitened and despised by the world, grant unto me to imitate Thee in despising the world, *for the servant is not greater than his lord, nor the disciple above his master.* Let Thy servant be exercised in Thy life, because there is my salvation and true holiness. Whatsoever I read or hear besides it, it refresheth me not, nor giveth me delight.

"My Son, because thou knowest these things and hast read them all, blessed shalt thou be if thou doest them. *He who hath My commandments and keepeth them, he it is that loveth Me, and I will love him, and will manifest Myself to him,* and I will make him to sit down with Me in My Father's Kingdom."

THE BELIEVER AND THE CROSS

O Lord Jesu, as Thou hast said and promised, even so let it be unto me, and grant me to prove worthy. I have received the cross at Thy hand; I have carried it, and will carry it even unto death, as Thou hast laid it upon me. Truly the life of a truly devoted servant is a cross, but it leadeth to paradise. I have begun; I may not return back nor leave it.

Come, my brothers, let us together go forward. Jesus shall be with us. For Jesus' sake have we taken up this cross, for Jesus' sake let us persevere in the cross. He will be our helper, who was our Captain and Forerunner.

Behold our King entereth in before us, and He will fight for us. Let us follow bravely, let no man fear terrors; let us be prepared to die bravely in battle, *and let us not so stain our honour,* as to fly from the cross.

CHAPTER LVII
THAT A MAN MUST NOT BE TOO MUCH CAST DOWN WHEN HE FALLETH INTO SOME FAULTS

"My Son, patience and humility in adversities are more pleasing to Me than much comfort and devotion in prosperity. Why doth a little thing spoken against thee make thee sad? If it had been more, thou still oughtest not to be moved. But now suffer it to go by; it is not the first, it is not new, and it will not be the last, if thou live long.

"Thou art brave enough, so long as no adversity meeteth thee. Thou givest good counsel also, and knowest how to strengthen others with thy words; but when tribulation suddenly knocketh at thine own door, thy counsel and strength fail. Consider thy great frailty, which thou dost so often experience in trifling matters nevertheless, for thy soul's health these things are done when they and such like happen unto thee.

"Put them away from thy heart as well as thou canst, and if tribulation hath touched thee, yet let it not cast thee down nor entangle thee long. At the least, bear patiently, if thou canst not joyfully. And although thou be very unwilling to hear it, and feel indignation, yet check thyself, and suffer no unadvised word to come forth from thy lips, whereby the little ones may be offended.

"Soon the storm which hath been raised shall be stilled, and inward grief shall be sweetened by returning grace. I yet live, saith the Lord, ready to help thee, and to give thee more than wonted consolation if thou put thy trust in Me, and call devoutly upon Me.

ENDURE TRIBULATION PATIENTLY

"Be thou more calm of spirit, and gird thyself for greater endurance. All is not frustrated, though thou find thyself very often afflicted or grievously tempted. Thou art man, not God; thou art flesh, not an angel. How shouldst thou be able to remain alway in the same state of virtue, when an angel in heaven fell, and the first man in paradise? I am He who lifteth up the mourners to deliverance, and those who know their own infirmity I raise up to my own nature."

O Lord, blessed be Thy word, sweeter to my mouth than honey and the honeycomb. What should I do in my so great tribulations and anxieties, unless Thou didst comfort me with Thy holy words? If only I may attain into the haven of salvation, what mat-

ter is it what things or how many I suffer? Give me a good end, give me a happy passage out of this world. Remember me, O my God, and lead me by the right way unto Thy Kingdom. Amen.

CHAPTER LVIII

OF DEEPER MATTERS, AND GOD'S HIDDEN JUDGMENTS WHICH ARE NOT TO BE INQUIRED INTO

"MY Son, beware thou dispute not of high matters and of the hidden judgments of God; why this man is thus left, and that man is taken into so great favour; why also this man is so greatly afflicted, and that so highly exalted. These things pass all man's power of judging, neither may any reasoning or disputation have power to search out the divine judgments.

"When therefore the enemy suggesteth these things to thee, or when any curious people ask such questions, answer with that word of the Prophet, *Just art Thou, O Lord, and true is Thy judgment,* and with this, *The judgments of the Lord are true, and righteous altogether.* My judgments are to be feared, not to be disputed on, because they are incomprehensible to human understanding.

PROPER REGARD FOR THE SAINTS

"And be not given to inquire or dispute about the merits of the saints, which is holier than another, or which is the greater in the Kingdom of Heaven. Such questions often beget useless strifes and contentions: they also nourish pride and vainglory, whence envyings and dissensions arise, while one man arrogantly endeavoureth to exalt one saint and another another. But to wish to know and search out such things bringeth no fruit, but it rather displeaseth the Saints, for I am not *the God of confusion but of peace;* which peace consisteth more in true humility than in self-exaltation.

"Some are drawn by zeal of love to greater affection to these saints or those; but this is human affection rather than divine. I am He Who made all the Saints: I gave them grace, I brought them glory; I know the merits of every one; *I prevented them with the blessings of My goodness.* I foreknew my beloved ones from everlasting, *I chose them out of the world;* they did not choose Me. I called them by My grace, drew them by My mercy, led them on through sundry temptations. I poured mighty consolations upon them; I gave them perseverance; I crowned their patience.

"I acknowledge the first and the last; I embrace all with inestimable love. I am to be praised in all My Saints; I am to be blessed above all things, and to be honoured in every one whom I have so gloriously exalted and predestined, without any preceding merits of their own. He therefore that shall despise one of the least of these My people, honoureth not the great; because I made both small and great. And he who speaketh against any of My saints speaketh against Me, and against all others in the Kingdom of Heaven."

"They are all one through the bond of charity; they think the same thing, will the same thing, and all are united in love one to another.

"But yet (which is far better) they love Me above themselves and their own merits. For being caught up above themselves, and drawn beyond self-love, they go all straightforward to the love of Me, and they rest in Me in perfect enjoyment. There is nothing which can turn them away or press them down; for being full of Eternal Truth, they burn with the fire of inextinguishable charity.

"Therefore let all carnal and natural men hold their peace concerning the state of the saints, for they know nothing save to love their own personal enjoyment. They take away and add according to their own inclination, not as it pleaseth the Eternal Truth.

AVOID VAIN BABBLING

"In many men this is ignorance, chiefly is it so in those who, being little enlightened, rarely learn to love any one with perfect spiritual love. They are still much drawn by natural affection and human friendship to these or to those: and as they reckon of themselves in lower matters, so also do they frame imaginations of things heavenly. But there is an immeasurable difference between those things which they imperfectly imagine, and these things which enlightened men behold through supernatural revelation.

"Take heed, therefore, My Son, that thou treat not curiously those things which surpass thy knowledge, but rather make this thy business and give attention to it, namely, that thou seek to be found, even though it be the least, in the Kingdom of God. And even if any one should know who were holier than others, or who were held greatest in the Kingdom of Heaven; what should that knowledge profit him, unless through this knowledge he should humble himself before Me, and should rise up to give greater praise unto My name? He who considereth how great are his own sins, how small his virtues, and how far he is removed from the perfection of the Saints, doeth far more acceptably in the sight of God, than he who disputeth about their greatness or littleness.

"They are altogether well content, if men would learn to be content, and to refrain from vain babbling. They glory not of their own merits, seeing they ascribe no good unto themselves, but all unto Me, seeing that I of my infinate charity have given them all things. They are filled with so great love of the Divinity, and with such overflowing joy, that no glory is lacking to them, neither can any felicity be lacking.

"All the Saints, the higher they are exalted in glory, the humbler are they in themselves, and the nearer and dearer are they unto Me. And so thou hast it written that they cast their crowns before God and fell on their faces before the Lamb, and worshipped Him that liveth for ever and ever.

AS LITTLE CHILDREN

"Many ask who is greatest in the Kingdom of Heaven, who know not whether they shall be worthy to be counted among the least. It is a great thing to be even the least in Heaven, where all are great, because all shall be called, and shall be, the sons of God. *A little one shall become a thousand*, but *the sinner being an hundred years old shall be accursed.*

"For when the disciples asked *who should be the greatest in the Kingdom of Heaven*, they received no other answer than this, *Except ye be converted and become as little children, ye shall not enter into the Kingdom of Heaven. But whosoever shall humble*

himself as this little child, the same shall be greatest in the Kingdom of Heaven."

Woe unto them who disdain to humble themselves willingly with the little children; for the low gate of the kingdom of Heaven will not suffer then to enter in. Woe also to them who are rich, who have their consolation here; because whilst the poor enter into the kingdom of God, they shall stand lamenting without. Rejoice ye humble, and exult ye poor, for yours is the kingdom of God if only ye walk in the truth.

CHAPTER LIX
THAT ALL HOPE AND TRUST IS
TO BE FIXED IN GOD ALONE

O LORD, what is my trust which I have in this life, or what is my greatest comfort of all the things which are seen under Heaven? Is it not Thou, O Lord my God, whose mercies are without number? Where hath it been well with me without Thee? Or when could it be evil whilst Thou wert near?

I had rather be poor for Thy sake, than rich without Thee. I choose rather to be a pilgrim upon the earth with Thee than without Thee to possess heaven. Where Thou art, there is heaven; and where Thou are not, behold there death and hell.

Thou art all my desire, and therefore must I groan and cry and earnestly pray after Thee. In short I can confide fully in none to give me ready help in necessities, save in Thee alone, O my God. Thou art my hope, Thou art my trust, Thou art my Comforter, and most faithful in all things.

All men seek their own; Thou settest forward only my salvation and my profit, and turnest all things unto my good. Even though Thou dost expose me to divers temptations and adversities, Thou ordainest all this unto my advantage, for Thou are wont to prove Thy beloved ones in a thousand ways. In which proving Thou oughtest no less to be loved and praised, than if Thou wert filling me full of heavenly consolations.

WE ARE HOPELESS APART FROM GOD

In Thee, therefore, O Lord God, I put all my hope and my refuge, on Thee I lay all my tribulation and anguish; because I find all to be weak and unstable whatsoever I behold out of Thee. For many friends shall not profit, nor strong helpers be able to succour, nor prudent counsellors to give a useful answer, nor the books of the learned to console, nor any precious substance to deliver, nor any secret and beautiful place to give shelter, if Thou Thyself do not assist, help, strengthen, comfort, instruct, keep in safety.

For all things which seem to belong to the attainment of peace and felicity are nothing when Thou art absent, and bring no felicity at all in reality. Therefore art Thou the end of all good, and the fulness of Life, and the soul of eloquence; and to hope in Thee above all things is the strongest solace of Thy servants. *Mine eyes look unto Thee*, in Thee is my trust, O my God, Father of mercies.

Bless and sanctify my soul with heavenly blessing that it may become Thy holy habitation, and the seat of Thy eternal glory; and let nothing be found in the Temple of Thy divinity which may offend the eyes of Thy majesty. According to the greatness of Thy goodness and the multitude of Thy mercies look upon me, and hear the prayer of Thy poor servant, far exiled from Thee in the land of the shadow of death. Protect and preserve the soul of Thy least servant amid so many dangers of corruptible life, and by Thy grace accompanying me, direct it by the way of peace unto its home of perpetual light. Amen.

The Fourth Book

OF THE SACRAMENT OF THE ALTAR
A DEVOUT EXHORTATION TO THE HOLY COMMUNION

"Come unto Me, all ye that labour and are heavy laden, and I will refresh you, saith the Lord. The bread that I will give is My flesh which I give for the life of the world. Take, eat: this is My Body, which is given for you; this do in remembrance of Me. He that eateth My flesh and drinketh My blood dwelleth in Me and I in him. The words that I speak unto you, they are spirit, and they are life."

CHAPTER I

WITH HOW GREAT REVERENCE CHRIST MUST BE RECEIVED

THESE ARE THY WORDS, O Christ, Eternal Truth; though not uttered at one time nor written together in one place of Scripture. Because therefore they are Thy words and true, I must gratefully and faithfully receive them all. They are Thine, and Thou hast uttered them; and they are mine also, because Thou didst speak them for my salvation. Gladly I receive them from Thy mouth, that they may be more deeply implanted in my heart.

Words of such great grace arouse me, for they are full of sweetness and love; but my own sins terrify me, and my impure conscience driveth me away from receiving so great mysteries. The sweetness of Thy words encourageth me, but the multitude of my faults presseth me down.

CHRIST'S INVITATION TO HIS DISCIPLES

Thou commandest that I draw near to Thee with firm confidence, if I would have part with Thee, and that I receive the food of immortality, if I desire to obtain eternal life and glory.

Come unto Me, sayest Thou, *all that labour and are heavy laden, and I will refresh you.* Oh, sweet and lovely word in the ear of the sinner, that Thou, O Lord my God, dost invite the poor and needy to the Communion of Thy most holy body and blood. But who am I, O Lord, that I should presume to approach unto Thee? Behold *the heaven of heavens cannot contain Thee,* and yet Thou sayest, *Come ye all unto Me.*

What meaneth this most gracious condescension, this most lovely invitation? How shall I dare to come, who know no good thing of myself, whence I might be able to presume? How shall I bring Thee within my house, seeing that I so often have sinned in Thy most loving sight?

Angels and archangels stand in awe of Thee, the Saints and just men fear Thee, and Thou sayest, *Come unto Me!* Except Thou, Lord, hadst said it, who should believe it true? And except Thou hadst commanded, who should attempt to draw near?

CONTEMPLATION OF HOLY MEN OF OLD

Behold, Noah, that just man, laboured for a hundred years in building the ark, that he might be saved with the few; and I, how shall I be able in one hour to prepare myself to receive the Builder of the world with reverence? Moses, Thy servant, Thy great and especial friend, made an ark of incorruptible wood, which also he covered with purest gold, that he might lay up in it the tables of the law, and I, a corruptible creature, shall I dare thus easily to receive Thee, the Maker of the Law and the Giver of life?

Solomon, the wisest of the kings of Israel, was seven years building his magnificent temple to the praise of Thy Name, and for eight days celebrated the feast of its dedication, offered a thousand peace offerings, and solemnly brought up the Ark of the Covenant to the place prepared for it, with the sound of trumpets and great joy, and I, unhappy and poorest of mankind, how shall I bring Thee into my house, who scarce know how to spend half an hour in devotion? And oh that it were even one half hour worthily spent!

O my God, how earnestly these holy men strove to please Thee! And alas! how little and trifling is that which I do! how short a time do I spend, when I am disposing myself to Communion. Rarely altogether collected, most rarely cleansed from all distraction. And surely in the saving presence of Thy Godhead no unmeet thought ought to intrude, nor should any creature take possession of me, because it is not an Angel but the Lord of the Angels, that I am about to receive as my Guest.

THE EXAMPLE OF THE ARK OF THE COVENANT

Yet there is a vast difference between the Ark of the Covenant with its relics, and Thy most pure Body with its ineffable virtues, between those sacrifices of the law, which were figures of things to come, and the true sacrifice of Thy Body, the completion of all the ancient sacrifices.

Wherefore then do I not yearn more ardently after Thy adorable presence? Why do I not prepare myself with greater solicitude to receive Thy holy things, when those holy Patriarchs and Prophets of old, kings also and princes, with the whole people, manifested so great affection of devotion towards Thy Divine Service?

The most devout king David danced with all his might before the Ark of God, calling to mind the benefits granted to his forefathers in days past; he fashioned musical instruments of various sorts, put forth Psalms, and appointed them to be sung with joy, played also himself ofttimes on the harp, being inspired with the grace of the Holy Ghost; he taught the people of Israel to praise God with the whole heart, and with unity of voice to bless and praise Him every day.

If so great devotion was then exercised, and celebration of divine praise was carried on before the Ark of the Testimony, how great reverence and devotion ought now to be shown by me and all Christian people at the ministering of the Sacrament, at receiving the most precious Body and Blood of Christ.

THOUGHTS ON VISITS TO SHRINES

Many run to diverse places to visit the memorials of departed saints, and rejoice to hear of their deeds and to look upon the beautiful buildings of their shrines. And behold, Thou art present here with me, O my God, Saint of saints, Creator of men and Lord of the Angels. Often in looking at those memorials men are moved by curiosity and novelty, and very little fruit of amendment is borne away, especially when there is so much careless trifling and so little true contrition.

But here in the Sacrament of the Altar, Thou art present altogether, My God, the Man Christ Jesus; where also abundant fruit of eternal life is given to every one soever that receiveth Thee worthily and devoutly. But to this no levity draweth, no curosity, nor sensuality, only steadfast faith, devout hope, and sincere charity.

GRACE IS CONVEYED BY HOLY COMMUNION

O God, invisible Creator of the world, how wondrously dost Thou work with us, how sweetly and graciously Thou dealest with Thine elect, to whom Thou offerest Thyself to be received in this Sacrament! For this surpasseth all understanding, this specially draweth the hearts of the devout and enkindleth their affections. For even Thy true faithful ones themselves, who order their whole life to amendment, oftentimes gain from this most excellent Sacrament great grace of devotion and love of virtue.

Oh admirable and hidden grace of the Sacrament, which only Christ's faithful ones know, but the faithless and those who serve sin cannot experience! In this Sacrament is conferred spiritual grace, and lost virtue is regained in the soul, and the beauty which was disfigured by sin returneth again. So great sometimes is this grace that out of the fulness of devotion given, not only the mind but also the weak body feeleth that more strength is supplied unto it.

GRATITUDE FOR THE HOLY COMMUNION

But greatly must we mourn and lament over our lukewarmness and negligence, that we are not drawn by greater affection to become partakers of Christ, in whom all the hope and the merit of those that are to be saved consist. For He Himself *is our sanctification and redemption.* He is the consolation of pilgrims and the eternal fruition of the saints. Therefore it is grievously to be lamented that many so little consider this health-giving mystery, which maketh heaven glad and preserveth the whole world. Alas for the blindness and hardness of man's heart, that he considereth not more this unspeakble gift, and even slippeth down through the daily use, into carelessness.

For if this most holy Sacrament were celebrated in one place only, and were consecrated only by one priest in the whole world, with what great desire thinkest thou, would men be affected towards that place and towards such a priest of God, that they might behold the divine mysteries celebrated? But now are many men made priests and in many places the Sacrament is celebrated, that the grace and love of God towards men might the more appear, the more widely the Holy Communion is spread abroad over all the world.

Thanks be unto Thee, O good Jesus, Eternal Shepherd, who hast vouchsafed to refresh us, poor and exiled ones, with Thy precious Body and Blood, and to invite us to partake these holy mysteries by the invitation from Thine own mouth, saying, *Come unto Me, ye who labour and are heavy laden, and I will refresh you.*

CHAPTER II

THAT THE GREATNESS AND CHARITY OF GOD IS SHOWN TO MEN IN THE SACRAMENT

TRUSTING in Thy goodness and great mercy, O Lord, I draw near, the sick to the Healer, the hungering and thirsting to the Fountain of life, the poverty-stricken to the King of heaven, the servant to the Lord, the creature to the Creator, the desolate to my own gentle Comforter. But whence is this unto me, that Thou comest unto me? Who am I that Thou shouldest offer me Thyself? How doth a sinner dare to appear before Thee? And how dost thou vouchsafe to come to the sinner?

Thou knowest Thy servant, and Thou knowest that he hath in him no good thing for which Thou shouldest grant him this grace. I confess therefore mine own vileness, I acknowledge Thy goodness, I praise Thy tenderness, and I give Thee thanks for Thine exceeding great love. For Thou doest this for Thine own sake, not for my merits, that Thy goodness may be more manifest unto me, Thy charity more abundantly poured out upon me, and Thy humility more perfectly commended unto me. Therefore because this pleaseth Thee and Thou hast commanded that thus it shall be, Thy condescension pleaseth me also; and oh that mine inquity hinder it not.

MAN'S UNWORTHINESS TO RECEIVE HOLY COMMUNION

O most sweet and tender Jesus, what reverence, what giving of thanks is due to Thee with perpetual praise for the receiving of Thy sacred Body and Blood, the dignity whereof no man is found able to express. But what shall I think upon in this Communion in approaching my Lord, whom I am not able worthily to honour, and nevertheless whom I long devoutly to receive? What shall be better and more healthful meditation for me, than utter humiliation of myself before Thee, and exaltation of Thine infinite goodness towards me? I praise Thee, O my God, and exalt Thee for evermore. I despise myself, and cast myself down before Thee into the deep of my vileness.

Behold, Thou art the Saint of saints and I the refuse of sinners; behold, Thou stoopest unto me who am not worthy to look upon Thee; behold, Thou comest unto me, Thou willest to be with me, Thou invitest me to Thy feast. Thou willest to give me the heavenly food and bread of Angels to eat; none other, in truth, than Thyself, *The living bread, which didst descend from heaven; and givest life to the world.*

THE MYSTERIES OF HOLY COMMUNION

Behold, whence this love proceedeth! what manner of condescension shineth forth herein. What great giving of thanks and praise is due unto Thee for these benefits! Oh how salutary and profitable Thy purpose when Thou didst ordain this! How sweet and pleasant the feast when Thou didst give Thyself for food! Oh how admirable is thy working, O Lord, how mighty Thy power, how unspeakable Thy truth! For Thou didst speak the word, and all things were made; and this is done which Thou hast commanded.

A thing wonderful, and worthy of faith, and surpassing all the understanding of man, that Thou, O Lord my God, very God and very man, givest Thyself altogether to us in a little bread and wine, and art so our inexhaustible food. Thou, O Lord of all, who hast need of nothing, hast willed to dwell in us through Thy Sacrament.

Preserve my heart and my body undefiled, that with a joyful and pure conscience I may be able very often to [celebrate, and]* receive to my perpetual health. Thy mysteries, which Thou hast consecrated and instituted both for Thine own honour, and for a perpetual memorial.

THE HOLY COMMUNION, CAUSE FOR GREAT REJOICING

Rejoice, O my soul, and give thanks unto God for so great a gift and precious consolation, left unto thee in this vale of tears. For so oft as thou callest this mystery to mind and receivest the body of Christ, so often dost thou celebrate the work of thy redemption, and art made partaker of all the merits of Christ. For the charity of Christ never groweth less, and the greatness of His propitiation is never exhausted.

Therefore, by continual renewal of thy spirit, thou oughtest to dispose thyself hereunto and to weigh the great mystery of salvation with attentive consideration. So great, new, and joyful ought it to appear to thee when thou comest to communion, as if on this self-same day Christ for the first time were descending into the Virgin's womb and becoming man, or hanging on the cross, suffering and dying for the salvation of mankind.

CHAPTER III

THAT IT IS PROFITABLE TO COMMUNICATE OFTEN

BEHOLD I come unto Thee, O Lord, that I may be blessed through Thy gift, and be made joyful in Thy holy feast which *Thou, O God, of Thy goodness hast prepared for the poor.* Behold in Thee is all that I can and ought to desire; Thou art my salvation and redemption, my hope and strength, my honour and glory. Therefore *rejoice the soul of Thy servant this day, for unto Thee, O Lord Jesus, do I lift up my soul.*

I long now to receive Thee devoutly and reverently; I desire to bring Thee into my house, so that with Zacchaeus I may be counted worthy to be blessed by Thee and numbered among the children of Abraham. My soul hath an earnest desire for Thy Body, my heart longeth to be united with Thee.

MAN'S NEED FOR THE REFRESHMENT OF HOLY COMMUNION

Give me Thyself and it sufficeth, for besides Thee no consolation availeth. Without Thee I cannot be, and without Thy visitation I have no power to live. And therefore I must needs draw nigh unto Thee often, and receive Thee for the healing of my soul, lest haply I faint by the way if I be deprived of heavenly food.

For so Thou, most merciful Jesus, preaching to the people and healing many sick, didst once say, *I will not send them away fasting to their own homes, lest they faint by the way.* Deal therefore now to me in like manner, for Thou left Thyself for the consolation of the faithful in the Sacrament.

For Thou art the sweet refreshment of the soul, and he who shall eat Thee worthily shall be partaker and inheritor of the eternal glory. Necessary indeed it is for me, who so often slide backwards and sin, so quickly wax cold and faint, to renew, cleanse, en-

---

*The words in brackets are only suitable for a priest.

kindle myself by frequent prayers and pentinences and receiving of Thy sacred Body and Blood lest haply by too long abstinence, I fall short of my holy resolutions.

For the imaginations of man's heart are evil from his youth, and except divine medicine succour him, man slideth away continually unto the worse. The Holy Communion therefore draweth us back from evil, and strengtheneth us for good. For if I now be so negligent and lukewarm when I communicate [or celebrate], how should it be with me, if I receive not this medicine, and sought not so great a help? [And though I am not every day fit nor well prepared to celebrate, I will nevertheless give diligent heed at due season, to receive the divine mysteries, and to become partaker of so great grace.] For this is the one principal consolation of a faithful soul, so long as it is absent from Thee in mortal body, that being continually mindful of its God, it receiveth its Beloved with devout spirit.

PRAISE FOR THE HOLY COMMUNION

Oh wonderful condescension of Thy pity surrounding us, that Thou, O Lord God, Creator and Quickener of all spirits, deignest to come unto a soul so poor and weak, and to appease its hunger with Thy whole Deity and Humanity. Oh happy mind and blessed soul, to which is granted devoutly to receive Thee its Lord God, and in so receiving Thee to be filled with all spiritual joy!

Oh how great a Lord doth it entertain, how beloved a Guest doth it bring in, how delightful a Companion doth it receive, how faithful a Friend doth it welcome, how beautiful and exalted a Spouse, above every other Beloved, doth it embrace, One to be loved above all things that can be desired! Oh my most sweet Beloved, let heaven and earth and all the glory of them be silent in Thy presence; seeing whatsoever praise and beauty they have it is of Thy gracious bounty; and they shall never reach unto the loveliness of Thy Name, *Whose Wisdom is infinite.*

CHAPTER IV

THAT MANY GOOD GIFTS ARE BESTOWED UPON THOSE WHO COMMUNICATE DEVOUTLY

O LORD my God, prevent Thou Thy servant with the blessings of Thy sweetness, that I may be enabled to draw near worthily and devoutly to Thy glorious Sacrament. Awaken my heart towards Thee, and deliver me from heavy slumber. Visit me with Thy salvation that I may in spirit taste Thy sweetness, which plentifully lieth hid in this Sacrament as in a fountain. Lighten also mine eyes to behold this so great mystery, and strengthen me that I may believe it with undoubting faith.

For it is Thy word, not human power; it is Thy holy institution, not the invention of man. For no man is found fit in himself to receive and to understand these things, which transcend even the wisdom of the Angels. What portion then shall I, unworthy sinner, who am but dust and ashes, be able to search into and comprehend of so deep a Sacrament?

HOLY COMMUNION GIVES HEALTH TO THE SOUL

O Lord, in the simplicity of my heart, in good and firm faith, and according to Thy will, I draw nigh unto Thee with hope and reverence, and truly believe that Thou art here present in the Sacrament, God and man. Thou willest therefore that I receive Thee and unite myself to Thee in charity.

Wherefore I beseech Thy mercy, and implore Thee to give me Thy special grace, to this end, that I may be wholly dissolved and overflow with love towards Thee, and no more suffer any other consolation to enter into me. For this most high and most glorious Sacrament is the health of the soul and the body, the medicine of all spiritual sickness, whereby I am healed of my sins, my passions are bridled, temptations are conquered or weakened, more grace is poured into me, virtue begun is increased, faith is made firm, hope is strengthened, and charity is enkindled and enlarged.

For in this Sacrament Thou hast bestowed many good things and still bestowest them continually on Thine elect who communicate devoutly, O my God, Lifter up of my soul, Repairer of human infirmity, and Giver of all inward consolation. For Thou pourest into them much consolation against all sorts of tribulation, and out of the deep of their own misery Thou liftest them up to the hope of Thy protection, and with ever new grace, dost inwardly refresh and enlighten them; so that they who felt themselves to be anxious and without affection before Communion, afterwards being refreshed with heavenly food and drink, find themselves changed for the better.

And even in such wise Thou dealest severally with Thine elect, that they may truly acknowledge and clearly make proof that they have nothing whatsoever of their own, and what goodness and grace come to them from Thee; because being in themselves cold, hard of heart, indevout, through Thee they become fervent, zealous, and devout. For who is there coming humbly to the fountain of sweetness, carrieth not away thence at the least some little of that sweetness? Or who standing by a large fire, feeleth not from thence a little of its heat? And Thou art ever a full and overflowing fountain, a fire continually burning, and never going out.

COME AND I WILL REFRESH YOU

Wherefore if it is not suffered to me to draw from the fulness of the fountain, nor to drink unto satisfying, yet will I set my lips to the mouth of the heavenly conduit, that at least I may receive a small drop to quench my thirst, that I dry not up within my heart. And if I am not yet able to be altogether heavenly and so enkindled as the Cherubim and Seraphim, yet will I endeavour to give myself unto devotion, and to prepare my heart, that I may gain if it be but a little flame of the divine fire, through the humble receiving of the life-giving Sacrament. But whatsoever is wanting unto me, O merciful Jesus, Most Holy Saviour, do Thou of Thy kindness and grace supply, who hast vouchsafed to call all unto Thee, saying, *Come unto me, all ye that are weary and heavy laden, and I will refresh you.*

I indeed labour in the sweat of my face, I am tormented with sorrow of heart, I am burdened with sins, I am disquieted with temptations, I am entangled and oppressed with many passions, and there is none to help me, there is none to deliver and ease me, but Thou, O Lord God, my Saviour, to whom I commit myself and all things that are mine, that Thou mayest preserve me and lead me unto life eternal.

Receive me unto the praise and glory of Thy name, who hast prepared Thy Body and Blood to be my meat and drink. Grant, O Lord God my Saviour, that with coming often to Thy mysteries the zeal of my devotion may increase.

CHAPTER V

OF THE DIGNITY OF THIS SACRAMENT, AND OF THE OFFICE OF THE PRIEST

"IF thou hadst angelic purity and the holiness of holy John the Baptist, thou wouldst not be worthy to receive or to minister this Sacrament. For this is not deserved by merit of man that a man should consecrate and minister the Sacrament of Christ, and take for food the bread of Angels. Vast is the mystery, and great is the dignity of the priests, to whom is given what is not granted to Angels.

"For priests only, rightly ordained in the church, have the power of consecrating and celebrating the Body of Christ. The priest indeed is the minister of God, using the Word of God by God's command and institution; nevertheless God is there the principal Author and invisible Worker, that to whom all that He willeth is subject, and all He commandeth is obedient.

A CHARGE TO PRIESTS

"Therefore thou must believe God Almighty in this most excellent Sacrament, more than thine own sense or any visible sign at all. And therefore with fear and reverence is this work to be approached. Take heed therefore and see what it is of which the ministry is committed to thee by the laying on of the Bishop's hand. Behold thou art made a priest and art consecrated to celebrate. See now that thou do it before God faithfully and devoutly at due time, and shew thyself without blame.

"Thou hast not lightened thy burden, but art now bound with a straiter bond of discipline, and art pledged to a higher degree of holiness. A priest ought to be adorned with all virtues and to afford to others an example of good life. His conversation must not be with the popular and common ways of men, but with Angels in Heaven or with perfect men on the earth.

"A priest clad in holy garments taketh Christ's place that he may pray unto God with all supplication and humility for himself and for the whole people. He must always remember the Passion of Christ. He must diligently look upon Christ's footsteps and fervently endeavour himself to follow them. He must bear meekly for God whatsoever ills are brought upon him by others. He must mourn for his own sins, and for the sins committed by others, and may not grow careless of prayer and holy oblation, until he prevail to obtain grace and mercy. When the priest celebrateth, he honoureth God, giveth joy to the Angels, buildeth up the Church, helpeth the living, hath communion with the departed, and maketh himself a partaker of all good things."

CHAPTER VI

AN INQUIRY CONCERNING PREPARATION FOR COMMUNION

WHEN I consider Thy dignity, O Lord, and mine own vileness, I tremble very exceedingly, and am confounded within myself. For if I approach not, I fly from life; and if I intrude myself unworthily, I run into Thy displeasure. What then shall I do, O my God, Thou helper and Counsellor in necessities.

Teach Thou me the right way; propound unto me some short exercise befitting Holy Communion. For it is profitable to know how I ought to prepare my heart devoutly and reverently for Thee, to the intent that I may receive Thy Sacrament to my soul's health [or it may be also for the celebrating this so great and divine mystery].

CHAPTER VII
OF THE EXAMINATION OF CONSCIENCE, AND PURPOSE OF AMENDMENT

"ABOVE all things the priest of God must draw nigh, with all humility of heart and supplicating reverence, with full faith and pious desire for the honour of God, to celebrate, minister, and receive this Sacrament. Diligently examine thy conscience and with all thy might with true contrition and humble confession cleanse and purify it, so that thou mayest feel no burden, nor know anything which bringeth thee remorse and impedeth thy free approach.

"Have displeasure against all thy sins in general, and specially sorrow and mourn because of thy daily transgressions. And if thou have time, confess unto God in the secret of thine heart, all miseries of thine own passion.

CONFESS THY SINS

"Lament grievously and be sorry, because thou art still so carnal and worldly, so unmortified from thy passions, so full of the motion of concupiscence, so unguarded in thine outward senses, so often entangled in many vain fancies, so much inclined to outward things, so negligent of internal; so ready to laughter and dissoluteness, so unready to weeping and contrition; so prone to ease and indulgence of the flesh, so dull to zeal and fervour; so curious to hear novelties and behold beauties, so loth to embrace things humble and despised; so desirous to have many things, so grudging in giving, so close in keeping; so inconsiderate in speaking, so reluctant to keep silence; so disorderly in manners, so inconsiderate in actions; so eager after food, so deaf towards the Word of God; so eager after rest, so slow to labour; so watchful after tales, so sleepy towards holy watchings; so eager for the end of them, so wandering in attention to them; so negligent in observing the hours of prayer, so lukewarm in celebrating, so unfruitful in communicating; so quickly distracted, so seldom quite collected with thyself; so quickly moved to anger, so ready for displeasure at others; so prone to judging, so severe at reproving; so joyful in prosperity, so weak in adversity; so often making many good resolutions and bringing them to so little effect.

PRESENT THYSELF AS A SACRIFICE TO GOD

"When thou hast confessed and bewailed these and thy other shortcomings, with sorrow and sore displeasure at thine own infirmity, make then a firm resolution of continual amendment of life and of progress in all that is good. Then moreover with full resignation and entire will offer thyself to the honour of My name on the altar of thine heart as a perpetual whole burnt-offering, even by faithfully presenting thy body and soul unto Me, to the end that thou mayest so be accounted worthy to draw near to offer this sacrifice of praise and thanksgiving to God, and to receive the Sacrament of My Body and Blood to thy soul's health.

"For there is no oblation worthier, no satisfaction greater for the destroying of sin, than that a man offer himself to God purely and entirely with the oblation of the Body and Blood of Christ in the Holy Communion. If a man shall have done what in him lieth, and shall repent him truly, then how often soever he shall draw nigh unto Me for pardon and grace, *As I live, saith the Lord, I have no pleasure in the death of a sinner, but rather that he should be converted, and live. All his transgressions that he hath committed, they shall not be mentioned unto him.*

CHAPTER VIII
OF THE OBLATION OF CHRIST UPON THE CROSS, AND OF RESIGNATION OF SELF

"As I of My own will offered Myself unto God the Father on the Cross for thy sins with outstretched hands and naked body, so that nothing remained in Me that did not become altogether a sacrifice for the Divine propitiation; so also oughtest thou every day to offer thyself willingly unto Me for a pure and holy oblation with all thy strength and affections, even to the utmost powers of thine heart.

"What more do I require of thee than thou study to resign thyself altogether unto Me? Whatsoever thou givest besides thyself, I nothing care for, for I ask not thy gift, but thee.

GIVE THYSELF WHOLLY TO GOD

"As it would not be sufficient for thee if thou hadst all things except Me, even so whatsoever thou shalt give Me, if thou give Me not thyself, it cannot please Me. Offer thyself to Me, and give thyself altogether for God, so shall thy offering be accepted. Behold I offered Myself altogether to the Father for thee, I give also My whole body and blood for food, that thou mightest remain altogether Mine and I thine. But if thou stand in thyself, and offer not thyself freely to My will, thy offering is not perfect, neither shall the union betwixt us be complete.

"Therefore ought the freewill offering of thyself into the hands of God to go before all thy works, if thou wilt attain liberty and grace. For this is the cause that so few are inwardly enlightened and made free, that they know not how to deny themselves entirely. My word standeth sure, *Except a man forsake all, he cannot be My disciple.* Thou therefore, if thou wilt be My disciple, offer thyself to Me with all thy affections."

CHAPTER IX
THAT WE OUGHT TO OFFER OURSELVES AND ALL THAT IS OURS TO GOD, AND TO PRAY FOR ALL

LORD, *all that is in the heaven and in the earth is Thine.* I desire to offer myself up unto Thee as a freewill offering, and to continue Thine for ever. Lord, *in the uprightness of mine heart I willingly offer* myself to Thee to-day to be Thy servant for ever, in humble submission and for a sacrifice of perpetual praise. Receive me with this Holy Communion of Thy precious Body, which I celebrate before Thee this day in the presence of the Angels invisibly surrounding, that it may be for the salvation of me and of all Thy people.

CLEANSE ME

Lord, I lay before Thee at this celebration all my sins and offences which I have committed before Thee and Thy holy Angels, from the day whereon I was first able to sin even unto this hour; that Thou mayest consume and burn them every one with the fire of Thy charity, and mayest do away all the stains of my sins, and cleanse my conscience from all offence, and restore me to Thy favour which by sinning I have lost, fully forgiving me all, and mercifully admitting me to the kiss of peace.

What can I do concerning my sins, save humbly to confess and lament them and unceasingly to beseech Thy propitiation? I beseech Thee, be propitious unto me and hear me, when I stand before Thee, O my God. All my sins displease me grievously: I will never more commit them; but I grieve for them and will grieve so long as I live, steadfastly purposing to repent me truly, and to make restitution as far as I can.

Forgive, O God, forgive me my sins for Thy holy Name's sake; save my soul, which Thou hast redeemed with Thy precious blood. Behold I commit myself to Thy mercy; I resign myself to Thy hands. Deal with me according to Thy lovingkindness, not according to my wickedness and iniquity.

ACCEPT MY GOODNESS

I offer also unto Thee all my goodness, though it is exceedingly little and imperfect, that Thou mayest mend and sanctify it, that Thou mayest make it well pleasing and acceptable in Thy sight, and ever draw it on towards perfection; and furthermore bring me safely, slothful and useless poor creature that I am, to a happy and blessed end.

Moreover I offer unto Thee all pious desires of the devout, necessities of parents, friends, brothers, sisters, and all who are dear to me, and of those who have done good to me, or to others for Thy love; and those who have desired and besought my prayers for themselves and all belonging to them; that all may feel themselves assisted by Thy grace, enriched by consolation, protected from dangers, freed from pains; and that being delivered from all evils they may joyfully give Thee exceeding thanks.

PREPARE US, GOD, FOR ETERNAL LIFE

I offer also to Thee prayers and Sacramental intercessions for those specially who have injured me in aught, made me sad, or spoken evil concerning me, or have caused me any loss or displeasure; for all those also whom I have at any time made sad, disturbed, burdened, and scandalized, by words or deeds, knowingly or ignorantly; that to all of us alike, Thou mayest equally pardon our sins and mutual offences.

Take away, O Lord, from our hearts all suspicion, indignation, anger, and contention, and whatsoever is able to injure charity and diminish brotherly love. Have mercy, have mercy, Lord, on those who entreat Thy mercy; give grace to the needy; and make us such that we may be worthy to enjoy Thy grace, and go forward to the life eternal. Amen.

CHAPTER X

THAT HOLY COMMUNION IS NOT LIGHTLY TO BE OMITTED

"THOU must frequently betake thee to the Fountain of grace and divine mercy, to the Fountain of goodness and all purity; to the end that thou mayest obtain the healing of thy passions and vices, and mayest be made stronger and more watchful against all temptations and wiles of the devil. The enemy, knowing what profit and exceeding strong remedy lieth in the Holy Communion, striveth by all means and occasions to draw back and hinder the faithful and devout, so far as he can.

HINDRANCES TO AVOID

"For when some set about to prepare themselves for Holy Communion, they suffer from the more evil suggestions of Satan. The very evil spirit himself (as is written in Job), cometh among the sons of God that he may trouble them by his accustomed evil dealing, or make them over timid and perplexed; to the intent that he may diminish their affections, or take away their faith by his attacks, if haply he may prevail upon them to give up Holy Communion altogether, or to come thereto with lukewarm hearts.

"But his wiles and delusions must not be heeded, howsoever wicked and terrible they be; but all his delusion must be cast back upon his own head. The wretch must be despised and laughed to scorn: neither must Holy Communion be omitted because of his insults and the inward troubles which he stirreth up.

"Often also too much carefulness or some anxiety or other touching confession hindereth from obtaining devotion. Do thou according to the counsel of wise men, and lay aside anxiety and scruple, because it hindereth the grace of God and destroyeth devotion of mind. Because of some little vexation or trouble do not thou neglect Holy Communion, but rather hasten to confess it, and forgive freely all offences committed against thee. And if thou hast offended any man, humbly beg for pardon, and God shall freely forgive thee.

LET NOTHING HINDER YOU FROM TAKING HOLY COMMUNION

"What profiteth it to put off for long time the confession of thy sins, or to defer Holy Communion? Cleanse thyself forthwith, spit out the poison with all speed, hasten to take the remedy, and thou shalt feel thyself better than if thou didst long defer it. If to-day thou defer it on one account, to-morrow perchance some greater obstacle will come, and so thou mayest be long time hindered from Communion and become more unfit.

"As soon as thou canst, shake thyself from thy present heaviness and sloth, for it profiteth nothing to be long anxious, to go long on thy way with heaviness of heart, and because of daily little obstacles to sever thyself from divine things: nay it is exceeding hurtful to defer thy Communion long, for this commonly bringeth on great torpor. Alas! there are some, lukewarm and undisciplined, who willingly find excuses for delaying repentance, and desire to defer Holy Communion, lest they should be bound to keep stricter watch upon themselves.

"Alas! how little charity, what flagging devotion, have they who so lightly put off Holy Communion. How happy is he, how acceptable to God, who so liveth, and in such purity of conscience keepeth himself, that any day he could be ready and well inclined to communicate, if it were in his power, and might be done without the notice of others.

"If a man sometimes abstaineth for the sake of humility or some sound cause, he is to be commended for his reverence. But if drowsiness have taken hold of him, he ought to rouse himself and to do what in him lieth; and the Lord will help his desire for the good will which he hath, which God specially approveth.

TAKE HOLY COMMUNION REGULARLY

"But when he is hindered by sufficient cause, yet will he ever have a good will and pious intention to communicate; and so he shall not be lacking in the fruit of the Sacrament. For any devout man is able every day and every hour to draw near to spiritual communion with Christ to his soul's health and without hindrance.

"Nevertheless on certain days and at the appointed time he ought to receive the Body and Blood of his Redeemer with affectionate reverence, and rather to seek after the praise and honour of God, than his own comfort. For so often doth he communicate mystically, and is invisibly refreshed, as he devoutly calleth to mind the mystery of Christ's incarnation and His Passion, and is inflamed with the love of Him.

"He who only prepareth himself when a festival is at hand or custom compelleth, will too often be unprepared. Blessed is he who offereth himself to God for a whole burnt-offering, so often as he celebrateth or communicateth!

"Be not too slow nor too hurried in thy celebrating, but preserve the good received custom of those with whom thou livest. Thou oughtest not to produce weariness and annoyance in others, but to observe the received custom, according to the institution of the elders; and to minister to the profit of others rather than to thine own devotion or feeling."

CHAPTER XI

THAT THE BODY AND BLOOD OF CHRIST AND THE HOLY SCRIPTURES ARE MOST NECESSARY TO A FAITHFUL SOUL

O MOST sweet Lord Jesus, how great is the blessedness of the devout soul that feedeth with Thee in Thy banquet, where there is set before it no other food than Thyself its only Beloved, more to be desired than all the desires of the heart? And to me it would verily be sweet to pour forth my tears in Thy presence from the very bottom of my heart, and with the pious Magdalene to water Thy feet with my tears.

But where is this devotion? Where the abundant flowing of holy tears? Surely in Thy presence and in the presence of the holy Angels my whole heart ought to burn and to weep for joy; for I have Thee in the Sacrament verily present, although hidden under other form.

CHRIST IS HIDDEN IN THE SACRAMENT

For in Thine own Divine brightness, mine eyes could not endure to behold Thee, neither could the whole world stand before the splendour of the glory of Thy Majesty. In this therefore Thou hast consideration unto my weakness, that Thou hidest Thyself under the Sacrament. I verily possess and adore Him whom the Angels adore in heaven; I yet for a while by faith, but they by sight and without a veil.

It is good for me to be content with the light of true faith, and to walk therein until the day of eternal brightness dawn, and the shadows of figures flee away. But when that which is perfect is come, the using of Sacraments shall cease, because the Blessed in heavenly glory have no need of Sacramental remedy. For they rejoice unceasingly in the presence of God, heholding His glory face to face, and *being changed from glory to glory* of the infinite God, they taste the Word of God made flesh, as He was in the beginning and remaineth for everlasting.

When I think on these wondrous things, even spiritual comfort whatsoever it be becometh sore weariness to me; for so long as I see not openly my Lord in His own Glory, I count for nothing all which I behold and hear in the world. Thou, O God, art my witness that nothing is able to comfort me, no creature is able to give me rest, save Thou, O my God, whom I desire to contemplate everlastingly. But this is not possible, so long as I remain in this mortal state. Therefore ought I to set myself unto great patience, and submit myself unto Thee in every desire.

For even Thy Saints, O Lord, who now rejoice with Thee in the kingdom of heaven, waited for the coming of Thy glory whilst they lived here, in faith and great glory. What they believed, that believe I; what they hoped, I hope; whither they have attained to, thither through Thy grace hope I to come. I will walk meanwhile in faith, strengthened by the examples of the Saints. I will have also holy books for comfort and for a mirror of life, and above them all Thy most holy Body and Blood shall be for me a special remedy and refuge.

TWO NECESSARY THINGS

For two things do I feel to be exceedingly necessary to me in this life, without which this miserable life would be intolerable to me; being detained in the prison of this body, I confess that I need two things, even food and light. Thou hast therefore given to me who am so weak, Thy sacred Body and Blood, for the refreshing of my soul and body, and hast set *Thy Word for a lantern to my feet.* Without these two I could not properly live; for the Word of God is the light of my soul, and Thy Sacrament the bread of life.

These may also be called the two tables, placed on this side and on that, in the treasury of Thy holy Church. One table is that of the Sacred Altar, bearing the holy bread, that is the precious Body and Blood of Christ; the other is the table of the Divine Law, containing holy doctrine, teaching the true faith, and leading steadfastly onwards even to that which is within the veil, where the Holy of Holies is.

Thanks be unto Thee, O Lord Jesus, Light of Light everlasting, for that table of holy doctrine which Thou has furnished unto us by Thy servants the Prophets and Apostles and other teachers. Thanks be to Thee, O Creator and Redeemer of men, who to make known Thy love to the whole world had prepared a great supper, in which Thou hast set forth for good not the typical lamb, but Thine own most

Holy Body and Blood; making all Thy faithful ones joyful with this holy banquet and giving them to drink the cup of salvation, wherein are all the delights of Paradise, and the holy Angels do feed with us, and with yet happier sweetness.

THE GRAVE RESPONSIBILITY OF PRIESTS

Oh how great and honourable is the office of the priests, to whom it is given to consecrate the Sacrament of the Lord of majesty with holy words, to bless it with the lips, to hold it in their hands, to receive it with their own mouth, and to administer it to others!

Oh how clean ought those hands to be, how pure the mouth, how holy the body, how unspotted the heart of the priest, to whom so often the Author of purity entereth in! From the mouth of the priest ought naught to proceed but what is holy, what is honest and profitable, because he so often receiveth the Sacrament of Christ.

His eyes ought to be single and pure, seeing they are wont to look upon the Body of Christ; the hands should be pure and lifted towards heaven, which are wont to hold within them the Creator of heaven and earth. To priests is it specially said in the Law, *Be ye holy, for I the Lord your God am holy.*

A PLEA FOR DIVINE ASSISTANCE

Assist us with Thy grace, O Almighty God, that we who have taken upon us the priestly office, may be able to converse worthily and devoutly with Thee in all purity and good conscience. And if we are not able to have our conversation in such innocency of life as we ought, yet grant unto us worthily to lament the sins which we have committed, and in the spirit of humility and full purpose of a good will, to serve Thee more earnestly for the future.

CHAPTER XII
THAT HE WHO IS ABOUT TO COMMUNICATE WITH CHRIST OUGHT TO PREPARE HIMSELF WITH GREAT DILIGENCE

"I AM the Lover of purity, and Giver of sanctity. I seek a pure heart, and *there is the place of My rest.* Prepare for Me *the larger upper room furnished,* and *I will keep the Passover at thy house with My disciples.* If thou wilt that I come unto thee and abide with thee, *purge out the old leaven,* and cleanse the habitation of thy heart. Shut out the whole world, and all the throng of sins; sit *as a sparrow alone upon the house-top,* and think upon thy transgressions with bitterness of thy soul. For everyone that loveth prepareth the best and fairest place for his beloved, because hereby the affection of him that entertaineth his beloved is known.

ON PREPARING TO TAKE HOLY COMMUNION

"Yet know thou that thou canst not make sufficient preparation out of the merit of any action of thine, even though thou shouldest prepare thyself for a whole year, and hadst nothing else in thy mind. But out of My tenderness and grace alone art thou permitted to draw nigh unto My table; as though a beggar were called to a rich man's dinner, and had no other recompense to offer him for the benefits done unto him, but to humble himself and to give him thanks.

"Do therefore as much as lieth in thee, and do it diligently, not of custom, nor of necessity, but with fear, reverence, and affection, receive the Body of thy beloved Lord God, who vouchsafeth to come unto thee. I am He who hath called thee; I commanded it to be done; I will supply what is lacking to thee; come and receive Me.

"When I give the grace of devotion, give thanks unto thy God; it is not because thou art worthy, but because I had mercy on thee. If thou hast not devotion, but rather feelest thyself dry, be instant in prayer, cease not to groan and knock; cease not until thou prevail to obtain some crumb or drop of saving grace.

"Thou hast need of Me, I have no need of thee. Nor dost thou come to sanctify Me, but I come to sanctify thee and make thee better. Thou comest that thou mayest be sanctified by Me, and be united to Me; that thou mayest receive fresh grace, and be kindled anew to amendment of life. See that thou neglect not this grace, but prepare thy heart with all diligence, and receive thy Beloved unto thee.

PROPER BEHAVIOUR FOLLOWING HOLY COMMUNION

"But thou oughtest not only to prepare thyself for devotion before Communion, thou must also keep thyself with all diligence therein after receiving the Sacrament; nor is less watchfulness needed afterwards, than devout preparation beforehand: for good watchfulness afterwards becometh in turn the best preparation for the gaining more grace. For hereby is a man made entirely indisposed to good, if he immediately return from Communion to give himself up to outward consolations. Beware of much speaking; remain in a secret place, and hold communion with thy God; for thou hast Him whom the whole world cannot take away from thee. I am He to whom thou oughtest wholly to give thyself; so that now thou mayest live not wholly in thyself, but in Me, free from all anxiety."

CHAPTER XIII

THAT THE DEVOUT SOUL OUGHT WITH THE WHOLE HEART TO YEARN AFTER UNION WITH CHRIST IN THE SACRAMENT

WHO shall grant unto me, O Lord, that I may find Thee alone, and open all my heart unto Thee, and enjoy Thee as much as my soul desireth; and that no man may henceforth look upon me, nor any creature move me or have respect unto me, but Thou alone speak unto me and I unto Thee, even as beloved is wont to speak unto beloved, and friend to feast with friend?

For this do I pray, this do I long for, that I may be wholly united unto Thee, and may withdraw my heart from all created things, and by means of Holy Communion and frequent celebration may learn more and more to relish heavenly and eternal things.

Ah, Lord God, when shall I be entirely united and lost in Thee, and altogether forgetful of myself? *Thou in me, and I in Thee;* even so grant that we may in like manner continue together in one.

PERFECT PEACE AND TRUE REST

Verily Thou art my Beloved, the choicest among ten thousand, in whom my soul delighteth to dwell all the days of her life. Verily Thou art my Peacemaker, in Whom is perfect peace and true rest, apart from Whom is labour and sorrow and infinite misery. Verily *Thou art a God that hidest Thyself,* and Thy counsel is not with the wicked, but Thy Word is with the humble and the simple.

O how sweet, *O Lord, is Thy spirit,* who that Thou mightest manifest Thy sweetness towards Thy children, dost vouchsafe to refresh them with the bread which is full of sweetness, which cometh down from heaven. Verily *there is no other nation so great, which hath its gods drawing nigh to them, as Thou, our God, art present unto all Thy faithful ones,* unto whom for their daily solace, and for lifting up their heart unto heaven, Thou givest Thyself for their food and delight.

MY WHOLE DESIRE

For what other nation is there so renowned as the Christian people? Or what creature is so beloved under heaven as the devout soul to which God entereth in, that He may feed it with His glorious flesh? O unspeakable grace! O wonderful condescension! O immeasurable love specially bestowed upon men!

But what reward shall I give unto the Lord for this grace, for charity so mighty? There is nothing which I am able to present more acceptable than to give my heart altogether unto God, and to join it inwardly to Him. Then all my inward parts shall rejoice, when my soul shall be perfectly united unto God. Then shall He say unto me, "If thou wilt be with Me, I will be with thee." And I will answer Him, "Vouchsafe, O Lord, to abide with me, I will gladly be with Thee; this is my whole desire, even that my heart be united unto Thee."

CHAPTER XIV

OF THE FERVENT DESIRE OF CERTAIN DEVOUT PERSONS TO RECEIVE THE BODY AND BLOOD OF CHRIST

O HOW great is the abundance of Thy sweetness, O Lord, which Thou hast laid up for them that fear Thee. When I call to mind some devout persons who draw nigh to Thy Sacrament, O Lord, with the deepest devotion and affection, then very often I am confounded in myself and blush for shame, that I approach Thine altar and table of Holy Communion so carelessly and coldly, that I remain so dry and without affection, that I am not wholly kindled with love before Thee, my God, nor so vehemently drawn and affected as many devout persons have been, who out of the very earnest desire of the Communion, and tender affection of heart, could not refrain from weeping, but as it were with mouth of heart and body alike panted inwardly after Thee, O God, O Fountain of Life, having no power to appease or satiate their hunger, save by receiving Thy Body with all joyfulness and spiritual eagerness.

MAKE MY HEART ARDENTLY BURN WITHIN

O truly ardent faith of those, becoming a very proof of Thy Sacred Presence! For they verily know their Lord *in the breaking of bread,* whose heart so *ardently burneth within them* when Jesus walketh with them by the way. Ah me! far from me for the most part is such love and devotion as this, such vehement love and ardour.

Be merciful unto me, O Jesus, good, sweet, and kind, and grant unto Thy poor suppliant to feel sometimes, in Holy Communion, though it be but a little, the cordial affection of Thy love, that my faith may grow stronger, my hope in Thy goodness increase, and my charity, once kindled within me by the tasting of the heavenly manna, may never fail.

But Thy mercy is able even to grant me the grace which I long for, and to visit me most tenderly with the spirit of fervour when the day of Thy good pleasure shall come. For, although I burn not with desire so vehement as theirs who are specially devout towards Thee, yet, through Thy grace, I have a desire after that greatly inflamed desire, praying and desiring to be made partaker with all those who so fervently love Thee, and to be numbered among their holy company.

CHAPTER XV
THAT THE GRACE OF DEVOTION IS ACQUIRED BY HUMILITY AND SELF-DENIAL

"THOU oughtest to seek earnestly the grace of devotion, to ask it fervently, to wait for it patiently and faithfully, to receive it gratefully, to preserve it humbly, to work with it diligently, and to leave to God the time and manner of heavenly visitation until it come.

"Chiefly oughtest thou to humble thyself when thou feelest inwardly little or no devotion, yet not to be too much cast down, nor to grieve out of measure. God ofttimes giveth in one short moment what He hath long time denied; He sometimes giveth at the end what at the beginning of prayer He hath deferred to give.

"If grace were always given immediately, and were at hand at the wish, it would be hardly bearable to weak man. Wherefore the grace of devotion is to be waited for with a good hope and with humble patience. Yet impute it to thyself and to thy sins when it is not given, or when it is mysteriously taken away. It is sometimes a small thing which hindereth and hideth grace (if indeed that ought to be called *small* and not rather *great*, which hindereth so great a good); but if thou remove this, be it small or great, and perfectly overcome it, thou wilt have what thou hast asked.

SEEK GOD WITH ALL THINE HEART

"For immediately that thou hast given thyself unto God with all thine heart, and hast sought neither this nor that according to thine own will and pleasure, but hast altogether settled thyself in Him, thou shalt find thyself united and at peace; because nothing shall give thee so sweet relish and delight, as the good pleasure of the Divine will. Whosoever therefore shall have lifted up his will unto God with singleness of heart, and shall have delivered himself from every inordinate love or dislike of any created thing, he will be the most fit for receiving grace, and worthy of the gift of devotion.

"For where the Lord findeth empty vessels, there giveth He His blessing. And the more perfectly a man forsaketh things which cannot profit, and the more he dieth to himself, the more quickly doth grace come, the more plentifully doth it enter in, and the higher doth it lift up the free heart.

"Then shall he see, and flow together, and wonder, and his heart shall be enlarged within him, because the hand of the Lord is with him, and he hath put himself wholly in His hand, even for ever. Lo, thus shall the man be blessed, that seeketh God with all his heart, and receiveth not his soul in vain. This man in receiving the Holy Eucharist obtaineth the great grace of Divine Union; because he hath not regard to his own devotion and comfort, but, above all devotion and comfort, to the glory and honour of God."

Chapter XVI

THAT WE OUGHT TO LAY OPEN OUR NECESSITIES TO CHRIST AND TO REQUIRE HIS GRACE

O MOST sweet and loving Lord, whom now I devoutly desire to receive, Thou knowest my infirmity and the necessity which I suffer, in what evils and vices I lie; how often I am weighed down, tempted, disturbed, and defiled. I come unto Thee for remedy; I beseech of Thee consolation and support.

I speak unto Thee who knowest all things, to whom all my secrets are open, and who alone art able perfectly to comfort and help me. Thou knowest what good thing I most stand in need of, and how poor I am in virtues.

TRANSFORM ME INTO THYSELF

Behold, I stand poor and naked before Thee, requiring grace, and imploring mercy. Refresh the hungry suppliant, kindle my coldness with the fire of Thy love, illuminate my blindness with the brightness of Thy presence. Turn thou all earthly things into bitterness for me, all grievous and contrary things into patience, all things worthless and created into contempt and oblivion.

Lift up my heart unto Thee in Heaven, and suffer me not to wander over the earth. Be Thou alone sweet unto me from this day forward for ever, because Thou alone art my meat and drink, my love and joy, my sweetness and my whole good.

Oh that Thou wouldest altogether by Thy presence, kindle, consume, and transform me into Thyself; that I may be made one spirit with Thee, by the grace of inward union, and the melting of earnest love! Suffer me not to go away from Thee hungry and dry; but

deal mercifully with me, as oftentimes Thou hast dealt wondrously with Thy saints. What marvel if I should be wholly kindled from Thee, and in myself should utterly fail, since Thou art fire always burning and never failing, love purifying the heart and enlightening the understanding.

Chapter XVII

OF FERVENT LOVE AND VEHEMENT DESIRE OF RECEIVING CHRIST

WITH the deepest devotion and fervent love, with all affection and fervour of heart, I long to receive Thee, O Lord, even as many Saints and devout persons have desired Thee in communicating, who were altogether well pleasing to Thee by their sanctity of life, and dwelt in all ardent devotion. O my God, Eternal Love, my whole Good, Happiness without measure, I long to receive Thee with the most vehement desire and becoming reverence which any saint ever had or could have.

A CONSUMING DESIRE FOR GOD

And although I be unworthy to have all those feelings of devotion, yet do I offer Thee the whole affection of my heart, even as though I alone had all those most grateful inflamed desires. Yea, also, whatsoever things a pious mind is able to conceive and long for, all these with the deepest veneration and inward fervour do I offer and present unto Thee. I desire to reserve nothing unto myself, but freely and entirely to offer myself and all that I have unto Thee for a sacrifice.

O Lord my God, my Creator and Redeemer! with such affection, reverence, praise, and honour, with such gratitude, worthiness, and love, with such faith, hope, and purity do I desire to receive Thee this day, as Thy most blessed Mother, the glorious Virgin Mary, received and desired Thee, when she humbly and devoutly answered the Angel who brought unto her the glad tidings of the mystery of the Incarnation. *Behold the handmaid of the Lord; be it unto me according to Thy word.*

And as Thy blessed forerunner, the most excellent of saints, John Baptist, being full of joy in Thy presence, leapt while yet in the womb of his mother, for joy in the Holy Ghost; and afterwards discerning Jesus walking amongst men, humbled himself exceedingly, and said, with devout affection, *The friend of the bridegroom, who standeth and heareth him, rejoiceth greatly because of the bridegroom's voice;* even so I wish to be inflamed with great and holy desires, and to present myself unto Thee with my whole heart.

Whence also, on behalf of myself and of all commended to me in prayer, I offer and present unto Thee the jubilation of all devout hearts, their ardent affections, their mental ecstasies, and supernatural illuminations, and heavenly visions, with all the virtues and praises celebrated and to be celebrated by every creature in heaven and earth; to the end that by all Thou mayest worthily be praised and glorified for ever.

PRAISE THE LORD

Receive my prayers, O Lord my God, and my desires of giving Thee infinite praise and unbounded benediction, which, according to the multitude of Thine unspeakable greatness, are most justly due unto Thee. These do I give Thee, and desire to give every day and every moment; and with beseechings and affectionate desires I call upon all celestial spirits and all Thy faithful people to join with me in rendering Thee thanks and praises.

Let all peoples, nations, and tongues praise Thee, and magnify Thy holy and sweet-sounding Name, with highest jubilations and ardent devotion. And let all who reverently and devoutly celebrate Thy most high Sacrament, and receive it with full assurance of faith, be accounted worthy to find grace and mercy with Thee, and intercede with all supplication for me a sinner; and when they shall have attained unto their wished-for devotion and joyous union with Thee, and shall depart full of comfort and wondrously refreshed from Thy holy, heavenly table, let them vouchsafe to be mindful of me, for I am poor and needy.

CHAPTER XVIII

THAT A MAN SHOULD NOT BE A CURIOUS SEARCHER OF THE SACRAMENT, BUT A HUMBLE IMITATOR OF CHRIST, SUBMITTING HIS SENSE TO HOLY FAITH

"THOU must take heed of curious and useless searching into this most profound Sacrament, if thou wilt not be plunged into the abyss of doubt. *He that is a searcher of Majesty shall be oppressed by the glory thereof.* God is able to do more than man can understand. A pious and humble search after truth is to be allowed, when it is always ready to be taught, and striving to walk after the wholesome opinions of the fathers.

"Blessed is the simplicity which leaveth alone the difficult paths of questionings, and followeth the plain and firm steps of God's commandments. Many have lost devotion whilst they sought to search into deeper things. Faith is required of thee, and a sincere life, not loftiness of intellect, nor deepness in the mysteries of God.

"If thou understandest not nor comprehendest the things which are beneath thee, how shalt thou comprehend those which are above thee? Submit thyself unto God, and humble thy sense to faith, and the light of knowledge shall be given thee, as shall be profitable and necessary unto thee.

SATAN CAUSES DOUBTS

"There are some who are grievously tempted concerning faith and the Sacrament; but this is not to be imputed to themselves but rather to the enemy. Care not then for this, dispute not with thine own thoughts, nor make answer to the doubts which are cast into thee by the devil; but believe the words of God, believe His saints and prophets, and the wicked enemy shall flee from thee.

"Often it profiteth much, that the servant of God endureth such things. For the enemy tempteth not unbelievers and sinners, because he already hath secure possession of them; but he tempteth and harasseth the faithful and devout by various means.

TRUST GOD

"Go forward therefore with simple and undoubting faith, and draw nigh unto the Sacrament with supplicating reverence. And whatsoever thou art not enabled to understand, that commit without anxiety to Almighty God. God deceiveth thee not; he is deceived who believeth too much in himself.

"God walketh with the simple, revealeth Himself to the humble, giveth understanding to babes, openeth the sense to pure minds, and hideth grace from the curious and proud. Human reason is weak and may be deceived; but true faith cannot be deceived.

"All reason and natural investigation ought to follow faith, not to precede, nor to break it. For faith and love do here especially take the highest place, and work in hidden ways in this most holy and exceeding excellent Sacrament.

"God who is eternal and incomprehensible, and of infinite power, doth great and inscrutable things in heaven and in earth, and His wonderful works are past finding out. If the works of God were of such sort that they might easily be comprehended by human reason, they should no longer be called wonderful or unspeakable."

The Practice of the Presence of God

Brother Lawrence

Introduction

A FRIEND OF MINE likes to say that the biggest problem with the Christian life is that it is so daily.[1] Most believers have times when God seems very close. Some people experience God's presence during life's high points: the birth of a child, a wedding day, walking alongside a beautiful mountain stream, or any moment when it looks like all their dreams may come true. But other people feel closest to God during life's low points: the death of a friend, a serious illness, the loss of a job, or those moments when they feel trapped in their worst nightmares. Even then—some might say, especially then—one can have a "peace that passes all understanding" (Phil. 4:7).

Life at the extremes—in the best and worst of times—is where most people experience God's presence most easily. For many believers, however, finding God is much more difficult during the in-between times. For most of us, it is the daily grind that wears us out and does us in. Many Christians cannot locate God in the sameness of every day responsibilities and in the unending cycles of what we do most of the time.

The big question, then, for us is this: Where is God when one day seems pretty much like another, when nothing much seems to be happening in our lives? Where is God in the dullness of daily living? At least part of the answer to that question can be found in the thoughtful life-experience of Brother Lawrence, a seventeenth-century Frenchman, who learned how to "practice the presence of God" in a kitchen.

BROTHER LAWRENCE (c. 1605–1691)

Not much is known about the early life of Brother Lawrence. We believe that he was born Nicholas Herman in about 1605 in the French province of Lorraine. His parents were poor but respectable; and they raised Nicholas as a devout Catholic.

Like much of Europe, France had been deeply divided by the Protestant Reformation of the sixteenth century. French Protestants, who were called Huguenots, had grown rapidly after the 1530s, prompting the Catholic monarchy to take strong measures against them. After decades of religious strife and even armed conflict between French Catholics and Huguenots, in 1598 the Edict of Nantes created an uneasy peace between the warring parties.

By the time Nicholas was born, then, the Catholic majority had guaranteed the Huguenots certain rights, including possession of a number of fortified cities to call their own. Huguenot security actually depended on who was in control of the French government. Fearing their growing strength, in 1629 Cardinal Richelieu, King Louis XIII's most powerful adviser, drove the Huguenots from their fortified cities, then rather surprisingly granted them extensive religious and civil toleration. The next king, Louis XIV, was much less accommodating. He demanded that Huguenots re-convert to Catholicism or be driven from France. To that end, in 1685 the king issued the Edict of Fontainebleau, which abolished the religious guarantees of the Edict of Nantes and outlawed Protestantism throughout the realm.

In short, because Nicholas Herman was a Roman Catholic, he did not experience religious persecution himself; but his religious loyalties did not keep him completely out of harm's way. According to our sketchy sources, Nicholas may have been a soldier in the French army during the Thirty Years' War (1618–1648), in which Catholic France sided with German Protestants against the Hapsburgs, the Catholic dynasty that ruled both Spain and the Holy Roman Empire. In a fierce battle fought near Lorraine, Nicholas was severely wounded.

After a slow and painful recovery which left him partially disabled, he became a footman for a local official, Mr. Fieubert. Nicholas later described himself as "a great awkward fellow who broke everything." Nevertheless, during his years of service for Mr. Fieubert, his relationship with God began to grow. In 1623, when Nicholas was eighteen, he had experienced a religious conversion. "In the winter, seeing a tree stripped of its leaves, and considering that within a little time the leaves would be renewed, and after that the flowers and fruit appear, he received a high view of the providence and power of God, which has never since been effaced from his soul." This personal experience of God's sovereignty and power "set him loose from the world, and kindled in him such a love for God" that its impact never left him.[2]

Over the years, Nicholas became dissatisfied with his life in the world. Some historians believe that he may have tried his hand at living as a hermit. One thing is certain: when he was about fifty years of age, he decided to enter the Discalced Carmelite monastery in Paris. Looking back years later, Nicholas was quite honest about his motives. Because of his love for God, he wanted to sacrifice his life and all its pleasures in order to serve Him. He also hoped that in the rigors of monastic life he would "be made to smart for his awkwardness and the faults he should commit."[3]

The Carmelites were a religious order that had been founded in the thirteenth century and named after Mount Carmel in Israel. For a while, the Carmelites had been known for their strict discipline; but over the years standards declined. In the early sixteenth century, the order was reformed by St. Theresa of Avila. New Carmelite convents and monasteries were founded, and much of the old discipline returned. The strictest of the Carmelites broke off from the main body and established their own separate order in 1593. They called themselves barefoot (discalced) Carmelites because they preferred sandals to shoes and socks.

Nicholas joined the Carmelites as a lay brother, which meant that he was part of the work force that allowed the rest of the community to study, teach, preach, and copy manuscripts. As part of the monastery, the lay brothers prayed and kept regular hours of devotion, to be sure; but they were there mainly to work hard for everyone else. When Nicholas Herman entered the community, he received a new name and got a new job: he was now Brother Lawrence and was put in charge of the kitchen.

Because Brother Lawrence had no natural inclination for such work, he figured that it was God's way of making him "smart for his awkwardness" and his faults. He had come to the monastery to learn discipline, so spending the rest of his life up to his elbows in dirty pots and pans seemed like a fitting venue for self-sacrifice. But, he said years later, in this God disappointed him. Instead of being a life-long penance for his sins, over time the kitchen work brought him "nothing but satisfaction." Much to his surprise, slaving over a hot stove taught him how to practice the presence of God.

It took him a while to figure it out, however. For the first four years, Brother Lawrence did not like his work; in fact, he had a great aversion to it. He also anguished over the condition of his soul, convinced that if there were any justice in the world, God should damn him. Despite his best efforts, he was miserable. Finally he had a breakthrough. To put it simply, he evaluated his condition to find out where he had gone wrong. Eventually he understood that he was spending too much time and energy worrying about himself. He decided to get back to basics and focus his life on loving God. Years later, he put it this way: "I engaged in a religious life only for the love of God, and I have endeavored to act only for Him; whatever becomes of me, whether I be lost or saved, I will always continue to act purely for the love of God. I shall have this good at least, that till death I shall have done all that is in me to love Him."[4]

That is what made all the difference in his life. From that time on, he found joy in his work. He was "pleased when he could take up a straw from the ground for the love of God." Even the most menial and unwelcome tasks took on new meaning. When he consciously decided to do everything out of his love for God, his life changed. In fact, he became famous, at least after a fashion.

Other people in the community noticed that something had happened to the lay brother in charge of the kitchen. When they asked him about it, he told them about practicing the presence of God in life's little duties. There was no real trick to it, he said, nothing all that mysterious. All one had to do was remember God as one went around one's work. Of course, it was a bit more complicated than that, but for Brother Lawrence experiencing God's presence in daily life consisted of thinking about God all the time.

Over the years, then, Brother Lawrence's life proved that he had discovered something of enormous importance. He never promoted himself, but he was eager to share what he had learned. Fellow Carmelites consulted with him about practicing God's presence, as did people from outside the monastery. Religious leaders came to him for advice; and other people wrote him letters seeking spiritual counsel. What he learned in the kitchen he practiced until he died in Paris, in his mid-eighties.

THE PRACTICE OF THE
PRESENCE OF GOD

The book that has become a Christian spiritual classic consists of a summary of four conversations between Brother Lawrence and the Abbot of Beaufort, the Grand Vicar to Monsieur de Chalons, which occurred in 1666–67, and fifteen letters whose dates are uncertain, but may extend to just before his death in 1691. These materials were edited by the Abbot of Beaufort and published in Paris during the mid-1690s.

Despite the fact that the conversations and letters were intensely personal in nature, they contain very little autobiographical information. Brother Lawrence was much more interested in telling what he had learned than the story of his own life. As a result, the book includes few details about monastic life and virtually nothing about what was going on in the outside world. Brother Lawrence's focus was on his personal experience with God and little else. "I renounced, for the love of Him, everything that was not He, and I began to live as if there was none but He and I in the world."[5]

Possibly that is the reason why *The Practice of the Presence of God* still speaks to people three hundred years after it was first published: much of modern religious life remains centered on the self and the quest for an intensely personal experience of God. Pollsters keep finding evidence of deep religious longings in modern life. Americans are the most church-going

people in the western, industrialized world; and even among those who have sworn off religious institutions, there is widespread interest in "spirituality." Similarly, modern people demand that religion be practical, that it speak to personal needs. In short, in most circles today, the emphasis is on relevance, not religious dogma or denominational loyalty.

Naturally, not everyone is happy about this individualistic and even consumeristic approach to things spiritual. Religious experience cut off from religious communities can easily become eccentric and self-absorbed. But Brother Lawrence was intensely personal about religion without being self-centered. After all, to practice the presence of God, one needed to concentrate on God, not on one's self. How one felt and what one experienced were always secondary to loving and remembering God during one's daily routine.

In a world awash with twelve-step programs for breaking old addictions and how-to manuals on everything from losing weight to getting everything we want in life, one is struck by Brother Lawrence's almost total lack of concern with *methodology*. Modern readers will not find any clearly-spelled-out, step-by-step process for experiencing the presence of God. According to this kitchen saint, experiencing God's presence is not a program; it is a practice, a way of life. There is nothing all that complex about it. One has to set priorities, eliminate distractions, and decide to think about God—a lot. In one of his letters, Brother Lawrence put it this way: "Pray remember what I have recommended to you, which is, to think often on God, by day, by night, in your business, and even in your diversions. He is always near you and with you; leave Him not alone. You would think it rude to leave a friend alone who came to visit you; why, then, must God be neglected?"[6]

What about distractions? Some people are surprised to learn that there were any in monasteries: Did not people join religious communities in order to serve God without any diversions? True enough, but it is much easier to take the monk out of the world than it is to take the world out of the monk. The history of Christianity is filled with stories of exasperated monastic men and women who lived behind cloistered walls or even in hermit caves, only to be consumed with thoughts of the life they left behind.

Brother Lawrence struggled here too. He did not find structured times of prayer and devotion all that helpful at first. Like many others, he discovered that the more he tried to rid his mind of wandering thoughts, the more he had them. So he took another approach: He worked, he stayed busy, he kept his hands occupied, and he thought about God while he went about his business in the kitchen. In this way, much to his surprise, he could concentrate more easily on God. The harder he worked, the better he prayed.

Dr. Wayne Oates, one of the pioneers of pastoral counseling, finds real wisdom in Brother Lawrence's approach. He notes that sometimes manual labor is the best way to reconnect with the life of the spirit. "As a minister-teacher, I have times of unproductive doldrums of spirit as I search for some new revealing of the Spirit. I have found that to clean a basement room, to paint a door, to fix a bothersome piece of tile in the kitchen releases many unaccustomed sources of thought and revelation."[7] Most monastic leaders who drew up the rules that monks and nuns lived by understood that to keep spiritual lives healthy, there must be a balance between prayer and work.

But by itself, Brother Lawrence discovered, hard work was never enough. One also had to keep one's mind fixed on God while working. He said that it was easier to keep his mind from wandering during prayer if he had not let it wander too far at other times: "You should keep it strictly in the presence of God; and being accustomed to think of Him often, you will find it easy to keep your mind calm in the time of prayer, or at least to recall it from its wanderings."[8] Would Brother Lawrence find life's distractions more numerous today than in his time? Probably. No seventeenth century lay brother could have imagined the flood of distractions competing for our attention. Nevertheless, one suspects that his advice to us would be the same: Eliminate distractions whenever possible and remember that the still, small voice of God's presence is hard to hear over blaring televisions and CD players.

What about sin? How does practicing the presence of God relate to the problem of sin in one's life? Brother Lawrence was no sinless saint. He sinned and he knew it. But he did not dwell on his sins. By faith he got over his fear of damnation. He confessed his sins and moved on, confident of the love and grace of God.[9] In the Second Conversation Brother Lawrence said "that all possible kinds of mortification, if they were void of the love of God, could not efface a single sin. That we ought, without anxiety, to expect the pardon of our sins from the blood of Jesus Christ, only endeavoring to love Him with all our hearts. That God seemed to have granted the greatest favors to the greatest sinners, as more signal monuments of His mercy."

Does practicing the presence of God come easily? Not according to Brother Lawrence. One has to work at it. In the First Letter, he described how he developed "that habitual sense of God's presence." Practicing God's presence must become a habit (*habitus* in Latin), a regular and disciplined way of life that in time becomes a natural and almost involuntary response. But even Brother Lawrence had to start slowly; over time he learned to see God in everything he did and everything that happened to him. But it took practice.

In the long run, maybe that is what separates Brother Lawrence from most people. Over 90 percent of Americans polled say they believe in God. But how many of them think about God, look for those signs of God's presence in their work, in the daily grind, in the middle of exhausting family or business obligations? How many people go through their daily lives without giving God a second thought? They say they believe in God, but they never pay God any mind. Anyone interested in living daily with a keen sense of God's presence cannot go through life that way. According to the author of Hebrews, "Without faith it is impossible to please God, because anyone who comes to him must believe that he exists and that he rewards those who earnestly seek him" (11:6).

Conversations

THE FIRST TIME I saw Brother Lawrence was upon the 3rd of August, 1666. He told me that God had done him a singular favor in his conversion at the age of eighteen.

BROTHER LAWRENCE'S CONVERSION AND EARLY LIFE

That in the winter, seeing a tree stripped of its leaves, and considering that within a little time the leaves would be renewed, and after that the flowers and fruit appear, he received a high view of the providence and power of God, which has never since been effaced from his soul. That this view had perfectly set him loose from the world, and kindled in him such a love for God that he could not tell whether it had increased during the more than forty years he had lived since.

That he had been footman to M. Fieubert, the treasurer, and that he was a great awkward fellow who broke everything.

That he had desired to be received into a monastery, thinking that he would there be made to smart for his awkwardness and the faults he should commit, and so he should sacrifice to God his life, with its pleasures; but that God had disappointed him, he having met with nothing but satisfaction in that state.

That we should establish ourselves in a sense of God's presence by continually conversing with Him. That it was a shameful thing to quit His conversation to think of trifles and fooleries.

THE NEED OF DEDICATION TO GOD

That we should feed and nourish our souls with high notions of God; which would yield us great joy in being devoted to Him.

That we ought to *quicken*—i.e., to *enliven—our faith*. That it was lamentable we had so little; and that instead of taking *faith* for the rule of their conduct, men amused themselves with trivial devotions, which changed daily. That the way of faith was the spirit of the church, and that it was sufficient to bring us to a high degree of perfection.

That we ought to give ourselves up to God, with regard both to things temporal and spiritual, and seek our satisfaction only in the fulfilling of His will, whether He lead us by suffering or by consolation, for all would be equal to a soul truly resigned. That there needed fidelity in those drynesses or insensibilities and irksomenesses in prayer by which God tries our love to Him; that *then* was the time for us to make good and effectual acts of resignation, whereof one alone would oftentime very much promote our spiritual advancement.

LAWRENCE'S VIEW OF SIN

That as for the miseries and sins he heard of daily in the world, he was so far from wondering at them that, on the contrary, he was surprised that there were not more, considering the malice sinners were capable of; that, for his part, he prayed for them; but knowing that God could remedy the mischiefs they did when He pleased, he gave himself no further trouble.

That to arrive at such resignation as God requires, we should watch attentively over all the passions which mingle as well in spiritual things as in those of a grosser nature; that God would give light concerning those passions to those who truly desire to serve Him. That if this was my design, viz., sincerely to serve God, I might come to him (Brother Lawrence) as often as I pleased, without any fear of being troublesome; but if not, that I ought no more to visit him.

SECOND CONVERSATION

THAT he had always been governed by love, without selfish views; and that having resolved to make the love of God the *end* of all his actions, he had found reasons to be well satisfied with his method. That he was pleased when he could take up a straw from the ground for the love of God, seeking Him only, and nothing else, not even His gifts.

LAWRENCE'S FEARS OF DAMNATION

That he had been long troubled in mind from a certain belief that he should be damned; that all the men in the world could not have persuaded him to the contrary; but that he had thus reasoned with himself about it: *I engaged in a religious life only for the love of God, and I have endeavored to act only for Him; whatever becomes of me, whether I be lost or saved, I will always continue to act purely for the love of God. I shall have this good at least, that till death I shall have done all that is in me to love Him.*

That this trouble of mind had lasted four years, during which time he had suffered much; but that at last he had seen that this trouble arose from want of faith, and that since he had passed his life in perfect liberty and continual joy. That he had placed his sins betwixt him and God, as it were, to tell Him that he did not deserve His favors but that God still continued to bestow them in abundance.

LAWRENCE'S APPROACH TO THE SPIRITUAL LIFE

That in order to form a habit of conversing with God continually, and referring all we do to Him, we must at first apply to Him with some diligence; but that after a little care we should find His love inwardly excite us to it without any difficulty.

That he expected, after the pleasant days God had given him, he should have his turn of pain and suffering; but that he was not uneasy about it, knowing very well that as he could do nothing of himself, God would not fail to give him the strength to bear it.

That when an occasion of practising some virtue offered, he addressed himself to God, saying, Lord, *I cannot do this unless Thou enablest me;* and that then he received strength more than sufficient.

That when he had failed in his duty, he only confessed his fault, saying to God, *I shall never do otherwise if You leave me to myself; it is You who must hinder my falling, and mend what is amiss.* That after this he gave himself no further uneasiness about it.

That we ought to act with God in the greatest simplicity, speaking to Him frankly and plainly, and imploring His assistance in our affairs, just as they happen. That God never failed to grant it, as he had often experienced.

DO ALL FOR THE LOVE OF GOD

That he had been lately sent into Burgundy, to buy the provision of wine for the society, which was a very unwelcome task for him, because he had no turn for business, and because he was lame and could not go about the boat but by rolling himself over the casks. That, however, he gave himself no uneasiness about it, nor about the purchase of the wine. That he said to God, *It was His business he was about,* and that he afterward found it very well performed. That he had been sent into Auvergne, the year before, upon the same account; that he could not tell how the matter passed, but that it proved very well.

So, likewise, in his business in the kitchen (to which he had naturally a great aversion), having accustomed himself to do everything there for the love of God, and with prayer, upon all occasions, for His grace to do his work well, he had found everything easy, during fifteen years that he had been employed there.

That he was very well pleased with the post he was now in; but that he was as ready to quit that as the former, since he was always pleasing himself in every condition by doing little things for the love of God.

OBSTACLES TO PRAYER

That with him the set times of prayer were not different from other times; that he retired to pray, according to the directions of his superior, but that he did not want such retirement, nor ask for it, because his greatest business did not divert him from God.

That as he knew his obligation to love God in all things, and as he endeavored so to do, he had no need of a director to advise him, but that he needed much a confessor to absolve him. That he was very sensible of his faults, but not discouraged by them; that he confessed them to God, but did not plead against Him to excuse them. When he had so done, he peaceably resumed his usual practice of love and adoration.

That in his trouble of mind he had consulted nobody, but knowing only by the light of faith that God was present, he contented himself with directing all his actions to Him, i.e., doing them with a desire to please Him, let what would come of it.

That useless thoughts spoil all; that the mischief began there; but that we ought to reject them as soon as we perceived their impertinence to the matter in hand, or our salvation, and return to our communion with God.

That at the beginning he had often passed his time appointed for prayer in rejecting wandering thoughts and falling back into them. That he could never regulate his devotion by certain methods as some do. That, nevertheless, at first he had *meditated* for some time, but afterward that went off, in a manner he could give no account of.

THE PLACE OF BODILY MORTIFICATION

That all bodily mortification and other exercises are useless, except as they serve to arrive at the union with God by love; that he had well considered this, and found it the shortest way to go straight to Him by a continual exercise of love and doing all things for His sake.

That we ought to make a great difference between the acts of the *understanding* and those of the *will;* that the first were comparatively of little value, and the others all. That our only business was to love and delight ourselves in God.

That all possible kinds of mortification, if they were void of the love of God, could not efface a single sin. That we ought, without anxiety, to expect the pardon of our sins from the blood of Jesus Christ, only endeavoring to love Him with all our hearts. That God seemed to have granted the greatest favors to the greatest sinners, as more signal monuments of His mercy.

That the greatest pains or pleasures of this world were not to be compared with what he had experienced of both kinds in a spiritual state; so that he was careful for nothing and feared nothing, desiring only one thing of God, viz., that he might not offend Him.

That he had no scruples; for, said he, when I *fail* in my duty, I readily acknowledge it, saying, *I am used to do so; I shall never do otherwise if I am left to myself.* If I fail not, then I give God thanks, acknowledging that the strength comes from Him.

THIRD CONVERSATION

HE told me that the *foundation of the spiritual life* in him had been a high notion and esteem of God in faith; which when he had once well conceived, he had no other care at first but faithfully to reject every other thought, *that he might perform all his actions for the love of God.* That when sometimes he had not thought of God for a good while, he did not disquiet himself for it; but, after having acknowledged his wretchedness to God, he returned to Him with so much the greater trust in Him as he had found himself wretched through forgetting Him.

GOD'S GRACE

That the trust we put in God honors Him much and draws down great graces.

That it was impossible not only that God should deceive, but also that He should long let a soul suffer which is perfectly resigned to Him, and resolved to endure everything for His sake.

That he had so often experienced the ready succors of divine grace upon all occasions, that from the same experience, when he had business to do, he did not think of it beforehand; but when it was time to do it, he found in God, as in a clear mirror, all that was fit for him to do. That of late he had acted thus, without anticipating care; but before the experience above mentioned, he had used it in his affairs.

LAWRENCE'S DESIRE FOR GOD

When outward business diverted him a little from the thought of God, a fresh remembrance coming from God invested his soul, and so inflamed and transported him that it was difficult for him to contain himself.

That he was more united to God in his outward employments than when he left them for devotion and retirement.

That he expected hereafter some great pain of body or mind; that the worst that could happen to him was to lose that sense of God which he had enjoyed so long; but that the goodness of God assured him He would not forsake him utterly, and that He would give him strength to bear whatever evil He permitted to happen to him; and therefore that he feared nothing, and had no occasion to consult with anybody about his state. That when he had attempted to do it, he had always come away more perplexed; and that as he was conscious of his readiness to lay down his life for the love of God, he had no apprehension of danger. That perfect resignation to God was a sure way to heaven, a way in which we had always sufficient light for our conduct.

HINDRANCES TO SPIRITUAL GROWTH

That in the beginning of the spiritual life we ought to be faithful in doing our duty and denying ourselves; but after that, unspeakable pleasures followed. That in difficulties we need only have recourse to Jesus Christ, and beg His grace; with that everything became easy.

That many do not advance in the Christian progress because they stick in penances and particular exercises, while they neglect the love of God, which is the *end*. That this appeared plainly by their works, and was the reason why we see so little solid virtue.

That there needed neither art nor science for going to God, but only a heart resolutely determined to apply itself to nothing but Him, or for *His* sake, and to love Him only.

FOURTH CONVERSATION

HE discoursed with me frequently, and with great openness of heart, concerning his manner of *going* to God, whereof some part is related already.

ENGAGE IN A CONTINUAL CONVERSATION WITH GOD

He told me that all consists *in one hearty renunciation* of everything which we are sensible does not lead to God. That we might accustom ourselves to a continual conversation with Him, with freedom and in simplicity. That we need only to recognize God intimately present with us, to address ourselves to Him every moment, that we may beg His assistance for knowing His will in things doubtful, and for rightly performing those which we plainly see He requires of us, offering them to Him before we do them, and giving Him thanks when we have done.

That in this conversation with God we are also employed in praising, adoring, and loving Him incessantly, for His infinite goodness and perfection.

WHY GOD'S GRACE "FAILS"

That, without being discouraged on account of our sins, we should pray for His grace with a perfect confidence, as relying upon the infinite merits of our Lord Jesus Christ. That God never failed offering us His grace at each action; that he distinctly perceived it, and never failed of it, unless when his thoughts had wandered from a sense of God's presence, or he had forgotten to ask His assistance.

That God always gave us light in our doubts when we had no other design but to please Him.

That our sanctification did not depend upon *changing* our works, but in doing that for God's sake which we commonly do for our own. That it was lamentable to see how many people mistook the means for the end, addicting themselves to certain works, which they performed very imperfectly, by reason of their human or selfish regards.

LAWRENCE'S APPROACH TO PRAYER

That the most excellent method he had found of going to God was that of doing our common business without any view of pleasing men, and (as far as we are capable) purely for the love of God.

That it was a great delusion to think that the times of prayer ought to differ from other times; that we are as strictly obliged to adhere to God by action in the time of action as by prayer in the season of prayer.

That his prayer was nothing else but a sense of the presence of God, his soul being at that time insensible to everything but divine love; and that when the appointed times of prayer were past, he found no difference, because he still continued with God, praising and blessing Him with all his might, so that he passed his life in continual joy; yet hoped that God would give him somewhat to suffer when he should grow stronger.

FAITH, HOPE, AND CHARITY

That we ought, once for all, heartily to put our whole trust in God, and make a total surrender of ourselves to Him, secure that He would not deceive us.

That we ought not to be weary of doing little things for the love of God, who regards not the greatness of the work, but the love with which it is performed. That we should not wonder if, in the beginning, we often failed in our endeavors, but that at last we should gain a habit, which will naturally produce its acts in us, without our care, and to our exceeding great delight.

That the whole substance of religion was faith, hope, and charity, by the practice of which we become united to the will of God; that all besides is indifferent, and to be used as a means that we may arrive at our end, and be swallowed up therein, by faith and charity.

That all things are possible to him who *believes;* that they are less difficult to him who *hopes;* that they are more easy to him who *loves,* and still more easy to him who perseveres in the practice of these three virtues.

THE PLACE OF SELF-EXAMINATION

That the end we ought to propose to ourselves is to become, in this life, the most perfect worshipers of God we can possibly be, as we hope to be through all eternity.

That when we enter upon the spiritual life, we should consider and examine to the bottom what we are. And then we should find ourselves worthy of all contempt, and not deserving indeed the name of Christians; subject to all kinds of misery and numberless accidents, which trouble us and cause perpetual vicissitudes in our health, in our humors, in our internal and external dispositions; in fine, persons whom God would humble by many pains and labors, as well within as without. After this we should not wonder that troubles, temptations, oppositions, and contradictions happen to us from men. We ought, on the contrary, to submit ourselves to them, and bear them as long as God pleases, as things highly advantageous to us.

That the greater perfection a soul aspires after, the more dependent it is upon divine grace.

BROTHER LAWRENCE'S PERSONAL EXPERIENCE

*Being questioned by one of his own society (to whom he was obliged to open himself) by what means he had attained such an habitual sense of God, he told him that, since his first coming to the monastery, he had considered God as the end of all his thoughts and desires, as the mark to which they should tend, and in which they should terminate.

That in the beginning of his novitiate he spent the hours appointed for private prayer in thinking of God, so as to convince his mind of, and to impress deeply upon his heart, the divine existence, rather by devout sentiments, and submission to the lights of faith, than by studied reasonings and elaborate meditations. That by this short and sure method he exercised himself in the knowledge and love of God, resolving to use his utmost endeavor to live in a continual sense of His presence, and, if possible, never to forget him more.

That when he had thus in prayer filled his mind with great sentiments of that infinite Being, he went to his work appointed in the kitchen (for he was cook to the society). There having first considered severally the things his office required, and when and how each thing was to be done, he spent all the intervals of his time, as well before as after his work, in prayer.

That when he began his business, he said to God, with a filial trust in Him: *O my God, since Thou art with me, and I must now, in obedience to Thy commands, apply my mind to these outward things, I beseech Thee to grant me the grace to continue in Thy presence; and to this end do Thou prosper me with Thy assistance, receive all my works, and possess all my affections.*

As he proceeded in his work he continued his familiar conversation with his Maker, imploring His grace, and offering to Him all his actions.

When he had finished he examined himself how he had discharged his duty; if he found *well,* he returned thanks to God; if otherwise, he asked pardon, and, without being discouraged, he set his mind right again, and continued his exercise of the *presence* of God, as if he had never deviated from it. "Thus," said he, "by rising

---

*The particulars which follow are collected from other accounts of Brother Lawrence.

after my falls, and by frequently renewed acts of faith and love, I am come to a state wherein it would be as difficult for me not to think of God as it was at first to accustom myself to it."

BROTHER LAWRENCE'S EXAMPLE

As Brother Lawrence had found such an advantage in walking in the presence of God, it was natural for him to recommend it earnestly to others; but his example was a stronger inducement than any arguments he could propose. His very countenance was edifying, such a sweet and calm devotion appearing in it as could not but affect the beholders. And it was observed that in the greatest hurry of business in the kitchen he still preserved his recollection and heavenly-mindedness. He was never hasty nor loitering, but did each thing in its season, with an even, uninterrupted composure and tranquillity of spirit. "The time of business," said he, "does not with me differ from the time of prayer, and in the noise and clatter of my kitchen, while several persons are at the same time calling for different things, I possess God in as great tranquillity as if I were upon my knees at the blessed sacrament."

Letters

SINCE YOU DESIRE so earnestly that I should communicate to you the method by which I arrived at that *habitual sense of God's presence*, which our Lord, of His mercy, has been pleased to vouchsafe to me, I must tell you that it is with great difficulty that I am prevailed on by your importunities; and now I do it only upon the terms that you show my letter to nobody. If I knew that you would let it be seen, all the desire that I have for your advancement would not be able to determine me to it. The account I can give you is [this.]

BECOMING HIS ALONE

Having found in many books different methods of going to God, and divers practices of the spiritual life, I thought this would serve rather to puzzle me than facilitate what I sought after, which was nothing but how to become wholly God's. This made me resolve to give the all for the all; so after having given myself wholly to God, that He might take away my sins, *I renounced, for the love of Him, everything that was not He, and I began to live as if there was none but He and I in the world.*

UNINTERRUPTED THOUGHTS OF GOD

Sometimes I considered myself before Him as a poor criminal at the feet of his judge; at other times I beheld Him in my heart as my Father, as my God. I worshipped Him the oftenest that I could, keeping my mind in His holy presence, and recalling it as often as I found it wandered from Him. I found no small pain in this exercise, and yet I continued it, notwithstanding all the difficulties that occurred, without troubling or disquieting myself when my mind had wandered involuntarily. I made this my business as much all the day long as at the appointed times of prayer; for at all times, every hour, every minute, even in the height of my business, I drove away from my mind everything that was capable of interrupting my thoughts of God.

A NATURAL, HABITUAL PRACTICE

Such has been my common practice ever since I entered in religion; and though I have done it very imperfectly, yet I have found great advantages by it. These, I well know, are to be imputed to the mere mercy and goodness of God, because we can do nothing without Him, and *I* still less than any. But when we are faithful to keep ourselves in His holy presence, and set Him always before us, this not only hinders our offending Him and doing anything that may displease Him, at least wilfully, but it also begets in us a holy freedom, and, if I may so speak, a familiarity with God, wherewith we ask and, that successfully, the graces we stand in need of.

In fine, by often repeating these acts, they become *habitual*, and the presence of God rendered as it were *natural* to us. Give Him thanks, if you please, with me, for His great goodness toward me, which I can never sufficiently admire, for the many favors He has done to so miserable a sinner as I am. May all things praise Him. Amen.

I am, in our Lord,
Yours, etc.

SECOND LETTER

To the Reverend ——

NOT finding my manner of life in books, although I have no difficulty about it, yet, for greater security, I shall be glad to know your thoughts concerning it.

In a conversation some days since with a person of piety, he told me the spiritual life was a life of grace, which begins with servile fear, which is increased by hope of eternal life, and which is consummated by pure love; that each of these states had its different stages, by which one arrives at last at that blessed consummation.

HOW THE "PRACTICE" DEVELOPED

I have not followed all these methods. On the contrary, from I know not what instincts, I found they discouraged me. This was the reason why, at my entrance into religion, I took a resolution to give myself up to God, as the best return I could make for His love, and, for the love of Him, to renounce all besides.

For the first year I commonly employed myself during the time set apart for devotion with the thought of death, judgment, heaven, hell, and my sins. Thus I continued some years, applying my mind carefully the rest of the day, and even in the midst of my business, *to the presence of God*, whom I considered always as *with* me, often as *in* me.

At length I came insensibly to do the same thing during my set time of prayer, which caused in me great delight and consolation. This practice produced in me so high an esteem for God that *faith* alone was capable to satisfy me in that point.*

BROTHER LAWRENCE'S EARLY STRUGGLES

Such was my beginning, and yet I must tell you that for the first ten years I suffered much. The apprehension that I was not devoted to God as I wished to be, my past sins always present to my mind, and the great unmerited favors which God did me, were the matter and source of my sufferings. During this time I fell often, and rose again presently. It seemed to me that all creatures, reason, and God Himself were against me, and *faith* alone for me. I was troubled sometimes with thoughts that to believe I had received such favors was an effect of my presumption, which pretended

I suppose he means that all distinct notions he could form of God were unsatisfactory, because he perceived them to be unworthy of God; and therefore his mind was not to be satisfied but by the views of *faith*, which apprehended God as infinite and incomprehensible, as He is in Himself, and not as He can be conceived by human ideas.

to be *at once* where others arrive with difficulty; at other times, that it was a wilful delusion, and that there was no salvation for me.

When I thought of nothing but to end my days in these troubles (which did not at all diminish the trust I had in God, and which served only to increase my faith), I found myself changed all at once; and my soul, which till that time was in trouble, felt a profound inward peace, as if she were in her center and place of rest.

HIS PRESENT STATE

Ever since that time I walk before God simply, in faith, with humility and with love, and I apply myself diligently to do nothing and think nothing which may displease Him. I hope that when I have done what I can, He will do with me what He pleases.

As for what passes in me at present, I cannot express it. I have no pain or difficulty about my state, because I have no will but that of God, which I endeavor to accomplish in all things, and to which I am so resigned that I would not take up a straw from the ground against His order, or from any other motive than purely that of love to Him.

I have quitted all forms of devotion and set prayers but those to which my state obliges me. And I make it my business only to persevere in His holy presence, wherein I keep myself by a simple attention, and a general fond regard to God, which I may call an *actual presence* of God; or, to speak better, an habitual, silent, and secret conversation of the soul with God, which often causes me joys and rap-

tures inwardly, and sometimes also outwardly, so great that I am forced to use means to moderate them and prevent their appearance to others.

BROTHER LAWRENCE'S VIEW OF HIMSELF

In short, I am assured beyond all doubt that my soul has been with God above these thirty years. I pass over many things that I may not be tedious to you, yet I think it proper to inform you after what manner I consider myself before God, whom I behold as my King.

I consider myself as the most wretched of men, full of sores and corruption, and who has committed all sorts of crimes against his King. Touched with a sensible regret, I confess to Him all my wickedness, I ask His forgiveness, I abandon myself in His hands that He may do what He pleases with me. The King, full of mercy and goodness, very far from chastising me, embraces me with love, makes me eat at His table, serves me with His own hands, gives me the key of His treasures; He converses and delights Himself with me incessantly, in a thousand and a thousand ways, and treats me in all respects as His favorite. It is thus I consider myself from time to time in His holy presence.

My most useful method is this simple attention, and such a general passionate regard to God, to whom I find myself often attached with greater sweetness and delight than that of an infant at the mother's breast; so that, if I dare use the expression, I should choose to call this state the bosom of

God, for the inexpressible sweetness which I taste and experience there.

If sometimes my thoughts wander from it by necessity or infirmity, I am presently recalled by inward motions so charming and delicious that I am ashamed to mention them. I desire your Reverence to reflect rather upon my great wretchedness, of which you are fully informed, than upon the great favors which God does me, all unworthy and ungrateful as I am.

HIS APPROACH TO PRAYER

As for my set hours of prayer, they are only a continuation of the same exercise. Sometimes I consider myself there as a stone before a carver, whereof he is to make a statue; presenting myself thus before God, I desire Him to form His perfect image in my soul, and make me entirely like Himself.

At other times, when I apply myself to prayer, I feel all my spirit and all my soul lift itself up without any care or effort of mine, and it continues as it were suspended and firmly fixed in God, as in its center and place of rest.

I know that some charge this state with inactivity, delusion, and self-love. I confess that it is a holy inactivity, and would be a happy self-love if the soul in that state were capable of it, because, in effect, while she is in this repose, she cannot be disturbed by such acts as she was formerly accustomed to, and which were then her support, but which would now rather hinder than assist her.

Yet I cannot bear that this should be called delusion, because the soul which thus enjoys God desires herein nothing but Him. If this be delusion in me, it belongs to God to remedy it. Let Him do what He pleases with me: I desire only Him, and to be wholly devoted to Him. You will, however, oblige me in sending me your opinion, to which I always pay a great deference, for I have a singular esteem for your Reverence, and am, in our Lord,

Yours, etc.

THIRD LETTER

WE have a God who is infinitely gracious and knows all about our wants. I always thought that He would reduce you to extremity. He will come in His own time, and when you least expect it. Hope in Him more than ever; thank Him with me for the favors He does you, particularly for the fortitude and patience which He gives you in your afflictions. It is a plain mark of the care He takes of you. Comfort yourself, then, with Him, and give thanks for all.

ADVICE FOR A FELLOW BELIEVER

I admire also the fortitude and bravery of Mr. ——. God has given him a good disposition and a good will; but there is in him still a little of the world and a great deal of youth. I hope the affliction which God has sent him will prove a wholesome remedy to him, and make him enter into himself. It is an accident which should engage him to put all his trust in *Him* who accompanies him everywhere. Let him think of Him as often as he can, especially in the greatest dangers. A little lifting up of the heart suffices. A little remembrance of God, one act of inward worship, though upon a march, and a sword in hand, are prayers, which, however short, are nevertheless very acceptable to God; and far from lessening a soldier's courage in occasions of danger, they best serve to fortify it.

ENGAGE IN LITTLE INTERNAL ADORATIONS

Let him then think of God the most he can. Let him accustom himself, by degrees, to this small but holy exercise. No one will notice it, and nothing is easier than to repeat often in the day these little internal adorations. Recommend to him, if you please, that he think of God the most he can, in the manner here directed. It is very fit and most necessary for a soldier who is daily exposed to the dangers of life. I hope that God will assist him and all the family, to whom I present my service, being theirs and

Yours, etc.

FOURTH LETTER

I HAVE taken this opportunity to communicate to you the sentiments of one of our society, concerning the admirable effects and continual assistances which he receives from *the presence of God*. Let you and me both profit by them.

ADMIRABLE EFFECTS OF PRACTICING THE PRESENCE OF GOD

You must know his continual care has been, for about forty years past that he has spent in religion, to be *always with God*, and to do nothing, say nothing, and think nothing which may displease Him, and this without any other view than purely for the love of Him, and because He deserves infinitely more.

He is now so accustomed to that *divine presence* that he receives from it continual succors upon all occasions. For about thirty years his soul has been filled with joy so continual, and sometimes so great, that he is forced to use means to moderate them, and to hinder their appearing outwardly.

WHEN THE SOUL DRIFTS

If sometimes he is a little too much absent from that *divine presence*, God presently makes Himself to be felt in his soul to recall Him, which often happens when he is most engaged in his outward business. He answers with exact fidelity to these inward drawings, either by an elevation of his heart toward God, or by a meek and fond regard to Him; or by such words as love forms upon these occasions, as, for instance, *My God, here I am all devoted to Thee. Lord, make me according to Thy heart.*

And then it seems to him (as in effect he feels it) that this God of love, satisfied with such few words, reposes again, and rests in the fund and center of his soul. The experience of these things gives him such an assurance that God is always in the fund or bottom of his soul that it renders him incapable of doubting it upon any account whatever.

Judge by this what content and satisfaction he enjoys while he continually finds in himself so great a treasure. He is no longer in an anxious search after it, but has it open before him, and may take what he pleases of it.

ON THE FAILURE TO ENJOY
THE INFINITE TREASURE
OF GOD'S PRESENCE

He complains much of our blindness, and cries often that we are to be pitied who content ourselves with so little. *God*, saith he, *has infinite treasure to bestow, and we take up with a little sensible devotion, which passes in a moment. Blind as we are, we hinder God and stop the current of His graces. But when He finds a soul penetrated with a lively faith, He pours into it His graces and favors plentifully; there they flow like a torrent which, after being forcibly stopped against its ordinary course, when it has found a passage, spreads itself with impetuosity and abundance.*

Yes, we often stop this torrent by the little value we set upon it. But let us stop it no more; let us enter into ourselves and break down the bank which hinders it. Let us make way for grace; let us redeem the lost time, for perhaps we have but little left. Death follows us close; let us be well prepared for it; for we die but once, and a miscarriage *there* is irretrievable.

A CHALLENGE TO ADVANCE SPIRITUALLY

I say again, let us enter into ourselves. The time presses, there is no room for delay; our souls are at stake. I believe you have taken such effectual measures that you will not be surprised. I commend you for it; it is the one thing necessary. We must, nevertheless, always work at it, because not to advance in the spiritual life is to go back. But those who have the gale of the Holy Spirit go forward even in sleep. If the vessel of our soul is still tossed with winds and storms, let us awake the Lord, who reposes in it, and He will quickly calm the sea.

I have taken the liberty to impart to you these good sentiments, that you may compare them with your own. It will serve again to kindle and inflame them, if by misfortune (which God forbid, for it would be indeed a great misfortune) they should be, though never so little, cooled. Let us then *both* recall our first fervors. Let us profit by the example and the sentiments of this brother, who is little known of the world, but known to God, and extremely caressed by Him. I will pray for you; do you pray instantly for me, who am, in our Lord,

Yours, etc.

FIFTH LETTER

I RECEIVED this day two books and a letter from Sister ——, who is preparing to make her profession, and upon that account desires the prayers of your holy society, and yours in particular. I perceive that she reckons much upon them; pray do not disappoint her. Beg of God that she may make her sacrifice in the view of His love alone, and with a firm resolution to be wholly devoted to Him. I will send you one of these books, which treat of *the presence of God*, a subject which, in my opinion, contains the whole spiritual life; and it seems to me that whoever duly practises it will soon become spiritual.

THE PLEASURE OF A CONTINUAL
CONVERSATION WITH GOD

I know that for the right practice of it the heart must be empty of all other things, because God will possess the heart *alone;* and as He cannot possess it *alone* without emptying it of all besides, so neither can He act *there,* and do in it what He pleases, unless it be left vacant to Him.

There is not in the world a kind of life more sweet and delightful than that of a continual conversation with God. Those only can comprehend it who practise and experience it; yet I do not advise you to do it from that motive. It is not pleasure which we ought to seek in this exercise; but let us do it from a principle of love, and because God would have us.

Were I a preacher, I should, above all other things, preach the practice of *the presence of God;* and were I a director, I should advise all the world to do it, so necessary do I think it, and so easy, too.

A PLEA TO PRACTICE GOD'S PRESENCE

Ah! knew we but the want we have of the grace and assistance of God, we should never lose sight of Him—no, not for a moment. Believe me, make immediately a holy and firm resolution nevermore wilfully to forget Him, and to spend the rest of your days in His sacred presence, deprived, for the love of Him, if He thinks fit, of all consolations.

Set heartily about this work, and if you do it as you ought, be assured that you will soon find the effects of it. I will assist you with my prayers, poor as they are. I recommend myself earnestly to yours and those of your holy society, being theirs, and more particularly,

Yours, etc.

SIXTH LETTER

(To the Same)

I HAVE received from Mrs. —— the things which you gave her for me. I wonder that you have not given me your thoughts of the little book I sent to you, and which you must have received. Pray set heartily about the practice of it in your old age; it is better late than never.

LAWRENCE'S EXPERIENCE OF GOD'S PRESENCE

I cannot imagine how religious persons can live satisfied without the practice of *the presence of God.* For my part, I keep myself retired with Him in the fund or center of my soul as much as I can; and while I am so with Him I fear nothing, but the least turning from Him is insupportable.

This exercise does not much fatigue the body; it is, however, proper to deprive it sometimes, nay, often, of many little pleasures which are innocent and lawful, for God will not permit that a soul which desires to be devoted entirely to Him should take other pleasures than with Him: that is more than reasonable.

LAY ASIDE ALL OTHER CARES

I do not say that therefore we must put any violent constraint upon ourselves. No, we must serve God in a holy freedom; we must do our business faithfully, without trouble or disquiet, recalling our mind to God mildly, and with tranquillity, as often as we find it wandering from Him.

It is, however, necessary to put our whole trust in God, laying aside all other cares, and even some particular forms of devotion, though very good in themselves, yet such as one often engages in unreasonably, because these devotions are only means to attain to the end. So when by this exercise of *the presence of God* we are *with Him* who is our end, it is then useless to return to the means; but we may continue with Him our commerce of love, persevering in His holy presence, one while by an act of praise, of adoration, or of desire; one while by an act of resignation or thanksgiving; and in all the ways which our spirit can invent.

Be not discouraged by the repugnance which you may find in it from nature; you must do yourself violence. At the first one often thinks it lost time, but you must go on, and resolve to persevere in it to death, notwithstanding all the difficulties that may occur. I recommend myself to the prayers of your holy society, and yours in particular. I am, in our Lord,

Yours, etc.

SEVENTH LETTER

I PITY you much. It will be of great importance if you can leave the care of your affairs to ——, and spend the remainder of your life only in worshiping God. He requires no great matters of us: a little remembrance of Him from time to time; a little adoration; sometimes to pray for His grace, sometimes to offer Him your sufferings, and sometimes to return Him thanks for the favors He has given you, and still gives you, in the midst of your troubles, and to console yourself with Him the oftenest you can. Lift up your heart to Him, sometimes even at your meals, and when you are in company; the least little remembrance will always be acceptable to Him. You need not cry very loud; He is nearer to us than we are aware of.

ENJOY GOD'S PRESENCE EVERYWHERE

It is not necessary for being with God to be always at church. We may make an oratory of our heart wherein to retire from time to time to converse with Him in meekness, humility, and love. Every one is capable of such familiar conversation with God, some more, some less. He knows what we can do. Let us begin, then.

Perhaps He expects but one generous resolution on our part. Have courage. We have but little time to live; you are near sixty-four, and I am almost eighty. Let us live and die with God. Sufferings will be sweet and pleasant to us while we are with Him; and the greatest pleasures will be, without Him, a cruel punishment to us. May He be blessed for all. Amen.

ACT WITH CONFIDENCE IN GOD

Accustom yourself, then, by degrees thus to worship Him, to beg His grace, to offer Him your heart from time to time in the midst of your business, even every moment, if you can. Do not always scrupulously confine yourself to certain rules, or particular forms of devotion, but act with a general confidence in God, with love and humility. You may assure —— of my poor prayers, and that I am their servant, and particularly

Yours in our Lord, etc.

EIGHTH LETTER

(Concerning Wandering Thoughts in Prayer)

YOU tell me nothing new; you are not the only one that is troubled with wandering thoughts. Our mind is extremely roving; but, as the will is mistress of all our faculties, she must recall them, and carry them to God as their last end.

When the mind, for want of being sufficiently reduced by recollection at our first engaging in devotion, has contracted certain bad habits of wandering and dissipation, they are difficult to overcome, and commonly draw us, even against our wills, to the things of the earth.

A REMEDY FOR WANDERING THOUGHTS

I believe one remedy for this is to confess our faults and to humble ourselves before God. I do not advise you to use multiplicity of words in prayer, many words and long discourses being often the occasions of wandering. Hold yourself in prayer before God like a dumb or paralytic beggar at a rich man's gate. Let it be *your* business to keep your mind in the presence of the Lord. If it sometimes wander and withdraw itself from Him, do not much disquiet yourself for that: trouble and disquiet serve rather to distract the mind than to recollect it; the will must bring it back in tranquillity. If you persevere in this manner, God will have pity on you.

KEEP STRICTLY IN THE PRESENCE OF GOD

One way to recollect the mind easily in the time of prayer, and preserve it more in tranquillity, *is not to let it wander too far at other times*. You should keep it strictly in the presence of God; and being accustomed to think of Him often, you will find it easy to keep your mind calm in the time of prayer, or at least to recall it from its wanderings.

I have told you already at large, in my former letters, of the advantages we may draw from this practice of the presence of God. Let us set about it seriously, and pray for one another.

Yours, etc.

NINTH LETTER

THE enclosed is an answer to that which I received from ——; pray deliver it to her. She seems to me full of good will, but she would go faster than grace. One does not become holy all at once. I recommend her to you; we ought to help one another by our advice, and yet more by our good examples. You will oblige me to let me hear of her from time to time, and whether she be very fervent and very obedient.

OUR ONLY BUSINESS IN LIFE

Let us thus think often that our only business in this life is to please God, and that all besides is but folly and vanity. You and I have lived about forty years in religion (i.e., a monastic life). Have we employed them in loving and serving God, who by His mercy has called us to this state, and for that very end? I am filled with shame and confusion when I reflect, on one hand, upon the great favors which God has done, and incessantly continues to do me; and on the other, upon the ill use I have made of them, and my small advancement in the way of perfection.

Since by His mercy He gives us still a little time, let us begin in earnest; let us repair the lost time; let us return with a full assurance to that Father of mercies, who is always ready to receive us affectionately. Let us renounce, let us generously renounce, for the love of Him, all that is not Himself; He deserves infinitely more.

Let us think of Him perpetually. Let us put all our trust in Him. I doubt not but we shall soon find the effects of it in receiving the abundance of His grace, with which we can do all things, and without which we can do nothing but sin.

THINK OF HIM OFTEN

We cannot escape the dangers which abound in life without the actual and *continual* help of God. Let us, then, pray to Him for it *continually.* How can we pray to Him without being with Him? How can we be with Him but in thinking of Him often? And how can we often think of Him but by a holy habit which we should form of it?

You will tell me that I am always saying the same thing. It is true, for this is the best and easiest method I know; and as I use no other, I advise all the world to do it. We must *know* before we can *love.* In order to *know* God, we must often *think* of Him; and when we come to *love* Him, we shall then also think of Him often, for our heart will be with our treasure. This is an argument which well deserves your consideration.

I am,
Yours, etc.

TENTH LETTER

I HAVE had a good deal of difficulty to bring myself to write to Mr. ——, and I do it now purely because you and Madam —— desire me. Pray write the directions and send it to him. I am very well pleased with the trust which you have in God; I wish that He may increase it in you more and more. We cannot have too much in so good and faithful a Friend, who will never fail us in this world nor in the next.

LOVE FOR GOD MUST EXCEED LOVE FOR FRIENDS

If Mr. —— makes his advantage of the loss he has had, and puts all his confidence in God, He will soon give him another friend, more powerful and more inclined to serve him. He disposes of hearts as He pleases. Perhaps Mr. —— was too much attached to him he has lost. We ought to love our friends, but without encroaching upon the love due to God, which must be the principal.

Pray remember what I have recommended to you, which is, to think often on God, by day, by night, in your business, and even in your diversions. He is always near you and with you; leave Him not alone. You would think it rude to leave a friend alone who came to visit you; why, then, must God be neglected?

Do not, then, forget Him, but think on Him often, adore Him continually, live and die with Him; this is the glorious employment of a Christian. In a word, this is our profession; if we do not know it, we must learn it. I will endeavor to help you with my prayers, and am, in our Lord,

Yours, etc.

ELEVENTH LETTER

I DO not pray that you may be delivered from your pains, but I pray God earnestly that He would give you strength and patience to bear them as long as He pleases. Comfort yourself with Him who holds you fastened to the cross. He will loose you when He thinks fit. Happy those who suffer with Him. Accustom yourself to suffer in that manner, and seek from Him the strength to endure as much, and as long, as He shall judge to be necessary for you.

A PROPER VIEW OF SICKNESS

The men of the world do not comprehend these truths, nor is it to be wondered at, since they suffer like what they are, and not like Christians. They consider sickness as a pain to nature, and not as a favor from God; and seeing it only in that light, they find nothing in it but grief and distress. But those who consider sickness as coming from the hand of God, as the effect of His mercy, and the means which He employs for their salvation—such commonly find in it great sweetness and sensible consolation.

THE SOVEREIGN PHYSICIAN

I wish you could convince yourself that God is often (in some sense) nearer to us, and more effectually present with us, in sickness than in health. Rely upon no other physician; for, according to my apprehension, He reserves your cure to Himself. Put,

then, all your trust in Him, and you will soon find we often retard by putting greater confidence in physic than in God.

Whatever remedies you make use of, they will succeed only so far as He permits. When pains come from God, He only can cure them. He often sends diseases of the body to cure those of the soul. Comfort yourself with the sovereign Physician both of the soul and body.

BE SATISFIED WITH YOUR CONDITION

Be satisfied with the condition in which God places you; however happy you may think me, I envy you. Pains and sufferings would be a paradise to me while I should suffer with my God, and the greatest pleasures would be hell to me if I could relish them without Him. All my consolation would be to suffer something for His sake.

I must, in a little time, go to God. What comforts me in this life is that I now see Him by *faith;* and I see Him in such a manner as might make me say sometimes, *I believe no more, but I see*. I feel what faith teaches us, and in that assurance and that practice of faith I will live and die with Him.

Continue, then, always with God; it is the only support and comfort for your affliction. I shall beseech Him to be with you. I present my service.

Yours, etc.

TWELFTH LETTER

IF we were well accustomed to the exercise of *the presence of God*, all bodily diseases would be much alleviated thereby. God often permits that we should suffer a little to purify our souls and oblige us to continue *with* Him.

HOW TO DEAL WITH PAIN

Take courage; offer Him your pains incessantly; pray to Him for strength to endure them. Above all, get a habit of entertaining yourself often with God, and forget Him the least you can. Adore Him in your infirmities, offer yourself to Him from time to time, and in the height of your sufferings beseech Him humbly and affectionately (as a child his father) to make you conformable to His holy will. I shall endeavor to assist you with my poor prayers.

God has many ways of drawing us to Himself. He sometimes hides Himself from us; but *faith* alone, which will not fail us in time of need, ought to be our support, and the foundation of our confidence, which must be all in God.

OUR NEED FOR GOD'S PRESENCE

I know not how God will dispose of me. I am always happy. All the world suffer; and I, who deserve the severest discipline, feel joys so continual and so great that I can scarce contain them.

I would willingly ask of God a part of your sufferings, but that I know my weakness, which is so great that if He left me one moment to myself I should be the most wretched man alive. And yet I know not how He can leave me alone, because faith gives me as strong a conviction as sense can do that He never forsakes us until we have first forsaken Him. Let us fear to leave Him. Let us be always with Him. Let

us live and die in His presence. Do you pray for me as I for you. I am,

Yours, etc.

THIRTEENTH LETTER

(To the Same)

I AM in pain to see you suffer so long. What gives me some ease and sweetens the feelings I have for your griefs is that they are proofs of God's love toward you. See them in that view and you will bear them more easily. As your case is, it is my opinion that you should leave off human remedies, and resign yourself entirely to the providence of God. Perhaps He stays only for that resignation and a perfect trust in Him to cure you. Since, notwithstanding all your cares, physic has hitherto proved unsuccessful, and your malady still increases, it will not be tempting God to abandon yourself in His hands and expect all from Him.

HOW TO PRAY IN TIME OF PAIN

I told you in my last that He sometimes permits bodily diseases to cure the distempers of the soul. Have courage, then; make a virtue of necessity. Ask of God, not deliverance from your pains, but strength to bear resolutely, for the love of Him, all that He should please, and as long as He shall please.

Such prayers, indeed, are a little hard to nature, but most acceptable to God and sweet to those that love Him. Love sweetens pains; and when one loves God, one suffers for His sake with joy and courage. Do you so, I beseech you; comfort yourself with Him, who is the only Physician of all our maladies. He is the Father of the afflicted, always ready to help us. He loves us infinitely, more than we imagine. Love Him, then, and seek no consolation elsewhere. I hope you will soon receive it. Adieu. I will help you with my prayers, poor as they are, and shall always be, in our Lord,

Yours, etc.

FOURTEENTH LETTER

(To the Same)

I RENDER thanks to our Lord for having relieved you a little, according to your desire. I have been often near expiring, but I never was so much satisfied as then. Accordingly, I did not pray for any relief, but I prayed for strength to suffer with courage, humility, and love. Ah, how sweet it is to suffer with God! However great the sufferings may be, receive them with love.

ADORE HIM INCESSANTLY

It is paradise to suffer and be with Him; so that if in this life we would enjoy the peace of paradise we must accustom ourselves to a familiar, humble, affectionate conversation with Him. We must hinder our spirits' wandering from Him upon any occasion. We must make our heart a spiritual temple, wherein to adore Him incessantly. We must watch continually over ourselves, that we may not do nor say nor think anything that may displease Him. When our minds are thus employed about God, suffering will become full of unction and consolation.

I know that to arrive at this state the beginning is very difficult, for we must act purely in faith. But though it is difficult, we know also that we can do all things with the grace of God, which He never refuses to them who ask it earnestly. Knock, persevere in knocking, and I answer for it that He will open to you in His due time, and grant you all at once what He has deferred during many years. Adieu. Pray to Him for me as I pray to Him for you. I hope to see Him quickly. I am,

Yours, etc.

FIFTEENTH LETTER

(To the Same)

GOD knoweth best what is needful for us, and all that He does is for our good. If we knew how much He loves us, we should always be ready to receive equally and with indifference from His hand the sweet and the bitter. All would please that came from Him.

The sorest afflictions never appear intolerable, except when we see them in the wrong light. When we see them as dispensed by the hand of God, when we know that it is our loving Father who abases and distresses us, our sufferings will lose their bitterness and become even matter of consolation.

TO KNOW GOD BETTER IS TO LOVE HIM MORE

Let all our employment be to *know* God; the more one *knows* Him, the more one *desires* to know Him. And as *knowledge* is commonly the measure of *love*, the deeper and more extensive our *knowledge* shall be, the greater will be our *love;* and if our love of God were great, we should love Him equally in pains and pleasures.

SEEK GOD BY FAITH

Let us not content ourselves with loving God for the mere sensible favors, how elevated soever, which He has done or may do us. Such favors, though never so great, cannot bring us so near to Him as faith does in one simple act. Let us seek Him often by faith. He is within us; seek Him not elsewhere. If we do love Him alone, are we not rude, and do we not deserve blame, if we busy ourselves about trifles which do not please and perhaps offend Him? It is to be feared these *trifles* will one day cost us dear.

LAWRENCE'S DESIRE TO SEE GOD

Let us begin to be devoted to Him in good earnest. Let us cast everything besides out of our hearts. He would possess them alone. Beg this favor of Him. If we do what we can on our parts, we shall soon see that change wrought in us which we aspire after. I cannot thank Him sufficiently for the relaxation He has vouchsafed you. I hope from His mercy the favor to see Him within a few days.* Let us pray for one another. I am, in our Lord,

Yours, etc.

---

*He took to his bed two days after, and died within the week.

Notes

THE CONFESSIONS, ST. AUGUSTINE
 1. The best biography of Augustine is Peter Brown, *Augustine of Hippo* (Berkeley and Los Angeles: University of California Press, 1967).
 2. Second Book.
 3. Tenth Book.

ON THE SONG OF SONGS, ST. BERNARD OF CLAIRVAUX
 1. Chapter 25.
 2. Chapter 3.

REVELATIONS OF DIVINE LOVE, JULIAN OF NORWICH
 1. Justo Gonzalez, *The Story of Christianity,* vol. 1 (San Francisco: Harper and Row, 1984), 324.
 2. Barbara Tuchman, *A Distant Mirror: The Calamitous 14th Century* (New York: Ballantine Books, 1978), 506.
 3. J.C.L.S. de Sismondi, quoted in *A Distant Mirror,* xiv.
 4. Louise Collis, *Memoirs of a Medieval Woman: The Life and Times of Margery Kempe* (New York: Harper Colophon Books, 1964), 29–30.
 5. Second Chapter of *Revelations of Divine Love.*
 6. Barbara MacHaffie, *Her Story: Women in Christian Tradition* (Philadelphia: Fortress Press, 1986), 43–60.
 7. Twelfth Chapter.
 8. Thirty-First Chapter.
 9. Sixty-Fifth Chapter.
10. Ninth Chapter.
11. Father John-Julian, O.J.N., in *A Lesson of Love* (New York: Walker and Company, 1988), xii.
12. Julian of Norwich, *Revelations of Divine Love,* translated with an introduction by Clifton Wolters (London: Penguin Books, 1966), 32.

THE IMITATION OF CHRIST, THOMAS À KEMPIS
 1. Second Book, chapter I.
 2. Third Book, chapter LIX.
 3. Fourth Book, chapter XVII.
 4. First Book, chapter I.
 5. Fourth Book, chapter I.
 6. Third Book, chapter LV.
 7. Third Book, chapter XXXII.

8. John Wesley, The Christian's Pattern, or an Extract of The Imitation of Christ (Nashville: Abingdon Press).

THE PRACTICE OF THE PRESENCE OF GOD, BROTHER LAWRENCE

1. The friend is Bruce Shelley, now senior professor of church history at Denver Seminary.
2. First Conversation in the text following.
3. Ibid.
4. Second Conversion.
5. First Letter.
6. Tenth Letter.
7. Wayne E. Oates's psychological commentary on *The Practice of the Presence of God* is found in E. Glenn Hinson, Seekers After Mature Faith: A Historical Introduction to the Classics of Christian Devotion (Nashville: Broadman Press, 1968), 158.
8. Eighth Letter.
9. Second and Fourth Conversations.